Family Law

EXAMPLES & EXPLANATIONS

ALLEN COUNTY

P9-BIG-348

EDITORIAL ADVISORS

Vicki Been
Elihu Root Professor of Law
New York University School of Law

Erwin Chemerinsky
Dean and Distinguished Professor of Law
University of California, Irvine, School of Law

Richard A. Epstein
James Parker Hall Distinguished Service Professor of Law
University of Chicago Law School
Peter and Kirsten Bedford Senior Fellow
The Hoover Institution
Stanford University

Ronald J. Gilson
Charles J. Meyers Professor of Law and Business
Stanford University
Marc and Eva Stern Professor of Law and Business
Columbia Law School

James E. Krier
Earl Warren DeLano Professor of Law
The University of Michigan Law School

Richard K. Neumann, Jr.
Professor of Law
Hofstra University School of Law

Robert H. Sitkoff
John L. Gray Professor of Law
Harvard Law School

David Alan Sklansky
Professor of Law
University of California at Berkeley School of Law

Kent D. Syverud
Dean and Ethan A. H. Shepley University Professor
Washington University School of Law

Elizabeth Warren
Leo Gottlieb Professor of Law
Harvard Law School

ASPEN PUBLISHERS

Family Law

Third Edition

Robert E. Oliphant
Emeritus Professor of Law
William Mitchell College of Law

Nancy Ver Steegh
Associate Professor of Law
William Mitchell College of Law

Wolters Kluwer
Law & Business

AUSTIN   BOSTON   CHICAGO   NEW YORK   THE NETHERLANDS

© 2010 Aspen Publishers. All Rights Reserved.

No part of this publication may be reproduced or transmitted in any form or by any means, electronic or mechanical, including photocopy, recording, or any information storage and retrieval system, without permission in writing from the publisher. Requests for permission to make copies of any part of this publication should be mailed to:

Aspen Publishers
Attn: Permissions Department
76 Ninth Avenue, 7th Floor
New York, NY 10011-5201

To contact Customer Care, e-mail customer.care@aspenpublishers.com, call 1-800-234-1660, fax 1-800-901-9075, or mail correspondence to:

Aspen Publishers
Attn: Order Department
PO Box 990
Frederick, MD 21705

Printed in the United States of America.

1 2 3 4 5 6 7 8 9 0

ISBN 978-0-7355-8828-8

Library of Congress Cataloging-in-Publication Data

Oliphant, Robert E., 1938–
    Family law / Robert E. Oliphant, Nancy Ver Steegh. — 3rd ed.
        p. cm.
    Includes bibliographical references and index.
    ISBN 978-0-7355-8828-8 (perfectbound : alk. paper)
    1. Domestic relations—United States—Outlines, syllabi, etc.
    I. Ver Steegh, Nancy, 1953– II. Title.

    KF505.Z9O43 2010
    346.7301'5—dc22   2009052600

About Wolters Kluwer Law & Business

Wolters Kluwer Law & Business is a leading provider of research information and workflow solutions in key specialty areas. The strengths of the individual brands of Aspen Publishers, CCH, Kluwer Law International and Loislaw are aligned within Wolters Kluwer Law & Business to provide comprehensive, in-depth solutions and expert-authored content for the legal, professional and education markets.

CCH was founded in 1913 and has served more than four generations of business professionals and their clients. The CCH products in the Wolters Kluwer Law & Business group are highly regarded electronic and print resources for legal, securities, antitrust and trade regulation, government contracting, banking, pension, payroll, employment and labor, and healthcare reimbursement and compliance professionals.

Aspen Publishers is a leading information provider for attorneys, business professionals and law students. Written by preeminent authorities, Aspen products offer analytical and practical information in a range of specialty practice areas from securities law and intellectual property to mergers and acquisitions and pension/benefits. Aspen's trusted legal education resources provide professors and students with high-quality, up-to-date and effective resources for successful instruction and study in all areas of the law.

Kluwer Law International supplies the global business community with comprehensive English-language international legal information. Legal practitioners, corporate counsel and business executives around the world rely on the Kluwer Law International journals, loose-leafs, books and electronic products for authoritative information in many areas of international legal practice.

Loislaw is a premier provider of digitized legal content to small law firm practitioners of various specializations. Loislaw provides attorneys with the ability to quickly and efficiently find the necessary legal information they need, when and where they need it, by facilitating access to primary law as well as state-specific law, records, forms and treatises.

Wolters Kluwer Law & Business, a unit of Wolters Kluwer, is headquartered in New York and Riverwoods, Illinois. Wolters Kluwer is a leading multinational publisher and information services company.

Summary of Contents

Summary of Contents

Contents

Contents

Contents

Chapter 8   Parenting Time and Visitation   177

Contents

Contents

Chapter 14   Premarital (Antenuptial or Prenuptial) Contracts — History, Requirements, and Restrictions   303

Contents

Contents

Contents

Chapter 22   Mediation, Collaborative Law, Parenting Coordination, and Arbitration   501

Contents

Preface

We are pleased to provide an updated and revised third edition of *Family Law: Examples & Explanations*. Each of the 24 chapters features recent developments in family law and the book includes 250 hypothetical examples and explanations, most of which are based on fact patterns taken from actual cases. Because new developments in family law often reflect underlying societal changes in family structure and demographics, this volume incorporates empirical research and census data that are likely to be of interest to the reader. We also highlight ways that the practice of family law and the role of attorneys have been transformed through the use of processes such as mediation and collaborative law.

This book contains a balanced and in-depth analysis of family law. Because the tapestry of family law is complex, and because we believe that focus is an essential ingredient to learning, we have separated the subject of family law into specific topics that are organized as chapters. Each chapter is subdivided into discrete sections that often include hypothetical examples and illustrative explanations. Wherever possible, we have based our analysis and the examples and explanations on nationally accepted legal principles. However, because family law is so often state specific, the text contains contrasting perspectives from various jurisdictions. To eliminate confusion and to assist with family law research, we have included hundreds of citations to relevant state decisions and legislation associated with the principles under consideration.

We believe that this book provides a clear, well-organized, and efficient learning platform that will assist readers in understanding and appreciating the subject of family law.

Robert E. Oliphant
Nancy Ver Steegh
January 2010

Acknowledgments

We are thankful for the hard work, assistance, and encouragement of the generous people who have helped us complete three editions of this book. Foremost among our supporters in the development of the first edition were Aspen editors Lynn Churchill and Eric Holt. Taylor Kearns was likewise instrumental in the preparation of the updated second edition and Peter Skagestad assisted with the third edition.

William Mitchell College of Law and its administration have remained solid supporters of the project since its beginning, and for that we are grateful. Faculty Publication Specialists Linda Thorstad and Cal Bonde were tireless in helping us create the first edition. Ms. Thorstad took the lead in the production of the second edition with substantial proofreading assistance from Ms. Jennifer Miller. Ms. Bonde helped produce the third edition with proofreading assistance from Maureen Long. For their commitment to the project, we say, "Thank you for all your efforts."

Several research assistants worked with us on the first edition, including Mr. Arthur Boylan, Mr. Peter Hendricks, Mr. Chris Iijima, Ms. Katherine Kelly, and Ms. Tammy Schemmel. They were tireless in their cite checking and research. We also want to thank former William Mitchell Library Director Ann Bateson and Reference Librarian William Jack for their assistance with the earlier editions.

Our respective book widow and widower spouses, Susan Oliphant and Jack Ver Steegh, have been patient, tolerant, and supportive as we worked on the manuscripts for these editions. Thank you!

Robert E. Oliphant
Nancy Ver Steegh
January 2010

EXAMPLES&EXPLANATIONS

Family Law

CHAPTER 1

Marriage — History

1.1. Introduction

Family law principles and practices have centuries of custom and tradition associated with them, which may explain why change in some areas, such as allowing same-sex couples to marry, has generated such a strong emotional reaction. Other, less controversial issues, such as those associated with consanguinity prohibitions, can be traced to 1400 B.C., when under Mosaic law, a man was barred from marrying his mother, stepmother, sister, half-sister, granddaughter, or granddaughter-in-law. Even today, Mosaic law may occasionally influence the outcome of an issue in a family dispute. *See, e.g., Burns v. Burns*, 538 A.2d 438 (N.J. Super. Ct. 1987) (court ordering spouse to obtain a "get" so party could enter into a Jewish contract of marriage known as a "ketubbah").

The Bible has, no doubt, played a considerable role in the early development of family law in the United States. It is said that the Bible was "nothing short of the underlying fabric upon which American society was founded" and helped form the earliest colonial laws. John W. Welch, *Biblical Law in America: Historical Perspectives and Potentials for Reform*, 2002 BYU L. Rev. 611, 619 (2002). The theory that, when a couple marry, they become one and that "one" is the husband, most likely derives from the book of Genesis (Genesis 2:24), which states that a husband must leave the home of his parents to be joined to his wife, and "they shall become one flesh." This Biblical view of marriage is repeated by Paul in his Epistle to the Ephesians (Ephesians 5:31).

Traces of principles and practices of present American family law can also be found in Roman law, the canon law as developed by the English Ecclesiastical courts, and the early common law.

1.2. Marriage Evolves

Some believe that the concept of marriage began to evolve into a social institution as early as the period of Roman domination of Europe. *See* John Witte, Jr., *From Sacrament to Contract: Marriage, Religion and Law in the Western Tradition* 3, 20-21 (1997). During that early period, marriages were viewed as private rather than public matters, and there is little historical evidence suggesting that there was significant concern or control by governmental authorities over them. A systematic theology of marriage began to emerge as the Church of Rome provided a shape for it in the fourth and fifth centuries. *Id.* at 19-21.

In England, marriage regulation eventually fell under the control of the Ecclesiastical or Church courts. The Church claimed exclusive jurisdiction over what pertained to one's soul, salvation, and sanctification, which led to its conclusion that it had jurisdiction to deal with marriage and separation. The Church's jurisdictional view and its understanding of marriage were solidified by the thirteenth century.

From 1200 to 1500 A.D., the Church was recognized as the one universal sovereign that governed all of Christendom, and the canon law was the one universal law. Despite numerous amendments over the centuries, the thirteenth-century sacramental model of marriage remains, in some aspects, reasonably close to the heart of Catholic theology today.

1.3. Reformation, Divorce, and Blackstone

The sixteenth-century Protestant Reformation made a significant impact on how marriage and divorce were viewed. The Reformers rejected the Church's view that marriage was a sacrament, even though the concept of the indissoluble marriage had to some extent been mitigated by the law of annulment. Catholic teaching and canon law held that divorce meant only separation from bed and board, a divorce *a mensa et thoro*. The decree of divorce *a mensa et thoro* did not sever the marital tie — the parties remained husband and wife. The parties could not remarry during the lifetime of their spouse, and the husband was normally required to provide his wife with permanent support. The Reformers rejected this view of marriage, believing that divorce meant the termination, for cause, of one valid marriage with the right to contract another.

The feud between the Church and Henry VIII may also have influenced how marriage and divorce were eventually viewed. In England the canon law had provided the foundation for family law until Henry VIII broke with the Church when it refused to grant him a divorce in 1529. However, after he had made himself the head of the Church of England, little changed except for the slowly emerging view that marriage may no longer be a union for life.

Divorces were rare, and marriage continued to be viewed from a religious perspective as a gracious symbol of the divine, a social unit of the earthly kingdom, and a solemn covenant with one's spouse. Patrick McKinley, *Of Marriage and Monks, Community and Dialogue*, 48 Emory L.J. 689, 710 (1999).

Blackstone viewed marriage as the unity of a man and a woman into a single unit. He observed that by marriage "the husband and wife are one person in law: that is, the very being or legal existence is suspended during the marriage, or at least incorporated and consolidated into that of the husband." William Blackstone, *Commentaries on the Laws of England*, 442 (W. Lewis ed., 1897).

Example 1-1

Assume that P and D were married in a sixteenth-century ceremony by the clergy in London, England. Unfortunately, the relationship broke down and each came to hate the other. P sought to divorce D in the Ecclesiastical court. D agreed to the divorce. Would the Ecclesiastical court grant the couple a divorce?

Explanation

The Ecclesiastical court would not grant an absolute divorce. The Church took the view that there was a solemn covenant between the parties to marry, and no divorce, on any grounds, would be granted. P might attempt to seek an annulment of the marriage or ask for a decree of judicial separation, called divorce *a mensa et thoro* (divorce from bed and board). The decree of divorce *a mensa et thoro* did not sever the marital tie; the parties remained husband and wife. If granted by the Church court, the parties could not remarry during the lifetime of their spouse, and the husband was normally required to provide his wife with permanent support.

1.4. Colonial American Model of Marriage

The English canon and civil laws were often imported to this country by the early settlers. The settlers were aware that problems associated with marriage and divorce were governed by canon law in England and were exclusively within the jurisdiction of the Church's Ecclesiastical courts. 2 Pollock & Maitland, *History of English Law* (2d ed.) 366, 392-396.

During America's colonial period, "the principle objectives of marriage were wealth, social position, and love — usually in that order." John C. Miller, *This New Man, The American* 414 (1974). Most parents considered marriage a matter too serious to be left to the individuals directly concerned. Consequently, it was not uncommon for a young man to seek permission from the parents of a single young woman before he dated her. *Id.* at 413. Legally, the father of the girl had the right to permit or deny consent to marry. Eric Foner & John A. Garraty, *The Reader's Companion to American History* 700 (1991). Unwanted suitors were often effectively discouraged when a daughter's father let it be known that he intended to withhold financial assistance should his daughter seek to marry the undesirable male.

For the most part, when one married in colonial America, the marriage was intended to last forever, and the law reflected this view by making it difficult for married couples to divorce or separate. Stuart A. Queen, Robert W. Habenstein & Jill S. Quadagno, *The Family in Various Cultures* 214 (1985). For example, to keep marriages secure, husbands were penalized by expulsion from the Connecticut colony if they were estranged from their wives for more than three years. Jessica Kross et al., *American Eras, The Colonial Era* 278 (1998).

Slaves were not generally allowed to legally marry in most colonies, and where they were permitted to marry, the ceremony had to be approved and performed by the slave owner. Foner & Garraty, *supra* at 701. Racial intermarriage in most states was prohibited. For example, in Massachusetts in 1705, a marriage between a white person and a black person or mulatto was prohibited, and a person who violated this law could be fined £50.

1.5. Nineteenth-Century Patriarchic Model of Marriage

A hundred years ago, marriage in America was driven by rigid customs and centuries of religious tradition. Marriage was often viewed as a process to consolidate wealth and resources; occasionally it was used to cement political alliances. Marriage provided men with legal authority over their wives and children and identified the husband's legal heirs. The husband was the legal head of the household, responsible for its support and its links to external society. The wife was the mistress of the home, responsible for the day-to-day management of its internal affairs and the care and education of children. Divorces were, of course, rare, as were paternity actions and adoptions. The family was viewed as a single unit consisting of the mother, the father, and the children, with each member playing a well-defined role.

Early decisions reflected the nineteenth-century view that a husband had a life-long duty of support toward his wife. Therefore, should a divorce occur and the wife not be at fault, an ex-husband was normally required to provide for her for the rest of her life.

1.6. Moving Toward the Twenty-first Century

By the middle of the twentieth century, marriage and divorce were firmly in the grasp of state and religious institutions. State marriage license laws provided a premarital fitness criterion and instituted waiting periods designed to prevent hasty marriages. While common law marriages continued to exist in a handful of states, they were slowly being eliminated by legislatures who viewed them as frustrating state efforts to determine who could marry. Divorce laws raised challenging barriers to unhappy couples seeking to terminate their relationship and tended to reflect centuries of Christian influence on marriage and divorce.

Most point to the decade of the 1960s as the period when American culture began its remarkable rebellion against rigid marriage and divorce laws, customs, and traditions. The changes dramatically altered the face of family law. Associated with the changes was an increased involvement of courts and legislatures into almost every facet of family life. As a consequence, the body of family law studied and applied by judges and lawyers today is complex, exceedingly large, and constantly changing. In some instances, the law's complexity has generated specialists who apply their skills to a narrow area of family law. Concomitantly, specialized courts have been created in most jurisdictions that deal exclusively with family law issues.

Few dispute that the definitions of what constitutes a "family" and a "parent" have been radically altered during the last few decades. During this period, divorce became progressively more available to unhappy couples, and a traditional marriage no longer necessarily symbolized a "family." State legislatures and state courts began to show an increasing willingness to recognize civil unions between cohabiting same-sex couples. Notably, at least six jurisdictions now allow same-sex couples to legally marry.

Another factor influencing how "family" and "parent" are viewed today is the growing acceptance of cohabitation between couples who do not formally marry but live together much as husband and wife. In jurisdictions where common law marriages are not recognized, legislation and court decisions have provided these couples with property rights once thought never possible.

Children today may grow up in a traditional nuclear family consisting of two biological parents who share their children. However, it is increasingly common for children to grow up in households where there is only one parent — usually, but not always, the biological mother. They may also grow up in households with each divorced adult bringing children from an earlier marriage to the new marriage. Or, they may reside in a household where the parents are of the same sex.

Volumes of data from a variety of sources reflect the changes that have occurred in America's family structure. For example, by the early 1990s an estimated 15.5 million children were no longer living with two biological parents, and as many as 8 to 10 million children may have been born into families with a gay or lesbian parent. *See Alison D. v. Virginia M.*, 569 N.Y.S.2d 586, 589 (Judge Kay dissenting) (N.Y. Ct. App. 1991). Fewer persons are marrying than ever before; those who do marry are doing so later in life; and more marriages are ended by divorce than by death. The Census Bureau estimates that 25-year-olds marrying for the first time face a 52.5 percent chance overall that their marriage will end in divorce. Moreover, "about 50 percent of first marriages for men under age forty-five may end in divorce, and between 44 and 52 percent [of first marriages for women under age forty-five] may end in divorce." U.S. Census Bureau, U.S. Dep't of Commerce, Number, Timing, and Duration of Marriages and Divorces 18 (1996), available at *http://www.sipp.census.gov/sipp/p70s/p70-80.pdf*.

THE PRESENT VALUE OF MARRIAGE

1.7. The Debate

Today, eminent scholars debate the question of the value of marriage to this society — a question to which an irrefutable answer appears somewhat elusive. Professor Lynn Wardle, for example, suggests that marriage "is the best, most promising foundation for lasting, growing, individual, and family happiness and security. It also is the very seedbed of democracy. Home is the place where we get our first ideas about ourselves, our attitudes toward other people, and our habits of approaching and solving problems." Lynn E. Wardle, *The Bonds of Matrimony and the Bonds of Constitutional Democracy*, 32 Hofstra L. Rev. 349, 371 (2003).

Maggie Gallaher, President of the Institute for Marriage and Public Policy, wrote that "[m]arriage is an important social good, associated with an impressively broad array of positive outcomes for children and adults." 4 Ave Maria L.R. 409, 421 (Summer 2006). She suggests that children whose parents remarry do not experience the same well-being as those living in intact married families. She also suggests that children living with cohabiting parents or children in a single-parent home experience the same lower level of well-being.

Professor Martha Albertson Fineman, however, appears unconvinced. She suggests that "for all relevant and appropriate societal purposes, we do not need marriage, *per se*, at all. To state that we do not need marriage to accomplish many societal objectives is not the same thing as saying that we do not need a family to do so for some. However, family as a social category should not be dependent on having marriage as its core relationship. Nor is family synonymous with marriage." Martha Albertson Fineman, *Why Marriage?*, 9 Va. J. Soc. Pol'y & L. 239, 245 (2001).

Marriage Contracts — Requirements and Restrictions

TYPICAL STATE MARRIAGE REQUIREMENTS

2.1. How Marriage Contracts Differ from Ordinary Contracts

A marriage contract is viewed in law as being different from an ordinary civil contract. The distinction was recognized and discussed by the United States Supreme Court over 100 years ago in *Maynard v. Hill*, 125 U.S. 190 (1888). In *Maynard* the Court explained that marriage is an institution of society, founded upon consent and contract of the parties. It stated that marriage contracts differed from ordinary contracts because the rights, duties, and obligations of the parties rested not upon their agreement but upon the general common or statutory law of the state, which defined and prescribed those rights, duties, and obligations. The Court observed that parties can neither modify nor change a marriage contract without state intervention and the contract binds them to a lifelong relationship. The Court emphasized that marriage contracts may not be terminated by virtue of a simple agreement made solely between the two parties to it. The state always remains a third party and sets the grounds for ending the relationship.

A marriage contract can be created either by following criteria established by a state legislature by statute or, in a dwindling number of jurisdictions, by the parties' conduct. In the latter jurisdictions, the relationship creates a common law marriage. Such relationships are discussed in greater detail later in the chapter, but it is useful to note here that the courts in states

9

that recognize such marriages will usually require (1) an agreement of marriage in *praesenti*, (2) made by parties competent to contract, (3) accompanied and followed by cohabitation as husband and wife, (4) subsequently holding oneself out as being married, and (5) gaining a reputation as being married.

2.2. Capacity — Generally

To marry, one must have the state of mind and the capacity to marry. State of mind consists of voluntarily entering into the relationship with the intent to marry at that time (not a sham). Capacity generally, except where same-sex marriages are allowed, requires that the parties be of opposite gender (male-female), not be married to someone else (bigamy), not be related as defined by local statute, be of the age at which local law permits them to marry, and be capable of understanding the nature of the act.

The *Uniform Marriage and Divorce Act* (UMDA), §208(a)(1), states that a marriage is invalid if "a party lacked capacity to consent to the marriage at the time the marriage was solemnized, either because of mental incapacity or infirmity or because of the influence of alcohol, drugs, or other incapacitating substances, or duress, or by fraud involving the essentials of marriage." The issues of capacity and intent are often litigated in the context of annulment actions.

Example 2-1

Assume that P married D when P was 83 and the marriage took place less than a month before P's death from lung cancer. At the time of the marriage, P was heavily medicated, undergoing chemotherapy, and required the daily assistance of an in-home nurse. P was also hooked up to an oxygen tank during the wedding. Following P's death, P's estate brings an action contesting the marriage, claiming it was void because P did not have the capacity to consent to the marriage. How will a court most likely rule?

Explanation

A court will examine all of the facts surrounding the alleged marriage. Given the facts of this example, it is most likely that a court will find that P lacked the capacity to consent and the marriage is void. *See* In re Estate of Santolino, 895 A.2d 506 (N.J. Super. 2005); In re Estate of Crockett, 728 N.E.2d 765 (Ill. App. 5 Dist. 2000).

2.3. Capacity — Guardian's Consent

A guardian may consent to a marriage when the applicant is incompetent or is not of age to consent. *See Knight v. Radomski*, 414 A.2d 1211 (Me. 1980).

2.4. Capacity — Age Restrictions

The state has an interest in preventing unstable marriages among those who lack capacity to act in their own best interests. Consequently, states have established a minimum legal age for marriage that varies from jurisdiction to jurisdiction. For example, in most jurisdictions, a man and a woman 18 or older can marry without parental consent. With permission of the underage person's parents, guardian, or juvenile court, a person 16 or 17 years old may also marry in many jurisdictions. A few jurisdictions have allowed persons at 15 to marry with parental permission. A handful of states have allowed parties younger than 15 or 16 to marry without parental consent when the female is pregnant.

The UMDA, §205, has influenced how states treat the minimum age of marriage. The UMDA allows a court, upon examination of the parties, to approve certain underage marriages. It declares that after a reasonable effort has been made to notify the parents or guardians of each underage party, the court may order the clerk to issue a marriage license and a marriage certificate form when a party is 16 or 17 and has no parent capable of consenting to marriage.

In most jurisdictions, when there is a court-approved marriage, the judge must first find that the underage party is capable of assuming the responsibilities of marriage and, second, that marriage will serve his or her best interest. Pregnancy alone does not necessarily establish that the best interest of the party will be served by allowing a marriage.

Statutory age barriers have withstood constitutional challenge. *See, e.g., Moe v. Dinkins*, 533 F. Supp. 623 (S.D.N.Y. 1981), *aff'd*, 669 F.2d 67 (2d Cir.), *cert. denied*, 459 U.S. 827 (1982). When state statutes have been challenged on constitutional grounds, courts have asked whether there is a rational basis for the means selected by the legislature to establish the minimum age to marry and have examined the state interests allegedly advanced by the law. This is the lowest level of constitutional scrutiny applied to a statute. For example, in *Moe v. Dinkins*, a New York law that required the consent of a parent before a minor between ages 14 to 18 could marry was challenged as violating the fundamental right to marry. The court rejected the challenge concluding that the age restriction was rational because of the state's concern with unstable marriages and the inability of minors to make mature decisions. The court explained that the age restriction in the statute does not bar a marriage between the two applicants forever; rather, it delays their marriage until they can marry without parental consent.

Example 2-2

Assume that P, age 15, who is pregnant, desires to marry X, age 50, who is the father of the child. P's mother consents to the marriage. P's father, D, objects and relies on a statute in this jurisdiction that states that a minor "between the ages of 16 and 18 may marry with the consent of one parent and district court authorization." Assume that common law marriages have been abolished. The trial court held without explanation that the statute limiting marriage by age was unconstitutional and permitted P, age 15, to marry. D challenged the ruling on appeal. How will an appellate court most likely rule?

Explanation

The law is well settled that states have the right and power to establish reasonable limitations on the right to marry. This authority is justified as an exercise of police power, which confers upon the states the ability to enact laws to protect the safety, health, morals, and general welfare of society. The U.S. Supreme Court has held that parents have a fundamental liberty interest in the care, custody, and management of their children. Even though these rights are fundamental, they are not absolute. The state also has an interest in the welfare of children and may limit parental authority. In this example, there exists a rational relation between the means chosen by the legislature and legitimate state interests in adopting and enforcing the age restriction. In light of the important state interest in promoting the welfare of children by preventing unstable marriages among those lacking the capacity to act in their own best interests, the restriction would most likely be upheld as constitutional and the alleged marriage would be viewed as void.

Example 2-3

Assume that a state statute set the age to marry without parental consent at 18 for women and 19 for men. P (a man), age 18, wants to marry D (a woman), age 18, but P's parents refuse to consent to the marriage. P challenges the state statute on gender grounds. Most likely, how will a court rule on P's challenge?

Explanation

There has been a long-standing gender difference in this society between the age when men/boys and women/girls may marry. The common law allowed girls age 12, and boys age 14, to marry. The gender distinction was carried from the common law and placed in an altered form into most early state marriage statutes. However, the Supreme Court in *Stanton v. Stanton*, 421 U.S. 7 (1975), held that there was no "compelling State interest which justifies treating males and females of the same age differently for the purpose of determining their rights to a marriage license." In this example, the statute would be struck down as unconstitutional because of the gender difference and P would most likely be able to marry D.

Example 2-4

Assume that P and D desire to marry. P is 15, and D is 18. The jurisdiction where they intend to marry has abolished common law marriages and has adopted UMDA §§203-204. The UMDA allows a minor age 15 to 17 to marry with either parent's consent or after a finding that the minor is capable of assuming the responsibilities of marriage and that the marriage would be in the minor's best interests. Both P's and D's parents are opposed to the marriage. Despite the opposition, P and D petition the juvenile court for permission to marry. At the juvenile court hearing, evidence is introduced that P is not pregnant; she insisted that the two marry; she lives with her parents; and she is regularly attending high school as a sophomore. There was also evidence that D recently graduated from high school and has a full-time job at a local fast food restaurant. He has his own apartment and owns an older-model car. He has no outstanding debts. He stated he wanted to get married because he loved P and she wanted to get married. Most likely, how will a court rule on the request to allow the couple to marry?

Explanation

The court will consider whether both applicants understood or appreciated the duties and responsibilities of married life. Studies indicate that teenage marriages have a high rate of instability; teen marriages lead to decreased educational attainment for girls; and teen fathers earn less in early adulthood than males who delay parenting until after age 20. A court may consider the fact that P had proposed marriage to D, and to some extent, he may appear gallant in accepting the proposal. The opposition of both families to the marriage, the fact that P is not pregnant, and D's current employment all suggest that granting a marriage at this time is not in P's best interests. Most likely, the court will not allow the marriage.

Example 2-5

D and P decide to marry. D is 21 and has recently inherited a large sum of money and extensive real estate. P is 14. Both families approve of the marriage. The jurisdiction where they intend to marry has abolished common law marriages and has adopted UMDA §§203-204, which allow a minor age 15 to 17 to marry with either parent's consent or after a finding that the minor is capable of assuming the responsibilities of marriage and that the marriage would be in the minor's best interests. P lies about his age in order to obtain a marriage license, and the two are married in a public marriage ceremony. On their honeymoon, they are involved in a serious automobile accident and D dies. P now seeks his portion of her estate as her husband. The administrator of the estate contends he is not entitled to any of the estate because D was never legally married to P. How will a court most likely rule?

Explanation

A court will most likely rule in favor of the administrator. Common law marriages were abolished, and there is no statutory authority allowing the marriage. The relationship is void. If D had survived the car accident, it is possible that she would face criminal sexual misconduct charges.

Example 2-6

Assume that X, age 16, wants to marry Y, her 28-year-old high school civics teacher. Assume that X and Y cannot marry in state A, where they are living, because it prohibits marriages on any basis of persons under age 17. After consulting a lawyer, X, Y, and X's mother drive to state B, where they establish a legal basis to obtain a marriage license. Assume that the relevant statute reads in this jurisdiction as follows: "A court is authorized to permit a marriage of a person under 16 years old with consent of only one parent, in extraordinary circumstances in which marriage would serve best interests of minor." X's mother submits an affidavit in support of the marriage. It reads that she has "seen no other couple so right for each other," that they "have very real life plans at home, in the town in which we all reside," and that "their partnership and their talents will be most effectively utilized by this marriage." They obtain a court order, which allows them to marry if one parent agrees to the relationship. They are married with X's mother consent.

When they return to their home state (A), X's father, P, is outraged and he seeks and obtains ex parte temporary restraining order in the district court for the state of A. P is awarded immediate legal and physical custody of his daughter, X. Four days later, however, the court rescinds its order because it finds that X's marriage was valid under the law of state B and that X was emancipated as a result of the marriage.

P then brings an action in state B challenging the marriage. P argues that because the statute allows the court to approve the marriage of a person under the age of 16 with the consent of only one parent, he has been deprived of his fundamental right to the parent-child relationship without a compelling reason. P also argues that his procedural due process rights under the Constitution were infringed because he was not provided with notice, with an opportunity to be heard, or with an opportunity to object to his daughter's marriage before the court authorized it. Most likely, how will a court rule on P's challenge?

Explanation

When a similar problem came to the Nevada Supreme Court, it held that a statute that allowed a court to authorize the marriage of a person under 16 years old with consent of only one parent, in extraordinary circumstances and where the marriage would serve best interests of minor, did not violate substantive or procedural due process rights of father. *Kirkpatrick v. Eighth Judicial Dist. Court*, 64 P.3d 1056 (Nev. 2003). It said that there was no constitutional requirement that both parents be notified of the marriage. *Hodgson v. Minnesota*, 497 U.S. 417 (U.S. 1990). The court said that even though the other parent may have an interest in the minor's decision, and full communication is desirable, "[t]he State has no more interest in requiring all family members to talk with one another than it has in requiring certain of them to live together."

The court observed that states have the right and power to establish reasonable limitations on the right to marry. It said that this power is justified as an exercise of the police power, which confers upon the states the ability to enact laws in order to protect the safety, health, morals, and general welfare of society. It also said that there is "no one set of criteria that can be set forth as a litmus test to determine if a marriage will be successful. Neither is there a litmus test to determine whether a person is mature enough to enter a marriage. Age alone is an arbitrary factor. . . . The statute provides a safeguard against an erroneous marriage decision by the minor and the consenting parent, by giving the district court the discretion to withhold authorization if it finds that there are no extraordinary circumstances and/or the proposed marriage is not in the minor's best interest, regardless of parental consent. The statute strikes a balance between an arbitrary rule of age for marriage and accommodation of individual differences and circumstances."

Id. at 1060-1061. Here, although it is somewhat questionable that there are extraordinary circumstances, a trial judge's decision allowing (or rejecting) the marriage would most likely not be overturned.

2.5. Marriage License

Most jurisdictions impose specific statutory requirements on persons who intend to marry. For example, in all jurisdictions a couple intending to marry must first obtain a marriage license, which usually requires that one of the two persons seeking the license go to the office of a county or district clerk of court.

Once a license is obtained, most states impose a short waiting period between the date the marriage license is sought and the date of the marriage ceremony. The UMDA, §204, states that a marriage license becomes effective 3 days after it is issued and expires 180 days later. The waiting period may be waived or modified by a judge in an emergency or under extraordinary circumstances.

A few states take the view that strict compliance with state marriage statutes is mandatory, reasoning that they must guard against recognition of informal relationships. However, in a majority of jurisdictions, only substantial compliance with state marriage statutes is required for a valid marriage. These states reason that they should recognize the parties' reasonable expectations, even though there may be an imperfection in the marriage license or official application.

Although the procedures vary from jurisdiction to jurisdiction, it is common for a clerk to provide a party with a detailed questionnaire to be answered under oath. Once the clerk is satisfied that there is no legal impediment, a fee for administering and sending the required reports to the state is paid. Courts will distinguish between voiding a marriage consummated after the issuance of a marriage license because it was not solemnized and a marriage duly solemnized but deficient for the lack of a marriage license. *Compare Hames v. Hames*, 316 A.2d 379 (Conn. 1972), *with Carabetta v. Carabetta*, 438 A.2d 109 (Conn. 1980). The distinction between outcomes generally rests upon the specific language found in state statutes directly related to these subjects.

Example 2-7

Assume that P and D prepare a detailed agreement that they believe contains the important provisions regarding their contemplated future "marriage." They call a group of friends together, then read the agreement and sign it as a part of their "wedding" ceremony. Although they do not obtain a license to marry, it is clear that they fully intend the relationship to be that of husband

and wife and the marriage agreement to act as proof of their formal relationship. When the relationship breaks down a few months after they have lived together as husband and wife, P brings an action to dissolve the marriage and seeks to utilize the state's divorce statutes. D responds by arguing that there is no marriage for two reasons: First, this state does not recognize common law marriages, which is true. Second, the parties failed to comply with any of the state's statutory marriage requirements such as obtaining a marriage license. P replies that the parties intended to marry, and that the marriage contract was complete when the last party exchanged vows. How will a court most likely rule?

Explanation

A court will most likely rule that there never was a marriage. For legal recognition of a marriage, the parties must comply with a state's general requirements regarding a marriage application. Here, there is only an agreement between the parties to which the state was never a party. Consequently, the parties were never legally married and cannot benefit from divorce statutes designed by the state to guide and protect the parties when a marital relationship breaks down. Note that if this state recognized common law marriages, P would have been considered married and would have been able to utilize the state's divorce statutes. *See, e.g., Yaghoubinejad v. Haghighi*, 894 A.2d 1173 (N.J. Super. A.D. 2006).

2.6. Solemnizing a Marriage

Solemnizing a marriage serves several purposes. It provides public notice of the impending marriage and creates a permanent public record of the event. Solemnizing a marriage may also satisfy a religious tradition and may act to impress on the couple the seriousness of marriage.

The UMDA states that "[a] marriage may be solemnized by a judge of a court of record, by a public official whose powers include solemnization of marriages, or in accordance with any mode of solemnization recognized by any religious denomination, Indian Nation or Tribe, or Native Group." UMDA §206(a).

The U.S. Supreme Court held that common law marriages are valid, notwithstanding statutes that require ceremonial marriages to be solemnized by a minister or a magistrate, if no specific provision to the contrary exists. *Meister v. Moore*, 96 U.S. 76 (1877). As the Court explained, "No doubt, a statute may take away a common law right; but there is always a presumption that the legislature has no such intention, unless it be plainly expressed." *See* J.M.H. *v. Rouse*, 143 P.3d 1116 (Colo. App. 2006); *State v. Ward*, 28 S.E.2d 785 (S.C. 1944).

Example 2-8

Assume that P and D have decided to marry while D, the proposed groom, is very ill and confined to the hospital. The hospital chaplain, after checking with authorities, informs the couple that, in order to get married immediately, they are required to get a waiver of the three-day waiting period from a judge so that the license can be promptly issued. The parties decide to proceed with a ceremony that very day, despite the absence of a license. They intend to complete the paperwork following the ceremony. The parties are married by the hospital chaplain in an elaborate hospital ceremony; however, D dies one day following the ceremony. A marriage license is never obtained. Following D's death, P seeks an intestate share of D's estate. The relevant statute in this jurisdiction reads: "Previous to any marriage in this state, a license for that purpose shall be obtained from the officer authorized to issue the same, and no marriage hereafter contracted shall be recognized as valid unless the license has been previously obtained, and unless the marriage is solemnized by a person authorized by law to solemnize marriages." D's estate contends that no marriage existed because a license as required by state law was not obtained. P argues that the parties were married, as evidenced by the ceremony, and all that was needed was the license. She states that the witnesses at the marriage ceremony will testify that she and the deceased clearly intended to obtain a license a day or so after the ceremony. How will a court most likely rule on the validity of the marriage?

Explanation

A court that strictly relies on the above statutory language will most likely hold that there was not a legal marriage. Had D survived and later obtained and recorded a license, the court would recognize the marriage. *See Yun v. Yun*, 908 S.W.2d 787 (Mo. App. W.D. 1995). The most difficult obstacle that P had to overcome was the complete absence of a license (or even a belief that one existed.). *See Barbosa-Johnson v. Johnson*, 851 P.2d 866 (Ariz. App. 1993).

Example 2-9

Assume P and D obtain a marriage license in state X. State X has a statute declaring that marriages solemnized in another state or country are invalid under X's law when parties residing in X intend to evade X's marriage laws by going to another state or country for solemnization. After obtaining a marriage license in state X, P and D fly to Puerto Rico for a vacation. During the vacation, they have their marriage solemnized by a local pastor. They then return to state X and file their license with the clerk of court. Three years later, P files a petition to divorce D in state X. D replies to the divorce petition that P and D were never married under the laws of X because the marriage was solemnized outside that jurisdiction. D asks that the action be dismissed. Other than the testimony regarding the intent to vacation in Puerto Rico, there is no evidence suggesting an effort to evade X's marriage laws. How will a court most likely rule on the validity of the marriage?

Explanation

A court will most likely take a practical approach to this problem and rule that the marriage is valid. From a judicial perspective, little is gained by ruling that the marriage was void after the parties lived together as husband and wife for three years. Moreover, there is nothing to suggest that the couple intentionally flew to Puerto Rico to evade the laws of X. *See McPeek v. McCardle,* 888 N.E.2d 171 (Ind. 2008) (where a couple complied with Indiana's statutory requirements regarding marriage licenses, certificates, and solemnization, such that the marriage would have been valid if solemnized in Indiana, Indiana will recognize the marriage as valid even if the marriage ceremony took place in another state and did not comply with that state's law or public policy); *Barbosa-Johnson v. Johnson,* 851 P.2d 866 (Ariz. Ct. App. 1993).

2.7. Premarital Medical Testing

The Supreme Court observed nearly 50 years ago that "[t]he blood test procedure has become routine in our everyday life. It is a ritual for those going into the military service as well as those applying for marriage licenses. Many colleges require such tests before permitting entrance and literally millions of us have voluntarily gone through the same . . . routine in becoming blood donors." *Breithaupt v. Abram,* 352 U.S. 432, 436, 448 (1957).

Several states require that a marriage license applicant file a health certificate with the licensing authority. The requirements vary among states, with some asking that applicants certify that they have submitted to a medical examination and do not have a venereal disease, or, if infected, that they are not in a communicable state. Some states also require tests for measles for female applicants. *See generally People v. Smith,* 23 Cal. Rptr. 5 (Cal. App. 1962); *Hall v. Hall,* 108 S.E.2d 487 (N.C. 1959); *Peterson v. Widule,* 147 N.W. 966 (Wis. 1914) (upon application for a marriage license the male party to such marriage must, within 15 days prior to the application, be examined by a physician of designated qualifications with reference to the existence or nonexistence of any venereal disease).

The issue of whether a couple may be compelled to undergo compulsory medical testing before they can marry remains open. The UMDA states that "[t]he premarital medical examination requirements serve either to inform the prospective spouse of health hazards that may have an impact on marriage, or to warn public health officials of venereal disease." UMDA §203. The UMDA, however, makes the requirement of a medical examination optional.

In 1987 the Illinois legislature mandated that all marriage license applicants be tested for exposure to the AIDS virus. A year after its enactment, the number of marriage licenses issued in the state dropped by 25 percent as many couples either went out of state to be married or simply declined to get married. Jana B. Singer, *The Privatization of Family Law*, 1992 Wis. L. Rev. 1443 n.115. "Of the 221,000 people married in Illinois during the first 18 months of the statute's operation, only 44 tested positive for HIV exposure. In June 1989, the legislature repealed the testing requirement." Isabel Wilkerson, *Prenuptial Tests for AIDS Repealed*, N.Y. Times, A6 (June, 24, 1989). Louisiana similarly mandated premarital AIDS testing for a brief period of time but repealed that requirement along with other medical testing requirements in 1988. *See* La. Rev. Stat. Ann. §9:230-31 (West Supp. 1988) (repealed 1988). *Id.*

A Utah statute that prohibited marriage by a person afflicted with AIDS was ruled invalid because it was in conflict with the Americans with Disabilities Act. *See T.E.P. v. Leavitt*, 840 F. Supp. 110 (D. Utah 1993). In *Matter of Kilpatrick*, 375 S.E.2d 794 (W. Va. 1988), a couple wishing to marry were ordained ministers of the Universal Life Church and challenged the constitutionality of a state statute requiring them to undergo serological tests, claiming that it violated the Free Exercise Clause because it required them to disobey the canon law of their church in order to marry. The state responded that there were three compelling reasons for the test: (1) detection of a communicable disease (syphilis); (2) protection of the health interests of prenuptial couples; and (3) protection of the interests of the future children of the married couple. The court held that the Free Exercise Clauses of the federal and state constitutions were not violated.

Example 2-10

Assume that P and P2 apply for a marriage license in state X. State X requires both to undergo a blood test to determine whether either has a venereal disease. P and P2 refuse to take the required test and challenge the requirement, arguing that this test violates the Free Exercise Clause of the First Amendment to the U.S. Constitution. They contend that because the test requires the removal of blood from the body, which is a violation of a canon law of their church, the state is barred from applying the statute to them. How will a court most likely rule?

Explanation

The court will most likely require that the parties take the test. A majority of jurisdictions have similar statutory provisions requiring tests for venereal disease, tuberculosis, mental incompetence, rubella immunity, or sickle cell anemia. *See* Homer H. Clark, *The Law of Domestic Relations in the United States* §2.11 (2d ed. 1987). These provisions have sustained constitutional attack.

2.8. Premarital Counseling and Education

The seriousness of marriage makes adequate premarital counseling and education for family living highly desirable. Premarital counseling is viewed as one way to prevent unwise, hasty marriages. Some jurisdictions have proposed reducing marriage license fees for couples who have received premarital education. Where premarital education legislation is in force, it will normally specify that the topics include a discussion of the seriousness of marriage, conflict management skills, and encouragement of counseling should the marriage fall into difficulty. The education is usually provided by a member of the clergy, a person authorized by law to perform marriages, or a marriage and family therapist.

2.9. Form of Marriage — Ministerial Act

"Ministerial" describes a governmental decision involving little or no personal judgment by the public official as to the wisdom or manner of carrying out the project. Absent specific legislation mandating that the claimed marital relationship is void, courts are reluctant to invalidate a marriage merely because certain formal ministerial requirements were not met. This is especially true when the couple have lived together for several years in the belief they were legally married.

Example 2-11

Assume that P and D decide to marry and that P obtains a marriage license, which must be completed and returned to the county clerk's office within 60 days of the wedding ceremony. After obtaining the license, they go through with their marriage ceremony, which is presided over by a minister. The license is signed, but P fails to return it to the local clerk's office for filing. Ten months later, the two break up. D seeks a divorce and

P responds that there was never a marriage because the license was never properly filed with the county clerk. How should a court rule on this question?

Explanation

A court will most likely rule that the failure to do a ministerial act, such as returning the marriage license to the county clerk within 60 days of its issuance, cannot render a marriage void and does not by itself defeat the existence of the alleged marriage. *See In re Estate of Mirizzi*, 723 N.Y.S.2d 623 (N.Y. Sur. 2001) (entry of judgment of divorce was mere ministerial act); *Barbosa-Johnson v. Johnson*, 851 P.2d 866 (Ariz. App. 1993) (pastor who performed marriage ceremony in Puerto Rico failing to file marriage license in violation of Arizona statute did not, alone, invalidate marriage under Arizona law); *Wright v. State*, 81 A.2d 602 (Md. 1951) (certified copy of an official record of a marriage is not the only means of establishing marriage); *In re Parson's Estate*, 59 A.2d 709 (Del. Super. 1948) (parties participated in ceremony with witnesses and "the possibility of the existence of a license may be surmised," said the court, "for she described the production and signing of certain documents and we cannot absolutely assume that because no record of the marriage exists, our system of records is so perfect as to preclude the possibility of error in recording the issuance of a license"); *Fryar v. Roberts*, 57 S.W.3d 727 (Ark. 2001) (failure to do a ministerial act, such as returning the marriage license to the county clerk within 60 days of its issuance, cannot, by itself, render a marriage void).

COMMON LAW MARRIAGES

2.10. Common Law Marriage Defined; Presumed

A common law marriage is usually defined as a marriage created by the express agreement of the parties without ceremony, and often without a witness. It is an agreement in words — not *in futuro* or *in postea*, but *in praesenti*, uttered with a view and for the purpose of establishing the relationship of husband and wife. No specific form of words is needed, and all that is essential is proof of an agreement to enter into the legal relationship of marriage at the present time. Capacity and mutual consent are essential to a common law marriage.

The elements of a common law marriage generally include: (1) an agreement of marriage *in praesenti*, (2) made by parties competent to contract, (3) accompanied and followed by cohabitation as husband and wife,

(4) subsequently holding oneself out as being married, and (5) gaining a reputation as being married. All five elements must usually be proven, although whether the proof must be clear and convincing or merely a preponderance varies among jurisdictions. *See, e.g., Nestor v. Nestor,* 472 N.E.2d 1091 (Ohio 1984) (clear and convincing); *Callen v. Callen,* 620 S.E.2d 59 (S.C. 2005) (preponderance). Although it is typically required that there be a holding out that the parties are married to those with whom they normally come in contact, a common law marriage will not necessarily be defeated if all persons in the community within which the parties reside are not aware of the marital arrangement. Note, however, that decisions have consistently held that merely living together for a period of time does not support the common law marriage relationship. *In re Thomas' Estate,* 367 N.Y.S.2d 182 (N.Y. Sur. 1975).

When the parties are otherwise disabled from testifying regarding the creation of a contract *verba in praesenti,* or when there is a conflict in the evidence regarding the agreement, courts may apply a rebuttable presumption favoring the marriage if sufficient proof is presented of cohabitation and reputation of marriage. *Jeanes v. Jeanes,* 177 S.E.2d 537, 539-540 (S.C. 1970). This presumption may be overcome by "strong, cogent" evidence that the parties in fact never agreed to marry. *Id.* at 540.

2.11. History of Common Law Marriage

"Common law marriage" is a misnomer. Common law marriage probably did not exist in England, the home of the common law. The concept arose in "English Ecclesiastical courts, which administered canon law, rather than in the English common-law courts." John B. Crawley, *Is the Honeymoon Over for Common Law Marriage: A Consideration of the Continued Viability of the Common Law Marriage Doctrine,* 29 Cumb. L. Rev. 399, 401 (1998/1999).

In medieval England and the American frontier it was often impossible for couples wanting to marry to find authorized persons to issue marriage licenses and perform ceremonies. *See Crawley, supra* at 403. Common law marriage was viewed as a means of solving these difficulties.

New York was apparently the first state to recognize that marriages that were not solemnized could be treated under certain circumstances as common law marriages. *See Fenton v. Reed,* 52 N.Y. Sup. (1809) (per curiam). By the end of the nineteenth century, a majority of states recognized unsolemnized, long-term sexual unions as common law marriages. *See* David F. Crabtree, *Development, Recognition of Common-Law Marriages,* 1988 Utah L. Rev. 273, 275 n.12 (listing 34 states, as of 1931, recognizing common law marriages).

The U.S. Supreme Court considered the validity of common law marriage in *Jewell's Lessee v. Jewell,* 42 U.S. 219 (1843). With only eight justices sitting, the Court evenly divided on whether the relationship between the deceased and the surviving companion constituted a valid marriage. Finally, in 1877, the Court recognized a growing acceptance among states of common law marriages and approved the concept. *Meister v. Moore*, 96 U.S. 76 (1877).

Where recognized, a common law marriage provides an informal marriage relationship with legal standing. Common law marriage generally involves a nonceremonial relationship that requires "a positive mutual agreement, permanent and exclusive of all others, to enter into a marriage relationship, cohabitation sufficient to warrant a fulfillment of necessary relationship of man and wife, and an assumption of marital duties and obligations." *Black's Law Dictionary* 277 (6th ed. 1990). When the requisites for common law marriage have been met, a common law spouse is considered a legal spouse. Common law marriages are nearly identical in legal standing to licensed formal marriages.

Only nine states (Alabama, Colorado, Kansas, Rhode Island, South Carolina, Iowa, Montana, Oklahoma, and Texas) and the District of Columbia recognize common law marriages contracted within their borders. National Conference of State Legislatures, *Common Law Marriage*, http://www.ncsl.org/programs/cyf/commonlaw.htm (last visited April 10, 2009). Five states have "grandfathered" common law marriage (Georgia, Idaho, Ohio, Oklahoma, and Pennsylvania) and recognize common law marriages established before a certain date. New Hampshire recognizes common law marriage only for purposes of probate, and Utah recognizes common law marriages only if they have been validated by a court or administrative order. *Id.*

Example 2-12

Assume that P and D reside in a jurisdiction that recognizes common law marriages. They never had a ceremonial marriage, did not live together on a regular basis, and generally kept the claimed relationship secret, although occasionally they told close friends they were married. They often had sexual relations. When D died, P sought his intestate share of her estate as her common law husband. Will P be successful?

Explanation

P will not be successful. A common law marriage requires that the parties agree to be married, live together after the agreement as husband and wife, and represent to others that they are married. P and D did not hold themselves out to the community as husband and wife, did not cohabit together on a regular basis, and apparently did not have a present agreement to marry. Isolated references to close friends that they were husband and wife, without more, will not persuade most courts that there was a common law marriage. *Matter of Estate of Giessel*, 734 S.W.2d 27 (Tex. App. 1987).

Example 2-13

P and D reside in a jurisdiction that recognizes common law marriages. They have agreed that they are husband and wife, and their reputation in the community is that of husband and wife. They are concerned, however, that without a proper church ceremony their relationship will not be legally recognized. They plan such a ceremony, but before it occurs D dies. P now seeks her intestate share of D's estate as his wife. Will P be successful?

Explanation

Most likely a court will recognize the relationship as a common law marriage. They had an agreement in *praesenti* to be husband and wife, lived together, and held themselves out to the community as such. There is no common law requirement that they go through a formal wedding ceremony before a court will recognize the relationship. P will most likely be successful in persuading a court that she is D's common law wife.

Example 2-14

Assume that college students P, age 19, and D, age 21, resided in a jurisdiction that recognizes common law marriages. When D unexpectedly died in a motorcycle accident, P sought her intestate share of D's estate as his common law wife. P testified at the probate hearing that they had agreed to be husband and wife and had been living together for six months. One of P's friends testified that P told her once or twice that P and D were secretly married. The estate produced evidence that P used her own name in school and publicly represented to her peers at school and at work that she was a single person. It also produced evidence that P usually stayed with D on weekends but had her own apartment. How will a court rule?

Explanation

In a case similar to these facts, the Supreme Court of Texas held that there was insufficient evidence to support a common law marriage. It found an absence of evidence indicating they had ever moved into or occupied publicly a common residence or room. They did not have a reputation in the community as husband and wife, and P continued using her own name and publicly represented to those at her school and at her place of work that she was a single person. She did not establish that the couple lived together as man and wife or that they held themselves out to the public that they were man and wife. *Ex parte Threet*, 333 S.W.2d 361 (Tex. 1960).

2.12. Common Law Age to Marry

Under the common law, males at the age of 14 and females at the age of 12 could marry. The consent of their parents was not necessary to the validity of the marriage. *See In re Pace*, 989 P.2d 297 (1999); *Bennett v. Smith*, 1856 WL 6412 (N.Y. Sup. 1856). A state legislature has a right, of course, to abrogate common law marriage and set the minimum age of consent to marry. *State ex rel. Schneider v. Liggett*, 576 P.2d 221 (1978).

Example 2-15

Assume that D, age 41, and P, age 15, fall in love and P moves in and begins living with D in state X. They declare that they intend to be "married the rest of our lives." Under the common law, the couple would be viewed as husband and wife. Also assume that state X enacted legislation regarding the age to marry that reads in part: "The Uniform Marriage Act of this State sets forth the rules and requirements for ceremonial marriages. The Act reflects the legislative purposes of strengthening and preserving the integrity of marriage and safeguarding meaningful family relationships." The legislation provides procedures for the solemnization and registration of marriages and contains a final section stating that "nothing in this section shall be deemed to repeal or render invalid any otherwise valid common law marriage between one man and one woman." The statutory age of consent for marriage under this legislation is 18. The legislation also allows persons between 16 and 18 years to marry if they obtain parental consent or, if that is not possible, judicial approval. Can D and P marry under the common law in this jurisdiction?

Explanation

Despite the statutory language, a court may well consider the parties married under the common law. The age of consent under the common law in most jurisdictions was set at 14 for a male and 12 for a female, so the ages of P and D pose no issue. P and D will argue that the statute fails to clearly modify or abrogate the existing common law in the state, and therefore common law marriages can continue. Those opposed to common law marriage will argue that the legislature intended to grandfather existing common law relationships but prevent future ones. Under this reading of the statute, P and D cannot marry under the common law. This question requires close scrutiny; however, because of the ambiguity of the language in the statute, P and D can most likely marry under the common law.

Example 2-16

Assume that P and D reside in a jurisdiction that *does not recognize* common law marriages. They consider themselves husband and wife. They give each other wedding anniversary gifts, they live together, and P takes D's surname. Their friends are all told they are married. When D dies, P seeks his intestate share of D's estate as a surviving spouse.

The evidence presented to the probate judge showed that the couple had annually visited another state on vacation for three weeks for 15 consecutive years. This state recognizes common law marriages. During these visits, they lived together and held themselves out as a married couple to their families and friends. Will a court recognize the out-of-state common law marriage and allow P to recover a portion of the estate as a surviving spouse?

Explanation

P will ask that the forum where the action is brought to apply the rule of *lex loci*. Under this rule, a marriage valid where performed is valid everywhere, and P relies on the three-week visits over a 15-year period to prove that P and D were married under the common law. P provides the judge with citations to cases where some courts have said that they will recognize common law marriages consummated in another state, even though such marriages cannot be consummated in the forum state. *Mission Ins. Co. v. Industrial Comm'n*, 559 P.2d 1085 (Ariz. 1976); *Jennings v. Jennings*, 315 A.2d 816 (Md. 1974); *Gallegos v. Wilkerson*, 445 P.2d 970 (N.M. 1968).

The estate will argue that the above decisions involved a situation where a common law marriage was consummated while the parties were residents of the common law state. Here, P and D were residents of the forum state at all times.

Both sides will present additional authority to support their positions. A few jurisdictions have concluded that residents of a state that prohibits common law marriages may temporarily leave the state without taking up a new residence and consummate a common law marriage elsewhere that will be recognized in the forum state. *See Lieblein v. Charles Chips, Inc.*, 32 A.D.2d 1016 (N.Y. 1969), aff'd 271 N.E.2d 234 (N.Y. 1971). On the other hand, a few jurisdictions have indicated they will not recognize common law marriages consummated while residents temporarily leave the state, where the law of the forum state invalidates common law marriages. *See Metropolitan Life Ins. Co. v. Chase*, 294 F.2d 500, 503 (3d Cir. 1961) (applying New Jersey law); *Peirce v. Peirce*, 39 N.E.2d 990 (Ill. 1942); *Winn v. Wiggins*, 135 A.2d 673 (N.J. Super. 1957). This is especially true if there is a statute in the forum state that expressly invalidates common law marriages entered into by residents while living temporarily in another state. *In re Vetas' Estate*, 170 P.2d 183 (Utah 1946); *In re Van Schaick's Estate*, 40 N.W.2d 588 (Wis. 1949).

A court may be persuaded to find for P by totaling the days the couple lived as husband and wife outside the forum and consider that the time is sufficient to potentially justify finding a common law marriage. Additional evidence will have to be produced showing that they cohabited the entire time and continually held themselves out as husband and wife. The outcome will turn on the particular view of the forum jurisdiction toward short-term stays in common law jurisdictions.

2.13. Common Law Marriage Concept Declines

It is believed that judicial recognition of common law marriages was a historical necessity because the social conditions of early pioneer society made access to clergy or public officials difficult. However, as social and economic conditions changed, so did the attitude of legislatures and courts toward common law marriages. They began to suggest that common law marriage claims were a fruitful source of fraud and perjury, condoning vice, debasing conventional marriage, and no longer necessary with increased access to clergy and justices of the peace. *See Furth v. Furth*, 133 S.W. 1037, 1038-1039 (Ark. 1911); *Owens v. Bentley*, 14 A.2d 391, 393 (Del. Super. 1940). Courts began to require higher degrees of proof when common law marriages were claimed to exist, and they examined a professed contract with "great scrutiny." Courts also began to place a "heavy burden" on the proponent of a claimed common law marriage to prove its existence. *See, e.g., Manifredi Estate*, 399 Pa. 285, 292 (Pa. 1960). In response to repeated criticism, legislatures began to eliminate them. Today, only a handful of jurisdictions recognize common law marriages.

2.14. Should the Common Law Marriage Concept Be Revived?

Proponents of reviving common law marriages claim that they protect the interests of poor and minority women more effectively than any of the theories suggested to address the problems created by its absence. They also claim that most of the original reasons used to support the abolition of common law marriage — fear of fraud, protection of morality and the family, racism, eugenics, and health-related reasons — no longer withstand careful scrutiny. Furthermore, proponents claim that recognition of common law relationships will protect children better than paternity actions. *See* Sonya C. Garza, *Common Law Marriage: A Proposal for the Revival of a*

Dying Doctrine, 40 New Eng. L. Rev. 541 (2006); Cynthia Grant Bowman, *Feminist Proposal to Bring Back Common Law Marriage*, 75 Or. L. Rev. 709 (1996).

Example 2-17

Assume that P and D lived together for five years in state X, which recognizes common law marriages. However, P and D did not hold themselves out as husband and wife. They moved to another state, and that state does not recognize common law marriages. When D died in an industrial accident two years after moving to the new state, P sought to claim workers' compensation benefits as a "surviving spouse and seeks a declaratory judgment that she and D were married under the common law of state X, which would then make her eligible for coverage under the state act. P testifies that she and D had agreed to be husband and wife "but didn't make a big deal about it." A witness testifies for the state that P and D never used the same last name, did not have any joint savings or checking accounts, and did not jointly own any real or personal property. How will a court most likely rule?

Explanation

A court will examine the facts carefully. Although the parties were apparently competent to make a common law marriage contract, the only evidence is P's testimony that such a contract was made in *praesenti*. However, much of the evidence indicates they were living more like boyfriend and girlfriend than husband and wife. In particular, the complete separation of funds suggests they were not husband and wife. Finally, it is conceded they did not hold themselves out to the community as husband and wife and were not treated and reputed in the community as husband and wife. Most likely, a court would find on these facts that a common law marriage did not exist. *See Smith v. Smith*, 966 A.2d 109 (R.I. 2009) (alleged wife failed to prove the existence of a common law marriage where majority of friends and family and those individuals that constituted their community did not believe they were married; none of alleged husband's family members testified they believed alleged husband and alleged wife were married; and, other than in alleged wife's business, in which she used alleged husband's surname, public records and private accounts were in parties' own names as single persons).

2.15. *Lex Loci*

The Full Faith and Credit Clause of the Constitution and the *lex loci* concept appear closely related. *Lex loci actus* is defined as "[t]he law of the place where the act was done." *Black's Law Dictionary* 911 (6th ed. 1990). For example, *lex loci* requires that the existence of a common law marriage be recognized outside the borders of states that do not otherwise recognize such relationships. This is important because, as a general principle, the validity of a marriage is determined by the law of the forum in which it was celebrated, the *lex loci*.

Furthermore, the U.S. Constitution requires that every state accord "Full Faith and Credit" to the laws of its sister states. Consequently, a common law marriage that is validly contracted in a state where such marriages are legal will be valid even in states where such marriages cannot be contracted. This is true even if there is a strong policy in the new state against common law marriage. *See, e.g., Kelderhaus v. Kelderhaus*, 467 S.E.2d 303 (1996); *Carpenter v. Carpenter*, 617 N.Y.S.2d 903 (1994); *Mott v. Duncan Petroleum Trans.*, 414 N.E.2d 657 (1980); *Netecke v. Louisiana*, 715 So. 2d 449 (La. App. 1998).

PUTATIVE SPOUSE DOCTRINE

2.16. Putative Marriage Doctrine — History

Most jurisdictions have adopted either by statute or by common law the "putative marriage doctrine." Under this doctrine, a spouse who believed in good faith that he or she was validly married, and who participated in a ceremonial marriage, is allowed to use a state's divorce provisions even though the marriage is found to be void because of an impediment. *See* Christopher L. Blakesley, *The Putative Marriage Doctrine*, 60 Tul. L. Rev. 1, 6 (1985). The putative marriage doctrine is intended to protect a party who is ignorant of an impediment that makes the marriage either void or voidable. In addition to putative spouse legislation found in many jurisdictions, the doctrine is recognized by the Social Security Act. *See Estate of Leslie*, 207 Cal. Rptr. 561, 567-568 (Cal. 1984). Courts normally grant equitable relief where putative spousehood is recognized.

Putative spousehood terminates upon a party's loss of a good-faith belief that he or she is married. A putative marriage is not a marriage; therefore, one normally need not seek an annulment or divorce to terminate a putative relationship.

2.17. Putative Marriage Doctrine — UMDA

The UMDA has been influential in the development of the putative marriage doctrine. The UMDA states that

> [a]ny person who has cohabited with another to whom he is not legally married in the good faith belief that he was married to that person is a putative

spouse until knowledge of the fact that he is not legally married terminates his status and prevents acquisition of further rights. A putative spouse acquires the rights conferred upon a legal spouse, including the right to maintenance following termination of his status, whether or not the marriage is prohibited or declared invalid. If there is a legal spouse or other putative spouses, rights acquired by a putative spouse do not supersede the rights of the legal spouse or those acquired by the other putative spouses, but the court shall apportion property, maintenance, and support rights among the claimants as appropriate in the circumstances and in the interests of justice.

UMDA §209, 9A U.L.A. 192 (1998).

Example 2-18

Assume that P and D begin living together at a time when D is still married to X. P is aware of D's marital status. P and D continue to live together for several years. D dies without ever having obtained a divorce from X. During the time P and D lived together in this jurisdiction, which is one that recognizes common law marriages, P and D held themselves out to the community as husband and wife. They used the same surname, jointly signed notes, opened joint bank accounts, and otherwise held themselves out as husband and wife. P asserts two arguments: First, she claims that she and D had a common law marriage and that she should participate in D's estate as his widow. Second, P claims that if the court rejects her initial argument, then it should view her as a surviving spouse under the putative spouse doctrine.

Explanation

D has a preexisting impediment to a common law marriage (D was married to X and never divorced), and P had knowledge of the impediment. P's argument that she was D's common law wife will fail. P will also fail in her second claim as D's putative spouse. Only if P did not have knowledge of the impediment and had lived with D in the good faith belief that they were married under the state's common law doctrine, could P claim a share of D's estate as a putative spouse. P cannot claim a share of the estate under the putative spouse doctrine because she was aware of the impediment. A court will most likely reject both claims.

Example 2-19

Assume that D marries X, joins the National Guard, and is dispatched for an eight-month assignment in Iraq. D meets P, a corporal in another Guard unit, and they marry. D never informs P that he is still married to X.

P becomes suspicious when certain benefits due the spouse of a person in the military do not arrive. After a little investigation, she discovers that D is still married. P brings a divorce action, and D brings a motion to dismiss. In a jurisdiction with a typical UMDA putative spouse statute, how will the court handle the matter?

Explanation

P should prevail as a putative spouse. P entered the marriage with D in good faith and without any knowledge that D was still married. P can inherit from D, receive support and marital property, and sue for the wrongful death of D. In making an award, the court will also consider X's interests as D's legal wife.

2.18. Putative Spouse — Community Property Jurisdictions

In a community property state such as California, as between a putative spouse and the other spouse, or as between the surviving putative spouse and the heirs of his or her decedent other than the decedent's surviving legal spouse, the putative spouse is entitled to share in the property accumulated by the partners during their void or voidable marriage. It is also settled that the share to which the putative spouse is entitled is the same share of the quasi-marital property as the spouse would receive as an actual and legal spouse if there had been a valid marriage; that is, it shall be divided equally between the parties. *Estate of Leslie*, 689 P.2d 133 (Cal. 1984). The proportionate contribution of each of the parties to the property acquired during the void or voidable union is immaterial in this state because it is divided as community property and would be divided upon the dissolution of a valid marriage. *See Estate of Hafner*, 229 Cal. Rptr. 676 (Cal. App. 1986) (as between a surviving, innocent wife and the children of bigamous husband, and the surviving, innocent putative spouse, one half of estate awarded to surviving wife and children of decedent for distribution pursuant to probate code and one half awarded to surviving putative spouse as quasi-marital property).

Example 2-20

Assume that P and D married in California. The relationship later broke down, the parties separated, and D informed P that he had begun their divorce. P answered D's dissolution petition and subsequently signed a Marital Termination Agreement. However, during the period of separation, the couple decided to get back together. D explained to P that the divorce was never finalized when in fact a judgment and decree had been entered divorcing them. They continued to live together as husband and wife for the next two years until D died. D's children from a former marriage challenge any right of P to share in D's estate. P argues that the state statute allows her to take her widow's share. The statute reads as follows: "Whenever a determination is made that a marriage is void or voidable and the Court finds that either party or both parties believed in good faith that the marriage was valid, the Court shall declare such party or parties to have the status of a putative spouse." How will a court most likely treat the challenge?

Explanation

Although the putative spouse principle is usually applied in situations in which a ceremonial marriage becomes void or voidable, most courts would interpret the language of the statute (or the common law if no statute exists) to allow P to recover. Here, P continued to live with a former spouse in good faith ignorance of a divorce and will most likely be deemed to be a putative spouse. *In re Marriage of Monti*, 185 Cal. Rptr. 72 (Cal. 1982); *Manker v. Manker*, 644 N.W.2d 522 (Neb. 2002).

Example 2-21

Assume that P and D reside in a jurisdiction that has enacted a Domestic Partner Act that "extends to registered domestic partners substantially all rights, benefits, and obligations of married persons under state law, with the exception of rights, benefits, and obligations accorded only to married persons by federal law, the State Constitution, or initiative statutes." P presented D with a partnership agreement required by state law, and P completed it. P relied on D to complete the registration process by filing it with the state after they signed and had notarized the necessary documents. However, D failed to do so and left the documents in the trunk of D's car. D dies several months later. P claims his right to property under the agreement as a putative spouse. D's estate opposes stating that the doctrine is only applicable to heterosexual allegedly married husbands and wives. Most likely, how will a court rule?

Explanation

In a decision similar to the facts of the above example, a California Court of Appeals ruled that a person in P's position could pursue his claim as a putative domestic partner and seek whatever benefits allowed by the Domestic Partner Act. The court concluded that a person with a reasonable, good faith belief in the validity of his or her registered domestic partnership is entitled to protection as a putative registered domestic partner, even if the domestic partnership was not properly registered. *In re Domestic Partnership of Ellis*, 76 Cal. Rptr. 3d 401 (Cal. App. 4 Dist. 2008).

FORMS OF MARRIAGE

2.19. Proxy Marriage

A proxy marriage has been defined as "[a] marriage contracted or celebrated through agents acting on behalf of one or both parties. A proxy marriage differs from the more conventional ceremony only in that one or both of the contracting parties are represented by an agent[,] all the other requirements having been met." *State v. Anderson*, 396 P.2d 558, 561 (Or. 1964). *Black's Law Dictionary* 995 (8th ed. 2004) defines a proxy marriage as "[a] wedding in which someone stands in for an absent bride or groom, as when one party is stationed overseas in the military."

Proxy marriage has an interesting history. The Catholic Church historically insisted that the parties to a marriage exchange consent face-to-face in the presence of the Church. However, the failure to observe this requirement did not render the marriage void because Pope Innocent III accepted the Roman view that marriage could be consented to by messenger. *See* Ernest G. Lorenzen, *Marriage by Proxy and the Conflict of Laws*, 32 Harv. L. Rev. 473, 474-475 (1919). Proxy marriages were recognized in the old continental law of Europe and in the American colonies through the old English common law.

Proxy marriages became a modern issue during World War I. Some servicemen wanted to marry while they were stationed abroad, and because of this, various states revived marriage by proxy.

Proxy marriages were more recently discussed in *Barrons v. United States* 191 F.2d 92 (9th Cir. 1951). There the court considered the validity of a proxy marriage that had taken place in Nevada. At the time of the marriage, the parties were under military orders; one was stationed in California and the other in Africa. Before entering the military, one party had resided in California and the other in Texas. The court found that there was no difference between California and Texas law for the purposes of determining whether the marriage in Nevada was valid. The court observed that a "marriage relationship validly created by a proxy ceremony is in no way different from the same relationship created in the more usual manner." It said that a proxy marriage furthered the statutory objectives of the formal solemnization requirements to ensure "publicity and certainty." Id. at 95, 96. The "remote possibilities" of fraud and lack of consent were considered "not sufficiently substantial" to render proxy marriages, which in some cases may be the only way in which a desirable legal and social status can be achieved, "at variance with the Nevada marriage laws." Id. at 97.

Section 206(b) of the UMDA permits proxy marriages. UMDA §206. The comments note that the authors saw no reason to outlaw proxy marriages. UMDA §206(b). Note that the final determination of whether a proxy marriage will be allowed in a particular jurisdiction rests with its legislature. See In re Estate of Crockett, 728 N.E.2d 765 (Ill. App. 5 Dist. 2000).

Example 2-22

Assume that P and D were married at a time when the D suffered from an inoperable malignant brain tumor. The county clerk's office had issued D and P a marriage license; however, D's physical condition prevented him from signing the application in the presence of either the county clerk or one of his deputies. D never appeared before the county clerk. Both an appearance and a signature in the presence of the county clerk are required. At the marriage ceremony, D did not respond because of his brain tumor, and a third party was used as a proxy to acknowledge the marriage vows. D died four days after the ceremony. P seeks her intestate share of the estate as D's widow. The estate challenges the marriage and the use of a proxy. How will a court most likely rule?

Explanation

The solution, of course, is pretty straightforward. This is not a case involving a soldier or a war, and a court would obviously be concerned about a marriage being solemnized when only one party obtained the marriage license, only one party spoke or acknowledged the vows in any manner at the ceremony, and a representative spoke for the other party with no evidence of a written proxy authorizing said representative. This is not a case analogous to proxy marriage during wartime, and it is not consistent with the requirements of the UMDA. A court will hold that there was never a valid marriage. See In re Estate of Crockett, 728 N.E.2d 765 (Ill. App. 5 Dist. 2000).

2.20. Confidential Marriages

In some jurisdictions, such as California, there are provisions for "confidential" or "secret" marriages. The marriage will be recorded but generally will not be open to the public. Cal. Fam. Code §511 (West 2006). These statutes were apparently enacted to encourage persons who are living together out of wedlock, much like husband and wife, to formalize the relationship. Where available, the statutes eliminate some of the procedural requirements such as filing a health certificate or obtaining a license. However, they do require ceremony of solemnization. *See, e.g.*, Cal. Fam. Code §§500-536 (2003).

2.21. Tribal Marriages

In some jurisdictions, tribal marriages, contracted in accordance with tribal laws or customs, are recognized. *See, e.g.*, Minn. Stat. §517.18, subd. 4 (2002) (marriages may be solemnized among American Indians according to the form and usage of their religion by an Indian Midé or holy person chosen by the parties to the marriage).

2.22. Covenant Marriages

Three states — Louisiana, Arizona, and Arkansas — have created a separate form of marriage termed "covenant marriage." Other states are considering similar proposals. *See generally* Lynne Marie Kohm, *A Comparative Study of Covenant Marriage Proposals in the United States*, 12 Regent U. L. Rev. 31 (1999). A covenant marriage is a purely elective status available only to different-sex couples that creates stringent requirements for both entry and exit. James L. Musselman, *What's Love Got to Do with It? A Proposal for Elevating the Status of Marriage by Narrowing Its Definition, While Universally Extending the Rights and Benefits Enjoyed by Married Couples*, 16 Duke J. Gender L. & Pol'y 37, 39 (Jan. 2009).

Louisiana was the first state to offer the option of entering into a covenant marriage contract. If a couple chooses a covenant marriage, they pledge to enter matrimony only after serious deliberation, including premarital counseling. They also agree to try to solve potential marriage conflicts through counseling, if either spouse requests it, before initiating divorce proceedings. Before a divorce is granted, there is either an agreed-upon two-year separation or an agreement with a limited number of grounds such as adultery, abuse, imprisonment for a felony, or abandonment. The covenant provisions permit married couples to renew their vows and to recast their marriage under terms of the covenant.

In 2004 approximately 36,391 marriage licenses were issued in Louisiana, and 2 percent, or about 728, may have been covenant marriages. *See* Katherine Shaw Spaht, *Covenant Marriage Seven Years Later: Its as Yet Unfulfilled Promise*, 65 La. L. Rev. 605, 618 (2005) (only 2% to 3% of couples choose this option).

Example 2-23

Assume that P and D marry in a jurisdiction that provides for a covenant marriage contract, and they execute such an agreement. After six months of marriage, the couple agree that the relationship is not working. P files for a "no-fault" divorce (which is ordinarily allowable), and D does not oppose the filing. The local court clerk, however, refuses to file the divorce action. P and D seek an order from the court requiring the clerk to file the divorce papers and place the matter on the divorce docket. Will a court in a covenant marriage jurisdiction grant P and D's request?

Explanation

Given the current state of the statutory provisions regarding covenant marriage, the answer is most likely a court will prevent the filing. Pursuant to their covenant, the parties would be required to engage in counseling and wait the appropriate amount of time they specified in their agreement before seeking to dissolve their marital relationship. It is doubtful that a constitutional argument would cause any difference in the outcome. *See generally*, *Sosna v. Iowa*, 419 U.S. 393 (1975).

HISTORIC RESTRICTIONS ON MARRIAGE REMOVED

2.23. Race

In *Loving v. Virginia*, 388 U.S. 1 (1967), the U.S. Supreme Court reversed the Virginia conviction of an African-American woman who married a white man. It ruled that statutes barring marriage between the races violated the Fourteenth Amendment Equal Protection and Due Process Clause and constituted invidious discrimination. The equal protection ruling was based on restricting the freedom to marry solely because of racial classification. The due process ruling was based on the proposition that the right to marry is a fundamental right, and one could not suppress the right to marry based on racial classification. This case established that the right to marry was a constitutionally protected fundamental right.

Example 2-24

Assume that P, who is white, and D, who is black, attempt to marry. Under a local ordinance, it is illegal for persons of different races to marry. When the clerk of court refuses to issue a license, P and D bring an action challenging the existing ordinance. Most likely, how will a court rule on their challenge?

Explanation

Clearly, the ordinance is unconstitutional. The Court made absolutely clear in *Loving v. Virginia* that a provision that bars marriage between persons of different race or nationality violates the Fourteenth Amendment's equal protection and due process provisions.

2.24. Do Outstanding Child Support Obligations Prevent Marriage?

In *Zablocki v. Redhail*, 434 U.S. 374 (1978), the Supreme Court held unconstitutional a Wisconsin statute that provided that members of a certain class of Wisconsin residents may not marry, within the state or elsewhere, without first obtaining a court order granting permission to marry. The class was defined by statute to include any "Wisconsin resident having minor issue not in his custody and which he is under obligation to support by any court order or judgment." The Court held that the statute violated the Equal Protection Clause of the Fourteenth Amendment to the U.S. Constitution. The Court found the state interest in providing counseling before marriage and protecting a child's welfare legitimate and substantial. However, on close examination, the statute did not require or provide counseling, and it barred an applicant from marrying without providing funds (child support) to the applicant's children. The Court felt that there were other reasonable avenues open to the state to obtain support for the children. Moreover, the statute failed to consider the possibility that through a new marriage, the applicant might be better able to meet prior support obligations.

Example 2-25

Assume that state X is concerned about the increasing amount of unpaid child support, the high divorce rate, and the large percentage of children born out of wedlock. To assist the state in collecting support, a statute is enacted providing that, before a person can marry, he or she must complete a section on the marriage application form that asks whether there are any outstanding child support obligations. The applicant must state the total amount owed and suggest how it will be paid. If the section is not completed, a license will not be issued. If it is completed, a license will be issued. P, who owes several thousand dollars in child support, refuses to complete this area of the license application, and a marriage license is denied. P challenges the provision, arguing that the provision discriminates against persons who are indigent. How will a court most likely rule?

Explanation

This provision is quite different from the one discussed in *Zablocki v. Redhail* because there is no actual barrier to the marriage, other than the requirement that an applicant complete the form. A court would most likely apply a rational basis test to the provision and conclude that the state's interest in obtaining information regarding child support obligations outweighs a citizen's interest in refusing to provide the information. This provision would most likely be upheld.

Example 2-26

Assume that a state legislature is concerned about the state's high divorce rate and its impact on children. To discourage second marriages, it raised the marriage license fee to $500 for anyone seeking to marry in the state. P, who is indigent, has been divorced and desires to remarry. P claims the statute is unconstitutional because he is indigent and without funds to pay the $500 filing fee. How will a court most likely rule?

Explanation

P will argue that the statute prevents a person from ever marrying if he or she cannot pay the filing fee. Because of the nature of the barrier, the court will most likely subject it to strict constitutional scrutiny, which means the state will have to demonstrate a compelling interest in charging the fee. P has considerable authority to support his view, including *Loving*, *Zablocki*, and *Boddie v. Connecticut*, 401 U.S. 371 (1971). In *Boddie* the Supreme Court held that Connecticut could not deny access to divorce courts to those persons who could not afford to pay the required filing fee absent a countervailing state interest of overriding significance. *See also Crocker v. Finley*, 459 N.E.2d 1346 (1984), and *Boynton v. Kusper*, 494 N.E.2d 135 (1986).

2.25. When May Prisoners Marry?

States have occasionally barred marriage by a person who is imprisoned for a crime. However, in *Turner v. Safely*, 482 U.S. 78 (1987), while affirming *Butler v. Wilson*, 415 U.S. 953 (1974) (holding that a marriage prohibition when an inmate has received a life sentence is constitutional), the Supreme Court declared that a state regulation barring all inmate marriages was not reasonably related to the state interests. In *Turner*, the state regulation barred marriages of inmates except when there were compelling reasons such as a pregnancy or a nonmarital child to be born, and then only with the warden's permission, which permission was usually given only in the prospect of illegitimacy. Prison officials unsuccessfully argued that the restriction was related to the state's interest in rehabilitation of the inmate and the prevention of prison security problems.

The Supreme Court in *Turner* stated that "several factors are relevant in determining the reasonableness of the regulation at issue," including (1) "a 'valid, rational connection' between the prison regulation and the legitimate governmental interest put forward to justify it," (2) "whether there are alternative means of exercising the right that remain open to prison inmates," (3) "the impact accommodation of the asserted constitutional right will have on guards and other inmates, and on the allocation of prison resources generally," and (4) "the absence of ready alternatives." *See also Kentucky Dep't of Corr. v. Thompson*, 490 U.S. 454, 461 (1989) (holding that prisoner has no due process right to particular visitors).

Example 2-27

Assume P is convicted of a crime involving the use of prohibited drugs. The trial judge sentences P to a six-month rehabilitative drug program, which requires that P be incarcerated at a minimum security prison. While incarcerated, P decides to marry X and seeks to obtain a marriage license without a personal appearance before the clerk of court — a requirement under local law. The prison refuses to transport P to the clerk's office so he can obtain the license with his fiancée. P brings an action against the clerk to require him to travel to the prison. P also contends that it is reasonable and feasible for the clerk or a representative to periodically visit area prisons for the purpose of issuing licenses. He claims that *Turner* requires the clerk to do so. How should a court rule?

Explanation

This is a close question. The issue not addressed by Turner is whether under the totality of all circumstances involved in operating a prison, a prisoner's fundamental right to marry can be enforced irrespective of the cost to the ancillary services, which have no statutory responsibility to ensure that the prisoner and his or her partner get to the marriage license bureau door. A court rejecting the prisoner's request would reason that the court clerk does not have a legal duty to ensure that a prisoner obtains a marriage license. It would say that for a court to direct the clerk to engage in an activity that would entail unknown expenditures of money, manpower, and security concerns and which would divert funds and resources beyond their statutory mandate is inappropriate. In re Coates, 849 A.2d 254 (Pa. Super. 2004). This court would likely conclude that Turner never intended that its ruling was to be extrapolated to provide that prisoners must be accommodated regardless of cost or security problems in order to comply with the ministerial requirements of obtaining a marriage license.

A court favoring the prisoner would most likely view the matter as one where there are low-cost alternatives available. For example, the clerk's office could schedule periodic trips to prisons within the county to conduct examinations and issue marriage licenses two or three times a year. Since the examinations would be performed at predetermined intervals rather than at the prisoners' request, the cost associated with this service would be minimal. Alternatively, the clerk could accept affidavits that were sworn, attested, and notarized at the prison and then mailed to the clerk's office.

EXISTING MARRIAGE RESTRICTIONS

2.26. Polygamy

Polygamous marriages have not been protected at any time by the laws of the United States. See Reynolds v. United States, 98 U.S. 145 (1878); In re State ex rel. Black, 238 P.2d 887 (Utah 1955). These relationships are viewed as void in all jurisdictions. See State v. Holm, 136 P.3d 726 (Utah 2006), denied, 549 U.S. 1252, 1257 (2007). Because a polygamous relationship is viewed as a type of bigamy, such a relationship is punishable by imprisonment in most jurisdictions. Polyandry is likewise prohibited. See Riepe v. Riepe, 91 P.3d 312 (Ariz. App. 2005).

"Polygamy has been a common theme found in Christianity, Judaism, Islam, and other religions." Michael G. Myer, Polygamist Eye for the Monogamist Guy: Homosexual Sodomy . . . Gay Marriage . . . Is Polygamy Next? 42 Hous. L. Rev. 1458-1459 (Spring 2006). "There are other religions, including Islam and

Hinduism, under which polygamy is merely an acceptable practice." Keith Jaasma, *The Religious Freedom Restoration Act: Responding to Smith; Reconsidering Reynolds,* 16 Whittier L. Rev. 211, 286 (1995) (citing Jeremy M. Miller, *A Critique of the Reynolds Decision,* 11 W. St. U. L. Rev. 165, 179 (1984)). Polygamous marriages are legally recognized in many African, Asian, and Muslim countries. There are several arguments made in support of polygamy: The Old Testament of the Bible gives religious authority to a man's having more than one wife. For example, King Solomon's son and ruler over Judah had 18 wives and 60 concubines. 2 Chronicles 11:17, 21 (King James Version). Polygamy is justified as in society's interests when the wife is infertile or unwell, and it allows a man to have children without divorcing his first wife or possibly leaving her when she is ill. Polygamy prevents immorality such as prostitution, rape, fornication, and adultery, and it prevents a high divorce rate that can destabilize a society. Polygamy protects widows and orphans and responds to the excess of women over men in a society in a time of war or other disasters. Polygamy offers women a viable solution to successfully balance a career, motherhood, and marriage. It reduces the incidence of extramarital sex and children born out of wedlock without support from fathers.

2.27. Bigamy

Bigamy is a statutory crime and is commonly defined as "the act of marrying one person while legally married to another." *Black's Law Dictionary* 172 (8th ed. 2004). The Utah Supreme Court has held that the term "marry" in the state's bigamy statute makes a married person guilty of bigamy when the person purports to marry another person. Furthermore, the concept of marriage includes both legally recognized marriages and those that are not state-sanctioned. *State v. Holm,* 136 P.3d 726 (Utah 2006) (defendant was legally married to one woman and participated in religious marriage ceremonies with others).

Example 2-28

Assume that X marries D1 and D2 outside the United States. In the country where X and D1 and D2 are married, there is no barrier to having two spouses. Assume X migrates to the United States with D1 and D2. Shortly after arriving in the United States, D1 begins divorce proceedings against X. The clerk of court (P) discovers that D1 and D2 are both married to X under the law of another country and refuses to file the papers. What arguments might P and D1 make to the court when D1 challenges P's refusal to allow the filing of the divorce papers? How will a court most likely rule?

Explanation

Most likely P will argue that the action should be dismissed because a polygamist relationship in every state in the United States is void, and in most states is a crime punishable by imprisonment. Furthermore, the Full Faith and Credit Clause of the Constitution does not apply to the laws of a foreign government. D1 will argue that because the marriage was valid where it was performed, it is valid everywhere. D1 will also argue that, because she was married first, her marriage is valid while the marriage to D2 is invalid. P will respond that, even though the rule of *lex loci* generally supports D1's position, the rule is tempered by the strong public policy in the forum state that bars bigamous marriages. Moreover, P will contend that the policy of the foreign government is contrary to that of the forum state, and a court should not, under these circumstances, parcel out the sequence of the marriage in order to allow a divorce (noting that, if the divorce is allowed to D1, D2 apparently remains the wife of X). On these facts, the clerk's decision to reject the divorce petition will most likely be upheld. As a possible alternative, D1 may consider using the jurisdiction's putative spouse statute, which permits a person who believed in good faith that he or she was married to another to be treated in an equitable manner. P may counter that the putative spouse doctrine was not intended to apply to polygamous relationships and that D1's ignorance of the forum law is not an excuse for not following it. Although the answer to this somewhat close question turns on the precise language of the forum state's putative spouse statute, a trial court will most likely not recognize D1 as a putative spouse.

2.28. Sham Marriages — Immigration Fraud

Sham marriages are those entered into without the intent to live together as a husband and wife. Sham marriages are sometimes used by foreign aliens in an attempt to gain citizenship in the United States. For example, in *Faustin v. Lewis*, 427 A.2d 1105 (N.J. 1981), the plaintiff seeking a marriage annulment came to this country on a temporary visitor's visa. At that time, the defendant was in the employ of persons engaged in the unlawful business of arranging sham marriages between U.S. citizens and Haitians for a fee of between $500 and $1,200 so that the latter could obtain permanent residence in this country. Defendant, using various names, had married a number of Haitians for this purpose, including the plaintiff. Although it was undisputed that plaintiff and defendant participated in the ceremony solely for the purpose of making plaintiff eligible for lawful permanent residence in the United States, the New Jersey Supreme Court remanded the case to the trial court to allow the plaintiff to seek an annulment.

In response to immigration problems, Congress enacted the Marriage Fraud Amendments Act, 8 U.S.C. §1154(h), 1255(e) (1986). Section 702 of the Act amends 8 U.S.C. §§1154(h) and 1255(e) to permit an alien who marries during deportation proceedings to establish that the marriage was entered into in good faith, in accordance with law, not for the purpose of procuring the alien's entry as an immigrant, and that no fee or other consideration was given. This amendment applies to marriages entered into before, on, or after the date of enactment. *See* 136 Cong. Rec. H 132334 (Oct. 26, 1990). Prior to this Act, any U.S. citizen claiming that his or her alien spouse was entitled to immediate relative status could seek an adjustment in status for the alien spouse simply by filing a petition with the Attorney General. The Immigration and Naturalization Service (INS) then conducted an inquiry into each petition to determine whether the marriage was bona fide or merely a sham entered into for the purpose of obtaining immigration benefits. If the INS concluded that the marriage was sincere, it granted the alien spouse permanent resident status. No adjustment was granted if the marriage was determined to be a fraud.

2.29. Consanguinity

In the early history of England, marriage was under ecclesiastical control, and the canon law was the source of the rules declaring what classes of persons should be prohibited from marrying on account of relationship by consanguinity or affinity. The ecclesiastical law originally followed the Jewish law as set out in the Old Testament, which prohibited to an equal degree the marriage of persons related by consanguinity and affinity. This restriction arises from the injunction against incest found in the Book of Leviticus 20:11-21.

A medical reason advanced for the enactment of consanguinity statutes rests upon the generally accepted theory that genetic inbreeding by close blood relatives tends to increase the chances that offspring of the marriage will inherit certain unfavorable physical characteristics. *See State v. Sharon H.*, 429 A.2d 1321 (Del. Super. Ct. 1981).

Consanguinity restrictions bar marriages between persons related by blood within certain degrees of kinship, with the scope of the prohibition varying from state to state. All jurisdictions bar marriages within the immediate family, that is, between a parent and child or brother and sister. These relationships, if they occur, are void. Most states bar marriage between an aunt and nephew or an uncle and his niece. A majority of jurisdictions bar marriage between first cousins, although courts have on occasion waived the application of this prohibition. For example, in an Indiana case, two first cousins had married in Tennessee, where such marriages were legal. Later, after moving to Indiana, where such marriages are illegal, they sought a divorce. The Indiana court found that there was not a strong public policy against such marriages, so the marriage was given comity in Indiana and a divorce granted. *Mason v. Mason*, 725 N.E.2d 706 (Ind. Ct. App. 2002).

Consanguinity statutes that expressly prohibit marriages between brother and sister are applied to bar marriages or sexual relations between blood relatives, including relatives of half-blood. *See State v. Skinner*, 43 A.2d 76 (Conn. 1945); *State v. Lamb*, 227 N.W. 830 (Iowa 1929); *State v. Smith*, 85 S.E. 958 (S.C. 1915).

Example 2-29

Assume that D1 and D2 were half-brother and half-sister by blood (born of the same mother, but of different fathers). When she was approximately ten days old, D2 was adopted by family X. D1 became a ward of the state and was raised in or by various state programs. D1 and D2 met, fell in love, and married, and subsequently discovered that they were half-brother and half-sister. When a friend of the couple happened to accidentally provide the local prosecutor with information about D1 and D2's relationship, she indicted them under the state's criminal statutes for entering into a prohibited marriage.

The defendants argued that by adoption, a child is given the status of a natural child to his or her adopted parents, and any legal relationship to the child's natural parents is ended. Therefore, the prohibition in the state statute barring the marriage of a half-brother or half-sister is inapplicable due to D2's adoption. How will a court most likely rule on their argument?

Explanation

A court will most likely reject their argument. In general, consanguinity statutes prohibit marriages between blood relatives in the lineal, or ascending and descending, lines. When they discovered they had the same mother, the marriage was clearly illegal because of their blood relationship.

Example 2-30

Assume that P and D are married in a state that allows marriage between first cousins. Following their marriage they move to jurisdiction X that prohibits such marriages. When P brings an action in state X for divorce, D counters that there was never a marriage because the relationship was void. Most likely, how will a court rule?

Explanation

The marriage of first cousins was not forbidden at common law and is lawful, and not held to be incestuous, in most of the states of the United States. Absent a strong public policy against such relationships, the court will most likely allow the marriage. It will reason that it should recognize marriages if valid where contracted, as valid in this jurisdiction. The court will most likely distinguish a marriage between first cousins and marriages contracted by more closely related collaterals, that is, uncle and niece, aunt and nephew, and siblings. See *Ghassemi v. Ghassemi*, 98 So. 2d 731 (La. App. 1 Cir. 2008).

2.30. Affinity

"Affinity" is defined, in part, as "[a]ny familial relation resulting from a marriage." *Black's Law Dictionary* 59 (7th ed. 1999). Courts have consistently defined "affinity" as "the relationship which arises by marriage." See *Chinn v. State*, 26 N.E. 986, 987 (1890). For example, a mother-in-law and son-in-law are related by affinity. Affinity relationships are terminated upon divorce. *Hamilton v. Calvert*, 235 S.W.2d 453 (Tex. Civ. App. 1951 writ ref'd).

The criminalization of affinity relationships as incestuous is explicitly rejected by the Model Penal Code. The Code criminalizes marriage, cohabitation, or sexual intercourse with "an ancestor or descendant, a brother or sister of the whole or half blood [or an uncle, aunt, nephew or niece of the whole blood]." Model Penal Code and Commentaries §230.2 (1980). The Code adds, "The relationships referred to herein include blood relationships without regard to legitimacy, and relationship of parent and child by adoption." *Id.* The commentaries to the Model Penal Code make clear that the drafters carefully considered and rejected affinity-based incest (with the exception of the adoptive parent-child relationship). *Com. v. Rahim*, 805 N.E.2d 13 (Mass. 2004).

2.31. Adopted Children Marrying Each Other

Although all states prohibit marriage of relatives within certain degrees of kinship, most, but not all, do not prohibit marriage if the relationship is due to adoption. See, e.g., *State ex rel. Miesner v. Geile*, 747 S.W.2d 757 (Mo. App. E.D. 1988) (statutory prohibition against marriage between uncle and niece did not prohibit marriage between uncle and niece related by adoption); *Bagnardi v. Hartnett*, 366 N.Y.S.2d 89, 91 (N.Y. 1975) (marriage between adoptive father and adopted daughter legally permissible); *see also Israel v. Allen*, 577 P.2d 762 (Colo. 1978); *In re Enderle Marriage License*,

1 Pa. D & C.2d 114 (Phila. Cy. 1954). In *Israel v. Allen*, the court held that the Colorado statute prohibiting marriage between a brother and sister related by adoption is unconstitutional. It stated that the statute violated the couple's equal protection rights because it does not satisfy minimum rationality requirements and failed to further a legitimate state interest in family harmony. *But cf. Rhodes v. McAfee*, 457 S.W.2d 522, 524 (Tenn. 1970) (marriage of stepfather to stepdaughter after his divorce of her mother was void *ab initio* under the laws of Tennessee and Mississippi).

Example 2-31

Assume that P, age 50, and D, age 18 are married. P has a brother X, who adopted D when she was 2 months old. The family views D as P's niece. P dies unexpectedly shortly after the marriage, and D seeks her widow's share of P's large estate. P's children from a former marriage object citing a statute in effect in this jurisdiction that reads as follows: "All marriages between parents and children, including grandparents and grandchildren of every degree, between brothers and sisters of the half as well as the whole blood, between uncles and nieces, aunts and nephews, first cousins, and between persons who lack capacity to enter into a marriage contract, are presumptively void." Most likely, how will a court most likely rule on the objection?

Explanation

While all states prohibit the marriage of relatives within certain degrees of kinship, not all prohibit that marriage if the relationship is due to adoption. The statute cited above does not include the word "adoption." If the legislature intended to bar adoptions between the parties to this action, it could have accomplished that by explicitly including relatives by adoption in the statute. For that reason, and because of the policy considerations discussed above, a court would most likely conclude that the marriage was not void and would allow the widow to pursue her action. *See State ex rel. Miesner v. Geile*, 747 S.W.2d 757, 758 (Mo. App. E.D. 1988); *see also Singh v. Singh*, 569 A.2d 1112, 1121 (1990) (according common meaning to terms "uncle" and "niece" and determining that half-blood relationships fall within incest statute); *State v. Sharon H.*, 429 A.2d 1321, 1326-1328 (Del. Super. 1981) (interpreting statute that prohibited marriage between a person and "his or her ancestor, descendant, brother, sister, uncle, aunt, niece, nephew or first cousin" to include half-blood relatives); *Commonwealth v. Ashey*, 142 N.E. 788 (Mass. 1924) (convicting a half-blood uncle and niece of violating statutes providing that "no man shall marry his . . . sister's daughter" and "no woman shall marry her . . . mother's brother"). Note that in the latter cases, a statute specifying prohibited relationships, with no mention of "half blood" or "whole blood," was interpreted as applying to half-blood relationships as well as whole-blood ones. Our example does not, of course, involve a relationship by the whole or half blood.

Example 2-32

Assume that P and D are brother and sister related by adoption and are not related by either half or whole blood. When both reach the age of majority, they attempt to marry. However, the clerk of court refuses to issue a license based on a provision in that jurisdiction's law that prohibits "[a] marriage between an ancestor and a descendant or between a brother and sister, whether the relationship is by the half or the whole blood or by adoption." P and D contend that the statute is unconstitutional. Most likely, how will a court rule?

Explanation

At least one court considering this issue has found that marriage is a fundamental right and that no compelling state interest is furthered by prohibiting marriage between a brother and sister related only by adoption. Such a provision was held unconstitutional as a denial of equal protection by the Colorado Supreme Court. *Israel v. Allen*, 577 P.2d 762 (Colo. 1978).

SAME-SEX RELATIONSHIPS

2.32. Religious Perspectives

Although many religions recognize same-sex marriage, such as Buddhists, Quakers, Unitarians, and Reform and Reconstructionist Jews, a majority of religious persons in the United States oppose same-sex marriage. *Varnum v. Brien*, 763 N.W.2d 862 (Iowa 2009), n.31. A 2003 survey by the Pew Research Center reported that 59 percent of Americans oppose and 32 percent favor same-sex marriage, a ratio of less than 2-1. Note, Ben Schuman, *Gods & Gays: Analyzing the Same-Sex Marriage Debate from a Religious Perspective*, 96 Geo. L.J. 2103, 2108 (August 2008). "The ratio jumps to more than 6-1 (80% to 12%) for those 'with a high level of religious commitment.'" *Id. at* 2109. The reason for this is that, as a general rule, religion views homosexuality as a sin and same-sex marriage as an unacceptable extension of that sin.

Religious persons will often point to the Bible, which describes how woman was made from the rib of man, and states that "[f]or this reason a man will leave his father and mother and be united to his wife, and they will become one flesh." Genesis 2:24 (New International Version). This statement is said to imply that such unity, or marriage, shall be between one woman and one man. *See* Matthew 19:4-5. History, however, suggests that marriage has taken many different forms and has assumed varying degrees of importance in different cultures. *See* James L. Musselman, *What's Love Got to Do with It? A Proposal for Elevating the Status of Marriage by Narrowing Its Definition, While Universally Extending the Rights and Benefits Enjoyed by Married Couples,* 16 Duke J. Gender L. & Pol'y 37 (January 2009); Lynn D. Wardle, *The "Withering Away" of Marriage: Some Lessons from the Bolshevik Family Law Reforms in Russia, 1917-1926,* 2 Geo. J. L. & Pub. Pol'y 469 n.3 (2004); Mary Ann Glendon, *State, Law and Family: Family Law in Transition in the United States and Western Europe* 7-14 (1977) (discussing alternative forms of marriage regulation and different meanings of marriage). The argument that homosexuality is immoral is based in part on passages from the Bible that promote opposite-sex relationships and condemn homosexuality. *See, e.g.,* Genesis 2:18-24; Leviticus 20:7-16, 20:22-27; Romans 1:18-19, 1:22-32; and 1 Corinthians 6:1-3, 6:7-11. There are, however, many biblical examples of marriages not following the "one man to one woman" implication of Genesis. One example is King Solomon, who, it is claimed, had 700 wives. See 1 Kings 11:3.

Proponents of same-sex marriage contend that government regulation of marriage should not be based on religious doctrine because the Constitution requires the separation of church and state. *See* John G. Culhane, *Uprooting the Arguments Against Same-Sex Marriage,* 20 Cardozo L. Rev. 1119 (1999).

2.33. Defense of Marriage Act

The Defense of Marriage Act of 1996 (DOMA) prohibits federal recognition of state domestic partnerships, civil unions, and same-sex marriages. 1 U.S.C. §7; 28 U.S.C. §1738C (1996). DOMA defines marriage as between a man and a woman and declares that states are not required to recognize any same-sex marriage or union formed in another state. DOMA prevents same-sex couples from gaining access to federal laws providing certain benefits that are available to heterosexual married couples. Comment, Amanda Alquist, *The Migration of Same-Sex Marriage from Canada to the United States: An Incremental Approach,* 30 U. La Verne L. Rev. 200, 205 (Nov. 2008). The benefits to heterosexual couples include favorable joint tax rates, social security spousal benefits, and pension rights. Nancy J. Knauer, *Same-Sex Marriage and Federalism,* 17 Temp. Pol. & Civ. Rts. L. Rev. 421, 425 (Spring 2008).

Forty-four states currently have either a DOMA statute, state constitutional amendment, or some other legislation prohibiting same-sex marriage. Bryan K. Fair, *The Ultimate Association: Same-Sex Marriage and the Battle Against Jim Crow's Other Cousin*, 63 U. Miami L. Rev. 269, 277 (Oct. 2008).

DOMA has survived constitutional challenges in the federal courts. *See, e.g., Wilson v. Ake*, 354 F. Supp. 2d 1298 (M.D. Fla. 2005) (finding DOMA "constitutionally valid" where same-sex couple who married in Massachusetts challenged DOMA in Florida); *Smelt v. County of Orange*, 374 F. Supp. 2d 861, 880 (C.D. Cal. 2005) (DOMA does not violate the equal protection or due process guarantees of the Fifth Amendment), *aff'd in part, rev'd in part*, 447 F.3d 673 (9th Cir. 2006); *In re Kandu*, 315 B.R. 123, 133 (Bankr. W.D. Wash. 2004) (concluding that "DOMA does not violate the principles of comity, or the Fourth, Fifth, or Tenth Amendments to the U.S. Constitution"). A constitutional challenge to DOMA has yet to reach the Supreme Court.

Example 2-33

Assume that P and D, a same-sex couple, are married in Massachusetts. They move to Minnesota, where the legislature had adopted a state DOMA. When their relationship breaks down, P seeks to use Minnesota's divorce statutes to obtain alimony and an equitable distribution of the couple's property. D contends P cannot bring a divorce action in this jurisdiction. How will a court most likely rule?

Explanation

A court will most likely agree with D. Under the federal DOMA, Minnesota is not required to recognize the same-sex marriage even though it is valid in Massachusetts. There is no requirement that Minnesota give full faith and credit to the out-of-state marriage. Because Minnesota has its own state DOMA, it has established a policy against recognition of same-sex marriages in other states. Absent the state DOMA, Minnesota might well recognize the same-sex marriage from Massachusetts.

2.34. *Bowers v. Hardwick* and *Lawrence v. Texas*

One major obstacle to same-sex marriages was the oft-criticized decision by the Supreme Court in *Bowers v. Hardwick*, 478 U.S. 186 (1986). In that decision, the Court affirmed a lower court ruling that found constitutional a criminal statute punishing sex between consenting adults. The Court rejected the claim that the right to privacy (*Griswald v. Connecticut*, 381 U.S. 479 (1965)) protected consenting adults from prosecution under the statute. Subsequent to the Supreme Court's decision, the Georgia Supreme Court held that the statute considered in *Bowers* violated the due process rights of consenting adults under its state constitution. *Powell v. State*, 510 S.E.2d 18 (Ga. 1988).

Seven years after *Bowers* was decided, the Court reconsidered the case in *Lawrence v. Texas*, 123 S. Ct. 2472 (2003). *Lawrence* involved a Texas criminal statute that made it a crime for consenting adults to engage in anal intercourse. Justice Kennedy, writing for the Court, held that the criminal statute violated a liberty interest guaranteed by the Due Process Clause of the Fourteenth Amendment and overruled *Bowers*. The Court reasoned that the liberty interest concerned behavior between two consenting adults, which is inherently private and should not be subject to government intervention. Justice O'Connor concurred in the opinion, finding that the statute violated the Equal Protection Clause. She would not have overruled *Bowers v. Hardwick*. Justice Scalia dissented and questioned whether homosexual sodomy is now a fundamental right entitled to strict scrutiny.

It has been suggested that *Lawrence* "acutely calls DOMA's constitutionality into question." Roger Severino, *Or for Poorer? How Same-Sex Marriage Threatens Religious Liberty*, 30 Harv. J. L. & Pub. Pol'y 939, 956 (Summer 2007).

Since the *Lawrence* ruling, several states have questioned the constitutionality of their adultery and fornication statutes. Because *Lawrence* held that individuals have a right to engage in private sexual behavior in their homes without government intrusion, and adultery and fornication statutes regulate similar private consensual behavior between adults, the statutes would not appear to survive scrutiny under *Lawrence*. *See, e.g., Martin v. Ziherl*, 607 S.E.2d 367, 370-371 (Va. 2005) (Virginia criminal fornication statute unconstitutional).

2.35. Common Benefits Relationships — Civil Unions

In *Baker v. State*, 744 A.2d 864 (Vt. 1999), the Vermont Supreme Court held that the limitation of state-recognized marriage to opposite-sex couples violated the common benefits clause of that state's constitution. It directed the Vermont legislature to fashion a remedy providing same-sex couples with the same benefits and security granted married couples. In response, the Vermont legislature passed a law extending the benefits and protections of marriage to same-sex couples through a system of civil unions. However, under the Vermont statute, "marriage" remains a union between a man and a woman.

In 2005 Connecticut became the first state to promulgate legislation without a court order that provides same-sex couples with the opportunity to enter into a civil union. Conn. Pub. Act 05-10. The law became effective October 1, and it extends to civil union partners "all the same benefits, protections and responsibilities under law . . . as are granted to spouses in a marriage." However, parties to a civil union under Connecticut law are not defined as spouses.

At least seven states and the District of Columbia have legislation creating "domestic partners": California, Colorado, District of Columbia, Hawaii, Maine, Maryland, Oregon, and Washington. Four states — Connecticut, New Hampshire, New Jersey, and Vermont — have legalized civil unions.

2.36. Will States Recognize Civil Unions? Domestic Partners?

Because of the widespread state and federal public policy disfavoring legal recognition of same-sex relationships, same-sex couples may encounter serious resistance when seeking legal relief in a jurisdiction other than the one in which the union or partnership occurred. For example, in *Burns v. Burns*, 560 S.E.2d 47 (Ga. 2002), in the context of a child visitation dispute, a Georgia court would not recognize a "civil union" entered into in Vermont as an act of marriage. Similarly, in *Langan v. State Farm Fire & Cas.*, 48 A.D.3d 76 (N.Y.S. 2007), the court held that a domestic partner was not a worker's legal spouse under New York's Workers' Compensation Law by virtue of having entered into a civil union with the worker in Vermont. It also held that neither the doctrine of comity nor the Equal Protection Clause of the Constitution require New York to recognize the relationship for compensation purposes.

Example 2-34

Assume that P and D, a same-sex couple, form a civil union in Vermont. They move to another state where the legislature had adopted a mini-DOMA. When their relationship breaks down, P seeks to use that state's divorce statutes to obtain alimony and an equitable distribution of the couple's property. D contends P cannot bring a divorce action in this jurisdiction because of the mini-DOMA. Most likely, how will a court rule?

Explanation

Depending upon the wording of the state DOMA, the court is most likely prohibited from recognizing the civil union and allowing P to proceed under its divorce statutes.

2.37. Connecticut, Massachusetts, Iowa, Vermont, Maine, and New Hampshire Permit Same-Sex Marriage

Although the number of nontraditional families is increasing in the United States, and several jurisdictions have expanded the rights of same-sex couples, only six jurisdictions have extended to same-sex couples the right to marry. Massachusetts was the first state to expand the marriage right when in a 4-3 opinion, *Goodridge v. Department of Public Health*, 798 N.E.2d 941 (Mass. 2003), it ruled that "barring an individual from the protections, benefits and obligations of civil marriage solely because that person would marry a person of the same sex violated the Massachusetts Constitution." The court held that the state limitation of protections, benefits, and obligations of civil marriage to individuals of opposite sexes lacked a rational basis and violated the state constitutional equal protection principles. However, the majority stayed the entry of judgment for 180 days to allow the Massachusetts legislature to "take such action as it may deem appropriate in light of this opinion." When the legislature took no action, the court's ruling became law.

Connecticut technically became the third state — after Massachusetts and California — to legalize same-sex marriage. *Kerrigan and Mock v. Connecticut Department of Public Health*, 957 A.2d 407 (Conn. 2008) (California permitted them for about six months before voters approved a ban in November 2008). The court in a 4-3 decision held that laws restricting civil marriage to heterosexual couples violated same-sex couples' state constitutional equal protection rights. Because the ruling relied on the Connecticut state constitution, it cannot be appealed to the U.S. Supreme Court.

The Iowa Supreme Court overturned a ban on same-sex marriage in a unanimous, 69-page decision. *Varnum v. Brien*, 763 N.W.2d 862 (Iowa 2009). Justice Cady wrote, "We are firmly convinced the exclusion of gay and lesbian people from the institution of civil marriage does not substantially further any important governmental objective. . . . We have a constitutional duty to ensure equal protection of the law."

Vermont in April 2009 became the fourth state to legalize gay marriage and the first to do so by legislative enactment. The measure was approved over the governor's veto.

In May 2009, Maine became the fifth state to legally sanction same-sex marriage. Both the Maine House and Senate approved the measure, and it was signed into law by the governor the first week in May. The new law authorizes a marriage between any two people rather than between one man and one woman, as state law allowed prior to the new legislation. The law takes effect in mid-September 2009, unless opponents of the law mount a successful veto process on the measure via a state referendum. None of the states that have recognized same-sex marriages compel religious institutions to recognize gay marriage.

New Hampshire became the sixth state in the nation to legally sanction same-sex marriages on June 2, 2009. The legislation signed by the governor allowed same-sex marriages to be performed in the state and provided that religious clergy and organizations and their employees will not be required to participate in the services or recognize the unions.

In *Strauss v. Horton*, 207 P.3d 48 (Cal. 2009), the California Supreme Court rejected a challenge to Proposition 8, which amended the California Constitution to define marriage as the union of a man and a woman. The court said that same-sex marriages that took place before Proposition 8 was enacted were still valid because the amendment could not apply retroactively. In describing the scope of Proposition 8, the court said it would prohibit recognition of out-of-state same-sex marriages and prevent issuance of marriage licenses to same-sex couples in California.

2.38. State Recognition of Same-Sex Marriage

As noted earlier, DOMA, 1 U.S.C. §7; 28 U.S.C. §1738C (1996), declares that states are not required to recognize any same-sex marriage or union formed in another state. However, it does not prevent them doing so.

New York recognized out-of-state same-sex marriages in *Martinez v. County of Monroe*, 850 N.Y.S.2d 740, 742 (2008). The rationale for the appellate court ruling was that because New York recognizes out-of-state opposite-sex marriages it should recognize same-sex marriages. This is an unusual ruling because New York does not extend relationship recognition to same-sex couples. *See Hernandez v. Robles*, 855 N.E.2d 1 (N.Y. 2006) (holding state constitution does not compel recognition of same-sex marriage).

In *Cote-Whitacre v. Department of Public Health*, 844 N.E.2d 623 (Mass. 2006), the court upheld a statute that prohibited nonresidents from contracting a marriage in Massachusetts if the nonresident intended to continue to reside in another state and that state did not recognize same-sex marriages. The court ruled that couples who resided in states where same-sex marriage had not been expressly prohibited were entitled to proceed to trial, on expedited basis, to present evidence to rebut the Commonwealth's claim that their home states would prohibit same-sex marriages.

The District of Columbia voted May 5, 2009 to recognize same-sex marriages performed elsewhere, although it does not itself give marriage licenses to gay or lesbian couples.

TRANSSEXUAL RELATIONSHIPS

2.39. Recognizing Transsexual Relationships

Courts and legislatures are not uniform in result when asked to recognize transsexual marriages. In M.T. v. J.T., 355 A.2d 204, 211 (N.J. App. Div. 1976), the petitioner underwent a sex change to become a woman and married. When the relationship broke down, she sought support from her husband. He countered that the marriage was void because a man could not marry another man, even one who had had a sex change. He contended that the petitioner was born a male and did not possess the internal organs of a woman. The court rejected the argument, saying that when one has a sex change, for purposes of the state's marriage laws, that person is a woman and entitled to support. Sex reassignment surgery, under that view, merely harmonizes a person's physical characteristics with that identity. It said that the transsexual's gender and genitalia are no longer discordant; they have been harmonized through medical treatment. Plaintiff has become physically and psychologically unified and fully capable of sexual activity consistent with her reconciled sexual attributes of gender and anatomy.

In Littleton v. Prange, 9 S.W.3d 223 (Tex. App. 1999), the court of appeals held that a ceremonial marriage between a man and a transsexual born as a man, but surgically and chemically altered to have the physical characteristics of a woman, was not valid. See In re Ladrach, 513 N.E.2d 828 (Ohio Prob. 1987) (postoperative male-to-female transsexual could not obtain marriage license to marry male). The Maryland Court of Appeals in In re Heilig, 816 A.2d 68 (Md. 2003), held that it would recognize a transsexual's gender change. However, in In re Estate of Gardiner, 42 P.3d 120 (Kan. 2002), the court held that a postoperative male-to-female transsexual is not a woman within the meaning of the statutes recognizing marriage, and a marriage between a postoperative male-to-female transsexual and a man is void as against public policy.

Annulment of Marriage

3.1. Introduction

This chapter will focus exclusively on annulment of a marriage, a concept that is already covered to some extent out of necessity in Chapter 2. It examines the history of annulment, the differences between marital relationships that are void and those that are voidable, and provides a series of examples and explanations that will enhance an understanding of how the law treats these relationships.

Annulment and divorce are different in nature. For example, an annulment may be granted when proof is presented that a marriage is invalid or void at the time it was performed. A divorce is granted when there was a valid marriage, and the relationship is being terminated. Although the grounds for an annulment were historically developed, today all states have generated statutes that provide grounds for an annulment.

A party seeking an annulment must produce evidence showing the invalidity of the relationship existed at the time of the marriage ceremony. Time limitations set by statute for bringing an annulment vary by jurisdiction and depend on the theory under which an annulment is sought. Although most annulment actions occur early in a relationship, on a rare occasion, a court may grant an annulment despite the fact the couple have lived together as husband and wife for several years.

Annulment actions today are few and often involve immigration and Social Security disputes, where a marriage either qualifies or disqualifies an individual from eligibility for certain benefits. *See, e.g., Everetts v. Apfel,* 214 F.3d 990 (8th Cir. 2000) (annulment of claimant's first marriage, entered by state court after date of claimant's second marriage to wage earner, could not relate back and validate the second marriage; therefore, claimant never had valid marriage to wage earner for purposes of Social Security Act, and she did not qualify for widow's benefits).

When a marriage is annulled, it is in theory considered to have never existed. Consequently, no marital property could have been acquired during the time the parties were together. Courts, however, will exercise equitable powers when considering annulment requests, and they may distribute property acquired during the time the parties were together in the purported marriage in a manner they believe to be just. Most state statutes provide the courts with the authority to distribute property between the parties in such situations. Note that there are older decisions that suggest that alimony is not awarded when a relationship is annulled. *See* 4 Am. Jur. 2d *Annulment* §102 (1964).

ORIGIN

3.2. Canon law

Annulment has its origin in the canon law of the Ecclesiastical Church in England and was recognized in those courts for centuries. *See* W. Scott, *Nullity of Marriage in Canon Law and English Law,* 2 U. Toronto L.J. 319 (1937-1938). Annulment jurisdiction was removed from the Ecclesiastical courts and placed in the English civil family court system around 1870.

"VOID" AND "VOIDABLE" ANNULMENT ACTIONS

3.3. Defining a Void Marriage

Annulment actions involve relationships that may be void or voidable. A void relationship is a nullity and is invalid from its inception. *See Black's Law Dictionary* 994-995, 1098 (8th ed. 2004). For example, a person who is already married may not marry another without obtaining a divorce from the first partner. Absent a divorce, the second relationship is considered void.

A marriage that is void typically is one that offends a strong public policy. Examples of void marriages include relationships involving bigamy, polygamy, and incest. A void marriage normally does not require a judicial declaration or action to establish that it is not valid. However, an action may be sought to provide a party to a relationship with certainty and to establish a public record of its invalidity.

3.4. Defining a Voidable Marriage

In contrast to a void relationship, a voidable relationship is one that is recognized as lawful until it is legally voided by a court order. *Flaxman v. Flaxman*, 273 A.2d 567 (1971). A voidable marriage may exist, for example, when a party lacked the capacity to consent to the marriage contract because of his or her age. Note that if the underage party could have married with consent of a parent, guardian, or court, the marriage continues unless the disabled partner brings an action to void it. Whether a court determines that an action is void or voidable may be of practical importance. *See, e.g., Patey v. Peaslee*, 111 A.2d 194 (N.H. 1955) (marriage was voidable, not void; therefore, spouse not barred from intestate share of estate).

3.5. Standing to Pursue an Annulment

Generally, either the disabled party or a third party to an alleged marriage may bring an annulment action to challenge its validity. For example, a legal representative of a decedent's estate may pursue an annulment action as long as it was commenced prior to the decedent's death. *See Hall v. Nelson*, 534 N.E.2d 929 (Ohio App. 1987). Obviously, an underage party has standing to seek an annulment of a marriage. However, a party who is of marriageable age and, therefore, not under a disability, may not attack the validity of the marriage to the underage person.

The Uniform Marriage and Divorce Act (UMDA) states that "[a] declaration of invalidity . . . may be sought by the underage party, his parent or guardian." UMDA §208(b).

Example 3-1

Assume that P married D while P was still legally married to X. When D discovered that P was married to X, D sought advice regarding an annulment action. Under these circumstances, is a formal court initiated annulment necessary?

Explanation

Because the relationship is void, a formal legal action is not necessary on the part of the innocent spouse. However, if the jurisdiction has promulgated a statute that sets forth how void relationships are to be treated, obviously the statute must be followed. Even in the absence of a statute, a party may be so concerned about the implications of the relationship that an action to void the relationship may be brought. The advantage of such an action is the existence of a public record stating the relationship is "void."

RETROACTIVITY

3.6. Relation Back

When a court declares that a marriage is annulled, a question remains regarding what date the order relates back to. Does the annulment order relate back to the date of the marriage, the date the party filed the annulment action or the date the court entered its order? If the marriage is void because it is prohibited, common sense suggests that an order (even though not required in a void relationship) relates back in most cases to the date of the claimed marriage.

When a marriage is voidable, courts will use a different relation back approach, which appears to depend somewhat on the nature of the annulment claim and the jurisdiction where the action is brought. For example, in *Seirafi-Pour v. Bagherinassab*, 197 P.3d 1097, 1102 (Okla. Civ. App. 2008), the court annulled a marriage on the basis that the husband's Iranian wife fraudulently induced him to marry her. In granting the annulment, the court stated that "An annulment is said to 'relate back' and erase the marriage and all its implications from the outset." *See In re Marriage of Liu*, 242 Cal. Rptr. 649 (Cal. App. 1987) (an annulment relates back and erases marriage and all its implications from outset; if marriage is annulled, there can be no community property). In *Levine v. Dumbra*, 604 N.Y.S.2d 207 (N.Y. 1993), the court ruled that a marriage is void from the date a court enters its order of nullification if one of the parties was incapable of consenting to the marriage for want of understanding. In *Fredo v. Fredo*, 894 A.2d 399 (Conn. Super. 2005), the court held that where a decree of dissolution provides that the payor's obligation to pay alimony terminates upon remarriage, a later annulment of that marriage does not relate back so as to revive the payor's obligation to pay. The better rule appears to be that the relation-back doc-trine should be employed to promote justice between parties to a voidable marriage. *See Hodges v. Hodges*, 578 P.2d 1001, 1003 (Ariz. App. 1978) (the legal fiction that an annulment decree relates back to destroy a marriage from the beginning is sometimes ignored "as the purposes of justice are deemed to require"); *Lang v. Reetz-Lang*, 488 N.E.2d 929 (1985); *Darling v. Darling*, 335 N.E.2d 708 (1975).

It should be noted that various state statutes concerning property division and maintenance obligations may not necessarily reflect the relation-back theory. *See, e.g., Falk v. Falk*, 462 N.W.2d 547 (Wis. App. 1990) (Wisconsin statutes concerning property division and maintenance obliga-tions do not reflect this relation-back theory. Rather, under Wisconsin law, annulments and divorces have the same practical purpose and legal effect).

3.7. Uniform Marriage and Divorce Act

UMDA, §208(e), states that

> unless the court finds, after a consideration of all relevant circumstances, including the effect of a retroactive decree on third parties, that the interests of justice would be served by making the decree not retroactive, it shall declare the marriage invalid as of the date of the marriage. The provisions of this Act relating to property rights of the spouses, maintenance, support, and custody of children on dissolution of marriage are applicable to non retroactive decrees of invalidity.

MENTAL CAPACITY, AGE, DRUGS, OR JEST

3.8. Mental Capacity

A valid marriage requires that both parties possess sufficient mental capacity to understand the nature of the contract and the duties and responsibilities it creates. Generally, a party lacks the mental capacity to enter into a contract for marriage if that party is "incapable of understanding the nature, effect, and consequences of the marriage." 4 Am. Jur. 2d *Annulment of Marriage* §30; *see also Johnson v. Johnson*, 104 N.W.2d 8 (N.D. 1960) ("[T]he best accepted test . . . is whether there is a capacity to understand the nature of the contract and the duties and responsibilities which it creates."). The relevant inquiry is whether mental incapacity existed at the time the parties entered into the marriage. *Johnson*, 104 N.W.2d at 14. The mental capacity necessary to enter into marriage requires the ability to exercise "clear reason, discernment, and sound judgment." *Beddow v. Beddow*, 257 S.W.2d 45 (Ky. 1953). *Guthery v. Ball*, 228 S.W. 887 (Mo. Ct. 1921).

Example 3-2

Assume that it is three months after P and D married and that P (the wife), with the help of her lawyer son who was the issue of a former marriage of P to X, and who was appointed guardian ad litem for P, brought an action to annul the marriage, claiming P did not have sufficient mental capacity to understand the nature of the marriage ceremony. Experts called by P testified that she suffered from a severe and irreversible mental illness long before and at the time of her marriage and agree that based on their examinations, she was not capable of understanding the nature, consequences, and effect of marriage. D did not call any experts. However, D argued that P had waived her claim by delaying bringing the action for three months. D asserted that the only action available to P was one for divorce. How will a court most likely rule?

Explanation

To obtain an annulment on the ground of lack of understanding, it must be shown that the party was incapable of understanding the nature, effect, and consequences of the marriage. Here, there is unrebutted expert evidence that the wife suffered from a severe and irreversible mental illness before and at the time of her marriage. The remaining question for the court is whether P waived her annulment claim by remaining in the relationship for three months before she initiated it. Absent a state statute guiding the judge, the court will most likely grant the annulment reasoning that three months does not represent a long-term period of cohabitation of the kind that should bar an annulment. *See Levine v. Dumbra*, 604 N.Y.S.2d 207 (N.Y. App. Div. 1993); *Faivre v. Faivre*, 128 A.2d 139 (Pa. Super. Ct. 1956). *Weinberg v. Weinberg*, 255 A.D. 366 (N.Y.A.D. 4 Dept. 1938) (presumption of sanity in favor of the validity of a marriage celebrated in due form prevails unless it is overcome by proof clear and satisfactory which stands the test of most careful scrutiny).

3.9. Age

The common law allowed a girl age 12, and a boy age 14, to marry without the consent of parents or the approval and order of a court. Today, most jurisdictions set the age to legally marry by statute, and the minimum age is around 15 or 16 years with parental or court consent. The UMDA requires parental or judicial consent for persons 16 and 17.

If an underage person marries without consent of a parent or the court, the marriage is voidable (assuming the marriage would have been recognized had the court or a parent given consent). If a person attempts a marriage where the law would not recognize the relationship under any circumstances, the marriage is void. An annulment action may be maintained by the minor and usually by either parent of the minor or by a guardian of the minor's person. However, an annulment action is usually not allowed at the suit of a party who was of the age of legal consent when it was contracted or by a party who, for any time after he or she attained that age, freely cohabited with the other party as husband or wife.

Example 3-3

Assume that P, age 23, and D, age 16, who lies about her age, marry in a jurisdiction that requires consent of a parent or a court order when a party is under 18 but over 15. D obtains neither. Three years later, at age 19, D, who continues to share an apartment with P, seeks an annulment of the marriage on the ground that it was void when entered. P defends the annulment action asserting that D waived whatever opportunity she might have had to obtain an annulment once she became an adult and continued cohabiting with D. How will a court most likely rule on the annulment request?

Explanation

The court will most likely deny the request for an annulment. Most courts take the view that, to obtain an annulment, D should have brought her action before reaching age 18. Here, D failed to do this. Moreover, she freely cohabited with P as his wife after reaching the legal age of an adult and was continuing to live with D at the time the annulment action was initiated.

Example 3-4

Assume that P, age 23, and D, age 16, marry in a jurisdiction that requires consent of a parent or a court order when a party is under 18 and older than 15. D obtains neither. A year later, P brings an action to annul the marriage. Most likely, how will a court rule on P's effort?

Explanation

The court will most likely reject P's action reasoning that P is not the party with the age disability. As a general rule, courts will not provide P with standing to bring the annulment action. Therefore, P's only remedy is to seek a divorce.

3.10. Under the influence of Drugs or Alcohol

Most jurisdictions have promulgated statutes providing that an annulment may be granted if a party lacked capacity to consent to the marriage at the time the marriage was solemnized, either because of mental incapacity or infirmity, or because of the influence of alcohol, drugs, or other incapacitating substances. *See, e.g.*, 13 Del. C. §1506(a)(1) (2009). An excessive use of intoxicants may render one incapable of contracting a marriage because of the inability to concentrate one's mental faculties or to understand the marital obligations. Absent a showing that the party ratified the marriage by continuing to voluntarily live with the other person following the ceremony, such a marriage may be annulled.

Example 3-5

P and D participated in a marriage ceremony in Nevada on a Sunday, while P was allegedly under the influence of intoxicating liquor and so inebriated that he did not understand the nature of the ceremony or its legal effect. Two days later, when P claimed he was still suffering from the effects of intoxication, D advised P of the marriage. The next day, having fully recovered from his inebriation, P left the hotel room he shared with D and had not since cohabited with her. P sought to have the marriage annulled.

At trial, P testified he drank intoxicants for five hours prior to the marriage and for several hours after the ceremony was performed. A friend of P's, X, testified that he was with P before and after the marriage ceremony and P was "drunk" the entire time. X testified that P could hardly walk down the aisle and passed out for a minute or two during the wedding dinner. D testified that she felt that P was drinking "an awful lot before the ceremony, but we had talked about getting married for six months before." D testified that P was "able to stand up during the ceremony" and was not "too strange." The trial court denied the annulment, stating in effect that it did not believe P or P's friend, X. The judge wrote in her order that she was "satisfied that there isn't any minister in the city or anywhere else that is ordained, who will marry a drunken person. Moreover, the couple had discussed getting married for several months." P appeals. How will an appellate court most likely rule?

Explanation

One who can prove participation in a marriage ceremony while under the influence of intoxicating beverages to such extent as to be of unsound mind and without knowledge of what is happening is entitled to an annulment of the marriage. *See* cases cited in 28 A.L.R. (1924) 648. Here P's testimony was corroborated by X; however, the trial judge, who is the arbiter of credibility, concluded that both P and X were not telling the truth. The fact that P and D separated after three days and did not have further relations favors P It is of little relevance that the couple may have discussed marriage because the issue is whether P was without knowledge of what was transpiring at the time of the ceremony. Because of the credibility issue, this is a tough decision for an appellate court. If the appellate court decides to reverse the trial judge, it must do so on the basis that as a "matter of law, the facts support P's annulment action." *See Dobson v. Dobson,* 193 P.2d 794 (Cal. App. 2d Dist. 1948). The court could go either way.

Example 3-6

Assume that P and D married, and P, who seeks an annulment, claims that he was intoxicated and can recall very little of the marriage ceremony. D concedes during her testimony that P's recollection of the marriage ceremony and his state of inebriation is probably correct. However, testimony shows that P continued to live with D as her husband for several months following the marriage. Furthermore, P contributed financially to D's support. How will a court most likely rule on P's request for an annulment?

Explanation

A court will most likely not grant an annulment. Although P was intoxicated to the degree that he cannot recall what happened at the time of the marriage, the facts are undisputed that P thereafter lived with D and contributed financial support when sober. The law will take the view that by this conduct, P effectively condoned the acts done while he was intoxicated as if they had been done when he was sober.

3.11. Marriage Made in Jest

As a general principle, when two people participate in a mock marriage ceremony as an act of jest, exuberance, hilarity, or dare and harbor no intention to be bound thereby, most courts permit an annulment. *McClurg v. Terry*, 21 N.J. Eq. 225 (1870). Courts reason that mutual consent and bona fide agreement of the parties, freely given and with the intention of entering into a valid status of marriage, are fundamental and essential elements, and without them the marriage is invalid. Courts also reason that the public interest would not be served by compelling the persons involved to accept the legal consequences of their imprudent conduct. *Mpiliris v. Hellenic Lines, Ltd.*, 323 F. Supp. 865 (D.C. S.D. Tex. 1969). *See Crouch v. Wartenberg*, 104 S.E. 117 (W. Va. 1920).

ACTIONS INVOLVING FRAUD

3.12. Misrepresentation

Most states provide that a marriage may be annulled as a result of a fraud that goes to the essence of the marriage reasoning that this particular type of fraud vitiates the parties' consent. To justify an annulment, the fraud must be of an extreme nature pertaining to one of the essentials of the marriage and must go to present, not future, facts.

Once a marriage is consummated, courts require a greater quantum of proof of fraud before granting an annulment. When the injured party discovers the fraud, an annulment usually will not be granted unless the couple immediately, voluntarily ceases living together as husband and wife.

The mere fact of lying is not a sufficient basis for a court to grant an annulment. Lies that involve the concealment of incontinence, temper, idleness, extravagance, coldness, or fortune are not recognized as a sufficient justification for annulling a marriage. A shoe salesman's false representation to his bride-to-be that he owned his own shoe store fell short of fraud sufficient to annul a marriage in *Mayer v. Mayer*, 279 P. 783 (Cal. 1929). A future husband's statement that he was a "man of means" when he was really "impecunious" was insufficient evidence on which to grant an annulment. *Marshall v. Marshall*, 300 P. 816 (Cal. 1931). An annulment action was rejected when the husband turned out to be, in the eyes of his wife, a lazy, unshaven disappointment with a drinking problem. Annulment was denied despite the fact the husband claimed that he was chaste prior to marriage, even though another woman was pregnant with his child. *Hull v. Hull*, 191 Ill.

App. 307 (1915). In each of these examples, the courts found that the claimed fraud did not impair the ability of the parties to live together and perform the obligations and duties of marriage.

Example 3-7

P and D marry. A month after the marriage, P discovers that D had an affair only weeks before the wedding with his best friend. Based on this information, P seeks an annulment arguing that D fraudulently concealed her moral character from him prior to the marriage. How will a court most likely rule?

Explanation

Most courts take the view that concealment of defects of character, morality, chastity, habits, and temper are not sufficient to justify an annulment unless there is also evidence of overreaching. Evidence of overreaching includes taking advantage of another because of disparity in age, experience, or knowledge. Here, it is unlikely that a court will grant an annulment. P's remedy is to seek a divorce.

Example 3-8

After a 20-month marriage, P sought to have her marriage to D annulled on the ground that her consent had been fraudulently obtained. D agreed that the marriage should be terminated but requested a divorce. At the trial to determine whether the action should be one of divorce or annulment, P testified she was not aware of D's severe drinking problem until after the marriage and that she was upset to discover this and disappointed in his refusal to seek help. P also testified that she knew before the nuptials that D was unemployed, but she did not realize he would refuse to work once they were married. P testified that her sex life with D after marriage was unsatisfactory and that D was dirty and unattractive. According to P, "D turned from a prince before marriage into a filthy frog after marriage." D testified to the contrary, but the trial court believed P. Is it likely a court will grant an annulment on the basis that the marriage was fraudulently obtained?

Explanation

A court will most likely not grant an annulment. Despite P's testimony, most courts will view D's behavior following marriage as mere character defects that do not go to the essence of the marriage. Another factor supporting the ruling is that P lived with D and his defects for 20 months. P's remedy is to seek a dissolution of the relationship.

3.13. Pregnancy Claims

Cases involving misrepresentations of pregnancy fall into two general categories. One category consists of a false claim of a pregnancy, which the woman knows does not in fact exist. Relief has been denied under these circumstances on the ground that a false representation of pregnancy does not go to the essence of the marital relationship because it does not prevent the future performance of the marital obligation to bear only the children of the spouse. *Hill v. Hill*, 398 N.E.2d 1048 (1979); *Husband v. Wife*, 262 A.2d 656, 657-658 (Del. Super. Ct.1970); *Gondouin v. Gondouin*, 111 P. 756 (Cal. 1910) (a man who has been having illicit intercourse with a woman prior to his marriage with her cannot have the marriage annulled on the ground that it was brought about by the woman falsely representing that she was pregnant by him). However, some jurisdictions, such as Wisconsin, have granted an annulment when a woman lied about her pregnancy before marriage. *See Masters v. Masters*, 108 N.W.2d 674 (Wis. 1961). Wisconsin and New York courts reason that the punishment inflicted by denying an annulment is out of proportion to the offense committed.

The other general category of cases consists of a true claim of an existing pregnancy coupled with a false representation that the prospective spouse is the child's father when, in fact, the father of the child is known or suspected to be another man. A majority of cases have held that such fraud goes to the essence of the marital relationship and vitiates the marriage contract. *Miller v. Miller*, 956 P.2d 887 (Okla. 1998). Relief has sometimes been denied on the theory of *pari delicto*, that is, the husband having engaged in premarital intercourse, he has created his own mess and should not expect the courts to clean it up. *Mobley v. Mobley*, 16 So. 2d 5 (1943). There are usually aggravated situations where the doctrine of *in pari delicto* has been applied.

3.14. Religious Claims

Older decisions suggest that courts were not overly enthusiastic about recognizing religious claims as the basis for annulment actions. *See Wells v. Talham*, 194 N.W. 36 (Wis. 1923); *Boehs v. Hanger*, 69 N.J. Eq. 10, 59 A. 904 (N.J. 1905). For example, it was held that an annulment would not be granted when a woman falsely represented that she was a good, religious woman when in fact she was a prostitute. *Beckley v. Beckley*, 115 Ill. App. 27 (1904). However, in recent years several jurisdictions have adopted a more liberal view of religion as a basis for annulling a marriage. For example, in *Jordan v. Jordan*, 345 A.2d 168 (N.H. 1975), an annulment was granted on claims that the plaintiff, a Roman Catholic, was unaware of the defendant husband's prior marriage and divorce at the time she married him, that she would not have married him had she known, and that she could not live with defendant because of her religious beliefs. Ten years earlier, the same court had denied an annulment request under similar circumstances. *See Fortin v. Fortin*, 208 A.2d 447 (N.H. 1965).

Today, most courts hold that misrepresentation of strong religious convictions goes to the essence of the marriage contract, particularly if the marriage has not been consummated. The rationale for this view is that religion has a significant impact on family life.

Example 3-9

Assume that P knew D was a deeply religious individual before they married. Once they were married, each went to his or her own church. After eight years of marriage, P filed suit for divorce on grounds of extreme and repeated mental cruelty. D was extremely upset by the divorce petition because D's religion, as P knew, did not approve of divorce. During discovery, P revealed for the first time that she had lied to D a few days before they were married about whether her former husband was alive or dead. She revealed that she told D before their marriage that her former husband was dead when in fact she had divorced him. She also stated that she believed that D "probably" would not have gone through with the marriage because of his religious conviction had she told him that she had divorced her former husband. "But, he seemed to love me an awful lot," testified P. After P's revelation, D filed a counter-complaint for an annulment on the ground that D had been induced to marry P by P's fraudulent representation that her former husband was dead when in fact he was alive and she was divorced from him. During the hearing, D claimed that his strong religious beliefs would have prevented him from marrying P, a divorced woman, while her former husband was living. D also asserted that P's false representation was made to induce a marriage and constitutes fraud that goes to the essence of the marriage relationship. P argues that whatever basis D may have had for an annulment is barred by the length of their marriage. How will a court most likely rule on the annulment request?

Explanation

The parties were married a long time, and a statute in a particular state may bar the annulment claim. However, without a statutory barrier, and given the liberal trend in this area, a court might conclude that the false representations on these facts provide a sufficient basis upon which an annulment may be predicated. To one who is deeply religious, his faith is the foundation on which he builds his life and conducts his everyday affairs. His religious commitment determines his attitudes and behavior toward others. When one partner has discovered that unwittingly he has been duped into a violation of his religious beliefs and that indeed he has been living in a state of calamitous and grievous sin, that discovery may well make continuation of the relationship impossible. In such an instance the fraud eliminates the innocent party's consent to the relationship and goes directly to the essence of the marriage relationship, which is not merely "flesh and bones" but heart and soul and mind as well. *See Wolfe v. Wolfe*, 378 N.E.2d 1181 (Ill. 1978).

DURESS

3.15. A Wrongful Threat

Duress is another ground that is occasionally used in some jurisdictions to seek an annulment of a marriage. Duress is broadly defined as "a threat of harm made to compel a person to do something against his or her will or judgment; esp., a wrongful threat made by one person to compel a manifestation of seeming assent by another person to a transaction without real volition." *Black's Law Dictionary* (8th ed. 2004). A marriage that is induced by duress is generally voidable. *Black's Law Dictionary* (8th ed. 2004). The duress must be of such a degree as to prevent the individual from acting as a free agent. Although physical duress is normally the evidence a court looks for in a party seeking an annulment on this ground, some courts will accept evidence of mental stress. To have a marriage annulled on the grounds of coercion or duress, most courts will require clear and convincing evidence of the duress. *Fluharty v. Fluharty*, 193 A. 838 (Del. Super. Ct. 1937).

PHYSICAL INCAPACITY

3.16. Impotence or Sterility

Impotence is defined as the want of power for copulation. *Dolan v. Dolan*, 259 A.2d 32 (Me. 1969); *Heller v. Heller*, 174 A. 573 (Me. 1934).

Historically, there were two reasons why sex was considered to be an "essential of marriage": procreation and pleasure. Twila L. Perry, *The "Essentials of Marriage": Reconsidering the Duty of Support and Services*, 15 Yale J.L. & Feminism 1, 30 (2003). First, courts viewed procreation as a primary purpose of marriage. *Baker v. Nelson*, 191 N.W.2d 185, 186 (Minn. 1971), *appeal dismissed*, 409 U.S. 810 (1972). Second, sexual relations were valued for sexual pleasure within marriage. Perry, *supra*. The latter reason finds support by the fact that while historically impotence was a ground for annulment, sterility was not a ground for annulment or divorce. *Id.*

Impotence has been held to render a marriage voidable if the condition was unknown to the parties, or at least to the party not under the disability, at the time of marriage. *Nakoneczna v. I & L Eisenberg*, 60 A.D.2d 403, 400 N.Y.S.2d 884 (3d Dep't 1977) (marriage is voidable on the grounds of impotence is not void *ab initio*). To constitute impotence rendering the marriage invalid, the condition must be permanent and incurable and show that the other spouse was, at the time of marriage, and still is, incurably impotent. *See Manbeck v. Manbeck*, 489 A.2d 748 (Pa. Super. Ct. 1985); *see generally*, Am. Jur. 2d, *Annulment of Marriage* §§27 et seq. Impotence "need not be purely physical or organic in nature but may be based on psychogenic causes, if the mental block or disturbance results in making the spouse physically incapable of performing sexual intercourse." *Id.*

The UMDA states that a court may annul a marriage entered into under circumstances where a party lacks the physical capacity to consummate the marriage by sexual intercourse, and at the time the marriage was solemnized the other party did not know of the incapacity. UMDA §208(a)(2).

Example 3-10

Assume that after three months of marriage, P sought an annulment in a jurisdiction with a statute that declared that an annulment will be granted when there is "[i]ncurable physical impotency, or incapacity for copulation, at the suit of either party; if the party making the application was ignorant of such impotency or incapacity at the time of the marriage." Assume that at the annulment hearing P's expert testified that D suffered from no physical defect of a sexually incapacitating nature; rather, it appeared that psychogenic causes had caused D's physical inability to copulate. The expert also testified that it was probable that even with counseling D would not overcome his inability to copulate with P. D's lawyer contends that the statute applies only to physical, not psychological, problems. She also contends that unless there is evidence that the condition is permanent, an annulment cannot be granted. P's lawyer argues that the statute should be construed broadly to include both physical and psychological causes and that P's expert testified that D's condition was most likely permanent. Will a court most likely grant P an annulment?

Explanation

The court will most likely grant the annulment. The court will reason that it is not relevant that D's impotence resulted from psychological rather than physical causes. What is important to the determination is that D was and is impotent. *See Rickards v. Rickards*, 166 A.2d 425 (Del. 1960); *Manbeck v. Manbeck*, 489 A.2d 748 (Pa. Super. 1985) (psychological or emotional disorder from which wife suffered, referred to by physicians as a sexual dysfunction and described as rendering her incapable of participating in normal sexual intercourse, was sufficient evidence on which to base a finding of "impotence" and to warrant an annulment of marriage given sufficient additional evidence to warrant an inference that impotence was incurable). The purpose of the statute is to allow an annulment where there is sufficient evidence to support a finding that the spouse of the party seeking the order is, in fact, impotent.

COHABITATION AS A DEFENSE

3.17. Continued Cohabitation

As a general rule, once a disability of a partner is discovered, and the parties continue to live together as husband and wife, courts are reluctant to grant an annulment. This rule reflects the strong public policy favoring marriage.

Example 3-11

Assume that P petitions for an annulment in a common law court, claiming duress as the basis for relief. She testifies that she was forced to marry D because he threatened to tell D's mother the two had intercourse many times while dating before marriage if she didn't. D admits that he made such threats but says they were made in jest. D's lawyer argues that the threats do not constitute duress, and even if they did, the fact the two lived together as husband and wife for two years following their marriage ceremony bars the annulment action. How will a court most likely rule?

Explanation

A court will be troubled by P's petition on two bases. First, the testimony, at best, provides only weak support for P's claim of duress. Second, because the two cohabited for two years following the marriage, this will act as ratification of it. The court will most likely rule that because of the cohabitation, the action should be dismissed. P may, of course, pursue a divorce action.

Example 3-12

Assume that the parties were married for four years when husband P sought an annulment of his marriage to D after she left the marital home to live with X, her new female partner. P learned that D had been involved in various "quiet" affairs during their marriage. P alleged that at the time of the marriage ceremony, he was unaware that D had engaged in a lesbian affair with another woman. P claimed that had he known of these facts at the time of the marriage, he would have refused to marry D. P's lawyer argued that the facts were material, touching upon vital aspects of the marital relationship, and that D, "in concealing these facts from P, acted in a fraudulent, malicious and willful manner with the specific intent to deceive and defraud P."

Explanation

A court will reject the annulment petition. D's same-sex activities have little, if anything, to do with the essential aspect of the marriage. Because the marriage was sufficiently consummated, the wife's lesbian activities did not interfere with her ability to engage in "normal" and "usual" sexual relations with her husband. Moreover, same-sex activities prior to marriage are similar to claims of unchastity, which a party need not disclose to another party prior to marriage. *Woy v. Woy*, 737 S.W.2d 769 (Mo. App. W.D. 1987).

SUPPORT AND PROPERTY DISTRIBUTION

3.18. Support

At common law, an annulment resulted in the bastardization of any children born during the marriage. However, modern-day courts have made vigorous efforts to protect children of marriages where the parties sought an annulment that would bastardize the children. Courts have denied relief where children were involved, leaving the only alternative remedy one of divorce. *Johnson v. Johnson*, 157 S.E. 689 (Ga. 1931); *Mackey v. Mackey*, 32 S.E.2d 764 (1945). Statutes in all jurisdictions have removed this harsh common law view. UMDA §207(c) provides that children born to a void marriage are legitimate.

3.19. Alimony and Property Division

When an annulment is granted, courts have historically not provided relief similar to that provided when a couple divorce. Consequently, in a traditional annulment situation, the court did not award alimony or divide property as though it were "marital" in nature. However, that view has dramatically changed. Today, legislatures frequently provide statutory authority for courts to grant alimony and effectuate property divisions in annulment matters. *See Sefton v. Sefton*, 291 P.2d 439 (Cal. 1955); *Jones v. Jones*, 296 P.2d 1010 (Wash. 1956).

OTHER ISSUES

3.20. Enoch Arden Statute

Enoch Arden statutes colloquially take their name from Alfred Lord Tennyson's 1864 poem, *Enoch Arden*. The statutes apply to situations where a person suddenly returns after a long absence from which he was not expected to return at all. In Tennyson's poem, Enoch married Annie, who was secretly loved by Phillip Ray, the miller's son. When Enoch did not return from a voyage, Annie and Phillip married, believing Enoch to be dead. Ten years after departing, Enoch returned.

Enoch Arden statutes provide a defense to bigamy when a spouse remarries with the good-faith belief that a former spouse is dead. However, the statutes do not necessarily validate the later marriage. For the later marriage to be upheld, some jurisdictions require an Enoch Arden divorce as a prerequisite to the later marriage. *See, e.g., Randolph v. Randolph*, 212 N.Y.S.2d 468 (N.Y. Sup. Ct. 1961). The effect of the Enoch Arden statute in some jurisdictions is to create an express statutory exception to the general rule that an annulment of marriage is retroactive. *Estate of Lemont*, 86 Cal. Rptr. 810 (Cal. App. 1970).

Example 3-13

Decedent (D) was P's first husband. They separated, and P never heard from her first husband again. Six years after the separation, and after her inquiries proved unavailing, P believed that D was dead, and P married X. (Had she believed that D was alive, she should have obtained an Enoch Arden divorce before remarrying.) However, D actually died ten years from the time the P and D had separated. When D died, P and X had been married for four years. P learned of D's death and his huge estate. P immediately began legal action and secured an annulment of her second marriage. P then asserted a claim that she was D's widow and was entitled to a portion of his estate. The Enoch Arden statute in this jurisdiction reads, in part, as follows:

> A subsequent marriage contracted by any person during the life of a former husband or wife of such person, with any person other than such former husband or wife, is illegal and void from the beginning, when such former husband or wife is absent, and not known to such person to be living for the space of five successive years immediately preceding such subsequent marriage, or is generally reputed or believed by such person to be dead at the time such subsequent marriage was contracted. In either of which cases the subsequent marriage is valid until its nullity is adjudged by a competent tribunal.

Given the language of the statute, may P make a claim as D's surviving widow that a court will recognize?

Explanation

P's claim will most likely not be recognized. Courts will take the view that a claimant's status must be determined as of the date of D's death, and as of that date, P's marriage to X remained valid. P's marriage to X could become invalid only as of the date of an annulment decree — necessarily at a time after her status in relation to the estate had been fixed. Courts will usually take the view that only if P had secured her annulment while D was still alive could she contend that her marriage to him had become revived so as to give her a widow's status. *See Estate of Lemont*, 86 Cal. Rptr. 810 (Cal. Ct. App. 1970); *Valleau v. Valleau*, 6 Paige (N.Y. 1836).

Who May Divorce? Restrictions and Requirements

4.1. Introduction

This chapter examines the history and development of divorce. It traces the important legal developments in this area of the law from ancient times to the present. Where appropriate, examples are included to explain the application of a legal principle to a practical legal problem.

HISTORY

4.2. Ancient History

Divorce has existed in some form since ancient times. Under Athenian law, Greek husbands and wives could go their separate ways after the mere filing of notice with a magistrate, with the parties free to marry, divorce, and remarry at will. Around 18 B.C. the act of divorce may have assumed a more formal requirement when the Roman emperor, Caesar Augustus, promulgated the *Lex Julia de Adulteris*, which required that a divorcing couple execute a writing that renounced their marriage — making divorce something more than an informal dissociation.

The pervasive influence of the Roman Catholic Church was being felt throughout England by the eleventh and twelfth centuries. During this period, the Church, through its Ecclesiastical courts and canon law, gained control over marriage and divorce. The Church viewed marriage as a sacrament and indissoluble except by death; not even the Pope could break the bonds of marriage. Church theology was fortified by a conviction that sexual indulgence outside marriage involved mortal sin and created a formidable barrier within marriage to the achievement of spiritual purity. These beliefs were founded, at least in part, on the Gospels. *See, e.g.*, Matthew 19:5-6, 19:3-9; Luke 16:18; Ephesians 5:30-31; I Corinthians 7:10-11; and Romans 7:2-4.

LEGAL SEPARATION: DIVORCE *A MENSA ET THORO*

4.3. Generally

Although the Church historically forbade absolute divorce, when the marriage vows were broken by adultery or acts of cruelty that rendered further cohabitation unsafe, the innocent spouse was permitted, by judicial decree of an Ecclesiastical court, to live apart from the wrongdoer. This relief was afforded by a decree of judicial separation called divorce *a mensa et thoro*, or a divorce from bed and board. The decree of divorce *a mensa et thoro* did not sever the marital tie, and the parties remained husband and wife. *See Schlagel v. Schlagel*, 117 S.E.2d 790, 793 (N.C. 1961). Neither party could remarry during the spouse's lifetime, and the husband was normally required to provide his wife with permanent support. *See Metcalf v. Metcalf*, 51 S.W.2d 675 (Ky. 1932).

4.4. Defined

A *divorce a mensa et thoro* is defined in *Black's Law Dictionary* 515 (8th ed. 2004) as "[a] partial or qualified divorce by which the parties were separated and allowed or ordered to live apart, but remained technically married. This type of divorce, abolished in England in 1857, was the forerunner of modern judicial separation."

4.5. Separate Maintenance: Limited Divorce

Separate maintenance proceedings today are, in part, the residue of the divorce *a mensa et thoro*. Separate maintenance actions are distinguishable from a proceeding for an absolute divorce, and even from a modern proceeding for a limited divorce. Unlike the ancient divorce *a mensa et thoro*, an action for separate maintenance does not expressly or necessarily authorize the wife to live apart from her husband. However, a decree of limited divorce allows the parties to live apart. *See Cregan v. Clark*, 658 S.W.2d 924 (Mo. App. Ct. 1983).

A separate maintenance decree is usually intended to provide only for the support of the wife and children. However, in some jurisdictions, when a legal separation or limited divorce is sought, a court may determine child custody and property division, in addition to child support and alimony. *See Anderson v. Anderson*, 382 N.W.2d 620, 621 (Neb. 1986).

"FAULT" EMERGES

4.6. Ecclesiastical Courts and "Fault"

In the context of divorce, the concept of fault has historically played a significant role in most divorce actions. The use of "fault" can be traced to the early Church and the Ecclesiastical courts' exercise of authority over domestic matters. Under the rules established by the Ecclesiastical courts, a person could ask for permission to live apart from a spouse. However, to gain permission from the court, the person seeking the separation had to prove fault on the part of the spouse. Generally, to determine if fault existed, the court asked whether the erring spouse had committed one of the sins recognized by the Church. Adultery, physical cruelty, and unnatural sexual practices were recognized as valid reasons for parties to live apart, although they were not permanently divorced.

Fault also played a role in determining whether support was to be ordered when a divorce *a mensa et thoro* was granted. For example, if a wife committed adultery during the marriage, she was considered "at fault," and the Ecclesiastical courts were not obligated to require that her husband support her.

ABSOLUTE DIVORCE BECOMES POSSIBLE

4.7. Sixteenth-Century Theory of Absolute Divorce

The theory that one could obtain a permanent divorce emerged during the sixteenth-century Protestant Reformation. The Reformers believed that marriage was not a sacrament in the Roman sense; rather, it was a natural and social institution. Therefore, marriage fell under the natural and civil law, not under Church law.

Another factor that may have influenced the view of divorce during the sixteenth century was the difficulty England's Henry VIII had in securing annulments of marriages to his various wives. When ten years of negotiations with the Pope broke down over a request for the annulment of his marriage to Catherine of Aragon, Henry had Thomas Cranmer, Archbishop of Canterbury, declare the marriage null and void, and he directed Parliament to enact two laws. The first declared Henry the head of the Church in England. The second made the Church of England a separate entity from the Church of Rome.

Despite the break with the Pope, the Protestant Reformation, and the substitution of the Church of England for the Church of Rome, not a great deal changed in England. The Church of England assumed the role of the state church and continued to monopolize the resolution of matrimonial disputes.

Example 4-1

Assume that P and D are English citizens living in the fifteenth century, and P seeks a divorce claiming that D has committed adultery on numerous occasions. D admits his adulterous conduct. P files a request with an Ecclesiastical court to grant an absolute divorce. The request, however, is denied. Was the denial appropriate under the existing law?

Explanation

The early Church forbade absolute divorce; therefore, the request was appropriately denied. Note, however, that when the marriage vow was broken by adultery or acts of cruelty that rendered further cohabitation unsafe, the innocent spouse was permitted, by judicial decree, to live apart from the wrongdoer, and Church courts would afford the injured party relief by allowing a decree of divorce *a mensa et thoro*.

PARLIAMENTARY DIVORCE

4.8. Parliamentary Divorce Becomes Available

Parliamentary power to dissolve marriages had become a fact by the seventeenth century in England. Parliamentary divorces were occasionally sought by English nobility who, unable to obtain a divorce or annulment from the

Ecclesiastical courts, turned to Parliament for assistance. *See Waite v. Waite*, 4 N.Y. 95 (N.Y. 1855). Parliamentary divorces were rare and, as a practical matter, available only to England's "great families" for "special cases." William J. Goode, *World Changes in Divorce Patterns* 136 (1993). The English Parliamentary divorce model was transported from England to some American colonies and adopted by some early state legislatures. *See, e.g., Maynard v. Hill*, 125 U.S. 190 (1888).

EARLY AMERICAN VIEW OF DIVORCE

4.9. Colonial Divorce

The American colonies rejected the establishment of Ecclesiastical courts. Although the colonies differed greatly in their specific approach to divorce, in general they vested power in colonial legislatures or courts of equity to handle divorce matters. Divorces were not allowed in some of the colonies. *See* Barbara Dafoe Whitehead, *The Divorce Culture* 13 (1997).

4.10. Divorce Following the American Revolution

Following the American Revolution, statutory divorce was introduced in most jurisdictions. During this period, divorce actions were rare and were treated in a manner similar to other civil disputes, that is, as a means of providing compensation to a person who had been wronged. For example, in most jurisdictions, a divorced wife could recover the dowry she brought to the marriage if she could prove to a jury that her husband was guilty of adultery. Furthermore, if she met her burden of proving she was wronged and her dowry did not adequately provide for her, her husband could be required to provide her with a limited means of support from his personal estate. *See Brown's Appeal*, 44 A. 22 (Conn. 1899).

4.11. Jury Trial

During the nineteenth and early twentieth centuries, the issue of whether a divorce should be granted was tried to a jury in most jurisdictions. *See, e.g., Gilpin v. Gilpin*, 21 P. 612 (Colo. 1889). However, today only a few states continue to use a jury in a divorce action. *See, e.g., Waits v. Waits*, 634 S.E.2d

799 (Ga. App. Ct. 2006) (jury's verdict awarded title and possession of the marital residence to Mrs. Waits); *Soldinger v. Soldinger*, 799 N.Y.S.2d 815 (N.Y.A.D. 2005) (testimony in jury trial where plaintiff who claimed abandonment by lockout as a ground for divorce failed to establish a *prima facie* case since, among other things, he admitted that he was not excluded from the marital residence, he retained the keys to the martial residence, and the defendant never changed the locks). In order to obtain a jury trial in a divorce action, the right to trial by jury must arise either by statute or under the state constitution. *See Brennan v. Orban*, 678 A.2d 667, 672 (N.J. 1996). Sometimes, only a specific issue such as custody of a minor child is submitted to a jury for a decision. *See, e.g., Hausman v. Hausman*, 199 S.W.3d 38, 41 (Tex. App. Ct. 2006) (after paternity decision, jury trial was held with regard to custody).

TYPICAL "OLDER" GROUNDS FOR DIVORCE

4.12. Adultery

One of the oldest grounds used to obtain a divorce is adultery. Although the crime of adultery in some jurisdictions was a felony and could be committed only by a man with a married woman, this gender-specific view was not extended to civil divorce actions. *See, e.g., Nelson v. Nelson*, 164 A.2d 234, 235 (Conn. Super. Ct. 1960) (husband's adulterous actions provided sufficient ground for divorce, notwithstanding the fact that under criminal statute, adultery relates only to sexual intercourse between a man and a married woman).

Example 4-2

Assume that P and D are citizens of a jurisdiction that requires proof of adultery as the ground for divorce. P has discovered that D is visiting chat rooms on the Internet and has been "carrying on an affair via the Internet with another woman, X." E-mail messages between D and X, seized from the family computer by P, are described by P as "intimate" and "embarrassing." P testifies that D and X have apparently never met each other in person but have exchanged revealing photos over the Internet. P seeks a divorce on the ground of adultery. D moves to dismiss the action. How will a jurisdiction that has adultery as its only legislative basis for divorce most likely rule?

Explanation

Most courts will likely dismiss the action because P has failed to produce sufficient evidence of sexual activity between D and X. "Adultery is committed whenever there is an intercourse from which spurious issue may arise. . . ." *State v. Wallace*, 9 N.H. 515, 517 (1838). *See also* In re Blanchflower, 834 A.2d 1010 (N.H. 2003) (adultery, as statutory ground for divorce, does not include homosexual relationships).

4.13. Cruel and Inhuman Treatment

Another basis for divorce found in most states under the common law was "cruel and inhuman treatment." To support a finding of cruel and inhuman treatment, the defendant's conduct had to be serious and not merely an indication of incompatibility. *See Hessen v. Hessen*, 308 N.E.2d 891 (N.Y. 1974) (a high degree of proof is required to establish cruel and inhuman treatment).

In a few jurisdictions, the cruel and inhuman conduct could be in the form of emotional abuse; however, the conduct must be something more than mere "unkindness, rudeness, or incompatibility." *Brooks v. Brooks*, 652 So. 2d 1113, 1124 (Miss. 1995). As a general rule, the claim of cruel and inhuman treatment must be founded on conduct that is continuous and not based on one isolated incident.

Example 4-3

Assume that P (husband) and D (wife) were married ten years and had three children. Assume that P brought an action against D for divorce, alleging cruel and inhuman treatment. P's proof consisted of D's public statements, which P claimed disparaged and embarrassed him. P said that D often would state that he was a "deadhead husband who cheated friends," a "lousy lover," and "couldn't balance a checkbook if it had two entries." These were uttered before professional colleagues and friends. P alleged he had a cold and indifferent personal and sexual relationship with D and that D's behavior had caused him to suffer depression. D conceded that she may have made the statements P claimed she made but explained that they were made in jest. P testified that their marital difficulties were attributable to P's problems with alcohol and the inability to live a family life with D and the children. As to P's claim of sexual problems, D denied a coldness or indifference and testified that their sexual problems stemmed from differing sexual appetites and drives. How will a judge mostly likely rule on P's petition for divorce where the only ground for the divorce is cruel and inhuman treatment?

Explanation

To prevail in most jurisdictions on this ground, P must produce evidence that demonstrates a course of conduct by D that is harmful to P's physical or mental health and that makes continued cohabitation unsafe or improper. The conduct must be serious and not just an indication of incompatibility. The proof of activities that are alleged to constitute cruel and inhuman treatment will be viewed in the scope of the entire marriage. Here, P and D were together some ten years and had three children before P moved to pursue a divorce. The marriage is of significant length, and the transgressions will be viewed in terms of the scope of the marriage, including the fact that it produced three children. The conflicting versions of alleged cruel and inhuman treatment rest entirely on the credibility of the parties. The length of the marriage and the weak nature of the evidence produced by P will probably result in the divorce being denied. *Spence v. Spence*, 930 So. 2d 415 (Miss. App. 2005) (divorce on ground of habitual cruel and inhuman treatment denied where the only evidence of bad circumstances in the marital home, which was corroborated, was that the spouses had arguments).

4.14. Mental Cruelty

Several jurisdictions established mental cruelty as a ground for divorce under the common law and have subsequently incorporated the concept into their statutes. Actual bodily harm or apprehension need not be shown. *Alfaro v. United States*, 859 A.2d 149 (D.C. 2004). The humiliation of another human by reducing him or her to tears is "cruel" in the commonly understood sense of the word. *Waltenberg v. Waltenberg*, 298 F. 842, 844 (D.C. App. 1924) (there must have been such treatment as to destroy the peace of mind and happiness of the injured party, and to endanger the health or utterly defeat the legitimate objects of the marriage). Mental cruelty could be inflicted by the use of words or acts, conduct that constitutes quarreling, or fault finding that affects the health, well-being, or peace of mind of either of the parties. *Copeland v. McLean*, 763 N.E.2d 941 (Ill. App. 4 Dist. 2002) (husband's actions toward terminally ill wife constituted mental cruelty as grounds for marital dissolution; husband treated wife badly, mocked her in front of others, shouted obscenities at her, and told her that he wished that she were dead); *Cochran v. Cochran*, 432 P.2d 752 (Colo. 1967). Incompatibility of temperament is not viewed as cruelty and a ground for divorce. *Neff v. Neff*, 192 P.2d 344, 345 (Wash. 1948). A drastic change in a partner because of a religious conversion may, depending on the facts, provide a basis for a mental cruelty claim. *Hybertson v. Hybertson*, 582 N.W.2d 402 (S.D. 1998) (Husband following religious conversion would tell wife that she would not live in paradise on earth if she was a nonbeliever and that she would "just lay in the dirt." Wife could no longer have a normal conversation with husband as he continually states he is there to teach her and the children and was always quoting Bible verses to her.).

4.15. Desertion or Abandonment

Desertion, sometimes labeled "abandonment," is a grounds for divorce found in a majority of American jurisdictions. Matthew Butler, *Grounds for Divorce: A Survey*, 11 J. Contemp. Legal Issues 164, 170, 172 (2000). Desertion has been defined as (1) cessation from cohabitation, (2) an intention on the part of the absenting party not to resume it, (3) the absence of the other party's consent, and (4) the absence of justification. *McCurry v. McCurry*, 10 A.2d 365 (Conn. 1939). There must be an intent to put an end to the marital condition and the intent to never renew it. *Tirrell v. Tirrell*, 45 A. 153, 154 (1900). Desertion consists of the cessation of cohabitation, coupled with a determination in the mind of the offending person not to renew it. Intent is the decisive characteristic, and the question of intent is a question of fact. *See Barnes v. Barnes*, 428 S.E.2d 294, 297 (1993); *Schubert v. Schubert*, 33 A.D.3d 1177 (N.Y.A.D. 3 Dept. 2006) (to establish cause of action for divorce on ground of abandonment, plaintiff must demonstrate that defendant unjustifiably and without plaintiff's consent abandoned plaintiff for a period of one or more years and refused repeated requests to resume cohabitation or conjugal relations).

Example 4-4

Assume that P and D were married for five years before the relationship broke down. P sued D for divorce, claiming desertion under the common law, which in this jurisdiction permits a divorce if the desertion is excess of one year. At the trial, unchallenged evidence was presented by P that for the last year P acted "more or less" like the marriage was over. During this period, D slept "on the couch, in the garage attached to the house, or at his mother's house," despite P's repeated requests that he resume the marital relationship. D testified that he was happiest sleeping in the garage or a his mother's home. By the time of trial, he testified he had moved in with his mother "for good." He said he intends to continue living with his mother unless "P changes her ways." P testified that she had never asked or forced D to leave their marital home. Does P have a sufficient basis to support a divorce on the ground of desertion?

Explanation

The evidence tends to support the conclusion that D's actions broke off marital cohabitation, and D apparently intends to remain apart from P permanently. The court will most likely rule that P has proven that D deserted her and grant the divorce petition. *See Skeens v. Skeens*, 2000 WL 1459867 (Va. Ct. App. 2000) (unpublished).

4.16. Constructive Desertion

Constructive desertion is a court-created cause of action and often has a specific period of time the parties must be apart to justify the desertion claim. The cause of action provides courts with a basis to grant relief on the ground of desertion to a spouse driven from the home by his or her partner. *Lynch v. Lynch*, 616 So. 2d 294 (Miss. 1993) (If either party, by reason of such conduct on the part of the other as would reasonably render the continuance of the marital relationship unendurable, or dangerous to life, health, or safety, is compelled to leave the home and seek safety, peace, and protection elsewhere, then the innocent one will ordinarily be justified in severing the marital relation and leaving the domicile of the other, as long as the conditions shall continue, and in such case as the one so leaving will not be guilty of desertion. The one whose conduct caused the separation will be guilty of constructive desertion, and if the condition is persisted in for a period of more than one year, the other party will be entitled to a divorce.); (*Hartner v. Hartner*, 75 Pa. Super. 342 Penn. 1921) (under Pennsylvania law, desertion must be "willful and malicious," and guilty intent is manifest when without cause or consent either party withdraws from the residence of the other, and the desertion is an actual abandonment of matrimonial cohabitation, with an intent to desert willfully and maliciously and persisted in for two years without cause).

4.17. Habitual Drunkenness

Habitual drunkenness is a ground for divorce in some states. It has been defined as a fixed habit of frequently getting drunk; it does not necessarily imply continual drunkenness. *Rooney v. Rooney*, 131 S.E.2d 618 (S.C. 1963). One need not be an alcoholic to be guilty of habitual drunkenness. It is sufficient if the use or abuse of alcohol causes the breakdown of normal marital relations. *Id.* In *McVey v. McVey*, 289 A.2d 549 (N.J. Super. Ct. 1972), the court held that the evidence established the ground of "habitual drunkenness" for a divorce. The husband had progressed from a social drinker to an inebriate who was regularly drunk four or five times a week both at home and in public. The condition existed for a period of 12 or more consecutive months subsequent to the marriage and preceding the filing of a complaint by the wife for divorce. *See Kessel v. Kessel*, 46 S.E.2d 792 (W. Va. 1948) (proof that defendant occasionally became intoxicated from drinking intoxicating liquors does not establish the allegation of habitual drunkenness within the meaning of West Virginia law); *Whitehorn v. Whitehorn*, 332, 36 P.2d 943 (Okla. 1934).

4.18. Indignities

"Indignities" once existed as a ground for divorce in some states. For a spouse to prevail, the evidence had to show a course of behavior toward the spouse that was sufficiently humiliating and degrading as to render the condition of "any woman of ordinary sensibility and delicacy" intolerable and her life burdensome. *Steinke v. Steinke*, 357 A.2d 674 (Pa. Super. Ct. 1975) (husband who for several months was in a program leading up to anticipated sex change and who adopted clothing and physical appearance of a woman entitled wife to divorce on ground of indignities, in absence of showing of mental illness).   ·

TRADITIONAL COMMON LAW DEFENSES TO A DIVORCE ACTION

4.19. Overview: Affirmative Defenses

The common law created a group of affirmative defenses to a divorce action. Most of these defenses were related in one way or another to a party's "fault." A majority of jurisdictions have abolished most of these defenses.

4.20. Unclean Hands

This defense imposed a burden on the petitioning party to enter court without serious fault. It was sometimes used as a defense in mental cruelty or desertion cases when the petitioner's own acts were questionable. It is still in use in some jurisdictions. *See, e.g., Price v. Price,* 5 So. 3d 1151 (Miss. App. 2009); *Hurston v. Hurston,* 635 S.E.2d 451 (N.C. App. 2006). The defense resembles the defense of recrimination.

Example 4-5

Assume that P came before a nineteenth-century common law court asking for a divorce from D. D, who was serving a long prison sentence for a felony conviction, was properly served but failed to answer the divorce petition. At the required default hearing where grounds for the divorce had to be proven, the court asked P several questions. The answers revealed that P had been living in a state of adultery during D's absence and had become the mother of an illegitimate child. When these facts were revealed, the court refused to grant P a divorce. Was the court most likely correct in its application of the law?

Explanation

Most divorce proceedings at common law were regarded as equitable in nature, and various defenses appropriate to courts of equity were available. "Unclean hands, within the meaning of the maxim of equity, is a figurative description of a class of suitors to whom a court of equity as a court of conscience will not even listen, because the conduct of such suitors is itself unconscionable, that is, morally reprehensible." *Pollino v. Pollino,* 121 A.2d 62 (N.J. Super. Ch. 1956). Here, although there was no opposition to the divorce, a common law court would most likely not permit the divorce action to proceed because of the petitioner's "unclean hands."

4.21. Recrimination

Recrimination as a defense to a divorce action under the common law meant that if the complaining party was guilty of an offense that would justify a divorce, then a court could not grant the party a divorce. *Courson v. Courson,* 117 A.2d 850 (Md. App. 1955). This defense is a variation on the clean hands defense. For example, if both parties were guilty of adultery, neither could obtain a divorce. However, in some jurisdictions, the guilt of both parties was weighed and had to be found equal in order to trigger the recrimination defense. For example, neither drunkenness nor cruelty would normally constitute a sufficient recriminatory defense when weighed against a charge of adultery. *Bast v. Bast,* 82 Ill. 584 (1876). *See also De Burgh v. De Burgh,* 250 P.2d 598 (Cal. 1952) (extensive discussion of history and application of the recrimination defense).

Example 4-6

Assume that P sued D seeking a divorce in a common law court and alleged as grounds that D committed adultery. D, while not denying the claim, asserted the defense of recrimination, that is, that P had deserted D. In a jurisdiction that recognizes recrimination as a defense but weighs the various guilty acts of the parties, how will a court most likely rule?

Explanation

A common law court in these circumstances would most likely allow P's claim to proceed. It would weigh both claims and conclude that P's desertion cannot exonerate D from the more serious charge of adultery.

4.22. Condonation

Condonation as a defense represented forgiveness, usually conditional, based on a promise not to repeat the offense. *Owens v. Owens*, 31 S.E. 72 (Va. 1898). The forgiveness could be either actually expressed or implied; in either case, spouses, the forgiver and the forgiven, continued their married life as before. An offense that is condoned cannot later be used as grounds for a divorce. *Chastain v. Chastain*, 672 S.E.2d 108 (S.C. App. 2009) (husband commenced a divorce action on the grounds of adultery; however, family court dismissed the action based on condonation, finding husband and wife engaged in sexual relations before the divorce hearing); *Schubert v. Schubert*, 823 N.Y.S.2d 282 (N.Y.A.D. 3 Dept. 2006) (wife testified that husband's conduct in having affairs caused her to suffer shingles and gain weight, such testimony was not supported by medical proof, and wife also testified that parties voluntarily cohabited subsequent to events in question); *See* Marvin M. Moore, *An Examination of the Condonation Doctrine*, 2 Akron L. Rev. 75 (1969).

Example 4-7

Assume that in this common law jurisdiction P (husband) learned of several adulterous affairs involving D (wife). After a family fight, D left the family home to stay with her mother. P filed an action for divorce, but dismissed it three days later at D's request. D then moved back into their home and they attempted to reconcile as husband and wife and were intimate on several occasions. However, the reconciliation lasted only a few weeks, after which P once again filed a petition alleging D's earlier adultery as the ground for the divorce. D answered and asserted the defense of condonation and asked the court to dismiss P's divorce action. Will a common law court be likely to recognize the defense of condonation on these facts?

Explanation

Condonation is the forgiveness of an antecedent matrimonial offense on the condition that it shall not be repeated, and that the offender shall thereafter treat the forgiving party with conjugal kindness. Under the common law, the condonation must be free, voluntary, not induced by duress or fraud, and not procured by unconscientious and fraudulent practices. Obviously, it cannot have been obtained by force and violence. Here, P, with knowledge of D's repeated acts of adultery, dismissed the initial divorce action and allowed D to move back in with him, and they were intimate. A common law court will reason that the acts of intercourse by P with D, with knowledge that D had earlier been guilty of adultery, indicate that P condoned the earlier behavior. A common law court would most likely dismiss P's divorce action. *See Tigert v. Tigert*, 595 P.2d 815 (Okla. App. 1979); *Panther v. Panther*, 295 P. 219, 221 (Okla. 1931).

4.23. Collusion

Collusion as a defense under the common law represented an agreement by the two parties to create a false-fact situation upon which a divorce could be granted when no ground existed. *Lurie v. Lurie*, 370 A.2d 739 (Pa. Super. 1976); *Nelson v. Nelson*, 24 N.W.2d 327 (S.D. 1946). For example, collusion occurred when the married partners, having decided that they would divorce, stage a fake adultery scene in an effort to create grounds for divorce. To carry out their scheme, the husband goes to a hotel room, where a paid co-respondent joins him and partially undresses. While the two of them sit on the edge of the hotel bed, the wife, as prearranged, walks in with a detective and photographer. The photographs and testimony of the detective provide the evidence of adultery, and this forms the basis for the divorce action. Because the incident was rigged, the divorce proceeding would be viewed as collusive and as a fraud on the court. A divorce action based on this evidence would be dismissed.

Example 4-8

Assume P sues D for divorce in a jurisdiction that requires proof of misconduct, even if the matter goes by default. In her divorce petition, P alleges that D was an adulterer. D does not answer the petition, and a default hearing is set where P must prove that D committed adultery. At the default hearing, only P appears. She produces a handwritten letter, allegedly written by D, in which he confesses to his adulterous behavior. Based on the letter and the testimony of P, who claims she was aware of D's behavior, will a common law court likely grant P a divorce from D?

Explanation

Common law courts would be concerned about the couple colluding to obtain a divorce. D's confession would be received in evidence. However, because of the potential for collusion, proceedings such as this were subject to close judicial scrutiny. In this hypothetical, a court would be suspicious of the evidence presented by P, and it would not be unusual for it to deny P a divorce. *See Grobin v. Grobin*, 55 N.Y.S.2d 32 (N.Y. Sup. 1945) (a divorce will not be granted on spouse's confession of adultery unsupported by any other evidence); *Zoske v. Zoske*, 64 N.Y.S.2d 819 (N.Y. Sup. 1946).

4.24. Connivance

Connivance was a defense under the common law that was sometimes used in divorce litigation where the claim was adultery. This defense was defined as consent by one party to the adulterous act of the other. For example, if the couples swapped spouses for a night at a party, this incident could not later be used as the basis for a divorce. Connivance is sometimes confused with collusion; however, the two are quite different. Collusion occurs when the parties collaborate to impose on the court by fabricating a ground for the divorce. Connivance is consent to an offense that is actually committed. *Farwell v. Farwell*, 133 P. 958 (Mont. 1913) (connivance is the corrupt consent of one party to the commission of the acts of the other, constituting the cause of divorce).

4.25. Laches (Undue Delay)

Laches is an equitable defense that has been applied in cases where, from delay, loss of evidence, and death, a judgment would be "conjectural and difficult to do justice." *Williamson v. Shoults*, 423 So. 2d 874 (Ala. Civ. App. 1982). It has also been applied where there has been such a neglect or omission to assert a right, when taken in conjunction with the lapse of time and other circumstances, causes the adverse party to be prejudiced. *Gover's Adm'r et al. v. Dunagan,* 184 S.W.2d 225, 226 (Ky. 1944). Laches will depend upon the special facts and circumstances as shown in each case. In an unusual situation, a court might apply the doctrine of laches when rejecting an effort to enforce a divorce judgment. *Wooddy v. Wooddy,* 261 A.2d 486 (Md. 1970); *see* Pryor v. Pryor, 213 A.2d 545 (1965) (laches barred wife's action, brought 13 years after the husband had obtained a divorce, to void divorce on the basis that he made false statement that he had been a resident of Maryland for 1 year prior to filing his bill of complaint); *Ross v. Ross,* 143 A.D.2d 429 (N.Y.A.D. 1988) (wife barred from amending divorce petition because of undue delay).

4.26. Insanity

Insanity as a defense to a divorce action was recognized by the common law under certain circumstances. *See Shaw v. Shaw,* 269 P. 80 (Wash. 1928). For example, where the ground for a divorce was a claim of cruel and inhuman treatment, the action would fail if it was based on acts attributable to the insanity of the defending party. *Bosveld v. Bosveld,* 7 N.W.2d 782, 785 (Iowa 1943) (insanity is not a ground for divorce and charge of "cruel and inhuman treatment" cannot be based on acts attributable to insanity). The common law view of this defense has been replaced in a majority of jurisdictions by statute.

4.27. Provocation

Provocation was also once a recognized defense to a divorce action in some jurisdictions. The theory was that one could not provoke physical retaliation on the part of his or her spouse and complain of such retaliation unless it was out of all proportion to the provocation. *Trenchard v. Trenchard,* 92 N.E. 243 (Ill. 1910); *De La Hay v. De La Hay,* 21 Ill. 251, 254 (1859); *Gress v. Gress,* 148 N.W.2d 166 (N.D. 1967) (when provocation is asserted as a defense, it is for the trial judge to determine whether sufficient provocation existed and whether the retaliatory action was out of proportion to the provocation).

RELIGION AS A DEFENSE TO DIVORCE

4.28. Defense Will Fail

A litigant who attempts to block a divorce proceeding on religious grounds will fail. Three United States Supreme Court cases have settled the issue.

First, in *Maynard v. Hill*, 125 U.S. 190, 210 (1888), the Court held that marriage was a social relationship governed by the laws of the individual states under their police powers. Second, in *Sherbert v. Verner*, 374 U.S. 398, 403 (1963), the Court reiterated the standard under which First Amendment infringements by state regulation are to be judged, stating that "any incidental burden on the free exercise of appellant's religion may be justified by a 'compelling state interest in the regulation of a subject within the State's constitutional power to regulate. . . . '" (citing *NAACP v. Button*, 371 U.S. 415, 438 (1963)).

The third case, *Reynolds v. United States*, 98 U.S. 145 (1878), asked whether freedom of religion made a federal law prohibiting polygamy unconstitutional. In rejecting the challenge to the prohibition, the Supreme Court observed that "[m]arriage, while from its very nature a sacred obligation, is, nevertheless, in most civilized nations, a civil contract, and usually regulated by law. Upon it society may be said to be built, and out of its fruits spring social relations and social obligations and duties, with which government is necessarily required to deal." 98 U.S. at 165. The Court also observed that "[l]aws . . . cannot interfere with mere religious belief and opinions, they may with practices. . . . Can a man excuse his practices to the contrary because of his religious belief? To permit this would be to make the professed doctrines of religious belief superior to the law of the land, and in effect to permit every citizen to become a law unto himself. Government could exist only in name under such circumstances." 98 U.S. at 165-167.

In *Williams v. Williams*, 543 P.2d 1401 (Okla. 1975), the appellant complained that her constitutional right to the free exercise of religion was violated when a divorce was granted over her religious objection. The appellate court observed that the trial court only dissolved the civil contract of marriage between the parties and that there was no attempt to dissolve it ecclesiastically. Consequently, there was no infringement of her constitutional right to freedom of religion. *See also Everson v. Board of Educ.*, 330 U.S. 1, 15 (1947); *Sharma v. Sharma*, 667 P.2d 395, 396 (1983); *Martian v. Martian*, 328 N.W.2d 844 (N.D. 1983); *Trickey v. Trickey*, 642 S.W.2d 47 (Tex. Ct. App. 1982).

Example 4-9

Assume that P brings an action to divorce D in a no-fault jurisdiction. D challenges the action on the basis of his religious beliefs. He claims that his faith does not allow a divorce. D asserts that a divorce decree will violate his rights under the First Amendment to the U.S. Constitution. His sincerity in his position and his devotion to his faith are apparent to the trial judge. Assume that there is sufficient evidence produced by P to justify issuing the divorce decree; however, the court is concerned with the First Amendment argument made by D. How will a court most likely rule?

Explanation

D will most likely fail in his constitutional argument. The court will view D's religious belief and practice as completely separate from the secular divorce proceeding. It finds support in this position from the Supreme Court cases discussed above.

THE MODERN DIVORCE REFORM MOVEMENT

4.29. Common Law Supplanted by Statutes

The statutory grounds for a divorce in American jurisdictions have developed at varying speeds over the past two centuries. It is interesting to note, for example, that South Carolina did not have a provision for an absolute divorce until well into the twentieth century. *Poteet v. Poteet*, 114 P.2d 91, 92 (N.M. 1941) (South Carolina constitutionally prohibits absolute divorce). For many years, New York held to the view that the only ground for divorce in that state was adultery. Some jurisdictions created early statutes that provided for divorce on a variety of grounds, including desertion and habitual drunkenness. Cruel and inhuman treatment and mental cruelty were added as grounds for divorce in many jurisdictions in the twentieth century and became a commonly used basis for a divorce because they covered a multitude of marital sins.

4.30. New Grounds: Irretrievable Breakdown of Marriage

In August 1970 the National Conference of Commissioners on Uniform State Laws approved the Uniform Marriage and Divorce Act (UMDA). It was subsequently amended, and in 1974 the American Bar Association's House of Delegates approved the revised Act. *See* Harvey L. Zuckman, *The ABA Family Law Section v. The NCCUSI: Alienation, Separation and Forced Reconciliation over the UMDA*, 24 Cath. U. L. Rev. 61 (1974).

The UMDA helped foster major statutory change in the grounds for divorce in the United States. Section 305 of the UMDA established that a divorce could occur when there was irretrievable breakdown of the marriage and both parties stated under oath or affirmed that this was the case. It also permitted a divorce when one party stated under oath that the marriage was irretrievably broken and the other did not deny it. If one party challenged the allegation, a court was required to make findings that an irretrievable breakdown had occurred or continue the matter for 30 to 60 days with an eye toward recommending that the parties seek counseling.

The phrase *irretrievable breakdown*, used as a ground for divorce in the UMDA, is very general. The phrase was the end product of intense debate and careful consideration toward accommodating a variety of contradictory interests. *See* Robert J. Levy, *Comments on Legislative History of Uniform Marriage & Divorce Act*, 7 Fam. L.Q. 405 (1973). The UMDA was intended to reduce the acrimony connected with such proceedings as well as the time devoted to such litigation in already overcrowded court calendars.

4.31. Emergence of "No-Fault" Divorce

Driven by changing societal values, various states became active participants in a nationwide family law revolution during the 1970s and 1980s. In response to these changes, states began promulgating versions of the UMDA, discussed above, that were colloquially referred to as "no-fault" grounds for divorce. For most judges and family lawyers, no-fault divorce was viewed as a dramatic and welcome reform. Under the former system, couples seeking a divorce had to prove that one partner was guilty of fault. Often, when the parties arrived at court, they had already divided their property, lived apart for many years, and had little to dispute. Nevertheless, to prove that grounds for the divorce existed, they were required to produce witnesses to corroborate their in-court sworn testimony proving that the other party was at fault. This procedure was followed even when the other party failed to appear at the hearing. The result was that many divorce proceedings were a sham. In other cases in which fault dictated the amount of property to be divided, moral judgments about which party was right or wrong ignored the complexity of the underlying causes of the marital dispute. The process also made the eventual outcome of a divorce action speculative rather than reasonably certain. Too often, husbands and wives were combatants, with each of their lawyers arguing that responsibility for the marriage breakup belonged solely to the other spouse.

The advent of no-fault legislation dramatically altered the matrimonial landscape. Under no-fault statutes, divorces were granted when it was clear there were irreconcilable differences. The no-fault statutes eliminated fault and wrong as a substantive ground for dissolution. They also required consideration of the marriage as a whole and made the possibility of reconciliation an important issue. The changes were intended to induce a conciliatory and uncharged atmosphere, which might facilitate resolution of the other issues and perhaps effect a reconciliation.

By the year 2000, virtually every jurisdiction with the exception of New York had adopted a provision that permitted a divorce without proof of fault. A typical ground involved a showing that the marriage was irretrievably broken. A statement to the court by either party that this was the case usually resulted in a divorce. Fault was retained in some jurisdictions as a significant feature in an award of maintenance, but in others it was completely removed from the law.

Example 4-10

Assume that P seeks to dissolve the marriage between P and D in a typical no-fault jurisdiction. P and D have been married for 21 years. P is a self-employed trucker, and P's job requires him to do a lot of traveling and to spend long periods away from home. P has asked D to accompany him on the trips, but D has refused. P claims that D has refused to be P's "partner in life." P testifies that there has been an irretrievable breakdown of the marriage and that the marriage is at an end. D responds that the marriage is not irretrievably broken and that all P needs to do is to engage in "some marriage counseling." D testifies that the two should reconcile, even though D is aware that P is involved in a relationship with another woman. The no-fault statute in this jurisdiction reads as follows:

> A dissolution of a marriage shall be granted by a county or district court when the court finds that there has been an irretrievable breakdown of the marriage relationship. A finding of irretrievable breakdown under this subdivision is a determination that there is no reasonable prospect of reconciliation. The finding must be supported by evidence that there is serious marital discord adversely affecting the attitude of one or both of the parties toward the marriage. If after a hearing the court determines that there is a reasonable prospect of reconciliation between the parties, the court should continue the matter for at least 90 days and require the parties to attend marriage counseling.

How will a court most likely rule?

Explanation

Every marriage relationship is unique; therefore, the court must look at the facts of each individual case to determine whether the marriage is irretrievably broken with no "reasonable prospect of reconciliation." Although it is commendable that D wishes to reconcile and is willing to forgive P for his adulterous affair, most courts will still find that the marriage is irretrievably broken. They will take the position that a healthy marriage can only be nurtured by the love of both husband and wife. The fact that P stated he did not want to be married to D and demonstrated this desire through his romantic relationship with another woman is sufficient evidence to persuade most courts that the marriage is irretrievably broken.

Example 4-11

Assume the existence of the same no-fault statute set out above in Example 4-10 and the facts as stated in that example. However, assume that there is additional testimony that on various occasions P asked D to accompany him on his trips so that they may attempt to reconcile, although she did not join him on any of those trips. D also asserts that P should have communicated in some way that their marriage was breaking down. How should a court rule?

Explanation

These additional facts will normally not make a difference in the trial court's decision to grant P a divorce. When P filed the divorce petition alleging irretrievable breakdown of their marriage, D should have been on notice that their marriage was in trouble. D was apparently aware of P's extramarital affair, and while D asserts that P had asked her to accompany him on trips in an attempt to reconcile, D did not join him on any of those trips. *See, e.g., Mackey v. Mackey*, 545 A.2d 362 (Pa. Super. Ct. 1988); *Liberto v. Liberto*, 520 A.2d 458, 461 (Pa. Super. Ct. 1987).

Example 4-12

Assume that P files a petition in a jurisdiction that provides alternative grounds for a divorce. In this jurisdiction, a divorce may be obtained on the basis of an irretrievable breakdown or adultery. P alleges that the marriage is irretrievably broken down and that D has committed adultery. At the conclusion of the hearing, the trial court finds that there has been an irretrievable breakdown of the marriage and grants the divorce. P objects to the judge's decision and moves to withdraw the count in P's petition regarding an irretrievable breakdown. P asserts that the court should have made a finding of adultery as the basis for the divorce. Is the trial judge likely to allow P to withdraw the count?

Explanation

Most courts will not allow P to withdraw the irretrievable breakdown count so that a court must make a finding that D was an adulterer. They will view the marriage as irretrievably broken when a husband moves out of the marital property to live with another woman. The policy of most courts is to make the law for legal dissolution of marriage effective for dealing with the realities of matrimonial experience and to give primary consideration to the welfare of the family rather than the vindication of private rights or the punishment of matrimonial wrongs. To allow P to proceed would be tantamount to allowing P to invoke the power of the court to vindicate a private right. *See, e.g., Rosenberg v. Rosenberg*, 39 Pa. D. & C.3d 549 1984 WL 2628 (Pa. Com. Pl. 1984).

4.32. State Recognition of *Ex Parte* Divorce: Full Faith and Credit

The availability of an *ex parte* divorce decree is limited by the Fourteenth Amendment, which provides that a person shall not be deprived of any interest in liberty or property without due process of law. This language has been interpreted to require adequate notice of the request for judicial relief and an opportunity to be heard concerning the merits of such relief. There are situations, however, where one of the parties to a divorce action cannot be located or refuses to respond after being properly served with notice of a divorce petition. In those cases, a court may grant an *ex parte* divorce.

The law surrounding whether a state must recognize an *ex parte* divorce decree issued in another state begins with the Full Faith and Credit Clause of the United States Constitution, Article IV, §1. It states, "Full faith and Credit shall be given in each State to the public Acts, Records, and judicial Proceedings of every other State. And the Congress may by general Laws prescribe the Manner in which such Acts, Records and Proceedings shall be proved, and the Effect thereof."

The Full Faith and Credit Clause of the Constitution requires that a state recognize the decrees of a sister state, provided that the sister state had jurisdiction. The Supreme Court has held that the judicial power to grant an *ex parte* divorce exists when at least one of the spouses is legally domiciled in the divorce granting state. *Williams v. State of North Carolina (Williams I)*, 317 U.S. 287 (1942). The decree granting state, however, cannot foreclose the subsequent readjudication of the question of domicile by another state. *Williams v. State of North Carolina (Williams II)*, 325 U.S. 226 (1945).

The burden of undermining an *ex parte* divorce decree "rests heavily upon the assailant." *Williams v. State of North Carolina (II), supra*, 325 U.S. at page 233. Specifically, that burden is "to overthrow the apparent jurisdictional validity of the . . . divorce decree by disproving . . . intention to establish a domicile" in the granting state. *Id.*

After the *Williams* cases, a question about the scope of an *ex parte* divorce proceeding remained. For example, could a valid *ex parte* divorce entered at the domicile of only one party to the marriage automatically terminate the other spouse's right to support? This question was settled via the theory of divisible divorce set forth in *Estin v. Estin*, 334 U.S. 541 (1948). There the court held that an *ex parte* Nevada divorce procured by the husband did not terminate the wife's prior adjudicated right to separate maintenance. The result in *Estin* was to make the divorce divisible and give effect to the Nevada decree insofar as it affects marital status and to make it ineffective on the issue of alimony.

Finally, in *Vanderbilt v. Vanderbilt*, 354 U.S. 416 (1957), the court perfected the divisible divorce theory by its holding that even when the wife's right to support had not been reduced to judgment before the *ex parte* divorce, that divorce could not affect her support rights. The Due Process Clause forbids a divorce court from adjudicating an absent spouse's right to support. Consequently, a spouse cannot be deprived by that court of whatever rights of support the spouse had under the law of his or her domicile at the time of the divorce. An *ex parte* divorce may not impose child support obligations or set an amount of attorney fees to be paid by the absent spouse. To impose those personal obligations on the out-state absent spouse, the party obtaining the *ex parte* divorce must usually proceed to the state where the absent spouse is domiciled and bring a separate action that comports with the Due Process Clause of the Constitution.

Example 4-13

Assume that P and D marry and live together in state X. When their relationship breaks down, P travels to state Y and establishes residence there. P files for divorce on the ground of extreme mental cruelty. D receives notice of the action and retains counsel in state Y. D's lawyer denies the allegations and challenges the personal jurisdiction of the court in state Y to hear the matter. Despite the objections, the divorce is granted by the court in state Y. P returns to state X, where she marries her high school sweetheart. D brings an action in state X alleging that the decree issued by the court in state Y is invalid; therefore, P's subsequent marriage is void. How will a court in state X rule on D's challenge?

Explanation

The court will rule that the decree issued by the court in state Y is valid and comports with due process. In this case, D had his day in court in state Y, where, via his lawyers, he contested personal jurisdiction. Unlike the fact situation in *Williams* I, the finding of personal jurisdiction was made in a proceeding in state Y where D appeared and participated. Full Faith and Credit requires that state X recognize the decree rendered by the court in state Y, which gained personal jurisdiction over both parties. *Sherrer v. Sherrer*, 334 U.S. 343 (1948).

Example 4-14

Assume that after ten years of marriage, P and D's relationship breaks down. P, a lawyer, has been having an affair with his secretary and they decide he should obtain an absolute divorce from D. P writes to a lawyer friend in state X asking about the requirements for obtaining a divorce in that state. He is told that in order to obtain an *ex parte* divorce in state X, a petitioner must establish in good faith a domicile for a minimum of six weeks. P travels with his secretary to state X, where he rents a hotel room for the required six weeks. During this period he continues to conduct business in state Y, where his home is located. He uses the telephone, fax, and Internet facilities located in his hotel room. He does not change the address on his driver's license or checking account or submit a postal change-of-address form. After obtaining an *ex parte* divorce from a court in state X, P returns to state Y, where his marriage to his secretary is announced. D begins an action in state Y claiming that the *ex parte* decree issued by the court in state X is not entitled to Full Faith and Credit in state Y and, therefore, P and D are still married. Is P's divorce decree entitled to Full Faith and Credit in state Y?

Explanation

D will contend that P failed to establish a bona fide domicile in state X. Based on the Supreme Court decisions of *Williams* I and *Williams* II, state Y is entitled to determine for itself the jurisdictional facts upon which the decree issued by the court in state X was based. D never appeared in the state X proceeding, so the issue of personal jurisdiction over D was never litigated. D will contend that P was never domiciled in good faith in state X and that he never intended to abandon his domicile in state Y. D's evidence includes the following: P rented a hotel room (temporary residence); retained and continued working at his job in state Y through the use of e-mail, fax, and telephone; brought his secretary to live with him in a hotel room in state X; and P never changed the location of his residence for his bank account or his home mailing address. This is substantial evidence that P never intended in good faith to establish a domicile in state X. *See Huntington v. Huntington*, 262 P.2d 104 (Cal. App. 1953).

Example 4-15

Assume that P and D are married for five years and live in state X. When their relationship breaks down, D leaves P to live with her parents in state Y. P files a petition for divorce in state X based on the ground of desertion. However, P failed to have the divorce summons and petition served on D in state Y, even though he knows the mailing address of D's parents and believes she is living with them. P also failed to provide D with a notice of the date on which the divorce petition is to be heard by the court in state Y. Without D's knowledge, the court in state X enters an *ex parte* divorce decree. A few weeks after the divorce decree is entered, P dies. D learns of the divorce when she attends P's funeral. She then seeks her intestate share of P's estate as his wife. Will she be successful?

Explanation

D will claim that she was denied due process because P knew her mailing address and should have provided her with notice of the divorce proceeding. D's argument most likely will be successful and as a result, the *ex parte* divorce decree voided. A collateral attack may be made upon a divorce decree when it can be shown that the defendant in the divorce action was not served with process where the party seeking the divorce knew the residence of the defendant (respondent), the defendant (respondent) did not appear in the proceeding on the merits, and the defendant (respondent) did not waive any jurisdictional objections or consent to the court proceeding. *See Cook v. Cook*, 342 U.S. 126 (1951).

CHAPTER 5

Child Custody and Parenting Plans

5.1. Introduction

When it functions well, the child custody legal process meets three objectives: it protects the interests of children, assists parents in restructuring their relationships with the children, and leads to fair and predictable results for families. Courts and legislatures have historically struggled to achieve these goals against the backdrop of a constantly changing society. Consequently, child custody law has evolved significantly over the last century and has changed dramatically in recent years.

As a practical matter, today only a small percentage of child custody disputes are resolved through a trial in the adversarial system. Instead, the vast majority of cases are settled through processes such as mediation and cooperative negotiation. These processes are designed to avoid distributing blame between the parties and to empower parents to create parenting arrangements tailored to meet the needs of the child or children.

THE IMPACT OF DIVORCE

5.2. Effects of Divorce on Children

With nearly 50 percent of marriages ending in divorce, researchers estimate that 40 percent of children have experienced or will experience the divorce of their parents. *See* Stephen J. Bahr, *Social Science Research on Family Dissolution: What It Shows and How It Might Be of Interest to Family Law Reformers*, 4 J.L. & Fam. Stud. 5 (2002).

Much has been written about the effects of divorce on children. There is, for example, general agreement that a child's adjustment to divorce is directly related to the level of conflict between the parents before, during, and after the divorce. A child whose parents exhibit a continuing high degree of conflict experiences more difficulty adjusting than one whose parents have a better relationship. *See* Irwin Sandler, Jonathan Miles, Jeffrey Cookston & Sanford Braver, *Effects of Father and Mother Parenting on Children's Mental Health in High- and Low-Conflict Divorces*, 46 Fam. Ct. Rev. 282 (April 2008); Joan B. Kelly & Robert E. Emery, *Children's Adjustment Following Divorce: Risk and Resilience Perspectives*, 52(4) Fam. Rel. 352 (2003); Joan B. Kelly, *Children's Adjustment in Conflicted Marriage and Divorce: A Decade Review of Research*, 39(8) J. Am. Acad. Child Adolescent Psychiatry 963 (2000). One frequently cited study concludes that children's adjustment to divorce is linked to factors such as the absence of the noncustodial parent, the adjustment of the custodial parent, the conflict between the parents, economic hardship, and stressful life changes. *See* Paul R. Amato, *Children's Adjustment to Divorce: Theories, Hypotheses, and Empirical Support*, 55 J. Marriage & Fam. 23 (1993).

5.3. Impact on Parenting

Although the marital relationship ends at divorce, couples with children will continue to deal with each other as parents. Consequently, they must give careful thought to restructuring their parental alliance and renewing their commitment to the children at this critical time.

Divorce or the breakup of a relationship where the parties are not married is a stressful experience for parents as well as children. Parents must typically deal with their own emotional and financial pressures in addition to meeting the heightened needs of their children. The parents' ability to cope with change and minimize ongoing conflict bears directly on the well-being of the restructured family.

Researchers have found that 25 percent of parents ease into a co-parenting relationship, half disengage for a period of time and then become more cooperative, and 25 percent remain at odds indefinitely. *See* Carla B. Garrity & Mitchell A. Baris, *Caught in the Middle* 27 (1994). In fact, some 10 percent of divorcing couples demonstrate "unremitting animosity" as their children grow up. *See* Janet Johnston & Vivienne Roseby, *In the Name of the Child: A Developmental Approach to Understanding and Helping Children of Conflicted and Violent Divorce* 4 (1997). These high-conflict couples require tightly structured parenting arrangements designed to protect children from ongoing hostility. Janet R. Johnston, *Building Multidisciplinary Professional Partnerships with the Court on Behalf of High-Conflict Divorcing Families and Their Children: Who Needs What Kind of Help?* 22 U. Ark. Little Rock L. Rev. 453, 469 (2000).

DEFINING CUSTODIAL RELATIONSHIPS

5.4. Overview

Until recently, when a divorce was granted, one parent received custody of the child and the other parent was granted "reasonable" visitation. Visitation would typically occur on weekends and for a few weeks in the summer. However, due to changing sex roles and a heightened awareness of the importance of both parents in child development, a variety of custody arrangements have emerged over the last 40 years. Courts now place less emphasis on predefined labels and greater emphasis on creating workable day-to-day parenting schedules.

5.5. Legal Custody

Legal custody is a technical term used by courts to describe a parent's authority to make major decisions on behalf of the child. Decisions that the legal custodian might make include those about the child's religion, education, and medical treatment. Legal custody can be awarded to one parent, an arrangement that courts refer to as "sole legal custody," or it can be shared by the parents, referred to as "joint legal custody." The American Law Institute (ALI) refers to legal custody as "decision making responsibility." ALI, *Principles of the Law of Family Dissolution: Analysis and Recommendations* §2.03(4) (2002).

5.6. Physical Custody

Physical custody is a technical term that describes a parent's right to have the child reside with him or her and the obligation of that parent to provide for the routine daily care and control of the child. Physical custody can be awarded to one parent, which courts refer to as "sole physical custody," or it can be shared, in what courts term a "joint physical custody" arrangement.

5.7. Joint Legal and Physical Custody

When parents share "joint legal custody," which is a technical term used by the court, they agree to work together to make major decisions affecting the child. For example, they plan to agree on where the child should attend school, whether the child should have a major medical procedure, and what if any religious training the child should receive. Under a typical joint legal custody arrangement neither parent has a superior right to make such decisions. Consequently, a well-drawn joint legal custody agreement will include procedures for resolving conflicts (such as returning to mediation) short of returning to court.

In contrast, when parents share "joint physical custody," also a technical term used by the court, the child maintains a residence in both homes. Joint physical custody does not require precise 50-50 time sharing. In practice, it is sometimes difficult to distinguish a sole physical custody arrangement in which the noncustodial or nonresidential parent has liberal overnight parenting time from a joint physical custody arrangement.

Joint custody, as it is commonly practiced, encompasses a wide variety of parenting arrangements. Some couples share legal custody even though one of the parents is the sole physical custodian. Other couples share both legal and physical custody.

Example 5-1

P and D reached an agreement concerning the care of their children after divorce. They agreed to discuss and reach consensus on matters such as the children's religion and schooling. During the school year, they agree that the children are to reside with P Monday through Friday and spend every weekend living with D. During the summer, the children are to reside with D Monday through Friday and live with P every weekend. What technical legal description(s) or term(s) will a court most likely assign to this arrangement?

Explanation

A court will consider the agreement as constituting joint legal custody because P and D will share the major policy-making decisions regarding the children. P may claim to have sole physical custody because the children will reside with P the majority of the time during the school year and 60 percent of the time on an annual basis. D may argue that this arrangement constitutes joint physical custody because joint physical custody does not necessitate equal time sharing and, over the course of the year, the children will reside with D 40 percent of the time. A court would likely agree with D and consider these parents to have joint legal and physical custody.

However, P would be considered to have sole physical custody were it not for the fact that the children will reside substantially with D during the summer.

Example 5-2

P and D had one child, who was a preschooler at the time of their divorce. The parties resided 50 miles from each other, and both sought sole physical custody of the child. The court found that neither parent was an ideal custodian, and the evidence showed that their relationship was filled with strife and disagreement. On its own motion and to the surprise of the parents, the court ordered that primary physical custody of the child would alternate between them every year once the child started school. The court viewed this arrangement as a way for the child to have ongoing contact with both parents. P appealed the decision, believing that such an arrangement would not be in the child's best interest because the child would have to change schools every year. What is the likely result on appeal?

Explanation

In *Headrick v. Headrick*, 916 So. 2d 610 (Ala. Civ. App. 2005), the appellate court was concerned about the annually alternating custody arrangement, as are most courts. The court stated, "[T]he alternation of residence and primary physical custody guarantees a recurring, yearly disruption in this young child's life for which we find no justification in the record." *Id.* at 614. One of the concerns with a joint physical custody arrangement is that the child may feel as if he or she doesn't have a primary home. Such feelings could be exacerbated by alternating physical custody on a yearly basis. In addition, in this example, the trial court was not in the position of approving a parenting plan agreed to by the parties. Rather, it created the alternating arrangement on its own and without the agreement of the parents. Given the fact the parents had a history of conflict, this unorthodox arrangement would likely not benefit the child. *But see Mundy v. Devon*, 2006 WL 902233 (Del. Supr. Apr. 6, 2006) (court approved yearly alternating primary placement). Because of the difficulty of anticipating the needs of the child into the future, P and D would be well advised to attend mediation before the child starts school.

5.8. Parenting Plans

As a result of growing concern about the adversarial nature of some child custody proceedings, family law professionals have encouraged courts and legislatures to move away from reliance on custody labels and focus instead on creating detailed agreements built around the needs of the particular family. These parenting plans are frequently developed in mediation and typically cover topics such as parenting time schedules, decision-making protocols, parental cooperation and communication, dispute resolution, and financial support. *See* Andrew Schepard, *Children, Courts and Custody* (2004). Instead of using traditional custody labels, parents may create their own terms or use labels such as "on-duty" and "off-duty" parent or "residential" and "nonresidential" parent.

Consistent with this trend in terminology and perspective, the ALI replaced the terms *custody* and *visitation* with the concept of "custodial responsibility" in an effort to avoid the win-lose framework present in many custody disputes. ALI, *Principles of the Law of Family Dissolution: Analysis and Recommendations* §2.03(3), cmt. e (2002). Rather than awarding custody, the ALI encourages parents to allocate parenting responsibility and plan for dispute resolution through the use of detailed parenting plans. §2.05. However, exceptions are made for couples with a history of child maltreatment, domestic violence, substance abuse, or interference with the child's relationship with the other parent. §2.11.

Even when parents agree to provisions in a parenting plan, courts review them to ensure that they are in the best interests of the child. Using a slightly different standard, the ALI proposes that courts reject parenting plans agreed to by the parents in cases where the agreement is not "knowing or voluntary" or if the plan would be harmful to the child. §2.06.

PRESUMPTIONS

5.9. Overview

Faced with the difficult task of awarding custody, courts and legislatures have historically relied on various preferences and presumptions to lend predictability to decision making and give effect to societal beliefs about the nature of the family. Today such presumptions have largely, but not entirely, given way to individualized determinations of "the best interests of the child."

5.10. Historical Paternal Presumption

Under the English common law fathers maintained nearly absolute control over their children. At marriage, the wife's legal identity merged with her husband's, and she had no right to property or to custody of children born during the marriage. The paternal presumption benefited the child because the mother had no means of supporting the child in the father's absence. The father even had the right to appoint a guardian other than the mother in the event of his death. W. Blackstone, *Commentaries on the Laws of England* 446, 453 (9th ed. 1783).

Only if the father engaged in highly immoral conduct might a mother be awarded custody. This paternal presumption began to give way in 1873, when the English Parliament granted women the right to have custody of children who were under the age of 16. Early American decisions adopted the common law view initially, but the paternal preference began to wane by the end of the nineteenth century.

5.11. Historical Maternal Presumption

By the 1920s and 1930s, many American jurisdictions replaced the paternal preference with the "tender years" maternal presumption. Children of "tender years" included preschool children and sometimes children through the age of ten. These young children were seen as best cared for by mothers who would provide for their physical and emotional needs while the father was working away from home. As was stated in *Freeland v. Freeland*, 159 P. 698, 699 (Wash. 1916), the presumption could be overcome by showing that the mother was unfit:

> Mother love is a dominant trait in even the weakest of women, and as a general thing surpasses the paternal affection for the common offspring, and, more-over, a child needs a mother's care even more than a father's. For these reasons courts are loathe to deprive the mother of the custody of her children and will not do so unless it be shown clearly that she is so far an unfit and improper person to be instructed with such custody as to endanger the welfare of the children.

In *Freeland*, the presumption operated in favor of the mother even though she had been "indiscreet in her conduct with men." *See also Krieger v. Krieger*, 81 P.2d 1081 (Idaho 1938) (tender years presumption applied even over preference of eight-year-old child to live with father).

During the late 1960s and early 1970s, societal views shifted and fathers were viewed as being as competent as mothers in raising young children. As a result, courts and legislatures gradually became more concerned with the best interests of the child than with the sex of the parent seeking custody. In some jurisdictions, application of the tender years presumption was held to be unconstitutional. *Ex parte Devine*, 398 So. 2d 686 (Ala. 1981).

Example 5-3

Assume that P and D were married in 2006 and had one child, who was born in 2008. When P and D decided to divorce, they could not agree on a parenting arrangement, and the matter was set for trial. At the time of the custody hearing the child was 28 months old. The court determined that both P and D were fit parents, even though the father (D) showed some immaturity and worked long hours and the mother (P) had some psychological problems. The court granted physical custody to P, taking "personal notice of the natural bond that develops between infants and a mother, especially when the mother breast-feeds the infant" and finding that "by the very nature of the age and gender of the minor child (28-month-old female)," placement with the father "would be a negative aspect in the weighing of the positives and negatives." The father appealed, claiming that the court's reasoning amounted to an application of the historical tender years doctrine. The mother argued that this was a permissible consideration under the best-interests standard. What is the likely result of D's appeal?

Explanation

If this case had taken place in 1930, the mother of the young child would be the preferred custodian unless she was proven to be unfit. However, today the maternal presumption is no longer in effect, and courts do not award custody based on presumptions favoring either sex. Consequently, in *Greer v. Greer*, 624 S.E.2d 423 (N.C. App. 2006), on which this example is based, D prevailed on appeal. In that jurisdiction the "tender years presumption" had been abolished by statute, and the appellate court agreed with D's argument that the trial court improperly applied it in this case. It said that the best interests of the child is the appropriate test and is to be determined from the actual facts without reference to any presumptions.

5.12. Historical Primary Caretaker Presumption

Although most states adopted the sex-neutral "best interests of the child" standard during the 1970s, some states presumed that the interests of a young child are best served by placing him or her with the "primary caretaker." The primary caretaker was defined as the parent who performed the following types of tasks for the child:

- Bathing, grooming, and dressing
- Purchasing, cleaning, and caring for clothes

- Providing medical care, including caring for a sick child and taking him or her to doctor's appointments
- Arranging for social interaction with the child's peers
- Arranging for child care, putting the child to bed, attending to the child during the night, and waking the child in the morning
- Educating
- Disciplining
- Providing religious training
- Teaching elementary skills

The primary caretaker presumption was based on the child's need for a stable and continuous relationship with the primary parent. Preference was given to the parent who was most experienced in caring for the child and who had the strongest history of meeting the child's daily needs. *See Garska v. McCoy*, 278 S.E.2d 357 (W. Va. 1981); *Pikula v. Pikula*, 374 N.W.2d 705 (Minn. 1985); cf. Minn. Stat. §518.17, subd. 1(a) (2009) ("[t]he primary caretaker factor may not be used as a presumption in determining the best interests of the child").

Opponents of the primary caretaker presumption contended that despite the sex-neutral language, the presumption favored women. Courts sometimes had difficulty identifying a primary parent, and the preference had little application to older children such as teenagers.

States no longer use the primary caretaker preference as a presumption. However, some states use it as a factor to be considered among others in determining the best interest of the child. *See, e.g., Gianvito v. Gianvito*, 975 A.2d 1164 (Pa. Super. 2009) (a trial court is to give positive consideration to the parent who has acted as their child's primary caretaker).

The ALI has incorporated the primary caretaker tasks into its definition of caretakingfunctions. *See ALI, Principles of the Law of Family Dissolution: Analysis and Recommendations* (2002). The ALI suggests that, in the absence of an agreed upon parenting plan, post-divorce caretaking should mirror pre-divorce caretaking patterns. §2.03, cmt. g. In other words, caretaking should be allocated in a way that "approximates the proportion of time each parent spent performing caretaking functions" prior to separation. §2.08. If one parent performed the bulk of caretaking functions prior to divorce, the approximation standard would function similarly to the primary caretaker presumption. However, if caretaking tasks were shared more equally during the marriage, that past arrangement would be carried forward after the divorce. *See Katharine T. Bartlett, U.S. Custody Law and Trends in the Context of the ALI Principles of the Law of Family Dissolution*, 10 Va. J. Soc. Pol'y & L. 5, 18 (2002).

Example 5-4

P (father) sued D (mother) for divorce in 1986. They lived in a state that adopted the primary caretaker presumption. P and D had two children, who were two and five years old. D worked as an airline attendant and was consequently away from home overnight each week from Monday through Friday. She also worked one weekend per month. When she was at home, she helped care for the children by cooking meals, doing laundry, and entertaining them. P worked at home and was responsible for all of the children's care while D was away from home. A year before the divorce, P went into treatment for an alcohol problem, and although he did not drink after his release, D was afraid that P would relapse while caring for the children. Both P and D sought custody of the children. Who would have been likely to prevail if the court applied the primary caretaker presumption to this dispute?

Explanation

In a jurisdiction that applied the primary caretaker presumption, P would have prevailed as the primary caretaker of the couple's young children. He was the parent who spent more time feeding, disciplining, clothing, bathing, and generally caring for the children. D would probably argue that she performed these caretaking tasks when she was at home and that she should not be penalized for working long hours to meet the financial needs of the family. However, she would be unsuccessful because the primary caretaker presumption was intended to provide stability for the children, who in this case had been primarily cared for by their father. D would argue that because of his alcohol problem, P was not a fit parent and, consequently, the primary caretaker doctrine should not have applied. However, treatment for an alcohol problem would not be sufficient to show that D was not a fit parent. Here no facts are presented showing that D was currently drinking or that his alcohol use was detrimental to the children. Although some states use "primary caretaker" as one factor in determining the best interests of the child, it is no longer used as a custodial presumption. Today, P and D would be encouraged to create a parenting plan that would allow both of them to have strong continuing relationships with the children.

5.13. Natural Parent Presumption

As against third parties, natural parents are entitled to custody of their children unless there is clear evidence of unfitness. *McDermott v. Dougherty*, 869

A.2d 751 (Md. 2005). "Third parties" include stepparents and grandparents as well as others. *See State of N.M. ex rel. CYFD v. Lisa A.*, 187 P.3d 189 (N.M. App. 2008); *Eifert v. Eifert*, 724 N.W.2d 109 (N.D. 2006); *Webb v. Webb*, 546 So. 2d 1062 (Fla. Ct. App. 1989) (trial court abused discretion in awarding custody to stepparent without clear and convincing evidence that mother was unfit); *Brewer v. Brewer*, 533 S.E.2d 541 (N.C. Ct. App. 2000) (presumed that fit parent will act in best interests of child). *But see Bennett v. Jeffreys*, 356 N.E.2d 277 (N.Y. Ct. App. 1976) (extraordinary circumstances required consideration of best interests of child).

This preference in favor of natural parents remains in effect today. However, courts have struggled with situations in which the parent seeking custody has had little or no contact with the child and the child has lived with a third party for an extended period. *See* Elizabeth Barker Brandt, *De Facto Custodians: A Response to the Needs of Informal Kin Caregivers?* 38 Fam. L.Q. 291 (2004). The ALI has dealt with these situations by broadening the definition of parent to include parents by estoppel and *de facto* parents. ALI, *Principles of the Law of Family Dissolution: Analysis and Recommendations* §2.03(b), (c) (2002). A parent by estoppel is a person other than a legal parent who (1) is obligated to pay child support, (2) lived with the child and accepted parental responsibility for at least two years in the good-faith belief that he was the child's father, or (3) lived with the child since birth and acted as a parent pursuant to a parenting or co-parenting agreement. A *de facto* parent is a person other than a legal parent or parent by estoppel who for at least two years (1) lived with the child and (2) performed the bulk of caretaking functions or as many caretaking functions as the parent with whom the child resided (3) either by agreement or due to the failure or inability of the legal parent to do so.

Example 5-5

Assume that P (mother) and D (father) are the parents of one child, C. Because of severe alcohol dependency resulting in her incarceration, P was no longer involved with the child. D worked as a merchant seaman and was at sea for lengthy periods of time. Consequently, C's grandparents cared for C for the majority of a period of four years following his birth. The grandparents petitioned the court for custody of C, alleging that C needed stability and that it would be in C's best interest if custody were awarded to the grandparents. D promised to seek other employment and argued that he had acted responsibly in arranging for the child to be cared for in his absence. Without making a finding that D was an unfit parent, the court awarded custody of C to the grandparents, and D appealed. What will D argue and what is the likely outcome?

Explanation

D will argue that he is entitled to custody of C because he has not been found to be an unfit parent. Under the natural parent presumption, if D is fit, he is entitled to custody even if C might be "better raised" by the grandparents. In *McDermott v. Dougherty*, 869 A.2d 751 (Md. 2005), the court found that the father's employment at sea did not constitute an extraordinary circumstance sufficient to overcome the preference for the natural parent. The court stated:

> In the balancing of court-created or statutorily-created "standards," such as "the best interest of the child" test, with fundamental constitutional rights, in private custody actions involving private third-parties where the parents are fit, absent extraordinary (*i.e.*, exceptional) circumstances, the constitutional right is the ultimate determinative factor; and only if the parents are unfit or extraordinary circumstances exist is the "best interest of the child" test to be considered.

Id. at 808.

5.14. Joint Legal and Physical Custody Presumptions

Some legislatures have created presumptions that joint legal custody and, to a much lesser extent, joint physical custody are in the best interests of children. Some of the presumptions have limited application, such as when parents agree to share joint legal custody and/or joint physical custody, or when a parent requests a form of joint custody. In contrast, other states have adopted "preferences" for joint legal and/or physical custody or have decided to make joint legal and physical custody decisions based solely on the merits of each case. A few states disfavor joint custody, particularly joint physical custody. The ALI, in the absence of a parenting plan, presumes that joint decision making (joint legal custody) will be in the best interests of a child if each parent has performed a reasonable share of parenting tasks and there has been no domestic violence or child abuse. ALI, *Principles of the Law of Family Dissolution: Analysis and Recommendations* §2.09 (2002). Needless to say, careful reading of statutory language and relevant case law is necessary to determine the policy of any given state with respect to presumptions of joint legal and physical custody.

In a lengthy decision holding that recent statutory amendments did not create a presumption of joint physical care, the Iowa Supreme Court analyzed research on joint legal and physical custody arrangements and identified four factors for determining whether joint physical care is in the best interests of a child: (1) stability and continuity of care giving; (2) ability of parents to communicate and "show mutual respect"; (3) degree of parental conflict; and (4) parental agreement on approach to daily matters. In *re*

Marriage of Hansen, 733 N.W.2d 683 (2007). In addition, the court found "growing support" for the assertion that in terms of benefit to the child, the quality of contact with a nonresidential parent may outweigh the quantity of contact. *See also* Christy M. Buchanan & Parissa L. Jahromi, *A Psychological Perspective on Shared Custody Arrangements*, 43 Wake Forest L. Rev. 419 (2008).

Whether by presumption or not, joint legal and physical custody arrangements have become more common in recent years. Researchers estimate that joint legal custody is the final disposition in nearly 80 percent of cases, whereas joint physical custody is the result in 20 percent of cases. *See* Eleanor E. Maccoby & Robert J. Mnookin, *Dividing the Child: Social and Legal Dilemmas of Custody* 108, 113 (1997). Viewed positively, this trend signifies an increasing commitment to cooperative parenting after divorce. *See* Isolina Ricci, *Mom's House, Dad's House: Making Two Homes for Your Child* (1997). However, if underlying parental conflict is not resolved, such arrangements may exacerbate existing conflict. For this reason, joint custody is not favored in cases where the parties have a history of high conflict that may include domestic violence. Janet R. Johnston, *A Child-Centered Approach to High Conflict and Domestic Families: Differential Assessment and Interventions*, 12 J. Fam. Stud. 15 (2006); Janet R. Johnston, *Building Multidisciplinary Professional Partnerships with the Court on Behalf of High-Conflict Divorcing Families and Their Children: Who Needs What Kind of Help?* 22 U. Ark. Little Rock L. Rev. 453 (2000). Recent research from Australia indicates that shared care may work best for families with particular traits.

> It [shared care] was a parenting arrangement that proved viable for a small and distinct group of families, who shared the following profile: electing a shared arrangement, as opposed to having legally enforceable orders to adopt such an arrangement; geographical proximity (within a moderate car trip); the ability of parents to get along sufficiently well; a business-like working relationship between parents; child-focused arrangements; a commitment by everyone to make shared care work; family-friendly work practices for both mothers and fathers; financial comfort (particularly for women); and shared confidence that the father is a competent parent.

Jennifer E. McIntosh, *Legislating for Shared Parenting: Exploring Some Underlying Assumptions*, 47 Fam. Ct. Rev. 389 (2009).

MODEL ACTS

5.15. Uniform Marriage and Divorce Act

A majority of the states have adopted statutes providing that custody should be awarded based on the best interests of the child. Many of these statutes are patterned on §402 of the Uniform Marriage and Divorce Act (UMDA), which states,

> The court shall determine custody in accordance with the best interest of the child. The court shall consider all relevant factors including:
>> (1) the wishes of the child's parent or parents as to his custody;
>> (2) the wishes of the child as to his custodian;
>> (3) the interaction and interrelationship of the child with his parent or parents, his siblings, and any other person who may significantly affect the child's best interest;
>> (4) the child's adjustment to his home, school, and community; and
>> (5) the mental and physical health of all individuals involved.
>
> The court shall not consider conduct of a proposed custodian that does not affect his relationship to the child.

Some states have included additional factors to be considered in determining the best interests of the child. Examples include factors relating to the child's primary caretaker, the child's cultural background, the effect of domestic abuse on the child, and the propensity of each parent to encourage continuing contact between the child and the other parent.

Although widely used, the best-interest standard has been criticized because of its indeterminate nature. Despite the enumerated factors, judges must exercise substantial discretion in applying the standard, and this can lead to unpredictable and sometimes arbitrary results.

5.16. American Law Institute

The American Law Institute has created an alternative definition of the best interests of the child that makes fairness between the parents clearly secondary to the best interests of the child. *See* ALI, *Principles of the Law of Family Dissolution: Analysis and Recommendations* (2002). Under §2.02, the child's bests interests are served by parental planning and agreement, continuity in attachments, contact with both parents, caretaking by skilled and loving adults who place a priority on it, avoidance of conflict and violence, and "expeditious" decision making. The ALI favors the use of agreed parenting plans to achieve these goals. §2.05. However, if agreement is not reached, the ALI suggests allocating custodial responsibility to "approximate" the proportion of caretaking done by each parent prior to the divorce. §2.08. Exceptions may be made to accommodate the wishes of some children, to avoid separating siblings, to avoid harm to the child, and for other reasons listed in §2.08(1). Joint decision-making responsibility is presumed to be in the child's best interest unless a contrary showing is made. §2.09.

STANDARDS FOR DETERMINING THE BEST INTERESTS OF THE CHILD

5.17. Race

The Supreme Court has held that courts cannot use race as the sole or decisive factor in awarding custody. In *Palmore v. Sidoti*, 466 U.S. 429 (1984), the United States Supreme Court held that the lower court improperly failed to consider the relative qualifications of both parents and erred in depriving the mother of custody of her child because she had entered into an interracial marriage. Courts have consistently interpreted *Palmore* as not prohibiting the consideration of race in matters of child custody. *See, e.g., J.H.H. v. O'Hara*, 878 F.2d 240, 245 (8th Cir. 1989) (declining to read *Palmore* as "a broad proscription against the consideration of race in matters of child custody"); *Drummond v. Fulton County Department of Family & Children's Services*, 563 F.2d 1200, 1204-1206 (5th Cir. 1977) (en banc) (determining that use of race as merely one factor in making adoption decisions is constitutional), *cert. denied*, 437 U.S. 910 (1978); *Tallman v. Tabor*, 859 F. Supp. 1078 (E.D. Mich. 1994) (holding that race can be considered in determining custody so long as race is not the sole consideration); *In re Davis*, 465 A.2d 614, 621-629 (1983) (holding that trial court should have considered race as a factor in making foster placement decision); *Farmer v. Farmer*, 439 N.Y.S.2d 584, 588 (1981) (stating that "the general rule appears to be that race is simply one factor among many others which should be considered in determining what is in the child's best interest"). So long as race is not the sole consideration for custody decisions, but only one of several factors, it is not an unconstitutional consideration. The ALI prohibits court consideration of race or ethnicity. §2.12(1)(a).

5.18. Religion

If divorcing parents have religious differences, constitutional protections concerning the free exercise of religion may come into play. Consequently, courts cannot favor one religious tradition over another. However, courts can consider the compatibility of a parent's religious behavior with the health and well-being of the child. *See Hicks v. Cook*, 288 S.W.3d 244 (Ark. App. 2008) ("religious beliefs and practices are only material as they affect children's best interests"); *Sagar v. Sagar*, 781 N.E.2d 54 (Mass. App. Ct. 2003). The ALI prohibits consideration of a parent's religious practices other than as necessary to protect the child from harm or to allow the child to continue to practice a religion that is significant to the child. ALI, *Principles of the Law of Family Dissolution: Analysis and Recommendations* §2.12(1)(c) (2002).

Example 5-6

In the case of *Jones v. Jones*, 832 N.E.2d 1057 (Ind. App. 2005), P and D were the divorcing parents of one child. They both practiced Wicca, which is a form of paganism. The court awarded them joint legal custody and awarded D sole physical custody of their child. The judge directed the parents to "take such steps as are needed to shelter [the child] from involvement and observation of these non-mainstream religious beliefs and rituals." Both parents appealed the decision. What was the most likely outcome of the appeal?

Explanation

On appeal, the child's legal custodians (P and D jointly) were found to have the right to determine the child's religious upbringing. The appellate court found that there was no indication that the child would be endangered by Wiccan practice or that the parents disagreed about the choice of religion. Consequently, the appellate court held that the trial court lacked authority to limit the parents' direction with respect to religious practice. (The court did not reach the issue of the parents' constitutional right to control the religious training of the child.)

5.19. Disability

Under §102(5) of the UMDA, courts are instructed to consider the mental and physical health of all the parties. This does not give courts license to discriminate against parents with disabilities. Rather, this language has been interpreted to require the courts to make case-by-case determinations concerning the effect of the disability on the child. *See Arneson v. Arneson*, 670 N.W.2d 904 (S.D. 2003); *Schumm v. Schumm*, 510 N.W.2d 13 (Minn. Ct. App. 1993).

5.20. Child's Preference

Most courts will consider "the wishes of the child as to his custodians" as described in §402 of the UMDA. However, this broad language is tempered by the court's discretion to determine whether the child has sufficient maturity to express a meaningful preference. Although age is not the sole consideration in making this determination, teenagers are typically consulted.

See Joan B. Kelly, *Psychological and Legal Interventions for Parents and Children in Custody and Access Disputes: Current Research and Practice*, 10 Va. J. Soc. Pol'y & L. 129 (2002) (discussing ramifications of excluding children from the process); Andrew Schepard, *Children, Courts, and Custody* (2004); Randi L. Dulaney, *Children Should Be Seen AND Heard in Florida Custody Determinations*, 25 Nova L. Rev. 815 (2001) (discussing various state statutes regarding child preference). The ALI makes an exception to the "approximation" rule to accommodate the "firm and reasonable preference" of a child of a specific age. ALI, *Principles of the Law of Family Dissolution: Analysis and Recommendations* §208(1)(b) (2002).

When children are consulted, the court will evaluate the reasons behind the child's expressed preference. For example, in *In re Marriage of Mehlmauer*, 131 Cal. Rptr. 325 (Ct. App. 1976), the court did not defer to the preference of a 14-year-old boy who preferred to live with his father because the father allowed him to wear his hair longer and stay out later. However, in *McMillen v. McMillen*, 602 A.2d 845 (Pa. 1992), the court considered the preference of an 11-year-old child to live with his father where the two homes were equally suitable but the boy testified that his stepfather frightened and upset him and that he was left unattended by his mother and stepfather after school.

When a court is considering consultation with the child, §404 of the UMDA provides for two alternatives. First, the judge can interview the child in chambers and on the record with the attorneys present. Second, the court can "seek the advice" of a professional who can submit a written report to the court. Either way, care must be taken to avoid undue parental influence or coercion on the child being interviewed. *See Couch v. Couch*, 146 S.W.3d 923 (Ky. 2004) (mother entitled to access in camera interview tape). A child should not be interviewed in open court.

Section 310 of the UMDA provides that the court may appoint an attorney to act as an advocate for the child. However, this is relatively rare in most jurisdictions. In contrast, courts sometimes appoint a guardian *ad litem* who acts in the child's best interest as opposed to carrying out the child's wishes. Schepard, *supra; see also* ALI, *Principles of the Law of Family Dissolution: Analysis and Recommendations* §2.13 (2002).

5.21. Separating Siblings

Courts avoid separating biological siblings when making child custody arrangements. Siblings are kept together to maintain stability and promote sibling relationships unless there are compelling reasons to separate them. *See In re Marriage of Heath*, 18 Cal. Rptr. 3d 760 (Cal. App. 2004) (court improperly found detriment to one child based on sibling's disability). The ALI provides for an exception to the "approximation" standard in order to keep siblings together. ALI, *Principles of the Law of Family Dissolution: Analysis and Recommendations* §2.08(1)(c) (2002).

5.22. Parental Conduct Not Affecting the Child: The Nexus Test

Many states have adopted statutory language contained in §402 of the UMDA preventing courts from considering parental conduct that does not affect the parent's relationship to the child. Under the nexus test, evidence concerning parental behavior is relevant to a child custody decision only if the parental behavior affects the parent's relationship with the child; in other words, there must be a nexus between the parental activity and harm to the child. Whether parental conduct affects the child is a question of fact that the trial court must determine on a case-by-case basis. Questions of parental conduct are sometimes raised in cases involving gay and lesbian parents and cases involving cohabiting parents.

5.23. Gay and Lesbian Parents

The nexus test has been used in cases where one parent is gay or lesbian. While some courts have hesitated to award custody to gay or lesbian parents, other courts have considered what, if any, effect the parent's sexual orientation has upon the child or children. *See Hollon v. Hollon,* 784 So. 2d 943 (S. Ct. Miss. 2001); *Massey-Holt v. Holt,* 255 S.W.3d 603 (Tenn. Ct. App. 2007). The nexus test view is consistent with the position taken by the American Psychological Association in passing a resolution stating that sexual orientation should not be the sole consideration in making custody decisions. The ALI specifically prohibits court consideration of the sexual orientation of the parent. ALI, *Principles of the Law of Family Dissolution: Analysis and Recommendations* §2.12(1)(d) (2002).

5.24. Cohabitation

In the past, a parent's cohabitation with a member of the opposite sex would typically result in loss of custody. *See Jarret v. Jarret,* 449 U.S. 927 (1980). However, under §402 of the UMDA, cohabitation is relevant only to the extent that the parent's sexual relationship adversely affects the child or children. Similarly, the ALI prohibits consideration of a parent's extramarital sexual behavior unless it harms the child. ALI, *Principles of the Law of Family Dissolution: Analysis and Recommendations* §2.12(1)(e) (2002). *See* Margaret F. Brinig, *Feminism* and Child Custody Under Chapter Two of the American Law Institute's Principles of the Law of Family Dissolution, 8 Duke J. Gender L. & Pol'y 301, 312 (2001).

Example 5-7

P (mother) and D (father) are seeking a divorce. They separated in 2009, and they agreed that the couple's three children, ages four, six, and ten, would reside temporarily with D while the divorce was pending. D began cohabiting with C against the wishes of P, who strongly disapproves of cohabitation outside of marriage on moral grounds. P learns that C was twice convicted of shoplifting and that C drinks alcoholic beverages in the presence of the children. Assuming that D is otherwise a fit parent, will P be awarded physical custody based on D's cohabitation?

Explanation

D's cohabitation is relevant to the question of physical custody only if it adversely affects the children. P will argue that the shoplifting convictions and the drinking in front of the children show that C has poor moral character and will be a bad influence on the children. D will argue that P should not be awarded custody based on D's cohabitation with C unless P can prove specific adverse consequences to the children. Because the children were not involved with the shoplifting charges (and may not even be aware of them) and there is no indication that C drinks to excess or has placed the children in danger while drinking, P is not likely to be awarded physical custody of the children based solely on D's cohabitation with C. However, if P can show specific adverse consequences to the children, via expert testimony or otherwise, the cohabitation could become a factor in the outcome of the case. This is an example of a situation where the parties might benefit from creating a mediated parenting plan addressing ground rules for parenting.

5.25. Careers

Despite the gender-neutral language of the "best interests" test, working mothers sometimes fear that their careers could work against them in a custody dispute. This was the case in *Rowe v. Franklin*, 663 N.E.2d 955 (Ohio Ct. App. 1995), in which the trial court was found to have abused its discretion by focusing on a mother's behavior (including her enrollment in law school) rather than the best interests of the child. *See also Burchard v. Garay*, 724 P.2d 486 (Cal. 1986) (not permissible for court to award custody of child in day care based on economic advantage of father with new stay-at-home wife); *Linda R. v. Richard E.*, 162 A.D.2d 48 (N.Y. 1990) (mother who worked outside the home was not a "remote control" mother). Fathers also sometimes fear that their employment, particularly if they work long hours or travel frequently, may hinder their chances of being awarded sole or joint physical custody of their children. The ALI prohibits consideration of the relative earning capacity of the parents. ALI, *Principles of the Law of Family Dissolution: Analysis and Recommendations* §2.12(1)(f) (2002).

5.26. Cooperative Parent Provisions

Most states encourage or require courts to consider the extent to which a proposed custodial parent is likely to encourage ongoing contact between the child and the other parent. These are known as "cooperative" or "friendly" parent provisions, and the idea behind them is to encourage awards of custody to the parent who is most likely to support the child's relationship with the noncustodial parent. Such provisions have come under attack when applied to situations involving domestic violence and high-conflict cases. Consequently, some states make this factor inapplicable if there is a history of family violence. Peter G. Jaffe et al., *Child Custody and Domestic Violence: A Call for Safety and Accountability* 68 (2003). *See also* ALI, *Principles of the Law of Family Dissolution: Analysis and Recommendations* §2.11(1)(d) (2002).

Example 5-8

Assume that P and D live in a jurisdiction that has adopted UMDA (see Section 5.14 *supra*) and that the legislature has amended the Act to include the following additional factor: "(6) the disposition of each parent to encourage and permit frequent contact with the other parent by the child." Both P and D seek sole legal and physical custody of their child when P files for divorce. They are unable to agree on custodial arrangements and they have a history of conflict. The court awards P sole physical custody but, over P's objection, orders joint legal custody, stating that without such an order P would not "foster the relationship" between D and the child. Will P prevail on appeal?

Explanation

P is not likely to prevail on appeal because judges consider the proclivity of a proposed custodian to foster the child's relationship with the other parent when they award legal and physical custody. *Kay v. Ludwig*, 686 N.W.2d 619 (Neb. Ct. App. 2004). More typically, cooperative parent provisions are raised in connection with physical custody rather than legal custody awards. P and D may benefit from mediation addressing their decision-making process; otherwise, shared legal custody could result in an increased (rather than decreased) level of conflict.

5.27. Domestic Violence

In the past, as the states moved away from fault divorce and adopted provisions preventing courts from considering parental conduct that did not affect the child, some courts failed to view intimate partner abuse as relevant to child custody decisions. Unfortunately, in approximately half of families experiencing domestic violence, children are also physically abused. In other cases children are harmed by witnessing domestic violence. Jeffrey L. Edleson & Oliver J. Williams, *Involving Men Who Batter in Their Children's Lives*, in *Parenting by Men Who Batter: New Directions for Assessment and Intervention* 12-15 (Jeffrey L. Edleson & Oliver J. Williams eds., 2007). *See also* Janis Wolak & David Finkelhor, *Children Exposed to Partner Violence*, in *Partner Violence* 73 (Jana L. Jasinski et al. eds., 1998).

Today, nearly every state requires courts to consider the presence of domestic violence when awarding custody. *See Barry v. Barry*, 862 N.E. 2d 143, 146 (Ohio App. 2006) ("We cannot conceive how domestic violence by one spouse against another could not be relevant in a determination of an allocation of parental rights and responsibilities regarding their children."). Some states have gone so far as to create rebuttable presumptions against awards of custody to parents with a history of domestic violence. *See* Nancy K.D. Lemon, *Statutes Creating Rebuttable Presumptions Against Custody to Batterers: How Effective Are They?* 28 Wm. Mitchell L. Rev. 601 (2001); Nancy Ver Steegh, *Differentiating Types of Domestic Violence: Implications for Child Custody*, 65 La. L. Rev. 1379, 1422-1426 (2005). However, family courts and family law professionals continue to grapple with issues such as how to differentiate among families experiencing domestic violence, methods of screening and triage, safe participation in court processes and services, appropriate outcomes for children, and changing family court roles and resources. Nancy Ver Steegh & Clare Dalton, *Report from the Wingspread Conference on Domestic Violence and Family Courts*, 46 Fam. Ct. Rev. 454 (2008).

When domestic violence is an issue, special care must be taken in making child custody decisions and creating parenting plans. Researchers Peter G. Jaffe, Janet R. Johnston, Claire V. Crooks, and Nicholas Bala suggest consideration of the following priorities:

1. Protect children directly from violent, abusive, and neglectful environments;
2. Provide for the safety and support the well-being of parents who are victims of abuse (with the assumption that they will then be better able to protect their child);
3. Respect and empower victim parents to make their own decisions and direct their own lives (thereby recognizing the state's limitations in the role of *loco parentis*);

4. Hold perpetrators accountable for their past and future actions (i.e., in the context of family proceedings, have them acknowledge the problem and take measures to correct abusive behavior); and

5. Allow and promote the least restrictive plan for parent-child access *that benefits the child,* along with parents' reciprocal rights.

If all five goals cannot be simultaneously achieved, they recommend that the lower priorities (those with higher numbers on the list above) be successively abandoned. Peter G. Jaffe, Janet R. Johnston, Claire V. Crooks & Nicholas Bala, *Custody Disputes Involving Allegations of Domestic Violence: Toward a Differentiated Approach to Parenting Plans,* 46 Fam. Ct. Rev. 500, 509 (2008).

Example 5-9

Assume that P and D live in a jurisdiction that has adopted the UMDA (see Section 5.14 *supra*) and that the legislature amended the Act to add the following additional factors: "(6) the effect on the child of domestic abuse that has taken place between the parents; and (7) the disposition of each parent to encourage and permit frequent contact with the other parent by the child." D has been violent with P on several occasions, and D frequently uses tactics of intimidation to control P's behavior. When P files for divorce, P and D each seek custody of the two children. D has never physically harmed the children, but P claims that the children have witnessed the violence and that D should not have custody of the children. How is a court likely to analyze the situation with respect to child custody?

Explanation

Under the UMDA, the court is required to consider a number of factors in determining the best interests of the children. The court will exercise its discretion in determining which factors are most important in a given case. P will argue that the children are directly affected by the domestic violence because they have witnessed the physical abuse and intimidation. D will argue that D has never physically harmed the children and that if awarded custody, P will not be disposed to allowing D to have continuing contact with the children (P will not be a "cooperative" parent). Assuming that P has evidence of the abuse, a court is likely to award custody to P and carefully structure parenting time for D. If P lived in a jurisdiction that had adopted a rebuttable presumption against custody awards to perpetrators, P would be awarded custody if P could prove abuse of sufficient frequency and severity to trigger the presumption.

5.28. American Law Institute View of Domestic Violence and Custody

The ALI requires special written findings before a parent who has engaged in domestic violence is allowed to have custodial responsibility or decision-making responsibility for a child. The burden is placed on the parent who has committed domestic violence to show that such contact will not endanger family members. ALI, *Principles of the Law of Family Dissolution: Analysis and Recommendations* §2.11(3) (2002).

COURT SERVICES: TRIAGE, EDUCATION, AND INVESTIGATION

5.29. Differentiated Case Management

Recognizing that families have different needs, some courts customize the handling of dissolution cases using triage procedures and multidisciplinary screening teams. Once identified, high-conflict and violent families are referred to appropriate services. Even in jurisdictions where differentiated case management has been implemented, screening for domestic violence and high conflict is best accomplished when all family law professionals, including attorneys, actively participate. *See* Peter Salem, Debra Kulak & Robin M. Deutsch, *Triaging Family Court Services: The Connecticut Judicial Branch's Family Intake Screen*, 27 Pace L. Rev. 741 (2007).

5.30. Parenting Education Programs

In an effort to reduce conflict and help parents develop strategies to work cooperatively, some jurisdictions offer, and in some cases require, that parents attend sessions addressing the impact of divorce on children, co-parenting after divorce, and conflict resolution. The purpose of such classes is to ease the children's adjustment to divorce, prevent long-term emotional difficulties, and avoid relitigation of custody and visitation issues.

Some jurisdictions mandate attendance at educational sessions, and parents who fail to comply risk being held in contempt of court and other sanctions. Other states have implemented adult education programs but leave the issue of compulsory attendance to the discretion of the court. A few states make attendance entirely optional. *See* Solveig Erickson & Nancy Ver Steegh, *Mandatory Divorce Education Classes: What Do the Parents Say?* 28 W. Mitchell L. Rev. 889, 895 (2001).

Preliminary research indicates that attending parent education classes early in the divorce process is more valuable than attending them later on. Although early attendance has been linked to reduced rates of relitigation of custody, support, and visitation issues, few states require attendance within 45 days of service of the divorce complaint.

Do parental divorce programs work? So far, research indicates that participating parents may become more cooperative, parents may become more aware of the needs of the children, and some parental conflict levels may be reduced as a result of parent education programs. *See* Nancy Ver Steegh, *Family Court Reform and ADR: Shifting Values and Expectations Transform the Divorce Process*, 42 Fam. L. Q. 659 (2008).

Despite positive reviews from many parents, victims of domestic violence should not attend general parent education courses because of safety issues and because messages about co-parenting and enhanced communication can be dangerous for them. Instead, when domestic violence has occurred, specialized programs stressing safety planning and separate parenting should be provided. Geri S. W. Fuhrmann et al., *Parent Education's Second Generation: Integrating Violence Sensitivity*, 37 Fam. & Conciliation Cts. Rev. 24 (1999).

Example 5-10

P has filed for divorce from D. They have three young children. They live in a jurisdiction where the court has the discretion to order them to attend a parent education program. The judge assigned to their case orders them both to attend such a program. D does not want the divorce and refuses to attend the parenting sessions. What is likely to happen?

Explanation

By failing to attend the parent education program, D is in violation of a court order and is likely to be held in contempt of court. It appears that D understood the order, that it was clear, and that D failed to make a good faith effort to attend the educational program. D's conduct appears to be intentional. D may be allowed to "purge" the civil contempt citation by attending the program. Otherwise, D could be jailed for a period of time. In either event, P will be allowed to proceed with the divorce. *See In re Marquise EE*, 257 A.D.2d 699, N.Y.A.D. 1999).

5.31. Guardians ad Litem

Under various state statutes and depending on the resources available, a guardian *ad litem* may be appointed to represent the interests of the child.

The guardian *ad litem* investigates the child's situation, reports to the court, and advocates for the child's best interests. Although the guardian *ad litem* may be an attorney, this role differs from traditional attorney-client representation because the guardian *ad litem* formulates his or her own opinion concerning the best interests of the child rather than acting as an advocate of the child's expressed preference.

5.32. Neutral Mental Health Evaluators

Courts sometimes appoint neutral mental health professionals, such as child psychologists or social workers, to prepare custody evaluations containing specific recommendations for parenting arrangements. The investigation may be performed by a court agency, a state social services department, or a private practitioner. A report ordered by the court may be admitted into evidence. However, under §405 of the UMDA, any party can require the professional and those the professional has interviewed to testify.

Because courts frequently place substantial weight on the recommendations, commentators urge courts to scrutinize evaluator qualifications and report quality. *See* Andrew I. Schepard, *Children, Courts, and Custody* 152 (2004). In response to concerns about accountability and variations in practice, groups such as the Association of Family and Conciliation Courts have published model professional standards for custody evaluators. Task Force for Model Standards of Practice for Child Custody Evaluation, *Model Standards of Practice for Child Custody Evaluation*, 45 Fam. Ct. Rev. 70 (2007).

6

Modifying Custody — Relocating to Another Jurisdiction

6.1. Introduction

This chapter examines a variety of legal problems associated with two reasonably discrete types of custody modification actions. The first type of modification action involves the typical request for a change of custody from one parent to the other, after an initial order has been made and primary or sole custody has been awarded to one parent, and relocation is not an issue. The second type of modification action involves an analysis of issues associated with a custodial parent's request to relocate to another state or to a foreign country with the minor child or children after an initial order awarded primary or sole custody to the parent requesting the move.

JURISDICTION

6.2. Subject Matter Theory

States uniformly agree that they have subject matter jurisdiction to modify a custody order during the minority of the child or children if the modification request is made in the state where the original custody order was entered. This principle rests upon the well-accepted theory that the state always sits as a third party to divorce proceedings and carries the responsibility of ensuring that the best interest of a child is protected during minority. *See Troxel v. Granville*, 530 U.S. 57, 68-69 (2000) (so long as a parent adequately cares for his or her children (i.e., is fit), there will normally be no reason for the state to inject itself into the private realm of the family to further question the ability of that parent to make the best decisions concerning the rearing of that parent's children). The state always has a role as *parens patrie* as well as an interest in protecting a child where allegations of abuse, neglect, or abandonment are made. *Roth v. Weston*, 789 A.2d 431 (Conn. 2002).

6.3. *Res Judicata*; Presumption; Change in Circumstances Required

After a court enters a final judgment in a dissolution action that provides for the custody of a child, the judgment is *res judicata* of the facts and circumstances at the time the judgment became final. Once the judgment is entered, a presumption arises that favors its reasonableness. The presumption serves the practical purpose of providing stability and continuity to the original action because subsequent modification actions attacking the original judgment are considered potentially highly disruptive to children. *George v. Helliar*, 814 P.2d 238 (Wash. App. 1991). The presumption is rebuttable; however, a court usually places a heavy burden on the moving party to prove the circumstances necessary for modification. *Groves v. Groves*, 567 P.2d 459, 463 (Mont. 1977). The presumption may, of course, be overcome if a court is persuaded that a change in circumstances since the original judgment justifies such action. *See, e.g., Wade v. Hirschman*, 903 So. 2d 928 (Fla. 2005).

UNIFORM MARRIAGE AND DIVORCE ACT (UMDA)

6.4. Stability Is the Goal

The Uniform Marriage and Divorce Act (UMDA), §409(b), has influenced custody modification legislation in many jurisdictions. The UMDA reflects a desire to provide a minor child with stability once a custody ruling is issued, which is why §409(b) states that more than a change in circumstances must be shown if custody is to be modified. For example, when sole physical custody is awarded to one parent under this section of the UMDA, custody may be modified only upon a showing of changed circumstances, which are defined alternatively as follows: (1) the present custodial parent agrees to the custody change; or (2) the child has been integrated in the petitioner's family with the consent of the custodial parent; or (3) the child's present environment seriously endangers his physical, mental, moral, or emotional health, and the harm likely to be caused by a change of environment is outweighed by its advantages. UMDA §409(b); 9A U.L.A. 628 (1987 & Supp. 1996).

6.5. Time Barriers to Modification Actions

The UMDA recommends that states attach a time barrier to modification statutes, which usually becomes effective once an initial custody order has been entered. UMDA §§409(a)(b), 410. The purpose of the time barrier is to provide a minor child with as much stability as possible by preventing the noncustodial parent from bringing repeated or insubstantial motions for modification. See Pennington v. Marcum, 266 S.W.3d 759 (Ky. 2008) (if a change in custody is sought within two years of the decree, then the court must apply the statutory standard requiring either serious endangerment or abandonment, but visitation can be modified upon proper showing, at any time, having no two-year restriction); In re Marriage of Dorman, 9 P.3d 329 (Ariz. App. 2000); but see In re F.A.G., 148 P.3d 375 (Colo. App. 2006) (under the Colorado statute, the two-year bar is not based upon when the original decree was entered, but, instead, upon whether a previous motion to modify the original decree has been filed). Unless on the basis of affidavits a court believes that a prima facie case is established that there is reason to believe the child's present environment may seriously endanger his physical, mental, moral, or emotional health, the UMDA bars a custody modification action for two years following an initial decision. In re Weber, 653 N.W.2d 804 (Minn. App. 2002) (a prima facie case must establish four elements for an endangerment-based custody modification: (1) a change in circumstances since the prior custody order; (2) that a modification would serve the child's best interests; (3) that the child's present environment endangers her physical or emotional health; and (4) that the harm to the child likely to be caused by the change of environment is outweighed by any likely benefits of a change in custody). Most states have adopted some form of the UMDA limitations. See, e.g., Minn. Stat. §518.18(b) (1992) (motion to modify a custody order may not be brought earlier than two years after disposition of a prior motion on its merits, except when the child is endangered or the custodial parent has willfully denied visitation).

Example 6-1

Assume that P and D divorce, and the trial judge awards sole physical and legal custody of X, age 13, to D, his mother. Six months after the judgment is entered (and no appeal was taken), P brings an action asking that the judgment be modified so that P is awarded sole legal and physical custody of X. In the moving papers, P asserts that X has told P that D is drinking heavily and has a boyfriend who was once convicted of drunk driving. In an affidavit submitted to the court in response to P's moving papers, D denies that she is drinking heavily, saying that X has made up the story. She says that X is angry after being grounded for a month for bad behavior. D concedes that her boyfriend was convicted of drunk driving five years ago; however, affidavits are produced signed by him and his AA counselor stating that he has been "dry for two years."

Assume that this jurisdiction has adopted the UMDA and in addition requires a *prima facie* showing of endangerment before a modification hearing will be granted. The trial judge has two questions: Is the above action time-barred? If it is not, has the party moving for modification made out a *prima facie* showing of endangerment? How will most courts answer these two questions?

Explanation

The answer to the "time-barred" question is easy. Section 409 of the UMDA bars a change-of-custody hearing for two years following an initial custody decision. Here, the original custody order was entered only six months ago. Therefore, the action is time-barred unless the moving party can establish a *prima facie* case of endangerment. More formally stated, the moving party must show that that the child's present environment seriously endangers his or her physical, mental, or emotional health, and the harm likely to be caused by a change of environment is outweighed by its presumed advantages.

Most courts will find that the noncustodial parent's evidence in support of his allegations falls short of establishing a *prima facie* case that justifies reopening the original order. The noncustodial parent would have a better chance of a favorable decision had he produced evidence from experts and disinterested non-expert third parties to support his claims. The custodial parent countered the drinking allegations with her responsive affidavit and the affidavits of her boyfriend and the AA counselor. Furthermore, the claimed evidence of drinking doesn't appear to be something new; therefore, a judge could reasonably assume that if such evidence existed, it should have been produced at the original custody hearing held only six months earlier.

SELECTED STATE STANDARDS FOR CUSTODY MODIFICATION NOT INVOLVING RELOCATION

6.6. Overview of Procedures and Standards

The procedures and standards employed by courts considering a modification request vary among jurisdictions. As illustrated below, states use somewhat different procedures and standards when approaching this issue.

6.7. California: "Significant Change"

California has articulated a variation on the best-interest standard, known as the "changed circumstance" rule, which is applied when a parent seeks modification of a final judicial custody determination. In re Marriage of Brown and Yana, 127 P.3d 28 (Cal. 2006). Under the rule, custody modification is appropriate only if the parent seeking modification demonstrates a significant change of circumstances indicating that a different custody arrangement would be in the child's best interest. It is thought that this rule serves to protect the weighty interest in stable custody arrangements, and that it fosters judicial economy. In re Marriage of Lucio, 74 Cal. Rptr. 3d (Cal. App. 2008; In re Marriage of Seagondollar, 43 Cal. Rptr. 3d 575 (Cal. App. Ct. 2006).

6.8. Florida: No Proof of Detriment Needed

In Wade v. Hirschman, 903 So. 2d 928 (Fla. 2005), the Florida Supreme Court held that in a child custody modification proceeding, "satisfaction of the substantial change test is necessary in order to overcome the res judicata effect of the final judgment." Id. at 934. The substantial change test requires that the moving party prove "both that the circumstances have substantially, materially changed since the original custody determination and that the child's best interests justify changing custody." Id. at 931 n.2 (quoting Cooper v. Gress, 854 So. 2d 262, 265 (Fla. App. Ct. 2003)). In addition, "the substantial change must be one that was not reasonably contemplated at the time of the original judgment." Id. (quoting Cooper, 854 So. 2d at 265).

6.9. New York: Totality of Circumstances

In New York the legal standards for determining custody and visitation modifications are basically the same, although the extent and magnitude of the proposed modification have some bearing on the court's ultimate determination. *See Matter of Engwer v. Engwer*, 762 N.Y.S.2d 689 (N.Y. 2003). To modify an existing custody order, a petitioner must "demonstrate a change in circumstances warranting modification of the visitation or custody order to advance the best interest[s] of the children." *Matter of Reese v. Jones*, 671 N.Y.S.2d 170 (N.Y. 1998); *Matter of La Bier v. La Bier*, 738 N.Y.S.2d 132 (N.Y. 2002). A change-of-custody standard requires a clear demonstration of a significant change of circumstances, which, based on the *totality of circumstances*, warrants a modification of custody in the best interests of the children before moving them. *Renzulli v. McElrath*, 712 N.Y.S.2d 267 (N.Y. Sup. 2000).

6.10. Ohio: Change Can't Be Inconsequential

In Ohio, modification can occur if (1) there was a change in circumstances since the parties filed their parenting plan with the court; (2) a modification was deemed to be in the best interests of the parties' children; and (3) the harm likely to be caused by a change of environment is outweighed by the advantages of the change of environment to the children. *Rohrbaugh v. Rohrbaugh*, 136 Ohio App. 3d 599 (2000). Furthermore, the "change of circumstances" required to modify parental rights "must be a change of substance, not slight or inconsequential change." *Davis v. Flickinger*, 77 Ohio St. 3d 415, 418 (Ohio 1997).

6.11. Pennsylvania: Substantial Change Not Required

In Pennsylvania, a custody order is subject to modification without proof of a substantial change in circumstances when it is shown that change is in the best interests of the child. *Moore v. Moore*, 634 A.2d 163, 169 (Pa. 1993). Whenever a court is called upon to address the best interests of a child, traditional burdens or presumptions such as substantial change in circumstances, the fitness of one parent over another, or the tender years doctrine must all give way to the paramount concern: the best interests of the child. *Id.* In determining the best interests of a child, a court must consider all factors that legitimately affect the child's physical, intellectual, moral, and spiritual well-being. *Swope v. Swope*, 689 A.2d 264 (Pa. 1997).

6.12. Texas: Heightened Burden

To support modifying custody in Texas, a trial court must find that the modification would be in the best interest of the child and that the circumstances of the child have materially and substantially changed since the date of the original order. Tex. Fam. Code Ann. §156.101(1) (West Supp. 2005). The party seeking modification has the burden to establish these elements by a preponderance of the evidence. *Agraz v. Carnley*, 143 S.W.3d 547, 552 (Tex. App. 2004); In re T.D.C., 91 S.W.3d 865, 871 (Tex. App. 2002); *Considine v. Considine*, 726 S.W.2d 253, 255 (Tex. App. 1987). To prove that a material change in circumstances has occurred, the petitioner must demonstrate what material changes have occurred in the conditions existing at the time of the entry of the prior order as compared with the circumstances existing at the time of the hearing on the motion to modify.

One seeking to change custody within a year after an order was entered faces a heightened burden. *Burkhart v. Burkhart*, 960 S.W.2d 321, 322 (Tex. 1997). In such a circumstance, the petitioner must file an affidavit showing *inter alia* that "the child's present environment may endanger the child's physical health or significantly impair the child's emotional development." *See* Tex. Fam. Code Ann. §156.102(b)(1) (West Supp. 2005). If the court determines, based on the affidavit, that the facts stated are adequate to support such an allegation, the matter will be set for hearing. *Id.* §156.102(c).

Example 6-2

Assume that this jurisdiction does not have a time barrier for bringing modification actions similar to that found in the UMDA. Also assume that P and D were divorced and that D was awarded sole physical custody of child X. According to the findings made by the judge at the custody proceeding, she was concerned about X's mother's (P's) abuse of drugs and alcohol. A year after the original custody decision, P sought to modify custody so that she would have sole physical custody of X. At the first custody proceeding the Department of Social Services had been involved because of concerns over P's fitness to care for X, age ten. The concerns were prompted in large part by the mother's history of drug abuse. At the modification proceeding, P called a social worker, who testified that P was having "great success in overcoming her alcohol and drug dependence" and that X "would be better nurtured by P." D's lawyer argued that there had not been a change in circumstances, and even if there were, the change would not justify modifying custody. D testified that X was enrolled in school and was doing a good job (X's report cards supported D). D also testified that X had made friends in the neighborhood, that X attended church with D on a regular basis, and that X was on a Little League baseball team. D testified that X appeared to enjoy the home setting. How will a court likely rule?

Explanation

Jurisdictions will debate whether there has been a substantial change in circumstances since the initial custody order. Some may conclude there was a change, but it was not (material) substantial. That is, it was foreseeable at the first hearing that P would eventually bring her drug problem under control. Others may take the view that there has been a (material) substantial change since the original hearing because P now apparently has her drug problem under control. Regardless of the outcome of this debate, there is little evidence supporting a conclusion that the custodial parent consented to the modification to allow X to be integrated into the noncustodian's family, or that X was in physical or psychological danger while with D. Because stability and continuity are so important in considering a modification request, and D has produced evidence demonstrating X's relationship to D's neighborhood and school, most courts will conclude that P's evidence has failed to overcome the presumption favoring the custodial parent. *See Ardizoni v. Raymond*, 667 N.E.2d 885 (Mass. App. Ct. 1996). Even without a presumption, it is doubtful that a court would change custody based on the above facts.

TYPICAL MODIFICATION CLAIMS

6.13. Unwarranted Denial of Visitation

Although successful custody modification actions based solely on denial of visitation are rare, a majority of jurisdictions have by statute declared that unwarranted denial of or interference with duly established visitation constitutes contempt of court and may be sufficient cause for reversal of a custody ruling. *See, e.g.,* Iowa Code §598.23(2)(b) (2006); New Hampshire Code Rev. Stat. Ann. 458:17, V(a)(2) (2004) (modification allowed if court finds repeated, intentional, and unwarranted interference by a custodial parent with the visitation or custodial rights of the noncustodial parent). Unwarranted denial of or interference with visitation is not dispositive but is usually viewed as only one of several factors to be considered in contemplating a change of custody. *See, e.g., In re Marriage of Ciganovich,* 61 Cal. App. 3d 289 (1976); *Slinkard v. Slinkard,* 589 S.W.2d 635 (Mo. App. 1979); *Lopez v. Lopez,* 639 P.2d 1186 (N.M. 1981); *Lemcke v. Lemcke,* 623 N.W.2d 916 (Minn. App. 2001); *cf. Entwistle v. Entwistle,* 402 N.Y.S.2d 213 (1978) (custodial parent's interference with the other parent's visitation rights is so inconsistent with the child's best interests as to *per se* raise a strong probability that custodial parent is unfit).

6.14. Failure to Pay Child Support

A noncustodial parent is often required by a court order or an agreement between the parties to make child support payments. When the noncustodial parent fails to make such payments, the custodial parent will sometimes resort to a self-help method of enforcement. The self-help consists of withholding court-ordered visitation privileges from the noncustodial parent until that parent pays the support.

Courts are unwilling to support a custodial parent's withholding of visitation because support was not paid. As a general rule, courts will not terminate visitation solely for reasons unrelated to the welfare of the child, and a failure to pay support is usually not included within the scope of this principle. *See Stewart v. Soda*, 226 A.D.2d 1102 (N.Y. 1996). Note, however, that some "older" decisions have prevented visitation where an agreement between the parties conditioned visitation upon payment of child support. *See* 65 A.L.R. 1155 (1988).

Example 6-3

Assume when P and D divorce that P is awarded sole physical and legal custody of X and that D is ordered to pay P $1,000 per month in child support. When D fails to make three consecutive child support payments, P refuses to allow D to visit with their minor child. D reacts to P's withholding of visitation by bringing a motion to enforce the court-ordered visitation or, alternatively, to modify the custody decree and give D sole legal and physical custody of the child. P responds by asking the court to hold D in contempt because of his failure to pay child support and to deny D visitation on the ground that he has either forfeited or abandoned the child by failing to pay support. The court issues a contempt citation against D for failure to pay support as ordered. P then argues that the contempt order bars D from making a custody request of any kind; he does not have "clean hands." How will a court most likely rule on the motions by the parties?

Explanation

First, it is unlikely that a court will accept the abandonment argument because of the short period of time between the initial court order and P's action to deny visitation; moreover, D is seeking visitation with X. Second, some courts will not apply the clean-hands doctrine, reasoning that a child's best interests are at stake. Third, courts will apply the general rule that proof of unwarranted denial of or interference with established visitation rights may be sufficient cause for reversal of custody. However, as noted earlier in this chapter, courts view a denial or interference with visitation as not necessarily controlling in a custody modification proceeding; it is considered along with the other factors. Finally, the court will most likely keep custody with the custodial parent and order visitation with the noncustodial parent to be resumed. It will also likely continue to utilize its civil contempt power in an effort to force D to pay the ordered support.

6.15. Integration into Noncustodial Parent's Home

Most jurisdictions recognize that custody may be modified when the child has been integrated into the noncustodial parent's family with the consent of the custodial parent. *See* §409, 9A U.L.A. 62829 (1987). Consent has been defined as "a voluntary acquiescence to surrender of legal custody." *In re Marriage of Timmons*, 617 P.2d 1032, 1037 (Wash. 1980). Most courts view integration as more than expanded visitation. It includes the performance of normal parental duties such as washing clothes, providing meals, attending to medical needs, assisting with homework, and guiding the children physically, mentally, morally, socially, and emotionally. *See, e.g., In re Marriage of Wechselberger*, 450 N.E.2d 1385 (Ill. App. Ct. 1983). The time spent by the children with the proposed custodial parent must be of sufficient duration that they have become settled into the home of that parent as though it were their primary home. *See In re Marriage of Paradis*, 689 P.2d 1263 (Mont. 1984). Consideration may also be given to which residence the children consider to be their true home. *In re Custody of Thompson*, 647 P.2d 1049 (Wash. App. 1982); *See generally Annot.*, 35 A.L.R. 4th 61 (1985).

Example 6-4

Assume that upon dissolution of P and D's marriage, sole physical and legal custody of their three children was awarded to D (mother). P (father) was ordered to pay child support. Six years after the original judgment was entered, P filed a motion asking that the judgment be modified so that he is awarded sole physical custody of the three children. The testimony at the modification hearing showed that when the dissolution decree was entered, P was granted visitation consisting of alternating weekends and Wednesday afternoons. However, shortly after the divorce became final, P remarried and requested additional visitation with the children. Because the children enjoyed the time they spent with P, D informally agreed to additional visitation, although the original visitation order was not amended. At the time P filed the modification action, the evidence showed that the three children were spending about an equal percentage of time with P and D.

In opposition to the motion, D presented evidence that since the divorce she had continued to exercise daily control over the lives of the children, even when they stayed with P. She testified that she made the major decisions on their behalf and maintained other parenting duties, such as assisting with homework; attending parent-teacher conferences; transporting them to athletic activities and music lessons; assisting in their expenses; and providing love, support, and encouragement. P testified that he was working a great deal and found it difficult to attend many of the events and conferences involving his children, although his new wife attended many of them. D testified that it was never her intention to formally expand visitation to constitute a change in her capacity as sole legal custodian for the children. She testified that she had begun to reduce the amount of time the children spent with D, and it was her opinion that D was bringing the modification motion in an attempt to reduce his child support obligation. P testified that "the fact is, the children have been integrated" into his home with D's permission. How will a court most likely rule on P's claim that the children have been integrated into his home?

Explanation

A court will, of course, conduct a factual inquiry and will most likely conclude that there has been a change in circumstances, that is, the children are spending more time with P. The question at issue, however, is whether this is merely a change or a "material" or "substantial change." The Alaska Supreme Court has held that a material change of circumstances occurs when important facts unknown at the time of the initial custody judgment arise that impact the welfare of the child. *Cochran v. Cochran*, 5 So. 3d 1220 (Ala. 2008). Furthermore, while definitions vary as to what constitutes a "material" or "substantial" change in circumstances, the change generally must be of a continuing nature that makes the terms of the initial order unreasonable or unfair.

Regardless of the answer to the material/substantial change question, it appears that there was neither consent nor complete integration of the minor children into P's household. Moreover D continued to make the major decisions and exercise control of the children, although she agreed informally to the change in the amount of time to be spent with the non-custodial parent. The evidence produced by P will be viewed by most courts as falling short of the kind of knowing integration that statutes and case law require to support a modification request. *See, e.g., In re Marriage of Pontius*, 761 P.2d 247 (Colo. App. 1988).

6.16. Endangerment

One of the more common grounds for seeking modification of custody is a claim that the present environment endangers a child's physical or emotional health or impairs a child's emotional development and that the advantages of the change in environment will outweigh the harm of change to the child. *See Goldman v. Greenwood*, 748 N.W.2d 279, 284 (Minn. 2008) (a party must demonstrate "a significant degree of danger" to satisfy the endangerment element in Minnesota law).

Endangerment may be difficult to prove. For example, in *Molitor v. Molitor*, 718 N.W.2d 13 (N.D. 2006), the noncustodial father claimed endangerment following an incident in which the custodial parent had discovered her oldest child and her new husband's two children "huffing" gasoline in the basement of her house. In rejecting the noncustodial father's claim, the court concluded that the incident was the result of the behavior of the child's sibling and step-siblings in the mother's home, and that the child was not in danger. *See Sharp v. Bilbro*, 614 N.W.2d 260, 263 (Minn. App. 2000), *review denied* (Minn. Sept. 26, 2000) ("endangerment" implies a significant degree of danger or likely harm to the child's physical or emotional state); In re K.L.R., 162 S.W.3d 291 (Tex. App. 2005) (endangerment found where former wife was about to move child to house of unknown quality and environment, her physical condition was deteriorating, she had been arrested on two felony charges and subsequently spent time in jail, and noncustodial father feared she might flee jurisdiction with child).

6.17. Modifying (Parenting) Agreements Made by the Parties

When there is an agreement between the parties regarding a child custody arrangement, several jurisdictions will presume that the agreement is in the best interests of the child. *See, e.g., In re Marriage of Jennings*, 50 P.3d 506 (Kan. App. 2002). This presumption must be overcome when a modification motion is brought. Custody agreements are, of course, always subject to the overarching power of the court to determine the best interests of the child.

In Oregon a party seeking modification of a parenting plan does not have the obligation to demonstrate a substantial change of circumstances since the entry of the original dissolution judgment. *Cole v. Wyatt*, 116 P.3d 919, 921 (Or. App. 2005) ("[T]he modification of parenting time does not require a showing of a substantial change of circumstances.").

Some jurisdictions give priority to the first determination of custody in the belief that the stability produced by this policy is in the child's best interests. *Eschbach v. Eschbach*, 451 N.Y.S.2d 658 (N.Y. 1982).

Other jurisdictions treat a permanent custody order obtained by stipulation as little different from a permanent custody order obtained via litigation. *See, e.g., In re Marriage of Burgess*, 913 P.2d 473 (Cal. 1966). These jurisdictions apply the changed circumstance rule regardless of whether the initial determination of custody resulted from an agreement, default judgment, or litigation.

Example 6-5

Assume that a judgment of divorce was entered incorporating the terms of a stipulated agreement between the husband and wife. The judgment stated that "the parties agreed that P shall not remove the children outside the town of X until the youngest child shall have reached the age of eighteen (18) years." P was awarded sole legal and physical custody of the children.

Six months after the judgment was entered P asked the court that she be allowed to move the children from the town of X to a large metropolitan city 200 miles away. P argued that as the custodial parent, she is allowed to make major decisions regarding the family, including moving to another location. In addition, she argued that she intended to marry Y, who was employed in a "good job" in the city. D opposed P's motion, arguing that P's right to move the children had been clearly addressed in the divorce action and that the court should honor the agreement. On these facts, should the court enforce the stipulation restricting movement that was contained in the judgment?

Explanation

Although various jurisdictions approach the issue from somewhat different perspectives, most courts will uphold the stipulation. They will reason that P knowingly entered into an agreement that contained express and unmistakable relocation restrictions. Although P may be subject to financial and other advantages by moving to the big city, a court will most likely be unwilling to allow the change because of the stipulation made by the parties only a few months earlier. See *Zindulka v. Zindulka*, 726 N.Y.S.2d 173 (N.Y. App. Div. 3 Dept. 2001).

CHILD'S PREFERENCE

6.18. Maturity

Whether a child's preferences and feelings regarding custody and visitation will be given weight by the trial judge in a custody dispute necessarily depends on all the facts, including the child's age and ability to intelligently form and express those preferences and feelings. *Azia v. DiLascia*, 780 A.2d

992 (Conn. App. Ct. 2001). Although the express wishes of the child are not controlling at a modification proceeding, they are entitled to great weight, particularly where the child's age and maturity would make his or her input particularly meaningful. *McMillian v. Rizzo*, 817 N.Y.S.2d 679 (N.Y.A.D. 2006). Where the households of both parents were equally suitable, a child's preference to live with one parent "'could not but tip the evidentiary scale in favor' of that parent." *Bovard v. Baker*, 775 A.2d 835, 841 (Pa. Super. 2001). Obviously, when a child states a preference, a court will evaluate the opinion in light of a child's general susceptibility to influence, parental and otherwise. *See Clara L. v. Paul M.*, 673 N.Y.S.2d 657 (N.Y. App. Ct. 1998). The predominant importance of the choice of an older child is recognized in most jurisdictions. *See, e.g., State ex rel. Feeley v. Williams*, 222 N.W. 927, 928 (Minn. 1929) (preference of $12\frac{1}{2}$-year-old child given great weight in maintaining her custody with aunt and uncle); *David M. v. Margaret M.*, 385 S.E.2d 912, 920 (W. Va. 1989) (preference of child 14 years old or older is determinative); *Marcus v. Marcus*, 248 N.E.2d 800, 805 (Ill. App. 1969) (error to award custody of 14-year-old to mother against his stated preference to remain with grandmother); *Patrick v. Patrick*, 212 So. 2d 145, 147 (La. Ct. App. 1968) (award of custody of 17- and 18-year-old children to father reversed when they expressed a preference to remain with mother; from practical viewpoint, it would be "vain and useless act" to order children who are approaching age of majority to live with parent with whom they do not wish to live). While some courts have placed particular emphasis on a teenager's preference, terming it "an overwhelming consideration," all courts agree that a teenager's preference will not necessarily be controlling, regardless of the strength of the conviction.

Example 6-6

Assume that P and D divorced and that P was awarded sole physical custody of the two minor children of the marriage. Five years after the divorce, D began to suspect that P was having an affair. D hired private detectives to investigate P's behavior. After receiving various reports from the private detectives, who suggested that P was having an affair, D brought a motion to modify custody of the two minor children, then ages 16 and 17. D argued that the children were being raised in an immoral atmosphere by P and that he should have sole legal and physical custody of them. The evidence to substantiate the claim of the alleged adulterous acts was circumstantial and consisted of the testimony of the detectives, who had observed P enter a hotel on five occasions with a male and leave the hotel several hours later. The children appeared as witnesses and expressed their strong desire to remain with P. Despite the testimony, the trial judge ordered that custody be changed to D. P appealed and raised a number of issues, one of which was that the trial judge had failed to give sufficient weight to the children's testimony. How will an appellate court most likely treat the issue of the children's preference?

Explanation

On these facts, an appellate court might not even reach the issue of the children's preference because of a failure to show the kind of changed circumstances that most courts would recognize as significant. However, if the appellate court should consider their preferences, it is difficult to believe that, given the ages of the children, anyone can practically contradict their choice, even if their opinions are shown to be misguided (and there is no such showing). Because of the apparent maturity of the children, after weighing their opinions, the appellate court will most likely reverse the lower court ruling. P will retain custody.

RELOCATING (REMOVING) A CHILD TO ANOTHER STATE: SOLE PHYSICAL CUSTODY

6.19. The Relocation Debate

Relocation cases "present some of the knottiest and most disturbing problems that courts are asked to resolve." *Tropea v. Tropea*, 665 N.E.2d 145, 148 (N.Y. 1996). The interests of the primary residential parent in moving to a new location, where educational or work opportunities are better, are pitted against those parents who will be left behind and have a strong desire to maintain frequent and regular contact with the child. Cases involving the geographic relocation of the primary residential parent following dissolution of a marriage are intensely emotional, and the issues are extensively litigated. The remainder of this chapter will focus on relocation issues.

There is an ongoing debate among experts over the impact relocation of a custodial parent with a minor child has on the child's psychological development. Some social science experts have suggested that the psychological welfare of a child depends more on the well-being of the family unit with whom the child primarily resides than on maintaining frequent and regular contact with the other parent. *See, e.g.*, Janet M. Bowermaster, *Sympathizing with Solomon: Choosing Between Parents in a Mobile Society*, 31 U. Louisville J. Fam. L. 791, 884 (1992) (custodial parents should be allowed to relocate with their child in good faith to pursue "their best opportunities"); Judith S. Wallerstein & Tony J. Tanke, *To Move or Not to Move: Psychological and Legal Considerations in the Relocation of Children Following Divorce*, 30 Fam. L.Q. 305, 311, 318 (1996) (social science research on custody does not support the presumption that frequent and continuing access to both parents is in the child's best interests; therefore, a parent with primary physical custody generally should be able to relocate with the child). William G. Austin, *Relocation, Research, and Forensic Evaluation, Part II: Research in Support of the Relocation Risk Assessment Model*, Fam. Ct. Rev. 46(2), 347, 359 (Apr. 2008) (relocation continues to be an area of ongoing controversy in the field of child custody). Austin finds "convincing evidence" that relocation significantly expands the level of risk for children of divorce, but cautions that the research should not be interpreted as a basis for a bias or legal presumption against relocation. William G. Austin, *Relocation and Forensic Evaluation: Relocation, Research, and Forensic Evaluation, Part I: Effects of Residential Mobility on Children of Divorce*, Fam. Ct. Rev. 46(1), 137, 139 (Jan. 2008).

Other social science research suggests that children are better off if they have frequent contact and good relationships with both parents. *See, e.g.*, Marion Gindes, *The Psychological Effects of Relocation for Children of Divorce*, 10 J. Am. Acad. Matrimonial Law. 119, 132 (1998). Some experts believe that any move, even a relatively short one, is a stressful event for a child and can have a negative impact on the child's well-being. *See, e.g.*, Joan B. Kelly & Michael E. Lamb, *Using Child Development Research to Make Appropriate Custody and Access Decisions for Young Children*, 38 Fam. & Conciliation Cts. Rev. 297, 309 (2000) (regardless of who is the primary caretaker, a child benefits from extensive contact with both parents); David Wood et al., *Impact of Family Relocation on Children's Growth, Development, School Function, and Behavior*, 270 JAMA 1334, 1337 (1993) ("[a] family move disrupts the routines, relationships, and attachments that define the child's world"). This difference of opinion explains, at least in part, the disparate approaches among jurisdictions in considering relocation issues.

6.20. Relocation Law Is Nationally Diverse

As Americans began divorcing in larger numbers beginning in the late 1960s, they also began to ask courts to allow them to relocate with their children to cities and states located far from the other parent. The initial judicial trend was to impose more restrictions on the ability of the primary parent to move with the child or children. *See* Arthur B. LaFrance, *Child Custody and Relocation: A Constitutional Perspective*, 34 U. Louisville J. Fam. L. 1 (1995-96). However, during the late 1990s a number of jurisdictions began to articulate new standards for use in relocation cases. *See* Carol S. Bruch & Janet M. Bowermaster, *The Relocation of Children and Custodial Parents: Public Policy, Past and Present*, 30 Fam. L.Q. 245 (Summer 1996).

When examining relocation standards, one quickly discovers that the law applicable to interstate relocation of a child by a custodial parent is nationally diverse. For example, when a relocation request is made in

New York, all relevant facts are considered, but the predominant emphasis is placed on what outcome is most likely to serve the best interests of the child. *Friedman v. Rome*, 847 N.Y.S.2d 616 (N.Y.A.D. 2007); *Matter of Tropea v. Tropea*, 665 N.E.2d 145 (N.Y. 1996); *See also Fisher v. Fisher*, 137 P.3d 355 (Haw. 2006).

In California, the custodial parent has a presumptive right to relocate with the minor child, subject to the power of the court to restrain a change that would prejudice the rights or welfare of the child. *See, e.g., In re Marriage of LaMusga*, 88 P.3d 81, 98 (Cal. 2004); *In re Marriage of Burgess*, 913 P.2d 473, 482-483 (1996) (placing burden on noncustodial parent to show move will be harmful to child); *Kaiser v. Kaiser*, 23 P.3d 278, 282 (Okla. 2001) (custodial parent has presumptive right under Oklahoma statute to move with the child). In Arkansas and Colorado, it is presumed that a parent's choice to move with the children should generally be allowed. *Hollandsworth v. Knyzewski*, 109 S.W.3d 653 (Ark. 2003); *In re Marriage of Francis*, 919 P.2d 776, 784 (Colo. 1996). However, in Oregon the custodial parent does not enjoy a presumptive right to relocate with the child. *In re Marriage of Fedorov*, 206 P.3d 1124 (Or. App. 2009).

In some jurisdictions, such as Connecticut, the custodial parent seeking permission to relocate bears the initial burden of demonstrating, by a preponderance of the evidence, that the relocation is for a legitimate purpose and that the proposed relocation is reasonable in light of that purpose. Once the custodial parent has established a *prima facie* case, the burden shifts to the noncustodial parent to prove, by a preponderance of the evidence that the relocation would not be in the best interests of the child. *See, e.g., Ireland v. Ireland*, 717 A.2d 676 (Conn. 1998) (limited to post-judgment relocation matters); *Ford v. Ford*, 789 A.2d 1104 (Conn. 2002).

Florida's relocation statute, Fla. Stat. §61 13001 (2006), contains a provision defining what constitutes a change of residence. A change of residence means the relocation of a child to a principal residence more than 50 miles away from his or her principal place of residence at the time of the entry of the last order establishing or modifying the designation of the primary residential parent or the custody of the minor child, unless the move places the principal residence of the minor child less than 50 miles from the nonresidential parent. The statute declares that no presumption shall arise in favor of or against a request to relocate with the child when a primary residential parent seeks to move the child and the move will materially affect the current schedule of contact, access, and time sharing with the nonrelocating parent or other person. The parent wishing to relocate has the burden of proving, by a preponderance of the evidence, that relocation is in the best interest of the child. If that burden is met, the nonrelocating parent or other person must show by a preponderance of the evidence that the proposed relocation is not in the best interest of the child. The statute contains 11 factors a court must consider when making a relocation decision.

In *Baures v. Lewis*, 770 A.2d 214 (N.J. 2001), New Jersey held that a custodial parent may move with the children as long as the move does not interfere with the best interests of the children or the visitation rights of the noncustodial parent. *Baures*, 770 A.2d at 227. The court established essentially a two-part test requiring a good-faith reason for the move and proof that the child will not suffer from it. *See Baures*, 770 A.2d at 230.

In Pennsylvania a court, on its own motion or upon the motion of either party, may review the existing custody order when a relocation request is received. *Gruber v. Gruber*, 583 A.2d 434, 440 (1990). The custodial parent has the initial burden of showing that the move is likely to significantly improve the quality of life for that parent and the children. In addition, each parent has the burden of establishing the integrity of his or her motives in either desiring the move or seeking to prevent it.

Oregon requires that the parent seeking modification demonstrate a substantial change of circumstances. *Colson and Peil*, 51 P.3d 607 (Or. App. 2002) (in a relocation case, the party seeking the change of custody "has the burden to show that there [has] been a substantial change of circumstances since the time of the original custody award"). The parent must also demonstrate that the change of custody is in the best interests of the child. *Hamilton-Waller and Waller*, 123 P.3d 310 (Or. App. 2005).

In Texas, a party may demand a jury trial on the issue of primary residence. *Lenz v. Lenz*, 79 S.W.3d 10 (Tex. 2002); *see* Tex. Fam. Code §105.002(c)(1)(D). As a consequence, the analytical framework is different for a reviewing judge, even though much of the evidence will be similar to that brought to a judge in another jurisdiction where a jury trial is not allowed. When reviewing the jury verdict, the court conducts a legal-sufficiency review to determine whether the evidence supports the jury's verdict in favor of removing a residency restriction. Texas courts view the evidence relevant to the best-interest factors in a light that tends to support the jury's verdict. *See Bradford v. Vento*, 48 S.W.3d 749, 754 (Tex. 2001).

As noted in Section 6.17, *supra*, jurisdictions may distinguish parenting plan relocation requests from custody modification relocation requests without an agreement or plan in terms of applying presumptions and burdens of proof.

6.21. Right to Travel

The United States Constitution protects the fundamental right of U.S. citizens to travel freely from state to state and to reside in the state of their choice. *Jones v. Helms*, 452 U.S. 412, 418 (1981). Generally, state action penalizing a citizen for leaving or entering a state violates the citizen's right to travel. *Jones*, 452 U.S. at 419. However, a state may restrict a citizen's right to leave the jurisdiction when doing so is necessary to serve a compelling government interest. *Shapiro v. Thompson*, 394 U.S. 618, 634 (1969), *overruled on other grounds by Edelman v. Jordan*, 415 U.S. 651 (1974).

State courts cannot agree on the interplay of a parent's right to travel and a parent's right to the care and control of his or her child in the context of a best-interest analysis and *Shapiro v. Thompson*, *supra*. One jurisdiction reads *Shapiro* as tipping the scale in favor of the parent's right to travel. *Watt v. Watt*, 971 P.2d 608, 616 (Wyo. 1999). Others view the child's best interests as trumping the parent's right to travel. *LaChapelle v. Mitten*, 607 N.W.2d 151, 163-164 (Minn. Ct. App. 2000); *Ziegler v. Ziegler*, 691 P.2d 773, 780 (Idaho Ct. App. 1985). Some balance the relocating parent's right to travel with two other important interests: the best interests of the child and the nonrelocating parent's interest in the care and control of the child. *Baxendale v. Raich*, 878 N.E.2d 1252 (Ind. 2008) (*Shapiro* recognizes that a chilling effect on travel can violate the U.S. Constitution, but also acknowledges that other considerations, such as the child's interests, may outweigh an individual's interest in travel); *In re Marriage of Ciesluk*, 113 P.3d 135, 146 (Colo. 2005) (trial court is to balance custodial parent, child, and noncustodial parent concerns).

In *Brtosz v. Jones*, 197 P.3d 310 (Idaho 2008), the court held that protecting the best interest of a child is a compelling government interest. In making its ruling, it affirmed the trial judge's order changing primary custody from the mother to the father. The mother had sought to move with the child to Hawaii, where her new husband had been transferred by the military. *See Ziegler v. Ziegler*, 691 P.2d 773 (Ct. App. 1985) (residency restriction requiring the children to live within a 100-mile radius of town upheld on the ground that it was justified by a compelling government interest, namely, ensuring the best interests of the children).

In *In re Marriage of Guffin*, 209 P.3d 225 (Mont. 2009), the couple originally approved a joint parenting plan in which the mother was the primary custodian. When she decided to relocate about 700 miles away from the children's father in Montana, the trial court changed the plan so that the father was the primary custodian. In reversing the trial judge, whose expressed reason for changing custody was the mother's decision to move 700 miles across the state, the appellate court stated that the dispute implicated the constitutional issue of the right to travel. It observed that a custodial parent who bears the burdens and responsibilities of raising a child is entitled, to the greatest possible extent, to the same freedom to seek a better life for herself or himself and the children as enjoyed by the noncustodial parent. It said that a custodial parent has a fundamental, although qualified, constitutional right to migrate, resettle, find a new job, and start a new life; and the noncustodial parent bears a heavy burden to demonstrate a compelling interest on the part of a court to interfere with this right. *See Matter of Custody of D.M.G.*, 951 P.2d 1377 (Mont. 1998).

Some courts have held that removal cases do not implicate a parent's right to travel because removal statutes do not outright prohibit a parent's traveling, but prohibit only a parent's traveling with a child. *See, e.g., Lenz v. Lenz,* 40 S.W.3d 111, 118 n.3 (Tex. App. 2000), *rev'd on other grounds, Lenz v. Lenz,* 79 S.W.3d 10 (Tex. 2002).

MODEL RELOCATION DRAFTING EFFORTS

6.22. American Law Institute (ALI)

The American Law Institute (ALI) *Principles* reflect "the policy choice that a parent, like any other citizen, should be able to choose his or her place of residence, and that the job of rearing children after divorce should not be made too financially or emotionally burdensome to the parent who has the majority share of custodial responsibility." ALI, *Principles of the Law of Family Dissolution,* ch. 2, §2.17, cmt. d (2002).

Where physical custody is shared, the best-interest calculus pertaining to removal is appreciably different compared with those situations that involve sole physical custody. ALI, *Principles of the Law of Family Dissolution: Analysis and Recommendations,* §2.17(1), (4)(c) (2002). Where physical custody is shared, a judge's willingness to elevate one parent's interest in relocating freely with the children is often diminished. Edwin J. Terry et al., *Relocation: Moving Forward, or Moving Backward?* 15 J. Am. Acad. Matrimonial Law. 167, 212-213 (1998).

6.23. American Academy of Matrimonial Lawyers (AAML)

The American Academy of Matrimonial Lawyers (AAML) Model Act has 22 sections and covers notice, procedures for objection, and remedies. It "is meant to serve as a template for those jurisdictions desiring a statutory solution to the relocation quandary." *Perspectives on the Relocation of Children,* 15 J. Am. Acad. Matrimonial Law. 1, 2 (1998).

Among its recommendations, the Model Act identifies nonexclusive factors that courts should consider in determining relocation issues, which include the following: (1) the nature, quality, and extent of involvement, and the duration of the child's relationship with the person proposing to relocate and with the nonrelocating person, siblings, and other significant persons in the child's life; (2) the age, developmental stage, and needs of the child, and the likely impact the relocation will have on the child's physical, educational, and emotional development, taking into consideration any special needs of the child; (3) the feasibility of preserving the relationship between the nonrelocating person and the child through suitable [visitation] arrangements, considering the logistics and financial circumstances of the parties; (4) the child's preference, taking into consideration the age and maturity of the child; (5) whether there is an established pattern of conduct of the person seeking relocation, either to promote or to thwart the relationship between the child and the nonrelocating person; (6) whether the relocation of the child will enhance the general quality of life for both the custodial party seeking the relocation and the child, including but not limited to financial or emotional benefit or educational opportunity; (7) the reasons of each person for seeking or opposing the relocation; and (8) any other factor affecting the best interests of the child. 15 J. Am. Acad. Matrimonial Law. §405 (1998).

6.24. The "New Family" Theory

Some states have applied a theory that views a divorce with children awarded to one parent but not the other as the creation of a new family unit. Jurisdictions applying this theory have concluded that what is beneficial to the new family unit as a whole also benefits its individual members. *See, e.g., In re Marriage of Harris*, 96 P.3d 141 (Cal. 2004) (final custody order creates a new family unit now commonly referred to as a single-parent family); *Rebsamen v. Rebsamen*, 107 S.W.3d 871 (Ark. 2003) (court should balance the needs of the noncustodial parent with that of the new family unit); *Rosenthal v. Maney*, 745 N.E.2d 350 (Mass. App. Ct. 2001); *Anderson v. Anderson*, 56 S.W.3d 5 (Tenn. Ct. App. 1999); *D'Onofrio v. D'Onofrio*, 365 A.2d 27, 29-30 (N.J. Super. Ct. Ch. Div.), aff'd, 365 A.2d 716 (1976) (children belong to a different family unit after a divorce); Joan G. Wexler, *Rethinking the Modification of Child Custody Decrees*, 94 Yale L.J. 757, 808 (1985). The new family unit is entitled to a measure of constitutional protection against unwarranted governmental intrusion, which is similar to that accorded to an intact, two-parent family. *In re Marriage of Mentry*, 190 Cal. Rptr. 843, 848-849 (1983).

In a "new family unit" jurisdiction, a court will take the view that a custodial parent should be permitted to make the significant, life-influencing decisions affecting a child so long as the parent remains fit to have custody, although the noncustodial parent's interests retain great importance. *Ascuitto v. Farricielli*, 711 A.2d 708 (Conn. 1998) (recognizing importance of familial relationship between noncustodial parent and child in context of parent-child immunity). The courts theorize that a child's interests can become so intricately interwoven with the well-being of the new family unit that the determination of the child's best interest also requires that the interests of the custodial parent be taken into account. *See, e.g.*, *Mize v. Mize*, 621 So. 2d 417, 419 (Fla. 1993) (it follows that what is good for custodial parent's well-being is good for child's well-being).

Example 6-7

Assume that when P and D's marriage dissolved, the court awarded joint legal custody of their minor son to the parties but placed primary physical custody with P. The order allowed D to visit his son every other weekend, and D has exercised this right without missing a weekend. Assume that this jurisdiction has a relocation statute that provides that the custodial parent seeking permission to relocate bears the initial burden of demonstrating, by a preponderance of the evidence, that the relocation is for a legitimate purpose and that the proposed relocation is reasonable in light of that purpose. Once the custodial parent has established a *prima facie* case, the burden shifts to the noncustodial parent to prove, by a preponderance of the evidence, that relocating is not in the child's best interests. The jurisdiction has also accepted the "new family" theory in custody relocation disputes. At the time of the dissolution, P and D resided in state X. Three years after the divorce, P remarried. P's new husband is a computer consultant, and his major consulting contract ended when the company he was working with closed because of financial problems. He undertook a search for another job and secured a position in state Y. P informed D of her plan to join her husband in state Y with their son, age 11, and moved to modify the existing custody order so that she could relocate there with the child. Is the court likely to grant P's request to relocate?

Explanation

In this jurisdiction P bears the initial burden of showing by a preponderance of the evidence that the relocation is for a legitimate purpose and that the proposed relocation is reasonable in light of that purpose. Given the fact that P's new husband lost his job and found a new one in state Y, a court would most likely rule that P has carried her burden. Once the custodial parent (P) establishes a *prima facie* case, the burden then shifts to the noncustodial parent to prove, by a preponderance of the evidence that the relocation would not be in the best interests of the child. In this jurisdiction, which applies the "new family theory," significant weight will be given to the "new family" consisting of the custodial parent and child and the custodian's decisions. As a result, the noncustodial parent will have a great deal of difficulty preventing the relocation; it will most likely be allowed. Note, however, that there appears to be a slight movement away from the "new family" theory toward one that gives greater weight to the relationship established by fathers such as D.

Example 6-8

Assume that this dispute takes place in a jurisdiction that applies the "new family" theory discussed above. P and D dissolve their relationship. D (mother) is awarded sole legal and physical custody of their two children. Three months after the judgment is entered, D brings a motion to leave the forum state with the children, ages four and seven, and move to another state that is 1,000 miles away. D produces evidence that she has been accepted into law school in the distant state. She also produces a plan that outlines how the children will be cared for while she is in law school. D agrees that P may have extended visits with the children in the summer. P introduces evidence that since the divorce, P has exercised his visitation rights with the children on Saturday and Sunday of every other week and has seen them every Wednesday evening for two or three hours. The trial judge observes that P and D appear angry with each other over the divorce. P argues that D is seeking revenge because P just married his secretary, who is 15 years younger than he. Most likely, how will a court rule on D's request to relocate?

Explanation

Obviously, one must carefully analyze the problem because of the varying standards jurisdictions use to resolve this issue. However, a jurisdiction that applies the "new family" theory will most likely allow D to relocate to another state. The "new family" theory is, in reality, a presumption favoring the custodial parent. The party opposing relocation must offer reasonably strong evidence to establish that the relocation is not in the best interest of the child or that the relocation is intended to interfere with visitation. A judge in this jurisdiction will most likely conclude that there is not enough "strong" evidence presented by P to prevent the relocation.

JOINT PHYSICAL OR "SHARED" CUSTODY AND RELOCATION REQUESTS

6.25. Overview

When the parties following a divorce have joint physical custody of a child, many courts will view the situation as one in which there is no noncustodial parent. Therefore, when a joint-custody parent opposes relocation, that parent is normally not saddled with an initial burden to come forward with evidence opposing the move. *In re Marriage of Seagondollar*, 43 Cal. Rptr. 3d 575 (Cal. App. 2006). Once the parent seeking relocation files a motion or petition, the burden of showing that the move is in the best interests of the child remains with that parent. *See, e.g., Mason v. Coleman*, 850 N.E.2d 513 (Mass. 2006); *In re Marriage of Burgess*, 913 P.2d 473, 483 n.12 (Cal. 1996) (when parents have shared joint physical custody, relocation of one of them justifies modification of custody under a best-interest test); *Ayers v. Ayers*, 508 N.W.2d 515, 519 (Minn. 1993) (in shared custody cases, relocation amounts to a modification of the custody award, and thus must be justified by the relocating parent); cf. *Jaramillo v. Jaramillo*, 823 P.2d 299, 309 (N.M. 1991) (when parties share custody equally, neither has the burden of proof in removal matter). The burden normally does not shift to the parent resisting the move to prove that the change would adversely affect the child. *See Stringer v. Vincent*, 411 N.W.2d 474 (Mich. App. 1987); Edwin J. Terry et al., *Relocation: Moving Forward, or Moving Backward?* 15 J. Am. Acad. Matrimonial L., 167, 212-213 (1998).

Example 6-9

Assume that P and D have joint legal and physical custody of child C, with each parent sharing physical custody for one-half of the week. C is eight years old. Assume that three months after the divorce was final, P filed a motion asking for primary physical custody of C and for permission to relocate to another jurisdiction with C. In the motion to relocate, P maintained that as a result of her mother's recent death, she desires to return to her childhood home to be close to her siblings. P explained that she had inherited a substantial sum of money from her mother, as well as part ownership of her mother's house. Her siblings have agreed to permit her to live in the house, rent free, while she finishes college and earns a teaching license. P explained that her mother's death not only resulted in closer contact with her siblings, but also renewed the importance of this contact. P also explained that she had exhausted her career opportunities as a secretary in the city where she currently lives. She stated that teaching would offer her a career, rather than a "job," and because her hours would mirror the minor child's school schedule, C would no longer need outside day care.

D (father) opposed her motion, arguing that relocation offered no actual advantage to the child and would disturb the current, functioning joint custody arrangement. D asks the court to award him sole physical custody of the child. How will the court most likely rule on the relocation request?

Explanation

The court will not, of course, bar P from leaving the state. However, it may well consider giving sole physical custody to D if P decides to relocate. It may reason that the best interests of C are to keep him in as stable an environment as possible — a familiar neighborhood and school system. This is a close issue, but one P may likely lose.

RELOCATING TO A FOREIGN COUNTRY

6.26. Hague Convention

The law governing child custody disputes between the United States and foreign countries is found in the Hague Convention on the Civil Aspects of International Child Abduction, entered into force December 1, 1983, (for the United States July 1, 1988) and the International Child Abduction Remedies Act (ICARA), 42 U.S.C. §11601 *et seq.*, which is the statute that implements the Hague Convention and states that its provisions "are in addition to and not in lieu of the provisions of the Convention." 42 U.S.C. §11601(b)(2)(A).

The Hague Convention establishes legal rights and procedures for the prompt return of children who have been "wrongfully removed to or retained in" a nation that is a party to the convention. Hague Convention, art. 1; 42 U.S.C. §11601(a). The nations that have adopted the Hague Convention have as their purpose "to protect children internationally from the harmful effects of their wrongful removal or retention and to establish procedures to ensure their prompt return to the State of their habitual residence, as well as to secure protection for rights of access." Hague Convention, preamble. The Hague Convention is intended "to preserve the *status quo*" with respect to child custody and to deter feuding parents from "crossing international boundaries in search of a more sympathetic [custody] court." *Miller v. Miller*, 240 F.3d 392, 398 (4th Cir. 2001). The scope of a court's inquiry under the Hague Convention is limited to the merits of the claim for wrongful removal or retention. *See* 42 U.S.C. §11601(b)(4); Hague Convention, art. 16. Consequently, a court is not to examine the merits of any underlying custody case when determining which country should hear the matter. *See Miller*, 240 F.3d at 398; Hague Convention, art. 19.

ICARA established procedures for implementing the Hague Convention in the United States, and it defined and allocated the burdens of proof for various claims and defenses under it. *See* 42 U.S.C. §11601 *et seq.* ICARA requires that a petitioner under the Hague Convention establish, by a preponderance of the evidence, that the child whose return is sought has been "wrongfully removed or retained within the meaning of the Convention." 42 U.S.C. §11603(e)(1)(A).

When a citizen from a foreign country brings an action in the United States claiming that the matter should not be heard here, the individual petitioner must prove by a preponderance of the evidence (1) that the child was habitually resident in the foreign county at the time the child was retained by the other parent in the United States, (2) that the retention was in breach of the petitioner's custody rights under the laws of the foreign nation, and (3) that the petitioner had been exercising those custody rights at the time of retention. *See* Miller, 240 F.3d at 398; Hague Convention, art. 3.

The party opposing the return of a child may prevail if he or she establishes certain defenses designated by ICARA and available under the Convention. For example, the opposing party might prevail if it is established by clear and convincing evidence (1) that there is a grave risk that returning the child to the foreign country would expose the child to physical or psychological harm or otherwise place him or her in an intolerable situation (Hague Convention, art. 13b), or (2) that the return of the child would not be permitted by the fundamental principles of the United States "relating to the protection of human rights and fundamental freedoms" (Hague Convention, art. 20). The opponent might also prevail if it is established by a preponderance of the evidence that the petitioner "was not actually exercising the custody rights at the time of . . . retention" (Hague Convention, art. 13a) or if it is shown that "the child objects to being returned and has attained an age and degree of maturity at which it is appropriate to take account of [the child's] views." Hague Convention, art. 13, §2.

The distinction between a Hague Convention petition brought pursuant to ICARA and a petition to determine the legal custody of a minor is that a Hague Convention petition affects custody, but it is not a custody determination. *See* Hague Convention, art. 19. The Hague Convention states that courts "shall not decide on the merits of rights of custody until it has been determined that the child is not to be returned under this Convention." Hague Convention, art. 16. The intention and effect of the Hague Convention, then, is to "lend priority to the custody determination hailing from the child's state of habitual residence." Miller, 240 F.3d at 399. As a result, a state court of competent jurisdiction may proceed to determine legal custody only when that court or a federal district court first finds that the petitioner cannot prove wrongful removal or retention or when the respondent establishes one of the available affirmative defenses.

Courts struggle with various provisions of the Hague Convention, including the definition of "habitual residence." *See, e.g., Interest of J.J.L.-P.,* 256 S.W.3d 363, 372 (Tex. App. 2008) (the habitual residence inquiry proceeds on a case-by-case basis, and focuses not upon a child's domicile or legal residence but where the child physically lived "for an amount of time sufficient for acclimatization and which has a degree of settled purpose from the child's perspective). The determination of whether any particular place satisfies this standard focuses "on the child, not the parents, and examine[s] past experience, not future intentions." *Humphrey v. Humphrey,* 434 F.3d 243 (4th Cir. 2006) (father required to establish habitual residence by a preponderance of evidence); *but see Gitter v. Gitter,* 396 F.3d 124 (2d Cir. 2005) (courts must focus on parental intent when deciding habitual residence).

Note that cases brought pursuant to ICARA and the Hague Convention are tried to a judge, because neither ICARA nor the Hague Convention provides for trial by jury and the available remedy — return of the child — is equitable in nature. *See Silverman v. Silverman,* 333 F.3d 886 (8th Cir. 2003). Forty-four countries (including the United States) have joined the Hague Convention on the Civil Aspects of International Child Abduction.

Removing a child from the United States, or retaining a child who has been in the United States outside the United States with intent to obstruct the lawful exercise of parental rights, is a federal felony punishable by up to three years in prison. 18 U.S.C. §1204.

Interstate Custody Struggles: The Uniform Child Custody Jurisdiction Act and the Parental Kidnapping Prevention Act — History, Restrictions, and Requirements

7.1. Introduction

This chapter focuses on the history, development, and reform efforts of the state and federal governments to provide a uniform set of jurisdictional rules and guidelines for national enforcement of child custody orders. The ultimate goal has been to simplify jurisdictional conflicts that persisted when states adopted a wide variety of child custody jurisdiction standards in isolation from each other. The federal government's role has been to provide child custody enforcement legislation pursuant to the Full Faith and Credit Clause of the Constitution and to deal with a broad scope of jurisdictional issues, including those involving tribes. *Garcia v. Gutierrez*, 192 P.3d 275 (N.M. App. 2008) (under the PKPA, tribes are United States territories that are to be treated as states).

HISTORY

7.2. Overview

Because of a lack of uniformity over the answer to the question of which state has jurisdiction in interstate custody disputes, several attempts have been made during the last four decades to persuade states to adopt uniform laws. Various model acts have been proposed with the hope that they would stimulate the attainment of a standardized approach to thorny jurisdictional issues.

The first model act intended to resolve the interstate jurisdictional custody problems between states was the Uniform Child Custody Jurisdiction Act (UCCJA) of 1968. It was, unfortunately, unsuccessful in bringing about uniformity. Congress, impatient and frustrated with the failed effort by the states to reach agreement on how to handle interstate jurisdictional custody disputes, stepped in and enacted the Parental Kidnapping Prevention Act (PKPA) of 1980. Seventeen years after the PKPA became law, a third effort was undertaken to create a model act that would reconcile the PKPA with various state-driven interstate jurisdictional provisions. This model act is the Uniform Child Custody Jurisdiction Enforcement Act (UCCJEA). The 1997 effort appears to have been reasonably successful in persuading states to adopt uniform standards.

7.3. Traditional View of Custody Jurisdiction — "Domicile"

Before major efforts were launched at creating uniformity among the states when interstate custody jurisdiction was at issue, the traditional view of custody jurisdiction was that only a court of the state where a child was domiciled could issue a custody decree. *See, e.g., Restatement, Conflict of Laws* §§1, 17 (1934). The domicile rule was based on the theory that only the child's domicile state possessed a sufficient relationship with the child to give that state a legitimate interest in determining custody. The domicile rule was criticized by scholars as rigid and as failing to focus on the real issue in a custody dispute, that is, the best interests of the child. *See* George W. Strumburg, *The Status of Children in Conflicts of Laws*, 8 U. Chi. L. Rev. 42 (1940); Russell M. Coombs, *Interstate Child Custody: Jurisdiction, Recognition, and Enforcement*, 66 Minn. L. Rev. 711 (1982). It was also criticized as leaving states helpless to act when a child was in grave need of protection.

7.4. Supreme Court Modification Rulings Spawn Controversy

Decisions by the Supreme Court over the past 60 years have failed to effectively resolve child custody disputes among the states. In fact, they have tended to generate jurisdictional unrest.

For example, in one of its earliest efforts to consider this issue, the Supreme Court held that the Full Faith and Credit Clause did not prevent modification of a custody decree by other states. *New York ex rel. Halvey v. Halvey,*

330 U.S. 610 (1947). It declared that a New York court was free to modify a Florida custody decree to permit visitation by the father because, under Florida law, custody decrees are not *res judicata* ' except as to the facts before the court at the time of judgment." Stewart E. Sterk, *The Muddy Boundaries Between Res Judicata and Full Faith and Credit*, 58 Wash. & Lee L. Rev. 47, 79 (Winter 2001). In response to *Halvey*, state courts concluded that there was a custody exception to the Full Faith and Credit mandate of the Constitution. *Id.* at 80. They began to exercise their custody modification power liberally, which may have encouraged forum shopping among warring parents. *See also Kovacs v. Brewer*, 356 U.S. 604 (1958) (Court declined to rule Full Faith and Credit Clause applied to custody disputes; state court could modify a custody decree issued in a sister state if the issuing state would not consider the decree *res judicata*).

The Supreme Court injected additional uncertainty into interstate custody disputes when it decided *May v. Anderson*, 345 U.S. 528 (1953). In that case, when the mother failed to appear for a divorce and custody hearing in Wisconsin, the father obtained an *ex parte* Wisconsin divorce judgment that granted him custody of the couple's minor children. Subsequent to the decree, the mother refused to return the children to Wisconsin while they were visiting her in Ohio. The father's efforts to enforce the Wisconsin decree in Ohio were unsuccessful, and the matter came before the Supreme Court.

A plurality in *May* held that in an interstate custody dispute, personal service upon a nonresident defendant (Ohio mother) notifying her of a pending custody hearing in another state (Wisconsin), was not sufficient to confer *in personam* jurisdiction over her in Wisconsin insofar as custody of the minor children was concerned. Under these circumstances, Ohio was not bound to accord full faith and credit to the Wisconsin custody order, even though the domicile of the children at the time of the *ex parte* divorce was Wisconsin.

The decision in *May v. Anderson* has been the subject of considerable academic dialogue concerning its meaning and application. *See, e.g.*, Bridgette M. Bodenheimer & Janet Neeley-Kvarme, *Jurisdiction over Child Custody and Adoption after Shaffer and Kulko*, 12 U.C. Davis L. Rev. 229 (1979); Bridgette M. Bodenheimer, *The Uniform Child Custody Jurisdiction Act: A Legislative Remedy for Children Caught in the Conflict of Laws*, 22 Vand. L. Rev. 1207, 1232-1233 (1969).

Some scholars have argued that the better view of jurisdiction in interstate custody disputes is found in Justice Jackson's dissent in *May v. Anderson*. Justice Jackson argued that custody should be viewed not with the idea of adjudicating rights in the children, as if they were chattels, but rather with the idea of making the best disposition possible for the welfare of the children. He observed that personal jurisdiction of all parties to be affected by a custody proceeding is highly desirable. "But the assumption that it overrides all other considerations and in its absence a state is constitutionally impotent to resolve questions of custody flies in the face of our own cases." *May v. Anderson, supra* at 541.

Justice Frankfurter concurred in *May v. Anderson*, and wrote that although Ohio was not required to give full faith and credit to the Wisconsin order, the Due Process Clause did not prohibit Ohio from recognizing it "as a matter of local law" or comity. *Id.* at 535-536. The *Restatement (Second) of Conflict of Laws* seems to agree with the Frankfurter interpretation of the law. "Under this view, a state may, as a matter of local law, recognize the custody disposition made by another state, regardless of lack of personal jurisdiction." Bodenheimer & Neeley-Kvarme, *supra* at 251.

Another view of the *May* decision is that Wisconsin did not have language in its long-arm statute authorizing extraterritorial service of process over the mother, who was served with process in Ohio. Since the decision, most states have adopted long-arm statutes with specific language that makes them applicable to cases growing out of domestic custody difficulties. *See Mitchim v. Mitchim*, 518 S.W.2d 362 (Tex. 1975).

7.5. Status Theory Emerges

Several state courts have rejected the plurality view of personal jurisdiction found in *May v. Anderson*. Instead, they have seized upon a "status" theory approach. This theory allows a court to make a custody decision if the state where the proceeding is being held has the most significant connections with the child and the child's family at the time of the hearing. *See Burton v. Bishop*, 269 S.E.2d 417 (Ga. 1980); *Yearta v. Scroggins*, 268 S.E.2d 151, 153 (Ga. 1980); *McAtee v. McAtee*, 323 S.E.2d 611, 616-617 (W. Va. 1984); *Hart v. Hart*, 695 P.2d 1285 (Kan. 1985); *Genoe v. Genoe*, 500 A.2d 3, 8 (N.J. Super. Ct. App. Div. 1985); *In re Marriage of O'Connor*, 690 P.2d 1095, 1097 (Or. Ct. App. 1984); *In re Marriage of Hudson*, 434 N.E.2d 107, 117-118 (Ind. Ct. App. 1982); *McArthur v. Superior Court*, 1 Cal. Rptr. 2d 296 (Cal. App. 6 Dist. 1991).

Tennessee courts have rejected the plurality view expressed in *May v. Anderson*, saying that their interpretation of later decisions has led them to conclude that the Supreme Court "abolished the distinctions between *in rem* and *in personam*" jurisdiction, and "recognized that exceptions can be made to the 'minimum contacts' standard" in "status" cases, such as child custody decisions. *Fernandez v. Fernandez*, No. 85-194-II, 1986 WL 7935, at 1-2 (Tenn. Ct. App. July 15, 1986); *see also Brown v. Brown*, 847 S.W.2d 496, 499 n.2 (Tenn. 1993) (noting that the Supreme Court decision in *May v. Anderson* has largely been ignored and that neither the UCCJA nor the PKPA requires personal jurisdiction over the respondent). The court in *Fernandez* declared that a state "having the most significant connections with the child and his family will be permitted to make a custody adjudication even in the absence of personal jurisdiction over a parent who does not reside in the forum state." *Fernandez*, 1986 WL 7935, at 2. *See also Roderick v. Roderick*, 776 S.W.2d 533, 535-536 (Tenn. Ct. App. 1989) (noting that the UCCJA permits the courts of the state with the most significant contacts to make custody determinations even without personal jurisdiction over the nonresident parent).

A Texas court that took essentially the same view as Tennessee explained that "[u]nlike adjudications of child support and visitation expense, custody determinations are status adjudications not dependent upon personal jurisdiction over the parents. Generally, a family relationship is among those matters in which the forum state has such a strong interest that its courts may reasonably make an adjudication affecting that relationship even though one of the parties to the relationship may have had no personal contacts with the forum state." *In re Interest of S.A.V.*, 837 S.W.2d 80, 84 (Tex. 1992). *See In re Marriage of Los*, 593 N.E.2d 126, 129-130 (Ill. App. Ct. 1992) (status determinations do not require personal jurisdiction over the parents). In *S.A.V.*, *supra*, the court stated that "[t]o acquire jurisdiction over custody issues, no connection between the nonresident parent and the state is required." *Id.* at 84 of 837 S.W.2d.

Example 7-1

Assume that P and D were married and lived in state X. After five years of marriage, the relationship broke down, they separated, and D left state X and established his domicile in state Y. The children remained with P in state X. One year after P and D separated, P brought a divorce action in state X. D ignored the matter and made no appearance in state X in response to a summons and dissolution petition served on him in state Y. P asked in her legal papers for sole physical and legal custody of the children. In its default judgment, the state X court awarded sole physical and legal custody of the parties' children to P, observing that the children are domiciled in that state with P. A few months later, after the children visit with D in state Y, D refuses to return them to P in state X. D then brings an action in state Y asking that he be granted sole legal and physical custody of the children. P argues that only state X may resolve this issue. How might the outcome of the action differ in state Y, depending on which of the various theories previously discussed in this chapter the court may choose to apply?

Explanation

First, if the court in state Y applies the traditional domicile rule, it will rule that it lacks jurisdiction to litigate the issue because the children are domiciled in state X.

Second, even if state Y has a long-arm statute covering domestic matters, it will most likely find that P does not have sufficient contacts with state Y to satisfy constitutional requirements. (Review the jurisdiction chapter, *infra*, if you have trouble with this point.)

Third, should the court strictly follow the plurality view in *May v. Anderson*, it may refuse to enforce the state X ruling on the theory that state X lost personal jurisdiction over D before the divorce action was initiated, when D became a citizen of state Y. It will reason that without personal jurisdiction over both parties, the state X court was without power to enter an enforceable judgment regarding custody outside its borders.

Fourth, the court might apply the "status" theory and consider the custody request because D and the children are within the physical boundaries of state Y and before the court. Under this theory, a state may alter a child's custody status without having jurisdiction over both parties if at the time of the hearing it has the most significant connections with the child and the child's family. This theory suggests that "status" (custody) implies more than the state's concern with the relationship of the parties. It encompasses the right and obligation of the state in its *parens patriae* role to consider the welfare of the child subject to its jurisdiction and to make a determination that is in the best interests of the child. In re Marriage of Leonard, 175 Cal. Rptr. 903 (Ct. App. 1981).

Finally, under the UCCJEA, it appears that the only jurisdiction where the modification issue could be brought is state X, absent a state X court waiving its right to adjudicate the matter in that state. If state Y has adopted the UCCJEA, it will refuse to entertain a custody motion involving D and the children because state X has already considered that issue. Moreover, state X is the home state of the children and D is not alleging an emergency.

THE UNIFORM CHILD CUSTODY JURISDICTION ACT (UCCJA)

7.6. Overview

As discussed earlier in this chapter, because of the inability on the part of states to cooperate in interstate custody matters, an effort to encourage development of a uniform system to resolve these disputes was launched in 1968 by the National Conference of Commissioners on Uniform State Laws. It created a model act that it called the UCCJA. 9 U.L.A. (Part 1A) 261 (1998). The model act had several purposes: First, it sought to avoid jurisdictional competition and conflict among courts of different states in matters of child custody and to promote cooperation among them in matters of child custody. Second, by promoting cooperation among the courts of different states, the Act sought to achieve a custody decree rendered in the state best suited to determine the best interests of a child. Third, the Act was aimed at deterring abductions and other unilateral removals of children undertaken by parents seeking to obtain favorable custody rulings.

The UCCJA was subsequently adopted by all 50 states; however, the versions were not uniform. Because of the dissimilarities, tension among the states developed over the goal of achieving stability of custody decrees and providing a system with sufficient flexibility to accommodate the best interests of a child. The Oregon Supreme Court critically characterized the UCCJA as "a schizophrenic attempt to bring about an orderly system of decision and at the same time to protect the best interests of the children who may be immediately before the court." In re *Marriage of Settle*, 556 P.2d 962, 968 (Or. 1976), overruled, *Matter of Custody of Russ*, 620 P.2d 353 (Or. 1981). It became clear after a number of years that the initial effort to achieve uniformity among the states had fallen far short of the mark.

PARENTAL KIDNAPPING PREVENTION ACT (PKPA)

7.7. Overview

Frustrated by the failed efforts of the states to adopt uniform versions of the UCCJA, Congress enacted the PKPA in 1980. 23 U.S.C. §1738A (1988); *see* Russell M. Coombs, *Progress Under the PKPA*, 6 J. Am. Acad. Matrimonial Law. 59 (1990). Despite its title, the Act is not limited to matters involving parental kidnapping but applies broadly to civil interstate custody disputes. *See* Anne B. Goldstein, *Tragedy of the Interstate Child: A Critical Reexamination of the Uniform Child Custody Jurisdiction Act and the Parental Kidnapping Prevention Act*, 25 U.C. Davis L. Rev. 845 (Summer 1992). Unlike the UCCJA, the PKPA prioritizes the bases of jurisdiction. It gives priority to the "home state" of the child. It also provides that once a state has exercised jurisdiction, the initial decree-granting state retains exclusive continuing jurisdiction if it remains the residence of the children or any contestant.

7.8. Federal Standards

The effect of sections 1738A(d) and 1738A(f) of the PKPA is to limit custody jurisdiction to the first state to properly enter a custody order, as long as two sets of requirements are met. 28 U.S.C. §1738A(d)(f) (1998). First, the Act establishes a federal standard for continuing exclusive custody jurisdiction in the state that initially possessed jurisdiction over the parties at the time the custody order was entered pursuant to the criteria found in the Act. Second, the Act incorporates a state law inquiry. To retain exclusive responsibility for modifying a prior order, the first state must have retained custody jurisdiction as a matter of its own law. However even if the federal and state criteria for continuing jurisdiction are met, the first state can, if it decides to do so, relinquish jurisdiction in favor of a court in a different state that is better situated to assess a child's needs.

In addition to sorting out the civil jurisdictional issues between states, the Act contains criminal provisions. For example, persons who "snatch" children may be criminally prosecuted under the Act. *See* 28 U.S.C. §1738A (1988). In child snatching cases, the Act also provides for a federal warrant and permits the intervention of the Federal Bureau of Investigation.

The Supreme Court held in *Thompson v. Thompson*, 484 U.S. 174 (1988), that under the provisions of the PKPA, once a state properly exercises jurisdiction, other states must give full faith and credit to the determination and no other state may exercise concurrent jurisdiction, even if it would be entitled to under its own laws.

Example 7-2

Assume that P and D are divorced in state X at a time when state X has personal jurisdiction over both parties. P is awarded sole physical and legal custody of child C. Following the divorce, D moves to state Y, while P and C remain in state X. Assume that a year after the divorce, D becomes very concerned about the care and treatment afforded child C. During one of the periods that child C is visiting D in state Y, D brings an action in a state Y family court seeking to modify the custody decree originally issued in state X. P responds to D's motion and asks the court to dismiss the action in state Y on the ground that only state X has jurisdiction in this matter. Most likely, how will a court rule?

Explanation

A court will most likely rule in favor of P. Here, state X has retained jurisdiction under its own laws. State X possessed initial custody jurisdiction when it entered its first order at a time when it had personal jurisdiction over both parties. State X has remained the residence of C and P since the original custody order was entered. Under the PKPA, a custody modification action must be brought in state X, unless state X declines to exercise jurisdiction, which in this hypothetical is unlikely. *See Matthews v. Riley*, 649 A.2d 231 (Vt. 1994).

7.9. Continuing Jurisdiction — Application

It is useful to examine more closely the concept of "continuing jurisdiction" under the PKPA. Under the Act, the court that is asked to modify an existing custody order determines whether the rendering court has continuing jurisdiction under the law of the rendering state. *See Cann v. Howard*, 850 S.W.2d 57, 60 (Ky. Ct. App. 1993); *Pierce v. Pierce*, 640 P.2d 899, 903 (Mont. 1982).

In determining continuing jurisdiction under section 1738A(d), the Act does not mandate a home state preference. Once a court acquires jurisdiction under the PKPA, whether it retains jurisdiction is wholly a matter of state law and the residence of one contestant. 28 U.S.C. §1738A(d); *see* §1738A(c)(2)(E) (determinations made by courts with continuing jurisdiction are consistent with PKPA and are entitled to interstate recognition and enforcement). The Act "does not affect the discretion of a state to limit its own continuing jurisdiction. The statute only curtails the freedom of another state to modify the decree for the period of time the rendering state's jurisdiction continues under its own law." Russell M. Coombs, *Interstate Child Custody: Jurisdiction, Recognition, and Enforcement*, 66 Minn. L. Rev. 711, 852 (1982). The possibility of continuing jurisdiction beyond the home state discourages parties from relocating to reestablish a home state only for the purpose of modifying what is perceived as an unfavorable custody arrangement. In providing for continuing jurisdiction, the PKPA seeks to foster a stable home environment and family relationship for a child, promote "negotiated settlement of custody disputes, and facilitate visitation between a child and the other noncustodial parent." Matthews, *supra* at 239.

7.10. Private Right of Action

Prior to 1988, some state courts had concluded that the PKPA gave warring parents in different states an implied private cause of action in federal court, where, they contended, their custody contest could be resolved. *See, e.g., Meade v. Meade*, 812 F.2d 1473 (4th Cir. 1987). In *Thompson v. Thompson*, 484 U.S. 174 (1988), the Supreme Court held that the Act did not create an implied private right of relief. It reasoned that the language of PKPA and its legislative history indicated that Congress did not intend to create a new cause of action and did not intend federal courts to "play an enforcement role" in custody disputes. *Id.* at 184.

UNIFORM CHILD CUSTODY JURISDICTION AND ENFORCEMENT ACT

7.11. Overview

In 1997, 17 years after Congress enacted the PKPA, another effort to create a uniform approach among the states regarding interstate custody disputes was launched by the National Conference of Commissioners on Uniform State Laws when the commissioners promulgated the Uniform Child Custody Jurisdiction Enforcement Act (UCCJEA), 9 U.L.A. (Part 1A) 649

(1997). The goal of the UCCJEA was to reconcile differences between the UCCJA found in all states in some form and the PKPA. Since its release, some version of the UCCJEA has been adopted in all jurisdictions.

The general objectives of the UCCJEA remained the same as those found in the UCCJA, including the goal to address problems associated with the growing number of custody disputes between geographically separated parents. *See Phillips v. Beaber*, 995 S.W.2d 655, 659 & n.2 (Tex. 1999). Like its predecessor, the UCCJEA is concerned with the refusal of some courts to give finality to custody decrees issued by other states, and it seeks to discourage the use of the interstate system for continuing controversies over child custody. It also is intended to deter the abduction of children.

Unlike the UCCJA, the UCCJEA prioritizes among the four bases of jurisdiction and follows the PKPA by giving priority to the child's home state. It also restricts the use of emergency jurisdiction to the issuance of temporary orders. The Act permits the exercise of emergency jurisdiction to protect a child, the child's siblings, or the child's parents. *See* Joan Zorza, *The UCCJEA: What Is It and How Does It Affect Battered Women in Child-Custody Disputes*, 27 Fordham Urb. L.J. 909, 917 (2000). The UCCJEA is consistent with the PKPA in that a modification action can be brought only in the state that made the initial custody determination so long as a child or parent involved in the original custody ruling remains in that state.

7.12. Scope

There are four areas where the UCCJEA may play an important role in the outcome of an interstate custody dispute: (1) in initial child custody determinations; (2) when continuing jurisdiction exists because the action is brought in the court that originally possessed personal jurisdiction over the parties to the action; (3) when a modification motion is brought to change an existing custody determination; and (4) in situations where an emergency exists and a court must act to protect the child.

In general, the UCCJEA applies to the following: custody, modification of custody, visitation disputes that arise in divorce and separation proceedings, domestic violence matters, and paternity disputes. It may also apply, depending on how a state legislature promulgates its version of the UCCJEA, to neglect, dependency, guardianship, termination of parental rights, and grandparental visitation. It has not been applied to adoption proceedings. *See* UCCJEA *prefatory note*, §4, 9 U.L.A. (Part 1A) 649 (1997).

7.13. Subject Matter Jurisdiction — Waiver

Adjudication under the UCCJEA requires that a court possess subject matter jurisdiction. Subject matter jurisdiction cannot be conferred by waiver, consent, or estoppel. *See In re Marriage of Arnold and Cully*, 222 Cal. App. 3d 499, 504 (1990). The subject matter jurisdictional requirements of the UCCJEA must be satisfied whenever a court makes a custody determination.

7.14. Exclusive Continuing Jurisdiction

Continuing jurisdiction was not specifically addressed in the UCCJA. Its absence caused considerable confusion, particularly because the PKPA, in §1738(d), required states to give full faith and credit to custody determinations made by the original decree state, pursuant to the decree state's continuing jurisdiction, so long as that state has jurisdiction under its own law and remains the residence of the child or any contestant.

Section 2 of the UCCJEA provides the rules of continuing jurisdiction and establishes a jurisdictional hierarchy to provide guidance to courts deciding child custody and visitation cases. At the top of the hierarchy is the court that possesses exclusive continuing jurisdiction. This is the most preferred jurisdictional basis and is applied if it is available, unless the court that has the preferred jurisdictional basis declines to exercise jurisdiction.

Once a court makes an initial custody determination consistent with the UCCJEA, that court is viewed as retaining exclusive continuing jurisdiction over the matter unless neither the child nor at least one parent or person acting as a parent has a significant connection with the state originally issuing the order and substantial evidence in that state is no longer available concerning the child. In general, the state issuing the original decree continues to have jurisdiction to decide a custody dispute regardless of the length of the absence of the child and the other parent from the jurisdiction.

If a court has entered a valid custody order and one of the parties or the child continues to live in the state, that court has the exclusive right to decide if the order should be modified. Courts of other states may not modify an order (assuming a parent or child continues to live in the state that issued an order) unless the court that issued the order gives permission to another state to decide the issue.

Example 7-3

Assume P and D divorce in state X, and P is awarded sole legal and physical custody of P and D's minor child. Following the divorce, P leaves state X with the child and has resided in state Y for one year. P brings an action in state Y to modify the order originally issued in state X and further restrict D's visitation with the minor child. D has never visited state Y. D argues that under the UCCJEA, the action can only be brought in state X, where D continues to reside. P argues that because she and the child are before the court in state Y, it can modify the original custody order. How will a judge most likely rule?

Explanation

A court that applies the typical language found in the UCCJEA will take the view that no other jurisdiction, other than the issuing court in state X, may modify a custody determination. Only if an issuing court in state X determines that it no longer has exclusive continuing jurisdiction may the matter be heard in state Y. Here, one of the parties, D, continues to live in state X, the state that issued the original custody order. State X does not appear to have lost jurisdiction or to be ready to give it up. It is unlikely that a court in state Y would ignore the PKPA and the UCCJEA and apply a status theory to resolve the dispute in state Y.

Example 7-4

Assume that D has brought a petition in state X seeking a change in his visitation schedule with child C, who is in P's custody in state Y. When the couple divorced in state X eight years ago, the court awarded sole physical custody of C to P, with D receiving two weeks visitation in the summer and one week at Christmas and Easter. P relocated with C to state Y and has resided there since the divorce. After the relocation, the parties arranged informally for C to visit D for an extended period in state X over the summer and during some of the child's spring, winter, and other holiday vacations. In July of this year P orally informed D that if he wanted to exercise any visitation with the child, now 16 years old, he would have to come to state Y and remain in that state to exercise said visitation. D has filed an action asking the court in state X to modify the former custody decree giving D a greater amount of visitation with C and requiring P to allow the child to visit D in state X. P argues that state X should refer the matter to state Y because it does not have jurisdiction over P and C as they are residents of state Y.

Without conceding the jurisdictional issue, P has submitted an affidavit to the family court in state X alleging that C has an attitude when he returns from visiting D and that D and his family are a bad influence on C. P also alleges that she would no longer send the child to state X for visitation due to D's alcohol and marijuana abuse and because of her concerns regarding the child's safety during visits. P claims that D's family members and his current girlfriend were the source of her information. P asserts that the overwhelming evidence concerning the child's care, protection, training, and personal relationships are in state Y and that it would be very inconvenient for the child and P to litigate the matter in state X. Will a court in state X dismiss D's petition?

Explanation

Under the UCCJEA, state X has exclusive, continuing jurisdiction unless a court in that state determines that neither the child nor the child and one parent have a significant connection with state X and that substantial evidence is no longer available in state X concerning the child's care, protection, training, and personal relationships. Before making a final decision, a judge in state X will consider that most, if not all, of the visitation between D and the child took place in state X. The child has an extended family in state X, and the primary witnesses regarding D's alleged alcohol abuse, use of marijuana, and any additional safety concerns (including any individual who may conduct a substance abuse evaluation), D's family members, and D's current girlfriend are located in state X. Basically, the most relevant information regarding the child's best interest and safety during visitation with D exists in state X. Because D still resides in state X and substantial evidence remains available in state X concerning the child's care, protection, and personal relationships during visitation, a court will most likely rule that state X has exclusive, continuing jurisdiction to modify the original visitation schedule.

On the question of whether the matter should be heard in state Y rather than state X because state Y is a more convenient forum, the evidence of alcohol and marijuana abuse involving D, if it exists, is located in state X. It also appears that the evidence that P intends to rely upon would include D's family members and D's current girlfriend. All those individuals are currently located in state X and most likely not subject to the subpoena powers of the state Y. State X would have a superior ability to compel, if necessary, the testimony of individuals having potentially relevant information regarding the child's safety.

The eight-year connection with state Y by the mother and child suggest that state X might elect to decline jurisdiction; however, because most of the evidence regarding P's allegations about D's behavior is located in state X, the eight-year period P and the child lived in state Y is not a compelling factor.

Other factors a court might consider are the distance P and the child will have to travel from state Y to state X and the mother's loss of income. However, because the child's best interest and safety during visitation is of paramount concern, a court would probably not rule that state X is an inconvenient forum.

7.15. Home State Jurisdiction

One of the considerations used by the UCCJEA to resolve jurisdictional disputes is a determination of whether the forum is the home state of the child. Home state is defined as the state where the child lived with a parent or a person acting as a parent for at least six consecutive months immediately before commencement of the proceeding. If the child is less than six months old, the home state is the state in which the child lived from birth. The definition of "home state" in the UCCJEA is identical to the definition found in the PKPA. UCCJEA §102(7); 28 U.S.C. §1738A(b)(4) (1994).

A court has jurisdiction to make an initial child custody determination if the state is the home state of the child on the date the proceeding is commenced. It also has such jurisdiction if the child no longer lives there, but the state was the home state of the child within six months before the proceeding commenced, and a parent or person acting as a parent continues to live in the state. A temporary absence from the forum state does not change the application of "home state" as found in the UCCJEA. In situations in which a parent has improperly removed a child from the home state, the home state may retain jurisdiction beyond six months.

Example 7-5

P and D divorced in state X, and the divorce judgment established D as the primary residential parent and acknowledged D's intent to relocate to state Y. P consented to D's relocation, and D relocated with the parties' three children to state Y, where she registered the divorce decree.

Five months after the divorce, P, who continued to reside in state X, filed a motion in state X for a change of custody of the two oldest children claiming endangerment. D filed a motion to dismiss P's post-decree motion asserting that the matter was within the jurisdiction of state Y because P resided in state Y with P's consent and had registered the divorce decree in state Y. The trial judge in state X agreed and dismissed P's modification motion. P has appealed. Most likely, how will an appellate court rule on the issue of jurisdiction under the UCCJEA?

Explanation

Despite P originally agreeing to allow D to relocate, an appellate court will most likely reverse the trial judge's ruling. The UCCJEA gives jurisdictional priority and exclusive continuing jurisdiction to the home state, which is X. Under the UCCJEA, the court in which a custody decree is originally issued retains continuing jurisdiction over issues of custody arising from that decree.

The UCCJEA defines the "home state" of a child, in relevant part, as "the state in which a child lived with a parent . . . for at least six consecutive months immediately preceding the commencement of a child custody proceeding." X was the "home state" of the children at the time the parties' divorce proceeding commenced and at the time of the modification motion brought five months later.

Because the trial court properly exercised jurisdiction in the initial determination of the parties divorce and because P still resides in state X, and the home state of the children is X, state X retains jurisdiction over the matter. If both parents had relocated out of state X, then there might have been a question as to X's exclusive and continuing jurisdiction, but that is not the case here.

D's assertion that because she "registered" the decree in state Y upon moving to that state, Y has jurisdiction to determine the children's custody under the UCCJEA, finds no support in the UCCJEA.

7.16. No "Home State"

If there is no home state, or the home state court declines to exercise jurisdiction, a court of another state may assume jurisdiction if it qualifies as one with "significant connections" to the action. UCCJEA §201(a)(2).

Example 7-6

Assume that D (mother) and P (father) were married in state X and a child was born to them. When the child was approximately six months old, the two divorced in state X. The trial court, at the request of the parties, did not make a custody determination or issue a custody order. D moved to state Y to live with her mother and child until this year when five months ago she moved from Y to state Z with the child. P moved from state X to state A about four months ago, where he now resides. The child is almost four.

Following their divorce, P had little contact with the child. However, in June of this year, the child visited P in state A for the first time for a three-week summer visit. P refused to return the child to D at the end of visitation. P commenced an action in state A asking for custody of the child. At the time the matter was commenced, P had been a resident of state A for four months, and the child had resided there for three weeks. P argued that because there was no "home state," A had jurisdiction to enter a custody order under the UCCJEA.

Assume that the UCCJEA, as adopted in state A by its legislature, provides a court in that state with jurisdiction to make child custody determination if

> A court of another state does not have jurisdiction, or a court of the home state of the child has declined to exercise jurisdiction on the ground that this state is the more appropriate forum because of inconvenient forum or "unjustifiable conduct" by the party seeking to invoke jurisdiction, and (a) the child and the child's parents, or the child and at least one parent . . . have a significant connection with this state other than mere physical presence, and (b) substantial

evidence is available in this state concerning the child's care, protection, training, and personal relationships. (c) All courts having jurisdiction have declined to exercise jurisdiction on the ground that a court of this state is the more appropriate forum to determine the custody of the child because of inconvenient forum or unjustifiable conduct by the party seeking to invoke jurisdiction]; or (d) No court of any other state would have jurisdiction.

The trial court in state A issued a custody order giving P primary custody of the child and reasonable visitation to D. D appeals challenging the jurisdiction of A to make this decision. Most likely, how will an appellate court in state A rule?

Explanation

First, it is clear that state A is not the home state of the child for purposes of jurisdiction as "home state" is defined by the UCCJEA. In this case, D and the child lived in state Y for substantially all of the child's life until D's recent move to state Z. D lived in state Z for five months prior to commencement of the state A proceedings. The child had resided in state A only three weeks and in state Z less than six months prior to this action. State X could not be the "home state" because the evidence shows that neither P, D, nor the child lived in state X at the time of the commencement of the custody proceeding. State Z could not be the "home state," as the evidence in this hypothetical shows that the child lived less than six months with D in that state and only three weeks with P in state A before P initiated the custody action.

Second, the language of the above statute permits a court in state A to exercise jurisdiction only if (1) a court of another state does not have "home state" jurisdiction or has declined to exercise jurisdiction; and (2) the child has significant connections with state A; and (3) there is available in state A substantial evidence concerning the child's welfare. Here, there is little evidence to establish either the child's significant connection with state A beyond the child's limited presence during three weeks this year, or the availability of substantial evidence concerning the child's past and future care, education, and safety. The child has, after all, lived with D in either state Y or state Z almost since birth.

Third, state A courts may exercise jurisdiction under the UCCJEA if no other state has jurisdiction. UCCJEA, §201, *comment*. Because neither state Y, state Z, nor state A could properly exercise "home state" jurisdiction, the trial court may have assumed jurisdiction under this default provision.

Fourth, the jurisdictional provisions of the UCCJEA seek to assure that litigation regarding custody of a child take place in the state with which the child and his family have the closest connection and where significant evidence concerning care and protection is readily available in order to provide a continuing stable environment for children. State A is not that state. While the trial court may not have erred in assuming jurisdiction, the spirit and intent of the UCCJEA is to protect the best interests of the child. It appears that P is left with a choice of state X, or state Z in which to bring the custody action. *See Wood v. Redwine*, 33 P.3d 53 (Okla. Civ. App. Div. 1 2001). State Z is the likely choice for P's modification action because D is residing there. State Y is most likely not available because it would be difficult to obtain personal jurisdiction over P in that state at this time.

7.17. Emergency Jurisdiction

A state court may assume temporary jurisdiction over a custody dispute if the child is present in the state and it is necessary to protect the child because he or she is subjected to or threatened with mistreatment or abuse. A trial court enjoys broad discretion in issuing orders for immediate protection of a child. UCCJEA §204, cmt. 9 U.L.A. (Part 1A) 677 (1997) (states' duties to recognize, enforce, and not modify custody determinations of other states do not take precedence over the need to protect child); *see Garza v. Harney*, 726 S.W.2d 198, 202 (Tex. Ct. App. 1987). States have a *parens patriae* duty to children within their borders, and the possibility that allegations of immediate harm might be true is generally sufficient for a court to assume temporary emergency jurisdiction in the best interests of the child under the UCCJEA. *In re Nada R.*, 108 Cal. Rptr. 2d 493, 500 (Ct. App. 2001); *Hache v. Riley*, 451 A.2d 971, 975 (N.J. Super. Ct. Ch. Div. 1982).

Any order issued under emergency circumstances must be temporary in nature and specify a period that the court considers adequate to obtain an order from the state with jurisdiction. The temporary order remains in effect only until proper steps are taken in the original forum state to adequately protect the children or until the specified period expires.

Once a court assumes temporary emergency jurisdiction, it has a duty to communicate with the other state that has asserted custody jurisdiction and it should retain a record of those communications. This mandatory duty of cooperation between the courts of different states is a hallmark of the UCCJEA, and the cooperation is intended to lead to an informed decision on custody. One of the reasons for consulting with the other state's court is to determine the duration of the temporary order. *In re C.T.*, 121 Cal. Rptr. 2d 897, 906 (Ct. App. 2002); *see also* Patricia M. Hoff, *The ABC's of the UCCJEA: Interstate Child-Custody Practice Under the New Act*, 32 Fam. L.Q. 267, 284 (1998).

Temporary emergency jurisdiction is reserved for extraordinary circumstances, and the trial court's assumption of temporary emergency jurisdiction does not include jurisdiction to modify the original court's child custody determination. UCCJEA §204, cmt. 9 U.L.A. (Part 1A) 677 (1997); *see Abderholden v. Morizot*, 856 S.W.2d 829, 834 (Tex. Ct. App. 1993) (holding that exercise of emergency jurisdiction does not confer authority to make permanent custody disposition or modify custody decree of court with jurisdiction). Because a court's exercise of emergency jurisdiction is temporary in nature, it may not be used as a vehicle to attain modification jurisdiction for an ongoing, indefinite period of time.

Example 7-7

Assume that in a paternity action, the state X trial judge awarded P (the father) custody of the minor child C who was born to D and P. C resided with P at P's parents' home in state X. D made an unannounced visit to P's home and abducted C. P tried to locate D and the minor child but he was unsuccessful.

Several months after D abducted C, a state Y County Department of Social Services (DSS) filed a petition alleging C to be a neglected and dependent juvenile. The petition asserted that she was not receiving proper care, supervision, or discipline from her parent, guardian, custodian, or caretaker; that she had been abandoned; and that she lived in an environment injurious to her welfare. Although the state Y trial judge knew of the state X order giving P custody, she made no effort to contact the state X court. At an adjudication hearing, the court found C to be a neglected and dependent juvenile and placed her in DSS custody. P, who eventually learned of the proceeding, filed an appeal and argued that the trial court should have granted full faith and credit to the state X order and returned C to his custody. How will an appellate court most likely rule, and of what relevance are the UCCJEA's emergency provisions to the resolution of this issue?

Explanation

The trial court's decision will most likely be reversed. The order finding C to be a neglected and dependent juvenile and placing her in custody of the county department of social services violated the emergency jurisdiction provisions of UCCJEA. The reasoning is that the order does not appear to be temporary, and although the state Y judge knew about the prior state X custody decree, there was no effort to immediately contact the state X court to determine that court's willingness to assume jurisdiction.

Example 7-8

Assume that P and D divorced in state X, and a court there awarded sole legal and physical custody of child C to D. Both parents were before the court when it issued the order. P subsequently moved to state Y. Also assume that about ten years following the entry of the divorce judgment, C called P from state X claiming that her new stepparent was abusing and mistreating her. P immediately sought an emergency order under the UCCJEA in state Y. P argued that state Y has jurisdiction to issue an emergency order regardless of whether the child is present in the state. How will a court most likely rule?

Explanation

A state Y court will most likely reject P's request. Section 204 of the UCCJEA codifies and clarifies several aspects of what has become common practice in emergency jurisdiction cases under the UCCJEA and PKPA. First, a court may take jurisdiction to protect a child even though it can claim neither home state nor significant connection jurisdiction. Second, the duties of states to recognize, enforce, and not modify a custody determination of another state do not take precedence over the need to enter a temporary emergency order to protect the child. However, section 204 of the UCCJEA must be read in context with the federal PKPA. The PKPA states a custody determination can be made by a state if it has jurisdiction under state law and the child is physically present in such state and if (1) the child has been abandoned or (2) it is necessary in an emergency to protect the child because he has been subjected to or threatened with mistreatment or abuse. 28 U.S.C. §1738A(c)(2)(C) (1994). This language is more explicit than the UCCJEA in defining that presence, as well as an additional emergency situation, is required. When the federal PKPA precludes exercise of UCCJEA jurisdiction, state courts "must give preemptive effect to the federal enactment." See McLain v. McLain, 569 N.W.2d 219, 224 (Minn. Ct. App. 1997). Because state Y meets none of the requirements for exercise of jurisdiction under either the UCCJEA or the PKPA, it is preempted from assuming jurisdiction. The action most likely must be brought in state X.

7.18. International Application of UCCJEA and Related Laws

International abduction of children by parents is a serious problem, and the UCCJEA has attempted, at least in part, to deal with it. Under the UCCJEA, another country is treated as if it were a state of the United States for purposes of applying Articles 1 and 2 of the Act. The Act provides that custody determinations of other countries will be enforced if the facts of the case indicate that jurisdiction was in substantial compliance with the requirements of the act. However, at least one jurisdiction has said that certain provisions of the UCCJEA do not apply to international custody disputes. See, e.g., Temlock v. Temlock, 898 A.2d 209 (Conn. 2006) (although

Connecticut adopted the provisions set forth in §§105(b) and (c) of the Model Act that address foreign judgments, it chose not to treat foreign countries as states for purposes of other provisions, including its *forum non conveniens* provision, by excluding §105(a) of the Model Act).

Congress addressed international child abduction in 1993 when it promulgated the International Parental Kidnapping Act (IPKA), 18 U.S.C. §1204 (2006). The Act imposes criminal penalties on parents who illegally abduct children. For example, the Act makes it a federal felony for a parent to wrongfully remove or retain a child outside the United States. Defenses to the criminal action include the following: (1) the defendant was granted custody or visitation pursuant to the UCCJEA; (2) the defendant is fleeing from domestic violence; or (3) the defendant was unable to return a child to the custodial parent because of circumstances beyond his or her control and the defendant made reasonable attempts to notify the other parent.

Another area of law relevant to international child abduction is the Hague Convention on the Civil Aspects of International Abduction. The United States began implementing the Convention in 1980 when Congress promulgated the International Child Abduction Remedies Act (ICARA), 42 U.S.C. §§11601-11610 (2006). The Hague Convention is intended to secure the return of children who are wrongfully removed from or retained in a signatory state and to return them to the country of their habitual residence, which must be another contracting nation, where the merits of the custody dispute can be decided.

Courts have disagreed on various provisions of the Hague Convention, including the definition of "habitual residence." *See, e.g., Humphrey v. Humphrey*, 434 F.3d 243 (4th Cir. 2006) (father required to establish habitual residence by a preponderance); *Gitter v. Gitter*, 396 F.3d 124 (2d Cir. 2005) (courts must focus on parents' intent when deciding habitual residence).

7.19. Is Canada a State for UCCJEA Purposes?

Canada is a "state" for the purposes of the UCCJEA. *See Atchison v. Atchison*, 664 N.W.2d 249 (2003). Canada has been a signatory to the Hague Convention since 1988, and has adopted specific and far-reaching legislation protecting the rights of noncustodial parents, including those who are not Canadian. *See generally Overview and Assessment of Approaches to Access Enforcement, Department of Justice, Canada*, 2001-FCY-8E; *Brausch v. Brausch*, —N.W.2d—, 2009 WL 1011206 (Mich. App. 2009).

Parenting Time
and Visitation

8.1. Introduction

When a divorce takes place, children's relationships with caring adults are restructured. Some of these relationships, such as those between parents and children, are legally protected and enforced. Other relationships, including those with grandparents and stepparents, may only be legally recognized under certain circumstances and conditions.

In most cases, continuing contact with both parents will promote a child's adjustment to his or her new family situation. If parents share joint physical custody, they will spend considerable effort scheduling time for the child with each parent. Alternatively, if one parent has sole physical custody, the noncustodial or nonresidential parent has traditionally been considered the "visiting" parent and is awarded "visitation rights" or "parenting time."

As sex roles became less rigid, society increasingly recognized the contribution of both parents in child rearing. As a result, family law professionals questioned the designation of one parent as a "noncustodial visitor" after divorce. Consequently, some jurisdictions no longer use the term *visitation* and have replaced it with *parenting time*. This shift in terminology shows recognition that from the child's point of view both former spouses remain parents throughout the child's life. The term *parenting time* is broad enough to encompass cases of joint physical custody (parents share roughly equal amounts of parenting time) as well as cases of sole physical custody (one parent exercises more parenting time). This approach is consistent with that taken in collaborative processes such as mediation, during which parents are encouraged to focus on the needs of the children instead of becoming fixated on winning a custody label.

Many children benefit from relationships with adults other than their natural parents. Interested people such as grandparents and stepparents have consequently turned to the courts to assure that their relationships with children will continue. Legislatures and courts struggle to set policy in this area, recognizing some relationships but not others.

MODEL ACTS

8.2. Uniform Marriage and Divorce Act: Reasonable Visitation

Section 407(a) of the Uniform Marriage and Divorce Act (UMDA) provides that a "parent not granted custody of the child is entitled to reasonable visitation rights unless the court finds, after a hearing, that visitation would endanger seriously the child's physical, mental, moral, or emotional health."

In practice, the "reasonable visitation" standard required parents to make parenting time arrangements on their own following a divorce. Although some parents were able to reach amicable agreements, many found this to be a source of serious and ongoing conflict. These couples frequently sought post-decree assistance from the court in defining "reasonable" and "unreasonable." Consequently, courts and legislatures now require specific and detailed visitation orders in most divorce decrees. In addition to scheduling hours for parenting time, final orders address issues such as transportation, holidays, and vacations.

In a situation in which one parent is given sole physical custody of the children, the nonresidential parent typically exercises parenting time every other weekend, one evening during the week, alternating holidays, and several weeks during the summer.

Example 8-1

Assume that P and D divorced and agreed that D would have sole physical custody of the children because P traveled extensively for work — she was out of the country for six to eight weeks at a time and then returned home for two to four weeks. P was granted "reasonable" parenting time with the two children. One child, X, was 16 years old, and another child, Y, was 3 years old. The couple experienced continued difficulty working out a parenting time arrangement. P claimed that she was entitled to have the children stay with her during the two to four weeks that she was in the United States. D argued that such an arrangement would amount to joint physical custody and would undermine the court's decision granting D sole physical custody of the children. He also argued that long blocks of parenting time would be disruptive to the children. If the couple does not reach an amicable agreement, what would a judge likely decide?

Explanation

The court is called on to interpret and enforce the divorce decree entitling P to reasonable parenting time. Because of P's unusual work schedule, she is not able to visit with the children every other weekend or have midweek face-to-face contact. The court will consider the best interests of the children when deciding what parenting time is reasonable under the circumstances However, this situation is complicated by the fact that one child is 3 and one child is 16. A very young child may particularly benefit from frequent physical contact with a nonresidential parent, whereas an older child might more easily supplement longer periods of face-to-face time with e-mail and phone conversations. Consequently, what is reasonable for one child may not be reasonable for the other. For example, the court might order that both children spend every weekend with P when she is in town and that the 3-year-old spend an additional overnight during the week with P.

8.3. American Law Institute

The American Law Institute (ALI) replaces the traditional use of *custody* and *visitation* with the term *custodial responsibility*. ALI, *Principles of the Law of Family Dissolution: Analysis and Recommendations* §2.03(3) (2002). Comment (e) to §2.03 explains,

> While any beneficial effects of this shift in terminology on people's perceptions of parenthood cannot be measured, it is assumed that the unified concept of custodial responsibility has some potential to strengthen the usual expectation that both parents have responsibility regardless of the proportion of time each spends with the child, and that neither parent is a mere "visitor."

Section 2.11 limits allocation of responsibility to parents who have abused, neglected, or abandoned a child; inflicted domestic violence; abused drugs and alcohol; and interfered with the other parent's access without cause. Limitations imposed can include reduction or limitation of custodial responsibility; supervision of custodial time; exchange of a child through an intermediary; restraints on communication and proximity; abstinence from prior drug and alcohol use; denial of overnight custodial responsibility; restrictions on persons present; requiring posting of bond; and completion of a treatment program.

STANDARDS FOR DENYING OR LIMITING PARENTING TIME

8.4. Court Denial or Suspension of Parenting Time

Because parents have a constitutional right to have contact with their children, courts will only deny parenting time in the most extreme and egregious cases. The burden is on the parent contesting the parenting time to show that the child would be seriously endangered by contact with the other parent. *See Sterbling v. Sterbling*, 519 N.E.2d 673 (Ohio Ct. App. 1987).

For example, in *Nelson v. Jones*, 781 P.2d 964 (Alaska 1989), supervised parenting time was denied to a father guilty of sexual abuse. Similarly, an incarcerated parent may be denied parenting time under some circumstances. In *Harmon v. Harmon*, 943 P.2d 599 (Okla. 1997), the court listed factors to be considered in deciding whether a father in a correctional facility should have parenting time. The factors included the age of the child, the distance to be traveled, the physical and emotional effect on the child, whether the parent had exhibited genuine interest in the child, past history of contact, and the nature of the crime committed. *See also Etter v. Rose*, 684 A.2d 1092 (Sup. Ct. Pa. 1996) (rebuttable presumption that visitation with incarcerated parent is not in the best interests of the child); *Mark C. v. Patricia B.*, 42 A.D. 3d 1317 (Sup. Ct. N.Y. 2007) (by itself incarceration does not make visitation inappropriate); Solangel Maldonado, *Recidivism and Paternal Engagement*, 40 Fam. L.Q. 191 (2006).

8.5. Restrictions on Parenting Time

Courts rarely deny a parent the right to see a child. However, with the proper showing, courts will place restrictions on the exercise of parenting time. For example, a parent might only be able to have contact with a child in a supervised setting (either formally supervised by professional staff at a visitation center or supervised more informally by friends or family), or a parent may be denied overnight contact.

In order to place restrictions on a parent's right to parenting time, the court must find that "visitation would endanger seriously the child's physical, mental, moral, or emotional health." *See* UMDA §407. Proof beyond mere allegations is required.

Research shows that when supervised parenting time is ordered to take place at a visitation center, it is usually in cases involving children who were severely traumatized. Typically these children have been abused or neglected, have witnessed domestic violence, have lived with a mentally ill parent, or have been abducted. *See* Janet R. Johnston & Robert B. Straus, *Traumatized Children in Supervised Visitation: What Do They Need?*, 37 Fam. & Conciliation Cts. Rev. 135 (1999). *See also* Elizabeth Barker Brandt, *Concerns at the Margins of Supervised Access to Children*, 9 J.L. & Fam. Stud. 201 (2007).

8.6. Child Abuse and Domestic Violence

When a parent has committed child abuse or is guilty of domestic violence, the other parent may be understandably frustrated by the court's insistence on allowing even limited parenting time. In such circumstances, if parenting time is going to occur, the parent and child are best protected if the court requires that the visitation be formally supervised. *See Mallouf v. Saliba*, 766 N.E.2d 552 (Mass. App. Ct. 2002); *Hollingsworth v. Semerad*, 799 So. 2d 658 (La. Ct. App. 2001). *But see Sevland v. Sevland*, 646 N.W.2d 689 (N.D. 2002) (allowing unsupervised visitation in a case involving domestic violence). Researchers have developed protocols for determining when restrictions such as supervised exchange, supervised access, or suspended contact are appropriate. Peter G. Jaffe, Janet R. Johnston, Claire V. Crooks & Nicholas Bala, *Custody Disputes Involving Allegations of Domestic Violence: Toward a Differentiated Approach to Parenting Plans*, 46 Fam. Ct. Rev. 500 (2008).

8.7. Alcohol and Substance Abuse

Supervised parenting time may be required if the visiting parent's alcohol or drug use makes parenting time unsafe for the child. *See Allen v. Allen*, 787 So. 2d 215 (Fla. Dist. Ct. App. 2001) (requiring supervision because of the mother's alcohol use); *see also Fine v. Fine*, 626 N.W.2d 526 (Neb. 2001) (requiring supervised visitation because of the parent's mental illness, history of domestic violence, and substance abuse); *White v. Nason*, 874 A.2d 891 (Me. 2005) (contempt action against father for violation of prohibition on substance use while children were in his care).

Example 8-2

Assume that P (mother) and D (father) are getting divorced. They have one child, X. D has been arrested several times for alcohol- and drug-related offenses, but he does not believe that he has a substance abuse problem. D argues that he neither drinks nor uses drugs in the presence of the child and that he should be entitled to spend unrestricted time with X. P asserts that D's drinking and drug use are out of control and that X would be in danger spending time alone with D. The trial court orders D to abstain entirely from alcohol and drug use at all times, whether he is with X or not. Will this restriction be upheld on appeal?

Explanation

Most likely, a court would order that parenting time with X take place in a supervised setting so that D is prevented from seeing the child if D is under the influence. By complying with the order for supervised parenting time and consistently appearing for parenting time in a sober state, D can establish his trustworthiness and possibly petition the court in the future to be allowed to spend unsupervised time with X. This example, which is based on *Cohen v. Cohen*, 875 A.2d 814 (Md. App. 2005), found the court going a step further and ordering the father to stop drinking and using drugs outside of the presence of the child. Although the court's order goes beyond ordering supervised parenting time, the appellate court upheld the trial judge who required the father to completely abstain from alcohol use.

8.8. Child Abduction

If there is credible evidence that a parent with court-ordered parenting time will abduct or has abducted the child, parenting time is likely to be supervised to prevent abduction from occurring. For example, in *Chandler v. Chandler*, 409 S.E.2d 203 (Ga. 1991), the court ordered supervised parenting time after one parent took the child out of state without notice. However, in *Abouzahr v. Abouzahr-Matera*, 824 A.2d 268 (N.J. Super. Ct. 2003), a parent was allowed to exercise visitation in Lebanon so long as the parent gave four weeks' advance notice.

8.9. Cohabitation

If the visiting parent cohabits with a person of the opposite sex, the other parent may petition to limit overnight visits with the child. However, such a restriction is not likely to be granted unless the cohabitation has a serious adverse impact on the children. *See Higgins v. Higgins*, 981 P.2d 134 (Ariz. Ct. App. 1999); *Harrington v. Harrington*, 648 So. 2d 543 (Miss. 1994). *But see Muller v. Muller*, 711 N.W.2d 329 (Mich. 2006) (upholding order that "neither party shall have an unrelated member of the opposite sex overnight while having parenting time with the minor children").

8.10. Parent Who Is Gay or Lesbian

Although courts take opposing views on the issue, the emerging view is that a parent who is gay or lesbian is entitled to overnight parenting time unless the parent opposing it can show specific endangerment to the child's physical or emotional health. *See Morris v. Hawk*, 907 N.E.2d 763 (Ohio

App. 2009); *Miller-Jenkins v. Miller-Jenkins*, 661 S.E.2d 822 (Va. 2008); *Downey v. Muffley*, 767 N.E.2d 1014 (Ind. Ct. App. 2002); *T.B. v. L.R.M.*, 567 Pa. 222, 786 A.2d 913 (Pa. 2001); *In re Marriage of Dorworth*, 33 P.3d 1260 (Colo. Ct. App. 2001); *Boswell v. Boswell*, 701 A.2d 1153 (Md. App. 1997); and *Johnson v. Schlotman*, 502 N.W.2d 831 (N.D. 1993).

8.11. HIV-Positive Parent

There are few reported decisions concerning the effect, if any, of a parent's infection with the AIDS virus on the parent's visitation rights. The reason for this is that AIDS is not transmitted through casual household contact. It is doubtful that a parent's infection with the AIDS virus alone will result in the denial of custody. *See Doe v Roe*, 526 N.Y.S.2d 718 (N.Y Sup. 1988). At least one jurisdiction has refused to restrict overnight visits with HIV-positive parents. *See North v. North*, 648 A.2d 1025 (Md. App. 1994) (noting that a parent's HIV status is not a basis for parenting time restriction without a showing of endangerment to the child).

8.12. Religious Differences

A parent without legal custody can be restricted from imposing his or her religious views on a child during parenting time, and the nonresidential parent may be required to bring a child to religious services chosen by the legal custodian. *See Lange v. Lange*, 502 N.W.2d 143 (Wis. Ct. App. 1993) and *Zummo v. Zummo*, 574 A.2d 1130 (Pa. Super. Ct. 1990). *But see Shepp v. Shepp*, 906 A.2d 1165 (Pa. 2006) (a fundamentalist Mormon could not be prohibited from discussing polygamy with his minor daughter where such discussions did not jeopardize the child's health, safety, or pose a "grave threat" to the child). However, within limits, a nonresidential parent may take the child to religious services of his or her own choosing during parenting time. *See In re Nina R.*, 638 N.W.2d 393 (Wis. App. 2001); *In re Marriage of McSoud*, 131 P.3d 1208 (Colo. Ct. App. 2006). In order to restrict this activity, the objecting parent may need to show that the child would be physically or emotionally harmed by it. *Zummo v. Zummo*, 574 A.2d 1130 (Pa. Super. Ct. 1990).

Example 8-3

P (mother) was awarded legal and physical custody of X, and D (father) was awarded parenting time with X. As the sole legal custodian, P decided to raise X as a Jehovah's Witness, over D's objection. As a part of her faith tradition, P objected to D's giving gifts to X and to D's encouraging X to participate in various holiday activities. Because of ongoing conflict about the child's religious affiliation, the court entered an order prohibiting D from interfering with X's religious training—D could not visit X on Christmas Eve or Christmas Day or allow X to participate in holiday activities, including gift-giving and trick-or-treating. D objected to the court order as an improper restriction on his parenting time. Will such an order be upheld on appeal?

Explanation

As the sole legal custodian, P has the right to determine X's religious upbringing, even over the strong objection of D. In *A.G.R. ex rel. Conflenti v. Huff*, 815 N.E.2d 120 (Ind. Ct. App. 2004), the court upheld a similar order because the custodial parent's right to determine religious training could only be limited by a showing that the child's physical health or emotional development would be "significantly impaired." In this example, D did not allege any harm to the child resulting from the religious practice. The appellate court found that the trial court's order did not unreasonably interfere with the nonresidential parent's right to parenting time because the father received the same amount of time with the child that he otherwise would.

ENFORCEMENT OF PARENTING TIME

8.13. Overview

If parenting time arrangements are not carefully structured or if divorced parents have not resolved underlying emotional issues, parenting time can be an ongoing source of serious conflict. In such situations, the parties may negotiate or mediate their differences or return to court to seek enforcement of parenting time provisions. Some parents who engage in ongoing post-decree litigation benefit from marriage-termination counseling.

8.14. Contempt and Modification of Custody

If the parties cannot reach an amicable resolution through agreement, a parent being denied parenting time may bring a contempt action to enforce a parenting time order. *See Ellis v. Ellis*, 840 So. 2d 806 (Miss. Ct. App. 2003).

In extreme cases, the parent denying parenting time could lose custody. *See Egle v. Egle*, 715 F.2d 999 (5th Cir. 1983).

8.15. Compensatory Parenting Time

If a parent has wrongfully been denied parenting time, that parent may be entitled to "makeup" or compensatory parenting time. *See* Mich. Comp. Laws Ann. §552.642 (2003) and Minn. Stat. §518.175 subd. (6)(b) (2002).

Example 8-4

P was awarded sole physical custody of the parties' two children, and D was awarded parenting time every other weekend, alternate Monday evenings, and on some holidays. Six months after the divorce, based on a motion to modify and an action for contempt, the court ordered that P could not schedule any activities for the children during D's parenting time periods unless D agreed ahead of time in writing. Eighteen months later, after some consultation with D, P enrolled the children in a religious education class that took place on one of D's parenting time evenings. D brought a contempt action against P and sought additional parenting time. The trial court found P in contempt and awarded D an additional ten hours per month of parenting time. If P appeals, what is the likely outcome?

Explanation

In an analogous case, *In re Kosek*, 871 A.2d 1 (N.H. 2005), the appellate court upheld the lower court's finding of civil contempt and the award of additional parenting time. The appellate court reasoned that the increase in parenting time was an appropriate sanction for civil contempt and that the new parenting time schedule was not contrary to the best interests of the child.

8.16. Withholding Child Support

In most states, a parent cannot deny parenting time because the nonresidential parent has not paid child support. Similarly, a child support obligor must continue to pay child support even if parenting time is denied. *See Carter v. Carter*, 479 S.E.2d 681 (W. Va. 1996); *Seidel v. Seidel*, 10 S.W.3d 365 (Tex. Ct. App. 1999).

8.17. Wishes of the Child

Absent specific restrictions on parenting time, parents are expected to encourage and support a child's relationship with the other parent. Consequently, a parent cannot deny parenting time based on a child's desire not to visit. *Schutz v. Schutz*, 581 So. 2d 1290 (Fla. 1991). Nevertheless, parenting time is more difficult to enforce if teenagers are opposed to it. For example, in *Worley v. Whiddon*, 403 S.E.2d 799 (Ga. 1991), a 14-year-old's wishes were considered but were not dispositive.

Example 8-5

Assume that when P (mother) and D (father) divorce, they have a 16-year-old son, X. Father and son have a difficult relationship despite the fact that both have attended counseling. Because of their history and X's age, the judge orders that D's continuing contact with X be "contingent upon the contact being mutually requested." D appeals the order. What is the likely outcome?

Explanation

D will argue that the conditional order could have the effect of denying his right to parenting time and that parenting time cannot be restricted without a finding that visitation would endanger the child. P might argue that a 16-year-old should not and cannot be forced to spend time with a parent if the teenager is strongly opposed to doing so. In the final analysis, although a court may consider the child's wishes with respect to the scheduling of parenting time, courts do not generally allow children to choose whether or not to spend time with a nonresidential parent. *In re Marriage of Kimbrell*, 119 P.3d 684 (Kan. Ct. App. 2005).

Example 8-6

Assume that P (mother) and D (father) were divorced and that P was granted physical custody of their two children. A high level of conflict between P and D continued after the divorce, and they returned to court several times on post-decree motions. One summer, one of the children (age 11) wanted to participate in sports and a band program that conflicted with D's parenting time. Through her own attorney (hired by P), the 11-year-old filed a motion to modify parenting time in the parents' divorce. What is the likely result?

Explanation

Under similar facts in In re Marriage of Osborn, 135 P. 3d 199 (Kan. App., 2006), a father argued that no change in circumstances was shown and that, consequently, modification of the parenting time order was improper. He also argued that the child lacked standing to bring the modification action. The appellate court ultimately agreed with the father and held that the child lacked standing to file the motion to modify.

MODIFICATION OF PARENTING TIME

8.18. UMDA Provisions

Like custody and child support, parenting time orders can be modified. Section 407 of the UMDA allows for modification in the best interests of the child, "but the court shall not restrict a parent's visitation rights unless it finds that the visitation would endanger seriously the child's physical, mental, moral, or emotional health." Typical restrictions are those discussed in earlier sections.

ATTEMPTS TO EXPAND THE RIGHT TO VISITATION

8.19. Stepparent Visitation

After a divorce, some stepparents have sought visitation with their stepchildren. Visitation is sometimes granted if the stepparent has acted in loco parentis with the stepchild prior to the divorce. See Simmons v. Simmons, 486 N.W.2d 788 (Minn. Ct. App. 1992); Weinand v. Weinand, 616 N.W.2d 1 (Neb. 2000); In re Marriage of Riggs and Hem, 129 P.3d 601 (Kan. Ct. App. 2006); Visitation Rights of Persons Other than Natural Parents or Grandparents, 1 A.L.R.4th 1270 (1980). However under the common law, stepparents have no protected right to ongoing contact with stepchildren at divorce or upon the death of the biological parent-spouse. See Seyboth v. Seyboth, 554 S.E.2d 378 (N.C. Ct. App. 2001) (visitation by stepparent was denied because there was no showing that the natural parent was unfit); In re C.T.G., 179 P.3d 213 (Colo. App. 2007) (stepfather lacked standing to seek parenting time).

Example 8-7

Assume that after a father and mother divorce, the father has physical custody of their child, X. The father remarries, and X's new stepmother, S, functions as a parent to him. Approximately two years after the father's remarriage, he is killed in a car accident. Although X's biological mother assumes physical custody of X, the stepmother petitions for visitation with X. A state statute allows a person standing in *loco parentis* to a child to petition for visitation if it is in the child's best interest, and one of the legal parents is deceased. The statute defines in *loco parentis* as "a person who has been treated as a parent by the child and who has formed a meaningful parental relationship with the child for a substantial period of time." The biological mother opposes the visitation on the basis that X already has a biological and legal mother. The court agrees and denies the visitation on the grounds that the stepmother could not establish in *loco parentis* status unless she "stood in the place of either Father or Mother" before the father's death. What is the likely outcome on appeal?

Explanation

In *Riepe v. Riepe*, 91 P.3d. 312 (Ariz. Ct. App. 2004), the appellate court held that the statute did not require the stepmother to show that her relationship with the child was the same as or superior to the child's relationship with the biological parents in order to be awarded visitation. The case was remanded so that the stepmother could establish that she was treated as a parent by the child and that she had a meaningful relationship with the child for a substantial period of time as required under the statute. On remand in such a case, it is likely that the biological mother would argue that a two-year relationship did not amount to a substantial period of time and that the relationship was not a meaningful one. Note that if the parties lived in a state without an in *loco parentis* statute, the stepmother would likely not be awarded visitation because, under the common law, stepparents do not generally have an enforceable right to ongoing contact with a stepchild. *See Dodge v. Dodge*, 505 S.E.2d 344 (S.C. Ct. App. 1998) (where mother died, stepfather had no derivative right to visitation).

8.20. Visitation by Nonbiological Gay or Lesbian Co-parent

Historically, courts have not granted visitation to lesbian or gay nonbiological co-parents (who have not formally adopted the child) after the relationship between the adult partners ends. For example, in *Nancy S. v. Michele G.*,

279 Cal. Rptr. 212 (Cal. Ct. App. 1991), the court refused to recognize the nonbiological mother as a parent under the Uniform Parentage Act or as a de facto parent. *See Behrens v. Rimland*, 32 A.D. 3d 929 (N.Y. 2006) (former same-sex partner lacked standing); *Stadter v. Siperko*, 661 S.E.2d 494 (Va. App. 2008) (former same-sex partner did not prove by clear and convincing evidence that denial of visitation would harm child); *Jones v. Barlow*, 154 P.3d 808 (Utah 2007) (common law doctrine of *in loco parentis* did not grant standing). *See also Alison D. v. Virginia M.*, 572 N.E.2d 27 (N.Y. 1991); and Robin Cheryl Miller, *Child Custody and Visitation Rights Arising from Same-Sex Relationship*, 80 A.L.R.5th 1 (2000).

However, more recently, some courts have ordered visitation in an exercise of the court's equitable power or based on the specific language of a "third-party" visitation statute. *See In re Custody of H.S.H.-K.*, 533 N.W.2d 419 (Wis. 1995); *E.N.O. v. L.M.M.*, 711 N.E.2d 886 (Mass. 1999); *V.C. v. M.J.B.*, 748 A.2d 539 (N.J. 2000); and *Laspina-Williams v. Laspina-Williams*, 742 A.2d 840 (Conn. Super. Ct. 1999) (same-sex partner had standing under visitation statute). *See also* Deborah L. Forman, *Same-Sex Partners: Stranger, Third Parties, or Parents? The Changing Legal Landscape and the Struggle for Parental Equality*, 40 Fam. L.Q. 23 (2006); Jennifer L. Rosato, *Children of Same-Sex Parents Deserve the Security Blanket of the Parentage Presumption*, 44 Fam. Ct. Rev. 74 (2006).

Example 8-8

Assume that P (legal mother) and D (same-sex partner) lived in a committed relationship for more than ten years. Because same-sex couples were not allowed to adopt children, the child was adopted by P individually. Both P and D were extensively involved in parenting the child, and they shared all major parenting decisions, including those related to education, religion, and medical care. After P and D part ways, D seeks visitation with the child under a statute allowing such a proceeding by a person "who has had physical care of a child for a period of six months or more." If P opposes D's request, what is the likely outcome?

Explanation

D will argue that she has physically cared for the child for more than six months as required by the statute, and she will likely succeed with this argument. In a similar case, *In re E.L.M.C.*, 100 P.3d 546 (Colo. Ct. App. 2004), an adoptive legal mother, P, unsuccessfully argued that her former partner was required to establish a legal relationship to the child, that the visitation request must be incident to a dissolution proceeding, and that the legally recognized parent must have relinquished care of the child. Of course, D would have great difficulty obtaining parenting time over P's objection if D lived in a state that had not adopted a statute recognizing psychological parenthood.

8.21. Parents by Estoppel and De Facto Parents

Under the ALI's *Principles of the Law of Family Dissolution: Analysis and Recommendations* §2.18, individuals other than legal parents can be allocated parental responsibility either as a parent by estoppel (§2.03(b)) or as a de facto parent (§2.03(c)). A parent by estoppel is a person other than a legal parent who (1) is obligated to pay child support; (2) lived with the child and accepted parental responsibility for at least two years in the good-faith belief that he was the child's father; or (3) lived with the child since birth and acted as a parent pursuant to a parenting or co-parenting agreement. A de facto parent is a person other than a legal parent or parent by estoppel who for at least two years (1) lived with the child and (2) performed the majority of caretaking functions or as many caretaking functions as the parent with whom the child resided (3) either by agreement or because of the failure or inability of the legal parent to do so. Although a parent by estoppel has more rights than a de facto parent, both statuses require the adult in question to have significantly functioned as the child's parent and are consequently theoretically consistent with acting *in loco parentis*. However, the ALI analysis appears to be broad enough to encompass petitions for parenting time by stepparents, lesbian and gay parents, and some grandparents.

GRANDPARENT VISITATION

8.22. History

At common law, grandparents generally had no legally enforceable right to visit their grandchildren. However, as both the number of living grandparents and the divorce rate increased, more formal recognition was given to the grandparent-grandchild bond in hope of adding stability to the lives of children experiencing divorce. *See* Maegen E. Peek, *Grandparent Visitation Statutes: Do Legislatures Know the Way to Carry the Sleigh Through the Wide and Drifting Law?*, 53 Fla. L. Rev. 321 (2001). Thanks in large part to the efforts of organized grandparent groups, by 1994 every state had adopted a grandparent visitation statute. These statutes vary widely in scope — some apply only if the parents divorce, die, or have their parental rights terminated, and other statutes apply regardless of the status of the child's immediate family unit.

8.23. *Troxel v. Granville*

State statutes providing for grandparent visitation have been subject to reexamination since the United States Supreme Court decided *Troxel v. Granville*, 530 U.S. 57 (2000). In *Troxel*, the Court struck down a Washington statute allowing "any person" to petition for visitation rights "at any time" that "visitation may serve the best interests of the child." The Court held that the statute as applied was an unconstitutional infringement on a fit parent's fundamental right to make decisions about the care and custody of minor children. The Court determined that some deference or "special weight" must be given to parental decisions because it is presumed that fit parents will act in their children's best interests. The court's decision rested in part on the breadth of the Washington statute, but the court stopped short of holding that specific types of statutes would violate due process.

The somewhat ambiguous nature of the decision spawned additional litigation as state courts considered the constitutionality of their visitation statutes in light of *Troxel*. Examining courts focused on the extent to which statutes deferred to the decisions of fit parents and the presence of statutory factors in addition to the "best interests of the child." Some state statutes have been found constitutional, whereas others have been held unconstitutional facially or as applied. For a discussion of the cases decided subsequent to *Troxel, see* Kristine L. Roberts, *State Supreme Court Applications of* Troxel v. Granville *and the Courts' Reluctance to Declare Grandparent Visitation Statutes Unconstitutional*, 41 Fam. Ct. Rev. 14 (2003). *See also* Elizabeth Williams, *Cause of Action by Grandparent to Obtain Visitation Rights to Grandchildren*, 17 Causes of Action 2d 331 (2008); George L. Blum, *Grandparents' Visitation Rights Where Child's Parents Are Living*, 71 A.L.R.5th 99 (1999).

Example 8-9

Assume that mother (M) and father (F) are married, and they live together with their two children. They reside in a jurisdiction with a statute allowing grandparents reasonable visitation of grandchildren if such visitation would be in the child's best interest and if a substantial relationship has been established between the child and the grandparent. The grandparents had ongoing contact with the grandchildren from their birth until recently, including regular phone contact, holiday visits, and overnight visits. However, since the grandmother mistakenly alleged that one of the children had been sexually abused, M and F have refused to let the grandparents see the child. The grandparents sue for visitation with both children over the objection of M and F. M and F argue that they are fit parents in a continuing nuclear family and that it is their prerogative to deny visitation to the grandparents. The grandparents argue that the statute makes no distinction between intact families and those experiencing divorce or other disruption. What is the likely outcome?

Explanation

Because the mother and father are fit parents in a "continuing nuclear family," they argue that their decision not to allow visitation should be given absolute deference by the court. However, the grandparents argue that the statute makes no distinction between intact families and other families. In a recent case, *Davis v. Heath*, 128 P.3d 434 (Kan. Ct. App. 2006), a court faced with this situation awarded visitation to the grandparents, holding that the language of the statute did not distinguish between intact and other families, that the parents' decision to terminate visitation was unreasonable, that the evidence showed that the grandmother and grandchild had a substantial relationship, and that visitation was in the child's best interest. *But see Santi v. Santi*, 633 N.W.2d 312 (Iowa 2001) (statute permitting visitation without circumstance such as divorce, death of parent, or adoption declared unconstitutional).

Establishing Child Support

9.1. Introduction

This chapter examines many of the child support issues that arise at the time of divorce or between unmarried parents. Issues related to modification of an existing child support award are considered in Chapter 10.

Child support is traditionally defined as a payment by one parent (often the noncustodial or nonresidential parent) to the other parent for the support of their common child. As a general rule, the law takes the view that it is in the best interests of a child that both parents be obligated to pay support; therefore, the fact that a custodial parent is able to support a child without financial assistance from the noncustodial parent does not necessarily shield the noncustodial parent from making support payments. An order for child support transfers the income from one parent to the other so that the combined incomes of both parents are available for the child's support.

A child support order is typically part of a divorce decree or paternity judgment and is usually payable on a monthly basis. Many states require that child support be paid by wage assignment (automatic deductions from the paycheck) whenever available because this procedure reduces the need for subsequent enforcement actions.

HISTORY

9.2. Elizabethan Poor Laws

Evidence of one of the first efforts to create a formal obligation to provide child support is found in the Elizabethan Poor Laws that were passed at the beginning of the seventeenth century. Passage of the Poor Laws resulted from economic conditions that created a large class of landless, often destitute laborers with children. "The Poor Relief Act of 43 Eliz. Ch. 2 required the father and the mother, among other relatives, of every poor, old, blind, lame, and impotent person, or other poor person unable to work, to relieve and maintain such person at their own charges, if they were of sufficient ability to do so." M.C. Dransfield, Annotation, *Parent's Obligation to Support Adult Child*, 1 A.L.R.2d 910, 935 (1948). These laws transformed the moral duties of family members toward each other and of the community toward its members into legal obligations. They also provided the first public welfare program, funded through taxation, to assist needy members of the community whenever family support was unavailable.

9.3. Common Law

In America, the common law imposed the duty of supporting minor children on their parents. However, as a general rule, there was no obligation placed on a parent to support an adult child. M.C. Dransfield, *Parent's Obligation to Support Adult Child*, 1 A.L.R.2d 910, 914 (1948). The states eventually removed any doubt regarding parental responsibility for the support of their children by enacting laws making it a criminal offense for a parent to desert or willfully neglect to provide support for a minor child.

Some common law courts felt that "nature" provided an adequate parental incentive to support children born to a marriage should a divorce occur. For example, in *Plaster v. Plaster*, 47 Ill. 290 (1868), the court observed that:

> [N]ature has implanted in all men a love for their offspring that is seldom so weak as to require the promptings of law, to compel them to discharge the duty of shielding and protecting them from injury, suffering and want, to the extent of their ability. Hence the courts are seldom called upon to enforce the duty of parents. The law of nature, the usages of society, as well as the laws of all civilized countries, impose the duty upon the parent of the support, nurture and education of children.

Id. at 291.

Unfortunately, the hoped-for natural inclination of a parent to provide support for a child has not been entirely realized. Consequently, today extensive state and federal legislation drive a variety of programs intended to ensure that minor children receive financial support from their parents and, as a last resort, from the state.

9.4. European View

Contemporary American law reflects the view that the cost of raising children is primarily a private matter, with the parents having that responsibility. In contrast, some European countries play a more active role by subsidizing day care for children and providing state-supported health care for them.

The legal landscape in America, however, has dramatically changed in the last 40 years because of the federal government's involvement. Before the federal government acted, states had primary responsibility to award and enforce child support.

ROLE OF THE FEDERAL GOVERNMENT

9.5. Child Support Traditionally a State Issue

Historically, the issue of child support was primarily a matter of state law and judges exercised discretion in making child support determinations. The Uniform Marriage and Divorce Act (UMDA) provided that a parent or parents would pay a reasonable amount of child support based on their financial resources; the standard of living the child would have enjoyed; and the needs of the child. UMDA §309. Under such a standard, awards were difficult to predict, and similarly situated children might receive different amounts. In an effort to promote uniformity and reduce public assistance expenditures, the federal government became increasingly involved in creating national child support policy.

9.6. Child Support and Establishment of Paternity Act of 1974

The federal government began collecting national data regarding child support awards and payments because of concern over rising rates of single parenting and welfare dependence. Since this fledgling effort, a multitude of federal programs to deal with child support have been enacted.

One of the first federal efforts was the Child Support and Establishment of Paternity Act of 1974, 42 U.S.C. §§651-655. The law was aimed at recipients of public assistance and required that they cooperate in establishing and enforcing support orders and cooperate in locating potential obligors. The act had three primary objectives. The first objective was to reduce public expenditures on welfare by obtaining child support from noncustodial parents on an ongoing basis. The second objective was to help families obtain support so that they could move off of public assistance. The third objective was to stimulate state action to establish paternity for children born outside marriage and obtain child support for them.

Under this early federal legislation, basic responsibility for administering the support program was left to individual states and local governments. However, the federal government dictated the major features of the programs by linking funding to specific state legislative activity, providing technical assistance, and giving direct assistance to help states locate absent parents.

9.7. State Guidelines Mandated

In 1984 Congress mandated that every state seeking federal funding to support its welfare program establish advisory child support guidelines. Child Support Enforcement Amendments of 1984, Pub. L. No. 98-378, 98 Stat. 1305. States that rejected creating statewide guidelines risked losing a large percentage of federal funding for their Aid to Families with Dependent Children (AFDC) program. *See* 42 U.S.C. §§651, 667(a)-(b) (1984). The guidelines were intended to reduce widely differing amounts of child support from being ordered from courtroom to courtroom and to provide judges with a reasonably objective basis for determining support. The legislation also required that states enact statutes providing for expedited processes for obtaining and enforcing support orders.

Congress strengthened the guidelines in 1988 with the passage of the Family Support Act, which required that the state guidelines be applicable in all cases and operate as rebuttable presumptions of the correct support amount to be awarded in a divorce or paternity action. The Act also mandated that any deviation from the presumptive amount be supported by a decision maker's specific findings, in writing or on the record. 42 U.S.C. §667(b)(2). *See also* Helen Donigan, *Calculating and Documenting Child Support Awards Under Washington Law*, 26 Gonz. L. Rev. 13 (1990-1991); Ira Mark Ellman & Tara O'Toole Ellman, *The Theory of Child Support*, 45 Harv. J. on Legis. (2008).

9.8. Omnibus Budget Reconciliation Act of 1993

The Omnibus Budget Reconciliation Act of 1993 mandated that states adopt in-hospital programs to facilitate voluntary acknowledgment of paternity in cases of children born out of wedlock. 42 U.S.C. §666. It also required that states create a rebuttable or conclusive presumption of paternity when genetic testing indicated a man was the father of a child born out of wedlock. It modified the Employee Retirement Income Security Act (ERISA) to require that employers make group health care coverage available to the noncustodial children of their employees. This resulted in the implementation at the state level of Qualified Medical Child Support Orders (QMCSO), which ordered an employer and insurance carrier to include the child in the employer's insurance program.

9.9. Federal Enforcement Efforts

The federal government has also taken an active role in promoting interstate enforcement of child support orders. Relevant legislation is discussed in Chapter 10.

INCOME DEEMED AVAILABLE FOR SUPPORT

9.10. What Is Income?

All jurisdictions have adopted provisions to provide general guidance to judges when determining what resources should be considered income for the purpose of calculating child support. The phrase "income from any source," as used in most statutory child support guidelines, is broadly construed and normally includes all financial payments, whatever the source. The determination of income for child support purposes under statutory guidelines is not necessarily controlled by definitions of gross income used for federal or state income tax purposes.

The following are examples of resources that courts in many jurisdictions will consider as available income when calculating child support: (1) wage and salary income and other compensation for personal services (including commissions, overtime pay, tips, and bonuses); (2) interest, dividends, and royalty income; (3) self-employment income; (4) net rental income (defined as rent after deducting operating expenses and mortgage payments, but not including noncash items such as depreciation); and (5) other income actually being received, including severance pay, retirement benefits, pensions, trust income, annuities, capital gains, social security benefits, unemployment benefits, disability and workers' compensation benefits, interest income from notes regardless of the source, gifts and prizes, spousal maintenance, and alimony.

However, courts differ concerning what counts as income for the purpose of setting child support. Examples of resources that some courts do not include in their calculation include return of principal or capital, accounts receivable, or benefits paid in accordance with aid for families with dependent children.

In the final analysis, the duty to pay child support may extend not only to an obligor's ability to pay from earnings, but also to his or her ability to pay from any and all sources that may be available. The following sections illustrate some of the issues courts face when determining whether a particular resource is income for the purpose of calculating child support.

Example 9-1

P and D are divorcing, and they have two daughters who will be in the physical custody of P. D had recently started a landscaping business, and due to business exigencies he elected to defer some of his salary. D paid his living expenses out of his existing assets. D argues that child support should be established based on his actual take-home pay, but P believes that D's "deferred" income should be considered income for the purpose of calculating child support. What is a court likely to decide?

Explanation

In a similar case, *In re Marriage of Berger*, 88 Cal. Rptr. 3d 766 (Cal. App. 2009), the court held that D's deferred earnings should be regarded as income for the purpose of calculating child support. The court concluded that D could not avoid his duty to support his children by arranging his business affairs so that he lived off of assets and deferred income.

Example 9-2

Assume that P and D are divorcing and the court is calculating child support for their child. P will have sole physical custody of the child, and D will pay child support to P. P claims that D earns $15,000 per year and receives $46,000 in gifts and loans from his parents. D argues that the gifts and loans should not be viewed as "net income" under the statute and thus be available income for child support purposes. P alleges that the loans and gifts are "net income" and should not be excluded. What is the likely result?

Explanation

One of the key determinations in calculating child support is the determination of net income. The payor is likely to claim various deductions in order to lower child support liability. The payee will seek to have questionable income included for purposes of calculating child support. In a case with similar facts, *In re Marriage of Rogers*, 280 Ill. Dec. 726 (2003), the court held that the value of the gifts and loans could not be deducted from net income and that both were available for child support purposes. Given that D has more income from gifts and loans than from earnings, holding otherwise in this case would have substantially deprived the child of support.

9.11. Vested Stock Options

In *MacKinley v. Messerschmidt*, 814 A.2d 680 (Pa. Super. Ct. 2002), the court held that once vested, stock options constituted available income that had to be imputed to the parent holding them, for purposes of calculating the parent's child support obligation, regardless of whether the parent chose to exercise the options. When determining income available for child support, the court must consider all forms of income. *Blaisure v. Blaisure*, 577 A.2d 640, 642 (Pa. Super. Ct. 1990) (court must consider every aspect of parent's financial ability, including stocks). A stock option, typically a "form of compensation," is defined as "an option to buy or sell a specific quantity of stock at a designated price for a specified period regardless of shifts in market value during the period." *Black's Law Dictionary* 1431 (8th ed. 2004). An option is "vested" when all conditions attached to it have been satisfied, and it may be exercised by the employee.

9.12. Employer's Contribution to Pension Plan

In *Portugal v. Portugal*, 798 A.2d 246, 253 (Pa. Super. Ct. 2002), the court held that an employer's contributions to a pension plan constitute income for purposes of support "if the employee could access his employer's contributions (regardless of penalties) at the time of the support calculation." The court reasoned that children should not be made to wait for support and that parents should not be permitted to defer income to which they are entitled until they choose to avail themselves of it. But *see Bruemmer v. Bruemmer*, 616 S.E.2d 740 (Va. Ct. App. 2005) (mandatory deductions excluded from income for child support purposes).

9.13. Lump-Sum Payments and Commissions

Regular commissions and lump-sum payments may be used to set the amount of child support. Lump-sum payments may also be withheld from an obligor to pay past-due support or to pay future support if there is a history of willful nonpayment. *See In re Marriage of Heiner*, 136 Cal. App. 4th 1514 (Cal. App. 2006) (evaluating whether lump-sum personal injury award is income for the purpose of child support).

9.14. Seasonal Employment

Seasonally employed obligors are generally required to make equal monthly payments throughout the year. Because the expenses of raising a child are not seasonal, judges generally require equal monthly payments despite the seasonal nature of the income.

9.15. Overtime

The law in most jurisdictions does not impose an obligation on obligors to work overtime. However, if an obligor has a history of working overtime, the courts may conclude that overtime is a normal, regular source of income and consider it when setting support. Similarly, if the overtime is a condition of employment, it is normally considered an income. *See Markey v. Carney*, 705 N.W.2d 13 (Iowa 2005).

9.16. Military Retirement Pay and Allowances

A military member's entire pay and allowances may be considered in the determination of child support amounts. *See Alexander v. Armstrong*, 609 A.2d 183 (Pa. Super. Ct. 1992) (father's military allowances were included in his income for purposes of child support); *Hautala v. Hautala*, 417 N.W.2d 879 (S.D. 1988) (military allowances are a species of remuneration subject to child support payments); *Merkel v. Merkel*, 554 N.E.2d 1346 (Ohio Ct. App. 1988); *Jackson v. Jackson*, 403 N.W.2d 248 (Minn. Ct. App. 1987); *Peterson v. Peterson*, 652 P.2d 1195 (N.M. 1982).

Collection of child support through direct payment by the Defense Finance and Accounting Service is determined by individual military service rules, which differ among the branches of service. Involuntary attachment of child support payments is provided for under federal law, but requires a court order.

9.17. Imputation of Income

The amount of child support paid is related to the income of the parent or parents supporting the child. However, if a parent is unemployed or under-employed, courts will sometimes impute income to the parent and base the child support order on the imputed income. For example, income equivalent to the minimum wage may be imputed to a voluntarily unemployed obligor. Similarly, if a parent is voluntarily underemployed, the court may base the child support order on the net income that the obligor previously earned. *See Christofferson v. Giese*, 691 N.W.2d 195 (N.D. 2005) (imputation must be based on actual income over prior 12 months rather than an extrapolation). *See also Weinstein v. Weinstein*, 911 A.2d 1077 (Conn. 2007) (imputation of 2.96% rate of return on investment yielding 1.24%).

Example 9-3

Assume that during the marriage of the parties P was employed as a builder earning approximately $100,000 per year. After the parties separated P quit his job and lived on money he made at weekend flea market sales. D seeks a divorce and asks the court to base the child support award on P's former income. What is the likely result?

Explanation

Confronted with a similar situation, the court in *Bator v. Osborne*, 983 So. 2d 1198 (Fla. App. 2008), found that P was voluntarily underemployed and remanded the case so that income could be imputed to him based on his recent work history, occupational qualifications, and prevailing community earnings levels.

ESTABLISHING BASIC CHILD SUPPORT

9.18. Presumptive Guidelines

States adopted various models of child support guidelines in response to federal mandates. *See* 42 U.S.C. §§651-667 (1982 & 1984 Supp. II) and 45 C.F.R. §302.56 (1989). The guidelines differ from state to state, but two of the most common models are briefly described in the following sections.

The state statutory guidelines amount is rebuttably presumed to be the correct child support award. Courts do, however, exercise considerable discretion with respect to issues such as determining available income, granting deviations from the guidelines, and sometimes imputing income to obligors.

9.19. Income Shares Model

The income shares model has been adopted by a majority of jurisdictions and operates on the theory that a child involved in a divorce or paternity determination should receive the same proportion of parental income as if the parents had lived or continued to live together. *See, e.g., Voishan v. Palmer*, 609 A.2d 319 (Md. 1992). State guidelines dictate a support amount based on the combined incomes of the parents, and that amount is prorated between the parents based on the percentage of combined income attributable to each.

The income shares model, in its simplest form, requires three steps to calculate a child support award. First, using a statutory formula, the net incomes of both parents are calculated, combined, and then prorated. For example, assume that the particular statutory formula resulted in a determination that parent A had a net income for child support purposes of $1,000, and the same formula resulted in a determination that parent B had a net child support income of $3,000. The parents would then be viewed as contributing 25 percent and 75 percent, respectively, to the support of a single child.

The second step is to apply the combined income to a guideline chart that suggests the amount of support that should be paid. For example, a state-mandated chart might suggest that with one child, when the combined net income is $4,000, the appropriate total amount of support is $1,000. Parent A would be required to pay 25 percent ($250), and parent B would pay 75 percent ($750). Thus, the parents are viewed as sharing equally in achieving the living standard for the child.

The final step in the application of this model allows a court to consider extraordinary medical expenses incurred by the child and a custodial parent's work-related child care expenses.

Example 9-4

Assume that P and D are divorcing in a state using the income shares method of child support calculation. They have one child. Assume that, for the purpose of calculating child support, P has a net income of $2,000 and that D has a net income of $4,000. Imagine that the amount of child support to be paid at a net income level of $6,000 is $2,000. How much child support will P and D pay?

Explanation

P has one-third of P and D's combined income, and D has two-thirds of their combined income. Consequently, P will pay one-third of $2,000 ($666.67) per month, and D will pay two-thirds of $2,000 ($1,333.33) per month. Rather than exchanging checks every month, D will probably just pay the difference ($666.66) to P each month.

9.20. Percentage of Income Model

The percentage of income model is sometimes viewed as the easiest of the various models to apply because of the limited need for calculations. Basically, the nonresidential parent pays a state-mandated percentage of his or her income for child support. When one parent is awarded sole physical and legal custody of a child, the model looks only at the noncustodial obligor's net income, although when joint physical custody (or shared custody) is ordered, this model considers both parents' incomes.

To begin the calculation, one takes an obligor's gross income and determines his or her net income by deducting those items allowed under the statute. The list of deductions is short and usually includes only items such as taxes, medical insurance, social security, and reasonable pension payments. An obligor is not allowed to deduct living expenses, or other items not on the statutory list, For example, assume that A is awarded sole legal and physical custody of child C. B, the noncustodial parent, has a gross income of $5,000 per month. To arrive at a net income figure for child support, B is allowed by statute to deduct state and federal taxes, social security payments, health care payments, and reasonable pension payments from the $5,000. Assume for the sake of simplicity that the allowed deductions reduce B's income to $4,000. Once net income is calculated, that figure is applied to a guideline formula, which takes into account the number of children to receive support. For example, assume that application of the formula to an obligor's gross income resulted in a net monthly income child support figure of $4,000. Also assume that there was one child born of the marriage. Using a typical guideline chart (see Example 9-5), one would find the column headed by "1" (the number of children) and follow it down to $4,000 net income. Where the column and the $4,000 intersect, one finds 25 percent. This means that in this jurisdiction, monthly child support is 25 percent of $4,000, or $1,000.

Example 9-5

Assume that P and D divorce in a percentage of income jurisdiction, and they have two children. P is awarded sole legal and physical custody of the children, and D is ordered to pay child support in accordance with the following guidelines. After taking the deductions allowed by the statute, D's net income is $900 per month. Using the following table, calculate how much monthly child support D most likely will have to pay.

Net Monthly Income of Obligor	1	2	Number of Children 3	4	5	6	7 or more
			Percentage of Income				
$551-600	16%	19%	22%	25%	28%	30%	32%
$601-650	17%	21%	24%	27%	29%	32%	34%
$651-700	18%	22%	25%	28%	31%	34%	36%
$701-750	19%	23%	27%	30%	33%	36%	38%
$751-800	20%	24%	28%	31%	35%	38%	40%
$801-850	21%	25%	29%	33%	36%	40%	42%
$851-900	22%	27%	31%	34%	38%	41%	44%
$901-950	23%	28%	32%	36%	40%	43%	46%
$951-1,000	24%	29%	34%	38%	41%	45%	48%
$1,001-5,000	25%	30%	35%	39%	43%	47%	50%

Explanation

D will most likely be required to pay $243 per month. D's net income is between $851 and $900 per month, and D is supporting two children. D will pay 27 percent of D's net income in child support ($900 × .27 = $243).

Example 9-6

Assume that P and D live in a jurisdiction that calculates child support using the percentage-of-income method. Using the earlier chart, assume that P has sole legal and physical custody of the two children from P's marriage to D. D's net income after allowable statutory deductions is $3,000 per month, and P's net income after deductions is $4,000 per month. How much child support will each pay?

Explanation

D will pay $900 per month to P ($3,000 × .30 = $900). However, even though P has the higher income, P will not pay any child support to D. P is the physical custodian of the two children, and P will be providing food, clothing, shelter, and such directly to the children. P's contribution was taken into consideration when the percentage of income chart was developed by the legislature.

9.21. Joint Physical Custody

Child support guidelines, which were adopted by states before extended parenting time and joint physical custody arrangements became common, often do not contemplate such custodial arrangements. Consequently courts and legislatures have had to reconsider how to calculate child support awards under these new circumstances. Some states now provide for an "offset" to the guidelines amount if both parents spend substantial time with the child. Other states allow courts to deviate from the child support guidelines. *See* In re Seay, 746 N.W.2d 833 (Iowa 2008) (use of offset method to calculate child support in cases of joint physical care); *Plymale v. Donnelly*, 157 P.3d 933 (Wyo. 2007) (50% abatement for summer months when father had residential custody); *Rivero v. Rivero* 195 P.3d 328 (Nev. 2008) (consideration of calculation of child support in joint custody arrangement with unequal timeshare); *Cheverie v. Cheverie*, 898 So. 2d 1028 (Fla. Dist. Ct. App. 2005) (downward deviation from child support guidelines where parent has more than 40% of the overnights); Stephanie Giggetts, *Application of Child-Support Guidelines to Cases of Joint-, Split-, or Similar Shared-Custody Arrangements*, 57 A.L.R.5th 389 (2009).

Example 9-7

Assume that P and D divorce in a percentage of income state that uses the table shown in Example 9-5. They are awarded joint legal and joint physical custody of their only child. P's net monthly income after the statutorily allowed deductions is $4,000, and D's net monthly income after the statutorily allowed deductions is $1,000. Assuming that the child spends approximately equal time with each parent, how will child support be awarded using the above guidelines?

Explanation

Each parent will pay the amount established by the guidelines for the period of time that he or she does not reside with the children. Another way to think of it is that D will pay $1,000 per month for half of the year for a total of $6,000 (when the child is with P), and P will pay $240 per month for half of the year (when the child is with D) for a total of $1,440. ($4,000 × .25 × 6 = $6,000; $1,000 × .24 × 6 = $1,440.) P and D may regularize payments by having D pay P $380 per month for the entire year.

9.22. Deviation from Guidelines

Courts are given limited discretion to deviate from the guidelines, although as a practical matter, few judges stray very far from them. In most jurisdictions, the guidelines are strictly applied. When courts deviate from the presumed guidelines, most states require specific findings explaining and supporting the deviation.

Special circumstances, such as extraordinary medical expenses, special educational needs, unusual travel expenses incurred for parenting time, and sometimes the cost of basic living expenses for children from another relationship, can affect the amount of child support that is to be paid under the guidelines. But see Scott v. Scott, 879 A.2d 540 (Conn. App. 2005) (private boarding school was not "therapy," and parent was not required to pay additional cost).

Courts continue to grapple with cases involving high-earning child support obligors. See McKittrick v. McKittrick, 732 N.W.2d 404 (S.D. 2007) (improper to extrapolate upward from guidelines without showing of actual need and standard of living); In re Keon C., 800 N.E.2d 1257 (Ill. Ct. App.

2003) (court allowed upward deviation to an amount that exceeded the monthly expenses of the custodial parent's household).

Example 9-8

Assume that P and D divorce and that P is awarded sole legal and physical custody of the two children of the marriage. P does not work outside the home, and D's gross monthly income is $4,500. Assume that the guidelines set child support at $1,350 per month, leaving D with $3,150 net. D submits his monthly expenses and lists the following: $1,500 house payment, $500 car payment, $200 utilities, $300 attorney fees, $400 permanent maintenance, $500 on credit cards, $200 miscellaneous (total $3,600). D argues for a downward deviation in child support because he cannot make the payments. How will a court most likely rule?

Explanation

The court will most likely not grant a downward deviation. It is assumed that the plight of D and other similarly situated obligors was thoroughly explored by the legislature when the guidelines were enacted. The guidelines function as a presumption that can be overcome only in extraordinary circumstances. But *see Lozner v. Lozner*, 909 A.2d 728 (N.J. Super. A.D. 2006) (factors for consideration with respect to potential deviation based on student loans of payor).

ADDITIONAL SUPPORT

9.23. Medical Support

In 1988 the federal government mandated that the states enact provisions for "child[ren]'s health care needs, through health insurance coverage or other means." *See* 45 C.F.R. §302.56(c)(3).

State courts have found it within the trial court's discretion to require payment of uninsured medical expenses in addition to the child support award. *See generally Lulay v. Lulay*, 583 N.E.2d 171, 172 (Ind. Ct. App. 1991) (finding the commentary to the Child Support Guidelines allows for apportionment of uninsured medical expenses because the guidelines do not mandate any specific treatment of these expenses); *Holdsworth v. Holdsworth*,

621 So. 2d 71, 78 and n.1 (La. Ct. App. 1993) (holding medical and dental expenses not covered by insurance were properly apportioned half to each party in addition to the child support award as determined under the guidelines); *Jamison v. Jamison*, 845 S.W.2d 133, 136-137 (Mo. Ct. App. 1993) (holding it was within the court's discretion to order the obligor to pay half of the uninsured medical expenses, in addition to the child support award determined under the guidelines); *Lawrence v. Tise*, 419 S.E.2d 176, 183 (N.C. App. 1992) (holding ordinary medical expenses not covered by insurance are to be apportioned between the parties at the discretion of the trial court, in addition to the child support award as determined by the guidelines). But *see Hazuga v. Hazuga*, 648 N.E.2d 391, 395 n.1 (Ind. Ct. App. 1995) (noting that the guidelines had been amended and therefore declined to follow *Lulay v. Lulay*); *Family Services ex rel. J.L.M. by C.A.M. v. Buttram*, 924 S.W.2d 870, 871 (Mo. Ct. App. 1996) (ordering father to pay for medical insurance as well as 50% of all uncovered medical expenses was a deviation under the guidelines).

9.24. Child Care Costs

In addition to child support, costs associated with child care may be awarded to the parent with sole physical custody or the expense may be apportioned between the parents pursuant to a legislative formula.

There appears to be an increasing amount of litigation over child care expenses. *See, e.g., Guard v. Guard*, 993 So. 2d 1086 (Fla. App. 2008) (specific findings required); *Mace v. Mace*, 610 N.W.2d 436 (Neb. Ct. App. 2000) (ex-wife entitled to modification of dissolution decree in order to require former husband to pay proportionate share of her work-related day care expenses); *Hoplamazian v. Hoplamazian*, 740 So. 2d 1100 (Ala. Civ. App. 1999) (court improperly added mother's work-related child care costs to father's basic child support obligation when mother was not seeking employment); *Cupstid v. Cupstid*, 724 So. 2d 238 (La. Ct. App. 1998) (ex-wife proved change in circumstances justifying increase in former husband's child support obligation when she returned to work and began incurring child care expenses); *Rosen v. Lantis*, 938 P.2d 729 (N.M. Ct. App. 1997) (court had authority under guidelines to adjust child support obligation in post-dissolution proceeding based on mother's testimony that she was incurring child care costs because of her employment); *Gal v. Gal*, 937 S.W.2d 391 (Mo. Ct. App. 1997) (day care costs incurred while mother attending nursing school full-time could be included as an extraordinary expense in calculating father's child support obligation); *Sigg v. Sigg*, 905 P.2d 908 (Utah Ct. App. 1995) (court's decision requiring ex-wife to be solely responsible for one-third of day care costs, then splitting the remaining costs between ex-wife and ex-husband, was not based on fact and was an abuse of discretion).

OTHER SUPPORT CONSIDERATIONS

9.25. Duration of Child Support

The duration of child support depends on state law. All states require both parents to be financially responsible for their child during the child's minority. However, child support can be terminated in the event of the death of the child, if the child goes on active duty in the armed forces, or if the child becomes emancipated or self-supporting. In many jurisdictions, a support order ends either when the child turns 18 or when the child completes secondary school (secondary school must be completed before the child reaches age 20). However, support may continue indefinitely for a child incapable of self-support because of a physical or mental condition. *See* Sande L. Buhai, *Parental Support of Adult Children with Disabilities*. 91 Minn. L. Rev. 710 (2007).

Courts in some states have approved parental funding of a college education. For example, under an Iowa statute, parents can be ordered to provide financial support for children attending college. Iowa Code §§598.21(5A), 598.1(8); *In re Marriage of Moore*, 702 N.W.2d 517 (Iowa Ct. App. 2005); *In re Marriage of Mullen-Funderburk and Funderburk*, 696 N.W.2d 607 (Iowa 2005). *See also* Ind. Code §31-16-6-2 (educational support order). In states without statutes authorizing contribution, settlement agreements relating to college expenses may be enforced as contractual obligations. *See, e.g., Solomon v. Findley*, 808 P.2d 294 (Ariz. 1991) (parties' contract for post-majority support is enforceable in breach-of-contract action); *Nicoletti v. Nicoletti*, 901 So. 2d 290 (Fla. Dist. Ct. App. 2005); *Spalding v. Spalding*, 907 So. 2d 1270 (Fla. Dist. Ct. App. 2005). *See* ALI, *Principles of the Law of Family Dissolution: Analysis and Recommendations* §3.12 (2002) (discusses provision of postsecondary education under "Providing for a Child's Life Opportunities").

9.26. Monitoring Support

Courts do not generally allow the obligor (person making the support payments) to monitor how the support is used by the obligee. Should the obligee fail to meet the child's needs, the remedy could involve a charge of child abuse or neglect. In extreme cases, abuse or neglect would be a basis for a change in custody.

9.27. Obligee Withholds Parenting Time

As a general rule, if an obligor fails to make child support payments, the obligee cannot interfere with parenting time between the obligor and the minor child. *See Engrassia v. Di Lullo*, 454 N.Y.S.2d 103 (App. Div. 1982) (failure of noncustodial parent to make child support payments, without other evidence, was insufficient basis upon which to deny visitation). The child support obligation and the right to parenting time are viewed by most courts as separate issues. The reason for the distinction is that parenting time is ordered because it is in the best interest of the child to promote love and affection with both parents, residential and nonresidential. When the parties cannot effectuate parenting time, the appropriate remedy is to seek the assistance of the court. *Pierpont v. Bond*, 744 So. 2d 843 (Miss. Ct. App. 1999). Although the coercive effect of withholding child support may, when appropriate, be used to encourage the allowance of parenting time, its use is only available upon approval of the court. Child support is payment based on the financial needs of the child and the ability of both parents to provide for these needs; it is not viewed as directly related to the psychological needs of a minor child. *See Lindsay, v. Lindsay*, WL 197111 (Tenn. Ct. App. 2006) (father could not be ordered to pay an additional $50 in child support every time he missed visitation).

Example 9-9

Assume that P and D divorce and that P is awarded sole legal and physical custody of their child, C. D is awarded parenting time with C every other weekend and for four weeks during the summer. D is ordered to pay child support in the amount of $200 per month. D believes that P is using the child support money to go out drinking and to attend concerts with friends rather than for the benefit of C. Consequently, D asks P for proof that the money is being spent on C, and when P refuses to provide an accounting, D stops paying child support. P tells D that P can barely make ends meet financially and that C has been unable to participate in some school activities because P cannot finance them without the child support payments from D. In exasperation, P refuses to allow D to exercise parenting time with C until D resumes child support payments. D brings an action to enforce parenting time, and P brings an action for enforcement of the child support order. How will a court most likely rule?

Explanation

Sadly, both P and D could be held in contempt of court. In most states, the physical custodian is not required to provide an accounting concerning child support expenditures, and D wrongfully violated the support order by unilaterally stopping payment. The right to parenting time is not conditioned on payment of support, so P could not prevent D from visiting with C even though D's child support payments were in arrears. As described here, this is a situation where the parties might benefit from going to mediation to resolve the ongoing conflict between them.

9.28. Federal Income Tax Treatment

For federal income tax purposes, child support payments are not income to the obligee. The parent who makes the payments cannot deduct the amount as an expense on his or her federal tax return.

9.29. Stepparent Liability

The common law did not impose a legal duty on a stepparent to provide support for a minor stepchild. *See Ulrich v. Cornell*, 484 N.W.2d 545, 548 (Wis. 1992). It also took the view that one's standing in *loco parentis* is voluntary and temporary and may be abrogated at will by either person standing in *loco parentis* or by a child. Without a statute and absent an adoption or unusual circumstances, a stepparent is not responsible for providing support for a spouse's children.

Courts generally will not consider the income of a stepparent in calculating the presumptively correct child support amount for a child. *See Gina P. v. Stephen S.*, 33 A.D.3d 412 (N.Y. 2006). Courts are cautious about imposing an ongoing support obligation on a stepparent who voluntarily supports a child, because it is thought that stepparents might be generally discouraged from providing such support for fear of becoming permanently obligated to do so.

Despite the general rule, a few states have adopted provisions requiring a stepparent to support stepchildren as long as the stepparent is married to the children's natural parent. *See, e.g.*, Wash. Rev. Code §26.16.205, which reads as follows:

> The expenses of the family and the education of the children, including stepchildren, are chargeable upon the property of both husband and wife, or either of them, and they may be sued jointly or separately. When a petition for

dissolution of marriage or a petition for legal separation is filed, the court may, upon motion of the stepparent, terminate the obligation to support the step-children. The obligation to support stepchildren shall cease upon the entry of a decree of dissolution, decree of legal separation, or death.

See also Washington Statewide Org. of Stepparents v. Smith, 536 P.2d 1202 (Wash. 1975) (statute does not unconstitutionally impair marriage contracts or violate the Equal Protection Clause because cohabitants are not held to the same standard).

Under North Dakota law, a stepparent may be liable for necessaries for a spouse's dependent children if they are "received into the stepparent's family. . . . [T]he stepparent is liable, to the extent of his or her ability, to support them during the marriage and so long thereafter as they remain in the stepparent's family." N.D. Stat. §14-09-09 (West 2005).

When stepparents divorce, most jurisdictions take the view that the support obligation, if any, ends. *See Bagwell v. Bagwell*, 698 So. 2d 746 (La. Ct. App. 1997) (no obligation after divorce). But *see Johnson v Johnson*, 617 N.W.2d 97 (N.D. 2000) (stepparent liable on equitable adoption theory).

Example 9-10

Assume that P and D married in the state of Washington and that P brought two children from a former marriage into the relationship. Although the children regularly visited with their biological father, X, and received child support from him, D treated the children as though they were his biological children. During the last year of the marriage, X fell ill and died. About eight months later, P and D's marriage dissolved. P argues that under the Washington statute (Wash. Rev. Code §26.16.205 *supra*), D must continue to pay child support. How will the court most likely rule?

Explanation

The court will most likely reject P's claim. Although the statute mandates that D provide support to the children during D's marriage to P, there is no requirement that the support continue after the marriage. There is also no evidence presented that would equitably estop D from asserting that he is not the children's father. Therefore, he is not liable for their support.

Child Support Modification and Enforcement

10

10.1. Introduction

Agreements and court orders regarding child support may be modified as circumstances change. For example, if parents alter their custodial arrangements, the issue of child support will be revisited. Similarly, if the obligor loses his or her job, or if the obligor has a substantial increase in income, the amount of child support is likely to be readjusted. In the unfortunate event that an obligor does not pay child support as ordered, the order may be enforced through a variety of legal measures.

STANDARDS FOR MODIFYING EXISTING AWARD

10.2. Substantial Change in Circumstances

Most jurisdictions have statutory provisions that permit an order for child support to be changed or modified. Although the language used by state legislatures varies, in general, modification may occur when a "substantial change in circumstances" has taken place since the issuance of the support order, a change that makes enforcement of the existing award unfair. The parent seeking the change has the burden of proof.

A substantial change in circumstances can take many forms. The change may concern an alteration in a parent's financial situation, such as loss of a job, receipt of a large inheritance, or winning a lottery. The change in circumstance could be the result of a new situation for the child, such as large unanticipated medical expenses, the need for special education, or other unexpected requirements. A typical statute may read as follows:

> Support orders may be modified if there is: (1) a substantial increase or decrease in either parent's earnings, or (2) a substantial increase or decrease in the needs of a parent or child, or (3) a change in a child's or parent's cost of living, or (4) a change in custody, and any of these changes makes the terms of the original order unreasonable or unfair.

Example 10-1

Assume that in a paternity action, D was adjudicated the father of three children. At the time that the original child support order was entered, D was not employed, and the court imputed federal minimum-wage income to him and entered a child support order for $250 per month. D was later convicted of a federal crime and sent to prison. D moves for a reduction in child support, asserting that he lacks financial resources because of imprisonment. Will the support order be modified?

Explanation

D will argue that his incarceration is a substantial change in circumstances sufficient to reduce his child support obligation. One difficulty D has in making this argument is that D's *income* (or lack thereof) did not change when he went to prison. However, D will argue that his *ability* to earn income changed substantially. In the similar case of *A.M.S. ex rel. Farthing v. Stoppleworth*, 694 N.W.2d 8 (N.D. 2005), the court held that the statutory support guideline amount could not be rebutted through a showing of incarceration because the obligor had brought the situation upon himself. The North Dakota court found that imprisonment was not a circumstance beyond the control of the obligor and was consequently not the type of change that warranted modification of the child support order. Some state courts have held as a matter of law that incarceration can never be a justification warranting the modification of child support. However, other courts have reasoned that incarceration is not a voluntary act and that the imprisoned, indigent child support obligor should be relieved of the support obligation during incarceration. The rationale underpinning this line of cases is that the child will not presently benefit from imposing on the parent a continuing support obligation, beyond his or her ability to pay. Unlike the voluntarily unemployed parent, an incarcerated parent is not able to rectify his or her situation by obtaining employment. The obligor will rarely be able to pay the arrears upon release, and precious judicial resources and taxpayer funds will be expended in the attempt to collect. *See Commonwealth ex rel. Marshall v. Marshall*, 15 S.W.3d 396 (Ky. App. 2000).

10.3. Statutory Presumption — Substantial Change

Some jurisdictions have created rebuttable statutory presumptions for use in modification cases. Such presumptions typically provide that modification is warranted if the parent seeking the change establishes that the child support order would be increased or decreased by more than 20 percent. For example, in *MacLafferty v. MacLafferty*, 829 N.W.2d 938 (Ind. 2005), the obligor sought to modify a child support order because of an increase in the physical custodian's income. The relevant statute provided that modification could only be made upon a showing that (1) the current order was unreasonable because of substantial changed circumstances or (2) the support order had been in effect for more than one year and the modified guidelines payment would result in an increase or decrease of more than 20 percent. The modification was denied because the changed circumstance only resulted in a 14 percent difference in the child support order.

Example 10-2

Assume that P and D are the unmarried parents of a child, X. When child support was determined, P had a weekly income of $450, and D, an NBA player, had a weekly income of $121,327. Under the child support guidelines, D was ordered to pay $760 per week in child support. Three years later, P brings an action to modify child support because D's annual income has increased from $6,309,004 to $9,061,875. The relevant statute provides that modification requires a showing that (1) the current order is unreasonable because of substantial changed circumstances or (2) the support order has been in effect for more than one year, and the modified guidelines payment would result in an increase or decrease of more than 20 percent. D argues (correctly) that under the child support guidelines, his increased income would only result in a 1 percent increase ($7.15 per week). P argues that X is entitled to live at the standard of living X would have had if X resided with D and that a deviation from the guidelines is warranted. What is the likely result?

Explanation

This example is similar to the case of *Davis v. Knafel*, 837 N.E.2d 585 (Ind. App. 2005), in which the court denied the modification request. P failed to show that D's increased income would result in more than a 20 percent change in the guidelines support order. P also failed to establish substantial changed circumstances *occurring since the entry of the original support order* that would render the support order unreasonable. For example, the court was not persuaded that D's purchase of a $1,700,000 residence was a change in lifestyle, stating that P "fails to show how this is a change in lifestyle for a man who already owned two homes in two different states and who earns several million dollars per year." *Id.* at 589.

10.4. Cost-of-Living Adjustments

Most child support orders provide for a biennial adjustment in the amount to be paid based on a change in the cost of living. An order may direct that a trial court use a cost-of-living index published by the Department of Labor or provide for use of a local index that more accurately reflects the economy in a particular area of the country. *See, e.g., Fronk v. Wilson*, 819 P.2d 1275 (Mont. 1991) (American Chamber of Commerce Researchers' Association Cost of Living Index obtained from the State of Montana's Census and Economic Information Center was admissible).

The cost-of-living requirement may be waived if the court makes an express finding that the obligor's income or occupation does not provide for a cost-of-living increase. A cost-of-living provision providing for a biennial adjustment reflects an obligor's increase in income and the children's needs, which also are rising with inflation.

10.5. Retroactive Awards

The court has broad discretion to set the effective date of a support modification. *Borcherding v. Borcherding*, 566 N.W.2d 90, 93 (Minn. Ct. App. 1997). Typically, a modification of support or maintenance may be made retroactive from the date of service of the motion for modification on the responding party. *See also Kerby v. Kerby*, 164 P.3d 1049 (Okla. 2007) (date of motion is effective date of modification).

Example 10-3

Assume that P and D divorce and that D is ordered to pay $300 per month to P in child support. Five years later, P seeks to increase the child support award by $300 per month. The litigation and appeal concerning the increase last two years, from 2008 until 2010, as D unsuccessfully challenges the modification. When P wins on appeal, P believes that D owes P a lump-sum payment of $3,600 (the support increase over the two-year period). D argues that this is a windfall to P and that the increase should begin from the date of the appellate court's decision. How will a court most likely treat this dispute?

Explanation

A court will most likely reject D's argument. P has been required to support the parties' child for nearly two years without receiving all the assistance P was entitled to from D. For this reason, the back support now owed to P will not be considered a windfall, and the court will not abuse its discretion in making the modification retroactive to the time when D was served with the motion papers.

10.6. Obligor Employment Change

When a party voluntarily assumes a lower-paying job, courts will not automatically modify the support obligation. Furthermore, a party ordinarily will not be relieved of a child support obligation by voluntarily quitting work or by being fired for misconduct.

When seeking a reduction in child support payments because of a change in employment, the moving party must usually establish that the voluntary change in employment, which resulted in a reduction of income, was not made for the purpose of avoiding child support payments. The moving party must also show that a reduction is warranted based on efforts to mitigate any income loss. In effect, the moving party must present evidence as to why she or he voluntarily left the prior employment and also as to why the acceptance of a lower-paying job was necessary. Otherwise, for calculation of child support, the moving party will be considered to have an income equal to his or her earning capacity. *See Chen v. Warner*, 695 N.W.2d 758 (Wis. 2005) (mother's decision to forgo employment outside the home was "reasonable under the circumstances").

Courts have applied one of three tests to determine whether to modify a child support order when a parent voluntarily terminates employment. Each of the tests evidences its own strengths and weaknesses, and each reflects the public policy of its adopting jurisdiction. The first of these tests, the good-faith test, considers the actual earnings of a party rather than his or her earning capacity, so long as he or she acted in good faith and not primarily for the purpose of avoiding a support obligation when terminating employment. *In re Marriage of Horn*, 650 N.E.2d 1103, 1106 (Ill. App. Ct. 1995);

Giesner v. Giesner, 319 N.W.2d 718, 720 (Minn. 1982); *Schuler v. Schuler*, 416 N.E.2d 197, 203 (Mass. 1981); *Fogel v. Fogel*, 168 N.W.2d 275, 277 (Neb. 1969); *Thomas v. Thomas*, 203 So. 2d 118, 123 (Ala. 1967); *Lambert v. Lambert*, 403 P.2d 664, 668 (Wash. 1965); *Nelson v. Nelson*, 357 P.2d 536, 538 (Or. 1960). The good-faith test is criticized because it assumes that a divorced or separated party will continue to make decisions in the best overall interest of the family unit, when often, in fact, the party will not. The test is also criticized as focusing on the parent's motivation for leaving employment rather than on the parent's responsibility to his or her children and the effect of the parent's decision on the best interests of the children.

The second approach is the strict rule test, which disregards any income reduction produced by voluntary conduct and looks at the earning capacity of a party in fashioning a support obligation. Child support remains based solely on earning capacity. The strict rule test is viewed by some as too inflexible because it considers only one factor, the parent's earning capacity.

The third approach, which is referred to as the intermediate test, balances various factors to determine whether to use actual income or earning capacity in making a support determination. The intermediate balancing test considers a number of factors and places the obligation to pay child support first and other financial obligations second. The court asks whether the parent's current educational level and physical capacity provide him or her with the ability to find suitable work in the marketplace. If so, the decision to leave employment is less reasonable. If the parent leaves employment to seek additional training, and if the additional training is likely to increase the parent's earning potential, the decision is more likely to be found reasonable. A court will also consider the length of the parent's proposed educational program because it matters whether the children are young enough to benefit from the parent's increased future income.

Example 10-4

Assume that the marriage between P and D dissolved and that D was ordered to pay $1,200 per month for child support. When the support was ordered, D was employed by the Air Force, earning an annual salary of $48,000, plus benefits. D also holds a master's degree in business administration. D terminated his employment with the Air Force and entered law school. He earns a monthly reserve pay from the Air Force of $308, and his ex-wife, a full-time student/caretaker, earns about $1,000 per month. D alleged a substantial and continuing change in circumstances in that his income was reduced because he terminated his position with the Air Force and entered law school. In his petition, appellant requested a reduction in child support payments from $1,200 to $200 per month. P contended that D could move to a nearby state where night law school is offered and be employed during the day. D's children at the time were ages four and six.

Explanation

This is a close question and depends, at least in part, on the standard the court uses in reviewing the facts. A court could allow the order to be reduced to the guidelines amount based on D's lower income. It is reasonable to believe that a law degree would enable D to embark on a career that could well result in enhanced economic fortunes, and the increased income would inure to the benefit of his children, given their present ages. The suggestion that D attend night school in another state may be viewed as unreasonable because it would require relocation away from his children. The fact that D chose to stay in state near the children not only is reasonable, but also shows D's desire to remain active in his children's upbringing, an important consideration to D and his children. *See Little v. Little*, 969 P.2d 188 (Ariz. Ct. App. 1998). However, in this example, P would have a difficult time supporting two children on a total income of $1,200 per month, and the first obligation of the court is to assure that the children are cared for financially. Consequently, a court is unlikely to approve a reduction in child support based on a voluntary action of the obligor that leaves the children in need.

DURATION OF CHILD SUPPORT

10.7. Obligor's Death

Under the common law, a father's death terminated his obligation of support for his minor children. However, by statute, states have altered that perspective. *See, e.g.,* Ariz. Rev. Stat. §25-327(c) ("Unless otherwise agreed in writing or expressly provided in the decree, provisions for the support of a minor child are not terminated by the death of a parent obligated to support the child. If a parent obligated to pay support dies, the amount of future support may be modified, revoked or commuted to a lump sum payment"). A court also has the power to require a parent to obtain or maintain insurance on the parent's life for the benefit of the parent's children. *Pittman v. Pittman*, 419 So. 2d 1376 (Ala. 1982); *Wolk v. Wolk*, 464 A.2d 780 (Conn. 1983); *Allen v. Allen*, 477 N.E.2d 104 (Ind. Ct. App. 1985); *Krueger v. Krueger*, 278 N.W.2d 514 (Mich. Ct. App. 1979); *Stein v. Sandow*, 468 N.Y.S.2d 910 (N.Y. App. Div. 2d Dept. 1983). It is recognized that a child is no less dependent on a parent after the parent's death than before and that the burden of support may fall in total or in part on society if the surviving parent is unable to fully carry the burden.

The Uniform Marriage and Divorce Act (UMDA) repudiates the common law rule that an obligor's support obligation ends upon death by providing that a parent's child support obligation is terminated "by emancipation of the child but not by the death of a parent obligated to support the child. When a parent obligated to pay support dies, the amount of support may be modified, revoked, or commuted to a lump sum payment to the extent just and appropriate in the circumstances." UMDA §316(c).

The UMDA also states that the parties or the court may provide for the contingency of the premature death of the parent in the original decree. But even if no such provision is incorporated into the original decree, the act permits courts to modify the support provisions at a later time, even after the death of the parent. In providing for the death of the parent, the act requires courts to use the criteria considered in the court's original order and in modifying a child support order. The intent of these provisions is to encourage divorcing parents to provide support for their children during their entire minority. UMDA Commissioners' Note to §316(c). In the absence of the parents voluntarily making such provisions for their children, however, these provisions give the court the discretion and authority to *sua sponte* secure the children's support after the parent's death.

10.8. Emancipation of Child

A child support obligation may end when the minor child is emancipated. Emancipation of a child occurs when the fundamental dependent relationship between parent and child is concluded, the parent relinquishes the right to custody and is relieved of the burden of support, and the child is no longer entitled to support. Emancipation may occur by reason of the child's marriage, by court order, or by the child attaining a certain age. Although in most states there is a presumption of emancipation at age 18, that presumption is rebuttable. *Filippone v. Lee*, 700 A.2d 384 (N.J. Super. Ct. App. Div. 1997). The emancipation issue is fact-specific, and the essential inquiry is whether the child has moved "beyond the sphere of influence and responsibility exercised by a parent and obtains an independent status of his or her own." *Bishop v. Bishop*, 671 A.2d 644 (N.J. Super. Ct. 1995). *See In re Marriage of Heddy*, 535 S.W.2d 276, 279 (Mo. Ct. App. 1976). Consent of the custodial parent, either express or implied, is a prerequisite to emancipation. *Vinson v. Vinson*, 628 S.W.2d 376 (Mo. Ct. App. 1982). The mere fact that a child is employed and retains her earnings does not by itself establish that parental control has been relinquished or that the obligation to support has been terminated. *Id.* at 377.

A state may recognize constructive emancipation under the common law. *See, e.g., In re Marriage of George*, 988 P.2d 251 (Kan. Ct. App. 1999). In *Harris v. Rattini*, 855 S.W.2d 410, 412 (Mo. Ct. App. 1993), the Missouri Court of Appeals for the Eastern District held that a child who drops out of school before his or her eighteenth birthday, takes a part-time job, and has no mental or physical incapacity is emancipated, and child support is no longer required. By way of contrast, in *Detwiler v. Detwiler*, 57 A.2d 426 (Pa. Super. Ct. 1948), the Superior Court of Pennsylvania found that a 17-year-old who dropped out of school and earned his own income, but lived at home, was not emancipated. The court found that the parents had not relinquished control over the child. In *In re Marriage of Clay*, 670 P.2d 31 (Colo. Ct. App. 1983), the Colorado Court of Appeals held that a 16-year-old daughter who was dependent on her mother for financial support, who had not established a residence away from both her parents, who was not married to the father of her child, and who did not receive support from her child's father was not emancipated and was entitled to support.

An otherwise unemancipated teenager who is dependent on parental support is not disqualified from receiving it because she has become pregnant and she elected to give birth to a child as an unmarried mother. Her own motherhood in these circumstances does not render her emancipated. *See, e.g., Filippone v. Lee, supra; In re Marriage of Clay*, 670 P.2d 31, 32 (Colo. Ct. App. 1983); *Doerrfeld v. Konz*, 524 So. 2d 1115, 1116-1117 (Fla. Dist. Ct. App. 1988); *Hicks v. Fulton County Dept. of Family and Children Services*, 270 S.E.2d 254, 255 (Ga. Ct. App. 1980); *French v. French*, 599 S.W.2d 40, 41 (Mo. Ct. App. 1980); *Wulff v. Wulff*, 500 N.W.2d 845, 851 (Neb. 1993); *Thompson v. Thompson*, 405 N.Y.S.2d 974, 975 (Fam. Ct. 1978), *aff'd*, 419 N.Y.S.2d 239 (App. Div. 1979); *Griffin v. Griffin*, 558 A.2d 75, 80 (Pa. Super. Ct. 1989), *appeal denied*, 571 A.2d 383 (Pa. 1989).

Residing apart from a minor's parents does not by itself result in the minor's emancipation. *Quinn v. Johnson*, 589 A.2d 1077 (N.J. Super. Ct. 1991). A troubled minor's removal from his parents' home to a public or private institutional alternative or even to the home of friends or relatives does not relieve the parents of their support obligation during minority, provided the child is not entirely self-supporting. *See In re Marriage of Donahoe*, 448 N.E.2d 1030,1033 (Ill. App. Ct. 1983); *Quillen v. Quillen*, 659 N.E.2d 566, 576 (Ind. Ct. App. 1995), *vacated in part, adopted in part*, 671 N.E.2d 98 (Ind. 1996); *In re Marriage of Bordner*, 715 P.2d 436, 439 (Mont. 1986); *Hildebrand v. Hildebrand*, 477 N.W.2d. 1, 5 (Neb. 1991); *In re Owens*, 645 N.E.2d 130, 132 (Ohio Ct. App. 1994); *Trosky v. Mann*, 581 A.2d 177, 178 (Pa. Super. Ct. 1990); *In re Marriage of George*, 988 P.2d 251 (Kan. Ct. App. 1999).

Military service normally acts to emancipate a minor. However, in *Baker v. Baker*, 537 P.2d 171 (Kan. 1975), the father argued that when his son went into the Navy, he became emancipated, and that relieved the father of any further obligation of support. The court held that entry into the Navy was not grounds for automatically terminating child support but could be considered as a factor for reducing or terminating the support payments.

Example 10-5

Assume that P and D are divorced. They have one child, X, and D pays child support to P for the support of X. When X is 16, she marries Y, with the permission of P. However, X continues to live in P's home, and P continues to provide financial support for her. Seven months later, X's marriage is annulled on the ground of fraudulent inducement on the part of Y. D stopped paying child support when X married Y, believing her to be emancipated. However, after the annulment, P again seeks child support from D, arguing that X was returned to her unemancipated status and consequently is entitled to support. How will a court likely rule?

Explanation

In *State ex rel. Dept. of Economic Sec. v. Demetz*, 130 P.3d 986 (Ariz. Ct. App. 2006), the court considered a similar situation. D argued that X's marriage was voidable, not void, and that the marriage was consequently valid when it occurred, thus emancipating X. The court disagreed, holding that once the annulment became final, the marriage was "deemed invalid from its inception." The court found that D's obligation to support X was revived when X's marriage was annulled. *See also Thomas v. Campbell*, 960 So. 2d 694 (Ala. App. 2006).

10.9. Child Reaches Majority

Parents are responsible for support until a child turns 18 or completes secondary school. See Chapter 9 for discussion of support while a child attends college.

ENFORCEMENT EFFORTS

10.10. Child Support Debt

National child support debt currently exceeds $100 billion. According to recent research the majority of obligors (57%) are less than $5,000 in arrears. However, very-low-income obligors account for 70 percent of arrears. U.S. Department of Health and Human Services, Administration for Children and Families, Office of Child Support Enforcement, *The Story Behind the Numbers* (May 2008), available at *http://www.acf.hhs.gov/programs/cse/pol/IM/2008/im-08-05a.pdf* (last visited July 4, 2009).

The following sections discuss the growing number of mechanisms for enforcement of existing child support orders.

10.11. Contempt of Court

Although family courts have many tools with which to enforce orders, one of the most powerful is the ability to hold an obligor in civil or criminal contempt. The purpose of civil contempt is to obtain compliance with the court order. In a civil contempt action, the person being held in contempt is said to hold the keys to the jailhouse door in his or her pocket — jail is conditioned on nonpayment, and the obligor is released when payment is made. *See Branum v. State*, 829 N.E.2d 622 (Ind. Ct. App. 2005) (in civil contempt case, court was required to ascertain that the obligor had ability to pay and to advise that the obligor could obtain release from incarceration through compliance). The purpose of criminal contempt is to punish, and the obligor typically completes a determinate sentence. Despite the bright line between the two types of contempt, in practice, courts sometimes fail to distinguish between them.

When criminal contempt is sought, the defendant-obligor is entitled to additional constitutional protections. In *Hicks v. Feiock*, 485 U.S. 624 (1988), the obligor failed to make child support payments, and the issue was whether the Due Process Clause of the Fourteenth Amendment prohibited the state court from placing the burden on the obligor, rather than the state, to establish the obligor's inability to make payments. The Supreme Court held that shifting the burden to the defendant in a criminal case violated due process. However, if the proceeding had been civil in nature, the obligor would not have enjoyed this constitutional protection.

Courts are split over the question of whether appointment of counsel is constitutionally required for an indigent civil contempt defendant. *See Rodriquez v. Eighth Judicial Dist. Court ex rel.*, 102 P.3d 41 (Nev. 2004) (Sixth Amendment right to counsel not applicable in civil contempt). *But see Pasqua v. Council*, 892 A.2d 663 (N.J. 2006) (civil contempt obligors entitled to counsel under Due Process Clause and state constitution).

Most states provide explicit statutory authority for courts to use during contempt proceedings to enforce maintenance and child support obligations. In contrast, property settlements are categorized as ordinary debts and are not subject to enforcement through contempt. In most jurisdictions, property settlements are enforced through execution on the judgment.

10.12. Criminal Nonsupport

All states have statutes that punish an obligor who willfully fails to pay child support. For example, Wisconsin law declares that

> [a]ny person who intentionally fails for 120 or more consecutive days to provide spousal, grandchild or child support which the person knows or reasonably should know the person is legally obligated to provide is guilty of a Class I felony. A prosecutor may charge a person with multiple counts for a violation under this subsection if each count covers a period of at least 120 consecutive days and there is no overlap between periods.

Wis. Stat. §948.22(2).

Such provisions have withstood constitutional attack from obligors who have claimed that that being imprisoned for nonpayment of a debt is unconstitutional. In rejecting this argument, courts reason that unlike a debt arising from a contract, a child support obligation is based on a court order. *O'Connor v. O'Connor*, 180 N.W.2d 735, 738 (Wis. 1970). *See State v. Bren*, 704 N.W.2d 170 (Minn. App. 2005); *Cramer v. Petrie*, 637 N.E.2d 882 (Ohio 1994); *Lyons v. State*, 835 S.W.2d 715, 718 (Tex. Ct. App. 1992).

Example 10-6

Assume that the state of X charged D with criminal nonsupport. D and his ex-wife were divorced, there were three children born of the marriage, and D was ordered to pay child support in the amount of $150 per month. In a very brief jury trial, the ex-wife testified that from the date of the decree until the date of trial (two years), she had received no child support payments from D. D did not testify and was convicted of criminal nonsupport and sentenced to five years in prison. In this jurisdiction, the criminal nonsupport statute provides that "any person who intentionally fails, refuses, or neglects to provide proper support which he or she knows or reasonably should know he or she is legally obligated to provide to a spouse, minor child, minor stepchild, or other dependent commits criminal nonsupport."

In her instructions to the jury, the trial judge stated, "Regarding criminal non-support, the elements of the State's case are: (1) The alleged crime occurred on or about a certain date. The alleged crime occurred in this County, and this state. (2) The defendant then and there failed to provide proper support for his minor children when he knew or reasonably should have known he was legally obligated to provide support pursuant to the Order of the Court." D argues that the conviction should be reversed because the words "intentionally fails, refuses, or neglects" were not included in the court's instruction. The state argues that D did not properly object to the court's instruction. The trial transcript shows that D's counsel objected to the court's instruction in the following manner: "[T]he defendant does object concerning the elements." How will a court most likely treat D's argument?

Explanation

The conviction most likely will be reversed. Although the objection could have been more specific, it was sufficient to inform the court of the claimed defect. Intent is an essential element of the crime of criminal nonsupport. In this hypothetical case, the court did not instruct the jury on all of the essential elements of the crime charged. An instruction omitting an essential element is prejudicially erroneous. *State v. Noll*, 507 N.W.2d 44 (Neb. Ct. App. 1993). *See also State v. Nuzman*, 95 P.3d 252 (Or. Ct. App. 2004) (state had burden to show that nonpayment was without lawful excuse).

10.13. Interception of Tax Refunds

In 1981 the federal income tax refund offset program was enacted into law. Pub. L. No. 97-35, §2331, 95 Stat. 860-863 (1981). Initially, this program was restricted to public assistance cases and enforced delinquent child support obligations by intercepting part or all of the obligor's federal income tax refund. The program was expanded in 1984 to allow for its use in nonassistance cases.

The Debt Collection Improvement Act (DCIA) of 1996, Pub. L. No.104-134, was enacted into law on April 26, 1996. The primary purpose of the DCIA is to increase the collection of nontax debt owed to the federal government. The DCIA contains important provisions for use in the collection of past-due child support obligations.

The DCIA was further strengthened by Executive Order 13019 — *Supporting Families: Collecting Delinquent Child Support Obligations*, dated September 26, 1998. This order allows the Secretary of Treasury, in consultation with the Secretary of Health and Human Services, to develop and implement procedures necessary to collect child support debts by administrative offsets. *See* 31 C.F.R. §§285.1, 285.3.

10.14. Garnishment

The Child Support and Establishment of Paternity Act of 1974, 42 U.S.C. §659, made it possible for a federal employer to withhold child support and pay an obligor directly from the withheld funds.

10.15. Credit Bureau Reporting

In many jurisdictions, a report to a credit bureau may be triggered if a noncustodial parent owes $1,000 or more in past-due child support.

10.16. Driver's License Suspension

In a number of jurisdictions, when a noncustodial parent is behind in paying child support by a certain number of weeks or months, the obligor's license may be suspended. Before the suspension becomes effective, the obligor is entitled to due-process protections, including written notice and a reasonable period in which to rectify the arrearage. *See also Office of Child Support v. Stanzione*, 910 A.2d 882 (Vt. 2006) (suspension of license did not infringe free exercise of religion); *Wheeler v. Idaho Dept. of Health and Welfare*, 207 P.3d 988 (Idaho 2009) (driver's license not an exempt property interest).

10.17. Recreational License Suspension

Some jurisdictions suspend the hunting and fishing licenses of obligors who are behind in support payments for a certain period, usually six months.

10.18. Publication of a "Most Wanted" List of "Deadbeat Obligors"

When obligors generate substantial sums in arrears, some jurisdictions publish their names in a local newspaper or place their names and sometimes their photos on a government web site.

10.19. Occupational License Suspension

Some states have provisions that permit license suspension for obligors working in occupations that require a license from the state, county, or municipal board or agency. Persons subject to suspension may include realtors, barbers, doctors, and lawyers. For example, Georgia's *Code of Professional Responsibility* for lawyers incorporates state law and provides that when a court makes a finding that a member of the bar has willfully failed to timely pay a child support obligation, and such refusal continues for 30 days after the determination becomes final, the bar member "shall be deemed not to be in good standing and shall remain in such status until such time as the noncompliance is corrected." *See Matter of Carlson*, 489 S.E.2d 834 (Ga. 1997).

10.20. Passport Denial

Section 370 of the Personal Responsibility and Work Opportunity Reconciliation Act (PRWORA) of 1996 (Pub. L. No.104-193, 110 Stat. 2105) amended the Social Security Act by adding subsection 452(k). This subsection became effective October 1, 1997, and provides for the denial, revocation, and restriction of U.S. passports. A passport application may be denied when the noncustodial parent is $5,000 or more past due in a child support obligation. PRWORA §§312, 653(a). *See Dept. of Rev. v. Nesbitt*, 975 So. 2d 549 (Fla. App. 2008) (trial court lacked authority to lift federally mandated restrictions on basketball player's passport).

10.21. Seizing Awards

Reemployment insurance, workers' compensation payments, and lottery winnings may be seized. *See Torres v. Kunze*, 945 A.2d 472 Conn. App. 2008) (lottery winnings of delinquent parent will be reduced by amount of child support owed); *LeClair v. Reed ex rel. Reed*, 939 A.2d 466 (Vt. 2007) (lottery winnings).

10.22. Seizing Assets Held

A child support office may also take assets held in financial institutions or in retirement funds.

10.23. Obtaining a Wage Assignment

An obligee may seek to obtain an order that directs an employer to deduct the child support payment from the earnings of an employee-obligor parent and then make this payment directly to the obligee parent. Violation of a wage assignment order could result in the employer becoming responsible for such payment to the obligee parent. Assignment orders can be obtained through a relatively simple court procedure. Once obtained, the wage assignment order must be served on the employer of the obligor parent before it becomes effective. *See In re Marriage of Hopkins*, 92 Cal. Rptr. 3d 570 (Cal. App. 2009) (a wage assignment order required the Social Security Administration to withhold $750 per month for current and past-due child support from the benefits due the obligor).

Additional measures found in some states include the following: (1) *Freezing bank accounts* until support is paid. *See, e.g., Murry v. Watkins*, (WL 2980357 Ohio App. Dist. 2004). A bank is relieved from liability for damages, should it have acted inappropriately. Both the various state departments of revenue and the federal Internal Revenue Service can also seize funds from these accounts. (2) *Using traditional creditor's legal remedies* such as execution and garnishment against any other property the obligor may own. Some states will place liens on real estate owned by an obligor who is in arrears in child support payments. *See Les Realty Corp. v. Hogan*, 714 A.2d 366 (N.J. Super. Ch. 1998) (the Automated Child Support Enforcement System was enacted to help remedy the serious problem of unpaid child support by ensuring liens on real estate owned by the debtor).

10.24 Effect of Bankruptcy

Child support debt is not dischargeable in bankruptcy. *See* Janet Leach Richards, *A Guide to Spousal Support and Property Division Claims Under the Bankruptcy Abuse Prevention and Consumer Protection Act of 2005*, 41 Fam. L.Q. 227, 228 (2007); United State Government Accountability Office, *Bankruptcy and Child Support Enforcement* (2008).

FEDERAL COLLECTION EFFORTS

10.25. Partnership with States

As discussed in Chapter 9, in 1974 Congress enacted Title IV-D of the Social Security Act creating a federal-state partnership for the purpose of establishing and enforcing child support orders. 42 U.S.C. §651 *et seq.* Although originally available only to recipients of public assistance, enforcement services were later made available for the benefit of all children.

10.26. Federal Crime

The Child Support Recovery Act (CSRA) of 1992, 18 U.S.C. §228(a), made it a federal crime to willfully fail to pay a past-due support obligation, where the child was located in a state separate from that of the obligor. Congress intended to take the incentive out of the delinquent parent's attempts to avoid the processes of state courts by moving out of the child's home state. *United States v. Gill*, 264 F.3d 929, 933 (9th Cir. 2001). The Act, when triggered and thereafter applied by federal courts, enhances state enforcement efforts by providing a greater or more efficient jurisdictional reach than possessed by the states. *Giordano v. Giordano*, 913 A.2d 146 (N.J. Super. A.D. 2007).

Past-due support is defined in the Act as either an amount determined by a state court that remains unpaid for longer than one year or one that exceeds $5,000. An obligor who violates the federal statute can be fined and imprisoned for not more than six months for the first offense or two years maximum and can be ordered to make restitution for subsequent offenses. Support must have been unpaid for at least a year and exceed $5,000. But see U.S. v. Pillor, 387 F. Supp. 2d 1053 (N.D. Cal. 2005); and United States v. Morrow, 368 F. Supp. 863 (C.D. Ill. 2005) (holding that mandatory CSRA rebuttable presumption that the obligor has the ability to pay violates due process by shifting burden regarding willfulness).

In 1998 CSRA became the Deadbeat Parents Punishment Act (DPPA). See United States v. Edelkind, 525 F.3d 388 (5th Cir. 2008). Two new federal felony categories were created by DPPA that carry a maximum of two years in prison plus fines and restitution at the discretion of the court. Crossing state lines with the intent to evade child support payments is now a felony for parents owing $5,000 or more or for parents whose payments have remained unpaid for more than a year. Out-of-state parents owing $10,000 or more or who fail to pay for two years will also be subject to felony charges. See United States v. Klinzing, 315 F.3d 803 (7th Cir. 2003) (DPPA does not violate Commerce Clause, Equal Protection Clause, or Sixth Amendment to the Constitution).

10.27. Uniform Interstate Family Support Act (UIFSA)

The enforcement of a child support order, even when the parents and children are residents of the same state, is difficult. However, when the parents live in different states, enforcement is much more difficult.

Before the 1950s, a parent who wanted to ensure support against the other parent who lived in another state had to travel to the support debtor's state to take legal action. However, since that time, a uniform act has existed in one form or another allowing states that subscribe to it to enforce each other's support orders. In 1950 the National Conference of Commissioners on Uniform State Laws prepared a model act that was eventually adopted in some form in all jurisdictions, URESA, which is short for Uniform Reciprocal Enforcement of Support Act.

In 1968, URESA was amended, and the new act was called RURESA, short for Revised Uniform Reciprocal Enforcement of Support Act. By 1992, all of the states had enacted RURESA or URESA. Even American Samoa, Puerto Rico, Guam, and the Virgin Islands had adopted a version of either URESA or RURESA.

The purpose of URESA, and later, RURESA, was to address "the problem of interstate enforcement of duties of support," given "the increasing mobility of the American population." In re Marriage of Gerkin, 74 Cal. Rptr. 3d 188, 192 (Cal. App. 2008). The greatest difficulty in enforcing support where the parties are in different states is the expense of travel to a distant state to litigate the rights of the destitute obligee. Under RURESA it was thought that the expense could be reduced to filing fees plus a few postage stamps. However, a problem arose because state legislatures refused to adopt language in their individual RURESA statutes that was consistent with what other states were enacting. States were prone to adopt some of the provisions suggested by the National Conference of Commissioners on Uniform State Laws while ignoring others. In addition, it became evident that the process under RURESA was slow, with petitions taking from four to eight months with a considerable amount of paperwork and administration.

With state efforts falling short, the federal government sponsored the revision of the uniform interstate support legislation, which resulted in the Uniform Interstate Family Support Act, or UIFSA. In 1996, Congress enacted a law requiring all 50 states to adopt UIFSA by January 1, 1998. UIFSA was intended to replace URESA and RURESA provisions in the states.

When a party seeks to modify a support order issued by another state, UIFSA applies. *See* Kurtis A. Kemper, *Construction and Application of Uniform Interstate Family Support Act*, 90 A.L.R.5th 1 (2001). Consequently, a party seeking to modify a support order from another state must establish jurisdiction pursuant to the act.

There are nine articles to UIFSA:

- Article 1 contains general provisions, including definitions.
- Article 2 contains the provisions concerning jurisdiction.
- Article 3 contains the provisions relating to the duties of the state in a UIFSA action.
- Article 4 contains the provisions relating to the establishment of an order.
- Article 5 contains the provisions relating to direct enforcement of an order of another state without the need for registration.
- Article 6 concerns the enforcement and modification of support orders after registration.
- Article 7 concerns paternity actions.
- Article 8 concerns interstate rendition.
- Article 9 contains miscellaneous provisions.

The jurisdictional rules are set out in Part A of Article 2 of UIFSA, §§201 and 202. Section 201 establishes UIFSA's bases for jurisdiction over a nonresident — that is, its long-arm jurisdiction — by providing that a state may exercise jurisdiction over an individual if

1. the individual has been properly served in the state;
2. the individual submits to the jurisdiction of the court by entering a general appearance or by filing a responsive document;
3. the individual resided with the child for whom support is being sought within the state;

4. the individual provided prenatal expenses or child support while residing within the state;
5. the child resides within the forum state because of some activities of the individual;
6. the individual engaged in sexual intercourse in the state;
7. the individual asserted parentage in the state's registry or in another appropriate agency; or
8. there is any other basis consistent with the constitutions of this state and the United States for the exercise of personal jurisdiction.

One scholar has stated that the first basis is a codification of *Burnham v. Superior Court*, 495 U.S. 604 (1990), which affirmed the constitutionality of asserting personal jurisdiction based on personal service within a state (the tag rule). *See* John J. Sampson & Paul M. Kurtz, *UIFSA: An Interstate Support Act for the 21st Century*, 27 Fam. L.Q. 85, 114 (Spring 1993).

Jurisdiction under UIFSA rests on the concept of continuing, exclusive jurisdiction to establish and modify the levels of child support due a particular child. The state issuing a child support order retains continuing, exclusive jurisdiction as long as this state remains the residence of the obligor, the individual obligee, or the child for whose benefit the support order is issued. The concept of continuing, exclusive jurisdiction was created in order to end the practice, common before UIFSA, of out-of-state payors seeking downward modifications of their child support obligations in the states of their current residence. UIFSA allows for only one enforceable order in a case at any time. This is accomplished by limiting jurisdiction to modify the original order. "Thus, once a court enters a support decree with jurisdiction, it is the only body entitled to modify it so long as it retains continuing, exclusive jurisdiction under the Act. Another state, while required by the *Uniform Interstate Family Support Act* to enforce the existing decree, has no power under that Act to modify the original decree or enter a support order at a different level," as long as one of the parties remains in the issuing state. *Id.* at 88. *See* Tina M. Fielding, *UIFSA: The New URESA*, 20 U. Dayton L. Rev. 425, 461 (1994).

UIFSA requires that states recognize the continuing, exclusive jurisdiction of a tribunal of another state that issued a child support order. The trial court may modify the child support order (1) upon both parties' consent to the court assuming jurisdiction, section 205(a)(2), or (2) if after registration of the order, the trial court determines that the child, the individual obligee, and the obligor do not reside in the issuing state.

Under UIFSA, an issuing state loses continuing, exclusive jurisdiction to modify child support provisions of a divorce decree once both parents and all their children move away from that state. *See* Ventura v. Leong, 873 N.Y.S.2d 238 (N.Y. Sup. 2008). As noted above, UIFSA permits only one tribunal at a time to have jurisdiction to modify a child support order. If the parties and their child no longer reside in the state that issued the original child support order, and one party seeks to modify an existing child support order, they must bring the action in the state where the nonmoving party resides, except for modification by agreement.

Example 10-7

Assume that P and D dissolve their marriage in Iowa and that a trial judge with jurisdiction over both parties issues a child support order in 2008. P is the custodial parent or obligee, and D is the obligor. P and the minor child move to Texas in 2009. D moves to New York in 2010. P seeks legal advice as to which state she should bring a modification of support action in under UIFSA. What advice will you give P?

Explanation

Under UIFSA, Iowa lost jurisdiction to modify its own order when D moved to New York, unless P and D consented in writing to Iowa retaining modification jurisdiction. Iowa retains jurisdiction to enforce any amount of arrears owed because of the Iowa order. However, P should be advised to bring her modification action in Texas.

Example 10-8

Assume that P and D dissolve their marriage in Iowa and that a trial judge with jurisdiction over both parties issues a child support order in 2009. P is the custodial parent or obligee, and D is the obligor. P and the minor child move to Texas in 2010. D remains in Iowa. P seeks legal advice as to which state she should bring a modification of support action in under UIFSA. What advice will you give P?

Explanation

Iowa retains modification jurisdiction as long as D is a resident, and Iowa has enforcement jurisdiction because it never lost it.

Example 10-9

Assume that P and D dissolve their marriage in Iowa and that a trial judge with jurisdiction over both parties issues a child support order in 2009. P is the custodial parent or obligee, and D is the obligor. P and the minor child remain in Iowa when D moves to New York in 2010. P seeks legal advice as to which state she should bring a modification of support action in under UIFSA. What advice will you give P?

Explanation

If D is the person who moved, but P and the child remained in Iowa, Iowa retains enforcement jurisdiction and modification jurisdiction because P and the child remained in that jurisdiction. Because D was originally a resident of Iowa at the time of the initial order, or consented to personal jurisdiction, Iowa retains the ability to modify this order, provided that at least one parent remains in that state.

10.28. Full Faith and Credit Act of 1994

In a further effort to address interstate child support issues, Congress enacted the Full Faith and Credit for Child Support Orders Act (FFCCSOA) in 1994. This Act was intended to establish national standards to facilitate the payment of child support, discourage interstate conflict over inconsistent orders, and avoid jurisdictional competition. FFCCSOA, codified at 28 U.S.C. §1738B, requires that state courts afford full faith and credit to child support orders issued in other states and refrain from modifying or issuing contrary orders except in limited circumstances. Under §1738B(e), a child support order may be modified by a sister state only if the rendering state has lost continuing, exclusive jurisdiction over the child support order, which in turn occurs only if (1) neither the child nor any of the parties continues to reside in the state, or (2) each of the parties has consented to the assumption of jurisdiction by another state. 28 U.S.C. §1738B(e)(2) (2003). Under the Supremacy Clause of the United States Constitution, FFCCSOA is binding on all states and supersedes any inconsistent provisions of state law, including any inconsistent provisions of uniform state laws such as URESA. *See Spencer v. Spencer*, 882 N.E.2d 886, 889 (N.Y. 2008); *Superior Court v. Ricketts*, 836 A.2d 707 (Md. App. 2003).

10.29. The Welfare Reform Act of 1996

The Welfare Reform Act of 1996 mandated that states adopt a version of the Uniform Interstate Family Support Act by January 1, 1998, and required that they develop expedited procedures that move away from complaint-driven approaches to collection of support and toward more efficient and faster administrative provisions. It also encouraged states to use liens, seizures of funds, license suspension, and administrative subpoenas to collect outstanding child support.

10.30. Personal Responsibility and Work Opportunity Reconciliation Act of 1996

The Personal Responsibility and Work Opportunity Reconciliation Act (PRWORA) of 1996 required each state desiring to receive block grants to develop a state directory of new hires that met federal requirements by either October 1, 1997, or October 1, 1998, depending upon whether a state had a new hire reporting law in effect before August 22, 1996. 42 U.S.C. §§601 *et seq.* The law required the Department of Health and Human Services to develop a national directory of new hires by October 1, 1997. States were also required to adopt laws that allowed for the automatic placement of liens on an obligor's property when the obligor was in arrears.

Alimony and Necessaries

11.1. Introduction

Alimony is the obligation of one party to provide the other with support in the form of income. It is also commonly labeled *maintenance* or *spousal support*. However, for simplicity's sake, we have chosen to use the word *alimony* in this book. This chapter focuses on when and how alimony is awarded, either through a negotiated settlement or court order.

Societal views about alimony have changed significantly over the years due to the changed legal and economic status of women. Legislatures and courts have consequently struggled to shape relevant legal principles to meet modern day needs. Although relatively little data exists, researchers estimate that some form of alimony is awarded in about 20 percent of divorces. *See* Thomas Oldham, *Changes in the Economic Consequences of Divorces, 1958-2008*, 42 Fam. L.Q. 419, 429 (2008); ALI, *Principles of the Law of Family Dissolution* §5.04 cmt. a (2001).

The current law with respect to alimony has deep historical roots stretching back for centuries. Three historical "customs" have particularly shaped modern doctrine, and the chapter begins with an explanation of these. The first is the custom of the bride's family providing gifts to a husband to protect the future wife upon marriage. The second is the Unity Doctrine, and the third is the need for finding fault before a legal support obligation is considered.

HISTORY

11.2. Dowry

The Anglo-Saxon custom of transferring a wife's property to her husband upon marriage probably began around A.D. 800. When a couple married, the bride's parents and relatives gave a husband all her property (her dowry) in return for his promise of care and protection. This early custom was apparently absorbed into the canon law and later found its way in part into English and American common law.

11.3. Unity Doctrine

Another significant factor in the development of modern alimony is the Unity Doctrine, which arose from the early theological teachings of the Church that when a couple married, they became one person. As noted earlier, once a couple married, the wife's person was merged into the husband. The concept took many forms, and its effects were numerous. For example, because one could not sue one's self, neither married partner could sue the other, and a husband was responsible for defending his wife against any third-party actions involving her interests. It was not until the late 1800s, when Married Women's Acts were passed in most jurisdictions, that the law began to change.

11.4. Assignment of Fault

A third factor affecting how alimony was viewed is fault, which is linked to the early Church's teaching that marriage is indissoluble and divorce is a mortal sin. Although the Church banned absolute divorce, it created alternatives when faced with the practical problem of married couples who wanted to live apart. One option was to annul the marriage, a *divorce a vinculo*, thus avoiding a divorce and permitting remarriage. Another canonical option was a divorce from bed and board (*a mensa et thoro*). Under this early separation scheme, a couple could separate and live apart from each other without obtaining an absolute divorce. However, a separation was granted only if a wife could provide a good reason for living apart from her husband. The policy of the law, as administered by the English Ecclesiastical courts, looked toward a reconciliation of the parties and preservation of the marriage relation; therefore, the allowance was for the reasonable support of the wife only. The courts sometimes sought to do justice by increasing the allowance in cases where the property originally came from the wife; however, the alimony still remained based on the wife's reasonable support during the separation.

11.5. Fault Adopted by Secular Systems

The ancient Ecclesiastical fault concept was incorporated into the judicial thinking of most early secular family law in the United States. Divorce was a remedy available only to an innocent party who had been "wronged" by a guilty party. It was believed appropriate to punish a wife whose behavior constituted grounds for divorce by either denying alimony altogether or awarding a much smaller sum than she might otherwise receive. The law reasoned that by her wrongful misconduct, she had forfeited any claim to her husband's financial protection.

Conversely, a husband whose marital fault was serious may have had to pay additional alimony either as compensation to the wife for the wrongs done to her or as a means of punishing the husband who was at fault. Alimony awards reflected the judiciary's perceptions of public morality, and the sanctions were considered appropriate when a citizen breached the community's acceptable moral standards.

11.6. Common Law Disabilities and Duties

At common law, a woman entering marriage faced severe legal disabilities. The husband and wife were considered one person, and that one person was the husband. Once married, all of a wife's personal property came under the husband's control, and she had no legal right to her husband's real property.

Under the common law, a husband was under a duty to maintain his wife in accordance with his means; however, there was no corresponding duty placed on a wife. *See Cruickshank-Wallace v. County Banking and Trust Co.*, 885 A.2d 403 (Md. App. 2005). A husband was obligated to provide a suitable home and necessaries such as food and clothing.

A wife was normally not entitled to alimony in a separate home, absent good reason to live apart from her husband. A husband did not have a duty to maintain his wife if she deserted the marriage, although the duty was revived if she returned. If she committed adultery, which the husband did not condone or which had not been contrived, his duty of support normally ceased.

If a wife was living apart from her husband because of his desertion or misconduct, she was entitled to support, as long as she was free from misconduct herself. If a husband failed to provide for her, she could pledge his credit for necessaries that were suitable given their lifestyle prior to the separation. *See* Brenda M. Hoggett & David S. Peal, *The Family Law and Society, Cases and Materials* 81 (Butterworths 1983).

During the nineteenth century, the common law in the United States in jurisdictions that permitted a divorce recognized the unfairness of leaving a wife in near poverty following a divorce or legal separation. Courts began to require that an ex-husband provide support—sometimes by returning all or a portion of the wife's dowry and at other times by requiring that he provide her with a portion of his personal property. The common law reasoned that the award was supported by public policy, which declared that it was the duty of the husband to support his wife for life.

The common law limited a husband's support obligation and imposed no reciprocal support duty on the wife. While requiring the husband to support the ex-wife, that law did not necessarily require that he make periodic alimony payments or provide funds from his income. Divorces were, of course, rare and effectively discouraged by most religious institutions.

11.7. Alimony for Husbands

The lingering impact of the historical view that, should there be a divorce, a wife owed no reciprocal duty to support a husband continued in this country until the Supreme Court decided Orr v. Orr, 440 U.S. 268 (1979). The Court invalidated an Alabama statute that imposed alimony obligations on husbands but not on wives. The Court observed that because the statute provided that different treatment be accorded persons on the basis of sex, it established a classification subject to strict scrutiny under the Equal Protection Clause of the Fourteenth Amendment. To withstand such scrutiny, gender classifications must serve important governmental objectives and must be substantially related to achievement of those objectives. *Califano v. Webster*, 430 U.S. 313, 316-317 (1977).

Alabama argued that its interests included providing help for needy spouses and claimed that the statute used sex as a proxy for need. It also argued that the statute was intended to compensate women for past discrimination during marriage, which had left them unprepared to fend for themselves in the working world following divorce. These arguments did not persuade the Court. Though conceding that they were legitimate governmental objectives, the Court ruled that the statute was not "substantially" related to the achievement of those objectives. Orr, 440 U.S. at 286. It observed that even if gender were a reliable proxy for need, and even if the institution of marriage did discriminate against women, the state did not adequately justify the salient features of the statutory scheme.

The Court also observed that under the statute, individualized hearings at which the parties' relative financial circumstances are considered were already occurring, and therefore, no reason existed to use sex as a proxy for need. It reasoned that needy males could be helped along with needy females with little, if any, additional burden on the state. *But see In re Miltenberger Estate,* 737 N.W.2d 513 (Mich. App. 2007) (dower statutes were substantially related to an important governmental objective of cushioning the financial impact of spousal loss on the party disproportionately burdened by the loss and do not violate equal protection).

THE NECESSARIES DOCTRINE

11.8. Husband's Common Law Duty

At common law, it was the duty of the husband to provide for a wife's necessaries. In return, a wife was obliged to provide domestic services that pertained to the comfort, care, and well-being of her family and consortium to her husband. *See Ritchie v. White,* 35 S.E.2d 414, 416-417 (N.C. 1945).

As observed earlier, when a woman married, the common law took the view that she forfeited her legal existence and became the property of her husband, and her services and earnings belonged to him. *Cheshire Medical Center v. Holbrook,* 663 A.2d 1344 (N.H. 1995). Because the wife could not contract for food, clothing, or medical needs, her husband was obligated to provide her with such "necessaries," and if the husband failed to do so, the doctrine of necessaries made him legally liable for essential goods or services provided to her by third parties. Most courts viewed the husband's duty as arising from the fact of the marriage, not from any express undertaking on his part. The duty also rested on a recognition of the traditional status of the husband as the financial provider of the family's needs.

Passage of married women's acts around the close of the nineteenth century gave women additional rights, including that a married woman could carry on a trade or business and keep the earnings as her separate property. *Gaver v. Harrant,* 557 A.2d 210 (Md. 1989). The acts also provided that real and personal property brought into marriage by a woman remained her separate property after the marriage. The statutes were at first construed in a strained and grudging fashion. *See generally Condore v. Prince George's Co.,* 425 A.2d 1011 (Md. 1981).

11.9. Gender-Neutral Application

Most jurisdictions that have considered the issue of necessaries in the last three decades have held that the doctrine should be applied in a gender-neutral fashion. *See, e.g., Nicholson v. Hugh Chatham Memorial Hosp.*, 266 S.E.2d 818, 823 (N.C. 1980); *Jersey Shore Med. Ctr.–Fitkin Hosp. v. Baum's Estate*, 417 A.2d 1003, 1009 (N.J. 1980). In the alternative, some states have eliminated it altogether. *See, e.g., Condore v. Prince George's County*, 425 A.2d 1011, 1019 (Md. 1981).

All agree that the old notion that it is the man's primary responsibility to provide a home and its essentials is no longer justified. A female is also no longer destined solely for the home and the rearing of the family, and the male only for the marketplace and the world of ideas. *Orr, supra; Stanton v. Stanton*, 421 U.S. 7, 14-15 (1975). The traditional formulation of the necessaries doctrine, predicated on anachronistic assumptions about marital relations and female dependence, cannot withstand scrutiny under the compelling interest standard. *See Cheshire Med. Ctr. v. Holbrook*, 663 A.2d 1344 (N.H. 1995).

Example 11-1

Assume the years are 1830 and 2010 and that a husband and wife live in a jurisdiction that recognizes the necessaries doctrine. Assume that the husband is admitted to the hospital and that the wife signs a form authorizing medical treatment for him. However, the wife refuses to sign a form that guarantees payment for the medical treatment. Assume that the husband recovers and that the hospital seeks payment of the expenses from the wife. The wife replies that the doctrine of necessaries is limited to a husband providing for a wife. Furthermore, she claims that medical expenses are not encompassed within the doctrine. How would a court most likely rule in 1830? In 2010?

Explanation

Until recently, the wife's argument would have been sustained. Under the common law, the wife was usually dependent on her husband for financial support. However, a majority of jurisdictions have either abolished the doctrine or replaced it with one that makes both spouses equally liable for necessaries. Furthermore, medical expenses are viewed in most jurisdictions that retain the necessaries doctrine as encompassed within it. When both parties are viewed as liable for necessaries, in the absence of an agreement by a spouse to undertake a debt, the creditors may be required to seek initial redress from the spouse incurring the debt, and only if those assets are insufficient may the creditors then reach the other spouse's assets. In this example, therefore, the creditors would most likely be required to initially pursue their claim with the husband. If the husband failed to satisfy the debt, the wife would be liable.

UNIFORM ACTS

11.10. The Uniform Marriage and Divorce Act

During the 1970s, many states adopted all or a portion of the Uniform Marriage and Divorce Act (UMDA). The UMDA was originally ratified by the National Conference of Commissioners on Uniform State Laws in 1970, and after three additional drafts, the American Bar Association endorsed it in 1974. The UMDA was remarkable because it departed from awarding maintenance based on fault when a marriage relationship ended. For example, the commentary to section 308 of the Act reads in part, "Assuming that an award of maintenance is appropriate under subsection 308(a), the standards for setting the amount of the award are set forth in subsection 308(b). Here, as in Section 307, the court is expressly admonished not to consider the misconduct of a spouse during the marriage."

The UMDA also contained a provision regarding homemakers that has been adopted by statute in a majority of jurisdictions. The provision recognized the value of the contributions of a full-time homemaker to the marital partnership and upon divorce entitled the homemaker to share equitably with the wage-earning spouse in the marital property.

11.11. Standard for Determining Amount and Duration Under UMDA

The statutes in the various states provide criteria for judges to apply when determining whether a party is eligible for alimony, the amount to be awarded, and its duration. Considerable discretion is left with the judge in making the award. The Uniform Marriage and Divorce Act §308 (1970) contained a provision that has been adopted in whole or in part by many states:

> The maintenance order shall be in amounts and for periods of time the court deems just, without regard to marital misconduct, and after considering all relevant factors including: (1) the financial resources of the party seeking maintenance, including marital property apportioned to him, his ability to meet his needs independently, and the extent to which a provision for support of a child living with the party includes a sum for that party as custodian; (2) the time necessary to acquire sufficient education or training to enable the party seeking maintenance to find appropriate employment; (3) the standard of living established during the marriage; (4) the duration of the marriage; (5) the age and the physical and emotional condition of the spouse seeking

maintenance; and (6) the ability of the spouse from whom maintenance is sought to meet his needs while meeting those of the spouse seeking maintenance.

11.12. American Law Institute Standards

The American Law Institute (ALI) has proposed a "loss compensation" theory to use when alimony is to be considered. ALI, *Principles of the Law of Family Dissolution: Analysis and Recommendations* §5.05 (2002). Under this theory, one spouse makes compensatory spousal payments to the other spouse for certain losses that have been experienced by the second spouse. The ALI suggests that compensable losses include the loss of a standard of living and a loss incurred because the one spouse was primarily responsible for child care during the marriage. Under the ALI proposal, a spouse would be entitled at dissolution to compensation for the earning-capacity loss arising from his or her disproportionate share, during marriage, of the care of the marital children, or of the children of either spouse.

For example, assume that H and W were married for 20 years and that during that time their relationship was "traditional" in the sense that H worked at developing a business while W remained at home caring for their three children. If W proves that she provided a disproportionate share of the parental child care, the ALI proposal would create an inference that child care responsibilities adversely affected her earning capacity.

The ALI proposal states that a presumption of entitlement to compensation is rebutted by evidence that the claimant did not provide a disproportionate share of the parental child care; however, "the inference that child-care responsibilities adversely affected the claimant's earning capacity is not rebuttable. The reasons are partly pragmatic, and arise from the difficulty of establishing what an individual's earning capacity would have been had the individual made different life choices years earlier." *Id.*

A spouse would also be entitled at dissolution to compensation for earning-capacity losses arising from the care provided during marriage to a sick, elderly, or disabled third party, in fulfillment of a moral obligation of the other spouse or of both spouses jointly. An award is allowed only to a claimant whose earning capacity at divorce is substantially less than that of the other spouse. ALI, *Principles of the Law of Family Dissolution: Analysis and Recommendations* §5.11(1). For example, assume that H and W were married for 25 years before their marriage broke down. Also assume that H's mother M lived with H and W during the last five years of the marriage. In the twenty-first year of H and W's marriage, M was diagnosed with cancer but continued to live with H and W. W left her part-time employment to care for M at home. After a three-year struggle with cancer, M died. A year later,

H and W filed to dissolve their marriage. The ALI would view the care for M as H's moral obligation and, during their marriage, the shared moral obligation of both H and W. As a consequence, W would be entitled to dissolution compensation for earning-capacity losses arising during her care of M.

STATE GROUNDS AND STANDARDS FOR DETERMINING NEED FOR ALIMONY

11.13. Fault

Although no-fault divorce grounds are recognized in almost all states, approximately half of jurisdictions may consider marital fault when awarding alimony. Linda D. Elrod & Robert Spector, *A Review of the Year in Family Law 2007-2008: Federalization and Nationalization Continue*, 42 Fam. L.Q. 713, 757 (2009). Some states treat fault as one factor among several when considering whether to award alimony. *See Patterson v. Patterson*, 917 So. 2d 111 (Miss. App. 2005). Some preclude an award of alimony to a spouse who has been at fault. *See Brown v. Brown*, 665 S.E.2d 174 (S.C. App. 2008) (wife who committed adultery barred from receipt of alimony); *Washington v. Washington*, 846 So. 2d 895 (La. App. 2003); *Congdon v. Congdon*, 578 S.E.2d 833 (Va. 2003) (whether denial of alimony would result in manifest injustice is based on the parties' economic circumstances and their fault). But *see Mani v. Mani*, 869 A.2d 904 (N.J. 2005) (fault relevant only if it has affected the parties' economic life or where it "so violates societal norms that continuing the economic bonds between the parties would confound notions of simple justice").

A court in a jurisdiction that permits consideration of fault in awarding alimony is faced with the question of what type of conduct constitutes "fault." Although the standard varies, generally, to constitute legal fault, misconduct must be of a serious nature and must be an independent contributory or proximate cause of the separation. Such acts are often viewed as synonymous with the fault grounds that previously entitled a spouse to a separation or divorce and may include adultery, conviction of a felony, habitual intemperance or excesses, cruel treatment or outrages, public defamation, abandonment, an attempt on the other's life, status as a fugitive, and intentional nonsupport. Mutual incompatibility and general unhappiness with the marital relationship are generally not viewed as lawful causes for leaving the family home. Lawful cause sufficient to justify a spouse's departure from the marital domicile is equivalent to grounds for alimony.

Example 11-2

Assume P and D are divorcing after 18 years of marriage. D has been violent with P throughout the marriage, and D has been convicted of a domestic violence-related felony. Because of D's alcoholism and other personality problems, D is not self-supporting and would qualify for an alimony award under the alimony statute. However, the state where P and D reside also has a statute creating a rebuttable presumption against an award of spousal support to an abusive spouse. P claims that D is precluded from receiving alimony, but D argues that D will be destitute without it. What is the likely result?

Explanation

This example is based on the somewhat similar case of *In re Marriage of Cauley*, 41 Cal. Rptr. 3d 902 (Cal. App. 2006), where the court considered the effect of such a rebuttable presumption statute and held that D was precluded from receiving alimony under it. *But see In re Peirano*, 930 A.2d 1165, 1173 (N.H. 2007) (alimony awarded to husband guilty of domestic violence where fault is one factor in awarding alimony).

11.14. Two-Step Process to Determine Eligibility

A two-step process is usually used to determine whether alimony should be awarded. The first step involves an assessment of the ability of the parties to provide alimony and their need for such support. Once this threshold is met, the second step is to calculate an amount of alimony to be awarded, if any, and its duration.

Step 1 — Financial ability. Typically, a court must find that a party seeking alimony lacks sufficient property to provide for his or her reasonable needs and is unable to be self-supporting through appropriate employment. Appropriate employment usually means employment that is suited to the individual and employment that reflects the expectations and intentions established during the marriage. *See, e.g., In re Marriage of Olar*, 747 P.2d 676, 681-682 (Colo. 1987). The "reasonable needs and unable to support" criteria tend to be interpreted somewhat broadly. *Id.* at 681.

Step 2 — Amount and duration of alimony. Once it is determined that some alimony should be awarded, the next step is to establish the amount and duration. Most jurisdictions have created statutes that contain factors a court is to consider when setting the amount and length of an award. The following is a typical list:

- A spouse's capacities and abilities
- Business opportunities
- Education
- Relative physical conditions
- Relative financial conditions and obligations
- Disparity of ages
- Sizes of separate estates
- Nature of the property
- Disparity in earning capacities or income.
- Duration of marriage

As noted earlier, courts may consider marital fault in addition to whether one of the parties to the marriage has wasted community assets. The fact that a particular state statute may contain as many as en "non-fault" factors, and the fact that each factor on the list is considered nonexclusive, provides a court with broad discretion in making its ultimate determination.

Most courts view the duration of the marriage as particularly important because it is often the major factor creating the disparity in the parties' earning capacities. This is especially true in cases involving a homemaker spouse. Regardless of the spouses' respective roles, duration provides a benchmark for determining reasonable needs — the longer the marriage, the more precisely reasonable needs can be measured by the standard of living established during the marriage.

In addition to the length of the marriage, another critical factor is the role the recipient spouse played during the marriage and the income that spouse is likely to achieve in relation to the standard of living set during the marriage. The latter factor, in turn, is closely related to the recipient spouse's age, health, child care duties, and access to income-producing assets. Depending on the facts of a particular case, it may be appropriate for a court to award permanent maintenance in short-term marriages — those less than 10 to 15 years. *See Greene v. Greene*, 895 So. 2d 503 (Fl. Ct. App. 2005) (15-year marriage is a "grey area").

FORMS AND DURATION OF ALIMONY

11.15. Rehabilitative Alimony

Rehabilitative alimony is commonly viewed as a short-term award, which is ordered to enable the former spouse to complete the preparation necessary for economic self-sufficiency. It usually ceases when the dependent spouse is in a position of self-support.

Rehabilitative alimony may be appropriate if, for example, a spouse gave up or postponed her own education to support the household during the marriage and requires a lump-sum or a short-term award to achieve economic self-sufficiency. Its purpose is to enhance and improve the earning capacity of the economically dependent spouse. Its focus is on the ability of a dependent spouse to engage in gainful employment, combined with the length of the marriage, the age of the parties, and the spouse's ability to regain a place in the workforce.

11.16. Reimbursement Alimony

Reimbursement alimony is sometimes characterized as "not truly support but an equitable creation designed to eliminate injustice." Frank Louis, *Limited Duration Alimony*, 11 N.J. Fam. Law. 133, 137 (1991). It is intended to compensate a spouse who has made financial sacrifices, resulting in that spouse's reduced standard of living, in order to enable the other spouse to forgo gainful employment while securing an advanced degree or professional license to enhance the parties' future standard of living. Reimbursement alimony is usually limited to monetary contributions made with the mutual and shared expectation that both parties to the marriage would derive increased income and material benefits. Some have questioned whether reimbursement alimony is truly alimony, given that it is based primarily on past contributions rather than future needs.

11.17. Limited Durational Alimony

The focus of limited durational alimony is distinctly different from rehabilitative or reimbursement alimony. Limited durational alimony is not intended to facilitate the earning capacity of a dependent spouse or to make a sacrificing spouse whole. Instead, it is appropriate when an economic need for alimony is established, but the marriage was of short duration, and permanent alimony is therefore not appropriate. *See Gordon v. Rozenwald*, 880 A.2d 1157 (N.J. Super. A.D. 2005) (limited duration alimony appropriate for marriage of short duration). Those circumstances stand in sharp contrast to marriages of long duration in which economic need is also demonstrated. With respect to shorter marriages, limited durational alimony provides an equitable and proper remedy. However, in cases involving longer marriages, permanent alimony is appropriate, and an award of limited durational alimony is clearly circumscribed, by equitable considerations and often by statute.

An award of limited durational alimony should reflect the underlying policy considerations that distinguish it from rehabilitative and reimbursement alimony. Limited durational alimony is conceptually more closely related to permanent alimony than to rehabilitative or reimbursement alimony. The latter two types of alimony represent forms of limited spousal support for specified purposes; once the purpose is achieved, entitlement to that form of alimony ceases. Permanent and limited durational alimony, by contrast, reflect a policy of recognizing that marriage is an adaptive economic and social partnership, and an award of either validates that principle.

11.18. Incapacity Alimony

This is alimony that is granted when a court finds a spouse to be physically or mentally incapacitated to the extent that the ability of the incapacitated spouse to support himself or herself is materially affected. *See Ferro v. Ferro,* 796 N.Y.2d 165 (N.Y.A.D. 2005) (disability must prevent spouse from earning a living). Permanent awards are more likely in longer-term marriages where the recipient suffers from a disability or health concern. *See Brooks v. Brooks,* 257 S.W.3d 418 (Tex. App. 2008) (spousal maintenance award to wife of 30 years with "incapacitating" disability); *Stewart v. Stewart.* 152 P.3d 544 (Idaho 2007) (award to wife of 25 years with degenerative illness).

11.19. Caregiver Alimony

This is alimony that is granted when a court finds that a spouse must forgo employment to care for a child with a physical or mental incapacity. *See Marriage of Snow v. England,* 862 N.E.2d 664 (Ind. 2007) (Indiana courts may order incapacity, caregiver, or rehabilitation maintenance only under conditions specified by statute).

11.20. Permanent Alimony

Courts are most likely to award permanent alimony at the end of a long-term marriage, particularly where there will be a disparity in income after divorce. Unfortunately, there is no precise point at which a marriage is defined as long-term. In general, awards of permanent alimony may be made in marriages of more than 10 to 15 years. *See* Joan M. Krauskopf, *supra*, at 586, 579-580 (1988) (citing trend upholding permanent maintenance awards in cases involving marriages of 15 to 20 years); Marsha Garrison, *How Do Judges Decide Divorce Cases?*, 74 N.C. L. Rev. 401, 467 (1996) (spousal income and marital duration as predictors of alimony awards).

There are two commonly expressed rationales for making an award of permanent alimony in traditional long-term marriages. The first is to compensate the recipient spouse for benefits conferred on the other spouse by being responsible for homemaking and child rearing. The primary benefit conferred on the other spouse is increased earning capacity because, while enjoying family life, he or she was free to devote all productive time to income activity outside the home. The second rationale is to compensate for the lost opportunity costs associated with homemaking. Earning capacity may be reduced either by not being employed outside the home or by holding employment subject to the needs of the family. Courts recognize this lost opportunity cost when they refer to the fact that a claimant for alimony remained in the home in the traditional role of full-time homemaker during the marriage. *See In re Marriage of Olson*, 705 N.W.2d 312 (Iowa 2005) (long-term homemaker with health problems entitled to "traditional alimony" for life or as long as incapable of self-support). A transfer of earning power occurs during a traditional marriage in which the homemaker spouse's efforts have increased the other's earning capacity at the expense of the homemaker. Alimony is an award formulated to compensate for that transfer by sufficiently meeting reasonable needs for support not otherwise met by property division and personal income. *See* Joan M. Krauskopf, *Rehabilitative Alimony: Uses and Abuses of Limited Duration Alimony*, 21 Fam. L.Q. 573 (1988).

Example 11-3

Assume that P and D were married for 30 years before their marriage ended in divorce. P is 50, and D is 48, and both are in good health. During the marriage, P managed the household and was the primary caretaker for the three children. The youngest of the three children was emancipated one year before the divorce action was initiated. Testimony at trial indicates that P is a high school graduate with limited employment prospects. An expert testified that P could earn from $18,000 to $24,000 annually. D has worked outside the home for the last 25 years as an assembly line worker in a car factory. D has gross annual income of approximately $58,000. P's lawyer has asked the trial judge to award P permanent alimony. D's lawyer argues that D should pay nothing or that the court should award rehabilitative or durational alimony. What will P's lawyer argue, and how will a court most likely decide the alimony issue?

Explanation

P's lawyer may concede that rehabilitative and limited durational maintenance awards are intended to assist a recipient spouse in becoming self-
supporting but will contend they are not appropriate in this case. P's lawyer
may argue that this is a long-term marriage and that alimony serves to
compensate a homemaker for contributions to family well-being not
otherwise recognized in the property distribution.

P's lawyer may also argue that the compensatory aspect of alimony
reflects the reality that when one spouse stays home and raises the children,
not only does that spouse lose future earning capacity by not being
employed, but that spouse also increases the future earning capacity of
the working spouse. In addition, the working spouse, while enjoying family
life, is free to devote productive time to career enhancement. When determining the extent of the compensatory component of an alimony award, a
court should give particular consideration to the role of the recipient spouse
during the marriage and to the length of the marriage. It is likely that
permanent maintenance will be awarded to P.

Example 11-4

Assume that P and D live in a jurisdiction with a statute that allows an award
of alimony, either rehabilitative or permanent, to a spouse where the court
finds that (1) the spouse lacks sufficient income and/or property to provide
for his or her reasonable needs and (2) the spouse is unable to support
himself or herself through appropriate employment at the standard of living
established during the marriage. The alimony must be in the amount and for
the duration the court deems just, based on the consideration of seven
nonexclusive factors. Part of the purpose of the statute is to provide spousal
support in relation to the standard of living established during the marriage.
Another purpose is to recompense a homemaker for contributions made
during the marriage.

Also assume that P and D had been married for ten years when their
marriage ended. At the time of the divorce, there were no children. P is
55 years old, had back problems for which she received disability benefits,
and has not worked outside the home for many years. During the marriage,
P helped D obtain a college degree by mail, particularly by typing papers.
At the time of the separation, P had an independent income of $670 per
month, the bulk of which came from the disability payment. Despite receipt
of disability benefits, P is capable of working and earning an income of
approximately $800 per month. Her monthly living expenses are about
$1,000 per month, including mortgage payments on her home. D's gross
income from his work is $45,000 per year and is expected to increase in the
future. D's monthly living expenses at the time of the divorce hearing were

about $1,800 per month. What are the likely prospects of P being awarded permanent alimony?

Explanation

In addition to the length of the marriage, the critical factors in determining the duration of an alimony award are the role the recipient spouse played during the marriage and the income that spouse is likely to achieve in relation to the standard of living established during the marriage. The latter factor, in turn, is closely related to the recipient spouse's age, health, child care duties, and access to income-producing assets. Although P is capable of employment, she is 55 years of age and has not worked outside the home for many years. Furthermore, she has a back problem for which she receives the disability payments. In addition, P was the homemaker, and she supported D's efforts to obtain a degree, which has allowed him to obtain the earning capacity he now enjoys. A permanent alimony award is probably necessary to keep P in the standard of living established during the marriage.

OTHER ISSUES REGARDING ALIMONY

11.21. Percentage Formulas

In general, courts have not favored the use of formulas for determining alimony awards. *See, e.g., Kunkle v. Kunkle*, 554 N.E.2d 83, 89-90 (Ohio 1990) (citing cases in other jurisdictions). Particularly disfavored are awards requiring one spouse to pay a percentage of gross or net income to the other spouse. *See, e.g., McClung v. McClung*, 465 So. 2d 637, 638 (Fla. Dist. Ct. App. 1985) (reversing award requiring husband to pay 50% of combined net incomes of parties); *Bourassa v. Bourassa*, 481 N.W.2d 113, 115 (Minn. App. 1992) (disallowing award requiring husband to pay 40% of his gross monthly income to wife); *Kunkle*, 554 N.E.2d at 88-90 (overturning award requiring husband to pay wife one-third of his gross earned income). When percentage awards are allowed, the cases often involve unusual circumstances. *See, e.g., Hefty v. Hefty*, 493 N.W.2d 33, 36 (Wis. 1992) (considering fluctuation of husband's bonus income, court properly awarded wife fixed monthly sum plus 20% of any bonus pay).

11.22. Alimony Guidelines

Unlike child support, alimony awards are based in large part on court discretion. This makes awards difficult to predict and results in potentially different outcomes for similarly situated couples. Because of such concerns, a few jurisdictions have begun to experiment with adoption of alimony guidelines. *See* Twila B. Larkin, *Guidelines for Alimony: The New Mexico Experiment,* 38 Fam. L.Q. 29 (2004); *Cullum v. Cullum,* 160 P.3d 231 (Ariz. App. 2007).

11.23. Life Insurance

Some courts have held that requiring the obligor to provide security, such as life insurance, to the recipient against the risk of the obligor's death violates the rule that the obligation to pay alimony normally ends with the obligor's death. *See, e.g., Eagan v. Eagan,* 392 So. 2d 988 (Fla. Dist. Ct. App. 1981); *Perkins v. Perkins,* 310 So. 2d 438 (Fla. Dist. Ct. App. 1975); *Putnam v. Putnam,* 154 So. 2d 717 (Fla. Dist. Ct. App. 1963). But cf. *Stith v. Stith,* 384 So. 2d 317 (Fla. Dist. Ct. App. 1980) (policies of life insurance may be awarded as lump-sum alimony).

11.24. Tax Treatment of Alimony

A payment to a spouse under a divorce or separation instrument is alimony if the spouses do not file a joint return and the payment meets both of two requirements. First, the payment must be based on the marital or family relationship; second, it must not be child support. In addition, the spouses must be separated and living apart for a payment under a separation agreement or court order to qualify as alimony.

For federal income tax purposes, alimony payments are included in the income of the payee and deductible from the income of the payor if, among other things, "there is no liability to make any such payment for any period after the death of the payee spouse and there is no liability to make any payment (in cash or property) as a substitute for such payments after the death of the payee spouse." 26 U.S.C.A. §§71(b)(1)(D), 215(b). As a result, in cases where a high-income payor pays alimony to a low-income recipient, some tax savings may result.

11.25. Alimony Distinguished from Property Division

Although alimony and property division are sometimes confused, alimony differs from property division in a variety of ways. First, alimony obligations cannot be discharged in bankruptcy, whereas some property obligations may be the object of discharge. Second, alimony is considered taxable income to the recipient and is deductible by the payor. Property settlements have no similar tax treatment. Third, alimony awards may be modified in the future, but property settlements are viewed as final. Fourth, alimony awards traditionally terminate upon the remarriage of the recipient, in contrast to property awards, which are not affected by remarriage. Finally, failure to pay alimony can be enforced by contempt proceedings, and enforcement of property awards generally occurs through traditional debtor-creditor remedies.

CHAPTER 12

Modification of Alimony

12.1. Introduction

This chapter examines the principles used by courts when considering whether to modify an existing alimony award. An award may generally be modified, even if it has been denominated as "permanent" in the decree, based on a substantial change in financial status or circumstances. Linda D. Elrod & Robert G. Spector, *A Review of the Year in Family Law: Redefining Families, Reforming Custody Jurisdiction, and Refining Support Issues*, 34 Fam. L.Q. 607, 618 (2001). The issue of modification typically arises in cases where the obligor's income has increased, the recipient's income has decreased, the recipient has remarried, or one of the parties has died.

When an alimony award is made, and a substantial change in circumstances later occurs in the life of either the obligor or the obligee, a court may be confronted with the question of whether to increase, decrease, or eliminate an alimony award or leave it untouched. What constitutes a change in circumstances is a factual inquiry that is said to rest within the trial court's discretion. In general, a trial court's modification decision will not be overturned on appeal absent an abuse of that discretion.

UNIFORM MARRIAGE AND DIVORCE ACT (UMDA)

12.2. UMDA's Unconscionability Standard

The Uniform Marriage and Divorce Act (UMDA) suggests that an existing spousal support award can be modified only if a change in circumstances has occurred that is so substantial and continuing as to make the terms of the original agreement unconscionable. UMDA §316(b) (1974). This standard has not gained widespread acceptance among the states, which appear to have adopted a less restrictive view.

12.3. State Standards

Courts and legislatures are not uniform in their approach; therefore, the particular standards of each jurisdiction must be examined to determine when modification is appropriate. For example, Colorado was greatly influenced by the UMDA and originally adopted a standard declaring that an award may be modified "only upon a showing of changed circumstances so substantial and continuing as to make the terms unconscionable." However, in 1986 it amended the statute by replacing "unconscionable" with "unfair." Colo. Rev. Stat. §14-10-122 (1986 Supp.). This made modifying an existing award less burdensome.

PRELIMINARY PROCEDURAL CONSIDERATIONS

12.4. Existing Order or Reservation of Jurisdiction

Courts can generally modify an alimony award only if there is an order currently in effect or if the court reserved subject matter jurisdiction over the issue at the time of the divorce. *See Midzak v. Midzak*, 697 N.W.2d 733 (S.D. 2005) (court expressly reserved jurisdiction); *Hartley v. Hartley*, 889 N.E.2d 1087 (Ohio App. 2008) (no "implied" reservation of jurisdiction). If a court did not award alimony in the original proceeding and failed to reserve jurisdiction, most courts hold that alimony cannot be awarded at a later date. Similarly, once an alimony order has expired, most courts hold that it cannot be reinstated or modified.

Example 12-1

Assume that P and D were divorced in 2005 and that D was ordered to pay alimony until November 30, 2009. D made the final alimony payment on October 15, 2009, approximately six weeks early. On October 30, 2009, P moved to modify the judgment, seeking a permanent alimony order. D moved for summary judgment on the grounds that the court no longer had jurisdiction over the issue of alimony because the order had been fully paid. P argued that D's voluntary early payment did not alter the due date and that the alimony order remained in effect because the final payment had not yet accrued. What is the likely result?

Explanation

This example is based on the situation in *In re Marriage of Harkins*, 115 P.3d 981 (Or. App. 2005), *review denied*, 136 P.3d 742 (2006). In that case, the court agreed with D and held that the court no longer had authority to modify the alimony award because payment had been made in full. Although some courts may take different view, a wise practitioner will advise his or her client to petition for modification well in advance of the termination of the alimony order.

12.5. Burden of Proof and Standard for Change

The party seeking modification normally bears the burden of proving that a change in circumstances has occurred — that is, that there have been changes in the needs of the recipient and in the financial abilities of the obligor. *In re Marriage of Logston*, 469 N.E.2d 167, 176 (Ill. 1984); *Rice v. Rice*, 528 N.E.2d 14, 15 (Ill. App. Ct. 1988). For example, a former spouse's otherwise unsupported assertion that inflation had affected her ability to support herself was not sufficient to warrant modification of an existing alimony award. *Hillier v. Iglesias*, 901 So. 2d 947 (Fla. App. 2005). However, a showing of inability to obtain health insurance was a substantial change in circumstances for purposes of modification. *Metz v. Metz*, 618 S.E.2d 477 (W. Va. 2005).

States differ concerning how substantial the change in circumstances must be in order to warrant modification. *See, e.g., Kamenski v. Kamenski*, 15 So.3d 842 (Fla. App. 2009) (change is material, permanent, and involuntary); *Tsai v. Tien*, 832 N.E.2d 809 (Ohio App. 2005) (change need not be substantial or drastic but must be more than a nominal change); *Metz v. Metz*, 618 S.E.2d 477 (W. Va. 2005) (substantial change in circumstances); *Withers v. Withers*, 390 So. 2d 453 (Fla. Dist. Ct. App. 1980), *cert. denied*, 399 So. 2d 1147 (Fla. 1981) (substantial change not contemplated at time of judgment); *Zan v. Zan*, 820 N.E.2d 1284 (Ind. App. 2005) (change so substantial and continuing that original terms are unreasonable); *Beard v. Beard*, 751 N.Y.S.2d 304 (App. Div. 2002) (current order creates an "extreme hardship").

12.6. "Bad Bargain" Not a Reason for Modification

Before a court may exercise its discretion to modify an alimony award, a change in circumstances existing at the time of the original decree must have occurred. As a general rule, the court is not to reflect on whether the decree was "equitable" when it was entered, but only on whether the economic circumstances of the parties have changed since the award such that the original award is now either insufficient or excessive. Most agree that it is not the role of trial courts to relieve a party of his or her bad bargain where the parties had agreed to an amount of alimony.

IMPACT OF AGREEMENTS ON SUBSEQUENT MOTIONS FOR MODIFICATION

12.7. Stipulations — Non-modification Agreements

Some potential obligors are reluctant to agree to pay time-limited alimony because of the potential for later modification extending the payments or making them permanent. Consequently, in settlement negotiations parties will sometimes agree that an alimony award cannot be later modified, even in the event of a substantial change in circumstances. In essence, the obligee waives the right to seek subsequent modification of the award.

Although courts have struggled with the issue of whether to enforce non-modification agreements, the UMDA strongly supports their approval and enforcement. Section 306(b) binds courts to agreements regarding alimony unless they are unconscionable. UMDA §306(f) states that "[e]xcept for terms concerning the support, custody, or visitation of children, the decree may expressly preclude or limit modification of terms set forth in the degree if the separation agreement so provides."

Courts usually enforce non-modification agreements, although they may review agreements for fraud, duress, or unconscionability. *See*

Maxwell v. Maxwell, 650 S.E.2d 680 (S.C. App. 2007) (alimony "non-modifiable and shall continue until the death of the Husband"); *In re Marriage of Waldren*, 171 P.3d 1214 (Ariz. 2007) (statute providing for non-modification agreements prevents court from exercising jurisdiction); *In re Marriage of Hulscher*, 180 P.3d 199 (Wash. App. 2008) (non-modifiability provision valid and enforceable). Enforcement rests on a freedom of contract theory, which, it is thought, will produce mutually acceptable accords, to which parties will voluntarily adhere. It also reflects a belief that the actual purpose behind any particular provision of a settlement agreement made by the parties may remain forever hidden from the trial judge.

OBLIGOR'S CHANGE IN CIRCUMSTANCES

12.8. Obligor's Unanticipated Increased Income

An unanticipated large increase in the obligor's income may constitute a substantial, material change in circumstances. However, if the increase does not make the original alimony award unfair, and the original award maintains the original standard of living, most jurisdictions will not grant an increase in alimony.

When assessing increases in the recipient's need for alimony, the trial court will usually consider both increases in the actual expenses of the recipient and changes in the recipient's nonsupport income. The trial court will balance the relative economic circumstances of both parties at the time of the request for modification against any increase in the recipient's earnings. The fact that the recipient's income has increased does not necessarily indicate that the recipient's long-term economic circumstances have been improved to such an extent that alimony is no longer required or should be reduced. A court, of course, should not speculate about the equities of the original award, but should confine its evaluation to increases in the recipient's needs since the divorce.

Example 12-2

Assume that P and D divorced after a 20-year marriage. At the time of the divorce, they were both unemployed; however, D was receiving $3,000 each month from a trust. The court ordered that D pay P $500 per month in permanent alimony. A year after the divorce, D obtained a position that paid $5,000 a month. P remained unemployed and moved to increase alimony to $1,000 a month. How will a court most likely treat the motion?

Explanation

P will argue that D's financial worth has increased substantially and that D can afford to pay additional alimony. P will explain that P cannot make ends meet on $500 per month and that P should be entitled to a standard of living more commensurate with that of the marriage. D will argue that P's needs haven't increased since the original alimony order was entered and that one of the purposes of divorce is to end the parties' financial interdependency. However, if P can clearly establish need, the court most likely will grant the request. See Irwin v. Irwin, 539 So. 2d 1177 (Fla. App. 1990).

12.9. Obligor's Retirement

When the retirement of an obligor is voluntary or foreseeable at the time of the divorce, several jurisdictions have denied a modification of alimony request. See Wheeler v. Wheeler, 548 N.W.2d 27 (N.D. 1996); Leslie v. Leslie, 827 S.W.2d 180, 183 (Mo. 1992); Ellis v. Ellis, 262 N.W.2d 265, 268 (Iowa 1978); Deegan v. Deegan, 603 A.2d 542 (N.J. Ct. App. 1992) (retirement should have been considered when parties originally divorced). Although most courts take the view that traditional standards regulating modification of support agreements should be applied to motivate parties to provide for such contingencies in their dissolution agreement, strict application of these standards in the retirement context can create unreasonable hardships. See, e.g., Sifers v. Sifers, 544 S.W.2d 269, 269-270 (Mo. Ct. App. 1976) (denying modification when obligor "voluntarily" retired, even though he was 62, had a malignant kidney removed, and was unable to find employment in the industry in which he had worked all his life). Courts have also said that at some point, parties must recognize that just as a married couple may expect a reduction in income because of retirement, a divorced spouse cannot expect to receive the same high level of support after the supporting spouse retires. See Silvan v. Sylvan, 632 A.2d 528 (N.J. Super. 1993) (concluding that a good faith retirement at age 65 may warrant a finding of changed circumstances); In re Marriage of Reynolds, 74 Cal. Rptr. 2d 636, 640 (Ct. App. 1998).

Courts caution that although bona fide retirement after a lifetime spent in the labor force is somewhat of an entitlement, an obligor cannot merely utter the word "retirement" and expect an automatic finding of a substantial and material change in circumstances. Rather, a court should examine the totality of the circumstances surrounding the retirement to ensure that it is objectively reasonable. In Ebach v. Ebach, 700 N.W.2d 684 (N.D. 2005), the court considered the following nonexclusive list of factors in determining the totality of the circumstances:

> A court may consider, for instance, the age gap between the parties; whether at the time of the initial [spousal support] award any attention was given by the parties to the possibility of future retirement; whether the particular retirement was mandatory or voluntary; whether the particular retirement occurred earlier than might have been anticipated at the time [spousal support] was awarded; and the financial impact of that retirement upon the respective financial positions of the parties. It should also assess the motivation which led to the decision to retire, i.e., was it reasonable under all the circumstances or motivated primarily by a desire to reduce the [spousal support] of a former spouse. A court may also wish to consider the degree of control retained by the parties over the disbursement of their retirement income, e.g., the ability to defer receipt of some or all. It may also wish to consider whether either spouse has transferred assets to others, thus reducing the amount available to meet their financial needs and obligations.

Id. at 689.

The burden of establishing that the retirement is objectively reasonable is on the party seeking modification of the award. *Seal v. Seal*, 802 S.W.2d 617, 620 (Tenn. Ct. App. 1990).

Example 12-3

Assume that P and D had been married for 25 years before they divorce. The court ordered that D pay P $1,500 a month permanent alimony. Following the divorce, P lived on the alimony payment plus a few hundred dollars she took from her IRA each month. The IRA had a value of about $50,000. At the time of the divorce, D was earning about $5,000 a month. When he reached age 60, D voluntarily retired because he was offered a retirement package that would guarantee him $2,000 per month for life. He was also suspicious that he would be laid off or fired, and he felt that coping with the boss was getting increasingly difficult. D now moves to reduce his alimony obligation. How will a court most likely treat D's motion?

Explanation

D may have a difficult time obtaining a reduction, even though D acted in good faith. P will argue that she has relied on the alimony and that early retirement should have been addressed at the time of divorce. A court may reduce the obligation if D has only the $2,000 to live on. Otherwise, the award may well stand. *See Deegan v. Deegan*, 603 A.2d 542 (N.J. App. 1992).

12.10. Obligor's Change of Occupation

Generally, when a party voluntarily assumes a lower-paying job, there will be no recomputation of the alimony payment. Courts have consistently ruled that obligors act in bad faith when they voluntarily leave steady employment without alternate plans for income or for positions that are less likely to provide sufficient income. *See Curtis v. Curtis*, 442 N.W.2d 173, 177-178 (Minn. Ct. App. 1989) (holding obligor acted in bad faith when he voluntarily left his employment of ten years without alternative employment plans); *Warwick v. Warwick*, 438 N.W.2d 673, 678 (Minn. Ct. App. 1989) (holding obligor acted in bad faith by resigning from his job, unjustifiably limiting his income); *Juelfs v. Juelfs*, 359 N.W.2d 667, 670 (Minn. Ct. App. 1984) (holding obligor acted in bad faith by voluntarily quitting longtime employment in favor of running business that had little chance of producing similar income).

A party ordinarily will not be relieved of an alimony obligation by voluntarily quitting work or by being fired for misconduct. When seeking a reduction in alimony payments because of a change in employment, the obligor must establish first that the voluntary change in employment, which resulted in a reduction of income, was not made for the purpose of avoiding alimony payments and, second, that a reduction in alimony is warranted based on the party's efforts to mitigate any income loss. In effect, the moving party must present evidence as to why he or she voluntarily left the prior employment and also as to why the acceptance of a lower-paying job was necessary. Otherwise, for calculation of a maintenance obligation, the moving party will be considered to have an income equal to his earning capacity.

Some courts may grant a temporary reduction or suspension in alimony when the obligor has suffered a reduction in income without deliberately seeking to avoid paying alimony and is acting in good faith to return his income to its previous level. However, a reduction in alimony will be denied when the moving party has not made a good-faith effort to obtain employment commensurate with his or her qualifications and experience. *See, e.g., Yepes v. Fichera*, 230 A.D.2d 803 (N.Y. App. Div. 1996).

An award of alimony may be based on the obligor's ability to work as distinguished from actual income. In some states, such as California, the court considers the spouse's ability to work, willingness to work, and opportunity to work. When ability and opportunity are present, and willingness is absent, the court has the discretion to apply the earnings capacity standard. Cf. *Pencovic v. Pencovic*, 287 P.2d 501 (Cal. 1955) (the earning capacity standard is properly used when the paying parent willfully refuses to seek or accept gainful employment).

A court is likely to reject the view that a finding of good faith prevents use of the earning-capacity standard. Although deliberate avoidance of family responsibilities is a significant factor in the decision to consider earning capacity, a trial court's consideration of earning capacity is not limited to cases in which a deliberate attempt to avoid support responsibilities is found. *See In re Marriage of Ilas*, 16 Cal. Rptr. 2d 345 (Cal. App. Dept. Super. Ct. 4 Dist. 1993).

Example 12-4

Assume that P and D divorced and that D was ordered to pay alimony to P based on D's employment as a computer hardware specialist earning $111,000 per year. D lost his job because of a reduction in work force, and one month later, he took a position as a massage therapist earning $300 per week (approximately $15,000 per year). D petitioned to reduce the alimony payment, arguing that the order should be based on his present lower income given that his change of position was involuntary. P argues that the alimony payment should be calculated based on the prevailing wage for computer service technicians because D elected to pursue a less lucrative career. What is the likely result?

Explanation

In the similar case of *Storey v. Storey*, 862 A.2d 551 (N.J. Super. 2004), the court imputed to D annual earnings of $60,000, the prevailing wage for a computer service technician. Although D's departure from his job was involuntary, the court held that because he had selected a less lucrative career, D had the burden of establishing that the resulting benefit to him substantially outweighed the disadvantages to P. The court found that D's decision was not reasonable under the circumstances.

Example 12-5

P and D's 15-year marriage was dissolved, and the court ordered D to pay $250 per month in alimony for 60 months. At the time of the dissolution, D was employed as a line technician earning about $24 per hour. He resigned from this position after about 18 years with the company. His resignation was precipitated by his failing a random drug test. A few months later, D also quit a second job because of a mutual disagreement with his employer. At D's request, the district court reduced his alimony obligation to $125 per month because he was now earning about half of what he had been earning at the time of the divorce. P appealed. How would an appellate court most likely treat the reduced alimony?

Explanation

As a general rule, a petition for modification will be denied if the change in financial condition is because of fault or voluntary wastage or dissipation of one's talents and assets. *See Grahovac v. Grahovac*, 680 N.W.2d 616 (Neb. App. 2004). It is undisputed that in this case, there has been a change in D's financial condition and that he is now earning approximately half as much as he once earned. However, the issue is whether the change was because of D's fault or voluntary wastage or dissipation of his talents and assets. Most courts would rule that the reduction in income was D's own fault and would not permit a modification on these facts. The appellate court would most likely reverse the trial court.

OBLIGEE'S CHANGE IN CIRCUMSTANCES

12.11. Obligee Takes a Job Outside the Home

Courts are sometimes asked to modify an alimony award when the obligee takes a job following a divorce. At least two factors are important in deciding the issue. First, was it foreseeable at the time of the divorce that the obligee would seek employment? Second, does the new job provide funds that will allow the obligee to live at the standard of living enjoyed during the marriage?

In *Block v. Block*, 717 N.Y.S.2d 24 (App. Div. 2000), the court rejected a modification request when the ex-wife procured employment before the expiration of durational alimony. The alimony award was scheduled to expire when the parties' youngest child entered kindergarten. The court observed that although the original order awarding alimony stated that it would be "difficult" for the wife to return to work before the parties' youngest child entered kindergarten, "that possibility was not ruled out, and it certainly was not an unforeseeable event that could not have been taken into account in setting the original award." *Id.* at 87. *See Matter of Hermans v. Hermans*, 547 N.E.2d 87 (N.Y. 1989) (particularized showing of facts concerning the personal and financial circumstances of the parties both at the time of the original divorce settlement and at the present time is required, and changes in the prevailing social and legal climate that may have occurred since the parties were divorced do not satisfy this standard); *Wheeler v. Wheeler*, 230 A.D.2d 844 (N.Y. App. Div. 1996) (court erred in terminating maintenance when obligee's earning potential increased as a result of her receiving a nursing degree when there was a substantial increase in the obligor's income between the time of the parties' divorce and the modification hearing).

TERMINATING ALIMONY

12.12. Remarriage

In most jurisdictions, alimony is automatically terminated upon remarriage, unless the parties' agreement or the divorce decree expressly provides that the flow of alimony is to remain unimpeded by the recipient spouse's remarriage. See Gibb v. Sepe, 690 N.W.2d 230 (N.D. 2004) (express agreement that alimony would continue after remarriage enforced). The theory is that remarriage is legally connected with need, and the link is broken because the new spouse has formed a legal relationship with another and has assumed a joint legal duty of support. See, e.g., Voyles v. Voyles, 644 P.2d 847 (Alaska 1982); Burr v. Burr, 353 N.W.2d 644 (Minn. Ct. App. 1984), Van Bloom v. Van Bloom, 246 N.W.2d 588 (Neb. 1976).

Some states, however, do not require automatic termination of an alimony award on remarriage of the recipient spouse. Instead, they hold that remarriage establishes a prima facie case for termination or reduction of the alimony payments. See, e.g., Oman v. Oman, 702 N.W.2d 11 (S.D. 2005); Keller v. O'Brien, 652 N.E.2d 589, 593 (Mass. 1995); Marquardt v. Marquardt, 396 N.W.2d 753, 754 (S.D. 1986). In these jurisdictions, the receiving spouse may continue to receive maintenance, but only in an extraordinary circumstance. See, e.g., In re Marriage of Gillilland, 487 N.W.2d 363, 366 (Iowa Ct. App. 1992) (extraordinary circumstance found when standard of living provided by new spouse with annual income of $30,000 would not meet standard of living during previous marriage to husband who earned $220,000 annually); Bauer v. Bauer, 356 N.W.2d 897, 898-899 (N.D. 1984) (extraordinary circumstance found when payor and recipient had large disparity in education and payor's unfulfilled agreement to pay for recipient's education was incorporated in original decree).

12.13. Recipient Cohabits

The majority rule regarding the effect of post-divorce cohabitation on alimony is that the right to receive alimony becomes subject to modification or termination only if the recipient spouse's need for the support decreases as a result of the cohabitation. See Gayet v. Gayet, 456 A.2d 102, 104 (N.J. 1983); Annotation, Divorced Woman's Subsequent Sexual Relations or Misconduct as Warranting, Alone or with Other Circumstances, Modification of Alimony Decree, 98 A.L.R.3d 453 (1980 & Supp. 1996). When there is a showing of financial dependence by the alimony recipient upon the third-party cohabitant, a court will likely reduce alimony. See Gayet, 456 A.2d at 104; Woodard v. Woodard, 696 N.W.2d 221 (Wis. App. 2005) (obligee benefited from cohabitant's income);

Miller v. Miller, 892 A.2d 175 (Vt. 2005) (cohabitation must improve financial circumstances enough to substantially reduce need for maintenance). Similarly, if alimony payments are used to benefit the cohabitant, most courts will reduce or eliminate them. See, e.g., In re Marriage of Tower, 780 P.2d 863, 866-867 (Wash. Ct. App. 1989). As stated by the New Jersey Supreme Court, "modification [of spousal support] for changed circumstances resulting from cohabitation [is warranted] only if one cohabitant supports or subsidizes the other under circumstances sufficient to entitle the supporting spouse to relief." Gayet, 456 A.2d at 104.

Of course, the amount of alimony that is reduced, if any, depends on a factual examination of the financial effects of the cohabitation on the recipient. See Ricketts, supra, at 154. Shared living arrangements, unaccompanied by evidence of a decrease in the actual financial needs of the recipient, are generally insufficient to call for alimony modification. See In re Marriage of Bross, 845 P.2d 728, 731-732 (Mont. 1993); Mitchell v. Mitchell, 418 A.2d 1140, 1143 (Me. 1980) (cohabitant's benefit from a recipient's expenditures on heating fuel, which would have a similar cost absent the shared living arrangements, does not show a decreased need for alimony). When a restriction regarding cohabitation is a part of a marital termination agreement, courts have tended to enforce the provision. See Bell v. Bell, 468 N.E.2d 849 (Mass. 1984).

Some jurisdictions, by statute or judicial decision, require elimination of alimony upon a showing of post-divorce cohabitation. See S.C. Code 1976 §20-3-150 (West 2005); Gayet, 456 A.2d at 103-104; Lucas v. Lucas, 592 S.E.2d 646 (interpreting statute providing for possible termination of alimony where a de facto marriage exists). Others have concluded that the mere fact of cohabitation is just a factor for the court to consider in the changed-circumstances assessment. See Alibrando v. Alibrando, 375 A.2d 9, 13-14 (D.C. 1977). See also Wallace v. Wallace, 12 So.3d 572 (Miss. App. 2009) (proof of cohabitation creates a presumption that a material change in circumstances has occurred; this presumption will shift the burden to the recipient spouse to come forward with evidence suggesting that there is no mutual support within his or her de facto marriage).

Example 12-6

Assume that P and D divorce after a traditional 20-year marriage. P is required to pay D $1,000 per month permanent alimony. Six months after the divorce is final, D moves in with X. P brings a motion to eliminate the alimony award, arguing that it is unfair to require him to pay alimony when his ex-wife and another man are living together much like husband and wife. P argues that cohabiting is so similar to remarriage that it terminates spousal support. D responds that X is not supporting her and has no legal obligation to do so. P also notes that there is not a provision in the final divorce decree that eliminates alimony should she move in with another person following divorce. How will the court most likely rule?

Explanation

The trend is to reject the argument that cohabitation alone can be the basis for terminating alimony. In determining the effect of post-divorce cohabitation on a recipient spouse's alimony entitlement, financial, rather than moral, aspects of the cohabitation should be the primary consideration.

In ruling on P's request, the trial court may consider what effect, if any, D's cohabitation with another person has had on D's financial circumstances. If X makes financial or other tangible contributions toward the living expenses of D, D's ability to support herself may be increased, her needs may be reduced, and the alimony award may in some cases be reduced accordingly; conversely, when the expenses of D are increased because of D's voluntary support of persons whom D is under no duty to support, a court may disregard those expenses to extent they are claimed by recipient as evidence of increased "need." Here, a court would have to conduct an evidentiary hearing to make these determinations. Only then could it make a sound decision. *See Gilman v. Gilman*, 956 P.2d 761 (Nev. 1998).

Example 12-7

At the time of divorce, P is awarded alimony "until P dies or remarries." Nine years after the divorce, P and her same-sex partner go through a marriage ceremony in a state that does not recognize same-sex marriages. D learns of the "marriage" and moves to terminate the alimony. What is the likely result?

Explanation

D will argue that P is married and that under the terms of the divorce decree, his obligation to make alimony payments is over. P will argue that since the state will not recognize her "marriage" to her same-sex partner, she is not legally married for the purpose of terminating the alimony payment. Based on the similar case of *In re Marriage of Bureta*, 164 P.3d 534 (Wash. App. 2007) the court would find that P is not legally married and would require D to continue making the payments. D could, however, alternatively argue that P's financial circumstances have changed as a result of the cohabitation.

Example 12-8

When P and D divorce, D agrees to pay alimony to P. The divorce decree provides that alimony is to terminate "upon cohabitation of the Wife with an unrelated male." A year after the divorce, D moves to terminate alimony payments based on his assertion that D and their children were living in a "commune" with another family. What is the likely result?

Explanation

In a case such as this, the court is called upon to determine what constitutes "cohabitation." In the similar case of *Clark v. Clark*, 827 N.Y.S.2d 159 (2006), the court found that sharing a house with another family was not sufficient to establish cohabitation under the divorce decree, especially since P had a certificate of occupancy for an "accessory apartment" and was paying rent to the owner. Courts are called on to make factual determinations about the definition of "cohabitation" with increasing frequency. *See Semken v. Semken*, 664 S.E.2d 493 (S.C. App. 2008) (statute defines continued cohabitation as residence for at least 90 consecutive days); *Graev v. Graev*, 898 N.E.2d 909 (N.Y. 2008) (reviewing multiple definitions of "cohabitation").

12.14. Death

Obviously, the recipient's death ends the need for support. However, when a lump-sum alimony award has been ordered, it is viewed by some courts as vested in the obligee, and a spouse's estate may receive the payment. *See, e.g., Maxcy v. Estate of Maxcy*, 485 So. 2d 1077, 1078 (Miss. 1986). When the obligor dies, the maintenance obligation generally terminates, unless stated otherwise in the court order. *See Findley v. Findley*, 629 S.E.2d 222 (Ga. 2006) (death of obligor terminates obligation to pay alimony); *Haville v. Haville*, 825 N.E.2d 375 (Ind. 2005) (order may continue spousal maintenance beyond the death of the obligor).

12.15. Annulment of Recipient's Remarriage

States may by statute view an annulment of the alimony recipient's remarriage like a divorce and prohibit reinstatement of the terminated alimony obligation of the previous spouse. *See, e.g., Hodges v. Hodges*, 578 P.2d 1001, 1005 (Ariz. Ct. App. 1978); Ferdinand S. Tinio, *Annulment of Later Marriage as Reviving Prior Husband's Obligations Under Alimony Decree of Separation Agreement*, 45 A.L.R.3d 1033 (1972).

12.16. Retroactivity

Most jurisdictions take the view that orders modifying alimony agreements can be made retroactive only to the date of filing a modification motion. However, the rule is not applied when the filing was delayed because of a misrepresentation by another party, so long as the motion is filed in a timely fashion on discovery of the misrepresentation. *See, e.g., Albert v. Albert*, 707 A.2d 234 (Pa. Super. Ct. 1998); *In re Marriage of Elenewski*, 828 N.E.2d 895 (Ill. App. 2005).

Dividing the Marital Estate upon Divorce

13.1. Introduction

When couples divorce and cannot amicably agree on how their marital property is to be divided, and they reject mediation or some form of arbitration to resolve their differences, the only recourse is to litigate the matter in family court. This chapter surveys the law and illustrates the application of the more common legal principles used by family courts to resolve marital property disputes.

When valuing and distributing marital property, a family court has three tasks. First, it gathers and classifies all the couple's assets and identifies those that are martial property and those that are nonmarital property. The nonmarital property will usually remain the separate property of each party.

Once the couple's property is identified, the second step is to place a reasonable value on those marital assets that are subject to distribution and those assets that are the separate nonmarital property of each spouse. Finally, the family court makes a decision about what in its judgment constitutes an equitable distribution of the martial assets. The distribution is included in the final judgment.

SEPARATE PROPERTY SYSTEM THEORY

13.2. Overview

During the past century, courts have applied three general theories when dividing marital assets upon divorce. *See* Stephen J. Brake, *Equitable Distribution vs. Fixed Rules: Marital Property Reform and the Uniform Marital Property Act*, 23 B.C. L. Rev. 761, 762 (1982). The three distribution theories or "systems" are the now-outdated separate property system; the community property system, which is used today in about eight jurisdictions; and the equitable distribution system, which is used today by a majority of jurisdictions.

13.3. Title Was Once Controlling

The separate property distribution theory, which is no longer used, was based on the view that each party was entitled to retain an asset to which that party had title. Should a couple divorce, although a rare occurrence, the property was returned to the title-holding spouse.

The separate property theory was criticized as unjust, especially in a traditional family setting where most of the marital property was titled in the husband's name. The separate property system refused to recognize a homemaker's nonfinancial contributions to the marriage. For example, where both spouses worked outside the home and the husband's income was placed into investments while the wife's earnings were devoted to family expenses, upon divorce, the husband usually received all of the investments. A divorced homemaker who did not work outside the home was often left with only a claim for alimony, which may have proved difficult to enforce.

Example 13-1

Assume that P sought to divorce D after 20 years of marriage in a jurisdiction that applied the separate property theory of dividing marital assets. During the marriage, D worked inside the home caring for P and their five children. P worked outside the home. The marital assets consisted of a home, purchased a few years after the couple married with a down payment of $10,000 made by P, now valued at $200,000and the family automobile, worth $10,000. The home and car were titled in P's name. When D sought an equitable share of the home and car, how would a court in a title jurisdiction most likely rule?

Explanation

The answer is self-evident, and the problem is used to illustrate the harsh realities of the literal application of the separate property theory to a divorce. Here, a court would most likely award P the home and the automobile reasoning that title was only in P's name; therefore, it was P's separate property. Most likely, D would receive child support and possibly alimony.

COMMUNITY PROPERTY THEORY

13.4. Background

In a community property jurisdiction, property acquired during the marriage is community property, and property acquired prior to marriage is separate property. These two property rights are of equal importance. A basic tenet of community property law is that property acquires its character as community or separate depending upon the marriage status of its owner at the time of acquisition. *Lawson v. Ridgeway*, 233 P.2d 459 (Ariz. 1951). "Time of acquisition" refers to the time at which the right to obtain title occurs, not to the time when legal title actually is conveyed. *Hollingsworth v. Hicks*, 253 P.2d 724 (N.M. 1953). Once identified, the status of community or separate becomes fixed and retains that character until changed by agreement of the parties or by operation of law. *Horton v. Horton*, 278 P. 370 (Ariz. 1929).

The community property theory rests upon a system of co-ownership of assets between spouses during marriage. The concept came from continental Europe and found its way to the American territories governed by Spain and France. In general all property, with the exception of that acquired by gift, devise, or descent, is community property and is owned equally by the spouses for purposes of division in the event of divorce or the death of one spouse. When a marital community no longer exists, there can be no community property because there is no longer any common enterprise to which each spouse is contributing.

Arizona, California, Idaho, Louisiana, New Mexico, Nevada, Texas, and Washington are currently recognized as community property states. Wisconsin closely aligned itself with the community property theory when it adopted the Uniform Marital Property Act. The community property laws in these states are not necessarily uniform. *See* John G. Brant, *Colorado: Now A Community Property State?*, Colo. Law., 55 (May 1996).

13.5. Marriage Is a Partnership

Jurisdictions that adhere to a community property theory of distributing assets upon divorce accept the view that a marriage is a partnership, and the partnership concept applies during the marriage as well as upon dissolution of the marriage. The theory behind such division is that in disposing of the property, a divorce should be treated much like the dissolution of a business partnership. "Regardless of the economic circumstances of business partners or of their moral conduct during the existence of the partnership, on dissolution the partners receive a portion of the assets commensurate with their respective partnership interests." In re Marriage of Brigden, 145 Cal. Rptr. 716, 723 (Cal. App. 1978).

As noted earlier in this chapter, in general, both spouses are vested in all of the property acquired during the marriage, other than property that by statute is specifically excluded from the community, such as a gift to one partner but not the other, or an inheritance to one partner but not the other. There are, of course, some limitations on the partnership theory in community property jurisdictions. For example, Arizona holds that a residence that is separate property does not change its character just because it is used as a family home and mortgage payments are made from community funds. See Drahos v. Rens, 717 P.2d 927, 928 (Ariz. App. 1985); Waldman v. Maini, 195 P.3d 850 (Nev. 2008) (although life insurance policies were purchased with community funds, Nevada's Uniform Simultaneous Death Act precluded the division of life insurance proceeds as community property).

Community property states also utilize presumptions. For example, in Texas, there is a presumption that property possessed by either spouse during or on dissolution of marriage is community property. If separate property and community property become so commingled as to defy resegregation and identification, the statutory presumption prevails. Jones v. Jones, 890 S.W.2d 471 (Tex. App. 1994). In Smith v. Lanier, 998 S.W.2d 324 (Tex. App. 1999), the court held that debts contracted during marriage are presumed to be on the credit of the community and are joint community obligations. The presumption is overcome if it is shown that creditor agreed to look solely to separate estate of contracting spouse.

13.6. Death of Partner

In a community property state, a spouse acquires a present vested undivided one-half interest in all property acquired during the existence of the marital relationship, regardless of the state of title. Carpenter v. Carpenter, 722 P.2d 230 (Ariz. 1986) (statutory death benefit was a community property interest, and ex-spouse entitled to one-half community share in the death benefit).

When a spouse dies intestate, the survivor is viewed by law as owning one-half of the community property. The remaining issue involves the division of the deceased's one-half interest in the community property. In contrast, when a spouse dies intestate in a non–community property jurisdiction, intestacy laws may provide the survivor with a portion of or all of the deceased's estate.

EQUITABLE DISTRIBUTION THEORY

13.7. Marriage as a Joint Enterprise

The separate property theory, discussed earlier in this chapter, has been rejected in all jurisdictions and replaced in 43 states with the equitable distribution theory. The remaining jurisdictions have adopted some form of the community property distribution theory.

The equitable distribution theory is a corollary of the principle that marriage is a joint enterprise whose vitality, success, and endurance are dependent on the conjunction of multiple components, only one of which is financial. *Mickey v. Mickey*, 974 A.2d 641 (Conn. 2009) (marriage is a shared enterprise or joint undertaking in the nature of a partnership to which both spouses contribute — directly and indirectly, financially and nonfinancially — the fruits of which are distributable at divorce). An equitable distribution jurisdiction views the nonremunerated efforts of raising children, making a home, performing a myriad of personal services, and providing physical and emotional support as important to a marriage. These contributions are entitled to substantial recognition. Courts applying the equitable distribution theory recognize that the extent to which each party contributes to the marriage is measured by a whole complex of financial and nonfinancial components. When a marriage ends, each of the spouses, based on the totality of the contributions, has a right to a share of the marital assets because they represent the capital product of what was essentially a joint enterprise.

Equitable distribution jurisdictions generally presume that both parties equally contributed to property acquired or income earned during the marriage. This presumption obviates the need to make factual determinations about the individual contributions of each party and effectuates the notion that marriage is a joint enterprise.

13.8. Nonmarital Property

Legislatures in equitable distribution jurisdictions have usually excluded from the definition of marital property the following: (1) property acquired before the marriage; (2) property acquired by inheritance or gift from a third party during the marriage; (3) property excluded by valid agreement between the parties such as found in a premarital contract; or (4) property that is directly traceable to any of these sources.

Example 13-2

Assume P and D were married in an equitable distribution jurisdiction. Before the marriage, D owned a home valued at $100,000, which did not have a mortgage on it. During the marriage, the couple lived in the home, and when they divorced, it was valued at $200,000. P argues that because this is an equitable distribution jurisdiction, P should receive an equitable interest in the home. P contends that the home is marital property, D disagrees. How will a court most likely rule?

Explanation

Assuming that D can meet the burden of proving her claim that the home was purchased before marriage and was free and clear of any mortgage before marriage, a court will most likely award the entire home to D. The home is exempt from consideration as marital property under most, if not all, equitable distribution statutes in the country. D is also entitled to the benefit of the increase in the value of the home because all the increase in the value is a result of market forces. D will most likely be awarded the home worth $200,000 free and clear of any claim by P to a portion of it.

13.9. Presumption of Equal Division

In an equitable distribution jurisdiction, a trial court will initially presume that all marital property is to be divided equally between the parties. *See Thompson v. Thompson*, 811 N.E.2d 888, 912 (Ind. Ct. App. 2004) (court presumes equal division of the marital property between the parties is just and reasonable — presumption may be rebutted by a party who presents relevant evidence that an equal division would not be just and reasonable); *James v. James*, 108 S.W.3d 1 (Mo. App. S.D. 2002) (all property acquired by either spouse after marriage and before decree of dissolution of marriage is presumed to be marital property); *Gantner v. Gantner*, 640 N.W.2d 565 (Wis. App. 2002) (court presumes that marital property is divided equally, and it is only in considering whether to deviate from this presumption that it looks to various other statutory factors). The presumption is applied regardless of how title is held — that is, regardless of whose name is on the legal document showing ownership. In an equitable distribution jurisdiction, equality is the cardinal precept, and it is assumed that all wealth acquired by the joint efforts of the husband and wife is common property.

Parties can overcome the presumption. For example, if a party can show that an asset was acquired in exchange for nonmarital property, the presumption is overcome. *Kottke v. Kottke*, 353 N.W.2d 633, 636 (Minn. App. 1984), *pet. for rev. denied* (Minn. Dec. 20, 1984); *see Hess v. Hess*, 475 A.2d 796, 799 (Pa. Super. 1984) (equitable distribution does not presume an equal division of marital property, and the goal of economic justice will often dictate otherwise). In several jurisdictions, the presumption may also be overcome by a finding that the property was acquired by one spouse and the purchase was not influenced directly or indirectly by the other spouse, that is, the other spouse contributed neither economically nor otherwise to the acquisition of the property. *See, e.g., In re Marriage of Kunze*, 92 P.3d 100 (Or. 2004) (although the inquiry into the "just and proper" division necessarily includes consideration of the statutory factors, including the court's determination under the presumption of equal contribution, that inquiry also takes into account the social and financial objectives of the dissolution, as well as any other considerations that bear upon the question of what division of the marital property is equitable).

While not uniform in their approach, to overcome the presumption, some courts may consider monetary contributions to marital property such as employment income, other earnings, and funds that were separate property. They may also consider nonmonetary contributions to marital property, such as homemaker services, child care services, labor performed without compensation, labor performed in the actual maintenance or improvement of tangible marital property, or labor performed in the management or investment of assets that are marital property. Courts may consider the effect of the marriage on the income-earning abilities of a party, such as contributions to the education or training of the other party or by either party forgoing employment and education.

Finally, courts in some jurisdictions may consider conduct that reduced the value of marital property as evidence in support of not applying the presumption that all marital property is to be divided equally between the parties. *See Somerville v. Somerville*, 369 S.E.2d 459, 460 (W. Va. 1988) (West Virginia statute permits court to consider the extent to which each party, during the marriage, may have conducted himself or herself so as to dissipate or depreciate the value of the marital property of the parties but may not consider fault or unrelated marital misconduct).

13.10. Mingled Marital and Nonmarital Property: Source-of-Funds Theory Applied

In the absence of a specific statute, some jurisdictions have adopted a "source of funds" or tracing theory of equitable distribution when there has been no joint titling after the marriage. *Hoffmann v. Hoffmann*, 676 S.W.2d 817, 825 (Mo. 1984). Under the source-of-funds theory, when property is acquired by an expenditure of both nonmarital and marital property, the property is characterized as part nonmarital and part marital. Therefore, a spouse who contributes nonmarital property to the marriage is entitled to maintain a proportionate nonmarital share in an otherwise marital asset. There are, however, differences among the states regarding exactly how to apply the source-of-funds theory.

For example, in *Hall v. Hall*, 462 A.2d 1179 (Me. 1983), the dispute was over a house and lots acquired by the husband prior to marriage, which were enhanced in value by expenditure of marital funds for improvements. He contended that the property was his separate, nonmarital property, arguing that that the improvements, although made after the marriage, are nonmarital because they fit within an exception to a provision of Maine law. The trial court agreed with him. However, the Maine Supreme Court rejected his argument. In doing so, the court applied its version of the source-of-funds rule. Under its approach, property is deemed to have been acquired as it is paid for, so that it includes both marital and separate ownership interests. The marital interest is ascertained by determining the ratio of marital and separate investment in the property. (Note that in Maine, although the source-of-funds theory is applied when characterizing property titled solely in one spouse as nonmarital or marital, it is not applied when characterizing property titled as tenants by the entirety.) *Carter v. Carter*, 419 A.2d 1018 (Me. 1980).

Courts in several equitable distribution states do not apply the source-of-funds theory in the same fashion as Maine, that is, property is deemed to have been acquired *as it is paid for*, when considering the definition of marital property with respect to property titled solely in one spouse. *Grant v. Zich*, 477 A.2d 1163 (Md. 1984); *Whitenton v. Whitenton*, 659 S.W.2d 542, 547-548 (Mo. Ct. App. 1983). Characterization of property as nonmarital or marital depends upon the source of contributions as payments are made, rather than the *time* at which legal or equitable title to or possession of the property is obtained. *Grant v. Zich, supra; Mitchell v. Mitchell*, 711 S.W.2d 572, 576 (Mo. App. 1986) (the designation of property as separate or marital, for distribution purposes, is governed by retroactive application of the source-of-funds rule; character of property is determined by the source of funds used for the purchase); *Wade v. Wade*, 372, 325 S.E.2d 260 (N.C. App. 1985) (when both the marital and separate estates contribute assets toward the acquisition of property, each estate is entitled to an interest in the property in the ratio its contribution bears to the total investment in the property); *Frank G.W. v. Carol M.W.*, 457 A.2d 715 (Del. 1983) (assets of corpus of trusts created prior to the marriage but distributed during the marriage were marital property, and distribution of trust which occurred after divorce was nonmarital property).

13.11. Mingled Nonmarital Property: Source of Funds Not Applied — Transmutation Through Commingling

Some jurisdictions have rejected application of the source of funds theory and in its place have adopted the theory of "transmutation through commingling." These jurisdictions may find that improved real property is entirely marital property. Under that theory, affirmative acts of augmenting separate property by commingling it with marital resources is viewed as indicative of an intent to transmute, or transform, the separate property to marital property. *In re Marriage of Smith*, 427 N.E.2d 1239 (Ill. 1981). This theory is particularly well developed in Illinois, where it was first adopted by judicial decision.

Adoption of the theory of transmutation and rejecting the source-of-funds theory has been justified on the perceived legislative preference for the classification of property as marital. Thus, if a jurisdiction has not adopted the source-of-funds theory, a spouse who commingles separate property with marital property may be viewed as causing the separate property to lose its nonmarital character. Courts in these jurisdictions may consider all of the commingled property as marital property and subject it to equitable distribution. *See, e.g., Smoot v. Smoot*, 357 S.E.2d 728 (Va. 1987) (Virginia's equitable distribution statute does not adopt source-of-funds doctrine and thus, when spouse fails to segregate and instead commingles separate property with marital property, chancellor must classify commingled property as marital property subject to equitable distribution).

Example 13-3

Assume that P and D divorce after 25 years of marriage in a jurisdiction that does not apply the source-of-funds theory. During the marriage, P received $20,000 cash as a gift from his mother. P placed the funds in P and D's joint bank account, which they use for household expenditures. When they divorce ten years after the money was placed into the account, P asserts that he is entitled to $20,000 from the account as his nonmarital property. How will a court in this jurisdiction most likely rule?

Explanation

A court in a jurisdiction that has not adopted a source-of-funds theory will most likely rule that when P commingled separate property with marital property, the commingled property became marital property subject to equitable distribution. *See Smoot v. Smoot*, 357 S.E.2d 728, 731 (Va. 1987). The court will view the evidence in this hypothetical as P failing to prove that he considered his interest to be composed of discrete, segregated shares.

The facts suggest that all of P's funds were commingled with D's and were considered to be an integral part of the marital estate. *See In re Marriage of Smith*, 27 N.E.2d 1239, 1245-1246 (Ill. 1981).

13.12. The Transmutation Doctrine

Transmutation has already been discussed, to some extent, in the source of funds sections above. Transmutation is a judicially created doctrine that is applied to prevent unfairness in the distribution of assets. When applied, property that was once classified as separate or nonmarital can be transmuted into marital property when a spouse with title to property represents to the other spouse that the property will be shared by the couple. *See Heustess v. Kelley-Heustess*, 158 P.3d 827 (Alaska 2007) (wife's house, which was originally separate, nonmarital property, transmuted into marital property through the husband's financial and personal contributions as well as the intent of both parties to use the home as the marital residence). Transmutation allows a spouse to transmute an item of nonmarital property into marital property by agreement, either express or implied, or by gift. For example, nonmarital property may be changed into marital property if a gift of nonmarital property is converted into co-tenancy with the other party. However, because technical application of the transmutation rule can result in unfair results, equitable considerations may take precedence over a mechanical application of the transmutation rule.

In most jurisdictions nonmarital property does not automatically become marital property solely because it may have become commingled with marital property. *D.K.H. v. L.R.G.*, 102 S.W.3d 93, 100 (Mo. App. 2003) (wife proved by clear and convincing evidence that real property was her separate property). Rather, courts will carefully examine the owner's intent to convert the property to marital property in deciding how to characterize it. *See Ker v. Ker*, 776 S.W.2d 873, 877 (Mo. App. 1989) (holding that "[n]onmarital property may lose its character as such if there is evidence of an intention to contribute the property to the community"); *Pirri v. Pirri*, 631 S.E.2d 279 (S.C. App. 2006) (wife failed to prove transmutation of husband's separate property); *Hanson v. Hanson*, 125 P.3d 299 (Alaska 2005). Nonmarital property cannot be transmuted to marital property based on evidence — oral, behavioral, or documentary — that is easily manipulated and unreliable. *In re Marriage of Benson*, 32 Cal. Rptr. 3d 471 (Cal. 2005); *Estate of MacDonald*, 272 Cal. Rptr. 153 (Cal. 1990).

Example 13-4

Assume that during their divorce hearing, stock acquired by P before and during his marriage to D was shown to be either a gift from his parents or purchased with nonmarital assets. However, the bank account through which P bought and sold stock and deposited dividends was occasionally used for marital purposes including household expenses and vacation trips. P argued that because this jurisdiction has adopted the source-of-funds theory, that the stock was his nonmarital property. D contended that, once P used an account that was occasionally used for marital purposes, the stock was transmuted into marital property. How will a court most likely rule?

Explanation

A court will most likely rule in favor of P. A court will observe that transmutation is a matter of intent to be gleaned from the facts of each case, and the mere use of separate properties to support the marriage without some additional evidence of intent to treat it as marital property is not sufficient to establish transmutation. In general, the spouse claiming transmutation must produce objective evidence showing that during the marriage, the parties themselves regarded the property as the common property of the marriage. Nonmarital property is transmuted into marital property when it becomes so commingled as to be untraceable. However, the mere commingling of funds does not automatically make them marital funds. Here, the facts tend to support P. *See Wannamaker v. Wannamaker*, 406 S.E.2d 180 (S.C. Ct. App. 1991).

Example 13-5

Assume that P and D married in a source-of-funds jurisdiction and that P brought $7,000 cash into the marriage. These funds and approximately $3,000 cash that D brought into the marriage were commingled in a joint account and used throughout the ten-year marriage for various expenses. When they divorce, P argues that she is entitled to the $7,000 as her nonmarital property. How will a court in a source of funds jurisdiction most likely rule?

Explanation

Although this is a source-of-funds jurisdiction, a court most likely will rule that the funds have lost their nonmarital character. The mere fact that the funds were placed in a joint account does not necessarily require that they be considered marital property. However, in many jurisdictions, a presumption arises that when deposits are made into a spousal joint bank account, the parties share a joint ownership in the funds on deposit. The presumption is rebuttable by either spouse if it can be shown that the account consists of his or her separate property only. Because everyone agrees that the premarital funds were contributed to a joint account, the account was used by both parties during the marriage, and there has been a significantly long passage of time since the deposit, a court will most likely rule that the funds were transmuted into marital property.

13.13. Mingled Marital and Nonmarital Property: Tracing

When a party claims that an asset is nonmarital, the burden of proof is placed on that party to trace the asset to its nonmarital source. *Kreilick v. Kreilick,* 831 N.E.2d 1046 (Ohio App. 2005) (party seeking to have certain property deemed separate for distribution in a divorce has the burden of proof by a preponderance of the evidence); *Hall v. Hall,* 462 A.2d 1179, 1181-1182 (Me. 1983); *Brandenburg v. Brandenburg,* 617 S.W.2d 871, 872 (Ky. Ct. App. 1981). When the original nonmarital asset is no longer owned, the nonmarital claimant must trace the previously owned asset to a presently owned specific asset. If the claimant is successful, the trial court assigns the asset, or an interest in it, to the claimant as his or her nonmarital property. *See In re Marriage of Wanstreet,* 847 N.E.2d 716 (Ill. App. 2006) (proponent, as the party claiming that property is nonmarital, must prove the elements of gift by the manifest weight of the evidence); *Terwilliger v. Terwilliger,* 64 S.W.3d 816 (Ky. 2002) (husband could not adequately trace $200,000 to a separate property source, and husband was an experienced businessman who was expected to have maintained detailed and accurate records of where the assets came from).

Example 13-6

Assume that P, an experienced businessperson, was injured in an accident prior to marriage to D. As a result of the accident, P received a $50,000 cash settlement. Approximately one year after the parties married, P purchased a parcel of land with the title only in his name.

The parties' marriage broke down after 20 years, and they were unable to agree on the division of property. The parcel of land purchased 19 years earlier was now valued at $500,000, and P asserted that it was his nonmarital property, and he was entitled to it. P testified that he used all of the $50,000 he received as compensation for injuries suffered in the accident he was involved in before his marriage to D to purchase the property. D disagreed. She testified that she recalled that some of the down payment on the land came from their joint bank account, estimating that it was as much as $15,000. She also testified that about $10,000 of the $50,000 came from an inheritance she had received when her father died. She also offered testimony that P purchased a new car for about $25,000, paying cash for it, in the first year of their marriage.

P produced a receipt at the hearing issued by the previous land owner, stating that P had paid $50,000. D's name was not on the receipt. The receipt also included a date showing it was issued one year after P and D married. P produced a copy of the release of his injury claim, which indicated that the claim was settled for $50,000 prior to the marriage. During cross-examination, P testified that he had years of experience as a businessperson, juggling the assets and liabilities of a number of corporations and orchestrating complex business deals.

D produced a copy of a $10,000 check given to her as a part of her father's estate a year after they married, and a photograph of the car P allegedly purchased just after they were married. No other evidence was introduced. Has P produced sufficient evidence to persuade a judge that the land is P's nonmarital property?

Explanation

While a close question, courts will most likely conclude that P has failed in meeting his burden of tracing the asset to its nonmarital source. P appears to be a skilled businessperson, with extensive recordkeeping experience, and not a person that a court would protect from stringent tracing requirements. It is reasonable to expect that P would keep detailed and accurate records, and be able to produce them at the hearing to establish his nonmarital property claim. D's check and the car photograph plus D's claim that some of the payment for the land came from their joint bank account raise as yet unanswered questions that place the burden on P to answer. Note that case law suggests that while tracing to a mathematical certainty is not always possible, a precise requirement is more appropriate for skilled businesspersons who are expected to maintain comprehensive records of their financial affairs than it would be for persons with lesser business skills or persons who are imprecise in their recordkeeping abilities. *See Terwilliger v. Terwilliger*, 64 S.W.3d 816 (Ky. 2002).

13.14. Mingled Marital and Nonmarital Property: Formula for Calculating Value of Nonmarital Assets (Home Example)

Courts face challenging situations when attempting to divide assets containing nonmarital and marital funds, particularly when the asset has increased (or decreased) in value. For example, one party may have purchased a house with nonmarital funds prior to the marriage, subsequent to the marriage the couple may have made mortgage payments out of marital funds, and by the time of divorce the house may have increased in value. How should the increase in value be apportioned?

In an equitable distribution jurisdiction, a court determines the present value of a nonmarital asset used in the acquisition of marital property by calculating the proportion the net equity or contribution at the time of acquisition bore to the value of the property at the time of purchase, multiplied by the value of the property at the time of separation. The remainder of the equity increase is characterized as marital property and is equitably distributed. *Woosnam v. Woosnam*, 587 S.W.2d 262 (Ky. Ct. App. 1979). *See Keeling v. Keeling*, 624 S.E.2d 687 (Va. App. 2006) (trial court erred in failing to apply the *Brandenburg* formula, which would have apportioned the marital and nonmarital contributions of hybrid property in the same percentages as their respective contributions to the total equity in the property, to ascertain the current value of husband's separate contributions toward the purchase of the marital residence).

Example 13-7

Assume that P and D were married in an equitable distribution jurisdiction. Before the marriage, D owned a home, which on the day of her marriage was valued at $100,000 with a $50,000 mortgage. During the marriage, the couple lived in the home, and D made all of the house payments. When they divorced, the home was valued at $200,000, and the mortgage was paid off. P argues that because this is an equitable distribution jurisdiction, he should receive an interest in the home. D argues that because she owned the home before P and D married and made all the mortgage payments after they were married that she should receive 100 percent of the home, that is, the home with a value of $200,000 free and clear of any claim to it by P. How will a court most likely resolve this dispute?

Explanation

A court will begin by recognizing that on the day the couple married, D had a 50 percent equitable interest in the home, that is, $50,000 is 50 percent of $100,000. During the marriage, the value of the home increased as a result of market forces. Consequently, D's equitable interest in the home because of her initial cash investment increased in value, and most courts believe that D should receive a fair return on the investment. A court will calculate that on divorce, D should receive $100,000 as her nonmarital interest in the homestead (50% of $200,000 is $100,000). A court will then divide the remaining $100,000 equitably between P and D, with each most likely receiving about $50,000. D will most likely receive a total of $150,000. Note that most courts will not consider the fact that D made all of the mortgage payments during the marriage as altering the outcome of the final division of property because the payments, in the eyes of the court, were made with marital funds.

Example 13-8

Assume P and D were married in an equitable distribution jurisdiction. Also assume that on the date of their marriage, P owned real estate then valued at $30,000, but subject to a $20,000 mortgage. A few months after they married, the couple, using marital funds and doing a lot of the work themselves, built an addition to the home and increased its value by $10,000 — from $30,000 to $40,000. During the course of the marriage, the parties used marital funds to pay the mortgage balance down to $4,000. At the time of the divorce, the market value of the home was $100,000. P and D seek a determination of their marital and nonmarital interests in the $100,000.

Explanation

The court will begin its analysis by recognizing that the home contains both marital and nonmarital interests. It will recognize that there are three types of "increases" involved in the example: (1) the increase in value attributable to the physical improvement of the property through application of marital funds and marital effort; (2) the increase in value attributable to the increase in equity by application of marital funds to reduce the mortgage indebtedness; and (3) the increase in value attributable to inflation and market forces. The hypothetical assumes an investment of cash and of property and services having a cash value in the total amount of $40,000. The amount P invested in the property prior to the marriage, as valued on the date of the marriage, is P's nonmarital equity in the property. In this example, P's nonmarital equity was $10,000 (33⅓% of the total value on the date of the marriage). During the marriage, the parties contributed marital funds and labor when they built an addition to the home. In this problem, the addition increased the value of the property by $10,000. The parties also undertook to pay off the $20,000 mortgage with marital funds, which at the time of the divorce reduced the unpaid mortgage balance to $4,000.

The court will reason that the present value of P's nonmarital interest is the proportion his net equity at the time of marriage ($10,000) bore to the aggregate of the value of the property on the date of the marriage ($30,000) plus the value of the addition on its completion ($10,000). The interests will then be apportioned as follows:

1. $10,000/$40,000 = 25 percent
2. $100,000 × .25 = $25,000 (P's nonmarital interest)
3. $100,000 − $25,000 = $75,000 (marital interest)

The net value of the property, however, is $96,000 ($100,000 − $4,000 mortgage balance).

Because the parties undertook payment of the mortgage debt with marital funds, reduction of the marital interests by the amount of the mortgage balance ($75,000 − $4,000 = $71,000) is appropriate. Thus, $71,000 is marital property, and $25,000 is P's nonmarital property. *See Nardini v. Nardini*, 414 N.W.2d 184, 193 (Minn. 1987). The $71,000 will be equitably divided between P and D.

13.15. Mingled Marital and Nonmarital Property: Active and Passive Appreciation (Stock Example)

In an equitable distribution jurisdiction, courts apportion the increase (or decrease) in value of an asset combining marital and nonmarital property using the theory of active and passive appreciation. The increase in value of an asset attributable to the efforts of one or both of the parties is characterized as "active appreciation" and is treated as marital property. Active appreciation occurs when marital funds or marital efforts cause a spouse's separate property to increase in value during the marriage. The time and energy of both spouses during the marriage is to be considered in dividing marital property.

Under this theory, "an asset's value at the inception of the marriage retains its separate character, but any subsequent increase in value is treated as marital property to the extent that it results from active marital conduct." *Harrower v. Harrower*, 71 P.3d 854, 858 (Alaska 2003). A finding of active appreciation requires application of a three-part test: First, the court must find that the separate property in question appreciated during the marriage. Second, it must find that the parties made marital contributions to the property. Finally, the court must find a causal connection between the marital contributions and at least part of the appreciation. *Id.* (quoting Brett R. Turner, *Equitable Distribution of Property* §5.22, at 236 (2d ed. 1994); *Hanson v. Hanson*, 125 P.3d 299 (Alaska 2005). The spouse seeking to classify the appreciation as active has the burden of proving the first two elements — an increase in value and marital contribution — while the burden of showing the absence of a causal link lies with the owning spouse. 125 P.2d 299, *citing* Turner, *supra*, n.13. *See Mayhew v. Mayhew*, 519 S.E.2d 188 (W. Va. 1999) (court sets out a five-step process for conducting active and passive appreciation test).

Passive appreciation occurs without any significant contribution being made toward that increase by either spouse. *Odom v. Odom*, 141 P.3d 324, 335 (Alaska 2006). If an increase in value of an asset is attributable to inflationary forces, general economics, and market conditions beyond the spouse's control, the increase in value is considered "passive appreciation" and is treated as nonmarital property. *Middendorf v. Middendorf*, 696 N.E.2d 575, 578 (Ohio 1998) (if the evidence indicates that the appreciation of the separate property is not due to the input of either spouse's labor, money, or in-kind contributions, the increase in the value of the property is passive appreciation and remains separate property). Should the asset increase in value because of these forces, the entire increase is attributed to the partner holding the asset.

For example, if one party owns stock prior to the marriage and it increases in value during the marriage, a court will make a determination concerning whether the increase in value resulted from the active effort of one or both of the parties (marital property) or whether the increase in value was passive in nature (nonmarital property).

Example 13-9

Assume that on the day of her marriage to P, D owned 300 shares of XYZ Company. On the date of marriage, the market value of the publicly traded, unencumbered shares was $25 per share, or $7,500. At the time of the divorce, D owned 800 shares of XYZ Company, which then had a market value of $40 per share or $32,000. The increase in the number of shares was the result of a 2-for-1 split during the marriage, which increased D's holdings from 300 to 600 shares. The additional 200 shares were acquired through the reinvestment by D of cash dividends paid during the marriage.

D claims all 800 shares of XYZ Company as her nonmarital property. P argues that the increase in value of the shares during the marriage and the additional shares received during the marriage are marital property. How will a court most likely resolve the dispute?

Explanation

If the court applies the intent of the drafters of the Uniform Marriage and Divorce Act, §307, comment at 204 (1970), a stock split is considered nonmarital property. The theory is that when stock splits, the value is determined by market forces and does not increase the shareholder's proportionate ownership interest in the corporation. Therefore, its increased value is passive and not considered income generated actively by the parties. The 600 shares would be awarded to D.

A court will treat the remaining 200 shares as having been purchased with marital funds and, therefore, as being marital property. The 200 shares would be equally divided between P and D.

13.16. "Egregious Fault"

Most, if not all, jurisdictions have no-fault grounds for a divorce. A majority have rejected application of fault when dividing marital property. However, if there is "egregious fault" by a party, some courts will consider the conduct when dividing property. See Alford v. Alford, 478 N.Y.S.2d 717, 718 (N.Y. App. Div. 1984) ("In the absence of egregious circumstances marital fault is not a proper factor to be considered under equitable distribution."). Those courts that allow a consideration of fault in some aspect of a divorce limit its application to an award of alimony—not a division of property. See, e.g., Fisher v. Fisher, 648 S.W.2d 244 (Tenn. 1983) (permitting consideration of fault when awarding alimony; barring consideration of fault when dividing marital property); compare Wilbur v. Wilbur, 498 N.Y.S.2d 525 (N.Y. App. Div. 1986) ("[M]arital fault is, generally, a proper consideration in awarding maintenance.") with Dusenberry v. Dusenberry, 326 S.E.2d 65 (N.C. Ct. App. 1985) (finding an adulterous affair on the part of a wife was an irrelevant and inappropriate matter in determining equitable distribution of marital property). In Charlton v. Charlton, 413 S.E.2d 911, 915 (W. Va. 1991), the West Virginia court stated that in enacting that state's equitable distribution statute, the legislature did not intend fault to be considered as a factor in determining the division of marital property. Note, however, that the West Virginia legislature did designate marital fault as a factor to be considered in awarding alimony under the provisions of West Virginia Code 48-2-15(i).

UNIFORM ACTS

13.17. Uniform Marriage and Divorce Act (UMDA)

The Uniform Marriage and Divorce Act (UMDA) addresses the disposition of property upon divorce. As originally drafted, §307(a) of the UMDA provided that the court "shall assign each spouse's property to him" and then divide the marital property in just proportions. The Act states that marital property does not include property acquired by gift, property acquired in exchange for property acquired by gift, or increase in value of property acquired before marriage. UMDA §307(b)(1), (2), (5). According to the *Commissioners' Note* to §307 and judicial interpretations of §307, appreciation in value of nonmarital property is not marital property. However, income from nonmarital property is treated as marital property. *See Wierman v. Wierman*, 387 N.W.2d 744, 748 (Wis. 1986).

In 1973, §307 of the UMDA was amended to provide two alternatives to dividing property upon divorce. Alternative A proceeds upon the principle that all property of the spouses, however acquired, should be regarded as assets of the married couple, to be apportioned equitably between the spouses. Alternative B is intended for community property states and allows courts to divide community property after considering a certain criteria. Both of these alternatives recognize that the spouses have been partners in the marriage and require courts to look beyond title in deciding how much each spouse should share in the distribution of marital assets. *See* Elizabeth A. Cheadle, Comment, *The Development of Sharing Principles in Common Law Marital Property States*, 28 UCLA L. Rev. 1269, 1287 (1981).

Note that courts in some jurisdictions that have adopted property distribution statutes based upon the UMDA have held that income derived from nonmarital property during the marriage is marital property. *In re Marriage of Reed*, 427 N.E.2d 282, 285 (Ill. App. Ct. 1981); *Sousley v. Sousley*, 614 S.W.2d 942, 944 (Ky. 1981); *In re Marriage of Williams*, 639 S.W.2d 236 (Mo. Ct. App. 1982); *See Brodak v. Brodak*, 447 A.2d 847, 855 (Md. 1982).

13.18. Uniform Marital Property Act (UMPA)

The Uniform Marital Property Act (UMPA) provides that income received during the marriage is marital property, regardless of its source. *See* UMPA §4 cmt., 9A U.L.A. 110 (1987). In Wisconsin, where the UMPA was adopted, property acquired with income generated by an excluded asset is also considered marital property. *Arneson v. Arneson*, 355 N.W.2d 16, 19 (Wis. Ct. App. 1984).

13.19. American Law Institute (ALI) Recommendations

The American Law Institute *Principles of the Law of Family Dissolution: Analysis and Recommendations* is the result of 11 years of work. The following is a summary of several sections of the ALI *Principles* that are associated with property division.

Section 4.03 contains the definition of marital and separate property, which follows standards used in community property and most equitable distribution jurisdictions. *See* David Westfall, *Unprincipled Family Dissolution: The American Law Institute's Recommendations for Spousal Support and Division of Property*, 27 Harv. J.L. & Pub. Pol'y 917 (2004). The section defines nonmarital property as property acquired either before marriage or as gifts (or inheritances) from third parties during marriage as the separate property of the acquiring spouse and hence not subject to division on divorce. Section 4.04 defines income and appreciation in the value of separate property as nonmarital property unless its value has been enhanced by spousal labor or it is impacted by section 4.12, which provides for gradual recharacterization of nonmarital property in marriages that last a minimum of five years. *Id.* at 947. Section 4.05(1) provides that a portion of any increase in the value of separate property is marital property whenever either spouse has devoted substantial time during marriage to the property's management or preservation.

Section 4.07 declares that occupational licenses and educational degrees should not be subject to division on divorce, and section 4.07 so provides. Section 4.09(1) mandates an equal division of marital property and marital debts, but section 4.09(2)(b) and section 4.09(2)(c) allow a court under certain circumstances to order an unequal division of debts. Section 4.09(1) exceptions provide that a court may deviate from equal division if it determines that a spouse is entitled to alimony and chooses to provide for the alimony by means of a larger property settlement. It may also deviate if a party is guilty of misappropriating marital property by making substantial gifts to third parties within a specified time period; by losing, expending, or destroying marital property by intentional misconduct within a specified time period; or by negligently losing or destroying marital property after service of the dissolution petition. A court may deviate from equal division if marital debts exceed marital assets, and it is just and equitable to unequally allocate the excess debt because of financial capacity, participation in the decision to incur the debt, or the purpose of the debt. Finally, a court may deviate from equal division if an existing debt was incurred to finance a spouse's education.

Section 4.10 allows an unequal division of property when one of the spouses has committed some sort of financial misconduct. The misconduct may involve (1) certain gifts made without the other party's consent; (2) property lost, expended, or destroyed through intentional misconduct; and (3) property lost or destroyed through negligence after the service of the dissolution petition. The suggested time period during which the conduct described is relevant is either six months — in the case of (1) or (2) — or a year prior to the service of the dissolution petition.

PENSION AND RETIREMENT BENEFITS

13.20. Qualified Domestic Relations Order (QDRO)

A qualified domestic relations order (QDRO) is a state court order in a domestic relations case that requires pension or retirement plan benefits to be used to provide alimony or child support, or to divide marital property upon a divorce. Under federal law, the administrator of the pension plan that provides the benefits affected by an order is the individual (or entity) initially responsible for determining whether a domestic relations order is a QDRO.

A QDRO allows a state court to order a pension-plan administrator to distribute a portion of a pension to the other spouse. A recipient may also "roll over" a pension received as a result of a QDRO into a qualified pension account without tax consequences. Note that a QDRO is a "special order after final judgment," and it must be denominated a "judgment" to be appealable. *Brooks v. Brooks*, 98 S.W.3d 530, 532 (Mo. en banc 2003).

QDROs were relatively ineffective until 1984 because of the Employment Retirement Income Security Act (ERISA) of 1974 anti-alienation provisions. ERISA was drafted primarily to protect the interests of employees who participated in employer-sponsored pension plans and was not concerned about the financial consequences associated with distribution of a pension upon divorce.

With the passage of the Retirement Equity Act of 1984 (REA) the concerns related to distributing pensions upon a divorce were addressed. This Act was intended to assure a greater and more equitable opportunity for women working as employees or homemakers to receive private pension income. REA focused on the division of pension benefits in marital dissolution or dependent support situations. Prior to the 1984 amendments, a spouse was denied a right to pension benefits upon divorce, regardless of how many years the spouse may have served as an economic partner to a married partner who was covered by a pension plan. Even in cases in which the state domestic relations court was willing to consider the pension an asset of the marriage and award the ex-spouse a share of it, the spouse's rights were thwarted. Pension plan trustees refused to honor state court orders claiming that they required an impermissible assignment of benefits and were preempted by ERISA.

The amendments to REA have made it clear that by honoring a legitimate state court order, a QDRO, awarding an ex-spouse some or all of a worker's pension does not violate the anti-alienation clause of ERISA. In addition, the legislation creates an exception from ERISA's broad preemption of state laws for QDROs. See 29 U.S.C.A. §§1056(d)(3)(A) (excepting QDROs from the prohibition against assignment or alienation). The Supreme Court has recognized that ERISA enforcement of QDROs effectively provides an exception to the general rule that administrators rely solely upon plan documents. See Kennedy v. Plan Administrator for DuPont Savings and Investment Plan, 555 U.S. (2009), 2009 WL 160440, at 9 (U.S.) (quoting from §1056(d)(3)(J) and stating, "But this in effect means that a plan administrator who enforces a QDRO must be said to enforce plan documents, not ignore them").

The Retirement Equity Act of 1984 did not resolve all of the federal-state conflicts over pension rights. One of the important issues concerned whether federal law preempts state testamentary law. In Boggs v. Boggs, 520 U.S. 833 (1997), the Supreme Court held that ERISA preempts a state community property law, which allowed a nonparticipant spouse to transfer by testamentary instrument an interest in undistributed pension plan benefits. The ruling directly applies to California and the other eight community property jurisdictions. The Court rested its ruling on the Supremacy Clause of Article 6 of the Constitution and the preemption provision of 29 U.S.C. §1144(a). The Court explained that the principal purpose of ERISA was "to protect plan participants and beneficiaries." Id. at 845. That purpose would be frustrated by testamentary transfers of pension benefits to third parties having no relation to the participant.

Example 13-10

Assume that X and Y live together as husband and wife for 30 years when Y dies. When Y's will is probated, it transfers all of her interest in X's undistributed pension plan benefits to their two children. X marries Z a year after Y's death. X dies three years after the marriage to Z. Z seeks a survivor annuity under X's pension plan. The two children from X and Y's earlier marriage, A and B, seek a portion of the surviving annuity based upon Y's testamentary transfer of Y's rights to them in Y's will under state law. How will a court most likely apportion the annuity among A, B, and Z?

Explanation

To the extent a state law might provide A and B with a right to a portion of Z's survivor's annuity, it is preempted by ERISA. The annuity is a qualified joint and survivor annuity mandated by §1055 of ERISA, the object of which is to ensure a stream of income to surviving spouses. ERISA's solicitude for the economic security of such spouses would be undermined by allowing a predeceasing spouse's heirs and legatees to have a community property interest in the survivor's annuity. Even a plan participant cannot defeat a nonparticipant surviving spouse's statutory entitlement to such an annuity. See §1055(c)(2). Nothing in ERISA's language supports the conclusion that Congress decided to permit a predeceasing nonparticipant spouse to do so. Testamentary transfers such as the one at issue could reduce the annuity below the ERISA minimum. See §1055(d)(1). Perhaps even more troubling, the recipient of the transfer need not be a family member; for example, the annuity might be substantially reduced so that funds could be diverted to support an unrelated stranger. In the face of a direct clash between state law and ERISA's provisions and objectives, the state law cannot stand. *Boggs v. Boggs*, 520 U.S. 833 (1997); *See Gade v. National Solid Wastes Management Assn.*, 505 U.S. 88, 98 (1992). A court will most likely award the annuity to Z and nothing to A or B.

13.21. Pension Benefits

Pensions are an asset in the nature of deferred compensation and are subject to equitable division because they are presently earned, although not presently possessed. Pension benefits are considered marital property and often constitute a substantial percentage of the marital property to be distributed by a family court. When considering a pension, the court will determine whether it is vested or nonvested and its value.

A vested pension is one that is not subject to forfeiture should the employee terminate employment or be terminated by an employer. A pension that is nonvested is subject to forfeiture should the employee quit or the employer terminate employment.

Courts are in agreement that vested pension rights should be considered marital property at the time of divorce. They are not, however, in agreement that nonvested pension rights should be included as a marital asset. Those that refuse to recognize nonvested pension rights as property reason that they are a mere expectancy, and thus, not an asset subject to division upon dissolution of a marriage. However, the trend in this country appears to be toward holding that pension rights, vested or nonvested, are a property interest, and to the extent that such rights derive from employment during coverture, they constitute an asset subject to division in a dissolution proceeding. *See, e.g., Shaver v. Shaver*, 165 Cal. Rptr. 672 (Cal. App. 1982); *In re Marriage of Brown*, 544 P.2d 561 (Cal. 1976); *See Shanks v. Treadway*, 110 S.W.3d 444 (Tex. 2003) (nonvested pension rights are a contingent interest in property, and to the extent that such rights derive from employment during coverture, they constitute a community asset subject to division in a dissolution proceeding); *Kendrick v. Kendrick*, 902 S.W.2d 918, 920 (Tenn. App. 1994) (nonvested pension rights accruing during a marriage are marital property subject to equitable division in divorce cases); *Swanson v. Swanson*, 583 N.W.2d 15 (Minn. App. 1998) (nonvested pensions are included within the definition of marital property).

13.22. Social Security

In *Hisquierdo v. Hisquierdo*, 439 U.S. 572 (1979), the U.S. Supreme Court held that Railroad Retirement Act benefits, which are analogous to social security benefits, may not offset an award of marital property to the other spouse in a community property state. Consequently, a wife did not have a community property interest in her husband's expectation of receiving railroad retirement benefits. The Court, in so holding, expressly pointed to the similarities between the railroad retirement benefits and benefits under the Social Security Act. Note that Congress subsequently extended benefits to divorced spouses who have been married to the railroad employee for at least ten years. 45 U.S.C. §231a(c)(4)(i-iii) (1996).

However, *Hisquierdo* is subject to varying interpretations around the country. Some state courts do not read *Hisquierdo* as barring consideration of social security benefits in a jurisdiction where the family court is charged with dividing the marital property equitably. *See, e.g., Stanley v. Stanley*, 956 A.2d 1 (Del. Super. 2008).

More than a dozen states have found that social security benefits may be considered as part of a trial court's fashioning of an equitable distribution of marital property. *See In re Marriage of Morehouse*, 121 P.3d 264, 267 (Colo. App.); *In re Marriage of Boyer*, 538 N.W.2d 293, 293-294, 296 (Iowa 1995); *In re Marriage of Brane*, 908 P.2d 625, 626, 628 (Kan. 1995); *Pongonis v. Pongonis*, 606 A.2d 1055, 1058 (Me. 1992); *Depot v. Depot*, 893 A.2d 995, 998 (Me. 2006); *Pleasant v. Pleasant*, 632 A.2d 202, 206, 207 n.3 (Md. App. 1993); *Mahoney v. Mahoney*, 681 N.E.2d 852, 856 (Mass. 1997); *Rudden v. Rudden*, 765 S.W.2d 719, 720 (Mo. App. 1989); *Dinges v. Dinges*, 743 N.W.2d 662, 671 (Neb. App. 2008); *Neville v. Neville*, 791 N.E.2d 434, 437 (Ohio 2003); *Powell v. Powell*, 577 A.2d 576, 580 (Pa. 1990); *Johnson v. Johnson*, 734 N.W.2d 801, 808 (S.D. 2007); *Olsen v. Olsen*, 169 P.3d 765, 772 (Utah App. 2007); *In re Marriage of Zahm*, 978 P.2d 498, 502 (Wash. 1999).

At least eight states have concluded that they cannot be considered. *See Johnson v. Johnson*, 726 So. 2d 393, 396 (Fla. App. 1999); *In re Marriage of Crook*, 813 N.E.2d 198, 204 (Ill. 2004); *In re Marriage of Berthiaume*, 1991 WL 90839 (Minn. App.); *English v. English*, 879 P.2d 802, 808 (N.M. App. 1994); *Wolff v. Wolff*, 929 P.2d 916, 921 (Nev. 1996); *Olson v. Olson*, 445 N.W.2d 1, 11 (N.D. 1989); *In re Marriage of Swan*, 720 P.2d 747, 752 (Or. 1986); *Reymann v. Reymann*, 919 S.W.2d 615, 617 (Tenn. App. 1995); *Mack v. Mack*, 323 N.W.2d 153, 157 (Wis. 1982).

In those jurisdictions where social security benefits are considered, a trial court examines the parties' future social security benefits in relation to all marital assets in arriving at an equitable distribution of marital property. *See Litz v. Litz*, 288 S.W.3d 753 (Mo. App. 2009). In *Neville v. Neville*, 791 N.E.2d 434 (Ohio 2003), the court stated that although social security benefits are not subject to division, they may be considered when making an equitable distribution of marital property in a divorce proceeding in relation to all marital assets. *See Flemming v. Nestor*, 363 U.S. 603, 609-610 (1960) ("To engraft upon the Social Security system a concept of 'accrued property rights' would deprive it of the flexibility and boldness in adjustment to ever changing conditions which it demands.").

13.23. Military Retirement Benefits

In *McCarty v. McCarty*, the Supreme Court held that military retirement benefits were the separate property of the retiree. The decision was subsequently overruled by the Uniform Services Former Spouses Protection Act (USFSPA), 10 U.S.C. §1408 (1982). The Act allows states to apply their own laws when determining the divisibility of military retirement benefits upon divorce.

SPECIAL PROPERTY CHARACTERIZATION AND VALUATION ISSUES

13.24. Advanced Degrees

Courts throughout the country take a variety of approaches when attempting to place a property value on an advanced degree or professional license obtained during a marriage. The issue most commonly arises when one partner works outside the home while supporting the other partner who achieves an advanced degree or professional license.

The New York Court of Appeals, in *O'Brien v. O'Brien*, 489 N.E.2d 712 (1985), concluded that a professional license is "marital property" within the context of the governing New York statute. The New York Appellate Division, relying on the rationale of *O'Brien*, subsequently also concluded, in *McGowan v. McGowan*, 518 N.Y.S.2d 346 (1987), that a professional degree is marital property.

In *O'Brien*, the working wife supported the student husband through medical school only to have the husband file for divorce two months after obtaining a medical license. The court concluded that New York's unique statutory scheme was broader than those of other states that had declined to consider degrees and licenses marital property, and that, unlike other states, "our statute recognizes that spouses have an equitable claim to things of value arising out of the marital relationship and classifies them as subject to distribution by focusing on the marital status of the parties at the time of acquisition. . . . [T]hey hardly fall within the traditional property concepts because there is no common-law property interest remotely resembling marital property." 489 N.E.2d. at 715. The court further acknowledged that "the New York Legislature deliberately went beyond traditional concepts when it formulated the Equitable Distribution Law. . . ." *Id.*

Under *O'Brien*, a court must determine the present value of projected future earnings of the spouse holding the degree at the time of divorce. In *O'Brien*, the court reasoned that although there may be problems fixing the present value of enhanced earning capacity, the problems are not insurmountable and no more difficult than computing tort damages for wrongful death or diminished earning capacity resulting from injury. The court said that fixing a value on a professional license differs only in degree from the problems presented when valuing a professional practice for purposes of a distributive award, something the courts have not hesitated to do. *See Procario v. Procario*, 623 N.Y.S.2d 971 (N.Y. Sup. 1994) (former husband's increased earning capacity as result of completion of surgical residence was marital property); *Parlow v. Parlow*, 548 N.Y.S.2d 373 (N.Y. Sup. 1989) (defendant's teaching license is marital property subject to equitable distribution).

A majority of jurisdictions refuse to treat professional licenses and degrees that represent one spouse's enhanced earning capacity as marital property and provide a number of reasons to support their position. They contend that a professional license is not property at all; rather, it represents a personal attainment in acquiring knowledge. It is also neither physically nor metaphysically property and does not have an exchange value or any objective transferable value on an open market. Moreover, an attempt to place a value on it is speculative. It is also personal to the holder, terminates on death of the holder, is not inheritable, and cannot be assigned, sold, transferred, conveyed, or pledged. An advanced degree is a cumulative product of many years of previous education, combined with diligence and hard work. It may not be acquired by the mere expenditure of money. It has none of the attributes of property in the usual sense of that term. *See Nelson v. Nelson*, 736 P.2d 1145 (Alaska 1987); *Wisner v. Wisner*, 631 P.2d 115 (Ariz. App. 1981); *In re Marriage of Sullivan*, 184 Cal. Rptr. 796 (Cal. App. 1982); *vacated*, 691 P.2d 1020 (1984) (statute amended to provide for the community to be reimbursed for community contributions to education of a party); *Graham v. Graham*, 574 P.2d 75 (Colo. 1978) (husband's master's degree in business administration, which was obtained during marriage and while wife was providing approximately 70% of the spouses' income, was not "property" subject to division); *Simmons v. Simmons*, 708 A.2d 949 (Conn. 1998) (husband's medical degree was not property subject to equitable distribution); *Hughes v. Hughes*, 438 So. 2d 146 (Fla. App. 1983); *In re Marriage of Weinstein*, 470 N.E.2d 551 (Ill. App. 1984); *Drapek v. Drapek*, 503 N.E.2d 946 (Mass. 1987) (spouse's professional degree and enhanced earning capacity, acquired during marriage, are not marital assets); *Geer v. Geer*, 353 S.E.2d 427 (N.C. 1987) (while professional license is separate property, contribution to spouse's career is compensable); *Ruben v. Ruben*, 461 A.2d 733 (N.H. 1983); *Mahoney v. Mahoney*, 453 A.2d 527 (N.J. 1982); *Hodge v. Hodge*, 520 A.2d 15 (Pa. Sup. Ct. 1986) (medical license is not marital property; doctor's increased future earning capacity cannot be considered for purposes of equitable distribution); *Wehrkamp v. Wehrkamp*, 357 N.W.2d 264 (S.D. 1984); *Petersen v. Petersen*, 737 P.2d 237 (Utah Ct. App. 1987) (medical degree not a marital asset; compensatory alimony award may be proper). Although a majority of jurisdictions reject treating a professional degree obtained during a marriage as marital property, it is not ignored. For example, some jurisdictions suggest that the future value of a degree acquired by one of the parties during the marriage, although not subject to division or transfer upon divorce, should be considered an element when reaching an equitable award of alimony. *See, e.g., Stevens v. Stevens*, 492 N.E.2d 131, 136-137 (Ohio 1986) (veterinary degree was not marital property; future value of veterinary degree was element to be considered in reaching alimony award); *Downs v. Downs*, 574 A.2d 156 (Vt. 1990) (future value of professional degree is relevant factor to be considered in reaching just and equitable maintenance award).

Rather than place a specific present and future value on a degree or license and treat it as a divisible asset, some courts will apply a cost-value theory to the parties' relationship, which recognizes the contributions a supporting spouse made to the person who obtained the degree while that person was obtaining it. In a cost-value jurisdiction, a court calculates the value of the supporting spouse's contributions, not only in terms of expenditures of money for education and living expenses, but also in terms of personal services rendered during the marriage. *See, e.g., De La Rosa v. De La Rosa*, 309 N.W.2d 755 (Minn. 1981) (wife awarded restitution for financial contributions made to husband during his medical schooling).

Some courts might select what is referred to as a "lost opportunity costs" theory. This theory considers the income the supporting spouse and family may have sacrificed because the student spouse attended school rather than accepting employment. If, for example, the student spouse could have earned $50,000 a year at a job for eight years rather than enter school with the goal of obtaining a medical license, the loss of income to the family unit is considered lost opportunity costs.

Still another possible theory involves compensating the supporting spouse according to the present value of the student spouse's enhanced earning capacity. This theory recognizes the supporting spouse's lost expectation of sharing in the enhanced earning capacity of the partner. It provides the supporting spouse with a return on his or her investment in the student spouse, measured by the student spouse's enhanced earning capacity. For example, assume the estimated enhanced earning capacity of the husband after graduating from medical school and completing his residency was estimated at $266,000. The figure is arrived at as "the product of multiplying the husband's after-tax annual enhanced earnings of $13,000 (the difference between the husband's annual salary as a physician and the mean salary for college-educated males in his age group) by 32.3 (estimated years remaining in the husband's expected working life) discounted to its present value." *Haugan v. Haugan*, 343 N.W.2d 796, 803 (Wis. 1984) (suggesting several possible approaches to problem of compensating supporting spouse for costs and opportunities forgone while student spouse was in school).

Example 13-11

Assume that P and D were married and that D immediately embarked on an accelerated medical school program to obtain a medical degree. P testified that while D attended medical school, she worked as a waitress five or six nights a week, earning between $30 and $40 a night. In the summers, P also was employed as recreational assistant. Previous to the marriage, she had worked as a nurse's aide. The monies P earned were used to support the family and to some extent D's medical school tuition and expenses. D received his medical degree after several years of study and notified P on graduation night that he wanted a separation. They separated for two years, and then P began divorce proceedings because D was living with a female doctor. P testified that during the separation, she had obtained a nursing certificate, and at the time of the divorce, she was earning about $50,000 a year. It was estimated that D was earning about $150,000 a year. Because the parties had not accumulated marital property of any significant value at the time of separation, P could not be reimbursed for her contributions to her husband's education through a distribution of property. P also waived a request for alimony. An expert placed a present value on D's medical degree at $1 million, and P sought a one-third share of it. In a majority of jurisdictions, how will a court most likely treat P's argument?

Explanation

A court in a majority of jurisdictions will not place a value on the medical degree but will distribute it to P. It will recognize that shortly after the degree was received, the marriage failed, and P was unable to see any benefit for her years of sacrifice while D was able to pursue a professional medical degree and became a physician. Many courts will conclude that P should be compensated in some fashion for the financial support she gave D while he was a student. Any one of the several theories discussed earlier in this section might be selected by the court. When the compensatory theory is selected and an award made, it will not be viewed as alimony. Rather, it will be considered compensation for P's contribution to attainment of the degree while they were married. *See Lehmicke v. Lehmicke*, 559, 489 A.2d 782 (Pa. Super. 1985); *Mahoney v. Mahoney*, 453 A.2d 527 (N.J. 1982). If alimony were awarded (P waived alimony), courts have a tendency to adjust the compensation to recognize the contributions made by the supporting spouse. A court on the facts of the hypothetical is faced with a very challenging problem. One of the more favored theories is the cost-value approach, described earlier, and it might well be selected as an equitable method of resolving the dispute. *See, e.g., De La Rosa v. De La Rosa*, 309 N.W.2d 755 (Minn. 1981).

13.25. Workers' Compensation and Personal Injury Awards

Courts have not been uniform in their treatment of workers' compensation and personal injury awards. Some courts appear to categorize them as benefits to the marital corpus, whereas others view them as a personal injury recovery and the separate property of the injured party. *See Weisfeld v. Weisfeld*, 545 So. 2d 1341, 1344-1345 (Fla. 1989) (analytical, rather than mechanistic or unitary, approach was to be used in deciding how to treat workers' compensation award upon dissolution). The various perspectives are summarized below.

Some courts take a mechanistic approach when considering how workers' compensation and personal injury awards should be distributed between a married couple. In these jurisdictions, if a personal injury or workers' compensation award was acquired during the marriage, it is considered marital or community property and is divided as such, unless it falls within specific but limited statutory exceptions. Arkansas, Colorado, Illinois, Michigan, Missouri, Nebraska, Pennsylvania, and Vermont appear to have adopted this view. *See Liles v. Liles*, 711 S.W.2d 447 (Ark. 1986); *In re Marriage of Fieldheim*, 676 P.2d 1234 (Colo. App. 1983); *In re Marriage of Dettore*, 408 N.E.2d 429 (Ill. App. Ct. 1980); *Hagen v. Hagen*, 508 N.W.2d 196 (Mich.

1993) (division of payments on workers' compensation claim for injury that occurred during the marriage found proper); *Jobe v. Jobe*, 708 S.W.2d 322 (Mo. Ct. App. 1986); *Maricle v. Maricle*, 378 N.W.2d 855 (Neb. 1985); *Platek v. Platek*, 454 A.2d 1059 (Super. Ct. 1982); *Condosta v. Condosta*, 395 A.2d 345 (Vt. 1978).

A growing number of courts have adopted the analytical theory, which requires an analysis of the nature of a workers' compensation or personal injury damage award to determine whether the property is separate and belongs to the injured spouse or is marital property subject to distribution. Under this theory, the damage award is allocated along the following lines. First, a court identifies the separate property of the injured spouse, which includes the noneconomic compensatory damages for pain, suffering, disability, and loss of ability to lead a normal life. Separate property also includes the economic damages that occur subsequent to the termination of the marriage, including the amount of the award for loss of future wages and future medical expenses. Second, a court identifies the separate property of the noninjured spouse, which includes loss of consortium. Third, the court identifies the marital property subject to distribution, which includes the amount of the award for lost wages or lost earning capacity during the marriage of the parties and medical expenses paid out of marital funds during the marriage.

Although community property states originally followed the mechanistic approach and treated a personal injury award as part of a marital couple's community property, Texas was one of the first to alter its approach and adopt the analytical approach in *Graham v. Franco*, 488 S.W.2d 390 (Tex. 1972). With the exception of California, all community property states and a number of equitable distribution states have adopted the analytical theory. *See Jurek v. Jurek*, 606 P.2d 812 (Ariz. 1980); *Rogers v. Yellowstone Park Co.*, 97 539 P.2d 566 (Idaho 1974); *Placide v. Placide*, 408 So. 2d 330 (La. Ct. App.1981); *Frederickson & Watson Constr. Co. v. Boyd*, 102 P.2d 627 (Nev. 1940); *Luxton v. Luxton*, 648 P.2d 315 (N.M. 1982); *Graham v. Franco*, 488 S.W.2d 390 (Tex. 1972).

A growing number of equitable distribution jurisdictions have also adopted the analytical theory: *See Campbell v. Campbell*, 339 S.E.2d 591 (Ga. 1986); *Van de Loo v. Van de Loo*, 346 N.W.2d 173 (Minn. App. 1984); *In re Marriage of Blankenship*, 682 P.2d 1354 (Mont. 1984); *Rich v. Rich*, 483 N.Y.S.2d 150 (Sup. Ct. 1984); *Johnson v. Johnson*, 346 S.E.2d 430 (N.C. 1986).

Another issue, raised on rare occasions, involves a divorce that is about to be finalized while an unsettled personal injury or workers' compensation claim is pending. Courts take two approaches; some courts view the existence of the uncertainty surrounding the question of whether a plaintiff spouse may win or lose the claim as speculative and not constituting marital property. However, a majority of courts view a pending claim as potentially constituting marital property, which is subject to later determination and possible distribution once the pending claim is resolved. In these jurisdictions, a divorce decree will include provisions allowing an examination of any proceeds later awarded from the unsettled claim to determine what portion is marital property.

Example 13-12

Assume that P is injured in an industrial accident during his marriage to D, loses his right arm, and is out of work for six months. P and D divorce in a jurisdiction that applies the analytical approach to workers' compensation awards. Six months after the divorce settlement, P receives a lump-sum payment of $100,000. P argues that compensation for an injury resulting in the loss of his right arm is a benefit and not property acquired during the marriage to be considered for distribution as marital property. P also argues that as an individual, he brought his body into the marriage, and on dissolution of the marriage, he is entitled to take it with him. He contends that his body is his separate property, and compensation received for damage or loss to it is his separate property. P also argues that a spouse's health, life, limb, personal security, and so on can be viewed as property acquired prior to marriage and later exchanged for compensation. Finally, he argues that because the final award was speculative at the time of divorce, it cannot be considered as marital property now. How will a court most likely treat these arguments and distribute the property?

Explanation

A court is likely to view the award as encompassing earnings lost both before and after the divorce and as involving individual pain and suffering. If a portion of the award is for income lost before divorce and while the couple was married, a court would hold that the pre-divorce portion is marital property subject to division. The post-divorce portion related to loss of income will likely be viewed as nonmarital property that belongs exclusively to P. *See Miller v. Miller*, 739 P.2d 163, 165 (Alaska 1987); *Queen v. Queen*, 521 A.2d 320, 324 (Md. 1987). The court would also consider that the noneconomic compensatory damages for pain, suffering, disability, and P's loss of ability to lead a normal life are P's nonmarital property and not subject to distribution.

13.26. Goodwill

Goodwill is an intangible asset of a marriage and may be valued and distributed upon divorce. Goodwill is defined as "the benefits that accrue to a business as a result of its location, reputation for dependability, skill or quality, and any other circumstances resulting in probable retention of old or acquisition of new patronage." Goodwill value is a transferable property right that is generally defined as the amount a willing buyer would pay for a going concern above the book value of the assets.

When the future earning capacity of a business has been enhanced because of its reputation, this leads to probable future patronage from existing and potential clients, and goodwill may exist and have value. When that occurs, the resulting goodwill is property subject to equitable distribution. *Spayd v. Turner, Granzow & Hollenkamp*, 482 N.E.2d 1232 (Ohio 1985).

Essentially, goodwill in a dissolution context is a portion of the value of the business as a going concern. *In re Marriage of Rives*, 181 Cal. Rptr. 572 (Cal. App. 1982).

RELATED AREAS OF LAW

13.27. Premarital Contracts

Premarital contracts or settlements validly executed and in conformity with local statutes and common law of a particular jurisdiction may determine what rights each party has in the nonmarital property upon dissolution of marriage, upon legal separation, or after the marriage's termination because of death and may bar each party of all rights in the respective estates not secured to them by their agreement. *See Gentry v. Gentry*, 798 S.W.2d 928 (Ky. 1990). By entering into a premarital contract, a couple waives the right to have a court consider how to divide their marital property. Instead, the contract sets out the terms of a property division should they divorce. Note that premarital contracts are given extensive analysis in Chapter 14.

13.28. Bankruptcy

Congress changed the bankruptcy law in 1994 and again in 2005 so that divorce-related property obligations are not always dischargeable. Note that a debt owed to a spouse, former spouse, or child in connection with a court order is not dischargeable in bankruptcy. 11 U.S.C. §523(a)(5). This includes any liability that "is actually in the nature of alimony, maintenance, or support." 11 U.S.C. §523(a)(5)(B). Nondomestic support obligations, such as property settlements, are dischargeable in Chapter 13 bankruptcies to the extent provided in the confirmed Chapter 13 plan. 11 U.S.C. §1328(a). *See also In re Douglas*, 369 B.R. 462, 465 (Bankr. E.D. Ark. 2007); Janet Leach Richards, *A Guide to Spousal Support and Property Division Claims*

Under the Bankruptcy Abuse Prevention and Consumer Protection Act of 2005, 41 Fam. L.Q. 227 (Summer2007).

13.29. Tax Treatment: Heterosexual and Same-Sex Marriages

As a result of the Tax Reform Act of 1984, the recipient of property in a heterosexual divorce takes the transferor's adjusted basis for the property. Prior to the 1984 reform, when property was transferred from one spouse to another as a result of a divorce settlement, and the fair market value exceeded the asset basis, the Internal Revenue Service considered this a taxable event, and taxes were due. If property that was transferred had lost value, this was also considered a taxable event. United States v. Davis, 370 U.S. 65 (1962). For an overview of tax policy and family law, see Patricia Cain, Taxing Families Fairly, 48 Santa Clara L. Rev. 805 (2008).

Because federal tax law does not recognize same-sex marriages, it will not apply its divorce provisions to a same-sex couple who dissolve their relationship, even if they were legally married in a jurisdiction that allows same-sex couples to marry. The outcome is the same where civil unions are concerned. Note that in July 2009, Massachusetts, the first state to legalize gay marriage, challenged the constitutionality of the Defense of Marriage Act of 1996, which defines marriage as the union of a man and woman. The lawsuit contends that the Act violates the U.S. Constitution by interfering with the state's right to define the marital status of residents. The suit also says the law forces the state to discriminate against same-sex married couples with respect to certain health benefits and burial rights or risk losing federal funding. There had not been any rulings ultimately resolving the Massachusetts lawsuit when this edition of this book went to press.

Premarital (Antenuptial or Prenuptial) Contracts — History, Requirements, and Restrictions

14.1. Introduction

This chapter surveys the legal issues confronted by practitioners and courts concerning drafting and enforcement of premarital contracts. A premarital contract is referred to in various jurisdictions as a *premarital, antenuptial,* or *prenuptial* agreement or contract. The words are used interchangeably but they all have the same definition. *See Black's Law Dictionary* 1220 (8th ed. 2004) (stating a prenuptial agreement is also termed as an antenuptial or premarital agreement). If validly created, a premarital contract permits the parties to agree before they marry to waive or limit certain "rights" or "benefits" that generally flow from the marital relationship via state law.

Premarital contracts are presently used to control property distribution upon the occurrence of two events: the death of a spouse or a divorce. They are also used in some jurisdictions to limit alimony. That was not always the case.

HISTORY

14.2. Courts Limit Use to a Party's Death

Premarital contracts first appeared during the sixteenth century in England. Judith T. Younger, *Perspectives on Antenuptial Contracts*, 40 Rutgers L. Rev. 1059, 1061, nn.2, 5 (1988); W. Holdsworth, *A History of English Law* 310-312

(3d ed. 1945). Both chancery and law courts passed on their validity, and by the mid-seventeenth century, they were of sufficient importance to be included in the original Statute of Frauds. *Id.* at nn.3, 4.

Historically, a premarital contract settled property rights at the time of the death of one of the parties to the relationship. A contract was often executed when the parties were contemplating a second marriage, and one or both had substantial property and children from a first marriage to whom they wanted their property to go upon their death. Without a premarital contract, in most jurisdictions, a surviving spouse had the option of taking property under a will or taking a statutory share of the marital estate and ignoring the will.

Premarital contracts that were limited to enforcement upon death of a party were "favored by the law as promoting domestic happiness and adjusting property questions which would otherwise often be the source of fruitful litigation." *Buffington v. Buffington*, 51 N.E. 328, 329 (Ind. 1898). *See Williamson v. First Nat. Bank of Williamson*, 164 S.E. 777 (W. Va. 1931) (premarital contracts tend to adjust family disputes). They were viewed as a legal mechanism by which a party could facilitate the transfer of certain property upon death to his or her children from a prior marriage, without it being subject to a claim by a surviving second family member.

State courts did not recognize the use of premarital contracts in the event of a divorce until the latter part of the twentieth century. Prior to that time, courts uniformly held that a contract between a husband and wife, which attempted to limit a court's power to distribute marital property upon divorce, was contrary to public policy, illegal, and void because it promoted the dissolution of the marriage. *Cohn v. Cohn*, 121 A.2d 704 (Md. 1956) (rule is well established that a contract that provides for, facilitates, or tends to induce a separation or divorce of the parties after marriage is contrary to public policy and void); *Stratton v. Wilson*, 185 S.W. 522, 523 (1916) (antenuptial agreements contemplating divorce and separation are void because they tended to promote, or at least predict, marital instability); *In re Estate of Appleby*, 111 N.W. 305 (Minn. 1907) (contracts that tend to induce a separation of husband and wife are, upon the same principle of public policy that discountenances contracts in restraint of marriage, utterly void and of no force or effect).

14.3. Courts Expand Premarital Contracts to Divorce

By the 1970s, the public's perspective on marriage and divorce had markedly changed. Freed & Walker, *Family Law in the Fifty States: An Overview*, 19 Fam. L.Q. 331, 438 (1985-1986). The country was experiencing major cultural changes, and views toward marriage and divorce were being radically altered. With the advent of no-fault divorce laws and the changes in societal norms, the traditional rule regarding the limits on the use of premarital contracts was being challenged.

The decision by the Florida Supreme Court in *Posner v. Posner*, 233 So. 2d 381 (Fla. 1970), marks a turning point in the use of premarital contracts upon divorce. When *Posner* was decided, the court took judicial notice of the fact that the ratio of marriages to divorces has

> reached a disturbing rate in many states. . . . With divorce such a commonplace fact of life, it is fair to assume that many prospective marriage partners whose property and familial situation is such as to generate a valid premarital contract settling their property rights upon the death of either, might want to consider and discuss also — and agree upon, if possible — the disposition of their property and the alimony rights of the wife in the event their marriage, despite their best efforts, should fail.

Id. at 384. After *Posner*, jurisdictions steadily retreated from the common law view that a premarital contract is limited to use only upon death. *See Rinvelt v. Rinvelt*, 475 N.W.2d 478 (Mich. App. 1991) (concluding that the outdated policy concerns that once led courts to refuse to enforce antenuptial agreements are no longer compelling); *Brooks v. Brooks*, 733 P.2d 1044 (Alaska 1987) (no-fault divorce laws and societal changes have given way to the more realistic view that prenuptial agreements are not void *ab initio*).

Example 14-1

Assume that P and D execute a premarital contract in 1890 containing a provision that limits the amount of marital property D would receive should the couple divorce. In a typical common law jurisdiction, how is such a provision treated? In a twenty-first century jurisdiction that applies the *Posner* perspective, how would such a provision be treated?

Explanation

In a common law jurisdiction, the 1890 contract provision related to dividing marital property would not be enforced. Common law courts viewed a contract to distribute property upon divorce as contrary to public policy on the theory that it encouraged a breakdown of the marriage relationship. In a jurisdiction today that has adopted the *Posner* view of premarital contracts, assuming the agreement was arrived at fairly, it would be upheld. *See Snedaker v. Snedaker*, 660 So. 2d 1070 (Fla. App. 1995) (provisions in premarital contract that neither spouse acquired any interest in property of other as a result of marriage, provisions that set the amount of the wife's support payments on escalating scale based on the length of marriage, and provisions that specifically waived a spouse's right to receive any further alimony, support, or maintenance payments were fair and reasonable to wife, given the circumstances of the spouses).

COMPARING COMMERCIAL AND PREMARITAL CONTRACTS

14.4. Difference Between Premarital and Commercial Contracts

There are three basic differences between a premarital contract and an ordinary civil contract. Judith T. Younger, *Perspectives on Antenuptial Contracts*, 40 Rutgers L. Rev. 1059, 1061 (1988). First, the state has a greater interest in a premarital contract than in a commercial contract. Because of its interest, the state assumes the role of *parens patriae* with respect to protecting the children of the relationship and, in some cases, protecting against an unfair distribution of marital and nonmarital property and an improper waiver of spousal support. Second, the relationship between the parties is different from that found in an ordinary business contract because, at the time a premarital contract is executed, courts view the relationship between the parties as confidential and not as an arm's-length one. Furthermore, unlike most business contracts, the parties to a premarital contract may not be evenly matched in bargaining power. Finally, a premarital contract is to be performed in the future, in the context of a personal relationship that the parties have yet to experience.

UNIFORM ACTS

14.5. Uniform Premarital Contract Act

In 1983 the National Conference of Commissioners on Uniform State Laws promulgated the Uniform Premarital Contract Act (UPA). The UPA was written to provide state legislatures with a model statute governing premarital contracts. The UPA addresses the formalities for execution and enforcement of premarital contracts. A majority of jurisdictions have legislation dealing with premarital contracts and have been influenced by the UPA.

The UPA creates a presumption that premarital contracts are valid and enforceable and places on the party seeking to void the contract the burden of proving the contrary. A comment to the UPA states that the marriage itself acts as consideration for a premarital contract. To invalidate a premarital contract, the party challenging it must prove that the contract was unconscionable, a somewhat amorphous concept.

The UPA has been adopted in some form in at least 29 states and the District of Columbia. Among the states are Arizona, Arkansas, California, Connecticut, Delaware, Hawaii, Idaho, Illinois, Indiana, Iowa, Kansas, Maine, Minnesota, Mississippi, Montana, Nebraska, Nevada, New Jersey, New Mexico, North Carolina, North Dakota, Oregon, Rhode Island, South Dakota, Texas, Utah, Virginia, West Virginia, and Wisconsin. More states are expected to adopt the Act.

14.6. American Law Institute Premarital Principles

The American Law Institute included provisions for drafting and evaluating premarital contracts in its *Principles of Family Dissolution*. *See Principles of the Law of Family Dissolution: Analysis and Recommendations* (Tentative Draft No. 4 2000). The *Principles* set out procedural requirements that are already required by most states. These requirements include that a contract be signed and in writing, that there be full financial disclosure, and that consent not be obtained under duress. There is a presumption of informed consent and the absence of duress if the contract was executed at least 30 days before the parties' marriage and if the parties were advised to obtain legal counsel and had an opportunity to do so.

The burden of proving the lack of duress and the presence of consent is placed on the party who is trying to enforce the contract, which is intended to "caution" the stronger party against overreaching. Judith T. Younger, *Antenuptial Contracts*, 28 Wm. Mitchell L. Rev. 697, 700, 718 (2000). Should one party fail to retain independent counsel, the informed-consent presumption will not go into effect unless the contract contains understandable language explaining the significance of its terms and the fact that the parties' interests may be adverse with respect to them. *Id.*

The American Law Institute omits any requirement of substantive fairness at the time of execution. However, at the time the contract is to be enforced, the *Principles* provide for "a wider substantive review of these contracts" than allowed under the UPA. *Id.*

STANDARDS FOR CREATION OF PREMARITAL CONTRACTS

14.7. Common Requirements and Restrictions

Most jurisdictions have attempted to reduce the uncertainty surrounding the use of premarital contracts by promulgating statutes that replace the common law and set forth specific procedures, which must be followed when drafting them. *See, e.g.,* N.J.S. §37:2-38 (2009) (enforcement of premarital or pre-civil union agreement, generally); Tenn. Code §36-3-501 (2009) (enforcement of antenuptial agreements); Minn. Stat. §519.11 (2005) (antenuptial and postnuptial contracts). For a contract to be valid, it must be fair, equitable, and reasonable in view of all of the surrounding facts and circumstances. There must be proof that it was entered into voluntarily by both parties, with each understanding his or her rights and the extent of the waiver of such rights.

Note that the fact that one party to the contract apparently made a bad bargain is not a sufficient ground, by itself, to vacate or modify a premarital contract. *Micale v. Micale,* 542 So. 2d 415, 417 (Fla. App. 1989) (while wife made a bad bargain for herself in entering into agreement dividing various businesses between her and her husband, the evidence failed to support claim of fraud).

14.8. Special Duty to Disclose — Waiving Property Rights

Where property rights are concerned, premarital contracts are viewed as giving rise to a special duty of disclosure not required in ordinary contract relationships. It is common, for example, to find courts and statutes adhering to the principle that each person signing a premarital contract has an affirmative duty to disclose to the other the nature of his property interests so that the effect of the contract can be understandingly assessed and waived. Disclosure is important because it underscores that each party is exercising a meaningful choice when he or she agrees to give up certain rights found in statutes to protect married persons should they divorce or should one of them die during the marriage. *See Ortel v. Gettig,* 116 A.2d 145 (Md. 1955) (refusing to uphold contract where there was no disclosure or discussion of the net worth of the parties).

The requirement of disclosure is intimately connected to the concept of waiver. The relationship is particularly important given the perspective of a majority of jurisdictions that consider the relationship as confidential, that is, not an arm's-length transaction. Courts reason that without full and truthful disclosure of the nature, extent, and worth of the real and personal property involved in the agreement, the party who contractually waives statutory protections cannot know what is in fact being waived. *See Newman v. Newman,* 653 P.2d 728, 732 (Colo. 1982) (if stringent tests of full disclosure and lack of fraud or overreaching are met, parties are free to agree to any arrangement for division of their property, including a waiver of any claim to the property of the other); *Burtoff v. Burtoff*, 418 A.2d 1085, 1089 (D.C. App. 1980) (prospective spouses may contractually define their rights in property and waive rights that otherwise would arise as a matter of law). The full disclosure rule also helps level the bargaining field for the party in the weaker bargaining position. *Kosik v. George*, 452 P.2d 560, 563 (Or. 1969) (invalid contract where decedent was man of extensive business background, knowledge, and financial worth, and widow was woman with high school education, very limited business experience, and limited financial worth; such wide disparity between decedent and widow invoked responsibility on decedent and his attorney to fully inform widow regarding consequences of executing prenuptial agreement, but only advice given widow before she signed agreement was that purpose of agreement was to avoid dower and curtesy, and agreement instead acted as bar to her right to claim property exempt from execution).

The extent of what constitutes "full and fair" disclosure varies from case to case, depending on a number of factors, which may include the parties' respective sophistication and experience in business affairs; their respective worth, ages, intelligence, and literacy; their prior family ties or commitments; the duration of their relationship prior to the execution of the contract; the time of the signing of the contract in relation to the time of the wedding; and their representation by, or opportunity to consult with, independent counsel. *See, e.g., Randolph v. Randolph*, 937 S.W.2d 815 (Tenn. 1996) (former wife did not enter antenuptial agreement knowledgeably, even though she had lived with husband for about a year before marriage, was aware of nature of former husband's business but was not aware of nature or extent of his assets, had no prior business experience or knowledge, he was shrewd businessperson, and she had no opportunity to study the agreement or to seek advice from her own attorney or others close to her). Although disclosure need not reveal precisely every asset owned by an individual spouse, at a minimum, full and fair disclosure requires that each contracting party be given a clear idea of the nature, extent, and value of the other party's property and resources. *See, e.g., Pajak v. Pajak*, 385 S.E.2d 384, 388 (Va. 1989) (contract upheld where wife knew husband was a successful businessman and she was aware that he owned a number of businesses, had real estate holdings, and lived reasonably well; unnecessary parties execute a detailed, written financial statement such as is required by a bank before making a loan). *See Hartz v. Hartz*, 234 A.2d 865, 871, n.3 (Md. 1967).

If parties wish to insulate a contract from subsequent challenge on the basis of overreaching, full, frank, and truthful disclosure is essential. *See Annot., Failure to Disclose Extent or Value of Property Owned as Ground for Avoiding Premarital Contract*, 3 A.L.R.5th 394 (1993).

14.9. Waiving Child and Spousal Support

Although there is a strong public policy favoring individuals ordering and deciding their own interests through contractual arrangements, including premarital contracts, child support, custody, and visitation trump such interests. In the context of child support, custody, and visitation, a court will act as *parens patriae*, and retains jurisdiction to act in the child's best interests. In all jurisdictions, absent extraordinary circumstances, a provision in a premarital agreement eliminating a party's child support obligation is void as against public policy. *See Serio v. Serio*, 830 So. 2d 278 (Fla. App. 2002) (parents may not waive their children's right to support because that right belongs to the children). Likewise, when determining child custody, the best interest of the children, rather than the parents, is the court's paramount concern. Even if the premarital agreement mandated joint custody, this would not affect the trial court's authority, indeed, obligation, to determine custody and parenting time in accordance with the best interests of the children. *See Edwardson v. Edwardson*, 798 S.W.2d 941, 946 (Ky. 1990) (holding that antenuptial agreements are ineffectual in determining child custody and visitation issues).

Historically, common law courts assumed provisions regarding waiver of spousal support were unenforceable and void as against public policy. The courts felt that if a husband were permitted to limit the amount of alimony the wife could receive at divorce, he would have an economic incentive to obtain a divorce. Another concern was that a man should not be able to contract before marriage against the liability to his wife that he would incur should he commit offenses against the wife during the marriage. Some courts were also concerned that such agreements tended to limit the rights of an unsophisticated prospective spouse.

Today, much of the common law policy barring spousal waiver of support in a premarital contract has disappeared. An estimated 41 jurisdictions have abandoned the common law restrictions on premarital waivers of spousal support. In 29 jurisdictions, premarital waivers of spousal support are authorized by statutes that adopt either all or substantially all of the provisions of the Uniform Premarital Agreement Act (UPAA).

In some jurisdictions, such as Iowa, legislation exists declaring that "[t]he right of a spouse or child to support shall not be adversely affected by a premarital agreement." Iowa Code §596.5(2) (1991). Therefore, the waiver of spousal support in a prenuptial agreement in Iowa is not binding. *In re Marriage of Regenmorter*, 587 N.W.2d 493, 495 (Iowa Ct. App. 1998). In South Dakota, provisions in a prenuptial agreement purporting to limit or waive spousal support are void and unenforceable because they are contrary to public policy. *Sanford v. Sanford*, 694 N.W.2d 283 (S.D. 2005) (legislature did not enact those portions of UPAA that allowed parties to a prenuptial agreement to contract with respect to the modification or elimination of spousal support).

In In re Marriage of Pendleton & Fireman, 5 P.3d 839 (Cal. 2000), the court held that provisions limiting alimony were not per se unenforceable. It upheld a waiver of spousal support "executed by intelligent, well-educated persons, each of whom appears to be self-sufficient in property and earning ability, and both of whom have the advice of counsel regarding their rights and obligations as marital partners at the time they execute the waiver" as not violating public policy. Id. at 848-849. Frey v. Frey, 471 A.2d 705, 711 (Md. 1984) (antenuptial agreement settling alimony upon divorce is not per se against public policy and may be specifically enforced).

The Massachusetts Supreme Court held that it is permissible for parties contemplating marriage to enter into an antenuptial contract settling their alimony rights in the event their marriage should prove unsuccessful. Osborne v. Osborne, 428 N.E.2d 810 (Mass. 1981). The court noted, however, that the freedom to limit or waive alimony in the event of divorce is not unrestricted, and it set forth guidelines to be used in determining the extent to which such agreements should be enforced. The court also held that the contract must be fair and reasonable at the time of entry of the divorce judgment.

The provision of an antenuptial contract by which parties waived alimony was held unconscionable at the time of enforcement by the Kentucky Supreme Court. Lane v. Lane, 202 S.W.3d 577 (Ky. 2006). Factors leading to this conclusion included that the marriage was the first for both parties, they were in their twenties when they married, two children were born of marriage, and the wife quit her job to care for children while her husband rapidly progressed in his career. The significant disparity in parties' incomes grew exponentially during marriage because the husband was able to concentrate on his career while the wife stayed home to care for the children and home, and parties maintained an affluent lifestyle during marriage.

In Missouri, if a spouse knowingly signs a waiver of alimony in a premarital contract, it will usually be upheld. In re Marriage of Thomas, 199 S.W.3d 847 (Mo. App. 2006) (agreement was not unconscionable where wife waived maintenance, attorney fees, and any interest in corporation husband owned); Gant v. Gant, 329 S.E.2d 106 (W. Va. 1985) (wife's waiver of alimony in prenuptial agreement was valid, reversing trial judge who found contract invalid because it was executed the day before parties were married, wife was not represented by counsel, agreement was not carefully prepared, and trial judge concluded it was unfair, inequitable, and overreaching, and failed to consider the size of the parties' separate estates).

Example 14-2

Assume that P and D execute a premarital contract that provides that should a divorce occur, and children are born to the marriage of P and D, that P will receive sole legal and physical custody of them. After ten years, the couple divorce and P seeks to enforce the terms of the contract over D's objection.

At the hearing on the matter, both P and D admit that at the time they signed the premarital contract they completely understood its terms including the provision regarding child custody. How will a court most likely resolve the dispute?

Explanation

The court will not enforce the provision in the contract relating to custody of the children. The state has a very strong interest in protecting the children of a marriage and assumes the role of *parens patriae* with respect to them if a divorce action is brought. The state will not abrogate that responsibility, even if the couple clearly understood the terms contained in a premarital contract about how custody would be handled should a divorce occur. Here, the court will decide how the best interests of the child will be served, and the contract provision will be ignored.

Example 14-3

Assume that P and D execute a premarital contract that provides that should a divorce occur, and children are born to the marriage, that D will be relieved of any child support responsibility for the children. At the time the couple signed the premarital contact, D was an airline pilot with a major airline, and P was a physician in a local clinic. After ten years, the couple divorce and D, whose airline has merged and recently terminated D's employment, uses the terms of the contract to defend against a child support claim made by P. At the hearing on the matter, both P and D admit that at the time they signed the premarital contract they completely understood its terms, including the child support provision. How will a court most likely resolve the support issue?

Explanation

The court will not enforce the provision in the contract relating to child support. The state has a very strong interest in protecting the children of a marriage and assumes the role of *parens patriae* with respect to them in a divorce action. The state will not abrogate that responsibility, even if the couple clearly understood the terms contained in a premarital contract about how child support would be handled should a divorce occur. The court will protect the children at a support hearing from an earlier contract in which one parent agreed the other did not have to pay child support should a divorce occur. The court will consider the financial circumstances of both parents. The fact that D lost a job with the airline and P is a physician will not cause a court to enforce a support provision in a premarital contract against the interests of the minor children. A court will most likely ignore the support provision in the premarital contract.

14.10. Prior Understanding — Duress

Courts have held that the lack of negotiations prior to execution of an agreement or insufficient notice about the desire of one party for an agreement, standing alone, is seldom enough to invalidate an antenuptial agreement. Courts generally have treated such claims as a degree of duress and have held that transactions between such parties must be free of undue influence and duress.

For example, in *Rose v. Rose*, 526 N.E.2d 231, 235-236 (Ind. Ct. App. 1988), the court upheld a premarital contract that was presented to the bride-to-be only two days before the marriage. The husband testified that he would not marry the bride if she did not sign it. The court was swayed in its decision to enforce the agreement encompassing marital assets of $1 million dollars because it believed the husband's testimony that the two had discussed the necessity of a contract several times months before the marriage. *See Matter of the Marriage of Adams*, 729 P.2d 1151 (Kan. 1986) (contract enforced where husband approached wife the morning of wedding and asked her to sign the contract; the contract was identical to one wife reviewed earlier with her attorney); *Taylor v. Taylor*, 832 P.2d 429, 431 (Okla. Ct. App. 1991) (agreement essentially upheld where wife knew prior to marriage that husband owned several businesses and had assisted husband in business in personal matters prior to marriage and had been conversant with general business practices and was in possession of the agreement for three months prior to its execution); *Shepherd v. Shepherd*, 876 P.2d 429, 432 (Utah Ct. App. 1994) (agreement upheld where parties discussed it for period of four months prior to marriage, each party had opportunity to review and make changes to agreement, and husband, who was challenging validity of agreement, was a competent and able attorney who understood, or who should have understood, content and effect of agreement); *Lee v. Lee*, 816 S.W.2d 625 (Ark. App. 1991) (agreement enforced where there had been full disclosure of parties' financial conditions, wife had entered the agreement freely and voluntarily, and the provisions were fair and equitable, despite wife's contention that she had been rushed into signing an hour before wedding and had not read agreement or been aware of extent of husband's property).

In *Liebelt v. Liebelt*, 801 P.2d 52 (Idaho Ct. App. 1990), the court stated that the threat of a refusal to marry if a premarital agreement is not signed is not wrongful in the eyes of the law. The court said that such a threat received from a proposed marriage partner should put the potential spouse on notice that the agreement was of a serious nature and should be dealt with in a serious manner.

Example 14-4

Assume that this action is brought in a jurisdiction that recognizes the use of premarital contracts upon death or divorce. Also assume that it is a jurisdiction that does not allow the use of presumptions. Assume that one day before their marriage, the parties entered into a contract prepared by P's lawyer. The contract provided, in part, that in the event of divorce or death, each party released all marital rights in the separate property of the other, and the division of marital property was to be based upon the amount of money each party had invested in the property during the marriage. Also assume that at the time the contract was signed, D owned no assets, except personal belongings, while P, a successful businessperson, had substantial real estate holdings that were valued at approximately $8,000,000. In addition, assume P had CDs and cash of approximately $500,000.

The marriage broke down after ten years, and P filed for divorce, asking that the premarital contract be enforced. D testified that she did not see the contract until one day before the parties were to be married. On cross examination, D admitted that she reviewed the contract before signing it on the drive to P's attorney's office, but claimed that no one explained the meaning of the document to her. She said that because she was responsible for a minor child and suffering from breast cancer at the time, her only choices were to sign the contract or be kicked out of the residence she and her son had shared with P for the year prior to their marriage. D conceded that P had told her about some of his property, but she insisted that she was not aware of, nor did anyone disclose to her, the full extent and value of his assets and holdings.

D was not represented by counsel when she signed the contract. However, P's attorney, who drafted the contract, was present at the hearing on the validity of the contract and testified that it is his normal practice to explain such contracts to both parties to ensure a mutual understanding of the terms. He could not specifically recall following that practice with D and acknowledged that he did not provide D with a copy of P's financial statement prior to execution of the contract. He testified he discussed P's assets in general terms with D.

P conceded that he never specifically advised D of his net worth prior to signing the contract, but asserted that she must have been aware of them because they had lived together for more than one year before the contract was signed, and she had accompanied him to many of his properties to collect rent. P testified that D had also reviewed the contract before signing it and had made suggestions for changes, including a provision relating to a watch. Although D conceded that she read that provision before signing the contract, she denied that the provision was included at her suggestion. Will a court most likely uphold the contract on these facts?

Explanation

This is a close question; however, a court will most likely not uphold the contract for the following reasons. Although all agree that D resided with P for about a year before their marriage, P conceded that he failed to reveal the extent or value of his holdings and further agreed that D's knowledge of P's property was only general in nature. D's testimony regarding her general knowledge of P's holdings was corroborated by P and his attorney. Although specific appraisal values are not required to sustain the validity of a premarital contract, greater knowledge of the proponent spouse's overall net worth is usually necessary. In terms of the comparative sophistication and business experience of the parties, P was apparently a learned businessman, whereas D possessed no prior business experience or knowledge. Moreover, the contract was executed only one day before the parties were married, and D was presented with it on the way to P's attorney's office. Because of the short period of time between the presentation of the contract and the marriage, there was little time for D to personally study the contract or to contact her own attorney. For all of the above, a court will most likely not enforce the terms of the contract. *See Randolph v. Randolph*, 937 S.W.2d 815 (Tenn. 1996).

14.11. Right to Counsel

Most jurisdictions view the presence of independent counsel as one factor among many in determining whether to enforce a premarital contract. They have said that the lack of representation alone is not sufficient to void a premarital contract. *See, e.g., In re Estate of Kinney*, 733 N.W.2d 118, 124 (Minn. 2007) (the opportunity to consult with independent counsel is not a requirement, but is one of several relevant factors that courts may consider when determining whether an antenuptial agreement is fair and equitable); *Panossian v. Panossian*, 569 N.Y.S.2d 182 (N.Y.A.D. 1991) (absence of independent counsel during the transaction does not, under the circumstances presented here, warrant setting aside the agreement). However, in *Hoag v. Dick*, 799 A.2d 391 (Me. 2002), a premarital agreement was held invalid where it eliminated the wife's rights to receive a share of marital property and to recover any amount of spousal support upon divorce. The agreement was presented to wife on her wedding day, which deprived her of any opportunity to obtain advice from independent legal counsel.

Some jurisdictions, such as California and Arkansas, have enacted statutory provisions to strengthen the independent counsel requirement. *See, e.g.,* Cal. Fam. Code §1615(c) (2002) ("For the purposes of subdivision (a), it shall be deemed that a premarital agreement was not executed voluntarily unless the court finds in writing or on the record all of the following: (1) The party against whom enforcement is sought was represented by independent legal counsel at the time of signing the agreement or, after being advised to seek independent legal counsel, expressly waived, in a separate writing, representation by independent legal counsel."); Ark. Code §9-11-406. *Enforcement* (2002).

14.12. Imposition of Marital Duties and Obligations

Occasionally, parties will incorporate provisions into a premarital contract that attempt to impose various duties and obligations on each other. Courts, generally, will not enforce such provisions. The reason for the reticence to enforce them begins with the principle that when a marriage occurs, it creates a status in which the state is vitally interested and under which certain rights and duties incident to the relationship come into being, irrespective of the wishes of the parties. *Graham v. Graham*, 33 F. Supp. 936 (D. Mich. 1940) (former husband attempted to enforce agreement wife would pay him $300 a month during marriage to adjust financial matters between them so in the future there would be no further arguments as to what money the husband would receive). A private contract between persons about to be married that attempts to change the essential obligations of the marriage contract is seen as contrary to public policy and unenforceable. *Michigan Trust Co. v. Chapin*, 64 N.W. 334 (Mich. 1895) (contract in which husband promised to pay his wife a specified sum per year for keeping house is contrary to public policy). *See Restatement of the Law of Contracts*, §587 (a bargain between married persons or persons contemplating marriage to change the essential incidents of marriage such as to forgo sexual intercourse is not enforceable). A premarital contract that contains a provision stating that the parties will not live together after marriage is not enforceable, although practically, it seems useless. *Mirizio v. Mirizio*, 140 N.E. 605 (Mich. 1926); *Franklin v. Franklin*, 28 N.E. 681 (Mass. 1891) (validity of a marriage entered into in regular form is unaffected by a preliminary agreement of the parties not to live together).

Courts will not enforce provisions that control the sharing of expenses between spouses during the marriage because this would negate one spouse's statutory duty to support the other. Other matters such as who does the cleaning and cooking or how often to have sex are likewise unenforceable.

Example 14-5

Assume that P and D agree in a premarital contract stating that during their marriage, P will pay D $2,500 a month in return for D accompanying P on her business travels. D gives up his job in reliance on this written contract, which in part reads, "P hereby agrees to pay to D the sum of Two Thousand

Five Hundred ($2,500.00) Dollars per month each and every month hereafter until the parties hereto no longer desire this arrangement to continue." After five years, the couple separates, and P stops making the monthly payment. D brings an action to enforce the contract, and P responds that the contract is without consideration. Alternatively, P contends that under its express provisions, the contract was to continue only until the parties no longer desired the arrangement to continue, and thus, it was terminated when they separated. How will a court most likely treat this contract?

Explanation

A court will most likely refuse to uphold this premarital contract because it will be viewed as altering by private contract the personal relationships and obligations assumed upon marriage. The court will reason that, if P and D were permitted to regulate by private contract where the parties are to live and whether the husband is to work or be supported by his wife, there would seem to be no reason why they could not contract as to the allowance the husband or wife may receive, the number of dresses she may have, the places where they will spend their evenings and vacations, and innumerable other aspects of their personal relationships. Recognizing the existence of such a right would open an endless field for controversy and bickering and would destroy the element of flexibility needed in making adjustments to new conditions arising in marital life. A wife can voluntarily pay her husband a monthly sum, and the husband by mutual understanding can quit his job and travel with his wife. The objection is to putting such conduct into a binding contract, tying the parties' hands in the future and inviting controversy and litigation between them. *Graham v. Graham*, 33 F. Supp. 936 (D. Mich. 1940).

ENFORCEMENT OF PREMARITAL CONTRACTS

14.13. Burden of Proof

Jurisdictions are not in agreement over which party carries the initial burden of proof in premarital disputes. Does the spouse who allegedly waived rights have the initial burden of proving the invalidity of the contract, or does the party who relies on the contract have the initial burden of proving its validity? As noted earlier, the Uniform Premarital Contract Act and the ALI *Principles of Family Law* differ over which of the parties should bear the burden.

A party seeking to set aside a premarital agreement bears a very high burden of showing that it is manifestly unfair and that this unfairness was the result of overreaching on the part of the other party to the agreement. *Panossian v. Panossian*, 569 N.Y.S.2d 182 (N.Y.A.D. 1991). Moreover, in New York a duly executed prenuptial agreement is given the same presumption of legality as any other contract, commercial or otherwise, and is not, regardless of the fairness and reasonableness of the agreement, "burdened by a presumption of fraud arising from the subsequent confidential relationship of the parties." *Id.* at 184 of 569 N.Y.S.2d.

In the following decisions, courts have placed the burden of proof in the usual dispute on the attacking spouse to prove the invalidity of the contract. Statutes in some jurisdictions, may, however, have altered where the burden is placed. *In re Estate of Kinney*, 733 N.W.2d 118 (Minn. 2007) (common law placed burden of proof on proponent of an agreement when the parties stand in a confidential relationship and the agreement is not supported by adequate consideration; when the parties stand in a confidential relationship and the court finds that the antenuptial agreement is supported by adequate consideration, the burden is on the party challenging the agreement); *Linker v. Linker*, 470 P.2d 921 (Colo. Ct. App. 1970) (party contesting validity of antenuptial agreement has burden of proving fraud, concealment, or failure to disclose material information); *Christians v. Christians*, 44 N.W.2d 431 (Iowa 1950) (one assailing an antenuptial contract has burden of establishing its invalidity); *Howell v. Landry*, 386 S.E.2d 610 (N.C. App. 1989) (party claiming the invalidity of the agreement for reasons of undue influence, duress, fraud, unconscionability, or inadequate disclosure has the burden of proof — defenses of undue influence, duress, fraud, unconscionability, and inadequate disclosure are all affirmative in nature, they must be affirmatively pled).

In the following decisions, courts would ordinarily have placed the burden of proof on the attacking spouse. However, because of the unusual facts in each dispute, the burden of proof shifted to the proponent of the contract. *Del Vecchio v. Del Vecchio*, 143 So. 2d 17 (Fla. 1962) (ordinarily, burden of proving invalidity of a prenuptial agreement is on the wife alleging it, but if, on its face, the contract is unreasonable, a presumption of concealment arises, and the burden shifts, and it is incumbent upon husband to prove validity); *Matter of Greiff*, 703 N.E.2d 752, 755 (N.Y. 1998) (court should ask whether, based on all of the relevant evidence and standards, the nature of the relationship between the couple at the time they executed their prenuptial agreements rose to the level to shift the burden to the proponents of the agreements to prove freedom from fraud, deception, or undue influence).

Although not entirely clear, it appears that in the following cases, courts have placed the *initial* burden on those relying on the contract to prove its validity: *Harbom v. Harbom*, 760 A.2d 272 (Md. App. 2000) (when there is neither full disclosure or actual knowledge and the allowance to the party waiving rights is unfairly disproportionate to the worth of the property involved, the party seeking to uphold the agreement must shoulder the burden to prove that it was entered into voluntarily, freely, and with full knowledge of its meaning and effect); In re Estate of Harbers, 449 P.2d 7 (Ariz. 1969) (after will admitted to probate, executor must defend and uphold it against subsequent attack; coexecutors failed to prove by clear and convincing evidence that property division agreement was not fraudulent or coerced, or that it was not unfair or inequitable); Seuss v. Schukat, 192 N.E. 668 (Ill. 1934) (burden of proving antenuptial agreement rests on party alleging its existence); Truitt v. Truitt, 162 S.W.2d 31 (Ky. Ct. App. 1942) (defendants had burden of proving existence of lost contract); Hartz v. Hartz, 234 A.2d 865 (Md. 1967) (where neither proper disclosure of worth of property and waiver of rights in whole or in part exists and the allowance made to the one who waives rights is unfairly disproportionate to the worth of the property involved at the time agreement is made, burden is on party who relies upon the agreement to prove that it was entered into voluntarily, freely, and with full knowledge of its meaning and effect); In re Estate of Strickland, 149 N.W.2d 344 (Neb. 1967) (burden on husband, or representatives, to show that antenuptial contract apparently unjust to wife was fairly procured).

14.14. Presumptions

In some jurisdictions, where a premarital statutory provision has not been promulgated concerning this issue, and in those jurisdictions that previously applied the common law to premarital contracts, a presumption of fraud may arise when an agreement contains inadequate consideration for the waiver of a spouse's rights. See Seebecker v. Seebecker, 368 N.W.2d 846 (Wis. App. 1985) (presumption of fraud may arise where prospective husband obtains from his intended wife waiver in consideration of marriage containing a manifestly inadequate pecuniary provision; here wife failed to produce sufficient evidence to create presumption); In re Mosier's Estate, 133 N.E. 202 (Ohio 1954) (wife received $7,000 for giving up interest in estate worth $40,000, amount not so disproportionate as to give rise to presumption of fraud); In re Neis' Estate, 225 P.2d 110 (Kan. 1950) (in proceedings to enforce antenuptial contracts, it is only where fraud, deceit, or unreasonable inadequacy or disproportion appear that presumption of fraud is raised and burden put on husband, or those claiming under him, to show that wife was fully informed as to his property); Davis v. Davis, 116 S.W.2d 607 (Ark. 1938) (provision secured for wife by contract in event of husband's death is disproportionate to husband's means, presumption is that husband's means were designedly concealed, and persons claiming in husband's right have burden of proving full knowledge by wife of all that materially affected the contract).

Where fraud is presumed because of a disproportionate division of property, the burden of proving the absence of fraud may shift to the proponent of the contract to show that it was voluntarily entered with full and fair disclosure of the nature, extent, and value of the other spouse's property and knowledge of the rights that were being waived. *See In re Estate of Kinney*, 733 N.W.2d 118, 126 (Minn. 2007); *Cf. In re Estate of Stephenson*, 503 N.W.2d 540, 546 (Neb. 1993) (one alleging fraud must prove fraud; rejecting previous case law that held that if the contract is unjust and unreasonable to the prospective wife on its face, a presumption of fraud arises, the burden shifts, and it is incumbent on the husband to prove the validity of the contract).

The inadequate consideration and the confidential relationship enjoyed by a married couple are usually considered sufficient justification for applying the presumption. *See Hill v. Hill*, 356 N.W.2d 49, 53 (Minn. App. 1984), *pet. for rev. denied* (Feb. 19, 1985) (common law presumption of fraud was applicable to antenuptial agreement entered into before statute authorizing such agreements was enacted, because husband and wife had confidential relationship by virtue of their contract to marry, and $20,000 was inadequate consideration to support wife's waiver of all rights upon dissolution of marriage or her husband's death).

Example 14-6

Assume that this common law jurisdiction will apply an automatic presumption of fraud theory upon a finding that there has been a disproportionate division of property in the premarital contract. Also assume that three weeks before P and D married, a premarital contract was executed at a time when P was 65 and without significant wealth; D was 68 and possessed substantial financial wealth. P agreed in the contract that D could make a will after their marriage, providing that, should D die before P, P's survivor's estate in D's marital property would be limited to $10,000 in cash. P waived her right to an intestate share of the marital property. A list of D's property with an approximate value of $7 million dollars was attached to the premarital contract. P testified that the list was not brought to her attention at the signing, and she did not read it. Note that P selected the attorney who drafted the premarital contract; however, it appears that the attorney was likely representing D, but giving some advice to P regarding the contract. Evidence at trial indicated that D paid the attorney $15,000 for her drafting and representation when the contract was signed. Following their marriage, a will incorporating the terms of the premarital contract was executed by both parties.

Fifteen years after their marriage, D died, leaving an estate valued at more than $10 million dollars. P challenged the premarital contract. The trial judge is asked to rule on the following: (1) Was the consideration for the contract adequate? (2) If not, which of the parties must prove the validity of the contract? (3) Ultimately, will the contract be upheld?

Explanation

Common law courts take two views on the issue of the adequacy of consideration. Some view the marriage itself as sufficient consideration for the contract. Others will consider the disparity in assets at the time the contract was signed, and if it is sufficiently great, will presume fraud. Here, if the latter courts are faced with the issue, it is pretty clear that they will hold that the consideration was inadequate. Therefore, on the facts of this hypothetical, fraud is presumed.

Once fraud is presumed, the burden of proof shifts to the proponent of the contract, in this hypothetical the estate. To overcome the presumption, the proponent (D's estate) must prove that P knew the extent, character, and value of the property involved and the nature and extent of the rights being waived.

D's estate will most likely prevail. There is little evidence to suggest that P was placed under undue duress at the time the premarital contract was signed, that is, the signing was voluntary. The fact that she signed a will after the contract was executed that incorporated the terms of the premarital contract suggests she was aware of the nature and extent of D's property and waived her marital rights to a share of it. The list that was attached to the contract is evidence that D was not withholding information about his worth. Although there is a question about legal representation, no one disagrees with the fact that P selected the lawyer, and it seems reasonable to infer that the lawyer may have provided P with some legal advice. There is no evidence to suggest that P was prevented from obtaining council. Despite the apparent unfairness of the division of property upon D's death, given the disclosures and absence of duress, a common law court will most likely uphold the contract. *See Estate of Serbus v. Serbus*, 324 N.W.2d 381 (Minn. 1982).

14.15. Procedural Fairness When Executed

What courts precisely intend when they examine premarital contracts at the time of execution for procedural fairness is often not easily distinguishable from an examination of substantive fairness at the time of execution. Procedural fairness could be interpreted as merely an examination to determine whether a statutorily mandated numbers of witnesses signed the contract, or that other specific statutorily mandated procedures were followed. However, procedural fairness examinations seem to go much further than this in that the courts usually consider the nature and extent of the disclosure, whether a signor was under duress, and whether the parties were represented by counsel. *See Fisher v. Koontz*, 80 N.W. 551 (Iowa 1899) (court considered procedural fairness in execution of agreement, apparently concluding contract terms were unjust and unreasonable); *Ryken v. Ryken*, 461 N.W.2d 122 (S.D. 1990) (agreement held invalid where presented to wife the night before the wedding, made no provision for the wife, and did not disclose the assets of either party); *In re Marriage of Shanks*, 758 N.W.2d 506 (Iowa 2008) (any doubt as to the conscionability of the agreement at issue in this case could have likely been avoided if both parties had been represented by competent Iowa-licensed counsel).

14.16. Substantively Fair: Unconscionable When Executed

The courts that examine a premarital contract for initial fairness may also examine it for substantive fairness. In some cases, this examination is translated into one to determine whether the contract when executed was unconscionable. To make matters more difficult, the meaning of the term *unconscionable* is far from clear. For example, in *Holler v. Holler*, 612 S.E.2d 469 (S.C. App. 2005), the court stated that under South Carolina law, unconscionability is the "absence of meaningful choice on the part of one party due to one-sided contract provisions, together with terms which are so oppressive that no reasonable person would make them and no fair and honest person would accept them." A New York court in *Clermont v. Clermont*, 603 N.Y.S.2d 923 (1933), defined unconscionable as involving a bargain "such as no [person] in his [or her] senses and not under delusion would make on the one hand, and as no honest and fair [person] would accept on the other."

The North Dakota Supreme Court held a contract unconscionable where the evidence indicated that the husband provided the wife with the contract only three days before their wedding, the wife did not have independent legal advice before signing the contract, the husband did not provide wife fair and reasonable disclosure of his property and financial obligations, the husband's representation of his income was not credible, and the wife did not waive her right to a fair and reasonable disclosure of husband's property or financial obligations. *Peters-Riemers v. Riemers*, 644 N.W.2d 197 (N.D. 2002).

One standard of unconscionability measured at the time of a contract's making is contained in the UPAA. Several states have adopted this standard. *See, e.g.*, *In re Marriage of Thomas*, 199 S.W.3d 847 (Mo. App. 2006) (conscionability is the same standard employed in commercial law, meaning protection against one-sidedness, oppression, or unfair surprise).

14.17. Fair and Reasonable Test When Executed

Some jurisdictions have discussed the validity of a premarital contract when it was signed using a fair and reasonable test. This test is not perceived as identical to unconscionability. *Upham v. Upham*, 630 N.E.2d 307 (Mass. App. 1994). Although there may be substantial overlap between the standards, a standard of unconscionability is generally thought to require a greater show-ing of inappropriateness. Several states appear to have adopted the fair and reasonable test. *See, e.g., Ex parte Walters*, 580 So. 2d 1352, 1354 (Ala. 1991) (nothing to indicate that the agreement was not fair, just, and equitable); *Harbom v. Harbom*, 760 A.2d 272 (Md. 2000), quoting *Hartz v. Hartz*, 234 A.2d 865 (Md. 1967) (contract upheld if it was "fair and equitable under the circumstances"); *Matter of the Estate of Crawford*, 730 P.2d 675 (Wash. 1986) ("if the contract makes a fair and reasonable provision for the party not seeking its enforcement, the contract may be upheld").

14.18. The "Second Look" Doctrine

Unlike commercial contracts, family courts in a few jurisdictions have adopted a contract theory that is unique to family law. This theory is collo-quially referred to as the *second look doctrine*. When considering an agreement, a judge will first determine whether the agreement was fair and reasonable at the time of execution. *See DeMatteo v. DeMatteo*, 762 N.E.2d 797 (Mass. 2002). Next, taking a "second look," the judge will inquire whether the agreement, at the time of the divorce, is "conscionable." *DeMatteo v. DeMatteo, supra* at 797 of 762 N.E.2d. If circumstances occurring during the course of the marriage would leave the contesting spouse "without sufficient property, maintenance, or appropriate employment to support" herself, enforcement will not occur. *Korff v. Korff*, 831 N.E.2d 385 (Mass. App. Ct. 2005).

Some jurisdictions ask whether, under the present circumstances, the contract is fair and reasonable or unconscionable. *See, e.g., Gross v. Gross*, 464 N.E.2d 500 (Ohio 1984) (in light of substantial increase in husband's assets during marriage, provisions in the antenuptial agreement that wife was entitled to receive maximum maintenance of $200 per month for ten years was unconscionable). Note that in Ohio the issue of an antenuptial agreement's fairness at the time of the divorce is only relevant to matters involving spousal support. *Gross v. Gross*, 464 N.E.2d 500 (Ohio 1984).

Whether the courts that employ the second look doctrine claim they are searching for "unconscionability," "unfairness and unreasonableness," "inequity," or something else, the judicial analysis appears remarkably sim-ilar in substance. *See* 1 H.H. Clark, Jr., *Domestic Relations in the United States* §1.9, at 52 n.51 (2d ed. 1987) ("Unconscionability seems to be defined as occur-ring when enforcement of the contract would leave the spouse without sufficient property, maintenance, or appropriate employment to support himself."). In *MacFarlane v. Rich*, 567 A.2d 585 (N.H. 1989), the court defined *unconscionable* as occurring when "provisions in a premarital contract may lose their vitality by reason of changed circumstances so far beyond the contem-plation of the parties at the time they entered the contract that its enforce-ment would work an unconscionable hardship."

The Wisconsin Supreme court, in *Button v. Button*, 388 N.W.2d 546 (Wis. 1986), held that "if there are significantly changed circumstances after the execution of a contract and the contract as applied at divorce no longer comports with the reasonable expectations of the parties, a contract which is fair at execution may be unfair to the parties at divorce." *See McKee-Johnson v. Johnson*, 444 N.W.2d 259, 267-268 (Minn. 1989) (contract must be substantively fair at the time of enforcement); *Gentry v. Gentry*, 798 S.W.2d 928, 936 (Ky. 1990) (premarital agreement, when viewed at time of dissolution, was not unconscionable as to wife).

Circumstances a court applying the second-look doctrine might use to deny enforcement of an otherwise valid premarital contract include an unanticipated mental or physical deterioration of the contesting party. The "second look" at a contract is to ensure that the contract has the same vitality at the time of the divorce that the parties intended at the time of its execution.

Example 14-7

Assume that P and D were employed outside the home and each represented by lawyers when they entered into a premarital contract that in part read as follows: "In the event that the Parties initiate dissolution of marriage proceedings, each Party waives and releases all rights and claims to receive alimony from the other Party." Also assume that ten years into their marriage, D was in a life-shattering automobile accident that caused her permanent disability. She underwent a dozen reconstructive surgeries and is slated to have many more. A year after the accident, P filed a petition to dissolve the marriage. At the time P filed the dissolution action, D had exhausted her insurance coverage and had only a few thousand dollars in assets. D asked for an equitable division of the marital assets and permanent alimony. Assume that a statute in this jurisdiction declares that "a premarital waiver of spousal support will not be enforced if enforcement would be unconscionable at the time sought." P asks the court to enforce their premarital contract. How will a court most likely rule?

Explanation

A court that has adopted the second-look doctrine will most likely apply an unconscionability test. As a general rule, courts applying the unconscionability test at the time the contract is to be enforced will examine what the parties could have anticipated when they married. The accident and consequential disability will persuade most of these courts that this is something the parties could not have anticipated and could not reasonably have been foreseen when the contract was executed. Furthermore, as a public policy matter, requiring P to support D is consistent with public policy as expressed in most state family code provisions. *See Borelli v. Brusseau*, 16 Cal. Rptr. 2d 16 (Cal. App. 1 Dist. 1993). P most likely will be required to provide D with alimony payments.

14.19. Jurisdictions Applying Strict Contract Principles

Pennsylvania is among a minority of jurisdictions that interpret premarital contracts using traditional contract law principles. *See, e.g., Simeone v. Simeone*, 581 A.2d 162 (Pa. 1990). The courts in that state believe that the law has advanced to recognize the equal status of men and women in our society and that paternalistic presumptions and protections that arose to shelter women from the inferiorities and incapacities, which they were perceived as having in earlier times, have appropriately been discarded. *Id.* at 165. From its perspective, it would be inconsistent to perpetuate the standards governing premarital agreements that were applied in earlier decisions, because these earlier decisions reflected a paternalistic approach "that is now insupportable." *Id.*

In *Simeone v. Simeone*, the court justified changing its position regarding applying a substantive fairness review to premarital contracts reasoning that such a review severely undermined the functioning and reliability of a contract and was not a proper subject for judicial inquiry. 581 A.2d at 166. It also rejected an inquiry into the substantive fairness of the contract at the time of enforcement. It reasoned that future events are reasonably foreseeable.

However, in *In re O'Brien*, 898 A.2d 1075 (Pa. Super. 2006), the court appeared to temper its view somewhat, stating that "in reorienting our standards for enforcing prenuptial agreements to the traditional principles of contract law, . . . we did not lose sight of the fact that parties to these agreements do not necessarily deal with each other at arm's length. Accordingly, we reaffirmed 'the longstanding principle that a full and fair disclosure of the financial positions of the parties is required.'" *Id.* at 1080.

RELATED ISSUES

14.20. Abandoning a Premarital Contract

In some jurisdictions, a premarital contract may be abandoned by mutual consent of the parties without consideration. *McMullen v. McMullen*, 185 So. 2d 191 (Fla. Ct. App. 1966). The abandonment of a contract may be effected when the acts of one party are inconsistent with the existence of the contract and are acquiesced in by the other party. This is tantamount to a rescission of the contract by mutual assent.

14.21. Tax Planning

Premarital contracts are sometimes related to the estate-planning wishes of one or both of the prospective spouses. Depending on the consideration being exchanged by the contract, there may be gift-tax or income-tax consequences involved.

15

Cohabitation Without Formal Marriage

15.1. Introduction

This chapter examines the legal issues involving disputes between unmarried cohabiting partners, who have lived together, much like married couples, and decide to terminate their relationship. Jurisdictions rely upon a variety of legal theories to resolve property division disputes between cohabiting couples and sometimes award support. Specific issues involving the children of cohabitants are discussed in Chapter 9 (child support), Chapter 10 (child support modification and enforcement), and Chapter 16 (parentage).

CHANGING LIFESTYLES

15.2. A Half-Century of Change

During the last 50 years or so, a revolution has occurred in the United States regarding how unmarried cohabiting couples are viewed. As the number of couples living together without the benefit of a marriage license increased, the social stigma associated with the once "shameful" behavior and the onus of bearing children out of wedlock gradually disappeared.

A variety of reasons are given for cohabiting instead of marrying. Some believe that a period of cohabitation provides a testing ground for the relationship; a period that provides couples contemplating marriage time to evaluate the relationship before obtaining a marriage license. The experience, they believe, may prevent an unwise marriage and the financial and emotional consequences associated with divorce. Others believe that cohabitation offers philosophical freedom from a marriage system dominated by traditional "outdated" societal values. A few cohabiting couples remain single because a formal marriage might end alimony payments from an earlier marriage or eliminate benefits provided by a public assistance program. Cohabitation critics argue that there is little hard statistical evidence to suggest that a "trial run" results in a greater chance of a successful marriage. They suggest that when a relationship ends, partners are often surprised to discover that courts are less than enthusiastic to assist them in sorting out property and support issues caused by the relationship. Critics also claim that the legal problems associated with a cohabitation arrangement can be as costly and as difficult to resolve as those associated with divorce. *See* Lynne Marie Kohm & Karen M. Groen, *Cohabitation and the Future of Marriage*, 17 Regent U. L. Rev. 261 (2005).

15.3. Cohabitation Data

The overall percentage of cohabiting couples is not great, although the number of unmarried-partner households has increased significantly since the late 1960s. By 1990, cohabitants constituted 3.5 percent of all households, and in 2000, unmarried-partner households accounted for 5.2 percent of all households. In 2007 the number of unmarried-partner households was reported at 5.4 percent of the population. *http://factfinder. census.gov* (last visited July 1, 2009). Of the 5.2 million cohabiting couples in 2000, 4.9 million were opposite-sex partners. According to the 2000 census figures, Vermont and Alaska had the highest percentage of unmarried-partner households (7.5%), and Alabama and Utah had the fewest (3.4%). *Census 2000 Briefs, Households and Families: 2000, http://www.census.gov/ population/www/cen2000/briefs.html* (last visited October 24, 2006).

Sixty-three percent of all households in Utah in 2000 were maintained by married couples, the highest in the country. *http://factfinder.census.gov* (last visited July 1, 2009). The states with less than one-half of their households maintained by married couples were geographically dispersed: Massachusetts, Rhode Island, New York, Louisiana, Mississippi, and Nevada. Only 23 percent of households in the District of Columbia were maintained by married couples. *Id.*

CONSTITUTIONAL ISSUES

15.4. Criminal Conduct

Most states have, or had, laws making it a criminal offense for unmarried persons to live together without benefit of marriage. These laws were originally intended to punish persons for sodomy, fornication, and cohabitation. The decision by the United States Supreme Court in *Lawrence v. Texas*, 539 U.S. 558 (2003), raised questions about the continued validity of many of these laws. In *Lawrence*, the Court held that a Texas statute making it a crime for two persons of the same sex to engage in certain intimate sexual conduct was unconstitutional, as applied to adult males who had engaged in consensual acts of sodomy in the privacy of their home. One may infer from this opinion that other laws prohibiting private intimate activity between consenting adults are likewise unconstitutional. *But see United States v. Thompson*, 458 F. Supp. 2d 730 (N.D. Ind. 2006) (holding prostitution is not a protected activity under *Lawrence*); *Muth v. Frank*, 412 F.3d 808, 817-818 (7th Cir. 2005) (no protected privacy interest for incestuous relationship), *cert. denied*, 546 U.S. 988 (2005); *United States v. Orellana*, 62 M.J. 595, 601 (N.M. Ct. Crim. App. 2005) (adultery not constitutionally protected conduct under *Lawrence* where offense is service discrediting or prejudicial to good order and discipline), *rev. denied*, 63 M.J. 295 (C.A.A.F. 2006); *Cawood v. Haggard*, 327 F. Supp. 2d 863 (E.D. Tenn. 2004) (adulterous, sexual activities with client in the confines of lawyer's private office do not fall within a right of privacy that is constitutionally protected from government intrusion where client made criminal complaint to authorities about lawyer's behavior).

Example 15-1

Assume that D was arrested after he solicited an undercover police officer for oral sodomy in violation of State Code §18.2-361 (crimes against nature). The arresting officer testified that D walked into a men's restroom located in a department store, which is freely accessible to members of the public, including children. Once in the restroom, D approached a stall occupied by the undercover police officer, leaned forward, and "peered" into the stall through the crack in the stall door. The undercover police officer, who was in a state of undress, engaged in a conversation with D. During the conversation D solicited the officer for oral sex, and the officer arrested D. Based on the holding of the U.S. Supreme Court in *Lawrence v. Texas*, D contends that Code §18.2-361 is unconstitutional because as applied to him, it prohibits private acts of consensual sodomy, in violation of the Due Process Clause of the Fourteenth Amendment. How will a court most likely rule on D's argument?

Explanation

A careful review of *Lawrence* indicates that the issue was whether the petitioners were free as adults to engage in the private conduct in the exercise of their liberty under the Due Process Clause of the Fourteenth Amendment to the Constitution. *Lawrence* does not apply because the restrooms are within stores open to the public and are not within the zone of privacy as contemplated by the U.S. Supreme Court. The trial judge will most likely reject D's motion. *See Singson v. Com.*, 621 S.E.2d 682 (Va. App. 2005) (Virginia's crimes against nature statute prohibiting oral sodomy did not violate due process as applied to defendant because he solicited oral sodomy in a public place).

THE COMMON LAW

15.5. Illicit Relationships

The common law took a dim view of enforcing agreements made between unmarried persons who were living together out of wedlock much like a husband and wife. If any part of an agreement, oral or written, rested upon the illicit relationship itself, the agreement would not be enforced. Common law courts objected to the parties' disregard of traditional moral values and were concerned that enforcement of such agreements might make meretricious relationships more attractive than marriage. The common law, it was said, should not allow a man to trade sexual services as consideration for contractual promises or make a woman's virtue an article of merchandise.

15.6. Decline of Common Law Marriage

During the early period of this country's growth, it was common for states to give legal recognition to couples who lived together much as husband and wife without obtaining a marriage license. The relationships were termed "common law marriages." *See State v. Bullman*, 203 P.3d 768 (Mont. 2009) (court did not err in instructing jury that four elements must be proved to establish a common law marriage: One, the parties must be competent to marry; two, the parties must assume the relationship by mutual consent; three, the parties must confirm their marriage by cohabitation; and, four, the parties must confirm their marriage by public repute); *Coleman v. U.S.*, 948 A.2d 534 (D.C. 2008) (the elements of common law marriage in this jurisdiction are cohabitation as husband and wife, following an express mutual agreement, which must be in words of the present tense; the existence of an agreement may be inferred from the character and duration of cohabitation).

However, as the nation moved well into the twentieth century, states began to eliminate common law marriages, justifying their abolition on various grounds. It was argued that the pioneering conditions that had fostered common law marriages disappeared and were not longer needed. There were concerns about the absence of public marriage records that would assist in verifying the property rights of spouses and a feeling in some quarters that recognition allowed spouses to completely avoid some of the state's objectives in enacting marriage statutes, such as obtaining medical examinations to prevent the spread of disease, collecting fee payments to finance recordkeeping, and requiring waiting periods to prevent impulsive unions. There was a practical difficulty of proving such marriages existed. Some criticized them as improperly sanctioning immorality and debasing formal marriage. Still others contended that the common law marriage concept encouraged perjury and fraud by unwed cohabitants hoping to gain the financial benefits of marriage.

With abolition of common law marriage in a majority of jurisdictions, the traditional nuclear family concept was thought to be relatively secure. However, cultural changes that emerged in the 1960s began to challenge the concept of "family" and the nonacceptance of couples living together without benefit of a marriage license.

Example 15-2

Assume that P and D were married to each other for ten years, when they separated and divorced. Following entry of the divorce judgment, they began living together in a home D purchased a few months following their divorce. P testified that they did not seek to obtain a new marriage license because this jurisdiction recognizes common law marriages. D testified that they did not get married because he "never wanted to be married again." The couple resided in the home for 15 years when their relationship again broke down. P claimed that despite the earlier divorce, P and D were common law spouses and that P was entitled to a marital portion of the house under the state's marital dissolution statute. The evidence during the trial showed that P and D did not consistently hold themselves out as husband and wife; they routinely filled out legal forms designating themselves as single people; they maintained separate bank accounts; and filed individual income tax returns stating they were single. P has identified one claim she intends to assert, that is, that P and D were common law spouses. How will a court most likely rule?

Explanation

If the only issue is whether a common law marriage exists, P will most likely lose her claim. Here, the evidence suggests that the couple never actually held themselves out to the community as husband and wife or intended to be married. *See In re Marriage of Martin*, 681 N.W.2d 612 (Iowa 2004) (there was no present intent or agreement to be married between former husband and wife who continued to cohabitate after divorce, and thus common law marriage did not exist).

Counsel for P might have explored the possibility of recovery on a cohabitation theory, because many courts have authority to adjudicate disputed property claims of unmarried persons who cohabitate. *See Metten v. Benge*, 366 N.W.2d 577 (Iowa 1985). However, P would have had to allege a recognized legal theory outside marriage to support the claim. Potential theories to support property claims between unmarried cohabitants include claims of contract, unjust enrichment, resulting trust, constructive trust, and joint venture. Unfortunately, P did not allege a legal cohabitation theory to support a possible division of property.

LEGAL RECOGNITION OF COHABITATION RELATIONSHIPS

15.7. *Marvin v. Marvin*

Legal recognition that partners in a cohabitating relationship may have enforceable rights is a byproduct of a phenomenon that began in the 1960s when increasingly large numbers of adults began openly living together without a traditional marriage ceremony or state license. The legal movement was sparked, at least in part, by the publicity following a decision by the California Supreme Court in *Marvin v. Marvin*, 557 P.2d 106 (Cal. 1976).

In *Marvin*, a woman sued a man with whom she had lived for approximately six years without marriage alleging that she and the defendant entered into an oral agreement that while the parties lived together they would combine their efforts and earnings and would share equally in any and all property accumulated as a result of their efforts, whether individual or combined; that they would hold themselves out to the general public as husband and wife; that the plaintiff would give up her career as an entertainer and singer in order to devote her full time to the defendant as his companion, homemaker, housekeeper, and cook; and that in return the defendant agreed to provide for all of the plaintiff's financial support and needs for the rest of her life. The plaintiff further alleged that after she had lived with the defendant for almost six years, he forced her to leave his household and refused to recognize her rights under the contract. The plaintiff demanded declaratory relief, asking the court to determine her contractual and property rights, and also to impose a constructive trust on half of the property acquired during the course of the relationship.

The defendant argued that the enforcement of the contract would violate public policy because it was so closely related to the "immoral" relationship of the parties. The trial judge granted the defendant's motion for judgment on the pleadings. The California Supreme Court reversed the judgment.

The court summarized its holding saying, "[W]e base our opinion on the principle that adults who voluntarily live together and engage in sexual relations are nonetheless as competent as any other persons to contract respecting their earnings and property rights. Of course, they cannot lawfully contract to pay for the performance of sexual services, for such a contract is, in essence, an agreement for prostitution and unlawful for that reason. But they may agree to pool their earnings and to hold all property acquired during the relationship in accord with the law governing community property; conversely they may agree that each partner's earnings and the property acquired from those earnings remains the separate property of the earning partner. So long as the agreement does not rest upon illicit meretricious consideration, the parties may order their economic affairs as they choose, and no policy precludes the courts from enforcing such agreements." Id. at 116 of 557 P.2d.

In determining whether a cohabiters' agreement rests upon illicit meretricious consideration, the court said that it would be guided by the following principle: "(A) contract between nonmarital partners, even if expressly made in contemplation of a common living arrangement, is invalid only if sexual acts form an inseparable part of the consideration for the agreement. In sum, a court will not enforce a contract for the pooling of property and earnings if it is explicitly and inseparably based upon services as a paramour." Id. at 114 of 557 P.2d.

The court declared that "[t]he fact that a man and woman live together without marriage, and engage in a sexual relationship, does not in itself invalidate agreements between them relating to their earnings, property, or expenses. Neither is such an agreement invalid merely because the parties may have contemplated the creation or continuation of a nonmarital relationship when they entered into it. Agreements between nonmarital partners fail only to the extent that they rest upon a consideration of meretricious sexual services." Id. at 113 of 557 P.2d.

The court held that the plaintiff has the same rights to enforce contracts and to assert her equitable interest in property acquired through her efforts as does any other unmarried person. However, it refused to extend to the plaintiff any rights that the California Family Law Act grants to valid or putative spouses.

Marvin v. Marvin was the first major decision by a state court that clearly held that unmarried adults who live together are free under general principles of contract law to make agreements concerning their property and earnings. The opinion received widespread recognition because of the scope of the contract principles it suggested could be employed when settling disputed live-in claims.

15.8. Response to *Marvin*

There were mixed reactions to Marvin v. Marvin. For example, states such as New Jersey and Minnesota appeared to accept and apply the Marvin principles. *See, e.g., Crowe v. De Gioia*, 495 A.2d 889 (N.J. Super. 1985) (so long as contract between unmarried cohabitants is not based on relationship proscribed by law, or on a promise to marry, agreements between cohabitants are enforceable); *Carlson v. Olson*, 256 N.W.2d 249, 255 (Minn. 1977) (courts should enforce express contracts between nonmarital partners except to the extent that the contract is explicitly founded on the consideration of meretricious sexual services. In the absence of an express contract, the courts should inquire into the conduct of the parties to determine whether that conduct demonstrates an implied contract, agreement of partnership or joint venture, or some other tacit understanding between the parties. The courts may also employ the doctrine of *quantum meruit*, or equitable remedies such as constructive or resulting trusts, when warranted). In other jurisdictions, there was a cautious application of selected principles enunciated in Marvin. Finally, a minority continued to adhere to the principle that cohabitation agreements under any circumstances involved immoral consideration; therefore, they are unenforceable as against public policy. *See, e.g., Liles v. Still*, 335 S.E.2d 168 (Ga. App. 1985) (proper to instruct jury that unmarried cohabitation constitutes immoral consideration so as to render contract between roommates unenforceable).

15.9. Separating Sexual Services/Consideration

A majority of jurisdictions now distinguish between oral or written contracts made by cohabiting couples that are explicitly and inseparably founded on sexual services and those that are not. Courts obviously will not enforce contracts for prostitution. However, a majority reject the proposition that an agreement between cohabitants is illegal merely because there is an illicit relationship between them. They consider a contract enforceable so long as the agreement is independent of the illicit relationship, the illicit relationship is not part of the consideration bargained for, and the relationship is not a condition of the agreement. *See Wilcox v. Trautz*,

693 N.E.2d 141(Mass. 1998) (unmarried cohabitants may lawfully contract concerning property, financial, and other matters relevant to their relationship, except to extent that sexual services constitute only, or dominant, consideration for agreement, or that enforcement should be denied on some other public policy ground); *Jones v. Daly*, 176 Cal. Rptr. 130 (Cal. App. 1981) (held court would not enforce alleged oral "cohabitors agreement" between two males where plaintiff's rendition of sexual services to decedent was an inseparable part of the consideration for the agreement). The courts holding to this view believe that if they refused to enforce contract and property rights between unmarried cohabitants, the result would often leave one party with all or almost of the assets accumulated during the relationship, while the other party, no more or less "guilty," would be deprived of assets that he or she helped to accumulate. Such a result is viewed as unduly harsh.

Courts appear to have little difficulty in finding consideration for most of these agreements. Although they will not enforce an agreement if the sole consideration for it is "the contemplation of out-of-wedlock sexual relations," most are willing to sever the sexual aspects of the contract from the intimate relationship. *See In re Estate of Eriksen*, 337 N.W.2d 671, 674 (Minn.1983). Services such as companionship, housekeeping, hostessing, and cooking may be sufficient consideration for a contract. In *Chiba v. Greenwald*, 67 Cal. Rptr. 3d 86 (Cal. App. 2007), one partner promised the other to provide for her "financial needs and support for the rest of her life" in exchange for her domestic services as his "homemaker, housekeeper, cook, secretary, bookkeeper and financial counselor," forgoing any independent career opportunities. The promise to perform these domestic services was held lawful and adequate consideration for a contract. See *Whorton v. Dillingham*, 248 Cal. Rptr. 405, 409-410 (1988) (holding that a same-sex, nonmarried cohabitant's alleged services as a chauffeur, bodyguard, secretary, and business partner were, if proven true, sufficient independent consideration for the formation of a contract).

Example 15-3

Assume that boyfriend P and girlfriend D agreed to share utilities and rent on an apartment while they were attending college. After three years of cohabiting, D purchased a small home in her name, paying $20,000 down and taking out a $150,000 mortgage. She also purchased insurance that would pay off her mortgage should she die prior to the final payment. While moving out of the apartment into the home, D suffered a sudden heart attack and died. The insurance company is ready to pay the $150,000 per the policy to the estate of D when P asserts that he has an interest in the money and the home. P claims that D orally promised him that should D die, that P would have the home as "his home."

At trial, D's estate produces all of the relevant real estate, loan, and insurance documents, and they contain only D's name and signature. The estate also produces evidence from D's bank showing that only D's name appears on the checking and savings accounts. P testifies that D expressly said the home was to be his should D die before P and introduces some checks showing that P, on occasion, purchased food for both P and D. P explains that he didn't want his name on any of the home purchase documents because he felt home ownership might jeopardize his ability to obtain future student loans since he was intending to pursue a graduate degree. How will a court most likely rule on P's claim?

Explanation

There appears at the outset to be little to support a conclusion that there is consideration for the agreement. P may argue that the intimate relationship of the couple provides the consideration for the contract. D's estate will counter that if contemplation of sexual relations was the sole consideration for the contract, that is insufficient consideration and should fail for public policy reasons.

P may fail for other reasons. P has never alleged he had any legal interest in the realty, that he ever conveyed any interest therein to D, or that he contributed any moneys toward the purchase of the property. There is no allegation of any unjust enrichment. At most, the pleading sets forth an unfulfilled expectation of P and nothing more. Compare the facts in this example with those in In re Estate of Eriksen, 337 N.W.2d 671 (Minn. 1983) (creation of constructive trust consisting of one-half interest in home was required to prevent unjust enrichment of estate). In Eriksen evidence was produced that the surviving cohabitant and the deceased each contributed money equally toward the expenses of purchasing and maintaining the home, and each contributed equally to the premiums for the credit life insurance policy, which ultimately paid $48,334.63 on the mortgage when the other cohabitant died. The court felt that the surviving cohabitant's claim was similar to a claim made by a joint venturer or partner. (Note that in some jurisdictions, the absence of an allegation of any writing that would satisfy the real property statute of frauds also might well cause a court to dismiss P's complaint).

15.10. Cohabitant's "Right" to Support and Compensation

It is, of course, axiomatic that cohabitation alone does not trigger a right to a future allowance or compensation. There is no right to temporary or permanent alimony, because this can only be claimed by a participant in a valid marriage or by a putative spouse. *See Combs v. Tibbitts,* 148 P.3d 430 (Colo. Ct. App. 2006). However, it appears that there is a growing trend among the courts to award financial support and compensation in cohabitation disputes. In other words, courts are not simply distributing real and personal property in "palimony" actions. (Note that *Black's Law Dictionary* defines palimony as "[a] court-ordered allowance paid by one member to the other of a couple that, though unmarried, formerly cohabitated." *Black's Law Dictionary* 1134 (7th ed. 1999).)

For example, in *In re Estate of Roccamonte,* 808 A.2d 838 (N.J. 2002), the court found that the female cohabitant's marital-type relationship with her male cohabitant, plus the evidence of her conduct during the relationship, was sufficient consideration for the now-deceased male cohabitant's promise to support her for life. In *Carney v. Hansell,* 831 A.2d 128 (N.J. Super. Ct. 2003), a cohabitant was held entitled to compensation under a theory of *quantum meruit* for services rendered as a key employee who assisted in building business and helping it grow but who had not been compensated for her contribution.

A recent decision by the Georgia Supreme Court is of significance because it allowed a trial judge to consider the length of time the couple lived together *before* marriage in making an alimony award. *Sprouse v. Sprouse,* 678 S.E.2d 328 (Ga. 2009) (under the catchall provision of OCGA §19-6-5(a)(8), the trial court is free to consider the parties' entire relationship, including periods of premarital cohabitation in determining alimony); *Harrelson v. Harrelson,* 932 P.2d 247 (Alaska 1997) (court is free to consider the parties' entire relationship, including periods of premarital cohabitation when deciding the amount of rehabilitative spousal support); *In re Marriage of Lind,* 139 P.3d 1032 (Or. App. 2006) (no reason to exclude length of the parties' premarital cohabitation when awarding alimony).

In *McCullon v. McCullon,* 410 N.Y.S.2d 226 (N.Y. Sup. 1978) (rejected on other grounds by *McCall v. Frampton,* 415 N.Y.S.2d 752 (N.Y. Sup. 1979)), the male defendant, with whom the female plaintiff had lived without marriage for 28 years, declared that he would always take care of her. The court held that the conduct of the defendant in supporting the female for all those years, together with his statement that he would always care for her, resulted in an enforceable implied contract for support between the parties, the consideration on her part being her forbearance of employment and providing of household services for him.

Example 15-4

Assume that P, a wealthy businessman, and D, his unmarried personal assistant, became romantically involved and maintained a somewhat erratic romantic relationship. The relationship continued for about 15 years, even after D married X. D remained married to X, and they had two children.

D unexpectedly suffered a serious stroke, and his financial affairs were taken over by his wife. She discovered that for the last 15 years D had been providing P with a monthly financial supplement that ranged from $100 to $1,000. When she refused to continue making payments, P brought a legal action alleging that D has orally promised that in consideration for the emotional and social support that D received from P, that he would provide financial support to her for life. How will a court most likely decide P's claim?

Explanation

This is a challenging problem. Some courts will view the agreement between P and D as based entirely on a sexual, immoral relationship and dismiss P's claim outright. A few jurisdictions may take a more analytical approach, similar to that used by the court in *Levine v. Konvitz*, 890 A.2d 354 (N.J. Super. A.D. 2006). There, the court held that "[i]n order to establish a *prima facie* case for palimony, a plaintiff must present competent evidence showing (1) that the parties cohabitated; (2) in a marriage-type relationship; (3) that during this period of cohabitation, defendant promised plaintiff that he/she would support him/her for life; and (4) that this promise was made in exchange for valid consideration." *Id.* at 354. If *Levine v. Konitz* is applied to the facts of this example, P's claim will most likely be dismissed because P has failed to prove the first element, that is, cohabitation. However, in a later decision, *Devaney v. L'Esperance*, 949 A.2d 743 (N.J. 2008), the court held that cohabitation was not an indispensable element of a palimony action, abrogating *Levine v. Konvitz*. The court said that cohabitation was but one element a court should consider when determining whether a marital-type relationship existed. Although the parties had a 20-year romantic relationship, the palimony claim was rejected because the evidence was insufficient to establish that the woman and the man had a marital-type relationship, as required to support the woman's palimony claim. The parties did not live together or spend significant periods of time together, did not commingle property, did not hold themselves out in public as husband and wife, and the man remained married to and continued to live with his wife.

15.11. American Law Institute

The American Law Institute approach to cohabitation issues contrasts with the principles established in *Marvin v. Marvin*. Rather than relying on contract and equitable remedies discussed in *Marvin*, it creates presumptive categories of "domestic partners" who are entitled to property and support in the same manner as legal spouses. Domestic partners are defined as two unmarried people (same- or opposite-sex) who "share a primary residence and a life together as a couple" for a significant period of time. ALI, *Principles of the Law of Family Dissolution: Analysis and Recommendations* §§6.01-6.06 (2002).

15.12. The State of Washington Adopts a "Meretricious Relationship Doctrine"

The state of Washington legally recognizes stable, cohabiting relationships, which it refers to as *meretricious relationships*, and provides these couples with remedies should the relationship dissolve. (Note that use of the term "meretricious" in this context denotes a committed intimate relationship rather than to describe an illicit relationship.) Cohabiting couples who claim a meretricious relationship must provide evidence on the following nonexclusive factors: (1) continuous cohabitation; (2) duration of the relationship; (3) purpose of the relationship; (4) services for mutual benefit; and (5) intent of the parties. Property acquired during such a relationship is presumed to belong to both parties, and the court may be guided by the state's dissolution statute in making a fair and equitable distribution. *In re Marriage of Pennington*, 14 P.3d 764 (Wash. 2000) (evidence failed to establish that relationship was meretricious); *Olver v. Fowler*, 126 P.3d 69 (Wash. App. 2006) (property acquired during relationship that would have been community property was subject to equitable division upon death of both man and woman in meretricious relationship).

15.13. Same-Sex Partners

The principles espoused in *Marvin v. Marvin* have been applied with equal force in some jurisdictions to agreements between same-sex partners. For example, in *Whorton v. Dillingham*, 202 Cal. App. 3d 447 (Cal. 1988), the court extended the *Marvin* principles to same-sex partners. In that case, the court allowed one partner to seek recovery on a breach of express oral contract theory based on allegations he provided the defendant with services as a chauffeur, bodyguard, secretary, and business partner. The court found that the oral agreement was supported by consideration independent of sexual services.

Example 15-5

Assume that P and D are a same-sex couple living in the state of Washington, and they had a close domestic relationship for ten years. During that time, they lived together continually, pooled their resources, acquired property as investments for their mutual benefit, and accumulated some debt. The real estate was held in D's name only; however, they used joint funds to make the payments. When they separated, D had significantly more income and legal title to more assets than P. P brought an action against D asking for an equitable distribution of their property. What is the most likely result in the state of Washington?

Explanation

Because the action is brought in a jurisdiction whose public policy recognizes that same-sex couples are to be viewed much like married couples, P should be able to use that state's statutes to provide evidence of the relationship. Given the ten years of living together as domestic partners, P should be able to prove that living together was for their mutual financial benefit and that they intended the relationship to be permanent when it was begun. Assuming P provides proof on these elements pursuant to the Washington statute, P will most likely receive equitable relief. *See Gormely v. Robertson*, 83 P.3d 1042 (Wash. App. 2004) (quasi-marital meretricious relationships should also apply to same-sex cohabitants). It is likely that outside the state of Washington, that a majority of jurisdictions court would grant P's request to divide the property.

A PANOPLY OF LEGAL THEORIES

15.14. Overview

Nationwide, jurisdictions have utilized a variety of legal theories when cohabiting couples have sought enforcement of agreements related to their relationship. As observed earlier, some jurisdictions have refused to provide any relief, viewing the relationship as immoral and illegal. Some jurisdictions will enforce an express agreement to share but reject recognition of an implied agreement. Still others will enforce an express or implied agreement to share based on the expectations of the parties. Others may allow a party to recover based on an unjust enrichment or *quantum meruit* theory. Some may apply gift law to avoid an inequitable result, and others may grant relief in the form of a constructive or resulting trust. A minority will consider the contract as similar to a commercial contract and reject application of equitable theories.

Regardless of the legal theory selected, a party alleging the existence of an agreement normally bears the burden of producing evidence to support it. *See Ball v. Smith*, 150 S.W.3d 889 (Tex. App. 2004) (plaintiff failed to produce more than "a scintilla of evidence" in support of claims for breach of contract and resulting trust).

15.15. Express Written Contracts

Courts are usually much more willing to enforce a written cohabitation contract than an oral one, assuming that the terms of the contract are independent of the parties' sexual relationship. A written contract will define the parties' expectations and understandings, and a signature on the contract by both parties indicates their understanding and acceptance of the terms. Although written contracts signed by both parties are seldom perfect, they are usually better than oral or implied contracts.

It has been suggested that an attorney should advise a client to never live together with a "romantic partner (or even a roommate) without a written cohabitation agreement." Elizabeth A. Pope, *Cohabitation: What to Do When Couples Cannot or Do Not Marry*, 20 DCBA Brief 22, 28 (Dec. 2007). Ms. Pope suggests that until a cohabitation agreement is effectuated for the client, an attorney should advise the client to never contribute money to an acquisition of a major asset, such as a house or car, which is held solely in the name of the other partner; never contribute money without keeping detailed records; and never put money into a joint account or hold title to other assets in joint names unless there is a written clear agreement of what is joint and what is separate. *Id.*

Note that in some states, only written agreements that comply with the state's statute of frauds will be enforced. Texas, for example, is one of those states. *Zaremba v. Cliburn*, 949 S.W.2d 822 (Tex. App. 1997) (failure to comply with statute of frauds bars all causes of action).

Example 15-6

Assume that D, a physician, and P, a nurse working at the same facility, developed a romantic relationship. When D decided to move her practice to another city, she wanted P to move with her. To induce P to quit her job, D made a number of requests and promises. She asked P to sell her home, and reside with D "for the remainder of P's life to maintain and care for their home." D agreed that she would provide essentially all of the support for the two, would make a will leaving her entire estate to P, and would "maintain bank accounts and other investments which constitute nonprobatable assets in P's name to the extent of 100 percent of her entire nonprobatable assets." The written agreement provided that P could cease residing with D if D failed to provide adequate support, if D brought a third person into the home for a period greater than four weeks without P's consent, or if D's abuse, harassment, or abnormal behavior made P's continued residence intolerable. D agreed to pay as liquidated damages the sum of $2,500 per month for the remainder of P's life, should one of the above contingences occur.

P required a written agreement as a condition of accompanying D to the new city. The agreement was drawn by a lawyer, properly witnessed, and

P moved to the new city and set up housekeeping for P and D. Four years after the parties had moved to the new city, D announced that she had developed a new relationship and wanted to move her new friend into the house. When P rejected D's efforts to bring her new companion into the house, D moved out and took up residence with the other woman. P now seeks to enforce the agreement that D will pay her $2,500 per month for the remainder of P's life. How will a court most likely rule?

Explanation

The fact that the agreement is in writing, prepared by a lawyer, and witnessed makes it much more likely that a family court judge will enforce it. Some courts may mistakenly view the $2,500 payment as a type of alimony and reject the effort to enforce the agreement on public policy grounds. However, a majority will enforce the agreement. They will reason that there is no impediment to parties agreeing between themselves to provide certain rights and obligations, including future financial support. *See Posik v. Layton*, 695 So. 2d 759 (Fla. App. 1997) (agreement for support between unmarried adults is valid unless agreement is inseparably based upon illicit consideration of sexual services). In *Marvin v. Marvin*, 557 P.2d 106 (Cal. 1976), the court observed that adults who voluntarily live together and engage in sexual relations are nonetheless as competent as any other persons to contract respecting their earnings and property rights, so long as the agreement does not rest upon illicit meretricious consideration. Here, the parties, represented by counsel, took pains to assure that sexual services were not mentioned in the agreement.

Although the parties undoubtedly expected a sexual relationship, the agreement suggests they contemplated much more. They contracted for a permanent sharing of, and participating in, one another's lives. The contract for permanent support is, therefore, much more likely enforceable in a majority of jurisdictions.

15.16. Oral Agreements

Few cohabitant disputes brought to family court involve an interpretation and enforcement of express written agreements; consequently, courts are often left to construe the meaning of claimed oral agreements, a difficult task at best. State statute of frauds provisions may bar such agreements, especially if they involve an attempt to enforce an agreement to make a will. A majority of jurisdictions take the view that an oral agreement to execute a will in favor of a cohabitant who was living with a decedent is void under the statute of frauds. In re *Gorden's Estate*, 168 N.E.2d 239 (N.Y. 1960) (noting that a meretricious relationship between decedent and companion would not prevent the companion from recovering for services rendered the decedent in maintaining a tavern he owned, or in maintaining his household, if there were an express agreement that she was to be paid, either a stipulated wage, or what the services were worth, and provided that the woman was not being paid to be decedent's mistress).

A Florida court held that an express oral contract in which a putative father agreed to support the mother of their child during pregnancy and for a reasonable time thereafter, in return for the mother quitting her job during pregnancy, was enforceable. *Crossen v. Feldman*, 673 So. 2d 903 (Fla. App. 1996). The court observed, "[T]hese parties entered into a contract for support, which is something that they are legally capable of doing." *Id.*

The Minnesota court in *In re Palmen*, 588 N.W.2d 493 (Minn. 1999), rejected application of the statute of frauds to an oral agreement reasoning that a claim by a cohabitant to recover, preserve, or protect his or her own property, which he or she acquired independent of any service contract related to cohabitation, is enforceable. An oral promise to leave a bequest to a cohabitant, although not binding under the statute of frauds, has been the basis for recovery in *quantum meruit* for the fair value of services rendered. *See Hastoupis v. Gargas*, 398 N.E.2d 745 (Mass. App. 1980) (although decedent's oral contract to bequeath to plaintiff one-half of his estate in return for plaintiff's performing services for him until his death was unenforceable by reason of statute of frauds, plaintiff, who fulfilled his part of the bargain, was entitled to recover in *quantum meruit* for fair and reasonable value of his services).

Partial performance of an oral contract may remove the contract from the statute of frauds requirements. *See Sullivan v. Porter*, 861 A.2d 625, 630 (Me. 2004) (holding that the part performance doctrine is an exception to the statute of frauds); *Turon State Bank v. Estate of Frampton*, 845 P.2d 79 (Kan. App. 1993) (true basis for the application of the doctrine of partial performance is that it is grossly unjust and inequitable for one party of the oral contract to rely on the contract and partially perform his obligations thereunder while the other takes advantage of the partial performance and repudiates the contract by invoking the statute of frauds); *Burke v. Fine*, 51 N.W.2d 818, 820 (Minn. 1952).

Example 15-7

Assume that boyfriend P and girlfriend D live together in an apartment for four years while attending college. Upon graduation, P takes a job in another state. D, relying on *Marvin v. Marvin*, brings an action against P asking that the court in count one award D temporary alimony under the state dissolution statute of $200 per month for six months. In count two, D seeks a $5,000 judgment against P. D alleges that P and D orally agreed to share rent and utility living expenses equally for their apartment but that P fell far behind and now owes D $5,000. P brings a motion to dismiss the complaint. How will a court most likely rule?

Explanation

Most, if not all, jurisdictions would dismiss the count in the complaint asking for temporary alimony. *Marvin* and its progeny have made clear that cohabiting parties may not use state statutes providing for temporary or permanent alimony because these provisions were specifically created for persons who were legally married and subsequently seek to dissolve their relationship.

The simple express oral agreement between the parties to share living expenses is not *per se* an illegal or an immoral contract. The consideration for the agreement was the mutual exchange of promises to pay one-half of the rent and utilities. A majority of jurisdictions would recognize that the two can make an express contract to share the rent as long as the contract is not explicitly and inseparably based upon services as a paramour. It does not appear that this is the case here.

In a minority jurisdiction, a court might reason that the evidence would also authorize a finding that the ultimate agreement as to sharing living expenses arose directly out of the parties' original agreement that they would find an apartment and live there together, the object being from the outset that the apartment to be rented would be the site of their meretricious rather than platonic relationship. See *Wellmaker v. Roberts*, 101 S.E.2d 712 (Ga. 1958) (where a contract grows immediately out of, and is connected with, an illegal or immoral act, a court of justice will not lend its aid to enforce it). A minority jurisdiction might not enforce any portion of the alleged contract; a majority of jurisdictions would most likely enforce it.

15.17. Implied-in-Fact Contracts

Some cohabitant disputes involve claims based on an implied-in-fact contract theory. The formation of such a contract requires proof of the existence of an agreement, which is supported by consideration. The facts supporting the formation of an implied contract are found in the conduct of the parties rather than in express written or oral statements made by them.

The New Jersey court held in *In re Estate of Roccamonte*, 808 A.2d 838 (N.J. 2002), that it would recognize implied palimony contracts. It reasoned that the existence of the terms of a contract between unmarried cohabitants is ordinarily not determinable by what was said. Rather, the terms are derived from the parties' actions and conduct in light of subject matter and surrounding circumstances. It found that the female cohabitant's marital-type relationship with her male cohabitant, plus the evidence of her conduct during the relationship, was sufficient consideration for the now-deceased male cohabitant's promise to support her for life. The court observed that unmarried adult partners, "even those who may be married to others, have the right to choose to cohabit together in a marital-like relationship and that if one of those partners is induced to do so by a promise of support given her by the other, that promise will be enforced by the court." Id. at 842. Because the subject of such a contract is intensely personal, rather than transactional in the customary business sense, the court said that special considerations must be taken into account when considering whether such a contract has been entered into and its terms. Id. at 843-844; See Kozlowski v. Kozlowski, 395 A.2d 913, (N.J. Super. Ch. 1978); Herring v. Daniels, 805 A.2d 718 (Conn. App. 2002) (where the parties have established an unmarried, cohabiting relationship, it is the specific conduct of the parties within that relationship that determines their respective rights and obligations, including the treatment of their individual property); Bayne v. Johnson, 957 A.2d 707 (N.J. Super. 2008) (rejecting as factually insupportable the trial judge's finding that while there was no express promise to support the partner for life, the facts established that the moneyed partner had made an implied promise to do so).

New York rejects application of the implied contract theory where unmarried cohabitants are concerned. For example, in Soderholm v. Kosty, 676 N.Y.S.2d 850, 851 (N.Y. Just. Ct. 1998), the court held that recognition of implied contracts was against New York's public policy as evidenced by the 1933 abolition of common law marriages because it runs too great a risk of error for a court, in hindsight, to sort out the intentions of the parties and to fix significance to conduct carried out within an essentially private and generally noncontractual relationship. See Morone v. Morone, 413 N.E.2d 1154 (N.Y. 1980).

The use of the implied contract theory is criticized because it is conceptually amorphous. Another concern is that because of the complex and varied relationships between men and women, once a relationship ends, one of the parties may be bitter and assert claims based on real or imaginary facts. There are concerns that personal service is often rendered by two people because they value each other's company or because they find it a convenient or rewarding thing to do — not as a contractual obligation. Without an express agreement, there is a substantially greater risk of emotion-laden afterthought and fraud when an effort is made to ascertain by implication what services, if any, were rendered gratuitously and what were rendered for compensation. See Elkins v. Ehrens, 251 N.Y.S.2d 560 (1964); Trimmer v. Van Bomel, 434 N.Y.S.2d 82 (N.Y. Sup. 1980).

Example 15-8

Assume that P and D do not marry, but have an ongoing romantic relationship for ten years preceding D's death. D initially supported P, however, when P moved into D's home early in their relationship, the payments stopped. D asked P not to work outside the home, and he assured her, "This is our house, and most of what I have is going to be yours anyway. I will make sure the house is yours in my will." Even though he orally promised to create a will providing for D before he died, he failed to do so. P contends that a court should enforce D's promise and is seeking advice regarding any possible legal action she may take to enforce the promise. What relief might P seek?

Explanation

Generally an agreement to enforce a promise to execute a will is not enforceable under the statute of frauds. See, e.g., Northrup v. Brigham, 826 N.E.2d 239 (Mass. App. Ct. 2005) (oral promise to execute a will unenforceable under the statute of frauds). However, P may pursue other avenues of relief such as enforcement of the express promise to transfer the house or a quantum meruit theory. P's testimony standing alone is probably not persuasive. However, evidence of her service to D over the past ten years will be given considerable weight by the court. A court will consider the fact that P and D lived together in a single residence as further evidence supporting the existence of a contract. Here, it appears the elements of a contract exist, that is, offer, acceptance, and exchange of consideration and a meeting of minds. There appear to be sufficient facts to at least withstand summary judgment. See Devaney v. L'Esperance, 949 A.2d 743 (N.J. 2008).

15.18. Quasi-Contracts; Palimony

Quasi-contracts are not contracts based on the apparent intention of the parties to undertake the performance in question, but are contracts created by law for reasons of justice. An action for recovery based on unjust enrichment is grounded on the moral principle that one who has received a benefit has a duty to make restitution when retaining such a benefit would be unjust. The remedy is based on the reasonable value of the benefit conferred by one party that enriched the other. The value of the benefit has two components: money expended and services or forbearance rendered. Several courts have held that unmarried cohabitants may raise claims of unjust enrichment following the termination of their relationships when one of the parties attempts to retain an unreasonable amount of the property acquired through the efforts of both.

Unlike express and implied contracts, the conduct of the parties is not critical to granting relief because no contract exists. Instead, a contract is imposed as a matter of law, not as a matter of fact. A party seeking to establish a quasi-contract must present evidence of the benefits conferred on the other party and services performed. In addition, the moving party must establish evidence of the reasonable value of those benefits and services.

15.19. Resulting Trusts

One will find claims involving two types of implied trusts in some cohabitation disputes: resulting trusts and constructive trusts. A resulting trust is imposed to implement the parties' intent; a constructive trust is imposed to prevent the unjust enrichment of another. More specifically, a "resulting trust" has been defined as "[a] remedy imposed by equity when property is transferred under circumstances suggesting that the transferor did not intend for the transferee to have the beneficial interest in the property." *Black's Law Dictionary* 1551 (8th ed. 2004). "Because the transferee . . . is not entitled to the beneficial interest in question, and because that beneficial interest is not otherwise disposed of, it remains in and thus is said 'to result' (that is, it reverts) to the transferor or the transferor's estate or other successors in interest." *Restatement (Third) of Trusts*, §7, cmt. a. The transferee "is said to hold the property upon a resulting trust for the transferor," and so "the beneficial interest that is held in resulting trust is simply an equitable reversionary interest implied by law." *Id.*

15.20. Constructive Trusts

Like a resulting trust, a constructive trust is also an equitable remedy that is imposed to prevent the unjust enrichment of another. *See Black's Law Dictionary* 1547 (8th ed. 2004). A constructive trust arises by operation of law against one who, through any form of unconscionable conduct, holds legal title to property when equity and good conscience demands that he should not hold such title. *Henkle v. Henkle*, 600 N.E.2d 791, 795-796 (Ohio App. 1991). A constructive trust closely parallels the equitable remedy of *quantum meruit*, with the primary difference being that the trust transfers title, whereas the *quantum meruit* remedy is based on value, not title. The facts in a particular case may permit a plaintiff to choose which remedy is most appropriate.

A constructive trust compels the restoration to another of property to which the holder thereof is not justly entitled. *Kraus v. Willow Park Public Golf Course*, 140 Cal. Rptr. 744 (Cal. 1977). One who gains a thing by fraud, accident, mistake, undue influence, the violation of a trust, or other wrongful act, is, unless he has some other and better right thereto, an involuntary trustee of the thing gained, for the benefit of the person who would otherwise have had it. Thus, a constructive trust may be imposed in practically any case where there is a wrongful acquisition or detention of property to which another is entitled. *Weiss v. Marcus* 124 Cal. Rptr. 297 (Cal. App. 1975).

In *Evans v. Wall*, 542 So. 2d 1055 (Fla. 3d DCA 1989), the female cohabitant sought imposition of a constructive trust asking for recovery of the reasonable value of her capital, materials, and labor invested over five-year period in the male cohabitant's residential and commercial property. She alleged she contributed income and household services, worked in male cohabitant's mango groves, assisted in construction of new dwelling on the land, and contributed money and materials for construction of barn. The court found in her favor, awarding her $8,000 as a constructive trust, which was imposed to do equity between the unmarried cohabitants. *Id.* at 1056.

RECOVERY LIMITS

15.21. Wrongful Death Claims

Because cohabitants are not married, they cannot avail themselves of direct relief, such as alimony, when the relationship dissolves. Cohabitants will also have difficulty receiving other benefits that commonly accrue to married people, including wrongful death awards and insurance recoveries.

In *Cole v. State Farm Ins. Co.*, 128 P.3d 171 (Alaska 2006), the court rejected a cohabitant's claim that her cohabiting partner was covered for an injury under his cohabitant's insurance policy. In *Ford v. American Original Corp.*, 475 F. Supp. 10 (E.D. Va. 1979), a cohabitant was held not entitled to any recovery as a beneficiary either under Death on the High Seas Act (DOHSA), the Jones Act, or Virginia's Wrongful Death Act). *See Lawson v. United States*, 192 F.2d 479 (2d Cir.), *cert. denied*, 343 U.S. 904 (1951) (holding that a putative wife was not a "legal" wife and therefore could not recover for wrongful death of her putative husband under DOHSA); *Tetterton v. Arctic Tankers, Inc.*, 116 F. Supp. 429 (E.D. Pa. 1953) (declaring that even if a valid common law marriage had been perfected under the law of Florida, which recognized common law marriages, the claimant still did not become a legal wife and was at most a common law wife, and the congressional intent of DOHSA was to permit the recovery of wrongful death damages only by "legal" spouses).

15.22. Loss of Consortium Claims

Courts will generally recognize loss of consortium actions brought by spouses, parents, and children. Spousal consortium has been held to be a right acquired through marriage, subject to forfeiture when the marriage is dissolved unless preserved in the dissolution decree.

A majority of jurisdictions have rejected allowing loss of consortium claims to be asserted by a cohabiting partner. *See, e.g., Mega Life and Health Ins. Co. v. Superior Court,* 92 Cal. Rptr. 3d 399 (Cal. App. 2009); *Charron v. Amaral,* 889 N.E.2d 946 (Mass. 2008) (loss of consortium cannot arise unless the family member has, *inter alia,* a legal relationship with the injured third party); *Biercevicz v. Liberty Mut. Ins. Co.,* 865 A.2d 1267 (Conn. Super. 2004) (fiancé was not "closely-related" to decedent so as to allow bystander emotional distress claim); *Weitl v. Moes,* 311 N.W.2d 259 (Iowa 1981) (children); *Tong v. Jocson,* 142 Cal. Rptr. 726 (Cal. 1977); *Barrow v. Curtis,* 209 So. 2d 699 (Fla. Dist. Ct. App. 1968); *Sostock v. Reiss,* 415 N.E.2d 1094 (Ill. 1980); *Angelet v. Shivar,* 602 S.W.2d 185 (Ky. App. 1980); *Sawyer v. Bailey,* 413 A.2d 165 (Me. 1980); *Rademacher v. Torbensen,* 13 N.Y.S.2d 124 (N.Y. 1939); *Booth v. Baltimore & Ohio Railroad,* 87 S.E. 84 (W. Va. 1915).

15.23. State and Federal Statutory Limits on Recovery

Courts have generally been unwilling to award benefits that flow from various state and federal statutes to cohabiting partners absent language that specifically recognizes the relationship. *See, e.g., Powell v. Rogers,* 496 F.2d 1248, 1250 (9th Cir. 1974), *cert. denied,* 419 U.S. 1032 (1974) (workers' compensation denied; federal law relied on state law defining whether claimant was married to decedent); *see Baldwin v. Sullivan,* 204 N.W. 420, 421-423 (Iowa 1925) (denying unmarried cohabitant's claim for workers' compensation).

The court in *Cato v. Alcoa-Reynolds Metals Co.,* 152 P.3d 981 (Or. Ct. App. 2007), refused to provide a cohabitant compensation under Oregon's workers' compensation statutes. Although the legislature provided for a survivor benefit to be paid to an unmarried partner with whom the deceased worker cohabited and had a child, because the couple did not have a child within the meaning of the statute, the surviving cohabitant could not collect the benefits. The cohabitants had a son who was past the age of maturity when his father died, and the court construed the language of the statute to mean a son or daughter who is 18 years or younger.

15.24. Insurance Policy Coverage

In *Ortiz v. New York City Transit Authority,* 699 N.Y.S.2d 370 (N.Y. App. Div. 1 Dept. 1999), the court ruled that the named insured's same-sex, live-in partner was not entitled to underinsured motorist coverage under the supplementary uninsured motorist clause in the named insured's automobile policy. The court held that the partner was neither a "spouse" nor a "relative" of the named insured and was not covered by the policy. *See Hartford Ins. Co. v. Cline*, 139 P.3d 176 (N.M. 2006) (excluding domestic partners from the definition of family member in an automobile insurance policy is not invalid as contrary to public policy); *Cole v. State Farm Ins. Co.*, 128 P.3d 171 (Alaska 2006); *Hedlund v. Monumental Gen. Ins. Co.*, 404 N.W.2d 371, 373-374 (Minn. App. 1987) (spouse is commonly known to mean husband or wife. The legal, as well as the ordinary, meaning of spouse is one's wife or husband — while many cohabiting relationships are permanent and analogous to marital relationships, they are not spousal relationships).

Example 15-9

P and D lived together for 14 years until D's death. They never married. Three children were born of this union, and the entire household was supported by D. In the words of P, her "marriage" was legal "in the sight of God, yes; but in the sight of man, no." P and D lived together in two states that did not recognize common law marriages and their statutes defined "wife" and "widow" as persons who were married under the laws of the states. When D died in an accident, P sought death benefits as a surviving wife or widow under the applicable federal law. How will a court most likely treat P's claim?

Explanation

In cases like this, the federal law usually turns to state law to determine the status of the couple, that is, does either of the two states that P and D lived in recognize P as a "surviving widow" on these facts? Unfortunately for P, neither jurisdiction recognizes common law marriages and both take a traditional approach to the definition of "wife" and "widow." Consequently, a court will not recognize P as D's lawful wife at the time of his death, and P will not receive any benefits.

Note that if the federal government created a federal common law marriage doctrine, there would be greater uniformity in terms of citizens qualifying for widow/widower benefits where federal statutes provided assistance or benefits. It would also eliminate the element of one state recognizing a common law marriage, thus allowing a claimant's benefits, while an adjacent state refuses to recognize common law marriages and the benefits are denied. As a practical matter, the courts have taken the position that these views are more properly directed to Congress. Furthermore, the creation of federal common law is said to be generally disfavored except where explicitly authorized by Congress. *See In re Consolidated Freightways Corp.*, 443

F.3d 1160 (9th Cir. 2006); *Commercial Union Ins. Co. v. Sea Harvest Seafood Co.*, 251 F.3d 1294 (10th Cir. 2001).

15.25. Housing

In *390 West End Associates v. Wildfoerster*, 661 N.Y.S.2d 202 (N.Y. App. Div. 1 Dept. 1997), the court awarded possession of a rent-controlled apartment to the landlord, finding that there was an insufficient familial relationship between tenant and companion to allow for transfer of the apartment to the companion under rent-control regulations. The companion and the deceased tenant had a 20-year relationship, during which they lived together from 1976 to 1978 and again for more than two years prior to the tenant's death from AIDS in 1993. The court found that the relationship lacked the normal indicia of a familial relationship. Although the tenant's close friends testified, and the trial court found, that the tenant and respondent had a very close, loving relationship, the trial evidence failed to sufficiently establish the respondent as a family member within the meaning of the applicable rent regulations.

The Supreme Court of California has held that California's Fair Employment and Housing Act's (FEHA) prohibition against discrimination because of "marital status" prohibits landlords from refusing to rent to prospective tenants because they are not married. The court also held that FEHA's prohibition against discrimination based on marital status does not "substantially burden" a landlord's religious exercise under the state constitution's free exercise and enjoyment of religion clause. *Smith v. Fair Employment & Hous. Comm'n*, 913 P.2d 909 (Cal. 1996).

Courts in states such as Minnesota and Washington have not followed California's lead. *See, e.g., State by Cooper v. French*, 460 N.W.2d 2, 5-6 (Minn. 1990); *McFadden v. Elma Country Club*, 613 P.2d 146, 150 (Wash. Ct. App. 1980). The Wisconsin Supreme Court declared a county ordinance similar to California's FEHA "invalid to the extent that it [sought] to protect 'cohabitants'". *County of Dane v. Norman*, 497 N.W.2d 714, 716 (Wis. 1993). The court reasoned that the county had no power to enact statutes that were "inconsistent with the public policy of Wisconsin, which seeks to promote the stability of marriage and family." *Id.* at 720.

15.26. Statute of Limitations

As a general principle, a *Marvin*-type agreement is breached when one of the partners ends the relationship. However, the limitations period is usually construed in light of the facts of a particular case. When no time for performance is specified, a person who has promised to do an act in the future and who has the ability to perform does not violate his or her agreement unless and until performance is demanded and refused. For example, if the parties have separated, but the obligor performs as required by the *Marvin* agreement, there has been no breach, no cause of action has accrued, and the statute of limitations has not begun to run. The statute of limitation only begins to run when the breach occurs. *See Cochran v. Cochran*, 66 Cal. Rptr. 2d 337 (Cal. Ct. App. 1997).

In *Whorton v. Dillingham*, 248 Cal. Rptr. 405 (Cal. App. 1998), the court observed that a cause of action for breach of contract accrues at the time of breach. *See* 3 *Witkin, Cal. Procedure* 402 (3d ed. 1985) *Actions*, §375. Consequently, a *Marvin*-type contract is breached when one partner terminates the relationship. The statute of limitations for an action upon a contract not founded on a writing in California is two years. *Code Civ. Proc.*, §339, subd. 1.

Example 15-10

Assume that P and D lived together in California for several years without getting married when D left the relationship to marry another. At some point in the relationship, D had orally promised P that should their relationship ever end, D would pay P $400 a month for life because she had given up her job and moved to the country to live with D. When D marries X, he continues to pay P $400 a month for the next three years and then stops payment. P brings an action to enforce the agreement six months after D stopped payments but three years and six months after they separated. D asserts that the two-year statute of limitations, similar to the California statute noted above, has run. How will a court most likely rule in this case?

Explanation

A court will most likely rule that the statute of limitations began to run when the defendant stopped making the monthly $400 payments. Normally, a *Marvin*-type contract is said to have been breached when one partner terminates the relationship. *Estate of Fincher*, 119 Cal. App. 3d 343, 352 (1981). The statute of limitations for an action upon a contract not founded on a writing in California is two years. (Code Civ. Proc. §339, subd. 1.) Because D continued making payments for three years after separating from P, and P brought the action only a few months after D stopped making the payments, a breach in the contract did not occur until he stopped making the payments. P is well within the two-year limitation. Note that support agreements between cohabitants are enforceable under *Marvin v. Marvin*, *supra*, *Friedman v. Friedman*, 20 Cal. App. 4th 876, 889 (1993). The above promise of support is similar to that of the defendant in *Marvin*, who allegedly "agreed to 'provide for all of plaintiff's financial support and needs for the rest of her life.'" *Marvin* held that this agreement supported a cause of action for breach of an express contract.

CHAPTER 16

Determining Parentage

16.1. Introduction

This chapter examines significant legal principles involved in determining legal parentage. Although the chapter primarily focuses on establishment of paternity, issues concerning establishment of maternity are also discussed.

Today there are many reasons for establishing parentage, some of which include the following: obtaining child support from the biological father; establishing the biological father's visitation and custodial rights; creating peace of mind; determining grandparentage; establishing inheritance rights; establishing insurance claims; obtaining social security benefits; establishing Native American tribal rights; determining the likelihood of being the biological sibling of a long-lost sister or brother; and helping a person seeking entry into the United States on the grounds that he or she is a biological relative of a citizen.

THE COMMON LAW

16.2. Disparate Treatment

Historically, establishment of paternity was important because it fixed the line of succession. In England, primogeniture, which passed property to the first-born male, made the determination of an heir very important.

Consequently, much of the early English law on this topic was inherited by America and was initially concerned with making a "legitimacy" determination. Note that courts today are more concerned with determining paternity than with issues of legitimacy.

The common law treated a child born during marriage and one born outside of marriage differently. If a child was born during a marriage, the common law was averse to declaring the child illegitimate — a result that could deprive the child of inheritance and succession and possibly make the child a ward of the state. It aided a child born during a marriage by applying a presumption that the child was the legitimate issue of the wife's husband. The presumption could be overcome only by evidence that the husband was incapable of procreation or had no access to his wife during the relevant period of conception.

Proof of illegitimacy was further complicated by the adoption in many jurisdictions of an evidentiary rule known as "Lord Mansfield's rule." The rule, developed in England and imported into this country, provided that neither the husband nor the wife were permitted to "bastardize" the issue of the wife after marriage by testifying to the nonaccess of the husband. *See Egbert v. Greenwalt*, 6 N.W. 654 (1880). The rule was apparently applied in some jurisdictions until the mid-twentieth century, when legislatures and courts abandoned its use. *See People v. C.*, 85 N.Y.S.2d 751 (N.Y. Child. Ct. 1949).

For children born out of wedlock, the common law was harsh. It labeled these children "bastards" and considered them *filius nullius* — the children of no one and the kin to nobody. In some jurisdictions, a child born out of wedlock remained illegitimate despite the marriage of the biological parents. Should a marriage be annulled, a child born during the relationship was considered illegitimate. Support for children born out of wedlock was almost nonexistent.

Example 16-1

Assume that 200 years ago, P and D were married, and a child was born to them in a common law jurisdiction. D suspects that the child was conceived during an affair his wife had with a neighbor, X, while P and D were separated for one year. D brings a legal action with the goal of proving that the child is the issue of X, or at least, not D's child. D is unable to produce any witnesses other than P and D. How would a common law court most likely rule on D's request that he be allowed to testify?

Explanation

The common law court most likely would reject the request, and the action would fail. In the common law jurisdiction that applied Lord Mansfield's rule, D would be barred from testifying to nonaccess.

SUPREME COURT MANDATES EQUAL TREATMENT

16.3. Overview

Discrimination against children born to unmarried parents was practiced in most jurisdictions in the United States until well into the 1960s. The United States Supreme Court, Congress, and the National Conference of Commissioners on Uniform State Laws all played a role in causing the states to abandon their unfair treatment of these children. One of the most important factors in changing society's views of these children was the Supreme Court, which invalidated a host of state statutes that treated children born outside of marriage differently from those born during marriage.

16.4. Child's Action for Wrongful Death of the Mother

The case of *Levy v. Louisiana*, 391 U.S. 68 (1968), helped close the gap between children born to unmarried parents and children born during marriage. The dispute involved five children born outside of marriage who sued for damages as the result of the wrongful death of their mother. Under a Louisiana statute, the children did not have a legally recognizable interest in her death if they were born out of wedlock. Although not finding that illegitimacy was a suspect classification, the Supreme Court struck down the statute on equal protection grounds, holding that it was invidious to discriminate against the children "when no action, conduct, or demeanor of theirs was relevant to the harm that was done in the matter." *See also* Annot.,

Discrimination on Basis of Illegitimacy as Denial of Constitutional Rights, 38 A.L.R.3d 613 (1971).

16.5. Child Claims Inheritance Rights

The Supreme Court has also aided children born out of wedlock in their efforts to inherit from their parents. For example, *Trimble v. Gordon*, 430 U.S. 762 (1977), involved Delta Mona Trimble, the nonmarital daughter of Jessie Trimble and the deceased biological father, Sherman Gordon. Gordon had provided support and had acknowledged the parent-child relationship; however, when he died without a will, Illinois probate law prohibited Delta Mona Trimble from collecting any portion of his estate. The statute declared that as an illegitimate child, she could only inherit if she had been legitimized by the subsequent marriage of her biological mother and father.

The Court held that a classification based on illegitimacy is not suspect so as to require strict scrutiny. However, using a mid-level or mid-tier analysis, the Court held that at a minimum, a statutory classification must bear some rational relationship to a legitimate state purpose. The Court explained that "in this context, the standard just stated is a minimum; the Court sometimes requires more. 'Though the latitude given state economic and social regulation is necessarily broad, when the state statutory classifications approach sensitive and fundamental personal rights, this Court exercises a stricter scrutiny.'" *Id.* at 767. The Court concluded that the statute bore only the most attenuated relationship to the asserted goal of family relationships and was unconstitutional.

In a subsequent decision, *Lalli v. Lalli*, 439 U.S. 259 (1978), the Court rejected a constitutional challenge to a New York intestacy statute that required illegitimate children seeking to inherit from their fathers to produce an order of affiliation made by a court of competent jurisdiction during the alleged father's lifetime. The Court observed that the statute was intended to soften the rigors of previous law, which permitted illegitimate children to inherit only from their mothers. It also believed that the statute provided for the just and orderly disposition of property at death and protected innocent adults, and those rightfully interested in their estates, from fraudulent claims of heirship and harassing litigation.

The Court distinguished *Trimble v. Gordon* on the grounds that the Illinois statute in *Trimble* was constitutionally unacceptable because it resulted in a total statutory disinheritance of children born out of wedlock who were not legitimated by the subsequent marriage of their parents. However, inheritance under the New York statute is barred only where there has been a failure to secure evidence of paternity during the father's lifetime. "This is not a requirement that inevitably disqualifies an unnecessarily large number of children born out of wedlock." *Id.* at 273. The Court concluded "that the requirement imposed by Section 4-1.2 on illegitimate children who would inherit from their fathers is substantially related to the important state interests the statute is intended to promote." *Id.* at 275.

Public policy debates concerning inheritance rights of children born to unmarried parents remain prevalent today. *See In re Estate of Farmer ex rel. Farmer,* 964 So. 2d 498 (Miss. 2007) (minor could inherit in case where deceased father had executed an acknowledgment of paternity); *In re Poldrugovaz,* 851 N.Y.S.2d 254 (N.Y. Sup. Ct. App. Div. 2008) (posthumous genetic marker testing ordered if decedent "openly and notoriously acknowledged" child). *See also* Paula A. Monopoli, *Nonmarital Children and Post-Death Parentage: A Different Path for Inheritance Law?,* 48 Santa Clara L. Rev. 857 (2008).

Example 16-2

Assume that P and D have a daughter, X, but they do not marry. D is not listed on X's birth certificate, but D was found to be X's father in a paternity action and was ordered to pay monthly child support. D paid the child support as ordered but had little contact with X. X was not included in family gatherings, many of D's friends did not know of her existence, and D described her as an "$18,000 mistake." Prior to X's birth, D executed a will disposing of his estate. He did not change the will after X's birth, and she was not included in it. D dies, and X seeks a share of the estate as an omitted child. The state where the parties live has a statute providing that an illegitimate child born after the date that a will is executed can take an intestate share of the decedent's estate if the testator "recognized" the child during his lifetime. What is the likely result?

Explanation

The other heirs will argue that D did not recognize X as his child because he did not treat her as his child or have a relationship with her. X will argue that if D had died intestate, she would have inherited from him based on the paternity judgment issued during D's lifetime. This example is based on the case of *In re Estate of Brewer,* 168 S.W.3d 135 (Mo. App. 2005), where the trial court found that X was not entitled to an intestate share of D's estate, but that decision was overturned on appeal. The appellate court reasoned that the paternity judgment constituted "recognition" within the meaning of the statute.

16.6. Child Claims Social Security Benefits

In *Mathews v. Lucas,* 427 U.S. 495 (1976), nonmarital children sought to obtain social security benefits after their biological father died. There was no dispute over the issue of the deceased being the biological father.

The Social Security Act provided that a child of an individual who died fully insured under the act is entitled to surviving child's benefits if the child is under 18, or a student under 22, and was dependent at the time of the parent's death. A child is considered dependent if the insured parent was living with the child or the parent was contributing to the child's support at the time of death.

The Court upheld the statute, holding that it did not violate the Equal Protection Clause of the Constitution, even though the statute treated children differently based at least in part on their parents' marital status. The Court said that the challenged statutory classifications are permissible because they are reasonably related to the likelihood of dependency at death. The Court concluded that although the act did not extend any presumption of dependency to illegitimate children as a group, it did not impermissibly discriminate against them when compared with legitimate children or those illegitimate children who are statutorily deemed dependent.

16.7. Child's Father Makes Wrongful Death Claim

In *Parham v. Hughes*, 441 U.S. 347 (1979), the Supreme Court rejected a claim by a father who had not legitimated his child and who sought to recover for the child's wrongful death. The relevant Georgia statute allowed a mother to bring a wrongful death action for the death of a child born out of wedlock and allowed the father, if he had legitimated the child, to bring an action if there was no mother. The Court found that "unlike the illegitimate child for whom the status of illegitimacy is involuntary and immutable, the [father] here was responsible for fostering an illegitimate child and for failing to change its status." *Id.* at 441. The Court indicated concern about proving the paternity of illegitimate children and the related danger of spurious claims against intestate estates. It also evinced additional concern that if paternity has not been established before the commencement of a wrongful death action, a defendant might face multiple lawsuits by individuals all claiming to be the father of the deceased child. Such uncertainty would make it difficult if not impossible for a defendant to settle a wrongful-death action because there would always exist the risk of a subsequent suit by another person claiming to be the father.

16.8. Tests to Determine Rights if Child Is Born Outside of Marriage

Since *Levy v. Louisiana*, the Supreme Court has used two tests to determine the rights of illegitimate children who are treated differently by a state statute than children born during marriage: (1) the "insurmountable barrier" test,

Gomez v. Perez, 409 U.S. 535, 538 (1973); *Labine v. Vincent*, 401 U.S. 532, 539 (1971); and (2) the less stringent "substantial relationship" test, *Lalli v. Lalli*, 439 U.S. 259 (1978); *Trimble v. Gordon*, 430 U.S. 762, 772-774 (1977).

Example 16-3

Assume that M and D are the biological parents of child P, who was born out of wedlock in state X. A month prior to P's birth, the biological father, D, was involved in an automobile accident. He remained in a coma for five months and died intestate. Under the law in state X, there are three means by which an illegitimate child may inherit from an intestate father: (1) the father may marry the mother and recognize the child as his own; (2) the father may legitimate the child by following the statutory procedure for legitimation by written declaration; or (3) a court may make a judicial determination of paternity during the father's lifetime. P argues that she was unable to qualify under any of these provisions because her biological father was fatally injured in an automobile accident that occurred before her birth and remained in a coma until his death some four months after her birth. P attacks the law in state X as unconstitutional. How will a court most likely rule?

Explanation

Obviously, after the accident, P's father could not have married her mother or acknowledged the child by written declaration. Nor did P have a meaningful opportunity to be legitimated through a paternity proceeding, which, under X's law, must be maintained during the father's lifetime. As a practical matter, X's intestacy scheme effectively denied P any means through which to become legitimated or qualify herself to inherit from her father's estate. On these facts, a court will most likely rule that the statute creates an insurmountable barrier and, as applied, is unconstitutional.

PROCEDURAL RIGHTS

16.9. Preponderance of Evidence Standard

In *Rivera v. Minnich*, 483 U.S. 574 (1987), the Supreme Court held that a paternity statute that provided proof by a preponderance of evidence did not violate the Due Process Clause of the Fourteenth Amendment to the United States Constitution. It concluded that the clear and convincing standard of proof for terminating a parent-child relationship established in *Santosky v. Kramer*, 455 U.S. 745 (1982), was not applicable.

16.10. Indigent's Right to Blood Tests

In *Little v. Streater*, 452 U.S. 1 (1981), the Supreme Court held that due process requires that an indigent defendant involved in paternity matters be entitled to blood testing at state expense to establish (or disprove) paternity. The importance of blood tests magnifies the necessity for the timely assistance of counsel, who can ensure that the defendant is apprised of his right to request blood tests and who can inform him of their significance.

16.11. Indigent's Right to Counsel in Paternity Proceeding

The Supreme Court has not mandated that counsel be afforded indigents who are accused of fathering a child out of wedlock. However, some state courts have required counsel either under the exercise of their supervisory power to ensure fairness or as a requirement of the state constitution. *Hepfel v. Bashaw*, 279 N.W.2d 342 (Minn. 1979) (supervisory power). In noncriminal cases in which a right to counsel has specifically been recognized (such as contempt or paternity cases), the court should exercise the same care in assuring the understanding of the right and voluntariness of the waiver, as in criminal cases.

Those jurisdictions that have determined that counsel should be provided reason that an adjudication of paternity can mean up to 18 years of child support payments and that paternity affects the distribution of defendant's estate upon death, Workers' Compensation benefits, social security benefits (42 U.S.C. §402(d)(1)), and insurance proceeds. A paternity adjudication can also seriously damage the reputation of the defendant and have a deleterious effect on an already established family of the defendant. The child's rights of support, inheritance, and custody are directly affected by a paternity proceeding, and a child's health interests are involved. An accurate family medical history can be critical in the diagnosis and treatment of a child's injuries and illnesses. *See Reynolds v. Kimmons*, 569 P.2d 799, 803 (Alaska 1977) (under state constitution); *Artibee v. Cheboygan Circuit Judge*, 243 N.W.2d 248, 250 (Mich. 1976); *Salas v. Cortez*, 593 P.2d 226, 234, *cert. denied*, 444 U.S. 900 (1979) (state constitution); *Wake Cty. ex rel. Carrington v. Townes*, 281 S.E.2d 765, 769 (N.C. App. 1981).

There is contrary state authority regarding the right to counsel. *State ex rel. Hamilton v. Snodgrass*, 325 N.W.2d 740 (Iowa 1982); *Sheppard v. Mack*, 427 N.E.2d 522, 528 (Ohio App. 1980) (no due process or equal protection right to appointed counsel); *State ex rel. Adult and Family Serv. Div. v. Stoutt*, 644 P.2d 1232, 1137 (Or. App. 1982) (no due process right to appointed counsel under federal or state constitutions); *State v. Walker*, 553 P.2d 1093, 1095 (Wis. 1976) (no due process or equal protection right to appointed counsel).

16.12. Putative Father's Standing to Bring Action — Michael H.

The best-known standing decision is *Michael H. v. Gerald D.*, 491 U.S. 110 (1988) (Stevens, J., concurring in the judgment; Brennan, J., with Marshall and Blackmun, J., dissenting; White, J., with Brennan, J., dissenting). Justice Stevens concurred in the judgment denying the putative father an opportunity to establish his paternity, only after concluding that under the California statute at issue, the putative father "was given a fair opportunity to show that he is [the child's] natural father, that he developed a relationship with her, and that her interests would be served by granting him visitation rights" *Id.* at 135-136. The dispute involved a child fathered by the wife's lover during the marriage and born while she was cohabiting with her husband. The child was conclusively presumed by statute to be a child of the marriage unless the husband was impotent or sterile. The husband's name was placed on the birth certificate, and he claimed the child as his daughter. Blood tests indicated, however, that the wife's lover, Michael H., was actually the child's biological father.

During the child's first three years, she and her mother intermittently lived with Michael, who consistently held himself out as her father. About 18 months after the child's birth, Michael filed a filiation action to establish his paternity and visitation rights, and during the course of this lawsuit, the constitutionality of the conclusive presumption was challenged.

The Court held that the biological father had no protected liberty interest in the parental relationship and that the state's interest in preserving the marital union was sufficient to support termination of his relationship with the child. The Court balanced the nonmarital father's rights against the rights of the married father. The plurality determined that the marital family and the marital father's rights are paramount and rested its holding on history and tradition. Five justices, however, refused to foreclose the possibility that the natural father might ever have a constitutionally protected interest in his relationship with a child, whose mother was married to and cohabiting with another man at the time of the child's conception and birth.

In addition to *Michael H. v. Gerald D.*, various state courts have considered a putative father's standing to bring a paternity action. *Barnes v. Jeudevine*, 2006 WL 2075648 (Mich. 2006) (biological father lacked standing to sue under Paternity Act); *Numerick v. Krull*, 694 N.W.2d 552 (Mich. App. 2005) (paternity action barred by marriage of mother to another man); *Lisa I. v. Superior Court*, 34 Cal. Rptr. 3d 927 (Cal. App. 2005) (biological father with no existing relationship with child lacks standing); *J.K. v. R.S.*, 706 So. 2d 1262 (Ala. Civ. App. 1997) (alleged biological father was not a parent for purpose of standing to bring custody action involving child born to a married couple); *S.B. v. D. H.*, 736 So. 2d 766 (Fla. Dist. Ct. App. 1999) (putative biological father could not maintain a paternity action concerning a child conceived by a married woman over the objections of the woman and her husband); *In re Paternity of S.R.I.*, 602 N.E.2d 1014 (Ind. 1992) (interpreting the relevant statute to allow a putative father to establish paternity without regard to the mother's marital status): *Pearson v. Pearson*, 182 P.3d 353 (Utah 2008) (putative father denied standing based on public policy of preserving marital stability and protecting children).

16.13. Alleged Father's Right to Jury Trial

A paternity action today is civil in nature, and most jurisdictions allow normal discovery such as interrogatories, depositions, requests for admissions, and requests for an adverse physical or psychological examination. The Personal Responsibility and Work Opportunity Reconciliation Act of 1996 (PRWORA) required states, as a condition of receiving federal funds, to preclude jury trials in contested paternity matters.

FEDERAL LEGISLATION

16.14. Overview

With an increasingly large number of children being born outside of marriage and the federal government providing support for some of them, more than three decades ago, Congress responded with legislation that reduced the government's financial burden by shifting it to the biological parents of the child—in particular, their fathers. To accomplish this objective, the federal government created a child support enforcement program that imposed requirements on states as a condition of receiving IV-D funding. The program, titled after IV-D of the Social Security Act, requires that the states comply with various requirements, including establishment of paternity, or risk losing up to two-thirds of support payments provided by the government.

Beginning in 1975, state and local IV-D agencies were required to establish the paternity of all children who were born to unmarried parents and who either received public assistance benefits or have applied for IV-D services. In 1984, Congress required that each state permit a paternity action to be brought at any time before a child's eighteenth birthday, rather than allowing shorter statutes of limitations, which had been the practice in some states.

16.15. The Omnibus Budget Reconciliation Act of 1993

The Omnibus Budget Reconciliation Act of 1993, Pub. L. No. 103-66 (1993), required that all states adopt an in-hospital, voluntary acknowledgment process as a condition of receiving federal IV-D funds. The Personal Responsibility and Work Opportunity Reconciliation Act of 1996 (PRWORA), Pub. L. No. 103-66 (1993), modified and expanded the required paternity acknowledgment procedures earlier established by Congress.

16.16. Personal Responsibility and Work Opportunity Reconciliation Act of 1996 (PRWORA)

The Personal Responsibility and Work Opportunity Reconciliation Act of 1996 (PRWORA) mandates that states have laws requiring that genetic testing be ordered in any contested case. The party requesting the testing must execute a sworn statement that either alleges paternity, with a showing of a reasonable possibility of sexual contact between the parties, or denies paternity. The tribunal can then compel genetic testing of the child and all parties. *See State ex rel. Dept. of Justice and Division of Child Support*, 120 P.3d 1 (Or. App. 2005) (requiring parentage testing was a reasonable "search" under state and constitutions).

UNIFORM PARENTAGE ACT (UPA)

16.17. Overview

The National Conference of Commissioners on Uniform State Laws (NCCUSL) first addressed parentage in 1922 with the Uniform Illegitimacy Act and continued to promulgate related acts such as the Uniform Blood Tests to Determine Paternity Act, the Uniform Paternity Act, the Uniform Probate Code, and the Blood Tests to Determine Paternity Act. One can see from the titles of the acts how societal and legal views of parentage have evolved over the last century.

The most influential current uniform law is the Uniform Parentage Act (UPA), which was originally approved in 1973 and most recently revised in 2002. The text of the Act can be found at http://www.law.upenn.edu/bll/ulc/upa/final2002.htm (last visited July 27, 2009). By December of 2000, the UPA had been adopted in 19 states and had influenced development of the law in a significant number of the remaining states. The 2002 revision has been adopted in nine states. *See* Legislative Fact Sheet at *http://www.nccusl.org/Update/ uniformact_factsheets/uniformacts-fs-upa.asp* (last visited July 27, 2009).

The UPA declared that the law should treat children equally, regardless of the marital status of their parents. UPA §202 (2002). Consequently, the title "illegitimate" was replaced with the term "child with no presumed father."

16.18. Genetic Testing

The UPA sets forth procedures and guidelines to expedite and regulate the use of genetic testing in paternity cases. A man may be rebuttably identified as the father of a child based on certain genetic testing results described in the Act. UPA §§501 *et seq.*; UPA §§621 *et seq.*

In the past, proving paternity scientifically was unreliable, and verdicts were unpredictable. Often, the evidence consisted of testimony about the mother's relationships with other men, the physical resemblance of the child to the alleged father, and the relationship of the mother and alleged father. When blood-type testing came into common use, it could not reliably identify the father of a child, but could exclude possible fathers.

Recent scientific advances have led to genetic testing that is able to identify a man as the father of a child to a reasonably high degree of accuracy. By testing blood and tissue, certain genes can be identified. If a test of a child reveals a gene that did not come from the mother, the gene was contributed by the child's biological father. If the DNA test shows the alleged father could not have contributed the gene, he is excluded. However, the fact that the alleged father could have contributed the gene does not automatically prove he is the father. Ronald J. Richards, *DNA Fingerprinting and Paternity Testing*, 22 U.C. Davis L. Rev. 609, 614 (1989).

Certain genes are more or less common in given human populations. If the test reveals that the child's father possesses uncommon genes also found in the child, but not found in the mother, it is probable that he is the biological father. The probability is expressed as a high paternity index or "probability of paternity." *DNA Fingerprinting and Paternity Testing, supra*, at 616-617. This probability exists because it is assumed that the man had access to the mother. *See, e.g.,* In re Paternity of M.J.B., 425 N.W.2d 404, 409 (1988). Regardless of the test results, if the alleged father is infertile or did not have access to the mother, he cannot be adjudicated as the father.

Example 16-4

Assume that P claims that D is the father of a child born out of wedlock. A genetic test reveals that D is the child's father to a probability of 97 percent or greater. In this jurisdiction, an individual is presumed to be the father of a child when genetic testing indicates a 96 percent or greater probability.

D insists he is not the father. What evidence, if any, might D be able to introduce that will overcome the presumption?

Explanation

Most likely, the only way to rebut the genetic test presumption is to discredit the test results (chain of custody, evidence) or to obtain a sample from another man who had access to the mother with a 97 percent or greater probability of paternity. Evidence that there was no sexual access for the 230 to 300 days preceding the birth is admissible; however, it must be clear and convincing. One-on-one testimony more than likely will not carry this burden. Evidence of promiscuity outside the period when conception might have occurred is usually not admissible.

16.19. Voluntary Acknowledgment

Under the PRWORA, states became required to facilitate a man's ability to voluntarily acknowledge paternity. To this end, a valid acknowledgment of paternity is sufficient to establish the father-child relationship. UPA §201(b)(2). The UPA sets forth detailed procedures for acknowledgment and denial. UPA §300 et seq.

Example 16-5

Assume that M gave birth to child, and D executed a voluntary acknowledgment of paternity two days later. The acknowledgment form informed D of his right to genetic testing and the legal consequences of signature. When sued for child support, D claimed that he is not the father of the child. He provided DNA testing showing that there was a 0 percent chance that he was the child's father. The state where M and D live has a statute providing that a voluntary acknowledgement becomes conclusive if it not timely rescinded, which D's was not. In contrast, D argues that if the marital presumption of paternity applied in this case, it could be rebutted by clear and convincing evidence. Will a court allow D to rescind the acknowledgement?

Explanation

This example is based on the case of *People ex rel. Dept. of Public Aid v. Smith*, 289 Ill. Dec. 1 (Ill. 2004), where the court found that the disparate treatment of the two groups of presumed fathers was logical and appropriate. The court reasoned that a man who signs an acknowledgement informing him of his rights and waiving them is in a very different position than a man assumed to be a father merely by virtue of his marital status. The court held that D could not rescind the voluntary acknowledgment of paternity.

365

Example 16-6

Assume that D had a sexual relationship with P, but they did not marry. One child, A, was born in 1999, and D signed a voluntary acknowledgment of paternity on the day that A was born. He did so based on assurances from P that he was the father of A. In 2000, D agreed to entry of a child support order, but several months later, he began to question whether he was actually A's father. After genetic tests were performed, it was determined that D was not A's biological father. In the state where P and D live, the statute dealing with voluntary acknowledgment provides that an acknowledgment can be overturned if based on a material mistake of fact. D claims that his belief that he was the father of A, based on P's assertions, was a material mistake of fact and that he should be allowed to rescind the acknowledgment. P claims that the acknowledgment should be enforced, and she alleges that D's error was caused by his "neglect of legal duty" because he signed the acknowledgment without insisting on genetic testing. What is the likely result?

Explanation

This example is based on *Department of Human Services v. Chisum*, 85 P.3d 860 (Okla. App. 2004), where the appellate court held that D had established a "material mistake of fact" as required under the statute. He was consequently allowed to rescind his prior acknowledgement of paternity. Note that the outcome likely would have been quite different were it not for the state statutory provision specifically providing for rescission of a voluntary acknowledgment based on a material mistake of fact.

16.20. Presumptions of Paternity

The UPA establishes five categories of presumed fathers, including the following: (1) the man is married to the mother, and the child is born during the marriage; (2) the man is married to the mother, and the child is born within 300 days of termination of the marriage; (3) the man and the mother attempted to marry, and the child is born within 300 days of the termination of the relationship; (4) after the child is born, the man and the mother marry or attempt to marry, and the man voluntarily asserts paternity through methods set forth in the Act; and (5) the man resides with the child for the first two years of the child's life and holds himself out as the father. UPA §204. An unrebutted presumption of paternity establishes a father-child relationship. UPA §201(b)(1).

The time limits and procedures for rebutting the presumptions are set forth in Article 6, *Proceeding to Adjudicate Parentage*. UPA §601 *et seq.* However, when the child has a presumed father, an action must generally be brought by the presumed father, the mother, or another individual within two years of the child's birth (unless the presumed father did not have sexual intercourse with the mother near the time of conception, and he never held the child out as his own). UPA §607. In the year 2000, 33 states had statutes or case law allowing rebuttal of the marital presumption. *But see Michael H. v. Gerald D.*, 491 U.S. 110 (1989) (bar on man suing to establish paternity in face of marital presumption).

Challenging issues arise when more than one man is the presumed father of a child. The UPA previously provided that the presumption founded on "the weightier considerations of policy and logic" should control. Although this provision is no longer contained in the UPA, it does appear in some state statutes.

Example 16-7

Assume that P and D were married but had some relationship problems. They separated but did not divorce. During the separation, P had a sexual relationship with X, which resulted in the birth of a child. X's name appeared on the birth certificate as the father, and he provided some financial support for the child. X brings a paternity action. D objects to the proceeding, claiming that he is the legal father of the child because he is the husband of the child's mother, and the child was conceived and born while P and D were married. X contends that under state law, the presumption of legitimacy can be rebutted if its application is "outrageous to common sense and reason." What is the likely result?

Explanation

This situation can be viewed in several different lights. Historically, the presumption that a child born during a marriage was the child of the husband was a strong and often impossible presumption to overcome. Particularly when the married couple opposed the paternity action, a man in X's position would have lacked standing to file suit. With the advent of genetic testing and changing views of the family, some states provide that the traditional marital presumption can be rebutted under some circumstances. This example is based in part on the case of *Lander v. Smith*, 906 So. 2d 1130 (Fla. App. 2005), where the court found for X, holding that the presumption of legitimacy could be rebutted in a circumstance where "common sense and reason are outraged" by its rigid application. The court was swayed by the fact that X was eager to embrace the responsibilities of parenthood.

367

Example 16-8

Assume that M was married to F1 but that during the marriage, she had an affair with F2. When a child was conceived, all of the parties believed that F1 was the father. However, routine hospital testing disclosed that F2 was the biological father of the child. F2 signed a support agreement, and F2's wife regularly cared for the child. F2 told family and friends that he was the father of the child. F2 brought an action to be declared the legal father of the child. F1 claimed to be the legal father of the child because he was M's husband at the time of conception and birth and was therefore the presumed father under state law. F1 claims that he is also a presumed father based on a state statute presuming paternity for a man who "receives the child into his home and openly holds out the child as his natural child." The state statute provides that "[i]f two or more presumptions conflict with each other, the presumption which on the facts is founded on the weightier considerations of policy and logic controls." What is the likely result?

Explanation

This example is based on the case of *Craig L. v. Sandy S.*, 125 Cal. App. 4th 36 (Cal. App. 2004), where the trial court's initial decision quashing F2's petition was reversed. The appellate court remanded the case for further consideration, giving the greatest weight to the well-being of the child. The court stated, "As we have indicated, in weighing the conflicting interests under [the statute] the trial court must in the end make a determination which gives the greatest weight to [the child's] well-being." *Id.* at 53. On remand, the court was instructed to consider the nature of F2's relationship with the child and the impact on the child of recognizing F2's paternity.

16.21. Statutes of Limitation

In order to retain federal subsidies for child support enforcement, states have extended their statutes of limitations for establishing paternity at least until the child reaches the age of 18. State statutes of limitation generally range from age 18 to age 23. However, nine states have no age limitation.

The UPA allows a child with no presumed, acknowledged, or adjudicated father to sue for determination of parentage until the alleged parent's estate has been closed. UPA §606. When the child has a presumed father, an action must generally be brought by the presumed father, the mother, or another individual within two years of the child's birth. However, an action to disprove the relationship with a presumed father may be brought at any time if the presumed father and mother did not cohabitate or have sexual intercourse with each other near the time of conception and if the presumed father never openly held the child out as his own. UPA §607.

States historically had statutes requiring that paternity actions be brought within a year or two of the birth of the child. For example, in Mills v. Habluetzel, 456 U.S. 91 (1982), the mother of an illegitimate child brought suit to establish paternity. The trial court dismissed the suit because the child was one year and seven months old when the suit was filed, and Texas law required a paternity action to be brought within one year of a child's birth. The Supreme Court held that the Texas statute effectively blocked legitimation by imposing such a short time limit on the initiation of paternity proceedings. The provision was unconstitutional under both the insurmountable barrier and the substantial relationship tests. The Court said that the statute denied equal protection to illegitimate children because a state that grants opportunity for legitimate children to obtain parental support must also grant that opportunity to illegitimate children, and this opportunity must be more than illusory.

In Clark v. Jeter, 486 U.S. 456 (1988), the mother of a child born out of wedlock waited ten years to seek support from the putative father. He claimed that Pennsylvania's six-year statute of limitations for bringing paternity actions barred the action to establish paternity. After reviewing Mills v. Habluetzel, 456 U.S. 91 (1982) (invalidating one-year statute of limitations) and Pickett v. Brown, 462 U.S. 1 (1983) (invalidating a two-year statute of limitations), the Court struck down the Pennsylvania limitation. The Court held that for a paternity limitation to pass intermediate scrutiny, the period must be sufficiently long to present a reasonable opportunity to be heard, and any limitation placed on that opportunity must be substantially related to the state's interest in avoiding litigation of stale or fraudulent claims.

There are, however, some state limits on bringing paternity actions. For example, in In re Estate of Smith, 685 So. 2d 1206 (Fla. 1996), the claim of a 60-year-old alleged daughter to the estate of her deceased father was denied on the basis that the Florida statute of limitations regarding adjudication of paternity had expired. But see R.A.C. v. P.J.S., 880 A.2d 1179 (N.J. Super. 2005) (man declared father of 30-year-old child after 23-year statute of limitations equitably tolled).

16.22. Registration to Receive Notice of Termination of Parental Rights

The UPA provides for the use of parentage registries in order to expeditiously free children for adoption. Any man who wants to receive notification of termination of parental rights and adoption proceedings concerning a child he may have fathered must enter his name on the registry. Failure to do so can result in termination of parental rights without notice. Approximately 33 states have enacted some form of a registry for putative fathers with an estimated 27 that are functional. Mary Joseph Beck, Wells Conference on Adoption Law, *A National Putative Father Registry*, 36 Cap. U. L. Rev. 295, 299-300 (Winter 2007).

The registration statutes have been the subject of numerous unsuccessful challenges. In *Lehr v. Robertson*, 463 U.S. 248, 264-265 (1983), the United States Supreme Court found New York's paternity registry an appropriate means of accommodating and protecting the existing, yet undeveloped rights of putative fathers. The Court stated, "Since the New York statutes adequately protected [the putative father's] inchoate interest in establishing a relationship with [the child], we find no merit in the claim that his constitutional rights were offended because the family court strictly complied with the notice provisions of the statute." *Id.* at 265. *See In re C.M.D.*, 287 S.W.3d 510 (Tex. App. 2009); *A.S.B. v. Dep't of Children & Family Servs.*, 688 N.E.2d 1215, 1220-1225 (Ill. App. 1997); *Heidbreder v. Carton*, 645 N.W.2d 355, 372-377 (Minn. 2002), cert. denied, 537 U.S. 1046 (2002); *Friehe v. Schaad*, 545 N.W.2d 740, 744-748 (Neb. 1996); *Robert O. v. Russell K.*, 604 N.E.2d 99, 101-105 (N.Y. 1992); *In re Baby Boy K.*, 546 N.W.2d 86, 90-101 (S.D. 1996); *Beltran v. Allan*, 926 P.2d 892, 897-898 (Utah Ct. App. 1996).

OTHER ISSUES IN DETERMINING PATERNITY

16.23. Equitable Parent Doctrine

The "equitable parent" doctrine, which is recognized by some states, permits an individual to assume the rights and responsibilities of a natural parent through a judicial determination. *See, e.g., In re Nicholas H.*, 46 P.3d 932 (Cal. 2002); *In re Marriage of Gallagher*, 539 N.W.2d 479 (Iowa 1995); *Atkinson v. Atkinson*, 408 N.W.2d 516 (1987). It allows a court to find that a husband who is not the biological father of a child born or conceived during the marriage may be considered the natural father of that child when (1) the husband and the child mutually acknowledge a relationship as father and child, or the mother of the child has cooperated in the development of such a relationship over a period of time prior to the filing of a complaint for divorce; (2) the husband desires to have the rights afforded to a parent; and (3) the husband is willing to take on the responsibility of paying child support. This doctrine has not been extended beyond the context of marriage. *See Killingbeck v. Killingbeck*, 711 N.W.2d 759 (Mich. App. 2005). Some states have rejected recognition of the doctrine. *See, e.g., Randy A.J. v. Norma I.J.*, 677 N.W.2d 630 (Wis. 2004).

Courts have refused to apply the doctrine to situations in which a child was not born or conceived during the marriage. *See Van v. Zahorik*, 597 N.W.2d 15 (Mich. 1999) (court refuses to apply doctrine to putative unmarried father); *People ex rel. J.A.U. v. R.L.C.*, 47 P.3d 327 (Colo. 2002) (man who waited 11 years before attacking a paternity judgment he stipulated to without demanding genetic testing waited too long); *W. v. W.*, 779 A.2d 716 (Conn. 2001) (court estopped the husband from denying his paternity when he had treated the child as his for 12 years); *In re Paternity of Cheryl*, 746 N.E.2d 488 (Mass. 2001) (man waited five years after acknowledging paternity to have genetic tests that showed his nonpaternity was not relieved of support obligation); *Huisman v. Miedema*, 644 N.W.2d 321 (Iowa 2002) (putative father's paternity action dismissed when it was brought seven years after child's birth, and mother and her husband raised child); *Killingbeck v. Killingbeck*, 711 N.W.2d 759 (Mich. App. 2005) (child not conceived or born within marital relationship).

Example 16-9

Assume P and D cohabited for five years but were never married. D claims that D and P continued their relationship for several years after they stopped living together, and P had two children in the course of this relationship. D alleges that P informed him that he was the father of the children, and he believes that he was named as the father on the birth certificates of both children. He also claims that he cared for and financially supported the children both during and after his relationship with P.

When D started a relationship with another woman, P refused to allow him to see the children. D filed a petition to establish paternity, and he alleged that he believed and continues to believe he is the father of the two children. P argued that D was not the biological father of either child and could not be an "equitable parent" to them because D and P were never married. D conceded that blood testing showed that he was not the biological father but argued that he was an "equitable parent" and that P was equitably estopped from denying that he is the father. The trial court decided for P and indicated that its ruling turned on two factors: (1) D apparently was not the biological father of the children, and (2) D and P were never married. The court noted that the state's public policy favored marriage and concluded that the doctrines of equitable estoppel, equitable parenthood, and equitable adoption require marriage. On appeal, how will the court rule most likely?

Explanation

The appellate court most likely will reject D's claim because D is not the husband of P and the children were not even born while P and D were cohabiting. Courts have been generally reluctant to apply the equitable parent doctrine to situations similar to this hypothetical.

ESTABLISHING MATERNITY

16.24. Uniform Parentage Act (UPA)

Traditionally, a woman who gives birth to a child is presumed to be the child's legal mother. However, societal changes and advances in reproductive technology, discussed more fully in Chapter 18, have made determination of maternity considerably more challenging.

Under the UPA the mother-child relationship is established when a woman gives birth, an adjudication of maternity is made, a woman adopts a child, or she is named as a parent under a validated or enforceable gestational agreement. UPA §201(a).

16.25. Same-Sex Partners

Questions of legal maternity sometimes arise when same-sex partners raise children together in states that do not recognize same-sex marriage or adoption. One partner may have legal rights to a child as the biological parent, but the other partner may not have traditional legal grounds for seeking custody or parenting time.

In such situations, courts have considered various theories for establishment of maternity. See In re Parentage of L.B., 122 P.3d 161 (Wash. 2005) (same-sex partner recognized as a common law de facto parent); Shineovich and Kemp, 2009 WL 2032113 (Or. App. 2009) (statute granting legal parentage to husbands of women who conceived by artificial insemination extended to cover same-sex domestic partner); Smith v. Gordon, 968 A.2d 1 (Del. 2009) (same-sex partner deemed not to be a legal parent under Delaware Uniform Parentage Act was found to be a de facto parent). But see Debra H. v. Janice R., 61 A.D.3d 460 (N.Y.A.D. 2009) (same-sex partner denied in loco parentis status despite the fact that the parties entered into a civil union in Vermont and registered as domestic partners in New York City).

16. Determining Parentage

In July of 2009, the District of Columbia passed legislation recognizing the legal parenthood of domestic partners of women who give birth. Both partners are required to consent in writing to the artificial insemination, but lack of written consent does not preclude a finding of intent to parent. 35 Fam. L. Rep. 1455 (2009).

Adoption

17.1. Introduction

This chapter reviews the history, development, and application of the law involving various forms of adoption. Over the last 20 years, the overall number of children adopted has not changed significantly — in 2000 and 2001, approximately 127,000 children were adopted each year in the United States. However, the proportion of adoptions characterized as kinship and private agency adoptions has decreased. In 2000 and 2001, 40 percent of adoptions were handled through publicly funded child welfare agencies, and 15 percent were intercountry adoptions. Child Welfare Information Gateway, How Many Children Were Adopted in 2000 and 2001? — Highlights, *http://www.childwelfare.gov/pubs/s_adoptedhighlights.cfm* (last visited August 2, 2009).

OVERVIEW

17.2. History

The law of adoption had its beginning early in civilization. It apparently existed in Greece and Rome and in portions of continental Europe that received Roman law. It also existed in the Middle East, Asia, and in the tribal societies of Africa and Oceania.

Adoption was unknown to the common law. The first instance in which a state legislature authorized adoption can be traced to 1847, when the Massachusetts House of Representatives ordered that the Committee on the Judiciary consider a law for adoption of children. An adoption bill was passed in 1851, and within 25 years most states followed Massachusetts' lead and passed adoption legislation.

When states first established adoption laws, adoptive children were commonly not accorded the same legal rights as children born during wedlock. For example, some states expressly provided that the relationship of parent and adopted child was to be without the right of inheritance.

During the early part of the twentieth century, states established laws requiring a pre-hearing investigation and a report by a local child welfare agency. They also required that adoption records be kept private and sealed. Secrecy was believed important because it assured anonymity, which protected the child from the stigma of illegitimacy and encouraged full integration of the child into the adoptive family.

During the 1970s, discussion in the adoption area focused on two issues: first, improving the policies and adoption practices so that special needs children could be placed in permanent homes; and second, determining the considerations under which certain persons would have access to adoption records. There emerged a movement during this period in which a small number of persons organized to provide support for others interested in searching for and meeting their biological parents. Two such organizations were the Adoptees Liberty Movement Association (ALMA) and the Concerned United Birth parents (CUB) group. The American Adoption Congress (AAC) was formed in 1980 to coordinate the efforts of those persons interested in legislative changes that would provide access to information that would lead to the discovery of biological parents. These organizations have been fairly successful in obtaining new legislation that permits adopted children, under limited circumstances, to locate their biological parents.

When conducting research, one will discover that adoption laws vary considerably among the states. Although efforts have been made to achieve uniformity among the states, only about a half dozen have enacted a version of the Uniform Adoption Act. As a result, one finds differences from state to state in terminology, organization, and procedure.

17.3. Abrogation of Adoption

In the past, many states allowed an adoption to be abrogated or annulled because the child was suffering from an undisclosed illness or disability. Some allowed the child to be returned to an orphanage because of the child's poor behavior. *See, e.g., In the Matter of the Abrogation of Anonymous*, 167 N.Y.S.2d 472 (N.Y. 1951) (adoptive parents abrogate adoption of 17-year-old emancipated boy whom they adopted when he was four years old). Similarly, in 1951, Minnesota passed a bill that gave parents of an adopted child five years from the time the child was adopted to annul the adoption if the child developed feeblemindedness, epilepsy, insanity, or venereal infection as a result of conditions existing prior to the adoption of which the adopting parent had no knowledge. The law was repealed in 1975.

Today, while some jurisdictions allow abrogation of an adoption on a limited basis (fraud), annulment is rare and will usually not be granted unless it is in the best interest of the child. *See, e.g.*, M.L.B. v. *Department of Health and Rehabilitative Services*, 559 So. 2d 87 (Fla. App. 1990).

17.4. Legal Effect of Adoption

Today, an adoption is viewed as completely severing the ties of a child with the child's biological parents. The child's new adoptive parents are substituted for the biological parents and may exercise the same rights toward the child as a natural parent. The child has the same right to support as a natural child born to the adoptive parents and may inherit as would such a child. The adoptive parents may bar visitation or any other contact between the child and his or her biological parents.

Example 17-1

Assume that M and D are a married couple who have three biological children. They farm land located in state X that has been in D's family for more than 100 years. They enjoy being parents, and they adopt another child, P. Unfortunately, P does not adjust well to the family and never adapts to rural living. P runs away from home repeatedly and does not develop close relationships with M, D, or the other children. M and D die suddenly in a plane crash without leaving a will. The biological children claim that, under the circumstances, P should not be allowed to inherit an interest in the family farm. Will P most likely inherit under the intestacy provisions of state X?

Explanation

P will most likely be allowed to inherit under the provisions of state X, because an adopted child is treated as a natural child of his adopted parent or parents. Just as with biological children, the quality of the adoptive parent-child relationship has no bearing on the right to inherit under intestacy provisions.

Example 17-2

Assume that P is adopted by M and D. Three years after the adoption, P learns that her natural parents, X and Y, were killed in an automobile accident and have left a sizeable estate. There is no will, and P seeks to inherit from her natural parents. What will be the likely outcome of P's effort to inherit from her natural parents?

Explanation

P will most likely be unsuccessful. The right to receive property by devise or descent is not a natural right but a privilege granted by the state, and absent a statutory provision allowing P to inherit from her natural parents, her claim will be unsuccessful. *See Hall v. Vallandingham*, 540 A.2d 1162 (Md. App. 1988). Because the states will treat P as a natural issue of M and D for intestacy purposes, it will not allow her to inherit from both her adoptive and biological parents.

FORMS OF ADOPTION

17.5. Agency Adoptions

Agency adoptions involve the placement of a child with adoptive parents by a public agency, or by a private nonprofit agency licensed or regulated by the state. The agency acts as an intermediary between potential adoptive parents and the child's natural parent or parents. Public adoption agencies generally place children who have become wards of the state as a result of abuse or because they have been abandoned. Private agencies are usually nonprofit organizations, and children placed by them are often obtained when a single mother is expecting a child and wants to give the child up for adoption.

17.6. Independent Adoption

An independent or direct adoption usually involves newborn infants, often born to young parents from 12 to 17 years of age. While the arrangements vary, sometimes there is a direct arrangement made between the birth parents and the adoptive parents. On other occasions, the arrangements are made through the use of an intermediary such as an attorney. A few states do not allow independent adoptions, and this form of adoption is carefully regulated in others.

Independent adoptions are used because the adoption can be accomplished faster than when working with an adoption agency. They are also viewed as advantageous to the natural parents of the child because they may participate in choosing the adoptive parents.

17.7. Stepparent Adoption

Stepparent adoption requires the consent of the spouse of the adopting stepparent (the child's mother or father) and the consent of or termination of the parental rights of the child's other legal parent. For example, if a couple with one child divorces and the mother remarries, the mother's new husband could not adopt the child unless the father consented or his parental rights were terminated. *See In re* R. M., 234 S.W.3d 619 (Mo. Ct. App. 2007) (stepfather's petition for adoption denied because of insufficient evidence to support termination of father's parental rights); *In re Adoption of* T.H., 171 P.3d 480 (Utah App. 2007) (termination of father's parental rights not in child's best interest); *In re* W.E.B., 980 So. 2d 123 (La. App. 2008) (father's failure to pay child support not sufficient grounds to terminate parental rights). However if the other legal parent consents, stepparent adoption is generally less complicated than other agency or independent adoption procedures.

17.8. Near Relative Adoption

The absence, inability, or incapacity of the natural parents to provide and care for their children may prompt other relatives to assume the benefits and responsibilities of that role. For example, grandparents may seek to adopt their grandchildren if the children's parents die while the children are minors. These adoptions are among the easiest to process.

While at one time judicial intervention was unnecessary, a body of common law developed according a custodial preference for near relatives. In most states, adoptive placement with a family member is presumptively in the best interests of a child, absent a showing of good cause to the contrary or detriment to the child. States may by statute create a preference for near relatives. *See, e.g.,* Minn. Stat. §259.57, subd. 2 (2009) ("authorized child placing agency shall consider placement, consistent with the child's best interests and in the following order, with (1) a relative or relatives of the child, or (2) an important friend with whom the child has resided or had significant contact").

17.9. Open Adoption

The concept of open adoption is a variation on the principle that upon the entry of an order of adoption, a child is the legal child of the persons adopting him or her, and they become the child's parents with all the rights and duties of natural parents. Once an adoption decree is entered, the natural parents of an adopted child are relieved of all parental responsibilities for the child, and may neither exercise nor retain any rights over the adopted child or his or her property. As a general rule, the adoptive parents may bar any contact between the minor child and the biological parents.

Several states have statutes that expressly address the issue of post-adoption contact between the adoptive and biological parents. *See, e.g.,* Cal. Fam. Code §8616.5 (West 2009) ("Post adoption contact agreements"); Mass. Gen. Laws Ann. ch. 210, §6C (West 2009) ("Agreement for Post-Adoption Contact or Communication"); Minn. Stat. Ann. §259.58 (West 2009) ("Communication or contact agreements"); Mont. Code Ann. §42-5-301 (2009) ("Visitation and communication agreements"); Neb. Rev. Stat. §43-162 (2009) ("Communication or contact agreement; authorized; approval"); Or. Rev. Stat. Ann. §109.305 (West 2009) ("Interpretation of adoption laws; agreement for continuing contact with birth relatives"). *See also* E. Gary Spitko, *Open Adoption, Inheritance, and the "Uncleing" Principle,* 48 Santa Clara L. Rev. 765 (2008) (proposing that adopted children who have "qualifying functional relationships" with birth parents be allowed to inherit from them). When there are no statutory provisions, the adoptive parents to an open adoption can most likely prevent future contacts at will between the child and the natural parents.

Example 17-3

Assume that a child was born out of wedlock to P. P meets with X and Y, who agree to adopt C, and the legal adoption becomes final when C is two months old. Prior to the adoption, the parties agree that on occasion P may visit with the child, but nothing is put in writing. P visits C several times each year. When C is five years old, X and Y overhear P using inappropriate language with C, and they hear P encouraging C to disobey household rules established by X and Y. X and Y conclude that P is upsetting the child, and they terminate the visits. P is shocked that X and Y would treat her this way after five years of contact with C, and P believes that X and Y are overreacting to innocent events. P consequently brings an action to enforce the oral visitation agreement. Will P be likely to succeed?

Explanation

X and Y will argue that as the legal parents of C, they have the obligation and prerogative to act in C's best interest, and a court would determine that X and Y are in the best position to know and understand C's needs. Especially in situations where there is no statute authorizing ongoing contact or a written agreement to that effect, P will not be able to enforce the oral agreement.

17.10. Subsidized Adoption

Children with special needs waiting for adoptive families are difficult to place because of the costs associated with caring for them. However, most states provide financial help to parents who adopt these children. The two sources of funds used to support such programs come from the federal Title IV-E program under the Social Security Act and each state's individual program, which will vary from jurisdiction to jurisdiction.

17.11. International Adoption

The Hague Convention on Protection of Children and Co-operation in Respect of Intercountry Adoption (commonly referred to as the Hague Convention on Intercountry Adoption) was adopted and opened for signature at the conclusion of the Seventeenth Session of the Hague Conference on Private International Law on May 29, 1993. By 2007 more than 70 countries, including the United States, had become parties to the Convention. Elizabeth Bartholet, *International Adoption: Thoughts on the Human Rights Issues*, 13 Buffalo Human Rts. L. Rev. 151 (2007). *See also* Hague Conference on Private International Law, Status Table, at *http://www.hcch.net/index_en.php?act=conventions.status&cid=69* (last visited August 2, 2009). The Convention sets out norms and procedures to safeguard children involved in intercountry adoptions and to protect the interests of their birth and adoptive parents. These safeguards are designed to discourage trafficking in children and to ensure that intercountry adoptions are made in the best interest of the children involved. Cooperation between Contracting States is facilitated by the establishment in each Contracting State of a Central Authority with programmatic and case-specific functions. The Convention also provides for recognition of adoptions that fall within its scope in all other Contracting States. It leaves the details of its implementation up to each Contracting State.

The United States ratified the Convention in 2007, and it took effect in 2008. The Central Authority for the purpose of implementation in the United States is the Department of State's Office of Children's Issues. Implementing legislation, the Intercountry Adoption Act was passed in 2000, and final regulations have been issued. Trish Maskew, *The Failure of Promise: The U.S. Regulations on Intercountry Adoption Under the Hague Convention*, 60 Admin. L. Rev. 487 (2008).

In an international adoption, the new parents must satisfy the adoption requirements of both the foreign country and the parents' home state in the United States. The adoptive parents must apply for U.S. citizenship for the child because it is not automatically granted.

PROCEDURES

17.12. Filing a Petition

In general, a petition for adoption is filed once consent is obtained from the child's natural parent or parents, or the adoption agency handling the matter. Once a petition is filed, in most jurisdictions the child is placed with the adoptive parents on a probationary basis. If the background checks, home study, and probationary period are satisfactory, a hearing is held in which the judge reviews the potential adoptive parents' qualifications. Once the adoption is approved, a permanent decree of adoption is filed.

17.13. Investigating Prospective Parents

In most cases, a home study is conducted to determine the suitability of the potential adoptive parents' home. The adoptive parents' background is investigated, including a criminal background check. The purpose of the criminal records check is to safeguard the well-being of foster and adoptive children by ensuring that persons seeking to care for or adopt a foster child have not been arrested for or convicted of criminal charges that would place the child at risk. *See In re Adoption of Paul Y.*, 696 N.Y.S.2d 796 (N.Y. Fam. Ct. 1999).

17.14. Sealing Adoption Records

Since the 1940s, states have sealed adoption records from the public due to the stigma historically associated with bearing a child out of wedlock and concern that the biological parents would interfere with the adoptive parents if their names became known. To ensure privacy, after the adoption, statutes typically provided for the issuance of a new birth certificate, which changed the adoptee's surname to that of the adoptive parents. The original birth certificate was then sealed.

Access to the sealed birth record is controlled by state statutes, which determine if, when, and how the information may be gained. *See* Shannon Clark Kief, *Restricting Access to Judicial Records of Concluded Adoption Proceedings*, 103 A.L.R.5th 255 (2002). While some state statutes provide adoptees with the opportunity to obtain the names of their biological parents from official records, a state may distinguish between a minor and an adult seeking access to the records, *Mills v. Atlantic City Dept. of Vital Statistics*, 372 A.2d 646 (N.J. Super. Ch. 1977) or may require an intermediary before access is allowed. *See In re* J.N.H., 209 P.3d 1221 (Colo. App. 2009). The statutes reflect an effort to balance the privacy concerns of the parties originally involved in the adoption with the desire or need for later knowledge, which is usually sought by the adopted child.

Some states will grant access when certain conditions are met. For example, some states will allow an adopted child to gain access to birth information when the biological family and the adoptive parents agree to allow access. Approximately six states grant adult adoptees full access to birth records. Elizabeth J. Samuels, *The Idea of Adoption: An Inquiry into the History of Adult Adoptee Access to Birth Records*, 53 Rutgers L. Rev. 367, 371-372 (2001). In In re *Adoption of S.J.D.*, 641 N.W.2d 794 (Iowa 2002), the adoptee's reasons for wanting adoption records unsealed, which included satisfaction of curiosity, thanking biological parents for what they did, and obtaining medical information, did not constitute sufficient good cause to entitle records to be unsealed, even though adoptee had been treated for manic depression. The adoptee presented no medical evidence that linked his manic depression to his status as an adopted child, and the adoptee was viewed as expressing more of a curiosity over whether manic depression was hereditary than any particular medical reason for wanting to know.

In In re *Long*, 745 A.2d 673 (Pa. Super. 2000), the adoptee sought disclosure of the identity of her biological parents and their medical histories. In support of her petition, she submitted a letter from her physician who stressed the importance of obtaining a complete family medical history to diagnose and treat her recent complicated medical issues. She also asserted that she suffered from depression, panic attacks, and similar psychological afflictions because of her lack of identity. The court said that an adoptee had the burden of showing by clear and convincing evidence that there is good cause for unsealing, given the overriding privacy concerns of the adoption process and this statute. It warned that unsealing adoption records is not to be lightly undertaken, and a court must consider the ramifications to those specifically affected by that unsealing, including the adoptive and biological parents and their families, as well as the impact on the integrity of the adoption process in general. Only if the adoptee's need for the information clearly outweighs the considerations behind the statute may the records be unsealed. *See In re Baby Boy SS*, 276 A.D.2d 226 (N.Y.A.D. 2001) (statute providing for unsealing of adoption records for purpose of addressing serious physical or mental illness does not require that party applying to unseal records must be adoptive child or adoptive parents).

QUALIFICATIONS OF POTENTIAL ADOPTIVE PARENT

17.15. Race

Race may be considered legitimately as one factor in making an ultimate adoption placement decision. *See, e.g., J.H.H. v. O'Hara*, 878 F.2d 240, 244 (8th Cir. 1989). Race may not, of course, be used in an automatic fashion to prescribe the appropriate adoptive placement. *See Palmore v. Sidoti*, 466 U.S. 429, 434 (1984). Race also may not be used as the sole basis for making long-term foster care placements or in determining who may adopt a child. *See In re Moorehead*, 600 N.E.2d 778, 786 (Ohio App. 1991) ("The difficulties inherent in interracial adoption justify consideration of race as a relevant factor in adoption, but do not justify race as being the determinative factor."). *See* David D. Meyer, *Palmore Comes of Age: The Place of Race in the Placement of Children*, 18 U. Fla. J.L. & Pub. Pol'y 183 (2007) (urging case-by-case determination of whether race should be a factor in placement). Under the Multiethnic Placement Act (MEPA), a person or government may not delay or deny placement for adoption on the basis of race, color, or national origin. 42 U.S.C. §1996b (West 2009).

17.16. Sexual Orientation

Lesbians, gay men, bisexuals, single people, and unmarried couples can and do adopt children. As with custody cases, approval may depend on the jurisdiction or judge. *See* generally, Karen Moulding and National Lawyers Guild, Lesbian, Gay, Bisexual, and Transgender Committee, 1 *Sexual Orientation and the Law* §1:20 (2009). The issue of whether gay and lesbian partners can adopt a child remains a matter of controversy. *See* Lynn D. Wardle, *The "Inner Lives" of Children in Lesbigay Adoption: Narratives and Other Concerns*, 18 St. Thomas L. Rev. 511, 513-515 (Winter 2005) (reviewing the current status of the legality of lesbigay adoption in the United States of America). Several states allow gay men and lesbians to adopt where it is in the bests interests of the child. *See* In re *Adoption of M.A.*, 930 A.2d 1088 (Me. Sup. Ct. 2007) (unmarried same-sex couple could petition for adoption despite statute authorizing married couples to adopt); In re *Infant Girl W.*, 845 N.E.2d 229 (Ind. App. 2006); *Sharon S. v. Superior Court*, 2 Cal. Rptr. 3d 699 (Cal. 2003). However, some states have legislated otherwise. *See* Sonja Larsen, *Adoption of Child by Same-Sex Partners*, 27 A.L.R.5th 54 (1995); Miss. Code Ann. §93-17-3 (West 2004) (prohibiting adoption by couples of the same gender); Conn. Gen. Stat. Ann. §45a-726A (West 2006) (child-placing agency may consider sexual orientation of adoptive or foster parent); Ark. Code Ann. §9-8-304 (West 2009) (child may not be adopted by person cohabiting outside of marriage).

Florida and Oklahoma, in particular, have been the settings for lengthy court battles concerning adoption by gay and lesbian persons. For example, a 1977 Florida statute prohibiting adoption by gay or lesbian petitioners survived a constitutional challenge on equal protection grounds. *Lofton v. Sec'y of Dept. of Children and Family Services*, 358 F.3d 804 (11th Cir. 2004). However, the statute was subsequently held by a Florida court to violate equal protection and infringe on the Adoption and Safe Families Act of 1997. In re *Adoption of Doe*, 2008 WL 5006172 (Fla. Cir. Ct. 2008). *See also* Embry v. Ryan, 2009 WL 1311599 (Fla. App. 2009) (holding that full faith and credit must be given to an out-state adoption judgment involving same-sex parents).

The Oklahoma legislature passed a statute denying recognition of final adoption orders from states permitting adoption by same-sex couples. However the Tenth Circuit Court of Appeals held the statute unconstitutional because it violated the Full Faith and Credit Clause. *Finstuen v. Crutcher*, 496 F.3d 1139 (2007). *See also* Adar v. Smith, 591 F.Supp.2d 857 (E.D. La. 2008) (requiring that full faith and credit be given to out-of-state adoption by same-sex parents).

17.17. Age of Adoptive Parents

The age of a potential adoptive parent may play a role in some adoption matters. For example, California requires that a prospective adoptive parent be at least ten years older than the child, unless the adoption is by a stepparent, sister, brother, aunt, uncle, or first cousin and the court is satisfied that adoption by the parent and, if married, by the parent's spouse is in the best interests of the parties and is in the public interest regardless of the ages of the child and the prospective adoptive parent. *See* Cal. Fam. Code §8601, subd. (a) (West 2006). Being elderly does not absolutely bar adoption. For example, in *Adoption of Michelle T.*, 117 Cal. Rptr. 856 (Cal. App. 1975), the court granted a petition to proposed parents, who were 71 and 55 years of age, who had a stable marriage, were financially secure, in good health, and had cared for the child for nine months prior to filing the petition. *See also* In re T.S., 7 Cal. Rptr. 3d 173 (Cal. App. 2003) (grandparents aged 58 and 61 allowed to adopt despite objections that they were too old and had not passed physical examinations).

WHO MUST CONSENT TO AN ADOPTION?

17.18. Consent of Birth Mother

All states mandate that consent to adoption be obtained from the natural mother after the birth of the child unless her rights are terminated. Most states mandate a waiting period following the birth of a child during which the natural mother may revoke her consent to the adoption. *See Sims v. Adoption Alliance*, 922 S.W.2d 213 (Tex. App. 1996) (legislation that required that a biological mother must wait 48 hours after the birth of the child before signing an affidavit of relinquishment is constitutional). This is to ensure that the consent is a fully deliberative act on the part of the biological parent and to provide a legal framework within which a future adoption can be undertaken with reasonable guarantees of permanence and with humane regard for the rights of the child, the natural mother, and the adoptive parents.

Occasionally, consent is obtained prior to the birth of the child, and the birth mother later seeks to void the adoption on the grounds that the pre-birth consent is void *ab initio*. Some courts that have examined this issue have concluded that in the case of a pre-birth consent, such consent is ratified by a post-birth act that sufficiently manifests a present intention to give the child up for adoption. *See, e.g., Matter of Pima City Juvenile Action*, 806 P.2d 892, 895 (Ariz. 1990). These courts have said that the statutory notice prerequisites and the mandate that consent must be executed after the birth of the child are aimed at safeguarding the rights and interests of the biological parents in adoption proceedings, rather than affording some kind of protection for the public at large. Under these statutes, the rights of a parent may be surrendered by a formally executed document. However, the purpose of the statute is to protect the parent's rights, and if this is done before birth and is after birth observed, recognized, and honored by all parties, the purpose of the law is fulfilled by the parent's ratification. *See In re Adoption of Krueger*, 448 P.2d 82 (Ariz. 1968);

Anonymous v. Anonymous, 530 N.Y.S.2d 613, 617 (N.Y. App. Div. 3 Dept. 1988); *In re Adoption of Long*, 56 So. 2d 450 (Fla. 1952).

Example 17-4

P arranged with an adoption agency to place her child for adoption as soon as the child was born. The state statute requires that a birth mother's consent be obtained not sooner than 48 hours after the birth of a child. However, P signed adoption consent forms two weeks before the child was born and once again on the day after the child was born. When the child is one month old, P changes her mind about the adoption and brings an action to void her consent. The adoptive parents argue that P waived the 48-hour requirement by giving consent both before and after the birth of the child. How will a court most likely rule?

Explanation

Because of the intimate nature of the proceeding, and the unambiguous language in the statute, it is likely that a court will consider the consent invalid. This is particularly likely if a statute provides for a waiting period. In some jurisdictions, a mother may recover a child legally placed for adoption if there has not been an adoption decree entered, if she is fit, and if returning the child to the mother is in the child's best interests. *See also In re Adoption of N.J.G.*, 891 N.E.2d 60 (Ind. App. 2008) (pre-birth consent void under statute providing that the "mother may not execute a consent to adoption before the birth of the child").

Example 17-5

P gave birth to a child, and two days after the birth she consented in writing to the adoption of the child. Within a week, she attempted to revoke her consent to relinquish the child for adoption on the grounds that it was involuntary. Prior to the birth of the child, P's boyfriend was killed in a car accident, her father died from cancer, and she lost her job and was unemployed. The child was the result of a rape. While in the hospital after the child's birth a psychological evaluation was performed, and she was diagnosed with "significant adjustment disorder," and follow-up therapy, without medication, was recommended. P expressed confusion over the significance of the forms she had signed. Would a court consider P's consent to be involuntary under these circumstances?

Explanation

This fact situation is similar to that found in *McCann v. Doe*, 660 S.E.2d 500 (S.C. 2008), where the court considered whether under the totality of the circumstances the signing of the consent was involuntary or done under duress or coercion and whether withdrawal of consent would be in the best interests of the child. After weighing conflicting evidence, the court determined that the mother was "incapable of giving a voluntary consent" and that relinquishment would be in the best interests of the child.

17.19. Minor Child's Consent

In most jurisdictions the consent of a child over the age of 12 to the adoption is necessary. For example, in the case of *In re Adoption of J.E.H.*, 859 N.E.2d 388 (Ind. App. 2006), the trial court "lacked authority" to allow a stepmother to adopt a 14-year-old without his written consent.

17.20. Putative Father's Consent

As the climate for children born out of wedlock has changed over the past 50 years, so has the treatment of unmarried biological fathers. Recognition of the biological fathers has provided them with a voice in adoption proceedings. In the leading case, *Stanley v. Illinois*, 405 U.S. 645 (1973), Stanley, an unwed father, lived with his children and their mother intermittently for 18 years prior to her death. When she died, under state law the children automatically became wards of the state, and Stanley was presumed unfit to care for them. The statutory presumption applied even though there had not been a hearing regarding his fitness or proof of neglect on his part. Stanley sought custody of the children, arguing that he should be afforded a hearing on his fitness. When the Illinois Supreme Court refused to provide him with a hearing, the United States Supreme Court granted review.

The Court held that a putative father's interest in the companionship, care, custody, and management of his children was greater than the state's interest in the children as long as the putative father was a fit parent. It ordered that a hearing be held to determine whether Stanley was in fact fit to have custody of the children. The Court did not, however, articulate the scope of the protection afforded an unwed father, especially when the state interests were more substantial. (On remand, the trial court found that Stanley was not a fit parent.)

Five years after *Stanley*, the Supreme Court clarified the principles articulated in *Stanley v. Illinois* in *Quilloin v. Walcott*, 434 U.S. 246 (1977), *reh', denied*, 435 U.S. 918 (1978). The Court held that a putative father who had little or no contact with his child did not have a constitutional right to veto the child's adoption. A unanimous Court rested its decision on the putative father's failure to seek actual or legal custody of the child and the fact he had played no part in the child's daily supervision, education, protection, or care. *Quilloin v. Walcott* established the principle that when there is no significant commitment on the part of the biological father to a child born out of wedlock, the state is not required to find anything more than that the adoption, and denial of legitimization, are in the best interests of the child.

In a third ruling, *Caban v. Mohammed*, 441 U.S. 380 (1979), both the mother and the putative father had emotionally and financially supported children born to them out of wedlock. When their relationship broke down, the mother married another man and then initiated proceedings asking the court to allow her new husband to adopt the children. The putative father filed a cross-petition in which he asked to adopt the children. Under New York law, a putative father could not adopt his children without the mother's consent. However, the mother could legally adopt the children without first obtaining the putative father's consent. The trial court permitted the mother and her new husband to adopt the children over their putative father's objection, and the Supreme Court granted review.

The Court reversed, holding that the New York statute had inappropriately created a gender-based distinction between unwed mothers and unwed fathers, which bore no substantial relation to any legitimate state interest. Because the putative father had demonstrated a substantial interest in his children, the Court said he had certain constitutionally protected rights that the state could not take from him.

In another significant decision, *Lehr v. Robertson*, 463 U.S. 248 (1983), the Court considered whether the Due Process and Equal Protection Clauses of the Fourteenth Amendment provided a putative father with the right to notice and an opportunity to be heard before a child is adopted, although he had not established a substantial relationship with his biological child born out of wedlock. Lehr had never lived with his child or its mother, had never registered with the state putative-father registry as the child's father, and had failed to provide any financial support for the child following birth. When the child was eight months old, the mother married, and her husband adopted the child.

The Court rejected Lehr's claim that he had a constitutional right to notice and a hearing before adoption. The Court reasoned that his rights had not been violated because he had failed to establish a substantial relationship with the child. The "mere existence of a biological link," wrote the court "does not merit equivalent constitutional protection."

The issue of consent by putative fathers remains a difficult one for courts seeking to balance the interests of the child, the adoptive parents, the putative father, and the mother. *See Helen G. v. Mark J.H.*, 175 P.3d 914 (N.M. 2007) (consent was not required as an "acknowledged father" where putative father knew of pregnancy and did not register or file a timely paternity action); *In re Pedro Jason William M.*, 847 N.Y.S.2d 17 (N.Y.A.D. 2007) (putative father who did not provide financial support, visit monthly, or communicate regularly "never acquired a constitutionally protected interest in his children"); *In re Adoption of Arthur M.*, 57 Cal. Rptr. 3d (Cal. App. 2007) (putative father's consent not required when "he did not show that he promptly came forward and demonstrated as full a commitment to his parental responsibilities as the biological mother allowed and the circumstances permitted within a short time after he learned or reasonably should have learned that the biological mother was pregnant with his child"). *But see In re Vanessa Ann G.-L.*, 856 N.Y.S.2d 657 (N.Y.A.D. 2008) (consent was required where father established paternity and paid child support).

Example 17-6

Assume that P is unmarried when she gives birth to C. The biological father, D, is aware of C's birth. However, he and P have a hostile relationship, and D avoids all contact with her. Consequently, D does not attempt to visit C and does not provide any financial support. P meets X, and she and X marry. After a year of marriage, when C is two years old, X moves to adopt C. When D learns of the adoption action, he appears in opposition to it, insisting that the court cannot terminate his rights to the child. How should a court rule?

Explanation

D has failed to manifest any "indicia of parenthood," which would provide him with constitutional protection of his parental rights. It is doubtful that his rights could be resurrected even with testimony that D is now ready to assume parental responsibilities for the child. D knew of the child's birth and could have played a role in the child's life well before the adoption action was begun. *See Caban, supra.*

17.21. Putative Father Consents by Failing to Use Adoption Registry

Some states have created a statutory adoption registry for the purpose of determining the identity and location of a putative father of a minor child who is, or who is expected to be, the subject of an adoption. The purpose of the registry is to provide notice to a putative father that a petition for adoption has been filed. States have adopted strict provisions regarding the registry. Some require that the putative fathers register within 30 days after the child's birth or the date the adoption petition is filed, whichever occurs later. If a father fails to do so, he is not entitled to notice of the child's adoption.

A putative father's failure to register not only waives his right to notice of the adoption but also irrevocably implies his consent. *See, e.g., In re Adoption of A.A.T.*, 196 P.3d 1180 (Kan. 2008); *In re J.D.C.*, 751 N.E.2d 747 (Ind. App. 2001) *Heart of Adoptions, Inc. v. J.A.*, 963 So. 2d 189 (Fla. 2007). Courts have held that a putative father was not entitled to notice of an adoption petition and that his consent was irrevocably implied when the biological mother did not disclose his identity or address and he failed to register with the putative father's registry until six months after the adoption petition was filed. *In re Paternity of Baby Doe*, 734 N.E.2d 281 (Ind. Ct. App. 2000). *See Robert O. v. Russell K.*, 604 N.E.2d 99 (N.Y. Ct. App. 1992) (putative father's notice or consent was not needed for the adoption when he failed to avail himself of the methods to qualify for notice until some ten months after the adoption became final); *Heidbreder v. Carton*, 645 N.W.2d 355 (Minn. 2002), *cert. denied*, 537 U.S. 1046 (2002) (requirement that putative father not otherwise entitled to notice of an adoption petition must register with the Minnesota Fathers' Adoption Registry no later than 30 days after birth of child to assert a claim to a child who is the subject of an adoption petition is not a statute of limitations that can be tolled by fraudulent concealment); *Petition of K.J.R.*, 687 N.E.2d 113 (Ill. App. 1 Dist. 1997) (birth mother's misrepresentation that another man was child's father did not excuse putative father's failure to register, and provision of Adoption Act that operated to deprive putative father of right to proceed with parentage petition did not deprive him of equal protection of the laws or due process); *M.V.S. v. V.M.D.* 776 So. 2d 142 (Ala. Civ. App. 1999) (requirements and procedures of Putative Father Registry Act to establish parental rights did not violate due process or equal protection).

These statutes and court decisions reflect a strong interest in providing stable homes for children early in their lives and a belief that permanent placement of children with adoptive families is of the utmost importance. If a father fails to register within the specified amount of time allowed under the statute, the state's obligation to provide the child with a permanent, capable, and loving family becomes paramount.

Example 17-7

Assume that P and D have a casual sexual relationship, and P becomes pregnant and gives birth. D, the biological father, does not know of P's pregnancy or the birth of the child until the child is six months old and is in the process of being adopted. D resides in a jurisdiction with an adoption registry requiring that registration take place within 30 days of the birth of the child, but D has no idea what an adoption registry is or how to go about registering. He consequently fails to do so. How will a court most likely treat D's effort to block the adoption?

Explanation

D most likely will not succeed. The adoption registry statute protects those putative fathers who have taken certain specified actions to preserve their rights. If the putative father has not so acted within the time limits provided by statute, the child's right to a stable environment and finality becomes paramount, and the putative father loses all right to intervene in adoption proceedings or to vacate a finalized adoption order. *See Lehr v. Robertson,* 463 U.S. 248 (1983). D's failure to register may well bar him from preventing the adoption.

UNIFORM ACTS

17.22. Uniform Adoption Act of 1994

The Uniform Adoption Act of 1994 was promulgated by the National Conference of Commissioners on Uniform State Laws (NCCUSL) as an attempt to codify and make uniform the current legal practice regarding adoption. However, only a half-dozen states have adopted some provisions of the proposed uniform act. *See* Uniform Adoption Act, online at *http://www.law.upenn. edu/bll/archives/ulc/fnact99/1990s/uaa94.htm* (last visited August 3, 2009).

FEDERAL GOVERNMENT'S ROLE

17.23. Indian Child Welfare Act (ICWA)

The Indian Child Welfare Act (ICWA), 25 U.S.C. §§1901 *et seq.,* governs the placement of Native American children for adoption. The ICWA contains procedural and substantive provisions that apply to Native American children. The ICWA protects the best interests of Indian children by promoting the survival and stability of Indian families and tribes. It is aimed at preventing wholesale separation of Indian children from their families through state court proceedings. The ICWA applies to any child who is either a member of an Indian tribe, or eligible to be a member, and the biological child of a member of a tribe.

State courts must follow the jurisdictional requirements of the ICWA, and an adoption decree entered in violation of the Act can be invalidated by the tribe or custodian. *See* 25 U.S.C. §1914 (West 2006); *Mississippi Band of Choctaw Indians v. Holyfield*, 490 U.S. 30 (1989). (Note that there is additional discussion regarding this Act in Chapter 24, Jurisdiction.)

Example 17-8

Assume that P and D are members of an Indian tribe living on a reservation, and they conceive a child. They do not want the child born on the reservation, and they prefer that the child be adopted and raised by non-Indians. The child is born off reservation, and within two weeks the child is adopted by non-Indian parents. The child is healthy and thriving in the adoptive home. When the tribe learns of the adoption four months later, it moves to vacate the adoption decree, claiming it had exclusive subject matter jurisdiction under the ICWA. How will a court most likely rule on the tribe's motion?

Explanation

Because the child's domicile is that of its mother, who apparently lives on the reservation, and there is no evidence the child was abandoned, a court most likely will vacate the judgment. One of the purposes of ICWA is to prevent Indian children from being adopted by non-Indians without the oversight of the tribe.

17.24. Multiethnic Placement Act (MEPA)

The Multiethnic Placement Act (MEPA), passed into law in 1994, allowed states to consider race as a factor when making adoptive placements. It also prohibited states from refusing to place children solely on the basis of the adoptive parents' race. The Act was amended in 1996 and made it illegal for a state to delay or deny an adoptive placement solely on the basis of race. Indian children were exempted from the MEPA; therefore, adoptions involving these children continue to be controlled by the ICWA. 42 U.S.C. §1996b(3) (West 2006). By statute, Congress has declared that no state or other entity receiving federal funds can deny to any individual the opportunity to become an adoptive or a foster parent on the basis of race, color, or national origin. 42 U.S.C. §1996b (West 2006).

17.25. Adoption and Safe Families Act (ASFA)

The Adoption and Safe Families Act of 1997 (ASFA) (Pub. L. No. 105-89, 111 Stat. 2115), enacted in November 1997, amended the foster care provisions of the Social Security Act. It was designed to promote and hasten the adoption of children in foster care and to facilitate the removal of children from abusive families. *See In re Karl H.*, 906 A.2d 898, 908 n.15 (Md. 2006). The increase in children in foster care during the two decades preceding its enactment, with the number nearly doubling since the mid-1980s to an estimated 520,000 children in 1998, was the catalyst for the Act. There was also concern that more children were entering foster care facilities each year than were leaving and that their stay in foster settings was getting much longer. *See N.J. Div. of Youth & Family Servs. v. S.F.*, 920 A.2d 652 (N.J. App. Div.) (emphasis has shifted from protracted efforts for reunification with a birth parent to an expeditious, permanent placement to promote the child's well-being. A child cannot be held prisoner to the rights of others, even those of his or her parents).

The Act was also passed to change a perception held by child welfare practitioners regarding the relationship between child safety and the requirement that a state make "reasonable efforts" to prevent removal of a child from a home or to return a child home. Long stays in foster care were often believed to be the result of well-intentioned efforts to preserve the family through prolonged and extensive services, without giving adequate consideration to the child's need for a permanent home. In these situations, adoption or an alternate permanent home was rarely considered until the child had been in out-of-home care for 18 months. *See In re D.P.*, 972 A.2d 1221 (Pa. Super. 2009) (best interests of the child, and not the interests of the parent, must guide the trial court, and the parent's rights are secondary).

Under the provisions of the Act, states no longer needed to pursue efforts to prevent removal from home or to return a child home if a parent had already lost parental rights to that child's sibling, committed certain felonies, including murder or voluntary manslaughter of the child's sibling, or had subjected the child to aggravated circumstances such as abandonment, torture, chronic abuse, and sexual abuse. In these egregious situations, the Act gave a court authority to determine that services to preserve or reunite the family — that is, the "reasonable efforts" requirement established in earlier law — are not required. Once the court makes such a determination, the state must begin within 30 days to find the child an alternate permanent home.

Under the Act, states begin termination proceedings if an infant has been abandoned, the parent has committed certain felonies, or the child has been in foster care 15 of the last 22 months. States may exempt a child from this requirement if the child is placed with a relative, the state has not provided services needed to make the home safe for the child's return, or there is a compelling reason why filing a petition to terminate parental rights is not in the child's best interests. As states begin the process of terminating parental rights, they must also find the child a qualified adoptive family. The Act authorized $20 million for bonuses to states for adoption of foster-care children, $5 million for health care for adopted children with special needs, and $11 million for subsidies for special-needs children if their adoptions are disrupted or their adoptive parents die.

CLAIMS

17.26. Fraud

Most states recognize a cause of action for fraud in the adoption setting. For example, in In re Lisa Diane G., 537 A.2d 131 (R.I. 1988), the court held that it possessed the authority to decide whether to vacate an adoption order based upon a claim of fraud or misrepresentation. In Allen v. Allen, 330 P.2d 151 (Or. 1958), Oregon recognized fraud as a cause of action in adoption matters while holding that the evidence was insufficient to support a determination that a decree of adoption was void by reason of fraud. Minnesota has ruled that if a party can demonstrate that an adoption decree was fraudulently obtained, the party is entitled to relief. In re Welfare of Alle, 230 N.W.2d 574, 577 (Or. 1975). Historically the Supreme Judicial Court of Massachusetts held that one may annul an adoption decree based on fraud, even after death. Tucker v. Fisk, 28 N.E. 1051 (Mass. 1891). The same court later held that if a person dominates his wife to such an extent that it amounts to "undue influence" and he thereby forces her to bring a petition for adoption of his son, he commits a "gross fraud" upon both her and the court. In such a case, the decree of adoption should be set aside. Phillips v. Chase, 89 N.E. 1049, 1051-1052 (Mass. 1909).

The elements of a cause of action for fraudulent misrepresentation require that one must show (1) a false statement of material fact, (2) known or believed to be false by the party making it, (3) intent to induce the other party to act, (4) action by the other party in reliance on the truth of the statement, and (5) damage to the other party resulting from such reliance. The party must be justified in his reliance; he must have a right to rely. See, e.g., Roe v. Catholic Charities of the Diocese of Springfield, 588 N.E.2d 354 (Ill. 1992).

17.27. Negligent Misrepresentation

Some states recognize claims against adoption agencies for negligent misrepresentation. The tort is based on the theory that an adoption placement agency owes prospective adoptive parents a duty of reasonable care to disclose information pertinent to the adoption. Courts find such a duty partly in a state's adoption statutes and partly in the existence of a "special relationship" between the agency and the prospective parents. Even if a state statute does not provide for such an action, the special relationship between adoption placement agencies and adopting parents may support recognition of a cause of action in tort. The purposes are not only to enable adoptive parents to obtain timely and appropriate medical care for the child, but also to enable them to make an intelligent and informed adoption decision. *See, e.g., Price v. State*, 57 P.3d 639 (Wash. App. Div. 2, 2002). The duty that emanates from the relationship of the potential adoptive parents and the agency is to exercise reasonable care in disclosing information pertinent to the adoption, thus enabling the adoptive parents to obtain timely and appropriate medical care for the child and make an intelligent and informed adoption decision. *See also Young v. Van Duyne*, 92 P.3d 1269 (N.M. App. 2004) (adoptive father whose wife was beaten to death by adoptive son could maintain wrongful death claim against agency regarding pre-adoption knowledge and conduct).

Example 17-9

Assume that P adopted a Russian baby girl who was discovered to be carrying the hepatitis C virus when the girl was examined by a pediatrician in the United States. P sued Adoption Center D for breach of contract, wrongful adoption/malpractice, and related counts. P adopted the child X in 1993. The contract between P and D reads as follows: "P understands that D cannot guarantee the health of the child, but will make best efforts to ensure that the child's health is known to the parent(s) prior to placement. However, P understand[s] that it is very difficult to know all of the health issues involved."

In addition to this contract language, P was made aware that even though D knew her highest priority was adoption of a healthy baby, no baby available for adoption would have a clean medical record because Russian law at that time prohibited foreign adoption of healthy Russian babies. Further, Russian orphanages rarely supplied prospective foreign parents with complete medical histories of children available for adoption. A photograph and a medical excerpt (three pages long when translated into English) were the only documentation made available to P or D, as was the standard practice in Russian adoptions at the time. The medical excerpt referenced one hospitalization for a respiratory infection, negative results on blood tests for HIV and hepatitis B, and some developmental delays, and a diagnosis that loosely translated as "encephalopathy."

When X was examined following the adoption in the United States, it was discovered that she contracted hepatitis C from blood transfusions when hospitalized in Russia, and also was suffering from fetal alcohol syndrome/fetal alcohol effect (FAS/FAE). Given these facts, which are not in dispute, D moved for summary judgment. How will a court most likely rule?

Explanation

Because Adoption Center D was not aware of X's hepatitis C status or of her transfusions prior to her diagnosis in the United States, the motion for summary judgment will most likely be granted. It is undisputed that none of the defendants withheld any medical information made available to them. P also adopted X knowingly in the face of incomplete information.

OTHER ISSUES REGARDING ADOPTION

17.28. Adults Adopting Adults

Cases involving adult adoptions are not necessarily consistent among jurisdictions. Many of them involve inheritance issues. The trend, however, is to allow adult adoption under limited circumstances. For example, in *Berston v. Minnesota Dept. of Public Welfare*, 206 N.W.2d 28 (Minn. 1973), the trial court's denial of the adoption of an adult woman by her natural son was reversed on public policy grounds. The court said that the broad language of Minnesota's adult adoption statute unequivocally foreclosed any limiting construction. In *Harper v. Martin*, 552 S.W.2d 690 (Ky. App. 1977), the court approved the adoption of a 47-year-old male by a terminally ill petitioner for the express purpose of making him the heir at law of a third person. In *Matter of Fortney's Estate*, 611 P.2d 599, 604-605 (Kan. App. 1980), the court upheld a trial court ruling allowing an adult adoption effectuated for purposes of inheritance. However, in *Matter of Griswold's Estate*, 354 A.2d 717 (N.J. Co. 1976), the court ruled that an adoption to make an adoptee a beneficiary of a trust was found to be an abuse of the adoption process. In *333 East 53rd Street Associates v. Mann*, 503 N.Y.S.2d 752 (N.Y. 1986), the petitioner adopted an adult woman to ensure that she would succeed to the tenancy of a rent-controlled apartment. The appellate court found nothing inherently wrong with an adoption intended to confer an economic benefit on the adopted person.

More recently, in *In re Trust Created by Nixon*, 763 N.W.2d 404 (Neb. 2009), a California court's decree granting a trust beneficiary's petition to adopt an adult was not contrary to the public policy of Nebraska, and entitled to recognition, even though the adoption would not have been allowed under Nebraska statutes. In *In re Adoption of Holland*, 965 So. 2d 1213 (Fla. App. 2007), the court allowed a grandfather to adopt his adult grandson to make the grandson eligible for financial aid available to the children of disabled veterans. However, in *In re P.B. for Adoption of L.C.*, 920 A.2d 155 (N.J. Super. L. 2006), the petition of an adult couple to adopt a 52-year-old woman who resided with them was denied because the woman was not more than ten years younger than the proposed adoptive couple, and there was no "pre-existing parent-child relationship."

The states are not in agreement on whether to allow gay and lesbian adults to adopt each other. The Delaware Supreme Court allowed such an adoption in *In re Adoption of Swanson*, 623 A.2d 1095 (Del. 1993). On the other hand, in *Matter of Adoption of Robert Paul P.*, 471 N.E.2d 424 (1984), the New York Court of Appeals ruled that a 57-year-old man could not adopt a 50-year-old man with whom he shared a relationship. The court reasoned that adoption is not a quasi-matrimonial device to provide unmarried partners with a legal imprimatur for their sexual relationship.

17.29. Adoption for an Illegal or Frivolous Purpose

Courts will not countenance an adoption for a fraudulent, illegal, or patently frivolous purpose. For example, the court in *In re Jones*, 411 A.2d 910 (R.I. 1980), rejected the adoption petition of an older married man who sought to adopt his 20-year-old paramour to the economic detriment of his wife and family.

CHAPTER 18

Alternative Reproduction — History, Restrictions, and Requirements

18.1. Introduction — History

The first hi-tech test tube baby was Louise Brown. She was conceived in 1978 from an embryo created in a British laboratory and implanted in a female who carried her to birth. Since then, scientific advancements have created a number of alternative methods of reproduction for those for whom infertility is a major problem.

The Centers for Disease Control and Prevention reported that of the approximately 62 million women of reproductive age in 2002, about 1.2 million, or 2 percent, had an infertility-related medical appointment within the previous year, and 8 percent had an infertility-related medical visit at some point in the past. (Infertility services include medical tests to diagnose infertility, medical advice and treatments to help a woman become pregnant, and services other than routine prenatal care to prevent miscarriage.) Additionally, 7 percent of married couples in which the woman was of reproductive age (2.1 million couples) reported that they had not used contraception for 12 months, and the woman had not become pregnant. http://www.cdc.gov/art/ (last visited July 1, 2009). In 2006, 483 fertility clinics reported that persons using their services resulted in 41,343 live births. http://www.cdc.gov/art/ (last visited July 1, 2009).

Data from 2002 indicated that 7.4 percent (2.1 million) of married women ages 15-44 were infertile (unable to get pregnant for at least 12 consecutive months). http://www.cdc.gov/nchs/fastats/fertile.htm (last visited July 1, 2009). It was also reported in 2002 that 11.8 percent of women 15-44 years of age and of all marital statuses, who were not surgically sterile,

399

found it difficult or impossible to get pregnant or carry a pregnancy to term. Statistics vary, but it would seem that around 30 percent of men are sub-fertile, and at least 2 percent of men are totally infertile.

Where normal impregnation, for whatever reason, is undesirable or cannot be achieved, several alternative reproduction methods may result in parenthood. For example, a wife could bear a child conceived from a third-party donor's egg and her husband's sperm. Or, a surrogate could carry a child to birth that was implanted in her after the child was scientifically conceived using the wife's egg and her husband's sperm. A child could also be conceived using a husband's sperm and a surrogate's egg. A surrogate or a wife could carry a child to term who was conceived using a donated third-party egg and the husband's sperm.

Although most states have provisions regarding sperm donors, there is a paucity of legislation dealing with numerous other procedures now available to achieve parenthood. The absence of clarifying legislation has left a cloud of uncertainty hanging over the legality of the process, and in some cases has erected legal barriers that are difficult, if not impossible, to overcome.

UNIFORM ACTS AND PROPOSALS

18.2. Uniform Parentage Act

The Uniform Parentage Act (UPA), as approved by the National Conference of Commissioners on Uniform State Laws in 1973, deals only superficially with parental rights of a child born as a result of artificial insemination. *See* Rodgers, *Equal Protection for the Illegitimate Child: Uniform Parentage Act of 1977*, 6 Colo. Law 1299, 1307 (1977). Eighteen states, including California, have adopted some form of the Uniform Parentage Act.

A California court drew upon that state's statutory version of the Act to recognize parentage rights in both gestational and genetic mothers. *K.M. v. E.G.*, 117 P.3d 673 (Cal. App. 2005). The Model Act provides support for extending the availability of paternity proceedings to genetic mothers. See UPA §106 (2000). The UPA §201 (2000) presumptively designates a child's gestational mother as her legal mother, but also allows for establishment of a legally recognized parental relationship by a genetic mother. *See Belsito v. Clark*, 644 N.E.2d 760 (Ohio Com. Pl. 1994) (interpreting Ohio's UPA). The UPA does not, itself, provide procedures for determining "maternity" other than by gestation but contains several provisions by which a man can establish paternity, including through proof of genetic parentage. UPA Article 5 (2000); UPA §12 (1973). Significantly, UPA §106 (2000) and UPA §21 (1973) state that any relevant sections of the UPA, presumably including UPA §204 (2000) and UPA §4(a) (1973), can be applied to establish maternity as well.

While treating husbands as natural fathers, the UPA also protects anonymous semen donors from liability for child support. *See* George P. Smith II, *The Razor's Edge of Human Bonding: Artificial Fathers and Surrogate Mothers*, 5 W. New Eng. L. Rev. 639, 652 (1983) ("obvious" purpose of §5 is "to protect anonymous [semen] donors from all legal responsibility for those children fathered as a consequence of their donation of semen"); Note, *Contracts to Bear a Child*, 66 Cal. L. Rev. 611, 614 (1978) (purpose of §5 "is clearly to protect anonymous donors from legal responsibility for any children fathered by the use of their semen"). *See also* Kern & Ridolfi, *The Fourteenth Amendment's Protection of a Woman's Right to Be a Single Parent Through Artificial Insemination by Donor*, 7 Women's Rts. L. Rep. 251, 256 (1982).

18.3. ABA Model Act Governing Assisted Reproductive Technology

The American Bar Association approved a new Model Act on Assisted Reproductive Technology (ART), in February 2008. *See* Charles P. Kindregan, Jr. & Steven H. Snyder, *Clarifying the Law of ART: The New American Bar Association Model Act Governing Assisted Reproductive Technology*, 42 Fam. L.Q. 203 (2008) (discussing the history of the Act and its provisions). The Act is intended to provide model provisions that can be considered in whole or in part by legislative bodies in the states and territories. *Ibid.* It is hoped that the Act will enable legislative committees considering the issues generated by the Act "to seek the input of diverse groups of professionals, including legal scholars, practicing attorneys, medical practitioners, scientists, and ethicists to review these proposals and to seek alternative proposals from such persons." *Id.* at 206. The Act appears to build upon the prior work done on parentage standards previously proposed in the Uniform Parentage Act, "especially in regard to gestational carrier agreements." *Id.* at 207. However, the ABA Model Act added an alternative method of determining such parentage issues by gestational carrier agreements that comply with specific requirements. "The Uniform Parentage Act focuses on parentage issues, whereas the Model Act is much broader in its legal proposals relating to existing and emerging reproductive technologies." *Id.* The Act is aspirational as it is viewed as serving as a mechanism to assist in resolving contemporary family controversies that now reach the courts with little legislative guidance or regulation. It goes beyond purely parentage issues and proposes standards intended to protect the legal interests of all concerned parties as these technologies are increasingly used to conceive children.

The Act encourages "intended parents" to enter into a written agreement prior to embryo creation and include the following in the agreement: (1) the intended use of the embryos; (2) disposition of embryos in the event of divorce, death, or incapacity; and (3) define and agree when the embryos will be deemed "abandoned." The Model Act clarifies which intended parent may control the embryos in the event of divorce, illness, or death. The Act suggests a mechanism to withdraw consent to the terms of the preembryo agreement to dispose of or transfer the embryos.

The Act includes a suggested default provision regarding abandonment of the frozen embryos, which is deemed to occur five years after the embryos are created. Where the parties cannot agree, the storage facility must obtain an order issued by a court of competent jurisdiction relating to disposition of the embryos. *See* Theresa M. Erickson & Megan T. Erickson, *What Happens to Embryos When a Marriage Dissolves? Embryo Disposition and Divorce*, 35 Wm. Mitchell L. Rev. 469, 470 (2009) ("It is through the debate of constitutional rights versus contract law, the debate over personhood versus property issues, and the use of the denial of the writ of certiorari in the case of *Roman v. Roman* that we can finally develop an enhanced legal landscape upon which the ART community and its patients can turn to without worrying about the legal implications of their actions in a world where having children is often their most important goal and desire.").

18.4. Uniform Putative and Unknown Fathers Act; Uniform Status of Children of Assisted Conception Act

The Uniform Putative and Unknown Fathers Act §2(a), 9B U.L.A. 80 (1996) (approved 1988), excludes the semen donor in cases of artificial insemination from being a putative father. Likewise, the Uniform Status of Children of Assisted Conception Act (USCACA) §4(a), 9B U.L.A. 191 (1966) (approved 1988), provides that a semen donor of a child conceived through assisted conception does not have parental status. The USCACA offers two alternative approaches to surrogacy. Alterative "A" allows surrogacy contracts if they have received court approval. Alternative "B" states that surrogacy contracts are invalid and makes the surrogate parent the mother and her husband the father.

INSURANCE

18.5. Who Is Covered?

Dealing with infertility is often traumatic and can be costly and time consuming. The average cost of one in vitro fertilization (IVF) cycle in the United States (and it frequently takes multiple cycles in order to succeed) has been estimated at $24,500-$32,000 at one Chicago clinic, and the cost is usually not covered by health insurance. *See Morrison v. Sadler*, 821 N.E.2d 15, 24 (Ind. App. 2005). In *Knight v. Hayward Unified School Dist.*, 33 Cal. Rptr. 3d 287 (Cal. App. 1 Dist. 2005), the provisions of a school district's health insurance were found to not include coverage of IVF treatment. The court rejected the argument that refusing IVF coverage constituted disability discrimination under the Fair Employment and Housing Act (FEHA) against the teacher and his wife. They were left to obtain IVF treatment at their own expense.

Some jurisdictions have statutorily required insurance carriers to provide coverage for diagnosing and treating infertility. *Goodridge v. Department of Public*, 798 N.E.2d 941 (Mass. 2003) n.31. In *Ralston v. Connecticut General Life Ins. Co.*, 617 So. 2d 1379 (La. Ct. App. 1993), the court held that in vitro fertilization procedures to induce pregnancy was treatment for a "sickness" and covered by a health insurance policy.

ARTIFICIAL INSEMINATION — STATE STATUTORY PROVISIONS

18.6. Typical Statutory Provisions

The most commonly used alternative method of reproduction to achieve parenthood is artificial insemination. This is the process where the sperm of a male is used to artificially impregnate the egg of a female.

Because of its prevalence, most states have legislation directed at settling legal issues created by the process. The legislation typically eliminates claims of adultery and illegitimacy while protecting the sperm donor from future child support obligations. The legislation usually provides that the husband of a woman who bears a child with donated sperm is automatically the legal father.

Artificial insemination legislation serves several purposes: First, it allows married couples to have children, even though the husband is infertile, impotent, or ill. Second, it allows an unmarried woman to conceive and bear a child without sexual intercourse. Third, it resolves disputes about parental rights and responsibilities; that is, the mother's husband, if he consents, is father of the child, and an unmarried mother is freed of any claims by the donor of parental rights. Fourth, it encourages men to donate semen while protecting them against claims by the mother or the child. *See, e.g., McIntyre v. Crouch*, 780 P.2d 239, 243 (Or. Ct. App. 1989) (statute barring donor of semen used in artificial insemination process from having rights or obligations with respect to resulting child applied even if, as alleged by donor, mother had agreed with him before he gave his semen that he would have such rights and responsibilities, and he acted in reliance on that agreement). Finally, it legitimizes the child that is born and gives it rights against the mother's husband, if he consents to the insemination.

Legislation typically requires that the artificial insemination occur under the supervision of a licensed physician and with the consent of the wife's husband. When a wife is inseminated artificially with semen donated by a man who is not her husband, the legislation treats the husband as if he were the natural father of the child. Statutes normally require that a husband's consent be in writing, and the physicians involved are required to certify their signatures, the date of the insemination, and file the husband's consent with the appropriate governmental authorities, where it remains confidential in a sealed file. Donor privacy is protected by provisions declaring that all papers and records pertaining to the insemination, whether part of the permanent record of a court or of a file held by the supervising physician or elsewhere, are subject to inspection only upon an order of the court for good cause shown.

Example 18-1

Assume that pursuant to a typical state artificial insemination statute, wife P, with husband D's express written permission, is impregnated under the supervision of a physician using the sperm of third party Y. The sperm is obtained from a local sperm donor clinic. Following the birth of a child using this sperm, the local prosecutor decides to put the sperm donor clinic out of business by bringing criminal charges of adultery against sperm donors and civil actions demanding that they pay child support for any children born to women who used their sperm. The prosecutor learns that Y was the sperm donor in the above matter and charges Y with adultery in criminal court and asks for a child support order in civil court. A motion to dismiss is brought in both courts by Y, the sperm donor. How will the criminal and civil courts most likely treat the motions?

Explanation

Although such claims have a possibility of success in a jurisdiction without a typical artificial insemination statute, they should have no possibility of success in a jurisdiction that has adopted one. Assuming a typical artificial insemination statute is in place, the criminal charge should be dismissed, and Y relieved of any responsibility to pay child support. *See* J.F. v. D.B., 848 N.E.2d 873 (Ohio App. 2006) (if a woman is the subject of a non-spousal artificial insemination, the donor shall not be treated in law or regarded as the natural father of a child conceived as a result of the artificial insemination, and a child so conceived shall not be treated in law or regarded as the natural child of the donor); *Levin v. Levin*, 645 N.E.2d 601, 604 (Ind. 1994) (child conceived during marriage through artificial insemination by third-party donor was "child of the marriage" — former husband stopped from denying obligation to support child).

Example 18-2

Assume that D is a sperm donor in a jurisdiction that does not have an artificial insemination statute. The sperm is used to artificially inseminate X, a single woman, and a child is born. X discovers the identity of the sperm donor (D) and brings an action seeking support from him. How will a court most likely rule on the child support request?

Explanation

The court may well grant the request for child support. Because the jurisdiction does not have a statute to guide the court in making a decision, there is little to help it to legally distinguish between artificial and natural conception. A court may likely reason that because the child is the genetic issue of D that D will be required to provide the child with financial support.

Example 18-3

Assume that P sues D, her former boyfriend, seeking to establish paternity and to impose support obligations for twin boys conceived through artificial insemination by an anonymous donor. They live in a jurisdiction that has a typical artificial insemination statute. At the trial, evidence was admitted showing that during their ten-year relationship, the parties discussed marriage, but D told P that he did not believe in marriage. They also discussed P's desire to have children with D, but it became apparent that D could not father children. P testified that D suggested that she be artificially inseminated by an anonymous donor as a means to have their child. P claims that D promised her that he would provide financial support for any child born by means of artificial insemination. According to P, with D's consent and active encouragement, she became pregnant through artificial insemination and twin children were born.

Evidence also showed that D had provided financial assistance for the insemination procedure, accompanied P to the doctor's office for examinations, injected P with medication designed to enhance her fertility, and participated in selecting the donor so that the offspring would appear to be a product of their relationship. D also participated in selecting names for the children, although he did not allow his name to be placed on their birth certificates. For three years following their birth, D provided the children with monthly payments of cash and the purchase of food, clothing, furniture, toys, and play equipment. When the children were three years old, the relationship broke down and P now wants to establish paternity and obtain child support. D states that he has no responsibility toward the children because they are not his genetic issue and he is not married to their mother. How will a court most likely rule?

Explanation

The court may view D's conduct as evincing actual consent and a demonstration of a deliberate course of conduct with the goal of causing the birth of the children. It will reason that if an unmarried man, who biologically causes conception through sexual relations without the premeditated intent of birth is legally obligated to support a child, the equivalent resulting birth of a child caused by the deliberate conduct of artificial insemination should receive the same treatment. Regardless of the method of conception, a child is born and needs support, and for a court to hold otherwise would deprive the children of financial support merely because of deception and a technical oversight. *See generally* In re Parentage of M.J., 787 N.E.2d 144 (Ill. 2003) (held that failure to obtain written consent of putative father to insemination precluded claim for paternity under Parentage Act but did not prohibit mother's action based on common law theories of oral contract or promissory estoppels).

18.7. Husband's Consent

As noted earlier, most artificial insemination statutes require the written consent of the wife's husband if the woman is married before he will be found the father of a child born of this procedure and required to provide financial support should the relationship break down. However, most courts agree that the best interests of children and society are served by recognizing that parental responsibility may be imposed based upon conduct evincing actual consent to the artificial insemination procedure. *See Gursky v. Gursky*, 242 N.Y.S.2d 406 (N.Y. Sup. Ct. 1963) (husband's declaration and conduct respecting the artificial insemination of his wife by means of a third-party donor, including the husband's written consent to the procedure, implied a promise on the husband's part to furnish support for any offspring resulting from the insemination, and, together with the wife's concurrence and submission to the artificial insemination, was sufficient to constitute an implied contract to support the child). A New Jersey court in *K.S. v. G.S.*, 440 A.2d 64, 68-69 (N.J. Super. Ch. 1981), found that oral consent of the husband to the artificial insemination process was effective at the time pregnancy occurs unless he can establish by clear and convincing evidence that consent was revoked or rescinded. The court in *In re Marriage of L.M.S.*, 312 N.W.2d 853, 855 (Wis. Ct. App. 1981), held that a man who was sterile must support a child born from this procedure. He had suggested to his wife that she become pregnant by another man and promised that he would acknowledge the child as his own and the legal obligation "to support the child for whose existence he is responsible." *See generally In re Baby Doe*, 353 S.E.2d 877 (S.C. 1987) (husband's consent to artificial insemination may be express or implied from conduct).

Example 18-4

Assume that wife P and husband D orally agree to have a child by artificial insemination because husband D is infertile. They live in a jurisdiction that will recognize a child born of this procedure as the child of P and D. The artificial insemination of P is successful. Two months before the child is born, husband D and wife P separate. Following the child's birth, husband D is listed as the father on the birth certificate. During divorce proceedings, D asks the court to declare that he is not the father of the child. Wife counterclaims asking for child support. D argues that under the language of the state statute his consent must have been in writing (it was not) and that he was not living with P when the child was born. How will a court most likely rule on P and D's claims?

Explanation

A court most likely will find the husband D to be the father of the child and order the payment of child support. D's knowledge of and assistance with his wife's efforts to conceive through artificial insemination will be viewed as constituting implied consent on his part, rendering him the legal father. *See In re Baby Doe*, 353 S.E.2d 877, 878 (S.C. 1987). The fact that D was not living with P at the time of the child's birth will most likely be considered irrelevant.

18.8. Do Artificial Insemination Statutes Apply to Wives?

Most state legislation has focused on protecting the male sperm donor from legal claims and providing the husband with a legal right to a child born to his wife using this alternative method of reproduction. A question often left open by the legislation is whether the provisions of an artificial insemination statute apply equally to both wives and husbands. In at least one jurisdiction, the answer to the question has been in the affirmative. In *In re Karen C.*, 124 Cal. Rptr. 2d 677 (2002), the court considered the scope of subdivision (d) of §7611 of the California Code, which states that a man is presumed to be the natural father of a child if "[h]e receives the child into his home and openly holds out the child as his natural child." The court held that the subdivision applies equally to women. This conclusion was echoed in *In re Salvador M.*, 4 Cal. Rptr. 3d 705 (2003), where the court stated, "[t]hough most of the decisional law has focused on the definition of the presumed father, the legal principles concerning the presumed father apply equally to a woman seeking presumed mother status."

18.9. Do Artificial Insemination Statutes Apply to Same-Sex Couples?

In *Shineovich and Kemp*, 214 P.3d 29 (Or. App. 2009), the petitioner, a lesbian, separated from her former same-sex domestic partner who had given birth to two children after being artificially inseminated twice, with petitioner's consent, during the course of their ten-year relationship, sought to be named a legal parent of the children. The petitioner filed an action for declaratory relief against her former partner, challenging the constitutionality of two Oregon statutes under which a married man is, by operation of law, deemed to be the legal parent of children born to his wife.

The Oregon Supreme Court ruled that the statute, which established legal parentage in the husband of a woman who gives birth to a child conceived by artificial insemination, without regard to the biological relationship of the husband and the child, improperly discriminates on the basis of sexual orientation. It stated that the constitutional infirmity of statute would be remedied by extending the privilege to the same-sex domestic partner of a woman who gives birth to a child conceived by artificial insemination.

The California Supreme Court held in *Elisa B. v. Superior Court*, 33 Cal. Rptr. 3d 46 (Cal. 2005), that under that state's version of the Uniform Parentage Act, a child may have two parents, both of whom are women. It ruled that a former partner in a lesbian relationship was obliged to pay child support where she had agreed to raise the children, supported the birth mother's artificial insemination using an anonymous donor, and received the resulting twin children into her home and held them out as her own.

18.10. Known Donors and Unmarried Recipients

The issue of whether known sperm donors are afforded the same protection from subsequent paternity claims as those afforded anonymous donors is often not addressed in state statues. For example, a Colorado court ruled that a state statute that extinguishes the parental rights of unknown donors of semen to any child conceived by artificial insemination does not necessarily apply to known semen donors and unmarried recipients who agree that the donor will be treated as the father of the child. In Interest of R.C., 775 P.2d 27 (Colo. 1989).

In C.M. v. C.C., 377 A.2d 821 (N.J. Sup. Ct. 1977), the known donor gave semen to an unmarried woman, who artificially inseminated herself without the aid of a licensed physician. The court held the donor was entitled to visitation rights with the resulting child. The court reasoned that the best interests of the child are served by recognizing the donor as its father, rather than by leaving the child with no father at all. The court found it significant that the woman and the donor had a long-standing dating relationship prior to her artificial insemination, that the child had "no one else who was in a position to assume the responsibilities of fatherhood when the child was conceived" because the woman was unmarried, and that the donor "fully intended to assume the responsibilities of parenthood" at the time of the insemination. Id. at 824. The New Jersey legislature subsequently enacted a statutory provision that provided that a donor of semen to someone other than his wife has no parental rights to a child conceived through artificial insemination unless the donor and the woman have entered into a written contract to the contrary. See N.J. Rev. Stat. §9:17-44(b) (2003).

In Jhordan C. v. Mary K., 224 Cal. Rptr. 530 (Cal. Dist. Ct. App. 1986), the court construed California's law precluding recognition of a sperm donor as a putative father as applying only when a physician performs the procedure or otherwise provides the semen. In Jhordan, the mother had self-inseminated, and the court declared that the sperm donor was the legal father of the child. The court also extended the protection it provided to married women (fear of a paternity lawsuit from sperm donor) to unmarried women. Id. at 392.

The Oregon Court of Appeals in McIntyre v. Crouch, 780 P.2d 239 (Or. Ct. App. 1989), held that Oregon's legislature had excluded a semen donor from the rights or obligations of fatherhood with respect to the resulting child, even though the insemination process was not conducted by a doctor and the recipient knew the donor. The court indicated, however, that should the parties agree that the man would be actively involved in the child's life, applying the artificial insemination statute to treat him solely as a donor, and not a father, would violate his constitutional rights. Id. at 244.

18.11. Using Husband's Sperm to Achieve Posthumous Reproduction

The law regarding the rights of posthumously conceived children is unsettled. Posthumous reproduction may occur if a married man and woman arrange for sperm to be withdrawn from the husband for the purpose of artificially impregnating the wife, and the woman is impregnated with that sperm after the man, her husband, has died.

In *Hecht v. Superior Court*, 20 Cal. Rptr. 2d 275 (Cal. Dist. Ct. App. 1993), the California Court of Appeals considered whether a decedent's sperm was "property" that could be bequeathed to his girlfriend. It answered in the affirmative, noting that under the provisions of California's Probate Code, "it is unlikely that the estate would be subject to claims with respect to any such children" resulting from insemination of the girlfriend with the decedent's sperm. *Id.* at 290.

In *Matter of Estate of Kolacy*, 753 A.2d 1257 (N.J. Super. Ct. Ch. Div. 2000), the plaintiff sought a declaratory judgment to have her children, who were conceived after the death of her husband, declared the intestate heirs of her deceased husband in order to pursue the children's claims for survivor benefits with the Social Security Administration. A Superior Court judge held that, in circumstances in which the decedent left no estate and an adjudication of parentage did not unfairly intrude on the rights of others or cause "serious problems" with the orderly administration of estates, the children would be entitled to inherit under the state's intestacy law. *Id.* at 1257.

Woodward v. Commissioner of Social Sec., 760 N.E.2d 257 (Mass. 2002), involved a dispute where the husband was informed that he had leukemia when the couple was childless. Because the husband's leukemia treatment might leave him sterile, the couple arranged for a quantity of the husband's semen to be medically withdrawn and preserved, in a process commonly known as "sperm banking." The husband subsequently died from cancer, and the wife was appointed administratrix of his estate.

The wife later gave birth to twin girls who were conceived through artificial insemination using the husband's preserved semen. She then applied for social security survivor benefits for the children. In rejecting her claim, the court said the question of recognition depends as a threshold matter upon a showing that the surviving parent or the child's other legal representative has a genetic relationship between the child and the decedent. Once that is shown, the survivor or representative must establish that the decedent affirmatively consented to posthumous conception and to the support of any resulting child. Even then, circumstances such as time limitations may preclude recognition of a claim for succession rights on behalf of a posthumously conceived child.

The court in *Woodward* also observed that because death ends a marriage, it viewed posthumously conceived children as nonmarital children. The court reasoned that because the parentage of such children can be neither acknowledged nor adjudicated prior to the decedent's death, under the intestacy statute, posthumously conceived children must obtain a judgment of paternity as a necessary prerequisite to seeking inheritance rights in the estate of the deceased genetic father.

Example 18-5

Assume that P and D are married and that D learns he has a serious heart problem and must undergo an operation. Because they have no children, P and D agree that a quantity of the D's semen will be medically withdrawn and preserved should D die during the surgery. P and D consult a lawyer regarding the most effective means of ensuring that any posthumous children will be eligible for social security benefits. What practical legal advice might the lawyer give P and D?

Explanation

The lawyer might advise them to draft a will that sets out in detail the sperm donor's intention of supporting such children. The lawyer might also advise P and D to inform the sperm bank in writing of the reason for banking D's sperm. The lawyer will note that special care must be exercised to retain all records showing D's intent so that, should D die and children be born posthumously, establishing paternity will be possible. The language in the will and testimony of the witnesses to the will should provide sufficient evidence to persuade a court that the children are D's issue and establish paternity that will make them eligible to receive social security benefits similar to those available to other children following the death of a parent.

IN VITRO FERTILIZATION

18.12. In Vitro Procedure Explained

The in vitro fertilization (IVF) procedure requires a woman to undergo a series of hormonal injections to stimulate the production of mature oocytes (egg cells or ova). The medication causes the ovaries to release multiple egg cells during a menstrual cycle rather than the single egg normally produced. The egg cells are retrieved from the woman's body and examined by a physician who evaluates their quality for fertilization. Egg cells ready for insemination are then combined with a sperm sample and allowed to incubate for approximately 12 to 18 hours. Successful fertilization results in a zygote that develops into a four- to eight-cell pre-embryo. At that stage, the pre-embryos are either returned to the woman's uterus for implantation or cryopreserved at a temperature of $-196°C$ and stored for possible future use.

In IVF programs, the embryo will be transferred to a uterus when it reaches the four-, six-, or eight-cell stage, some 48 to 72 hours after conception. It is also at this stage that the embryo would be cryopreserved for later use. About one in ten pre-embryos initiate a successful pregnancy.

Note that when cryopreservation is used, there is an estimated 70 percent rate of viability after having been frozen.

18.13. Pre-embryo Contracts: Emerging View

There is an emerging view that contracts entered into at the time of in vitro fertilization are enforceable so long as they do not violate public policy. *See Kass v. Kass*, 696 N.E.2d 174, 180 (N.Y. 1998) (stating agreements between donors "regarding disposition of pre-zygotes should generally be presumed valid and binding"); *Davis v. Tennessee*, 842 S.W.2d 588, 597 (Tenn. 1992) (holding agreement regarding disposition of embryos "should be considered binding"); *In re Litowitz*, 48 P.3d 261, 271 (Wash. 2002) (enforcing parties' contract providing for disposition of pre-embryos after five years of storage). In the absence of an agreement, courts will weigh the relative interests of the male and female providers of reproductive cells and the parties' intent. *In re C.K.G.*, 173 S.W.3d 714 (Tenn. 2005).

The Oregon Appellate Court in *In re Marriage of Dahl and Angle*, 572, 194 P.3d 834 (Or. App. 2008), considered an appeal by a husband involving a dissolution judgment that ordered the destruction of six cryopreserved embryos that were formed using the husband's sperm and the wife's eggs and that were stored at the Oregon Health and Science University. The court enforced the written contract made by the parties and ordered the pre-embryos destroyed as preferred by the wife. *See Roman v. Roman*, 193 S.W.3d 40, 50 (Tex. App. 2006), *rev. den.* (2007), *cert. den.*, 128 S. Ct. 1662 (2008) (ordering frozen embryos destroyed in accordance with IVF agreement); *cf. A.Z. v. B.Z.*, 725 N.E.2d 1051, 1057 (2000) (determining that the agreement was unenforceable for public policy reasons).

In *Davis v. Davis*, 842 S.W.2d 588 (Tenn. 1992), the issue was to determine who was entitled to control seven of the ex-wife's ova fertilized by the ex-husband's sperm through the IVF process. The fertilized ova were cryopreserved at the Fertility Center of East Tennessee in Knoxville. The ex-husband was vehemently opposed to fathering a child that would not live with both parents, in light of his boyhood experiences, and the ex-wife's only interest in the embryos was to donate them to another couple.

The Tennessee Supreme Court held that disputes involving disposition of pre-embryos produced by IVF should be resolved first by looking to the preferences of the progenitors. If their wishes cannot be ascertained, or if there is a dispute, their prior agreement concerning disposition should be carried out. If there is no prior agreement between the progenitors as to disposition of the pre-embryos, a court is to weigh the relative interests of parties in using or not using the pre-embryos. Ordinarily, the party who wishes to avoid procreation should prevail if there is a dispute as to custody of pre-embryos, assuming that the other party has a reasonable possibility of achieving parenthood by means other than use of the pre-embryos in question. However, if no other reasonable alternative exists, arguments in favor of using the pre-embryos to achieve pregnancy will be considered by the court. In resolving this dispute, the court ruled that because the ex-wife merely intended to donate them to another couple, the ex-husband had the greater interest and should prevail.

In J.B. v. M.B., 783 A.2d 707, 719 (N.J. 2001), the ex-husband sought to preserve the frozen embryos for his use or that of an infertile couple. The ex-wife wanted the frozen embryos destroyed. The trial court ruled in favor of the wife because the family unit was no longer intact. On appeal, the New Jersey Supreme Court held that the parties' consent agreement did not "manifest a clear intent by [the parties] regarding disposition of the pre-embryos in the event of a dissolution of their marriage." It then turned to a consideration of the constitutional rights of the parties concluding that, "[w]e will not force [the wife] to become a biological parent against her will." Id. at 717.

Note that at least one commentator has suggested that the gamete donation process that both husband and wife experience provides the consideration for an embryo contract. Marysol Rosado, *Sign on the Dotted Line: Enforceability of Signed Agreements, upon Divorce of the Married Couple, Concerning the Disposition of Their Frozen Preembryos*, 36 New Eng. L. Rev. 1041, 1069 (2002).

Example 18.6

Assume that during their marriage that wife P had a dozen of her ova fertilized by husband D's sperm through the in IVF process. They were cryopreserved by Clinic XYZ. When the couple divorced, the clinic was unable to locate an agreement in its files that the parties "thought" they had signed years earlier regarding the disposition of the fertilized ova. They could not recall the exact terms of the agreement. P sought custody of the frozen fertilized ova. At the hearing on the matter, D testified that he wanted them destroyed because he did not want children and if children were born from the ova, that he did not have sufficient funds to provide support for them. P testified that wished to donate them to her sister, who was having difficulty becoming pregnant. P admitted during cross-examination that she did not have any medical problems that would prevent her from becoming pregnant, should she decide to do so. How will a court most likely resolve this issue?

Explanation

The trial judge will most likely look to the reasoning used in *Davis v. Davis*, *supra*. Because the prior agreement that the parties "thought" might resolve the dispute cannot be located, and the parties cannot recall the terms, the judge will treat the matter as though there was no prior agreement. She will weigh the relative interests of parties in using or not using the fertilized ova. Under *Davis*, the party who wishes to avoid procreation should prevail if there is a dispute as to custody of the ova, assuming that the other party has a reasonable possibility of achieving parenthood by means other than use of the ova in question. P conceded at the hearing that she could achieve parenthood without the fertilize ova. Because P intends to donate the fertilized ova to her sister, D appears to have the greater interest and will most likely prevail.

SURROGACY

18.14. Surrogate Parent — History and Definition

Surrogacy is mentioned as early as Biblical times: Abram's wife Sara could not bear Abram any children so she gave her maid servant, Hagar, to Abram for this purpose, saying, "The Lord has kept me from bearing children. Have intercourse, then, with my maid; perhaps I shall have sons through her." Genesis 16:3. According to the Bible, a child, Ishmael, was born of this arrangement.

Black's Law Dictionary 1145(8th ed. 2006) defines a surrogate parent as "a person who carries out the role of a parent by court appointment or the voluntary assumption of parental responsibilities." It defines a surrogate mother as "a woman who carries out the gestational function and gives birth to a child for another; especially a woman who agrees to provide her uterus to carry an embryo throughout pregnancy, typically on behalf of an infertile couple, and who relinquishes any parental rights she may have upon the birth of a child." *Black's Law Dictionary* 1036(8th ed. 2006).

Some question the accuracy of the term *surrogate* when it is used to describe a woman who is in fact the actual biological mother of a child. One author expressed the opinion that "[t]he term 'surrogate' mother, coined by advocates of commercial surrogacy, is a misnomer. The woman who bears the child is an actual mother; she is a surrogate 'wife.' " Kathryn D. Katz, *The Public Policy Response to Surrogate Motherhood Agreements: Why They Should Be Illegal and Unenforceable*, N.Y. St. B. J. (May 1988).

18.15. Legislation Allowing and Banning Surrogacy

In contrast to artificial insemination statutes found in most states, only a handful of jurisdictions have legislation governing the subject of surrogacy. It appears that a majority of those jurisdictions that have promulgated legislation on the subject make surrogate contracts void if they involve money. *See, e.g., Doe v. Attorney General*, 487 N.W.2d 484 (Mich. App. 1992) (surrogate parentage contract entered into for compensation is unlawful — for-profit arrangements have the potential for demeaning women by reducing them to the status of "breeding machines"); cf *J.F. v. D.B.*, 879 N.E.2d 740 (Ohio 2007) (Ohio has no public policy in re surrogacy — such contracts for money are not unlawful).

18.16. Common Surrogacy Processes

There are two relatively common surrogacy processes currently being utilized. One process involves the artificial insemination of the surrogate mother with the sperm of a male, usually when the parties contemplate that the sperm-donor male and his spouse will raise the child as the child's "parents." *See, e.g., Matter of Baby M*, 537 A.2d 1227 (N.J. 1988). The second process, which is referred to as gestational surrogacy, involves couples who wish to have a child, and they provide the ovum and the sperm. The ovum and sperm undergo fertilization in a medical laboratory, which is called in vitro fertilization. Once an embryo is formed, it is placed in the uterus of a surrogate who is not the ovum donor. The surrogate mother carries and gives birth to the child.

18.17. Baby M

In re Baby M, 537 A.2d 1227 (N.J. 1988), is a leading surrogacy decision. In that dispute, William Stern and a surrogate, Mary Beth Whitehead, entered into a surrogacy contract. The contract recited that Stern's wife, Elizabeth, was infertile, that they wanted a child, and that Mrs. Whitehead was willing to provide that child as the mother with Mr. Stern as the father. The contract provided that through artificial insemination of Mrs. Whitehead's ovum, using Mr. Stern's sperm, Mrs. Whitehead would become pregnant, carry the child to term, bear it, deliver it to the Sterns, and thereafter do whatever was necessary to terminate her maternal rights so that Mrs. Stern could thereafter adopt the child. Mrs. Whitehead's husband was also a party to the contract, although Mrs. Stern was not. Mr. Whitehead promised to do all acts necessary to rebut the presumption of paternity under the New Jersey Parentage Act.

Following the birth of the child, Mrs. Whitehead refused to relinquish her rights to the baby according to the terms of the contract, and the Sterns brought an action to enforce the contract. The contract claim was rejected, with the court concluding it was in direct conflict with existing statutes and conflicted with the public policy of the state, as expressed in its statutory and decisional law. *Id.* at 422.

The court held that surrogacy contracts are directly contrary to the objectives of New Jersey's laws because they guarantee the separation of a child from its mother, allow adoption regardless of parental suitability, totally ignore the child, remove a child from the mother regardless of her wishes and her maternal fitness, and accomplish their goals through the use of money. The court indicated that money should not be used in a private adoption and feared that it was actually being paid to obtain an adoption and not for the personal services of Mrs. Whitehead. It felt that such conduct was similar to baby selling, was illegal, and was perhaps criminal.

The court found that there is coercion of contract when the natural mother's irrevocable agreement is obtained prior to birth, even prior to conception, to surrender the child to the adoptive couple. It felt that such agreements were totally unenforceable in private placement adoption. It observed that even where the adoption is through an approved agency, the formal agreement to surrender occurs only after birth.

The court noted that surrogacy arrangements focus exclusively on the parents' desires and interests. Because of this, it felt that the parties are apt to be insensitive to what would be in the child's best interests. It also felt that a child's best interests could not be protected because the child is placed without regard for whether the adoptive parents are suitable, the natural mother receives no counseling and guidance, and the adoptive parents may not be fully informed of the natural parents' medical history.

The agreement was thought to be contrary to termination statutes, which require a showing of intentional abandonment or a very substantial neglect of parental duties without a reasonable expectation of a reversal of that conduct in the future before a court will order the rights of a natural parent to be terminated.

The court in *Baby M* was also concerned that such surrogacy arrangements may result in the exploitation of women. It suggested that surrogacy-for-profit arrangements may demean women by reducing them to the status of "breeding machines." *See generally Doe v. Attorney General*, 487 N.W.2d 484, 487 (Mich. Ct. App. 1992).

In addition to the arguments found against surrogate contracts in *Baby M*, it is argued that if surrogacy contracts were recognized, every surrogate mother would soon be cast in the role of an "unfeeling, emotionless machine whose purpose is to create a life and then disappear." *See* Steven M. Recht, "M" *Is for Money: Baby M and the Surrogate Motherhood Controversy*, 37 Am. U. L. Rev. 1013, 1022 (1988).

Example 18-7

Assume that in this jurisdiction no surrogate statute exists. Also assume that P and X are sisters and that P, for medical reasons, cannot carry a child to term. P and X agree in writing that X will be artificially inseminated with P's husband's sperm and that X will carry the child to term and at birth, turn it over to P. When the child is born, X agrees to turn the child over to P. Before going through with the procedure, P consults a lawyer to determine the potential implications of the procedure. What advice might the lawyer provide P?

Explanation

The lawyer will most likely review all of the concerns expressed by the court in *Baby M*. She will note that *Baby M* is distinguishable on two grounds. First, the court in this jurisdiction may view the close family relationship as important; that is, the surrogate X is the biological sister of P, the woman seeking parenthood. Second, it will recognize that no money is being exchanged between the parties. Consequently, the concerns about baby selling and female exploitation are significantly reduced, if not eliminated. However, many other obstacles remain, such as terminating X's parental rights, dealing with state adoption requirements, and general considerations of the best interests of the child. While P may eventually achieve her goal, a lawyer could not provide such assurance with certainty.

GESTATIONAL SURROGACY

18.18. Gestational Surrogacy Defined

"Gestational surrogacy" is used to describe the process in which one woman agrees to be impregnated with an embryo formed from another woman's fertilized egg. Among the technologies related to gestational surrogacy are in vitro fertilization, embryo and gamete freezing and storage, gamete intra-fallopian transfer, and embryo transplantation. Gestational surrogacy is the result of two of these techniques: in vitro fertilization and embryo transplantation.

In vitro fertilization (IVF) is the fertilization of a human egg outside the human body in a laboratory. Children conceived in this way are often referred to as "test tube babies," because their actual conception may have occurred in a petri dish. A majority of states do not have gestational surrogacy statutes. At least three states have enacted legislation addressing frozen embryos. *See, e.g.,* Fla. Stat. Ann. §742.17 (couples must execute written agreement providing for disposition in event of death, divorce or other unforeseen circumstances); N.H. Rev. Stat. Ann. §§168-B:13-168-B:15, 168-B:18 (couples must undergo medical examinations and counseling; 14-day limit for maintenance of ex utero pre-zygotes); La. Rev. Stat. Ann. §§9:121-9:133 (pre-zygote considered "juridical person" that must be implanted); *see also* Tex. Fam. Code Ann. §160.102(2) (defining assisted reproduction), §160.706 (entitled "Effect of Dissolution of Marriage") (Vernon 2002), §160.754(e) (Vernon Supp. 2005) (stating that parties to gestational agreement must enter into agreement before the 14th day preceding the transfer of embryos); *Roman v. Roman*, 193 S.W.3d 40 (Tex. App. 2006) (husband complied with §160.706(a) of the Texas Family Code, which allows him to seek parental rights to any child born from the embryos).

18.19. State Gestational Surrogacy Theories

Johnson v. Calvert, 851 P.2d 776 (Cal. 1993), is a leading case on gestational surrogacy. In *Johnson v. Calvert*, a married couple supplied the egg and sperm and a surrogate agreed to carry and deliver the child. The surrogate was not related to the genetic providers, and was to be compensated for the surrogacy. When the child was born, a dispute arose over the compensation the surrogate was to be paid. She also asserted her claim as the legal parent of the child and refused to turn the child over to the gestational parents.

In its decision, the court concluded that either the gestational surrogate or the genetic parents could be recognized as the natural and legal parents. Recognition, however, depended upon which party intended to procreate and raise the child.

The court explained that when Anna Johnson had agreed to bear the genetic child, both Johnson (the surrogate) and Crispina Calvert (the genetic mother) had equal claims to the child. However, because the child would not have existed but for the surrogacy agreement, the tie was broken in favor of Calvert, the "intended" mother under the contract. Because the genetic mother intended to procreate, she was considered the natural parent.

In *McDonald v. McDonald*, 608 N.Y.S.2d 477 (N.Y. App. Div. 1994), the gestational surrogate received the egg from an anonymous donor, and her husband provided the sperm. The sperm of the husband was mixed with the eggs of a female donor, and the fertilized eggs were then implanted in the wife's uterus. The wife gave birth to the children, twin girls. When the relationship broke down, the husband brought an action challenging the right of his wife to consider the children her natural issue. The court rejected the claim, saying that in a true egg donation situation, where a woman gestates and gives birth to a child formed from the egg of another woman with the intent to raise the child as her own, the birth mother is the natural mother. *Id.* at 480.

In *Belsito v. Clark*, 644 N.E.2d 760 (Ohio Com. Pl. 1994), two fertilized eggs created through in vitro fertilization by the use of the wife's eggs and the husband's sperm were transferred into the wife's sister's uterus by her physician. The surrogate was to receive no compensation for her role, and she agreed that she planned to be no more than an aunt to the child or children.

When the wife spoke with the hospital about the birth certificate, she was told that the woman who gave birth to the child would be listed on the birth certificate as the child's mother. Furthermore, she was told that because the surrogate and the wife's husband are not married to each other, the child will be considered illegitimate. The husband and wife sought a declaratory judgment challenging the hospital's position.

The court held that because the husband and wife provided the child with their genetics, they should be designated as the legal and natural parents. It stated that individuals who provide the genes of a child are the natural parents if the genetic providers have not waived their rights and have decided to raise the child.

18.20. Same-Sex Issues

In *K.M. v. E.G.*, 33 Cal. Rptr. 3d 61 (Cal. 2005), a woman had donated her eggs so that her former lesbian partner, E.G., with whom she was registered in a domestic partnership, could bear a child through in vitro fertilization. K.M. filed a petition to establish parental relationship with E.G.'s twin children after the relationship ended.

The court reasoned that the couple in *Johnson v. Calvert* and the couple here intended to produce a child that would be raised in their own home. It observed that in *Johnson*, it was clear that the married couple did not intend to "donate" their semen and ova to the surrogate mother, but rather permitted their semen and ova to be used to impregnate the surrogate mother in order to produce a child to be raised by them.

The court observed that the couple in this dispute lived together, and intended to bring the children into their joint home. It concluded that K.M. did not intend to simply donate her ova to E.G., but rather K.M. provided her ova to E.G. so that E.G. could give birth to a child that would be raised in their joint home. It held that both lesbian partners were parents of the children and that the California statute providing that a sperm donor is treated as if he was not the natural father of a child so conceived did not apply to this situation.

In re Adoption of Sebastian, 879 N.Y.S.2d 677 (N.Y. Sur. 2009), involved Ingrid and Mona who were legally married in the Netherlands. They desired to establish a family that would reflect their ethnic and racial diversity. Mona donated her ova, which were fertilized in vitro by an anonymous sperm donor chosen for his similarities to Ingrid's Dutch Italian ethnicity.

The fertilized ovum was successfully implanted in Ingrid's uterus, and she gave birth to Sebastian. A birth certificate named Ingrid alone as Sebastian's parent. Since then Ingrid and Mona continued to live together and co-parent Sebastian, who they considered to be the child of each of them. Notwithstanding their marriage and Mona's unquestioned genetic relationship to Sebastian, Mona sought to adopt the child.

Ingrid and Mona's marriage in the Netherlands was recognized in New York with the executive branch of government extending full protection to same-sex couples validly married in other jurisdictions. Therefore, adoption was arguably unnecessary and impermissibly duplicative. They argued, however, that while New York recognized the relationship, the same recognition and protection of Mona's parental rights does not currently exist in the rest of this country, or in most other nations in the world. For this reason, only an order of adoption would ensure the portability of Sebastian's parentage, and further ensure that the federal government and other states would recognize Mona as Sebastian's legal parent.

The court held that adoption was the sole means by which Mona could legally establish parentage of the child born to Ingrid and was the sole means by which the rights and obligations relative to the child could be fully protected. Mona's petition to adopt Sebastian was granted.

Example 18-8

Assume that in this jurisdiction there is no surrogate statute, that a birth certificate can be prepared up to five days after the birth of a child, and that the adoption statutes provide that in recognition of the emotional and physical changes that occur at birth, voluntary surrenders are not valid if made within 72 hours after the birth of the child. Assume further that X is the unmarried sister of P. P and P's husband, D, entered into a gestational surrogacy contract with X. X, without financial compensation, agreed to have embryos implanted into her uterus that were created from the sperm of D and the ova of her sister, P. Assume that the child is due to be born in about two weeks at the county hospital when P and D file a complaint to declare the maternity and paternity of unborn Baby A. They seek a pre-birth court order that establishes them as the legal mother and father of unborn Baby A, and allows the hospital to place their names on the child's birth certificate. They argue that a pre-birth order is appropriate with a gestational surrogacy. How will a court most likely treat P and D's request?

Explanation

The court will most likely reject the request for a pre-birth order primarily because it is contrary to the existing 72-hour statute. The gestational mother may surrender the child 72 hours after giving birth. This leaves 48 hours in which the birth certificate may be prepared. If X chooses to surrender the infant, and she certifies that she wishes to relinquish all rights, the original birth certificate can list the two biological parents, P and D, as the baby's parents. However, because of the statute expressing this jurisdiction's public policy, if X changes her mind about turning the child over to P and D once the child is born, she will have an opportunity to litigate to protect her parental rights to the child. *See generally A.H.W. v. G.H.B.*, 772 A.2d 948 (N.J. Super. Ch. 2000). Absent the statute, a court would most likely uphold the agreement and require X to turn the child over to P and D.

18.21. Constitutional "Right" to Gestational Surrogacy?

Some argue that the use of processes such as gestational surrogacy are constitutionally protected and should be restricted only upon a showing of a compelling state interest. *See, e.g.,* John A. Robertson, *Procreative Liberty and the Control of Conception, Pregnancy, and Childbirth,* 69 Va. L. Rev. 405, 427 (1983); John A. Robertson, *Embryos, Families, and Procreative Liberty: The Legal Structure of the New Reproduction* 59 S. Cal. L. Rev. 939, 960 (1986). The theory is that procreation is protected under decisions of the United States Supreme Court that affirm the basic civil right to marry and raise children; therefore, the right to procreate should extend to persons who cannot conceive or bear children. Some contend, however, that the broad application of the right of privacy for all procreational techniques has been questioned by the Supreme Court in such decisions as *Michael H. v. Gerald D.*, 491 U.S. 110 (1989).

LIABILITY ISSUES

18.22. Physician's Tort Liability to Parents

Physicians or clinics involved in alternative reproduction may find themselves in court as defendants for a variety of reasons. For example, a doctor who counseled a childless couple about artificial insemination and agreed to perform the procedure on the wife using the husband's sperm was held subject to suit by the couple when he substituted his own sperm for that of the wife's husband. *See generally James v. Jacobson*, 6 F.3d 233 (4th Cir. 1993); *United States v. Jacobson*, 785 F. Supp. 563 (E.D. Va. 1992); *St. Paul Fire and Marine Ins. Co. v. Jacobson*, 826 F. Supp. 155, 158, n.3 (E.D. Va. 1993) (listing civil actions against physician for unauthorized use of physician's own semen).

In *Harnicher v. University of Utah Medical Center*, 962 P.2d 67 (Utah 1998), the Utah Supreme Court upheld the dismissal of a couple's claim against a medical center that used sperm from a donor other than the one the couple selected for artificial insemination, resulting in the birth of triplets. The court held that the parents failed to raise a triable issue of fact that they had suffered bodily harm, and had failed to show that the medical center's alleged negligence was of the type that was likely to cause severe and unmanageable mental distress in a reasonable person.

18.23. Wrongful Life

A California clinic was sued by a child who claimed its negligence had deprived the child of her legal parent because it failed to certify the signature of the mother's husband on a consent form used for artificial insemination. *Alexandria S. v. Pacific Fertility*, 64 Cal. Rptr. 2d 23 (Cal. Dist. Ct. App. 1997). The child claimed injury when the couple divorced and a divorce court ruled that the husband did not have a legal obligation to support the child born of the procedure. The child, who was now technically fatherless, sued the clinic.

The court rejected the child's claim, reasoning that the failure to certify the signature was not the proximate cause of any injury to the child. It said the certification was not required to establish the husband's consent under the statute that treated a husband who consents to a wife being inseminated artificially by a donor as the natural father of the child conceived.

18.24. Wrongful Death

In *Jeter v. Mayo Clinic Arizona*, 121 P.3d 1256 (Ariz. App. 2005), a couple alleged negligent destruction or loss of five of the couple's frozen pre-embryos that the clinic had agreed to cryopreserve and store. They brought claims for wrongful death, negligent loss of irreplaceable property, breach of fiduciary duty, and breach of bailment contract. The Arizona Court of Appeals held that cryopreserved, three-day-old eight-cell pre-embryos were not persons for purposes of recovery under the wrongful death statute. However, it allowed the couple to proceed on claims of negligent loss or destruction of pre-embryos and for breach of bailment contract.

The Arkansas Supreme Court in *Aka v. Jefferson Hospital Association, Inc.*, 42 S.W.3d 508 (Ark. 2001), held that the term "person" in the Arkansas wrongful death statute includes an unborn viable fetus, *overruling Chatelain v. Kelley*, 910 S.W.2d 215 (Ark. 1995). In this case, the administrator of the estates of a mother and an unborn viable fetus brought wrongful death and medical malpractice actions against a hospital and physicians. The plaintiffs alleged medical negligence in unnecessarily inducing mother's labor, failing to discontinue induction, failing to perform cesarean section, failing to resuscitate her or fetus, and failing to obtain informed consent, proximately causing mother's and fetus's deaths. The trial court was reversed on appeal because it had granted summary judgment to defendants by concluding that a fetus was not a person for the purposes of a tort action. Cf. *In re Marriage of Witten*, 672 N.W.2d 768 (Iowa 2003) (frozen embryo is not a "child" for purposes of Iowa's child custody laws).

18.25. Constitutional Issues

There have been a small number of constitutional challenges made to state statutes attempting to provide guidance in this area. For example, an Oregon court, in *dictum*, stated that, had its state statute prevented a sperm donor from exercising paternity rights, it would most likely be held unconstitutional in certain situations (as applied) under the Due Process Clause of the Fourteenth Amendment. *See McIntyre v. Crouch*, 780 P.2d 239, 244 (Or. Ct. App. 1989). The court also observed that the unconstitutionality of the barrier created by the statute becomes apparent in situations in which a sperm donor establishes that the donor and the woman inseminated with his sperm agree that he should have the rights and responsibilities of fatherhood, and in reliance on the agreement, he provides the sperm. *See generally, Lehr v. Robertson*, 463 U.S. 248 (1983) (held that where the putative father had never established a substantial relationship with his child, the failure to give him notice of pending adoption proceedings, despite the state's actual notice of his existence and whereabouts, did not deny the putative father due process or equal protection).

At least one court has held that a woman possesses a constitutional right to become pregnant by artificial insemination because she has a constitutional privacy right to control her reproductive functions. *Cameron v. Board of Educ. of Hillsboro*, 795 F. Supp. 228, 237 (S.D. Ohio 1991). The court relied on the Supreme Court's decisions in *Cleveland Board of Education v. LaFleur*, 414 U.S. 632, 640 (1974) (freedom of personal choice in matters of marriage and family life is one of the liberties protected by the Due Process Clause); *Roe v. Wade*, 410 U.S. 113, 153 (1973) (woman's right to privacy includes the right to terminate a pregnancy); and *Griswold v. Connecticut*, 381 U.S. 479, 485-486 (1965) (criminalizing purchasing contraceptives violates one's right to privacy).

18.26. "Imperfect" Child Is Born

In *Paretta v. Medical Offices for Human Reproduction*, 760 N.Y.S.2d 639 (N.Y. Sup. 2003), a New York court held that a right of recovery against a clinic for emotional distress did not exist for a child's birth with cystic fibrosis but that a right of recovery did exist for pecuniary expense for the infant's care and treatment. Evidence at trial indicated that it was the custom and practice of the program used by the clinic to screen donors for various diseases, including cystic fibrosis, and to inform the patient that a potential donor was a carrier. If a couple elected to go forward, they had the option or choice to be screened to see if there was a carrier status. No one remembered ever telling the plaintiffs that the available donor was a carrier of cystic fibrosis, and the husband was not tested to ascertain whether he was a carrier of the disease.

18.27. Liability When Genetic Material Mix-up Occurs

In *Robert B. v. Susan B.*, 135 Cal. Rptr. 2d 785 (Cal. Dist. Ct. App. 2003), a child, Daniel, was born to Susan B., a single woman, after a fertility clinic accidentally implanted embryos belonging to Robert and Denise B. into Susan. In an action to determine paternity, the trial court ruled that Susan was Daniel's mother, and Robert was his father. Denise was dismissed for lack of standing.

Robert and Denise B. had contracted with an anonymous ovum donor to obtain the donor's eggs for fertilization with Robert's sperm. The contract reflected the intent of the contracting parties that Robert and Denise would be the parents of any children produced from the resulting embryos. Susan went to the same fertility clinic with the intent of purchasing genetic material from "two strangers who would contractually sign away their rights" so that "there would be no paternity case against her, ever." She contracted with the clinic for an embryo created from anonymously donated ova and sperm.

About 13 embryos were produced for Robert and Denise, and some of them were implanted in Denise's uterus. Through an apparent clinic error, Susan received three of these embryos. When she became pregnant, Susan believed that the child she was carrying was the result of the anonymous donation procedure for which she had contracted. In February, ten days apart, Susan gave birth to Daniel, and Denise gave birth to Daniel's genetic sister, Madeline.

In December 2001, the fertility physician informed Robert and Denise that a mistake had occurred, in that the clinic had inadvertently implanted some of Robert and Denise's embryos in Susan's uterus, resulting in Daniel's birth. Robert and Denise promptly sought contact with Daniel. Susan was initially receptive, but after the three adults and two children met, she refused to relinquish custody, and Robert and Denise brought a parentage action. The trial court determined that Robert had standing to bring a paternity action under California law and ordered genetic testing. After receiving the test results, the court declared Robert to be the father of Daniel.

In resolving the dispute, the appellate court held that a wife who is not biologically related to the child is not an "interested party" and has no standing to bring a parentage action. It also held that California's statute providing that donor of semen for use in artificial insemination of woman who is not the donor's wife is treated as if donor is not natural father of conceived child did not apply and the genetic father was recognized as the child's father. *See Prato-Morrison v. Doe*, 126 Cal. Rptr. 2d 509 (Cal. App 2002) (evidence insufficient to show that plaintiffs were the genetic parents of defendants' twin teenage daughters, based on the facts that plaintiffs and defendants were clients of the same fertility clinic when the twins were conceived, and that the clinic had been found guilty of misusing abandoned genetic material such as plaintiffs).

Domestic Violence

19.1. Introduction

The existence of domestic violence has been traced as far back as ancient Rome, and as recently as the 1800s, an American husband could legally "chastise" his wife in the exercise of his property rights. Awareness of domestic violence has increased dramatically over the last half-century, and it is no longer explicitly approved under the law. However, courts and legislatures struggle to make policy concerning when and how to intervene in family matters.

UNDERSTANDING THE ISSUE

19.2. Risk Factors

Risk markers for domestic violence include growing up in a violent home, socioeconomic status, personality issues, substance abuse, biological factors, and situational dynamics. Rates of domestic violence may be higher when dating, in early marriage, during pregnancy, and at the time of divorce. Glenda Kaufman Kantor & Jana L. Jasinski, *Dynamics and Risk Factors in Partner Violence*, in *Partner Violence* 1, 41, 42 (Jana L. Jasinski et al. eds., 1998). Significant predictors of future male partner violence include past violence, past abuse, emotional dependency, relationship problems, mental health problems, control issues, and substance abuse. Desmond Ellis & Noreen Stuckless, *Domestic Violence, DOVE, and Divorce Mediation*, 44 Fam. Ct. Rev. 658 (2006).

19.3. Importance of Context

The impact and implications of domestic violence depend a great deal on the context in which it occurs. For example, consider three situations where partner A pushes partner B. In the first situation there has been no prior history of violence or intimidation. In the second situation there has been no previous physical violence, but partner A frequently threatens partner B and insists on knowing B's whereabouts at all times. In the third situation partner A has a history of violence, including cutting B with a knife and breaking B's jaw. Although the physical act of partner A pushing B is the same in each hypothetical situation, the impact on B and the risk level to B is significantly different. Consequently, it is important to consider the context of the violence in addition to the physical acts.

Families experiencing domestic violence differ significantly from each other, and researchers, practitioners, and courts are currently working to find appropriate and empirically valid ways to differentiate among them. Several prominent researchers suggest investigation of (a) the frequency, severity, and potential lethality of the violence; (b) the pattern of the violence, including signs of coercive control; and (c) whether there is a primary perpetrator of the violence. Peter G. Jaffe, Janet R. Johnston, Claire V. Crooks & Nicholas Bala, *Custody Disputes Involving Allegations of Domestic Violence: Toward a Differentiated Approach to Parenting Plans*, 46 Fam. Ct. Rev. 500 (2008).

Preliminary research indicates that families experience different patterns of domestic violence. In cases of *coercive controlling violence* or *classic battering*, the perpetrator (usually male) uses violence to control the victim. Accompanying tactics of control include emotional abuse, psychological abuse, isolation of the victim, economic control, and manipulation of children. The use of controlling tactics escalates over time. In contrast, *conflict-instigated violence* occurs when partners have poor conflict resolution skills and a disagreement leads to a violent incident. Conflict-instigated violence is not part of a larger pattern of control, and it does not usually escalate. It may be initiated by either partner; however, the female partner is more likely to suffer negative consequences. Other potential patterns may include *separation-instigated violence* and *violence resulting from severe mental illness*. Consideration of patterns of domestic violence is useful for generating hypotheses to be investigated, but patterns are not diagnoses and should not be used by lawyers to label individual families. *See* Joan B. Kelly & Michael P. Johnson, *Differentiation Among Types of Intimate Partner Violence: Research Update and Implications for Interventions*, 46 Fam. Ct. Rev. 476 (2008).

Although courts and legislatures have historically viewed domestic violence through a one-size-fits-all lens, important distinctions among families have emerged. Consequently it is important to tailor interventions such as parent education and dispute resolution processes to meet safety and other needs of family members. For some families these services may be dangerous, and they should not participate, but for other families, participation in a modified process may be safe and helpful. In the final analysis the specific needs of each individual family must be taken into account. Nancy Ver Steegh & Clare Dalton, *Report from the* Wingspread *Conference on Domestic Violence and Family Courts*, 46 Fam. Ct. Rev. 454 (2008); Nancy Ver Steegh, *Differentiating Types of Domestic Violence: Implications for Child Custody*, 65 La. L. Rev. 1379 (2005).

19.4. Impact on Children

Children who witness domestic abuse suffer a range of emotional and behavioral consequences. They are sometimes more fearful and inhibited, or they may act more aggressively than other children. Some children exhibit anxiety, depression, and trauma-related symptoms. Of course, the extent of the impact varies depending on the child's overall situation. Jeffrey L. Edleson, *Should Childhood Exposure to Adult Domestic Violence Be Defined as Child Maltreatment Under the Law?*, in Protecting Children From Domestic Violence 8, 10 (Peter G. Jaffe et al. eds., 2004). Approximately half of the children who witness domestic violence are themselves physically abused. *See* Evan Stark & Anne Flitcraft, *Women at Risk* 76 (1996); Lundy Bancroft & Jay G. Silverman, *The Batterer as Parent* 42 (2002) (finding 40-70% concurrent child abuse).

Special care must be taken when creating parenting plans and making child custody and access decisions in cases involving domestic violence. In order to keep children and other family members safe, supervised exchange, supervised access, or suspended contact may be advisable. Peter G. Jaffe, Janet R. Johnston, Claire V. Crooks & Nicholas Bala, *Custody Disputes Involving Allegations of Domestic Violence: Toward a Differentiated Approach to Parenting Plans*, 46 Fam. Ct. Rev. 500 (2008). Perpetrators of coercive-controlling violence frequently threaten, and manipulate children in an effort to control and intimidate the mother. Evan Stark, *Re-Presenting Woman Battering: From Battered Women Syndrome to Coercive Control*, 58 Albany L. Rev. 973, 40 (1995) (describing batterer's extension of coercive tactics to the children as "tangential spouse abuse").

19.5. Screening for Domestic Violence

Victims of domestic violence often downplay or deny the violence. Consequently, lawyers and professionals working with families must be alert for signs of abuse and should implement a screening protocol. Attorneys should use a written questionnaire or screening instrument in addition to asking questions about how the couple resolves conflict and whether a client is fearful. Throughout the proceeding lawyers must also listen carefully for indications of control and intimidation. *See* Margaret Drew, *Lawyer Malpractice and Domestic Violence: Are We Revictimizing Our Clients?*, 39 Fam. L.Q. 7 (2005) (exploring malpractice and ethical mistakes likely to occur when representing clients in cases involving domestic violence).

Family law attorneys routinely assist domestic violence victims with safety planning and make appropriate referrals to community resources. These are key aspects of providing competent representation.

DOMESTIC ABUSE STATUTES

19.6. History

During the 1960s, society became increasingly aware of the frequency and consequences of domestic violence, and more victims of domestic violence sought help. The need for safe shelter became immediately apparent, and volunteers cooperated to create safe homes and eventually to start shelters for victims. Shelter staff soon learned that the existing legal framework was inadequate to protect victims of domestic violence and their children. At a minimum, victims needed a way to remove the perpetrator from the home, establish child custody and support, and keep the perpetrator from contacting them. Even if the violence resulted in criminal prosecution, prospective relief was not readily available. Domestic abuse acts were developed to meet these needs.

Between 1975 and 1980, 45 states passed some type of civil domestic abuse legislation. Currently, every state has a statute granting prospective civil relief to victims of domestic violence.

19.7. Defining Domestic Violence

Although each state's domestic abuse statute defines domestic violence somewhat differently, the definitions usually focus on physical (as opposed to emotional or psychological) abuse. Section 102 of the Model Code on Domestic and Family Violence defines domestic violence in the following way:

> Domestic or family violence means the occurrence of one or more of the following acts by a family or household member, but does not include acts of self defense:
> a. Attempting to cause or causing physical harm to another family or household member;

b. Placing a family or household member in fear of physical harm; or
c. Causing a family or household member to engage involuntarily in sexual activity by force, threat of force, or duress.

Typical acts of violence falling within this definition include pushing, slapping, choking, punching, use of weapons, use of household objects as weapons, and rape. Thus, the definition of domestic violence encompasses a continuum of behavior from verbal threats to homicide.

Example 19-1

P and D decided to divorce. As they were separating, they had a heated argument about who should move out of the marital home. P heard D say that if he couldn't stay in the home, he would burn it down. P seeks an order for protection based on a statute allowing for an order of protection to be issued upon a showing of "actual or imminent domestic violence." D claims that he said that they should sell the house or burn it. The court issues an order for protection on P's behalf, and D appeals. What is the likely result?

Explanation

In a similar case, P obtained an order for protection from the trial court; however, that decision was overturned on appeal. In *Ficklin v. Ficklin*, 710 N.W.2d 387 (N.D. 2006), the court found that there was evidence that P was fearful that D would burn the house; however, the court ruled that the evidence was not sufficient to establish that she was in fear of *imminent* harm. The appellate court noted that the trial court erroneously focused on eliminating the mere possibility of harm.

Example 19-2

Assume P proves that D committed the following acts: (1) he shouted profanities at P, grabbed her hand, and pushed her against a bar; (2) he pushed a car door against P's arm; and (3) he yelled profanities at P's son. P alleges that she and her son are afraid of D. The domestic abuse act in P's state defines domestic and family violence as the occurrence of at least one of the following acts: (a) attempting to cause, threatening to cause, or causing physical harm to another family or household member; (b) placing a family or household member in fear of physical harm; (c) causing a family or household member to involuntarily engage in sexual activity by force, threat or force, or duress. D opposes entry of the order for protection, claiming that

431

P's testimony is insufficient to establish that these events occurred. Is the evidence sufficient to issue an order for protection?

Explanation

In *Aiken v. Stanley*, 816 N.E.2d 427 (Ind. App. 2004), the trial court issued the order for protection, and the court's decision was upheld on appeal. The appellate court found that the evidence outlined previously was sufficient to support issuance of the order for protection under the statute. The court noted that under the language of the statute, it was sufficient for P to show that she and her son were in fear of D. No particular threats or actions were specifically required as long as this showing was made.

Example 19-3

Assume that D attempted to isolate P from visitors, and he destroyed their DSL Internet connection so that P could not communicate with family and friends. He cut off power to their home and attempted to control P's actions through intimidation. P testified that she lives in fear of D and that their child would not be safe if left alone with D in part because D's conduct prevented the child from sleeping at night. D claims that no acts of physical abuse were alleged and that the trial court erred in issuing a protective order.

Explanation

D's behavior shows a pattern of attempting to control, intimidate, and isolate P, and she is consequently afraid for herself and her child. In the similar case of *Cole v. Cole*, 940 A.2d 194 (Me. 2008), the appellate court upheld the issuance of a protective order finding that such behavior fell within the statutory definition of "compelling a person by force, threat of force or intimidation to engage in conduct from which the person has a right or privilege to abstain or to abstain from conduct in which the person has a right to engage." Note that Maine's definition of domestic violence is different from that of most states in that it specifically addresses intimidation and compulsion of someone to abstain from conduct. Although D was clearly in danger, this hypothetical situation would present a closer call under the provisions of the Model Code on Domestic and Family Violence discussed in §19.7 above.

19.8. Who Is Covered?

State domestic abuse acts provide relief to spouses and former spouses of perpetrators. Most statutes extend coverage to children, other family members, household members, and unmarried parents of a common child. Many statutes include same-gender intimate partners and some include dating couples. *See Benjamin v. McKinnon*, 887 N.E.2d 14 (Ill. App. 2008) ("because ex-wife had been married to applicant's son, ex-wife's father and ex-wife's brother were applicant's relatives by collateral affinity" and were family members for purpose of seeking a protective order); *Smith v. Martin*, 2009 WL 2028403 (Ohio App. 2009) (unborn child falls outside statutory definition of "persons entitled to seek relief").

Example 19-4

P files for an order for protection after she is assaulted by her cohabiting boyfriend, D. P and D are not married. The domestic violence statute in their state extends to "a person living as a spouse." The state has amended its constitution to include a Defense of Marriage Amendment (DOMA) stating the following, "Only a union between one man and one woman may be a marriage valid in or recognized by this state and its political subdivisions. This state and its political subdivisions shall not create or recognize a legal status for relationships of unmarried individuals that intends to approximate the design, qualities, significance or effect of marriage." D asserts that applying the domestic violence statute to an unmarried couple violates the state constitution and that P is consequently not entitled to relief under the domestic violence statute. What is the likely result?

Explanation

In *State v. Ward*, 849 N.E.2d 1076 (Ohio App. 2006), the court agreed with D and held that the domestic violence statute provision extending protection to "a person living as a spouse" violated the state DOMA. However, due to a split among the Ohio courts, the Ohio Supreme Court considered the issue in *State v. Carswell*, 871 N.E.2d 547 (Ohio 2007), and held that the domestic violence statute did not conflict with the state DOMA. The court reasoned that the term "person living as a spouse" did not recognize or create a legal relationship but "merely identifies a particular class of persons for the purposes of the domestic-violence statutes."

19.9. What Relief Is Granted?

The workhorse of domestic abuse legislation is an injunctive order, which may be referred to as an order for protection, civil protective order, protective order, or restraining order. The relief available varies by state but typically includes a prohibition against further abuse, a no-contact order, award of exclusive possession of the residence, child custody and visitation arrangements, and/or a support order.

19.10. *Ex Parte* and "Permanent" Orders

Obtaining a protective order is usually a two-step process: first obtaining an *ex parte* order and then seeking a "permanent" order after notice and possibly a hearing. In many cases, the victim needs immediate relief, and giving notice to the perpetrator would subject the victim to additional harm. If the victim can demonstrate a substantial likelihood of abuse or an immediate and present danger of abuse, the victim can seek an *ex parte* order. In some jurisdictions this can be done by affidavit, but in other jurisdictions testimony is required. The relief available in an *ex parte* order is likely to be limited in scope. In many jurisdictions a full hearing is scheduled, and the defendant is served with the *ex parte* order and the hearing date. (If the defendant is served but fails to appear at the hearing, the judge may issue a default order.) In other jurisdictions, after the defendant is served, the defendant can request a hearing. If the defendant does not do so, the *ex parte* order becomes a permanent order. Final or permanent orders typically remain in effect for a year, although some states issue them for shorter or longer periods of time. *See Connolly v. Connolly*, 892 A.2d 465 (Me. 2006) (court required to conduct an evidentiary hearing and make findings); *Wright v. Wright*, 181 S.W.3d 49 (Ky. App. 2005) (court failed to hold evidentiary hearing as required by statute); *Nakamura v. Parker*, 67 Cal. Rptr. 3d 286 (Cal. App. 2007) (abuse of discretion to deny "facially adequate" application for temporary restraining order without a hearing).

Example 19-5

Assume that P lives in a jurisdiction that authorizes temporary (*ex parte*) and permanent orders for protection. In order to obtain a temporary order for protection under the statute P would be required to show "imminent danger." The statute authorizes issuance of a permanent order "If . . . the judge or magistrate is of the opinion that [a spouse] has committed acts constituting grounds for issuance of a civil protection order and that unless restrained will continue to commit such acts, the judge or magistrate shall order the temporary civil protection order to be made permanent or order a permanent civil protection order with different provisions from the temporary civil protection order." P seeks a permanent order, and after notice is given to D and a hearing is held, the court issues a permanent order without making a finding of imminent danger. D alleges that a finding of imminent danger was necessary, and D appeals on that basis. Will D succeed on appeal?

Explanation

In a similar case, the court held that although a showing of imminent danger was required to obtain a temporary order, it was not statutorily required for issuance of a permanent order. The court reasoned that temporary orders are issued under urgent circumstances and often without notice to the respondent, whereas permanent orders are designed to prevent future harm. *In re Marriage of Fiffe*, 140 P.3d 160 (Colo. App. 2005).

Example 19-6

P and D reside in Illinois. Due to domestic violence, P leaves Illinois to stay with family members in New Jersey. She obtains an *ex parte* temporary restraining order against D from a New Jersey court. D has never been to New Jersey, and D claims that the New Jersey court lacked personal jurisdiction over him. What is the likely result?

Explanation

In the similar case of *Shah v. Shah*, 875 A.2d 931 (N.J. 2005), the court held that it did not have personal jurisdiction over the defendant and that it consequently could not issue a final restraining order requiring the defendant to perform affirmative acts. However, the court determined that a temporary restraining order issued by the New Jersey court was valid to the extent that it provided prohibitory relief. In addition, the court ruled that the temporary restraining order could remain in effect indefinitely.

19.11. Due Process Constitutional Challenges

Respondents have challenged state domestic abuse acts, alleging that issuance of *ex parte* orders of protection violate their due process rights. However, these challenges have not been successful. *See State ex rel. Williams v. Marsh*, 626 S.W.2d 223 (Mo. 1982); *Baker v. Baker*, 494 N.W.2d 282 (Minn. 1992). In analyzing constitutional claims, courts have used the balancing test set forth in *Mathews v. Eldridge*, 424 U.S. 319 (1976). Although the defendant has a property interest in the home and a liberty interest in the children, the government has a strong interest in preventing future violence. Furthermore, procedural safeguards exist, including requiring affidavits, taking testimony, having a judge or referee make the decision, giving notice of rights, and holding an immediate hearing. *See also Crespo v. Crespo*, 972 A.2d 1169 (N.J. Super. 2009) (domestic violence act prohibition on possession of firearms did not violate Second Amendment); *Towner v. Ridgway*, 182 P.3d 347 (Utah 2008) (stalking injunction did not violate First Amendment rights).

Example 19-7

Assume that P and D have been married for five years. D is at work one day when he is served with an *ex parte* order of protection granting P exclusive possession of the residence, prohibiting D from contacting P, and barring D from seeing their children until after a hearing scheduled ten days later. In the petition, P accuses D of several acts of violence, which D denies, and P alleges that D has threatened to "kidnap" the children if P moves out of the marital home. D is outraged that he cannot go home, cannot see his children, and that all of this can happen to him without his having a chance to tell his side of the story. He contacts an attorney for advice. Have D's due process rights been violated?

Explanation

D's due process rights have not been violated. Although state action is involved and D clearly has a liberty interest in seeing the children and a property interest in the residence, this private interest is outweighed by the state's interest in preventing further abuse and possible parental kidnapping. D is protected by the requirement that P is required to file a verified affidavit and appear before a judge who assessed P's credibility and most likely took testimony on the record. The deprivation is temporary because D has received notice and will have a full hearing shortly.

Example 19-8

Assume that D assaults P, and P files for an order for protection. Under the state domestic abuse statute, before an order is issued, the court is required to make findings in an official record or in writing. In emergency situations, the court is required to examine the petitioner under oath and review a verified petition for relief. In this case, the court issued an order for protection but did not make findings or a record of testimony. D petitions to have the order overturned, arguing that significant provisions of the domestic abuse act were not followed. P argues that these were mere technicalities. What is the likely result?

Explanation

D is likely to have the order of protection overturned because D did not receive important procedural protections. In a similar case, *Hedrick-Korcll v. Bagley*, 816 N.E.2d 849 (Ill. App. 2004), the appellate court held that the trial court failed to comply with the Domestic Violence Act requirement of specific findings. The case was remanded for further proceedings.

19.12. Access to the Court Issues

A victim of domestic violence who is not represented by counsel may have difficulty procuring a protective order and obtaining other necessary relief. Some statutes require clerks of court to assist unrepresented victims seeking to file petitions. Domestic violence advocates also provide information and support, and in some jurisdictions their communications with the victim are privileged. *See People v. Turner*, 109 P.3d 639 (Colo. 2005). Nevertheless, legal representation for victims is a serious and ongoing problem. In an effort to make protection more readily available, a few courts provide for issuance of emergency orders outside of business hours. *See* Beverly Balos, *Domestic Violence Matters: The Case for Appointed Counsel in Protective Order Proceedings*, 15 Temple Pol. & Civ. Rts. L. Rev. 557 (2006).

19.13. Issuance of Mutual Orders

Either in settlement or at hearing, a respondent may request that an order for protection be issued against the victim as well as the defendant. This practice is known as issuing mutual or cross orders of protection. In *Deacon v. Landers*, 587 N.E.2d 395 (Ohio Ct. App. 1990), the trial court granted mutual orders over the objection of the victim and without any presentation of evidence showing that she had been violent. The appellate court overruled the trial court and held that issuance of mutual orders violated the victim's right to due process. *See Cooper v. Cooper*, 144 P.3d 451 (Alaska 2006) (no independent basis for issuance of mutual order).

Unless clearly warranted by the evidence, issuance of mutual orders of protection can be dangerous. Such orders empower the perpetrator, put the victim and children at additional risk, and confuse police, who are trying to enforce the orders.

Example 19-9

P and D cohabited for a period of years but did not marry. During this time, D committed several severe acts of domestic violence against P, and D was imprisoned three times for these assaults. P sought a restraining order against D, and D appeared at the hearing where P was granted a three-year restraining order. About a week later, D filed a separate action for a domestic violence temporary restraining order against P alleging that P harassed him while he was in prison by sending him letters, and that P later threatened to report him for stealing her ATM card. The court issued a temporary restraining order against P. The state where P and D reside has a statute stating that the court may not issue mutual restraining orders unless both parties personally appear in court to present evidence of abuse and the court makes detailed findings that both acted as primary aggressors and not in self-defense. P claims that mutual orders have been issued in violation of the statute. D claims that the requirements of the statute have been met because, with respect to both orders, the petitioner appeared personally and the court made detailed findings. Does this situation describe mutual orders within the meaning of the statute?

Explanation

In the similar case of *Conness v. Satram*, 18 Cal. Rptr. 3d 577 (Cal. App. 2004), the appellate court found that the term "mutual order" meant a single order imposing parallel requirements on each party. The orders issued against P and D were deemed to be separate orders that included findings of credibility by the trial court. Consequently, according to the appellate court, the orders were not "mutual" under the state statute, and both orders could remain in effect.

19.14. Enforcement of Orders

Most domestic abuse statutes make violation of a protective order a criminal offense, typically a misdemeanor, although some violations may be charged as a felony in some states. Despite such provisions, the Supreme Court has held that a domestic abuse victim who has obtained a restraining order does not have a constitutionally protected property interest in police enforcement of the order, even where there is probable cause to believe that the order was violated. *Town of Castle Rock, Colo. v. Gonzales*, 125 S. Ct. 2796 (2005).

In addition to being a criminal offense, violation of a protective order may constitute criminal contempt. Although both types of proceedings are useful, some commentators favor criminal contempt proceedings because victims have more control over the process, and contempt actions may proceed more quickly than criminal prosecutions. *See* David M. Zlotnick, *Empowering the Battered Woman: The Use of Criminal Contempt Sanctions to Enforce Civil Protection Orders*, 56 Ohio St. L.J. 1153 (1995).

Special enforcement issues can arise if the parties decide to reconcile but do not petition the court to dissolve an existing protective order. For example, in *Cole v. Cole*, 556 N.Y.S.2d 217 (Fam. Ct. 1990), the couple reconciled after issuance of a protective order and then separated again. Subsequent to the separation, the husband broke into the residence, choked the wife, and threatened to kill her. The police refused to enforce the order because of the intervening reconciliation. The court ultimately found that the order remained in effect and held the husband in contempt of court. In so doing, the court noted that the husband could have returned to court to vacate the order and that reconciliation did not license the husband to commit further abuse. *See Com. v. Brumbaugh*, 932 A.2d 108 (Pa. Super. 2007) (defendant held in contempt for violation of protective order even though the victim invited him to attend party).

Example 19-10

P and D had a history of domestic violence. After 20 years of marriage, P initiated divorce proceedings against D and obtained a no-contact order. Six months later, after another incident, D pleaded *nolo contendere* to charges of domestic disorderly conduct and violation of the no-contact order. D's probation officer met with him to explain the terms of the order, but shortly after the meeting D mailed two birthday cards to P. P claimed that D violated the no-contact order by sending the cards, but D claimed that the no-contact order did not specifically prohibit mailings. Did D violate the no-contact order?

Explanation

In the similar case of *State v. John*, 881 A.2d 920 (R.I. 2005), the court held that the order was reasonably clear and specific in restraining D from "any contact" with P. "Any contact" included sending mail to P. Consequently, D was in violation of the order. Although such a violation may sound trivial, coercive-controlling perpetrators commonly test the victim's resolve to enforce the protective order once it is obtained. Additionally, if there is a history of coercive control over the victim, gestures that seem innocent to an onlooker may actually have a threatening hidden meaning. *But see State v. Price*, 886 N.E.2d 852 (Ohio 2008) (court found implied exception to no-contact order to arrange visitation).

19.15. Effectiveness of Orders

Victims frequently report that protective orders have been helpful and empowering. However, researchers are still investigating how and when protective orders are most effective in preventing further abuse. For example, one study found that 60 percent of temporary orders of protection were violated within a year. Victims who had been more seriously abused suffered more serious violations, and abusers who objected to entry of the order were more likely to violate it. Adele Harrell & Barbara E. Smith, *Effects of Restraining Orders on Domestic Violence Victims*, in *Do Arrests and Restraining Orders Work?* (Buzawa & Buzawa eds., 1996). Protective orders may be less effective if the abuser has a past criminal history, the couple has minor children, and/or they have low incomes. *See* Eve S. Buzawa & Carl G. Buzawa, *Domestic Violence: The Criminal Justice Response* 242-245 (2003).

The decision about whether to obtain an order for protection must be made on a case-by-case basis. Victims should be counseled concerning the availability of relief and the costs and benefits of seeking an order in light of the victim's particular circumstances. Victims should be aware that jurisdictions vary in terms of the difficulty of obtaining an order and how seriously violations are viewed by police, prosecutors, and judges.

Example 19-11

Assume that P and D were married and that D was violent with P throughout the marriage. Most recently, D broke P's nose and threatened to kill her and take the children if she left him. P does not work outside the home and does not have relatives in the area. What factors should P be counseled about in deciding whether to obtain an order of protection?

Explanation

With respect to obtaining a protective order, P should be carefully counseled about the possibility that D might violate the order. P would probably have an accurate assessment of D's reaction to entry of the *ex parte* order — some respondents comply with orders and others become more violent. Also, some police departments respond more quickly, and some jurisdictions prosecute violations more vigorously than others. P's safety is more important than staying in the house. Consequently, P should seriously consider making a temporary move to a shelter or having someone stay at the house with P and the children. In any event, P and the children should have a detailed safety plan.

RELATED AREAS OF LAW

19.16. Violence Against Women Act

The federal Violence Against Women Act (VAWA) was originally passed in 1994 and was reauthorized in 2000 and 2005. Among other provisions, the Act requires states to enforce protective orders from different states so long as the issuing court had jurisdiction and provided due process. In cases in which mutual orders of protection were issued, only the order issued on behalf of the petitioner is enforceable unless the respondent filed a counter-petition and the court made specific findings. 18 U.S.C. §2265 (2003). *See* Emily J. Sack, *Domestic Violence Across State Lines: The Full Faith and Credit Clause, Congressional Power, and Interstate Enforcement of Protection Orders,* 98 N.W. U. L. Rev. 827 (2004). The VAWA also includes criminal penalties for crossing state lines to injure an intimate partner or violate a protective order, and the Act criminalizes possession of a firearm by respondents subject to protective orders. *See* 18 U.S.C. §§922(g)(8)(9); Lisa D. May, *The Backfiring of the Domestic Violence Firearms Bans,* 14 Colum. J. Gender & L. 1 (2005).

Example 19-12

Assume that after a full hearing, an order for protection is issued against D in the state of X. D continues to contact P in spite of a "no contact" provision in the order. P no longer feels safe at the residence, so P goes to stay with a friend who lives an hour away in state Y. D tracks P down and goes to the house where P is staying with the friend. P calls the police when D arrives. Can the police in state Y enforce the order?

Explanation

Prior to passage of the VAWA, only a few states recognized protective orders from other states. However, the VAWA requires states to give full faith and credit to protective orders issued by other states so long as due process was provided. Consequently, the police and the courts in state Y can enforce the order originally issued in state X.

19.17. Criminal Sanctions

Violence between intimate partners involves commission of crimes such as assault, battery, rape, and attempted murder. Police historically were trained not to arrest abusive partners, and domestic violence was, for the most part, not treated as a crime by prosecutors. This practice changed dramatically during the 1980s due to increased awareness of the issue, studies documenting the value of arrest as a deterrent, and lawsuits against police departments.

Arrest and criminal sanctions remain an important tool for victims of abuse — especially where police, prosecutors, and courts coordinate enforcement efforts. However, research indicates that arrest is less effective with some defendants than others. Eve S. Buzawa & Carl G. Buzawa, *Domestic Violence: The Criminal Justice Response* 104 (2003) (an excellent discussion of the history and effectiveness of arrest in cases of domestic violence). For example, arrest may not be as effective with unemployed defendants and may reduce violence only in the short run. Janell D. Schmidt & Lawrence W. Sherman, *Does Arrest Deter Domestic Violence?* in *Do Arrests and Restraining Orders Work?* (Buzawa & Buzawa eds., 1996). Clearly, more research is needed in this area.

19.18. Mandatory Arrest and No-Drop Policies

Some jurisdictions have adopted mandatory arrest (with probable cause) and/or no-drop policies so that the decision to press criminal charges is taken out of the hands of the victim. Such policies are designed to protect traumatized victims from pressure to drop charges by having the police and prosecutor bring the charges and subpoena the victim as a witness. Critics of these policies argue that they ignore the preferences of the victims and further disempower them. *See* David Hirschel, Eve Buzawa, April Pattavine & Don Faggiani, *Domestic Violence and Mandatory Arrest Laws: To What Extent Do They Influence Police Arrest Decisions*, 98 J. Crim. L. & Criminology 255 (2007) (preferred arrest policies increase arrest rates).

19.19. Confrontation Clause

Particularly if a victim does not testify at trial, prosecutors may seek to introduce statements made to police and medical personnel. However, under the Sixth Amendment, perpetrators facing criminal prosecution have the right to confront witnesses, and testimonial out-of-court statements cannot be admitted into evidence unless the witness is unavailable and the defendant had a prior opportunity to cross-examine. *Crawford v. Washington*, 541 U.S. 36 (2004). Recently, the United States Supreme

Court held that a domestic abuse victim's statements to a 911 operator were not subject to the Confrontation Clause because they were not testimonial in nature. In contrast, a victim's written statements in an affidavit provided to police were testimonial and thus subject to the Confrontation Clause. *Davis v. Washington*, 126 S. Ct. 2266 (2006). *See* John M. Leventhal, *The Admission of Evidence in Domestic Violence Cases After Crawford v. Washington: A National Survey*, 11 Berkeley J. Crim. L. 77 (2006) (courts continue to admit victims' out-of-court statements).

19.20. Tort Actions

In recent years, creative advocates have brought various tort actions on behalf of battered spouses. Such actions can be based on torts such as assault and battery, wrongful death, false imprisonment, defamation, wiretapping, and intentional infliction of emotional distress. *See* Clare Dalton, *Domestic Violence, Domestic Torts and Divorce: Constraints and Possibilities*, 31 New Eng. L. Rev. 319 (1997).

For example, in *Feltmeier v. Feltmeier*, 777 N.E.2d 1032 (Ill. Ct. App. 2002), aff'd, 798 N.E.2d 75 (Ill. 2003), the court upheld an action for intentional infliction of emotional distress based upon a finding of "extreme and outrageous" conduct. The husband unsuccessfully argued that a "reasonable wife" should have been able to endure 11 years of abuse. *See also Curtis v. Firth*, 850 P.2d 749 (Idaho 1993) (upholding damage award for intentional infliction of emotional distress); *Xiao Yang Chen v. Fischer*, 843 N.E.2d 723 (N.Y. 2005) (personal injury action for damages for physical and emotional abuse during marriage not barred by *res judicata*). *But see Hakkila v. Hakkila*, 812 P.2d 1320 (N.M. Ct. App. 1991) (husband's conduct did not meet "outrageousness" standard); *Pugliese v. Superior Court*, 53 Cal. Rptr. 3d 681 (Cal. App. 2007) (application of continuing tort doctrine in suit for damages for acts of domestic violence).

Neglect, Dependency, Child Abuse, and Termination of Parental Rights

20.1. Introduction — The Scope of the Problem

In the year 2007, 794,000 children were victims of some type of child maltreatment. Most (59%) suffered neglect, 10.8 percent were abused physically, 7.6 percent were abused sexually, 4.2 percent were abused psychologically, and less than 1 percent were medically neglected. Over 1,500 children died as a result of the abuse, and 75.7 percent of the children who were killed were younger than four years of age. U.S. Dept. of Health and Human Services, Administration for Children and Families, *Child Maltreatment 2007, http://www.acf.hhs.gov/programs/cb/pubs/cm07/index.htm* (last visited August 13, 2009).

State intervention into the family unit has historically focused on strengthening and reuniting the family unit. In cases of substantiated child abuse and neglect, the state child protection agency may have worked with the family, sometimes for years, with the goal of returning the child to the home. This approach was questioned in the 1990s as experts expressed concern that some children who might be made available for adoption were instead stranded in foster care without any realistic hope of reunification. Thus, in recent years, an emphasis has been placed on earlier termination of parental rights in order to free children in foster care for adoption.

As of 2006, 510,000 children were in foster care, and the average age of a child in foster care was 9.8 years old. Twenty-four percent were placed in the home of a relative, but others lived in placements including non-relative foster family homes (46%), institutions (10%), and group homes (7%). The mean length of stay in foster care was 28.3 months. In about half the

445

cases (49%) reunification was the stated case goal, and of children exiting foster care in 2006, 53 percent were reunited with their parent or primary caretaker. Adoption and Foster Care Analysis Reporting System (AFCARS) U.S. Department of Health and Human Services, Administration for Children and Families, Administration on Children, Youth and Families, Children's Bureau, *http://www.acf.hhs.gov/programs/cb/stats_research/afcars/tar/report14.htm* (last visited August 13, 2009).

STANDARDS FOR STATE INTERVENTION

20.2. Parents' Right to Privacy — Liberty Interests

The raising and disciplining of children has long been considered a private family matter, and this liberty interest has historically been given constitutional protection. *Meyer v. Nebraska*, 262 U.S. 390 (1923); *Pierce v. Soc'y of Sisters*, 268 U.S. 510 (1925); *Troxel v. Granville*, 530 U.S. 57 (2000). However, parents' prerogatives are not without limits. As the Supreme Court stated in *Prince v. Massachusetts*, 321 U.S. 158, 166 (1944),

> And neither rights of religion nor rights of parenthood are beyond limitation. Acting to guard the general interest in youth's well being, the state as *parens patriae* may restrict the parent's control by requiring school attendance, regulating or prohibiting the child's labor, and in many other ways.

Consequently, if there is compelling justification, such as when a child is "at risk of harm," the state may intervene in the family. *In re Juvenile Appeal (83-CD)*, 455 A.2d 1319 (Conn. 1983). However, statutes prescribing when intervention may occur may not be vague or overly broad. *Roe v. Conn*, 417 F. Supp. 769, 778 (D.C. Ala. 1976) (standard that "the child is in such condition that its welfare requires" is unconstitutionally vague and infringes on fundamental right); Scott A. Davidson, *When Is Parental Discipline Child Abuse? The Vagueness of Child Abuse Laws*, 34 U. Louisville J. Fam. L. 403, 409 (1996).

20.3. Indian Child Welfare Act (ICWA)

Special protections are provided for Native American children under the Indian Child Welfare Act (ICWA). The Act requires clear and convincing evidence of serious emotional or physical damage before a child is removed from the home. 25 U.S.C. §1912(e). In addition, absent good cause to the contrary, if an Indian child is removed from the home, the Act requires that the child be placed in foster care with an extended family, in a foster home approved by the tribe or a licensing authority, or in an institution approved of or operated by an Indian organization. 25 U.S.C. §1915(b).

20.4. Defining Abuse, Neglect, and Dependency

State statutes define the circumstances under which it will intervene in the family. States historically have separately defined abuse, neglect, and dependency. Abuse typically involves excessive corporal punishment, sexual abuse, or serious psychological abuse. Neglect is associated with failure to provide food or housing, or to meet medical or educational needs. Dependency is similar to neglect except that the lack of care occurs due to circumstances beyond the parent's control and without fault on the part of the parent.

Some states do not distinguish among abuse, neglect, and dependency but instead use a definition that includes all three. For example, as shown immediately below, the relevant California statute merges neglect and abuse into the definition of dependent child.

Cal. Welf. & Inst. Code §300 (West 2009). Children Subject to Jurisdiction . . .

Any child who comes within any of the following descriptions is within the jurisdiction of the juvenile court which may adjudge that person to be a dependent child of the court.

a. The child has suffered, or there is a substantial risk that the child will suffer, serious physical harm inflicted nonaccidentally upon the child by the child's parent or guardian. . . .

b. The child has suffered, or there is a substantial risk that the child will suffer, serious physical harm or illness, as a result of the failure or inability of his or her parent or guardian to adequately supervise or protect the child, or the willful or negligent failure of the child's parent or guardian to adequately supervise or protect the child from the conduct of the custodian with whom the child has been left, or by the willful or negligent failure of the parent or guardian to provide the child with adequate food, clothing, shelter, or medical treatment, or by the inability of the parent or guardian to provide regular care for the child due to the parent's or guardian's mental illness, developmental disability, or substance abuse. . . .

c. The child is suffering serious emotional damage, or is at substantial risk of suffering serious emotional damage, evidenced by severe anxiety, depression, withdrawal, or untoward aggressive behavior toward self or others, as a result of the conduct of the parent or guardian or who has no parent or guardian capable of providing appropriate care. . . .

d. The child has been sexually abused or there is substantial risk that the child will be sexually abused. . . .

e. The child is under the age of five and has suffered severe physical abuse by a parent, or by any person known by the parent, if the parent knew or reasonably should have known that the person was physically abusing the child. . . .

f. The child's parent or guardian caused the death of another child through abuse or neglect.

g. * * *

h. * * *

i. The child has been subjected to an act or acts of cruelty by the parent or guardian or a member of his or her household or the parent or guardian has failed to adequately protect the child from an act or acts of cruelty when the parent or guardian knew or reasonably should have known that the child was in danger of being subjected to an act or acts of cruelty.

j. The child's sibling has been abused or neglected. . . .

The following sections discuss how courts have interpreted and applied similar statutory provisions.

POSSIBLE FORMS OF ABUSE AND NEGLECT

20.5. Use of Unreasonable Force to Correct a Child

Parents can legally use reasonable force to correct a child. *See, e.g.,* MCL 750.135b(7) (parent or guardian, or other person permitted by law or authorized by the parent or guardian may take steps to reasonably discipline a child, including the use of reasonable force); *South Carolina Dept. of Soc. Servs. v. Father and Mother,* 366 S.E.2d 40, 42 (S.C. Ct. App. 1988) (force or violence of discipline must be "reasonable in manner and moderate in degree"); *State v. Lefevre,* 117 P.3d 980 (N.M. App. 2005) (discipline involves controlling behavior and correcting misbehavior for the betterment and welfare of the child, and physical force cannot be cruel or excessive if it is to be justified).

The Restatement (Second) of Torts §147 provides that "[a] parent is privileged to apply such reasonable force or to impose such reasonable confinement upon his child as he reasonably believes to be necessary for its proper control, training, or education. . . ." Section 150 lists factors to be considered in determining whether the action was reasonable:

a. whether the actor is a parent;

b. the age, sex, and physical and mental condition of the child;

    c. the nature of his offense and his apparent motive;

    d. the influence of his example upon other children of the same family or group;

    e. whether the force or confinement is reasonably necessary and appropriate to compel obedience to a proper command;

    f. whether it is disproportionate to the offense, unnecessarily degrading, or likely to cause serious or permanent harm.

20.6. Spanking

Spanking children is a matter of some controversy, and judges may be called upon to distinguish reasonable use of force from that which is excessive. For example, in *Raboin v. North Dakota Dept. of Human Servs*, 552 N.W.2d 329 (N.D. 1996), the court held that bruising on the buttocks resulting from the use of a wooden spoon, plastic spoon, or belt did not constitute child abuse. However, the concurring judge frowned upon the use of corporal punishment, stating that it "can only diminish a child's sense of self-worth, and thereby unnecessarily limit the resources that child can bring to life's battles." *Id.* at 335. *See generally In re J.L.*, 891 N.E.2d 778 Ohio App. 2008) (social worker testified that "developmentally, young children only understand that spanking means it's okay to hurt others").

However, in *State v. Denzel B.*, 192 P.3d 260 (N.M. App. 2008), the court stated that punishing a 16-year-old boy by beating him with a belt is not a reasonable use of force. It went on to say that where force is excessive or abusive, a child has a right to self-defense. *See State v. Lefevre*, 117 P.3d 980 (N.M. App. 2005). Similarly, the Georgia Supreme Court in *In re N.S.E.*, 666 S.E.2d 587 (Ga. App. 2008), upheld a trial court's ruling terminating a father's rights to his three children where he had disciplined them by spanking them with objects or slapping them, which resulted in bruises and marks on their bodies. He testified he was in charge of discipline and claimed that his mode of discipline was required by his religious beliefs. He asserted that "(a)ny sound spanking will leave a mark." He admitted that he began spanking one of the children at least one month prior to the child's death; that he had previously broken the child's femur due to slapping him; and that on the day the child was taken to the hospital, he had spanked and slapped the child, who he believed had exhibited "stubbornness."

Sweden, Norway, Denmark, Finland, and Austria have prohibited corporal punishment, and opponents of the practice have urged the United States to ratify the United Nations Convention on the Rights of the Child, which would prohibit its use. *See also* Alastair Nicholson, *Choose to Hug, Not Hit*, 46 Fam. Ct. Rev. 11 (2008); Benjamin Shmueli, *Who's Afraid of Banning Corporal Punishment? A Comparative View on Current and Desirable Models*, 26 Penn St. Int'l L. Rev. 57 (2007).

Example 20-1

Assume that a 13-year-old girl, X, comes home at 2:00 A.M. from a party even though she promised to be home by 11:00 P.M. Her father, D, is angry and frightened by X's failure to return home on time or call. He strikes the girl twice with his belt, leaving two large purple bruises, one on her thigh and the other on the back of her leg. D claims that X bruises easily and that he didn't use excessive force. X reports that D also struck her in the face with his hand, causing her ears to ring for the next 24 hours. D denies hitting X in the face and argues that X had no bruises on her face and no witnesses to support her claim. Assume that the jurisdiction has a civil dependency statute identical to the statute presented in Section 21.4 above. Is it likely that a court would declare X to be dependent?

Explanation

The state child protection agency will argue that X falls under paragraph (a) of the dependency statute because X has suffered serious physical harm inflicted nonaccidentally by her parent. D will argue that the bruises on X's thigh and leg do not constitute serious physical harm because X has no broken bones and no permanent disfigurement and that there is no evidence of a substantial risk that future serious harm will occur. Given that D struck X with a belt with enough force to leave physical marks, a court would likely rule that X is dependent under the statute. However, without more, the court will probably require that D participate in a parenting class or go to counseling rather than placing X in foster care. *See South Carolina Dept. of Soc. Servs. v. Father and Mother*, 366 S.E.2d 40 (S.C. Ct. App. 1988).

20.7. Sexual Abuse

Girls are three times more likely to be sexually abused than boys, and children from families with incomes below $15,000 per year are as much as 18 times more likely to be sexually abused. However, half of sexually abused children are abused by someone other than a parent or parent-substitute. U.S. Dept. of Health & Human Services, Administration for Children and Families, *Executive Summary of the Third National Incidence Study of Child Abuse and Neglect* (1996), http://www.healthieryou.com/cabuse.html (last visited August 13, 2009).

In *State v. J.Q.*, 617 A.2d 1196 (N.J. 1993), the court discussed behavioral indications of possible sexual abuse, known as the Child Sexual Abuse Accommodation Syndrome (CSAAS). These behaviors include overt or indirect disclosures, sexualized play, withdrawal, feelings of shame and guilt, falling grades, pseudo-mature personality development, sexual promiscuity, problems with peer relationships, attempted suicide, exhibiting positive relationship with the abuser, and being frightened or phobic.

Proving sexual abuse can be especially difficult because sexual abuse is rarely observed by a third party. Expert testimony is often required. *See State v. Waddell*, 504 S.E.2d 84 (N.C. Ct. App. 1998), *aff'd as modified*, 527 S.E.2d 644 (N.C. 2000) (discussion of issues related to child competency, hearsay, and use of anatomically correct dolls); *In re Jaclyn P.*, 179 A.D.2d 646 (N.Y. 1992), *aff'd*, 658 N.E.2d 1042 (N.Y. Ct. App. 1995). In cases of sexual abuse, some states specifically authorize the use of anatomically correct dolls to aid courtroom testimony. 42 Pa. C.S.A. §5987 (2009).

20.8. Failure to Protect from Harm

In addition to not harming children, parents have a legal obligation to protect children from known or reasonably anticipated danger. Thus a parent who fails to intercede to protect a child may be the focus of scrutiny by the child protection agency even though he or she did not affirmatively harm the child. For example, in *People v. T.G.*, 578 N.W.2d 921 (S.D. 1998), a mother knew that the stepfather was sexually molesting her daughters but ignored and concealed the abuse. Sadly, the mother herself had been "sold" to adoptive parents and sexually abused as a child. Nevertheless, her parental rights were terminated because of her failure to protect her daughters.

Example 20-2

Assume the same facts as in Example 20-1 except that M, X's mother, was present during the incident. M was extremely alarmed when X did not return home on time, and she began calling hospital emergency rooms, fearing that X had been in an accident. M feared that she was losing control of X, and she asked D, the father, to "lay down the law" to X. M saw D strike X multiple times with the belt and saw D hit X in the face. M told the child protection worker that D's use of force was appropriate and justified in order to "get X's attention." Assume that the statute found in Section 20.4 is in effect in this jurisdiction. Is M also likely to be the subject of the child protection investigation?

Explanation

The child protection agency could argue that M falls within paragraph (i) of the dependency statute under the theory that M witnessed X being subjected to acts of cruelty by D and that M failed to adequately protect X. M will argue that D acted reasonably to discipline X and that X was not subjected to acts of cruelty under the statute. Furthermore, no other incidents of abuse are alleged. In many cases where failure to protect is alleged, there is an ongoing pattern of abuse such as sexual abuse. However, under the terms of the statute, failure to protect can be shown based on one incident. In a case somewhat similar to this hypothetical, the court found that M was guilty of neglect because she did not intervene or report the incident. *South Carolina Dept. of Soc. Servs. v. Father and Mother*, 366 S.E.2d 40 (S.C. Ct. App. 1988). *See also In re Craig T.*, 744 A.2d 621 (N.H. 1999) (mother did not intervene to protect young child who was hit and shaken by father at shopping mall).

20.9. Failure to Protect from Harm: Domestic Violence

Removal of children for failure to protect has been especially controversial in cases of domestic violence. As noted in Chapter 19, there are many reasons why a victim of domestic violence may remain in the home, including the fact that the abuser may threaten to kill the victim or kidnap the children if the victim attempts to leave. Nevertheless, children growing up in violent homes suffer harm from witnessing abuse, and they may also be physically abused themselves. Consequently, if the victim does not leave the home, her children may be removed by the state on the basis that she failed to protect them. However, in a lawsuit regarding a New York policy, *Nicholson v. Scoppetta*, 820 N.E.2d 840 (Ct. App. N.Y. 2004), the court held that evidence that a caretaker allowed a child to witness domestic abuse was insufficient on its own to establish neglect. *See* Justine A. Dunlap, *Sometimes I Feel Like a Motherless Child: The Error of Pursuing Battered Mothers for Failure to Protect*, 50 Loy. L. Rev. 565 (2004); Beth A. Mandel, *The White Fist of the Child Welfare System: Racism, Patriarchy, and the Presumptive Removal of Children from Victims of Domestic Violence in Nicholson v. Williams*, 73 U. Cin. L. Rev. 1131 (2005); and Evan Stark, *A Failure to Protect: Unraveling the "Battered Mother's Dilemma,"* 27 W. St. U. L. Rev. 29 (1999-2000).

20.10. Prenatal Drug Abuse

Drug and alcohol use are frequently linked to child abuse and neglect. Many children are exposed to drugs and alcohol prior to birth. As a result, these children are likely to have special needs and be particularly difficult to parent. Unfortunately, a parent's ability to cope is likely to be severely compromised by continued substance abuse. Because this is a dangerous combination of dynamics, child protection workers frequently try to intervene in such cases. *See* Elizabeth Bartholet, *Nobody's Children* 68-69 (1999). However, intervention may be limited by the fact that some state courts hold that a fetus is not a "child" within the meaning of child protection statutes. *State ex rel. Angela M.W. v. Kruzicki*, 561 N.W.2d 729 (Wis. 1997). Policy makers also fear that criminal prosecution of substance-abusing mothers would discourage these women from seeking prenatal care and consequently bring more harm than benefit to unborn children. *Johnson v. State*, 602 So. 2d 1288 (Fla. 1992). *See also State of N.M. ex rel. CYFD v. Amanda H.*, 154 P.3d 674 (N.M. App. 2006) (no finding of neglect based on first trimester drug use because child was born healthy and without signs of exposure to drugs).

In contrast, other state courts have held that the term *child* includes a viable fetus and that a mother can be criminally liable for the death of a stillborn child related to drug use. *State v. McKnight*, 576 S.E.2d 168 (S.C. 2003). In addition, some state statutes include prenatal substance abuse in the definition of neglect. For example, Minn. Stat. §626.556(2)(f)(6) (2006) defines neglect to include prenatal exposure to a controlled substance as evidenced by withdrawal symptoms, toxicological testing, medical effects, or developmental delays during the first year of life. *See also* M. Suzanne Kerney-Quillen, *Fetal Abuse: The Societal Impact of Drug-Exposed Infants and the State's Interest in Preventing Child Abuse and Neglect by Expectant Mothers*, 3 Appalachian J.L. 81 (2004); Ellen M. Weber, *Child Welfare Interventions for Drug-Dependent Pregnant Women: Limitations of a Non-Public Health Response*, 75 UMKC L. Rev. 789 (2006).

In Illinois, mothers who give birth to babies with a controlled substance or metabolite thereof in their blood, urine, or meconium are presumed unfit without regard to the likelihood that the child will be placed for adoption. Ian Vandewalker, *Taking The Baby Before It's Born: Termination of the Parental Rights of Women Who Use Illegal Drugs While Pregnant*, 32 N.Y.U. Rev. L. & Soc. Change 423, 426 (2008). If another child of the mother has been adjudicated as neglected based on "positive toxicology" at birth, the presumption is not rebuttable. In Florida, the "use by the mother of a controlled substance or alcohol during pregnancy when the child, at birth, is demonstrably adversely affected by such usage" is "harm" and therefore constitutes child abuse if done willfully. *Id.* In Ohio, when a newborn child's toxicology screen yields a positive result for illegal drug due to prenatal maternal drug abuse, the newborn is, for the purposes of Ohio law, *per se* an abused child. R.C. 2151.031(D); *In re Baby Boy Blackshear*, 736 N.E.2d 462 (Ohio 2000).

Example 20-3

Assume that a 12-year-old boy resides with his mother and father. He was awake in his bedroom when law enforcement officers executed a search warrant based on the alleged drug use of his parents. The officers found one gram of marijuana in a trash can and another gram loose on a coffee table. They uncovered residual amounts of cocaine in the kitchen and other drugs in the parents' bedroom. The police called child protection, and the trial court found that the child was abused, neglected, and at imminent risk of being abused and neglected. The parents argued that there was no evidence presented that the child had come in contact with the drugs or paraphernalia and there was similarly no evidence that the child was denied food, clothing, or medical care. They appealed the decision. What is the likely outcome?

Explanation

In this case the appellate court reasoned that exposing a child to controlled substances is harmful if it occurs during the mother's pregnancy or when chronic drug use by a parent "demonstrably adversely" affects the child. The appellate court found that there was no evidence presented to support either assertion in this case. The court further reasoned that the child was not neglected because he was not deprived of food, clothing, shelter, etc. as defined under the statute. Finally the court found that the child was not in imminent danger of abuse or neglect because no nexus was shown between the parents' behavior and impending abuse or neglect of the child. J. B., III v. *Dept. of Children and Families*, 928 So. 2d 392 (Fla. App. 2006).

20.11. Emotional or Mental Abuse

Emotional abuse or neglect can be grounds for state intervention. Emotional abuse often accompanies physical abuse but can be more difficult to prove. Emotional abuse can also arise on its own. For example, in *In Interest of B.B.*, 500 N.W.2d 9 (Iowa 1993), a child suffered emotional harm when, because of his mother's obsession with his health, he was not allowed to attend school. Other examples of emotional abuse may include locking a child in barren rooms for extended periods of time, the existence of volatility and chaos in the home, or living with a parent who has a serious anger management issue.

Example 20-4

Assume that X is a five-year-old child who attends kindergarten. His teacher is concerned that he is very anxious and withdrawn. X has never spoken, and he cries easily. He is sometimes observed pinching himself until he has black and blue marks. The teacher contacts X's parents and asks them to attend a meeting about X. X's father comes to the meeting with X. At the meeting he calls X a "dummy" and tells the teacher that X is "nothing but trouble." The teacher urges the father to accept help for X, but the father refuses to do so. After the meeting, the teacher reports the situation to child protection. Assume that this hypothetical situation takes place in a jurisdiction with a statute identical to that found in Section 20.4. Is this the sort of case in which child protection services should intervene?

Explanation

The child protection worker could argue that X falls under paragraph (c) of the statute because X is suffering serious emotional damage evidenced by severe anxiety and withdrawal as a result of the belittling conduct of the father. The father might argue that X is merely having trouble adjusting to kindergarten and that X's behavior has nothing to do with the father's parenting style. Paragraph (c) of the statute is carefully drafted to focus on the impact of alleged emotional abuse on the child. In this case the teacher feels strongly that X is exhibiting behavior not normally seen in children adjusting to kindergarten. Although there is not a great deal of evidence linking the father's conduct to X's problems, the father's behavior at the meeting and his refusal to accept help for X would likely spur additional investigation by child protection.

20.12. Neglect

The term *neglect* refers to many situations and conditions that may occur separately or concurrently. Common themes include lack of food, lack of appropriate housing, lack of medical care, lack of supervision, failure to thrive, and irregular school attendance. Not surprisingly, findings of neglect are often linked to poverty. *See* Elizabeth Bartholet, *Nobody's Children*, 33 (1999) (noting that children from families with incomes under $15,000 annually are 44 times more likely to be neglected than children from families with annual incomes over $30,000).

Example 20-5

Assume that a father was incarcerated and left his three children in the care of his longtime girlfriend. She did not have legal custody over them, and the children were consequently taken briefly by their drug-using biological mother. Neglect proceedings were filed, and the state argued that an incarcerated parent *ipso facto* could not adequately care for children. The father argued that he had arranged for someone else (his girlfriend) to care for the children and that no nexus was shown between his unavailability and the condition of the children. What is the likely result?

Explanation

In *In re* T.T.C., 855 A.2d 1117 (D.C. 2004), the court agreed with the father that incarceration did not *ipso facto* constitute neglect. However, the court found that the father had put the children at risk by not granting his girl-friend (or someone else) legal authorization to care for the children and had consequently left them open to being taken by their unsuitable biological mother. The adjudication of neglect was affirmed.

20.13. Housing and Housekeeping

Children are sometimes removed from their parents' care because of housing problems. Critics allege that caseworkers may be overzealous in removing children from "dirty houses." However, courts commonly intervene in such cases.

Example 20-6

Assume that a child protection worker visits the home of a child while investigating a complaint of neglect. The worker finds that the apartment reeks of cat feces and urine and is filled with garbage and overflowing ash trays. Dirty dishes are stacked all over the kitchen, and the only food in the refrigerator is milk, eggs, and ketchup. Two litters of cats are living under the bed, and cats have defecated in the bathtub and on some of the child's clothing. Do these conditions constitute neglect? If so, should the child be placed in foster care?

Explanation

This fact situation is based on *In Interest of* N.M.W., 461 N.W.2d 478, 479 (Iowa Ct. App. 1990), in which the appellate court upheld the finding of neglect. The dissenting judge agreed that the mother was "an extremely poor housekeeper," but argued that the child's interest would have been better served by having the house cleaned instead of placing the child in foster care. *Id.* at 482. She argued that a wealthier mother would have been able to hire someone to clean and that there was no evidence that "only people in clean houses were good parents." *Id.* at 483.

20.14. Medical Treatment

Medical neglect occurs when parents fail to obtain necessary medical care. For example, in In re Seamus K., 33 A.D.3d 1030 (N.Y.A.D. 2006), the court found a father to have neglected a child by failing to obtain prompt medical care when his two-month-old child was "screaming, pale, acting strangely, vomiting, refusing to eat, and displaying seizure-like symptoms."

Difficult issues arise in both the civil and criminal context when parents withhold medical treatment for religious reasons. Some states have statutes providing that good-faith treatment by prayer does not constitute neglect. Del. Code Ann. tit. 10 §901(11) (2006). However, if the child dies, the parent may be subject to criminal prosecution. For example, in the case of Walker v. Superior Court, 763 P.2d 852 (Cal. 1988), a parent was criminally prosecuted for failure to seek medical care for a child who died of meningitis after being treated through prayer.

The dispute in In re Eli H., 871 N.Y.S.2d 846 (N.Y. Fam. Ct. 2008), involved the parents of an infant born with a hole between the lower chambers of his heart and a severe blockage between his right ventricle and his pulmonary artery, and New York's Department of Social Services. When the child's parents objected to the surgery to replace a shunt because the operation was against their religious beliefs, the Department of Social Services sought a court order finding the child neglected. The court found by a preponderance of the evidence that the child's physical condition was in imminent danger of being impaired as a result of the failure of his parents to exercise a minimum degree of care in supplying him with adequate medical care. It granted the petition reasoning that imminent risk to child's health justified the court's exercise of duty as *parens patriae* to order surgery without parents' consent. See In re D.R., 20 P.3d 166, 169 (Ok. App. 2001) (court upheld finding of medical neglect when the parents refused medical treatment based upon their religious beliefs, saying that the "state has an interest in protecting the lives of its children, which may override parental decisions which threaten a child's life"); In re McCauley, 565 N.W.2d 411 (Mass. 1991) (court authorized blood transfusion over contrary religious beliefs of parents). But see Marshall v. Sackett, 907 S.W.2d 925 (Tex. App. 1995) (a parent or guardian is not considered negligent if he fails to provide a child with specified medical treatment because of a legitimate practice of his religion. However, staff may still request a court order to provide medical services if the child's health requires it); In re E.G., 549 N.E.2d 322 (Ill. 1989) (minor whom court has determined to possess requisite degree of maturity has limited right to refuse life-sustaining medical treatment).

DISCOVERING ABUSE AND NEGLECT

20.15. Mandated Reporting

Professionals who come into frequent contact with children are required to make a report whenever the mandated reporter, in his or her professional capacity or within the scope of his or her employment, has knowledge of or observes a child whom the mandated reporter knows or reasonably suspects has been the victim of child abuse. Mandatory reporters typically include teachers, social workers, physicians, registered nurses, emergency medical technicians, and therapists, although clergy and attorneys may also be required to report. With respect to physical abuse occurring in 2007, 25.4 percent of incidents were reported by educators, 21.9 percent by law enforcement, and 13.3 percent by medical personnel. U.S. Dept. of Health & Human Services, Administration for Children and Families, *Child Maltreatment 2007, http://www.acf.hhs.gov/programs/cb/pubs/cm07/index.htm* (last visited August 13, 2009).

States may grant immunity for good-faith mistakes in making reports that turn out to be unfounded. *Lieberman v. Scully*, 709 N.Y.S.2d 583 (N.Y.A.D. 2000) (evidence in action for intentional infliction of emotional distress and defamation based upon unfounded report of physical and sexual child abuse made against the plaintiffs raised fact issues for jury as to whether defendant who had reported the alleged abuse was a mandated reporter under Social Services law and, if so, whether presumption of good faith to which such a reporter is entitled under immunity statute was rebutted). *See also Ouellet v. Tillitski*, 604 S.E.2d 559 (2004) (undisputed record showed that a mandated reporter had reasonable cause to believe that child abuse had occurred, and could therefore claim immunity, even if he had been negligent or exercised bad judgment). However, mandated reporters may be civilly or criminally liable for failing to report abuse and neglect. *See Landeros v. Flood*, 551 P.2d 389 (Cal. 1976).

20.16. Central Registry of Reports

Some states maintain a central registry of reports that can be used by some prospective employers. For example, a New York reporting statute required health care workers, social workers, education employees, law enforcement agents, and judicial officers to report child maltreatment. After investigation, if there was "some credible evidence" of maltreatment, the name of the alleged perpetrator was placed on a central register made available to child care employers. Noting a high risk of possible error, the Second Circuit found that the alleged perpetrators' due process rights were violated by the statutory scheme. *Valmonte v. Bane*, 18 F.3d 992 (2d Cir. 1994). *See Humphries v. County of Los Angeles*, 554 F.3d 1170 (9th Cir. 2009) (listing on Child Abuse Central Index violated parents' procedural due process rights). *See also Division of Youth and Family Services v. D.F.*, 781 A.2d 699 (N.J. Super. A.D. 2005) (mother's name placed on registry even though no child protective action filed), and *DuBray v. S.D. Dept. of Social Services*, 690 N.W.2d 657 (S.D. 2004) (removed mother's name from registry after it had been placed there based on hearsay evidence).

ADJUDICATION AND DISPOSITION

20.17. Two-Stage Proceedings

Civil juvenile proceedings usually involve a two-stage procedure. First, a jurisdictional hearing is held to establish that the child falls within the relevant state statutory definition of a neglected, abused, or dependent child. *People ex rel. U.S.*, 121 P.3d 326 (Colo. Ct. App. 2005) (court did not have statutory authority over a mother where there was no adjudication of dependency or neglect by her). Second, a dispositional hearing is held to determine whether the child should remain with the parent subject to conditions, should be placed in foster care, or should be sent to an institution. If the child is removed from the home, the state agency will begin to plan concurrently for the reunification of the family and the possibility of terminating parental rights.

20.18. Procedures When Child Is in Immediate Danger

In emergency situations, when a child is in immediate danger, the state may assume temporary custody of children. For example, Kentucky Revised Statutes, set out immediately below, provide as follows:

§620.060. Emergency Custody Orders

(1) The court for the county where the child is present may issue an *ex parte* emergency custody order when it appears to the court that removal is in the best interest of the child and that there are reasonable grounds to believe, as supported by affidavit or by recorded sworn testimony, that one (1) or more of the following conditions exist and that the parents or other person exercising custodial control or supervision are unable or unwilling to protect the child:

a. The child is in danger of imminent death or serious physical injury or is being sexually abused;

b. The parent has repeatedly inflicted or allowed to be inflicted by other than accidental means physical injury or emotional injury. This condition shall not include reasonable and ordinary discipline recognized in the community where the child lives, as long as reasonable and ordinary discipline does not result in abuse or neglect as defined in KRS 600.020(1); or

c. The child is in immediate danger due to the parent's failure or refusal to provide for the safety or needs of the child.

In Kentucky, a petition must be filed with the court within 72 hours of taking the child into custody. *See also Doe v. Kearney*, 329 F.3d 1286 (11th Cir. 2003) (upholding Florida statute permitting removal of children without court order when caseworker had probable cause to believe that children were in imminent danger of abuse). *See also* Mark R. Brown, *Rescuing Children from Abusive Parents: The Constitutional Value of Pre-Deprivation Process*, 65 Ohio St. L.J. 913 (2004).

Example 20-7

Assume that you are a judge in a jurisdiction with a statute identical to the Kentucky statute found in Section 20.18. On a Friday afternoon you are presented with an affidavit stating that a teacher has reported a fourth-grade student who came to school that day with bruises and what appear to be cigarette burns on her arms. The child told the investigating caseworker, who was called to the school by the teacher, that the bruises resulted from an accidental fall down the stairs and that the other marks were bug bites. The experienced caseworker does not believe the child and asserts that the child will be in danger over the weekend. Will you issue an *ex parte* removal order?

Explanation

The statute allows issuance of an *ex parte* custody order if it is in the best interests of the child and there are reasonable grounds to believe that the child is in danger of serious physical injury or the child is in immediate danger because of a parent's failure to provide for the child's safety. This is the sort of case that is difficult to resolve without expert medical evidence. However, a judge is likely to give more credence to physical indications and the opinions of the teacher and caseworker than the protestations of a child who may be afraid to disclose the possible abuse. The judge probably has reasonable grounds to believe that the child is in immediate danger.

20.19. Alternative Responses

Intervention of the state into the family system is inherently coercive in nature and can be upsetting to families in and of itself. Consequently, states are exploring innovative approaches aimed at establishing more positive relationships with struggling families. States such as Kentucky, Minnesota, Missouri, New Jersey, Oklahoma, and Wyoming authorize alternative approaches that are less confrontational and more assessment-oriented (and which may not require a formal finding of abuse or neglect) where children are at lower risk. Gila R. Shusterman et al., *Alternative Responses to Child Maltreatment: Findings from NCANDS*, http://aspe.hhs.gov/hsp/05/child-maltreat-resp/ (last visited August 13, 2009). *See also* U.S. Dept. of Health and Human Services, Administration for Children and Families, *Child Maltreatment 2007*, http://www.acf. hhs.gov/programs/cb/pubs/cm07/index.htm (last visited August 13, 2009) (during 2007 approximately 3.8 million children received preventive services); Clare Huntington, *Missing Parents*, 42 Fam. L.Q. 131 (2008) (urging focus on prevention).

20.20. Alternative Dispute Resolution

In order to promote better communication and planning, an increasing number of states offer mediation or some form of alternative dispute resolution in child protection and termination of parental rights cases. Recent research indicates that in 60-80 percent of the cases agreement is reached and that the treatment plans developed in mediation are similar to those developed outside of mediation. However, visitation arrangements tend to be more specific, and there is some indication that agreements involve more visitation. In mediation parents have more opportunity to be heard and to engage in finding solutions, and extended family members are more likely to participate. Compliance with agreements may also be higher in mediation. Nancy Thoennes, *What We Know Now: Findings from Dependency Mediation Research*, 47 Fam. Ct. Rev. 21 (2009). *See also* Bernie Mayer, *Reflections on the State of Consensus-Based Decision Making in Child Welfare*, 47 Fam. Ct. Rev. 10 (2009).

20.21. Foster Care: Safety and Accountability

In the well-known case of *DeShaney v. Winnebago County Dept. of Soc. Servs.*, 489 U.S. 189 (1989), a boy was beaten and permanently injured by his father after repeated involvement with the department of social services. The Supreme Court held that there was no due process violation because there was no special relationship giving rise to a duty to protect. The Court reasoned that because the boy was in the physical care of his father, the state had no obligation to protect him from abuse.

After the Supreme Court decided *DeShaney*, several state courts have recognized due process violations where the state has established a special relationship with the child or if the state affirmatively places an individual in danger. *Waubanascum v. Shawano County*, 416 F.3d 658, 665 (7th Cir. 2005) (civil rights case). *See also Radke v. County of Freeborn*, 694 N.W.2d 788 (Minn. 2005) (wrongful death action against workers for negligent investigation of abuse reports).

When a child is placed in foster care, the state is viewed as having a special relationship with that child, and the state may have a consequent duty to protect him or her while in foster care. *Lewis v. Anderson*, 308 F.3d 768 (7th Cir. 2002) (state must know or suspect likely abuse); *Nicini v. Morra*, 212 F.3d 798 (3d Cir. 2000) (conduct did not "shock the conscience"); *Lintz v. Skipski*, 25 F.3d 304 (6th Cir. 1994) (insufficient evidence of deliberate indifference); *Braam ex rel. Braam v. State*, 81 P.3d 851 (Wash. 2003) (whether state conduct falls substantially short of the exercise of professional judgment, standards, or practices); *Weatherford ex rel. Michael L. v. State*, 81 P.3d 320 (Ariz. 2003) (whether workers acted with deliberate indifference); *Miller v. Martin*, 838 So. 2d 761 (La. 2003) (state vicariously liable for intentional abuse by foster parents); *Mosher-Simons v. County of Allegany*, 783 N.E.2d 509 (N.Y. 2002) (court ordered home study "cloaked in judicial immunity").

Experts believe that frequent visits from caseworkers are key to keeping children safe in foster care. As a result of lawsuits, consent decrees, and collaborations with child advocacy groups, 43 states have adopted standards calling for monthly caseworker visits to children in foster care. However, 27 states have been cited as needing improvement in this area. Department of Health and Human Services, Office of Inspector General, *State Standards and Capacity to Track Frequency of Caseworker Visits with Children in Foster Care* (2005), http://oig.hhs.gov/oei/reports/oei-04-03-00350.pdf (last visited August 13, 2009).

CHILD WITNESSES (TRIAL CONSIDERATIONS)

20.22. Victim as Witness

Proving abuse, particularly sexual abuse, can be especially challenging because the abuse takes place in private, and a young child may be the only witness. Consequently, the state may call the child as a witness, seek to admit out-of-court statements, and/or attempt to use "syndrome" testimony.

20.23. Competency to Testify

Under the Federal Rules of Evidence Rule 601, children can testify without first establishing competence. While some states have adopted this approach, other states require inquiry about the child's understanding of the oath (truthfulness) or a full inquiry voir dire. Lucy S. McGough, *Child Witnesses: Fragile Voices in the American Legal System* 96 (1994); Nancy Walker Perry & Lawrence S. Wrightsman, *The Child Witness: Legal Issues and Dilemmas* (1991).

20.24. Right of Criminal Defendant to Confront Child

A child traumatized by abuse is likely to be traumatized again if required to testify in the presence of the abuser. On the other hand, a criminal defendant accused of abuse has a Sixth Amendment right to confront witnesses. In *Maryland v. Craig*, 497 U.S. 836 (1990), the Supreme Court considered Maryland's statutory procedure that permitted a child witness, who was alleged to be a victim of child abuse, to testify against a defendant by means of a closed circuit television. The court held that "if the State makes an adequate showing of necessity, the state interest in protecting child witnesses from the trauma of testifying in a child abuse case is sufficiently important to justify the use of a special procedure that permits a child witness in such cases to testify at trial against a defendant in the absence of face-to-face confrontation with the defendant." *Id.* at 855 of 497 U.S. The Court reaffirmed the preference for and importance of face-to-face confrontation with testifying witnesses but made clear that the right was not absolute. A physical, face-to-face confrontation at trial may be dispensed of only where denial of such confrontation is necessary to further an important public policy and only where the reliability of the testimony is otherwise assured.

The Court in *Maryland v. Craig* found it significant that the Maryland procedure preserved all other elements of the right to confrontation, namely the requirement that a witness testify under oath, the opportunity for contemporaneous cross-examination, and the opportunity for the triers of fact and defendant to observe the witness's demeanor during testimony. It determined that these features were sufficient to assure "reliability and adversariness" and, therefore, the "critical inquiry" was whether the procedure was "necessary to further an important state interest." *Id.* at 851-852 of 497 U.S.

The court noted that a state's interest in "the protection of minor victims of sex crimes from further trauma and embarrassment" is a "compelling" one. It concluded that "a State's interest in the physical and psychological well-being of child abuse victims may be sufficiently important to outweigh, at least in some cases, a defendant's right to face his or her accusers in court." *Id.* at 853 of 497 U.S.

The court fleshed out the meaning of an adequate showing of necessity and stated, "The requisite finding of necessity must of course be a case-specific one: The trial court must hear evidence and determine whether use of the one-way closed circuit television procedure is necessary to protect the welfare of the particular child witness who seeks to testify. The trial court must also find that the child witness would be traumatized, not by the courtroom generally, but by the presence of the defendant."

In a subsequent California case, an appellate court considered whether the trial court had infringed upon a defendant's right to confrontation by allowing the prosecutor to examine a child witness from a position that allowed the child to look away from the defense table so she would not have to look at defendant. *People v. Sharp*, 36 Cal. Rptr. 2d 117 (1994). The court found that this minor interference did not impermissibly impair defendant's right to face-to-face confrontation when weighed against the state's interests in obtaining a complete and accurate account and in protecting the young witness from unnecessary emotional trauma.

In some criminal prosecutions, the child victim may be deemed incompetent to testify. In such cases, prosecutors may attempt to introduce testimony about statements that the child made to medical personnel or investigators. In some situations this testimony may run afoul of the Supreme Court's holding in *Crawford v. Washington*, 541 U.S. 36 (2004), that testimonial out-of-court statements are not admissible in criminal cases unless the witness is unavailable and the defendant had a prior opportunity to cross-examine the witness. *See State v. Coates*, 950 A.2d 114 (Md. 2008) (statements of seven-year-old to pediatric nurse were not admissible). However, in *State v. Scacchetti*, 711 N.W.2d 508 (Minn. 2006), statements made by a three-and-a-half-year-old to a pediatric nurse were held not to be testimonial, and their admission into evidence did not violate the Sixth Amendment. In reaching its decision, the court placed particular emphasis on the identity (nongovernmental actor) and purpose (medical treatment) of the questioner. *See also* Kamala London et al., *Disclosure of Child Sexual Abuse: What Does the Research Tell Us About the Ways That Children Tell?*, 11 Psychol. Pub. Pol'y & L. 194 (2005) (exploring empirical data).

20.25. Syndrome Testimony

During the 1960s researchers labeled a cluster of symptoms as the "battered child syndrome." Battered child syndrome involves the infliction of multiple injuries over a period of time. When discovered, the injuries are in various stages of healing, and the parents' explanations of the injuries are inconsistent with the medical evidence. Expert knowledge is necessary to identify battered child syndrome. *Estelle v. McGuire*, 502 U.S. 62, 66 (1991) (battered child syndrome exists when "a child has sustained repeated and/or serious injuries by nonaccidental means"). *See also Commonwealth v. Rodgers*, 528 A.2d 610 (Pa. Super. 1987); *State v. Dumlao*, 491 A.2d 404 (Conn. App. 1985).

Significant controversy exists over the use of testimony concerning syndromes such as Child Sexual Abuse Accommodation Syndrome (CSAAS), Battering Parent Syndrome (BPS), and Battered Child Syndrome (BCS). *See* Sarah J. Ramsey & Robert F. Kelly, *Social Science Knowledge in Family Law Cases: Judicial Gate-Keeping in the Daubert Era*, 59 U. Miami L. Rev. 1 (2004). However, the trend appears to be increasing acceptance of the syndrome by the courts.

The defendant in *In re E.C.L.*, 278 S.W.3d 510 (Tex. App. 2009), a juvenile, was convicted after a jury trial of engaging in delinquent conduct for fatally shooting his father. The appellate court reversed the conviction in part because the trial judge excluded expert testimony that the juvenile suffered from battered child syndrome and believed his conduct was immediately necessary to avoid harm to himself or his brother.

Arizona recognized the syndrome in *State v. Hernandez*, 805 P.2d 1057, 1059-1060 (Az. App. 1990), where it upheld admission of expert testimony that a child's injuries most likely had been caused by violent shaking and were consistent with the battered child syndrome. *See State v. Poehnelt*, 722 P.2d 304, 318 (App. 1985) (expert witnesses' use of term "battered child syndrome" in describing injuries not improper). *See Estelle v. McGuire*, 502 U.S. 62, 70 (1991) (testimony regarding BCS did not violate defendant's right to due process); *People v. Peterson*, 537 N.W.2d 857 (Mich. 1995) (limited use of CSAAS testimony); *State v. MacLennan*, 702 N.W.2d 219 (Minn. 2005) (admissibility of BCS determined under rules of evidence).

TERMINATION OF PARENTAL RIGHTS

20.26. Legal Consequences of Termination

Termination of parental rights severs the parent-child relationship and makes the child available for adoption. The parent loses the right to see the child, and the child has no right to financial support from the parent or to inherit property upon the parent's death. *But see In re Stephen Tyler R.*, 584 S.E.2d 581 (W. Va. 2003) (under specially drafted statutory provision, terminated father ordered to pay child support), and Richard L. Brown, *Disinheriting the "Legal Orphan": Inheritance Rights of Children After Termination of Parental Rights*, 70 Mo. L. Rev. 125 (2005) (arguing for a change in the law to allow inheritance after termination). Because termination involves constitutional rights and is such a drastic remedy, special procedural precautions are required. In 2007, the parental rights to 84,000 children were terminated. *Trends in Foster Care and Adoption — FY 2000-FY 2007*, U.S. Department of Health and Human Services, Administration for Children and Families, Children's Bureau, *http://www.acf.hhs.gov/programs/cb/stats_research/afcars/trends.htm* (last visited August 13, 2009).

20.27. Grounds for Termination

Statutes typically provide specific grounds and requirements for termination of parental rights. *See In re Adoption/Guardianship of Rashawn H.*, 937 A.2d 177 (Md. 2007) (clear and specific findings required for each statutory factor). Termination may be sought when there has been chronic abuse and neglect, abandonment, parental incapacity, and abuse of a sibling or termination of parental rights of a sibling. As discussed below, with some exceptions states may seek termination of parental rights pursuant to the Adoption and Safe Families Act if a child has been placed outside of the home for 15 of the preceding 22 months. *See In re Parental Rights as to D.R.H.*, 92 P.3d 1230 (Nev. 2004) (upholding termination where child placed outside the home for 14 of 20 months).

20.28. Adoption Assistance and Child Welfare Act (AACWA)

In 1980 Congress passed the Adoption Assistance and Welfare Act (AACWA) as a result of concern about children languishing in foster care. The Act stressed reunification of the family but encouraged adoption in cases where reunification was not realistic. In order to receive matching funds, states were required to make "reasonable efforts" to prevent removal or reunify the family. States were also required to undertake "permanency planning" and make periodic case reviews. In *Suter v. Artist M.*, 503 U.S. 347 (1992), the Supreme Court held that there was no implied right of action to enforce the reasonable efforts language in AACWA.

20.29. Adoption and Safe Families Act (ASFA)

In 1997 Congress enacted the Adoption and Safe Families Act (ASFA) to limit the amount of time children spend in foster care (known as foster care drift) and to speed adoption. The Act requires states to pursue termination of parental rights if children have been in foster care for 15 of the preceding 22 months. (This provision does not apply if the child has been placed with a relative, if termination is not believed to be in the best interests of the child, or if reunification services have not been provided.) Permanency hearings are to occur within a year, but "reasonable efforts" to reunify are not required where there are "aggravated circumstances" (such as sexual abuse) or parental rights to a sibling have been terminated. *See* Stephanie Jill Gendell, *In Search of Permanency: A Reflection on the First Three Years of the Adoption and Safe Families Act*, 39 Fam. & Conciliation Cts. Rev. 25 (2001); Kurtis A. Kemper, *Construction and Application by State Courts of the Federal Adoption and Safe Families Act and Its Implementing State Statutes*, 10 A.L.R.6th 173 (2006).

Critics of ASFA believe that inadequate resources and the Act's aggressive timelines have worked to the detriment of children and families. William Wesley Patton & Amy M. Pellman, *The Reality of Concurrent Planning: Juggling Multiple Family Plans Expeditiously Without Sufficient Resources*, 9 U.C. Davis J. Juv. L. & Pol'y 171 (2005); Martin Guggenheim & Christine Gottliev, *Justice Denied: Delays in Resolving Child Protection Cases in New York*, 12 Va. J. Soc. Pol'y & L. 546 (2005); Catherine J. Ross, *The Tyranny of Time: Vulnerable Children, "Bad" Mothers, and Statutory Deadlines in Parental Termination Proceedings*, 11 Va. J. Soc. Pol'y & L. 176 (2004).

20.30. Reasonable Removal and Reunification Efforts

Under the Adoption Assistance and Child Welfare Act (ASFA), states are required to make "reasonable efforts" to prevent removal and reunify the family prior to terminating parental rights. *See In re Tiffany B.*, 228 S.W.3d 148 (Tenn. Ct. App. 2007) (factors to determine reasonableness of efforts include "(1) the reasons for separating the parents from their children, (2) the parents' physical and mental abilities, (3) the resources available to the parents, (4) the parents' efforts to remedy the conditions that required the removal of the children, (5) the resources available to the Department, (6) the duration and extent of the parents' efforts to address the problems that caused the children's removal, and (7) the closeness of the fit between the conditions that led to the initial removal of the children, the requirements of the permanency plan, and the Department's efforts"). However, under ASFA, such efforts are not required when there are "aggravated circumstances" or parental rights to a sibling have been terminated. *See* Anne Kathleen S. Bean, *Reasonable Efforts: What State Courts Think*, 36 Tol. L. Rev. 321 (2005).

If termination proceedings involve a Native American child, the Indian Child Welfare Act requires that "active efforts" be made to provide services designed to prevent removal of the child from the family, and this requirement is not overridden by AFSA. 25 U.S.C. §1912(d); *People ex rel. J.S.B., Jr.*, 691 N.W.2d 611 (S.D. 2005). However, in *J.S. v. State*, 50 P.3d 388 (Alaska 2002), the father was convicted of sexual abuse, and, citing the aggravating circumstances language in ASFA, the court held that active efforts to reunify the family were not required under ICWA.

Example 20-8

Assume that a four-and-a-half-year-old child, C, was placed in a foster home after her mother, D, developed cancer and was diagnosed with a schizoid personality disorder. At the time C was placed in foster care, she was dirty and hungry, and her mother characterized her as a defiant child. C was formally evaluated by a team of experts and was diagnosed with reactive attachment disorder, ADHD, and oppositional-defiant disorder. It was determined that she consequently needed a particularly high level of care. The child protection agency developed a case plan aimed at reunifying the family, and the plan was accepted by the court. The mother attended therapy sessions individually and with C in compliance with the treatment plan, but she failed to attend parenting classes, participate in a bonding study, or maintain regular contact with C. The therapist who saw C and her mother jointly strongly recommended termination of parental rights. In contrast, the foster parents coped well with C. After C had been in foster care for two and a half years, the state moved to terminate D's parental rights. In order to terminate, the state was required to show that reasonable efforts had been made to assist D in parenting and that there was little likelihood that the situation would change in the foreseeable future. D argued that, given her health and psychological problems, she had complied with as much of the treatment plan as she could and that she needed more assistance from child protection. At trial one of the experts described the mother as "an eccentric person with a 'crusty demeanor' and a tendency to 'shut down' when she is feeling defensive," but he did note some improvement in her interpersonal skills. Is a court likely to terminate parental rights under these circumstances?

Explanation

This fact situation is based on the case of *State ex rel. Children, Youth & Families Dept.*, 47 P.3d 859 (N.M. Ct. App. 2002), in which the court upheld termination of the mother's parental rights. The court considered the requirements of ASFA with respect to the state's obligation to make reasonable efforts to reunify the family and determined that the state had made reasonable, if not perfect, efforts to assist D. Because of the child's special needs and the mother's major parenting deficits, the court did not see any likelihood of change in the foreseeable future.

Example 20-9

Assume that three minor children were placed in foster care because their mother, due to drug use, had failed to protect them and they suffered serious emotional damage. As a part of the treatment plan, the mother was required to stop using drugs. However, she continued to use methamphetamine and was in fact arrested for drug use while the children were in foster care. The mother repeatedly sought visitation with the children but was prevented from seeing them because she failed to pass a drug test as required in the treatment plan. Pursuant to a statutory provision, after six months of no contact, the state ended reunification services and scheduled a permanency planning hearing likely to lead to termination of parental rights. The mother claimed that the department had actively prevented her from visiting the children despite her requests and was now accusing her of not maintaining contact with the children. She asserted that she was entitled to a full year of reunification services before her parental rights could be terminated. What is the likely result?

Explanation

In the similar case of *Sara M. v. Superior Court*, 116 P.3d 550 (Cal. 2005), the court found that the department made reasonable efforts to reunify the family. The appellate court upheld the trial court's finding that the mother was appropriately prevented from seeing the children while under the influence of drugs. Furthermore the court held that under California law, reunification services could be terminated where clear and convincing evidence showed that a parent had not contacted the children for six months after the start of services. But see In re O.S., 848 N.E.2d 130 (Ill. App. 2006) (termination reversed where department kept true identity of mother a secret from young son — she was introduced to the child as "Jenny" — but her parental rights were ultimately terminated in part because she had not established a parent-child bond with the boy).

Example 20-10

Assume that a child, X, was placed in foster care based on his mother's inability to deal effectively with his health and behavioral problems. As part of the family treatment plan, the mother was required to maintain appropriate housing, which she had some difficulty affording, and to work on her parenting skills. She did not attend a parenting class because it was some distance away and she had transportation problems, but she did meet with a family support worker who assisted her with parenting. The worker testified that the mother had made improvements that were evident when the worker made home visits. The worker also observed that the mother had a warm and playful relationship with X. The child protection agency seeks termination of parental rights under a statutory provision allowing termination of parental rights if a child is in foster care for more than 15 months of the most recent 22 months. The mother argues that she has made substantial progress with respect to her case plan and that the termination or parental rights is not in the best interests of the child. The family support worker testifies that the child would be harmed by the termination. However, the state argues that it is not in X's best interest to remain in foster care and that the mother has had sufficient time to make the required improvements. What is the likely outcome?

Explanation

In In re Interest of Aaron D., 691 N.W.2d 164 (Neb. 2005), the court held that, under the facts presented, termination based solely on length of stay in foster care was not in the child's best interest. The court stated as follows: "The 15-month condition set forth in [the statute] serves the purpose of providing a reasonable timetable for parents to rehabilitate themselves . . . [b]ut termination based on the ground that a child has been in out-of-home placement for 15 of the preceding 22 months is not in a child's best interests when the record demonstrates that a parent is making efforts toward reunification and has not been given a sufficient opportunity for compliance with a reunification plan. We do not mean to suggest that termination solely on the basis of [the statutory section] cannot be appropriate. Obviously, there will be cases in which clear and convincing evidence to that effect will be presented. But that may prove difficult in cases where the record is insufficient to prove any of the other statutory grounds, i.e., where the parent did not abandon the child, did not neglect to protect or provide for a child, was not unfit or unable to parent, did not fail to participate in necessary rehabilitation, and was not abusive." Id. at 261.

TERMINATION PROCEDURE

20.31. Standard of Proof

Because termination of parental rights is such a drastic remedy, the standard of proof is "clear and convincing evidence." In Santosky v. Kramer, 455 U.S. 745 (1982), the Supreme Court held that a New York statute requiring only a "fair preponderance of the evidence" violated a parent's right to due process in termination of parental rights proceedings. The Court found that parents have a fundamental liberty interest in the care and upbringing of children and that the state had an advantage over parents with respect to proof and expertise.

The Indian Child Welfare Act requires proof "beyond a reasonable doubt" when termination of parental rights is at issue. 25 U.S.C. §1912(f).

20.32. Right to Counsel?

In Lassiter v. Department of Soc. Servs., 452 U.S. 18 (1981), the Supreme Court ruled that due process does not require appointment of counsel for indigent parents in all termination actions. However, states generally appoint counsel in termination cases either as required by state statute or under state constitutional provisions. Once appointed, the question of which standard states are to use when assessing their competency is unsettled. *Compare In re R.E.S.*, — A.2d — , 2009 WL 2460891 (D.C. 2009) (appointed counsel in a proceeding where the termination of the parent and child relationship is under consideration has the statutory duty to competently represent client) with *In re Elysa D.* 974 A.2d 834 (Conn. App. 2009) (a parent "is constitutionally entitled to the effective assistance of counsel only if he had a constitutional right to appointed counsel in the termination proceeding). *See* Bruce A. Boyer, *Justice, Access to the Courts, and the Right to Free Counsel for Indigent Parents: The Continuing Scourge of Lassiter v. Department of Social Services of Durham*, 15 Temp. Pol. & Civ. Rts. L. Rev. 635 (2006).

Abortion

HISTORY AND BACKGROUND

21.1. Introduction

The history of abortion dates back to ancient times when unwanted pregnancies were terminated using such methods as the administration of abortifacient herbs, sharpened implements, the application of abdominal pressure, and other techniques. From the 1700s into the early 1800s, most states followed the British common law, which permitted an abortion before "quickening" but made abortion after "quickening" an offense. To "quicken" is generally defined as reaching the stage of pregnancy at which the child shows signs of life — when the initial motion of the fetus can be felt by the pregnant woman. This usually appears 16-20 weeks into pregnancy.

England passed its first antiabortion law in 1803. In the United States, the common law was slowly replaced by state statutory law during the early part of the nineteenth century, and by 1840 at least eight states had statutes dealing with abortion.

The earliest abortion laws were often criminal in nature and targeted those who performed abortions rather than the pregnant women who sought to have the procedure performed. The aim of these laws was to protect pregnant women and their fetuses from injury, not to prosecute them. At the time, abortion was an unsafe medical procedure for women. This was particularly true prior to the development of antisepsis.

After the War Between the States, more legislation emerged from various state legislatures concerning an abortion. In 1868, at least 28 of the then 37 states and 8 territories had statutes banning or limiting abortion. J. Mohr, *Abortion in America*, 200 (1978). The legislation tended to provide severe penalties should an abortion occur after quickening but was more lenient with an abortion that occurred before quickening.

Most state statutes punished attempted abortions equally with completed abortions. Many early statutes included an exception for an abortion thought by one or more physicians to be necessary to save the mother's life, but that provision soon disappeared, and the law typically required that the procedure actually be necessary for that purpose.

21.2. Twentieth Century

By the turn of the nineteenth century, the quickening distinction had disappeared from the statutory law of most states, and the degree of the offense and the penalties were increased. By the 1950s, a majority of jurisdictions had banned abortion unless done to save or preserve the life of the mother. The exceptions, Alabama and the District of Columbia, permitted an abortion to preserve the mother's health.

The widespread ban on abortions continued through the 1960s, although the American Law Institute's Model Code influenced several states to enact laws that allowed an abortion when it was necessary to save the life of the mother, in cases of rape or incest, if the fetus was deformed, or when continuation would impair a mother's mental or physical health (therapeutic abortion).

Colorado broadened the circumstances under which a woman could legally obtain an abortion in 1967. *The Pew Forum on Religion and Public Life,* http://pewforum.org/docs/?DocID=352 (last visited July 3, 2009). By 1970, 11 additional states had followed Colorado's lead by expanding the circumstances under which one could legally receive an abortion. Also, New York, Washington, Hawaii, and Alaska had completely decriminalized abortion during the early stages of pregnancy. *Id.*

Since the 1970s, federal courts, particularly the United States Supreme Court, have superseded state legislatures as the driving force in creating state abortion policy. A historic change in the legal landscape associated with abortion law occurred with the Supreme Court's decision in *Roe v. Wade,* 410 U.S. 113 (1973). Since the advent of *Roe,* state legislatures have encountered numerous constitutional limitations on how they may regulate abortion.

CONSTITUTIONAL PRIVACY

21.3. Roots of Privacy Theory

To understand current abortion law, it may be helpful to review the history of the treatment of privacy by the Supreme Court. Although privacy is not mentioned in the Constitution, most agree that the roots of the privacy theory are found in *Meyer v. Nebraska*, 262 U.S. 390, 400 (1923). In that decision, the Court said that the liberty interest protected by the Due Process Clause of the Fourteenth Amendment includes the right of parents "to control the education of their own children." In *Pierce v. Soc'y of Sisters*, 268 U.S. 510, 534 (1925), the Court said that "the liberty of parents and guardians" includes the right "to direct the upbringing and education of children under their control."

The privacy theory made its way into bedrooms of married couples under the guise of a liberty interest in *Griswold v. Connecticut*, 381 U.S. 479 (1965). In that decision, the Court held that the Constitution does not allow a state to forbid a married couple from using contraceptives. The majority asserted that "zones" of personal privacy are fundamental to the concept of liberty under the protected penumbra of specific guarantees of the Bill of Rights. The Court observed that although the word "liberty" is not defined in the Constitution, it includes at least the fundamental rights "retained by the people" under the Ninth Amendment. 381 U.S. at 484.

The right to privacy was not explicitly recognized by the Supreme Court until *Eisenstadt v. Baird*, 405 U.S. 438 (1972). In that case, the defendant was convicted under a criminal statute for exhibiting contraceptive articles in the course of delivering a lecture on contraception to a group of students at Boston University and for giving a young woman a package of vaginal foam at the close of his address. The defendant challenged the conviction claiming there was a certain "right to privacy" protected by the Constitution that shielded him from prosecution.

The state argued that the legislative purpose of the criminal statute was to promote marital fidelity and discourage premarital sex. The Supreme Court invalidated the statute saying that contraceptives may be made available to married persons without regard to whether they are living with their spouses or the uses to which the contraceptives are to be put. The Court reasoned that the legislation had no deterrent effect on extramarital sexual relations.

The *Eisenstadt* decision extended the "right of privacy" established in *Griswold v. Connecticut*, 381 U.S. 479 (1965), to all individuals regardless of marital status and explicitly recognized a constitutional right to privacy. *Eisenstadt* granted individuals the right "to be free from unwarranted governmental intrusion into matters so fundamentally affecting a person as the decision whether to bear or beget a child." 405 U.S. at 453. This decision is viewed by some as providing the foundation for *Roe v. Wade*.

Example 21-1

Assume that D, a druggist, stocks and sells contraceptives in direct violation of a state criminal statute that permits their sale only to married couples. D has regularly and knowingly provided contraceptives to unmarried adults. When the state brings criminal charges against D for selling contraceptives to unmarried couples, he defends on the basis that the criminal statute is unconstitutional. The state argues that the law is constitutional and that its purpose is to deter premarital sex and prevent unwanted out-of-wedlock pregnancies. Is it likely that D would be convicted under this statute after the decisions in *Griswold* and *Eisenstadt*?

Explanation

It is unlikely that D would be convicted of a crime. Here, the statute provides dissimilar treatment for married and unmarried persons who are similarly situated. This would clearly be considered a violation of the Equal Protection Clause.

The statute also appears to be exactly the type of legislation that the Court in *Eisenstadt* ruled was unconstitutional. Recall that *Eisenstadt* extended the "right of privacy" to all individuals regardless of marital status and explicitly recognized a constitutional right to privacy.

21.4. Protecting Personal Privacy

In *Whalen v. Roe*, 429 U.S. 589 (1977), the Supreme Court held that the right to privacy extends to both "the individual interest in avoiding disclosure of personal matters, and . . . the interest in independence in making certain kinds of important decisions." 429 U.S. at 599. *Whalen* recognized that information contained in medical records, for example, is constitutionally protected under the confidentiality branch of the privacy right.

The Court also held that in conjunction with its police power to regulate the distribution of dangerous drugs, the state of New York could maintain a data bank of all prescription sales of such drugs against a claim that such a recording was an impermissible invasion of the right of privacy. The Court noted that the case did not involve the "affirmative, unannounced, narrowly focused intrusions into individual privacy" protected by the Fourth Amendment. *Id.* at 604 of 429 U.S. n.32. It stated that a state was not absolutely barred from collecting information that was reasonably related to the important public purpose in regulating dangerous drugs and was protected against disclosure. *Id.* at 605 of 429 U.S.

Example 21-2

Assume that a high school swim team coach, suspecting that a teenage team member was pregnant, required the young woman to take a pregnancy test. She and her mother filed a civil rights action against the coach claiming *inter alia* that the pregnancy test unconstitutionally interfered with the daughter's right to privacy regarding personal matters. Most likely, how will a court rule on the challenge?

Explanation

The court in *Gruenke v. Seip*, 225 F.3d 290 (3d Cir. 2000), on which this example is based, held that the fact that the coach compelled the student to take the test, coupled with an alleged failure to take appropriate steps to keep the information confidential, infringed upon the young woman's right to privacy. Her claim fell squarely within the contours of the recognized right of one to be free from disclosure of personal matters as outlined in *Whalen v. Roe. See Sterling v. Borough of Minersville*, 232 F.3d 190, 196 (3d Cir. 2000) (it is difficult to imagine a more private matter than one's sexuality and a less likely probability that the government would have a legitimate interest in disclosure of sexual identity); *U.S. v. Westinghouse Elec. Corp.*, 638 F.2d 570 (3d Cir. 1980) (information about one's body and state of health is matter which the individual is ordinarily entitled to retain within the private enclave where he may lead a private life).

21.5. Statute Fails to Protect Fundamental Right to Privacy

Doe v. Bolton, 410 U.S. 179 (1973), was a companion decision to *Roe v. Wade.* The challengers argued that Georgia's abortion statute did not adequately protect a woman's right to an abortion. This is so, they contended, because it would be physically and emotionally damaging for Doe to bring a child into her poor, "fatherless" family, and because advances in medicine and medical techniques have made it safer for a woman to have a medically induced abortion than for her to bear a child. Therefore, a statute that requires a woman to carry an unwanted pregnancy to term infringes not only on a fundamental right of privacy but on the right to life itself.

She also argued that because her application for an abortion at a Georgia hospital was denied, she was forced either to relinquish her right to decide when and how many children she will bear or to seek an abortion that was illegal under the Georgia statute. This, she contended, invaded her rights of privacy and liberty in matters related to family, marriage, and sex, and deprived her of the right to choose whether to bear children. This was a violation of rights guaranteed her by the First, Fourth, Fifth, Ninth, and Fourteenth Amendments.

The Georgia statute under scrutiny required that abortions be performed only in a hospital accredited by the Joint Commission on Accreditation of Hospitals, that the procedure be approved by the hospital staff abortion committee, and that the performing physician's judgment be confirmed by independent examinations of the patient by two other licensed physicians. *Id.* at 192 of 410 U.S. The challengers argued *inter alia* that the provisions unduly restricted a woman's right of privacy. They also argued that by subjecting a doctor's individual medical judgment to committee approval and to confirming consultations, the statute impermissibly restricted the physician's right to practice his profession and deprived him of due process.

The Supreme Court held that the requirement that the abortion be performed in an accredited hospital was invalid because accreditation was not legitimately related to the state's objective of protecting the woman's life. It also invalidated the requirement that a woman secure advance approval from a hospital committee for an abortion because this would limit a woman's right to medical care and a physician's right to make medical decisions. The Court also rejected a provision that required consent from three physicians to justify the abortion and struck down a requirement that a woman be a citizen of Georgia in order to obtain an abortion there.

Example 21-3

Assume that state X is concerned that abortions should not threaten the life of the mother. To protect her health, state X promulgates a statute that allows abortions only in a state-accredited hospital and only after two doctors have concurred in the abortion decision. The statute is challenged on a constitutional basis.

Explanation

For the reasons outlined in *Doe v. Bolton* above, the statute would be held unconstitutional. The Supreme Court in *Bolton* held that requiring two Georgia-licensed physicians to confirm the recommendation of a pregnant woman's own physician, a procedure that is not required in any other voluntary medical or surgical procedure, has no rational connection with the patient's needs and unduly infringes on the physician's right to practice. It also held that a statute similar to that in this example requiring that abortions, unlike other surgical procedures, be done only in a hospital accredited by a private accreditation organization, is invalid because it is not based on differences reasonably related to the purposes of the act in which it is found, in the absence of a showing that only Georgia-licensed hospitals aid the state's interest in fully protecting a patient.

21.6. *Roe v. Wade*

In *Roe v. Wade*, 410 U.S. 113 (1973), the Supreme Court was asked to review a Texas criminal abortion statute that made an abortion illegal except for the purpose of saving a mother's life. The statute's challenger, Jane Roe, an unmarried pregnant woman, asserted that she was unable to obtain an abortion in Texas because under Texas law an abortion was allowed only if her life was threatened, and she did not have the funds to travel to another state where an abortion was legally permitted. She alleged that the Texas statute was unconstitutional.

The government argued that the statute was constitutional and provided three reasons to support its view: First, the statute discouraged illicit sexual conduct outside marriage. Second, it protected a pregnant woman from the dangerous nature of an abortion. Third, it protected the state's interest in potential life.

The Court found that the protection of a pregnant woman and the protection of potential life were compelling state interests and weighed those interests against a woman's right to privacy. It struck down the statute and created a trimester framework for reviewing abortion issues.

The Court held that no compelling state interest justifies a sweeping prohibition of abortion and concluded that during the first trimester of the pregnancy, little or no regulation is permissible. Even minor regulations on the abortion procedure may not interfere during the first trimester with physician-patient consultation or with the woman's choice between abortion and childbirth. The decision of whether to have an abortion is left with the woman in conjunction with her physician.

After the first trimester and until viability — viability defined as the point when a fetus is capable of survival outside the womb (*Roe*, 410 U.S. at 160, 163) — the state may regulate abortions but may not place an outright ban on them. It may, however, regulate the abortion procedure to protect the mother's health and safety.

During the third trimester, the state's interest in protecting potential life justifies regulating and banning abortions except when necessary for the preservation of life or health of the mother.

The Court relied primarily on the Ninth Amendment to the United States Constitution, declaring that "the Ninth Amendment's reservation of rights to the people, is broad enough to encompass a woman's decision whether or not to terminate her pregnancy." *Roe*, 410 U.S. at 153. It reasoned that from a practical perspective, modern medical techniques had significantly reduced the medical risks of an abortion, stating that prior to the end of the first trimester, although not without its risk, abortion is now relatively safe. 410 U.S. at 149.

Associate Justice Byron White and Chief Justice William Rehnquist joined in a vigorous dissent. Justice White wrote, "I find nothing in the language or history of the Constitution to support the Court's judgment. The Court simply fashions and announces a new constitutional right for pregnant mothers and, with scarcely any reason or authority for its action, invests that right with sufficient substance to override most existing state abortion statutes. The upshot is that the people and the legislatures of the 50 States are constitutionally disentitled to weigh the relative importance of the continued existence and development of the fetus, on the one hand, against a spectrum of possible impacts on the mother, on the other hand." 410 U.S. at 221-222.

Roe v. Wade prompted a national debate over abortion that continues today. The debate encompasses such questions as whether and to what extent abortion should be legal, who should decide the legality of abortion, and what tests the Supreme Court should apply to various state statutes involving abortion. The decision has had a significant impact on national politics, splitting the nation into pro-*Roe* (mostly pro-choice) and anti-*Roe* (mostly pro-life) groups.

21.7. Second-Trimester Issues

Questions involving an abortion ordinance dealing with second-trimester abortions and whether *Roe v. Wade* would be overturned came before the Supreme Court in *City of Akron v. Akron Center for Reproductive Health*, 462 U.S. 416 (1983). The Akron, Ohio, ordinance, *inter alia*, (1) required all abortions performed after the first trimester of pregnancy to be performed in a hospital; (2) prohibited a physician from performing an abortion on an unmarried minor under the age of 15 unless the physician obtained the consent of one of her parents or unless the minor obtained an order from a court having jurisdiction over her that the abortion be performed; (3) required that the attending physician inform the patient of the status of her pregnancy, the development of her fetus, the date of possible viability, the physical and emotional complications that may result from an abortion, and the availability of agencies to provide her with assistance and information with respect to birth control, adoption, and childbirth and also inform her of the particular risks associated with her pregnancy and the abortion technique to be employed. The ordinance also prohibited a physician from performing an abortion until 24 hours after the pregnant woman signed a consent form and required physicians performing abortions to ensure that fetal remains were disposed of in a humane and sanitary manner. A violation of the ordinance was punishable as a misdemeanor.

The court struck down as unconstitutional the provision requiring that all abortions be carried out in a hospital, saying it imposed a heavy and unnecessary burden on women's access to a relatively inexpensive, otherwise accessible, and safe abortion procedure. It also struck down a provision containing a blanket determination that all minors under the age of 15 are too immature to make an abortion decision or that an abortion never may be in the minor's best interests without parental approval. The Court said that the validity of an informed consent requirement rests on the state's interest in protecting the pregnant woman's health. However, this did not mean that a state has unreviewable authority to decide what information a woman must be given before she chooses to have an abortion. A state may not adopt regulations designed to influence the woman's informed choice between abortion and childbirth.

The Court also ruled that the requirement that the "attending physician" inform the woman of the specified information is unreasonable because there are nonphysicians who are competent to provide the information and counseling relevant to informed consent. Finally, it held that Akron had failed to demonstrate that any legitimate state interest is furthered by an arbitrary and inflexible waiting period. It said that there is no evidence that the abortion procedure will be performed more safely by requiring a 24-hour delay as a matter of course.

Of significance to the future trend of constitutional abortion law is the dissent's position in *Akron* that the trimester approach outlined in *Roe* was unworkable. Justice O'Connor, writing for the three dissenters, stated that "[i]t is not difficult to see that despite the Court's purported adherence to the trimester approach adopted in *Roe*, the lines drawn in that decision have now been 'blurred' because of what the Court accepts as technological advancement in the safety of abortion procedure. The State may no longer rely on a 'bright line' that separates permissible from impermissible regulation, and it is no longer free to consider the second trimester as a unit." 462 U.S. at 452. The solicitor general, in his *amicus curiae* brief in support of the City of Akron, argued that the Court should adopt the "unduly burdensome" standard when reviewing abortion regulations and in doing so, "accord heavy deference to the legislative judgment" in determining what constitutes an "undue burden." 410 U.S. at 465, n.10. The majority rejected application of the approach urged by the solicitor general; however, his view in this dispute was a precursor of future changes in the standard of review to be used by a majority on the Court.

It is important to note that several of the holdings just discussed in *Akron* were altered or overruled in *Planned Parenthood of Southeastern Pennsylvania v. Casey*, 505 U.S. 833 (1992). In *Casey* the Supreme Court held that a state may require that a pregnant woman be given truthful, nonmisleading information about the nature of the procedure, the attendant health risks and those of childbirth, and the probable gestational age of the fetus. The state may also require that the woman be informed of the availability of other materials if she chooses to look at them, in order to ensure that the woman is giving informed consent to the abortion. The Court held that to the extent there is anything to the contrary in *Akron v. Akron Center for Reproductive Health, Inc.*, it was now overruled.

The *Casey* majority also upheld the allowance of a 24-hour waiting period between the time information was provided about the abortion and the performance of the abortion. While the Court in *Akron* had invalidated the requirement of a similar waiting period, the *Casey* Court rejected *Akron*, stating that the idea that important decisions will be more informed and deliberate if they follow some period of reflection was not unreasonable, particularly where the statute directs that important information become part of the background of the decision. Although the Court indicated concern over the issue of whether the 24-hour waiting period was an undue burden on an abortion decision, the waiting-period rule was upheld because the record in the eyes of the Court failed to demonstrate that such a waiting period was a "substantial obstacle" to a woman seeking an abortion.

21.8. Wavering on *Roe*

Three years before *Casey*, the Supreme Court in *Webster v. Reproductive Health Services*, 492 U.S. 490 (1989), declined to overrule *Roe v. Wade*, but cast doubt on the reasoning of that decision. At issue was a Missouri statute that had been declared unconstitutional by the Eighth Circuit. The Missouri statute prohibited the use of public employees and facilities to perform or assist abortions not necessary to save the mother's life, and made it unlawful to use public funds, employees, or facilities for the purpose of "encouraging or counseling" a woman to have an abortion not necessary to save her life. The Court upheld the statute.

In the opinion (5 to 4 plurality), the Court, while recognizing the state's interest in protecting potential human life, pointed out that the interest does not come into existence only at the point of viability, but exists throughout pregnancy. It criticized the rigid trimester analysis found in *Roe* as having "proved to be unsound in principle and unworkable in practice." 492 U.S. at 494. It suggested that a less stringent standard of review be applied to its standard of review of state abortion statutes, which would result in allowing "more governmental regulation of abortion than was permissible before." 492 U.S. at 494. Because of this determination, the plurality concluded that there was no good reason for the rigid line allowing state regulation after viability but prohibiting it before viability as had been promulgated in the wake of *Roe v. Wade*.

21.9. A Further Departure from *Roe*

In *Planned Parenthood of Southeastern Pennsylvania v. Casey*, 505 U.S. 833 (1992), already discussed to some extent earlier, the Supreme Court clearly retreated from *Roe*. It relegated the right to an abortion from a fundamental right to one that involves a liberty interest. It also adopted the undue burden standard of review that had been suggested by the solicitor general in his *amicus curiae* brief in *City of Akron*, *supra*. It rejected the trimester analysis used in *Roe*.

In *Casey* a portion of the Pennsylvania Abortion Control Act was being challenged as unconstitutional. The Act required that women seeking abortions sign a statement 24 hours before the procedure giving their consent and, except in special cases, that a parent must consent before a minor child could obtain an abortion. Another section of the statute required a wife to sign a statement that she had notified her husband that she intended to get an abortion. There were also sections providing for a medical emergency exception and a reporting requirement for abortion facilities.

The Court upheld all of the statutory requirements except the spousal notification provision. Relying on the doctrine of *stare decisis*, the Court did not overrule the legality of abortions premised in *Roe v. Wade*. However, it said that in reviewing state statutes restricting abortions, that they were no longer *all* subject to review under the strict scrutiny standard. Rather, only those provisions in a statute that place an undue burden on a woman seeking an abortion would be reviewed under the strict scrutiny standard. 505 U.S. at 876.

The Court defined undue burden as "the conclusion that a state regulation has the purpose or effect of placing a substantial obstacle in the path of the woman." 505 U.S. at 877. According to the Court, neither the informed consent requirement nor the 24-hour provision found in the Pennsylvania statute created an undue burden for persons seeking abortion.

The Court stated that requiring a doctor to make certain information available to a woman in the first trimester is permissible as long as the information is truthful and not misleading and was not an undue burden. In overruling *Akron I*, and *Thornburgh*, at least in part, where the Court had determined statutes that mandated that such information be provided by a physician were unconstitutional, the Court wrote, "Requiring that the woman be informed of the availability of information relating to the consequences to the fetus does not interfere with a constitutional right of privacy between a pregnant woman and her physician, since the doctor-patient relation is derivative of the woman's position, and does not underlie or override the abortion right. Moreover, the physician's First Amendment rights not to speak are implicated only as part of the practice of medicine, which is licensed and regulated by the State. There is no evidence here that requiring a doctor to give the required information would amount to a substantial obstacle to a woman seeking an abortion." 505 U.S. at 838.

The Court also abandoned *Roe*'s reliance on the trimester approach, stating that it did not consider "the trimester framework . . . to be part of the essential holding of *Roe*." 505 U.S. at 873. The Court explained that "[t]he trimester framework no doubt was erected to ensure that the woman's right to choose not become so subordinate to the State's interest in promoting fetal life that her choice exists in theory but not in fact. We do not agree, however, that the trimester approach is necessary to accomplish this objective." 505 U.S. at 872. It continued, "Even in the earliest stages of pregnancy, the State may enact rules and regulations designed to encourage her to know that there are philosophic and social arguments of great weight that can be brought to bear in favor of continuing the pregnancy to full term and that there are procedures and institutions to allow adoption of unwanted children as well as a certain degree of state assistance if the mother chooses to raise the child herself." *Id.*

Example 21-4

Assume that a state statute requires that before an abortion is performed on a married woman, she must obtain written permission from her husband for the procedure. P, a married woman, challenges the statute as unconstitutional. How will a court most likely rule?

Explanation

A state may not require a spouse's prior written consent to an abortion. The Supreme Court has repeatedly invalidated both spousal notification and consent requirements. In *Planned Parenthood of Southeastern Pennsylvania v. Casey*, 505 U.S. 833, 837-838 (1992), the Court held that a husband notification provision in a state statute constitutes an undue burden on a woman seeking an abortion and is therefore invalid. It reasoned that a significant number of women would likely be prevented from obtaining an abortion by such a provision just as surely as if Pennsylvania had outlawed the procedure entirely. It observed that the fact that the provision may affect less than 1 percent of women seeking abortions does not save it from facial invalidity, since the proper focus of constitutional inquiry is the group for whom the law is a restriction, not the group for whom it is irrelevant. The Court also observed that it cannot be claimed that the father's interest in the fetus's welfare is equal to the mother's protected liberty, since it is an inescapable biological fact that state regulation with respect to the fetus will have a far greater impact on the pregnant woman's bodily integrity than it will on the husband's. Such a provision requiring notification of a husband before a woman has an abortion embodies a view of marriage consonant with the common law status of married women but repugnant to the Court's present understanding of marriage and of the nature of the rights secured by the Constitution.

DEFERENCE TO PHYSICIANS

21.10. Viability Determination

In *Colautti v. Franklin*, 439 U.S. 379 (1979), the Supreme Court held unconstitutionally vague a viability determination requirement in a Pennsylvania law. The challenged provision required that every person who performed or induced an abortion make a determination, "based on his experience, judgment or professional competence," that the fetus was not viable; if such person determined that the fetus was viable, or if "there was sufficient reason to believe that the fetus may be viable," then the person had to adhere to a prescribed standard of care. *Id.* at 391 of 439 U.S. It was not clear whether the statute contained a purely subjective standard or whether it imposed a mixed subjective and objective standard. *Id.* The Court emphasized that, while "viable" and "may be viable" presumably had different meanings, a physician could not know from the statute what they were. It said that the law provided no guidance and conditioned potential physician liability on "confusing and ambiguous criteria," and was, therefore, impermissibly vague. 439 U.S. at 394.

The Court also suggested that it favored providing broad discretion to physicians to make determinations as to "medical necessity" in the abortion context.

21.11. Physician's Duty to Inform

The approach of courts to defer to physicians may have reached its apex in *City of Akron v. Akron Center for Reproductive Health, Inc.*, 462 U.S. 416 (1983) (*Akron 1*), which has been discussed in a somewhat different context earlier in this chapter. In *Akron*, a local city ordinance required that a physician inform a woman of the status of her pregnancy, the development of her fetus, the date of possible viability, the physical and emotional complications that may result from an abortion, and the availability of agencies to provide assistance and information. 462 U.S at 442. The physician was also required to advise the woman of the risks associated with the abortion technique to be employed and other information. *Id.* The law was invalidated based on the physician's right to practice medicine in the way he or she saw fit. According to the Court, "[i]t remains primarily the responsibility of the physician to ensure that appropriate information is conveyed to his patient, depending on her particular circumstances." 462 U.S at 443. The ordinance was viewed by the Court as an unwarranted "intrusion upon the discretion of the pregnant woman's physician." 462 U.S at 445. The Court believed that a physician subject to this ordinance was being placed in an "undesired and uncomfortable straitjacket." *Id.*

Note that, even though the Supreme Court later overruled portions of *Akron I* in *Planned Parenthood of Southeastern Pennsylvania v. Casey*, 505 U.S. 833 (1992), *Casey* did not readdress the unconstitutionality of requiring second-trimester abortions to be performed in hospitals.

The Court in *Casey* rejected an argument that the Pennsylvania informed consent law violated the constitutional right to privacy between the pregnant woman and her physician. The *Casey* Court said that *Akron* was wrongly decided on this point and that the doctor-patient relationship was only "entitled to the same solicitude it receives in other contexts." 505 U.S. at 884. The Court referred to the law's provision allowing doctors to exercise their best medical judgment by permitting them not to furnish the required advisories if they could demonstrate by a preponderance of the evidence that they reasonably believed that making the disclosures would result in a severely adverse effect on the health of the patient. *See Planned Parenthood Minnesota, North Dakota, South Dakota v. Rounds*, 530 F.3d 724 (8th Cir. 2008) (abortion provider failed to demonstrate the requisite likelihood that disclosure which was statutorily required of physicians was untruthful or misleading); *Karlin v. Foust*, 188 F.3d 446 (7th Cir. 1999) (as long as a particular informed consent requirement is designed to further a legitimate state interest, whether it is protecting the life and health of the mother or the life of the fetus, it will not be considered a substantial obstacle to obtaining an abortion provided that the information that the state "requires to be made available to the woman is truthful and not misleading"; an informed consent provision that requires the distribution of false and misleading information places an unconstitutional burden on a woman's right to choose).

Example 21-5

Assume that state X passes an abortion statute providing that a woman's consent to an abortion is not voluntary or informed unless "the physician who is to perform the procedure, or the referring physician, has, at a minimum, orally, in person, informed the woman of described information." The XYZ Women's Center challenges the requirement on a constitutional basis. Both the center and a doctor handling abortions file affidavits in support of the challenge. The center's affidavit explains that first-trimester abortions, which compose the vast majority of its abortions, are done by two board-certified obstetrician/gynecologists three days each week. The information regarding the procedure, however, is given to the women primarily by counselors employed by the center. This is done during the first telephone call, which usually takes 10 to 15 minutes, but can last much longer. When a woman comes in for the abortion, she receives more extensive counseling and information from a counselor. It is not until after that counseling that the woman meets the physician, who ascertains whether the woman has any further questions. It is argued that if the physician performing the procedure must give the informed consent, it will increase the amount of time the physician has to spend in the clinic, will increase the cost of an abortion, and will disrupt the operation of the center. The doctor's affidavit states, among other things, that requiring the physician performing the abortion to give all of the informed consent information to women will "disrupt my practice, raise the cost of abortions, and burden women who seek to terminate a pregnancy." How will a court most likely treat the constitutional challenge?

Explanation

The court will most likely strike down the statute. The burden is on the state to demonstrate that this intrusion or restriction "serves a compelling state interest and accomplishes its goal through the use of the least intrusive means." Considering the fact that the state does not have a compelling interest in the health of a pregnant woman during the first trimester, or a fetus before it is viable, there is a substantial likelihood that the clinic will prevail. Even in the second trimester, where the state does have a compelling interest, this restriction will still have to meet the "least intrusive" standard. *See State v. Presidential Women's Center,* 707 So. 2d 1145 (Fla. App. 1998).

PERSONAL HISTORY, CONSENT, AND WAITING PERIOD

21.12. Consent, Reporting Requirement, Physician Duty to Inform, and Necessity of Second Physician Opinion

In *Thornburgh v. American Coll. of Obst. & Gyn.,* 476 U.S. 747 (1986), the Supreme Court considered a challenge to a number of provisions of a Pennsylvania abortion statute. The Court held that the requirement that a physician inform women of the detrimental physical and psychological effects and of all particular medical risks was unconstitutional. The provision was viewed by the Court as the antithesis of informed consent because it intruded upon a physician's exercise of proper professional judgment.

The Court also held that the statutory reporting requirements of the Pennsylvania statute were unconstitutional. It said that the scope of information required by the reporting provisions found in the Abortion Control Act, and the availability of the information to the public, belied any assertion by the Commonwealth that it was advancing a legitimate interest. The requirements went "well beyond the health related interests" that may justify reporting requirements in some cases. 476 U.S. at 766. Among the defects noted by the Court was the fact that the statute required information "as to the woman's personal history." Id. The Court also held that withholding a minor's name is not enough by itself to protect her anonymity where the publicly available information could identify the minor. 476 U.S. at 766-768. The Court reasoned that because the potentially identifying information is often so detailed, the absence of the minor's name will not protect her interests, and the use of a fictitious name does not adequately protect a pregnant minor's confidences. The Court felt that the reporting requirements raised the specter of public exposure and harassment of women who chose to exercise their personal, private right, with their physician, to end pregnancy.

Another provision that governed the degree of care for post-viability abortions was held facially invalid. The provision required that an abortion technique employed post-viability be one that provides the best opportunity for an unborn child to be aborted alive unless, in the physician's good-faith judgment, the technique "would present a significantly greater medical risk to the life or health of the pregnant woman." The Court said this provision was unsusceptible to construction that did not require the mother to bear an increased medical risk in order to save viable fetus.

Finally, the Court ruled that a provision requiring the presence of a second physician during an abortion, when viability is possible, was unconstitutional because it failed to provide a medical-emergency exception for situations where the mother's health was endangered by a delay in the second physician's arrival. The Court said that this section chilled the performance of a late abortion, which, more than one performed at earlier date, tends to occur under emergency conditions.

As noted earlier, Thornburgh was in part overruled by Planned Parenthood of Southeastern Pennsylvania v. Casey, 505 U.S. 833 (1992), in particular the portions of the decision that addressed the issue of informed consent. However, the Supreme Court left Thornburgh intact to the extent that it relied upon Roe's approach to post-viability regulation of abortions.

PICKETING

21.13. Buffer Zones

In Madsen v. Women's Health Center, 512 U.S. 753 (1994), anti-abortion protesters threatened to picket and demonstrate around a Florida abortion clinic. A state trial court permanently enjoined the petitioners from blocking or interfering with public access to the clinic, and from physically abusing persons entering or leaving it.

Later, when the clinic operators sought to broaden the injunction, the trial court found that access to the clinic was still being impeded, that petitioners' activities were having deleterious physical effects on patients and discouraging some potential patients from entering the clinic. The trial court also found that doctors and clinic workers were being subjected to protests at their homes. In response to these findings, the trial judge issued an amended injunction, which applied to the anti-abortion group and persons acting "in concert" with the group. The order excluded demonstrators from a 36-foot buffer zone around the clinic entrances and driveway and the private property to the north and west of the clinic. It also restricted excessive noisemaking within the earshot of the clinic, and the use of "images observable" by patients inside the clinic. It prohibited protesters within a 300-foot zone around the clinic from approaching patients and potential patients who do not consent to talk. It essentially created a 300-foot buffer zone around the residences of clinic staff.

The Florida Supreme Court upheld the amended injunction against anti-abortion proponents' claim that it violated their First Amendment right to freedom of speech, and the Supreme Court granted review.

The Supreme Court upheld the injunction. It said that, given the focus of the picketing on patients and clinic staff, the narrowness of the confines around the clinic, the fact that protesters could still be seen and heard from the clinic parking lots, and the failure of the first injunction to accomplish its purpose, the 36-foot buffer zone around the clinic entrances and driveway, on balance, burdens no more speech than necessary to accomplish the governmental interests in protecting access to the clinic and facilitating an orderly traffic flow on the street.

It held that the order under which the injunction was issued was content-neutral in terms of time, place, and manner regulation for First Amendment purposes. It also said that the injunction regulated only places where some speech could occur; applied equally to all demonstrators, regardless of viewpoint; and did not make any reference to content of speech. It concluded that the order issued as a part of the injunction provided the police with clear guidelines that were unrelated to the content of demonstrators' speech. The limited noise restrictions imposed by the injunction burdened no more speech than necessary to ensure the health and well-being of the clinic's patients.

However, the Court rejected the 300-foot buffer zone around staff residences as sweeping more broadly than is necessary to protect the tranquility and privacy of the home. The Court said that the record did not contain sufficient justification for so broad a ban on picketing

PARTIAL-BIRTH ABORTIONS

21.14. Partial-Birth Legislation: *Carhart I* and *II*

In *Stenberg v. Carhart*, 530 U.S. 914 (2000) (*Carhart I*), a physician who performed abortions brought suit on behalf of himself and his patients challenging the constitutionality of a Nebraska statute banning a "partial-birth abortion."

During a pregnancy's second trimester (12-24 weeks), the most common abortion procedure is "dilation and evacuation" (D & E). 530 U.S. at 914-915. This procedure involves dilation of the cervix, removal of at least some fetal tissue using nonvacuum surgical instruments, and (after the fifteenth week) the potential need for instrumental dismemberment of the fetus or the collapse of fetal parts to facilitate evacuation from the uterus. When dismemberment is necessary, it typically occurs as the doctor pulls a portion of the fetus through the cervix into the birth canal. 530 U.S. at 915.

The risks of mortality and the complications that accompany D & E are significantly less than those accompanying induced-labor procedures (the next safest mid-second-trimester procedures). *Id*. A variation of D & E, known as "intact D & E," is used after 16 weeks. "It involves removing the fetus from the uterus through the cervix 'intact,' i.e., in one pass rather than several passes. Intact D & E proceeds in one of two ways, depending on whether the fetus presents head first or feet first. The feet-first method is known as 'dilation and extraction' (D & X). D & X is ordinarily associated with the term 'partial birth abortion.' " *Id*.

The district court concluded that clear and convincing evidence established that Doctor Carhart's D & X procedure is superior to, and safer than, the D & E and other abortion procedures used during the relevant gestational period in the 10 to 20 cases a year that he handled.

The Court held that the Nebraska statute imposed an undue burden on women. Without deciding the issue of whether a statute that outlawed only intact D & E would be unduly burdensome, the Court held that an abortion ban that failed to differentiate in its statutory language between intact D & E and non-intact D & E unquestionably constituted an undue burden, because it would prohibit most second-trimester abortions. 530 U.S. at 938-946. As part of its analysis, the *Stenberg* Court provided legislatures with guidance about drafting statutes that would adequately distinguish between the two forms of D & E.

The Court explained that a legislature should make clear that a statute intended to regulate only intact D & E applies only to that form of the procedure by using language that "track[s] the medical differences between" intact and non-intact D & E or by providing an express exception for the performance of non-intact D & E and other abortion procedures. 530 U.S. at 939. In her concurring opinion, Justice O'Connor emphasized how, by employing the above approach, a legislature could make it clear that a statute intended to regulate intact D & E was in fact narrowly tailored to reach only that form of the D & E procedure. 530 U.S. at 950. Citing three state statutes prohibiting intact D & E that had specifically excluded from their coverage other abortion methods, Justice O'Connor described the language each statute used, providing legislatures wishing to prohibit only intact D & E with a clear roadmap for how to avoid the problems regarding the scope of coverage that undid the Nebraska statute. *Id.*

In the wake of *Carhart I*, Congress passed the Partial-Birth Abortion Ban Act of 2003, 18 U.S.C. §1531 (2003). Congress obviously intended the new Act to be a response to *Carhart I*. The Act was almost immediately challenged, and the matter eventually made its way to the Supreme Court. There, in a 5-4 ruling, the Court upheld the Act. *Gonzales v. Carhart (Carhart II)*, 550 U.S. 124 (2007).

Justice Kennedy, writing for the majority in *Carhart II*, stated that the new Act does not violate the constitutional right to abortion laid out in *Roe v. Wade*, or *Planned Parenthood of Southeastern Pennsylvania v. Casey*. The majority observed that the Act had responded to *Carhart I* in two ways. First, Congress had made its own factual findings for the Act. Second, the Act's language differs from that of the Nebraska statute struck down in *Carhart I* because it includes "anatomical landmarks" to describe the banned procedure and scienter requirements to prevent criminalization when intent is absent. 550 U.S. at 1627-1628.

The majority ruled that the lack of an exception in the Act for a woman's health was not fatal because medical uncertainty existed over whether the banned procedure was ever necessary to protect the health of the woman. Justice Thomas noted that although he joined the majority opinion, he believed that *Casey* and *Roe*, as well as the current abortion jurisprudence, are not rooted in the Constitution.

PARENTAL NOTIFICATION

21.15. Minor Notifying Parents

In *Hodgson v. Minnesota*, 497 U.S. 417 (1990), the Supreme Court considered a provision in Minnesota's abortion statute that required a physician to notify both parents at least 48 hours before performing an abortion on a minor. The Court held that the requirement did not reasonably further any legislative state interest and was unconstitutional. The Court said that "the requirement that both parents be notified . . . does not reasonably further any legitimate state interest." *Id.* The Court rejected as justifications for the two-parent requirement the parents' concern for the child's welfare and the state's interest in protecting the parents' independent right to determine and strive for what they believe best for their child. 497 U.S. at 452. Neither of these reasons, said the Court, can justify the two-parent notification requirement.

The Court recognized that the second parent may well have an interest in the minor's abortion decision, making full communication among all members of a family desirable in some cases, but the Court said that such communication may not be decreed by the state. The Court reasoned that the state has no more interest in requiring all family members to talk with one another than it has in requiring certain of them to live together. *Id.* The Court stated that to the extent a parental consent or parental notification provision legitimately supports the parents' authority to act in the minor's best interest, and thus "assures that the minor's decision to terminate her pregnancy is knowing, intelligent, and deliberate," that interest is fully served by notice to one parent. 497 U.S. at 450.

The Court further held, in an opinion by Justice Kennedy, that the provision of the statute that requires two-parent notification unless the pregnant minor obtains a judicial bypass was constitutional. *See Barnes v. State of Miss.*, 992 F.2d 1335 (5th Cir. 1993) (statute requiring consent of two parents but containing adequate judicial bypass mechanism is facially constitutional, and judicial bypass mechanism is constitutional).

21.16. Parent Notification Exceptions

In *Lambert v. Wicklund*, 520 U.S. 292 (1977), the constitutional challenge was to Montana's Parental Notice of Abortion Act. The Act prohibits a physician from performing an abortion on a minor unless the physician has notified one of the minor's parents or the minor's legal guardian 48 hours in advance. However, an "unemancipated" minor may petition the state youth court to waive the notification requirement, pursuant to the statute's "judicial bypass" provision. The provision gives the minor a right to court-appointed counsel, and guarantees expeditious handling of the minor's petition (since the petition is automatically granted if the youth court fails to rule on the petition within 48 hours from the time it is filed). The minor's identity remains anonymous, and the proceedings and related documents are kept confidential.

The physicians and other medical personnel challenged the third provision of the statute, alleging that "the notification of a parent or guardian is not in the best interests of the minor." The Supreme Court held that a judicial bypass provision that allowed waiver of the notice requirement if notification was not in minor's best interest was sufficient to protect a minor's right to abortion. Under the statute, a judge could waive the notice requirement if there was clear and convincing evidence that the minor was mature enough and well enough informed to make the abortion decision independently and the minor establishes that the abortion would be in her best interests. The Court observed that in *Bellotti v. Baird*, 443 U.S. 622 (1979), it struck down a statute requiring a minor to obtain the consent of both parents before having an abortion, subject to a judicial bypass provision, because the judicial bypass provision was too restrictive and unconstitutionally burdened a minor's right to an abortion. Here, however, the claim that there is a constitutionally significant distinction between requiring a minor to show that parental notification is not in her best interests and requiring a minor to show that an abortion (without such notification) is in her best interests is not supportable. Montana draws no such distinction.

Ayotte v. Planned Parenthood of New England, 546 U.S. 320 (2006), involved New Hampshire's Parental Notification Prior to Abortion Act, which prohibited physicians from performing an abortion on a minor until 48 hours following the delivery of written notice to the minor's parent or guardian. Although the Act did make an exception in cases where an abortion was necessary to preserve the life of the mother, it contained no corresponding health exception. The First Circuit invalidated the law in its entirety for want of the health exception. In a unanimous opinion, the Supreme Court held that because the parental notification law did not contain an exception allowing a minor to obtain an abortion without notice to her parent when necessary to preserve the minor's health, it was, as to that particular requirement, unconstitutional.

In *Akron v. Akron Center for Reproductive Health*, 497 U.S. 502 (1990) (*Akron II*), the Court observed that the statute under attack, which required a minor to notify one parent before having an abortion, contained a judicial bypass provision. The Court upheld the statute, concluding that its judicial bypass procedure complies with the Fourteenth Amendment; due process allowed the statute to require a minor to prove maturity or the minor's best interest by clear and convincing evidence when using judicial bypass procedure; and the statute could require parental notice to be given by physician performing the abortion. 497 U.S. at 508. The Court explicitly held that "the procedure must allow the minor to show that, even if she cannot make the abortion decision by herself, the desired abortion would be in her best interests." 497 U.S. at 511.

21.17. Mature Minor Exception

In *Bellotti v. Baird*, 443 U.S. 622 (1979), the Supreme Court, in separate opinions by Justice Powell and Justice Stevens, held that a Massachusetts statute that required a pregnant minor seeking an abortion to obtain the consent of her parents, or obtain judicial approval following notification to her parents, unconstitutionally burdened the right of the pregnant minor to seek an abortion. The Court stated that if a state decides to require that a pregnant minor obtain one or both parents' consent to an abortion, it must also provide for an alternative procedure whereby authorization for the abortion can be obtained.

The Court also ruled that a pregnant minor is entitled to show either that she is mature enough and well enough informed to make her own abortion decision, in consultation with her physician, independently of her parents' wishes, or that even if she is not able to make this decision independently, the desired abortion would be in her best interests. Such a procedure must ensure that the provision requiring parental consent does not in fact amount to an impermissible, absolute, and possibly arbitrary veto.

Example 21-6

Assume that state X enacts a statute that provides a two-step process to determine a minor's maturity to make an abortion decision. The statute mandates that the judge of the district court determine whether the minor is mature enough to make the abortion decision. If she is deemed mature, she is allowed to make the decision. In step 2, if the minor is not sufficiently mature to make the decision, the judge resolves the question of whether the abortion should occur. The challengers insist that undue burdens will result from the state's choice of the district court as the exclusive forum in which a minor may obtain judicial consent, arguing that the existence of a $250 filing fee in that court, the limited times during which it is in session, and the lack of easily utilized standard forms for such actions will in fact bar many minors from access to judicial consent. In response, the state asserts that there is a simple indigency form available to the minor that can be used in such a situation and that this form and an alternative one for nonindigents will provide immediate access to the court. How will a court most likely treat the challenge?

Explanation

The exclusive jurisdiction of the court could be troubling, but the availability of an indigency waiver form significantly reduces the possible burdensomeness of the filing fee. The provision for both immediate access to the court and a simple form for such actions makes the possible obstacles far less substantial. It is doubtful that a court will find the process so burdensome as to deny due process of law to minors seeking to use it. *Planned Parenthood League of Massachusetts v. Bellotti*, 641 F.2d 1006 (1st Cir. 1981) (state-prescribed consent form, which a woman was required to sign as prerequisite to obtaining abortion in Massachusetts, was not in itself violative of due process).

21.18. Written Consent of Parent

In *Planned Parenthood of Central Missouri v. Danforth*, 428 U.S. 52 (1976), a Missouri abortion statute required the written consent of a parent or person in *loco parentis* to an abortion of an unmarried woman under 18 during the first 12 weeks of pregnancy, unless a licensed physician certified that the abortion was necessary to preserve the mother's life. The Supreme Court held that such a provision was unconstitutional, at least insofar as it imposed a blanket parental consent requirement. Justice Blackmun wrote that "the State cannot 'delegate to a spouse a veto power which the [S]tate itself is absolutely and totally prohibited from exercising during the first trimester of pregnancy. . . . '" As stressed in *Roe*, "the abortion decision and its effectuation must be left to the medical judgment of the pregnant woman's attending physician." 424 U.S. at 53-54.

Example 21-7

Assume that in 1972 P, age 17, underwent an abortion. D, the physician who performed the abortion, obtained an informed consent signed by P's mother but did not obtain P's formal consent to the abortion. Also assume that the statute of limitations does not bar a civil action against D and that P sues D, alleging the physician was negligent in failing to consult with P prior to the abortion. In support of her claim, D responds that in 1972, D was not required to obtain the minor's consent. How will a court most likely rule on D's request that the lawsuit be dismissed?

Explanation

D's motion will most likely be granted. Even if the trial court had *Roe v. Wade* before it, a case decided a year after the alleged negligence occurred, *Roe* did not create a legal duty of a physician to obtain the consent of a minor patient before an abortion. Furthermore, at the time of the abortion, P was a minor who could not give effective consent. Given the purpose of requiring a physician to disclose information — that is, to help the person who will consent, or withhold consent, to make an informed decision — a physician was not required to make full disclosure to a minor, when the minor could not give legally effective consent. Consent from the minor's mother is sufficient. *See Powers v. Floyd*, 904 S.W.2d 713 (Tex. App. 1995) (physician, who obtained patient's mother's written informed consent prior to performing the abortion, had no duty in 1974 to obtain patient's consent).

Example 21-8

Assume that state X enacted a statute that allows only one petition per pregnancy for minors seeking a judicial bypass of the parental-consent requirement. P challenges the statute on its face as placing an undue burden on a woman seeking an abortion. Most likely, how will a court rule on the challenge?

Explanation

A state may regulate abortion before viability as long as it does not impose an "undue burden" on a woman's right to terminate her pregnancy. An "undue burden" exists when "a state regulation has the purpose or effect of placing a substantial obstacle in the path of a woman seeking an abortion of a non-viable fetus."

The statute as written prevents women from seeking a judicial bypass for an abortion where changed circumstances may exist. The changed circumstances that affect abortion-seeking minors include increased maturity, increased medical knowledge about abortion, and discovery that the fetus has a medical anomaly such as gastroschisis. A court will most likely decide that a single-petition rule places an undue burden on a woman seeking an abortion and is facially unconstitutional. *See Cincinnati Women's Services, Inc. v. Taft*, 468 F.3d 361 (6th Cir. 2006) (provision limiting minors seeking a judicial bypass of statutory parental-consent requirement to one petition per pregnancy was an undue burden on the constitutional right to an abortion).

ABORTION FUNDING

21.19. Medicaid Coverage

In 1977 the Supreme Court decided three cases involving laws that permitted states to refuse Medicaid coverage for nontherapeutic abortions. *Beal v. Doe*, 432 U.S. 438 (1977); *Mather v. Roe*, 432 U.S. 464 (1977); *Poelker v. Doe*, 432 U.S. 519 (1977). In *Beal v. Doe*, 432 U.S. 438 (1977), the Court held that Title XIX of the Social Security Act does not require a state Medicaid program to fund elective (nontherapeutic) abortions, declaring that states have broad discretion to determine the extent of medical assistance that is "reasonable" and "consistent" with the objectives of the Act. 432 U.S. at 444. The Court explained that it was "not unsympathetic to the plight of an indigent woman who desires an abortion, but the Constitution does not provide judicial remedies for every social and economic ill."

A majority in *Maher v. Roe*, 432 U.S. 464 (1977), found no "unduly burdensome interference" with a woman's abortion decision and that the exclusion of elective abortions from Medicaid did not violate the Equal Protection Clause. The Court treated the refusal to fund abortion as state inaction calling for the rational basis test rather than the strict scrutiny test applied in *Roe*. Because Connecticut encouraged childbirth over abortion, this was viewed as satisfying application of the rational basis test.

In *Harris v. McRae*, 448 U.S. 297 (1980), an action was brought challenging the statutory and constitutional validity of the Hyde Amendment, which severely limits use of federal funds to reimburse the cost of abortions under the Medicaid program. The Supreme Court held that a state that participates in the Medicaid program is not obligated under Title XIX of the Social Security Act to continue to fund those medically necessary abortions for which federal reimbursement was unavailable under the Hyde Amendment. It also held that funding restrictions of the Hyde Amendment violated neither the Fifth Amendment nor the Establishment Clause of the First Amendment. The Court said that the language in the Medicaid statute prohibiting the use of federal funds to reimburse the cost of abortions "except where the life of the mother would be endangered if the fetus were carried to term" was facially constitutional under the Equal Protection Clause.

21.20. Selective Funding of Programs in the Public Interest

In *Rust v. Sullivan*, 500 U.S. 173 (1991), recipients of family planning funds under Title X of the Public Health Service Act and doctors who supervised Title X funds brought two suits challenging regulations of the Department of Health and Human Services (HHS) that prohibit Title X projects from engaging in abortion counseling, referral, and activities advocating abortion as a method of family planning. The plaintiffs also challenged provisions of regulations requiring such projects to maintain an objective integrity and independence from prohibited abortion activities by the use of separate facilities, personnel, and accounting records.

The Supreme Court held that the regulations do not violate First Amendment free-speech rights of Title X fund recipients, their staffs, or their patients by impermissibly imposing viewpoint-discriminatory conditions on government subsidies.

The Court said that Congress may "selectively fund a program to encourage certain activities it believes to be in the public interest, without at the same time funding an alternative program which seeks to deal with the problem in another way." 500 U.S. at 193. In doing so, "the Government has not discriminated on the basis of viewpoint; it has merely chosen to fund one activity to the exclusion of the other." *Id.*; *see also Maher v. Roe*, 432 U.S. 464, 475 (1977) ("There is a basic difference between direct state interference with a protected activity and state encouragement of an alternative activity consonant with legislative policy"). *Rust's* holding has been limited to situations in which the government is itself the speaker, or instances in which the government used private speakers to transmit its own message.

21.21. Barring Use of Public Facilities

In *Webster v. Reproductive Health Services*, 492 U.S. 490 (1989), Missouri legislation prohibited the use of public facilities for abortion and required that a physician rigorously examine a pregnant woman seeking an abortion if the physician believes the woman's pregnancy to be past 20 weeks. The medical tests were to determine "the gestational age, weight, and lung maturity of the unborn child." 493 U.S. at 512.

The legislation was successfully challenged in the United States District Court for the Western District of Missouri, which held the statute unconstitutional. The Eighth Circuit Court of Appeals upheld the lower court decision, and review was granted by the Supreme Court. Although overturning *Roe v. Wade* was urged by the solicitor general, the Court did not do so. However, five of the nine justices agreed that restrictions such as Missouri's prohibition on the use of public facilities and funds for abortions and the state's required tests to determine viability do not burden procreational choice and are constitutional. In other words, the Court upheld a requirement that no public employees or facilities be used for nontherapeutic abortions.

21.22. State Constitutional Right to Privacy

Some believe that abortion rights may be obtained more successfully under some state constitutions than under the federal Constitution. For example, in *American Academy of Pediatrics v. Lungren*, 940 P.2d 797 (Cal. 1997), a California statute required that health care providers secure parental consent or judicial authorization before performing an abortion on a minor. The statute applied to a pregnant minor who is willing to seek parental advice and consent and to "a pregnant minor [who] is too frightened or too embarrassed to disclose her condition to a parent or to a court." 940 P.2d at 800. The court held that the statute violated the minor's right of privacy guaranteed by Article I, Section 1 of the California Constitution. The court reasoned that "[t]he statute significantly intrudes upon autonomy privacy by denying a pregnant minor the ability to obtain a medically safe abortion on her own, and instead requiring her to secure parental consent or judicial authorization in order to obtain access to the medical care she needs to terminate her pregnancy safely. In this respect, the statute denies a pregnant minor, who believes it is in her best interest to terminate her pregnancy rather than have a child at such a young age, control over her own destiny." 940 P.2d at 817. The majority found that under the California Constitution, a minor has the same privacy interest as an adult woman in deciding whether or not to bear a child.

Several jurisdictions are turning to their state constitutional provisions in considering a variety of abortion issues. *See generally Planned Parenthood League v. Attorney Gen.*, 677 N.E.2d 101, 103 (Mass. 1997) (held on state constitutional basis that statutory requirement that pregnant, unmarried minor obtain consent of both parents before obtaining abortion violated Due Process Clause); *In re T.W.*, 551 So. 2d 1186, 1194 (Fla. 1989) (parental consent provision statute invalid under the Florida Constitution); *Planned Parenthood of Central N.J. v. Farmer*, 762 A.2d 620, 626, 631-639 (N.J. 2000) (Act that conditions minor's right to obtain abortion on parental notification unless judicial waiver is obtained, but imposes no corresponding limitation on minor who seeks medical and surgical care otherwise related to her pregnancy, violates state constitution's equal protection provision); *State v. Planned Parenthood of Alaska*, 35 P.3d 30 (Alaska 2001) (state constitution's provision guaranteeing right of privacy from unwarranted governmental intrusion is self-executing); *Committee to Defend Reprod. Rights v. Myers*, 625 P.2d 779 (Cal. 1981) (funding restrictions violated privacy, due process, and equal protection provisions of California Constitution); *Women of the State v. Gomez*, 542 N.W.2d 17, 19 (Minn. 1995) (using strict scrutiny to rule that "a pregnant woman . . . cannot be coerced into choosing childbirth over abortion by a legislated funding policy" under privacy sections of Minnesota Constitution); *Right to Choose v. Byrne*, 450 A.2d 925 (N.J. 1982) (ruling that restrictions violate fundamental right protected by equal protection provisions of New Jersey Constitution); *Planned Parenthood Ass'n, Inc. v. Department of Human Resources*, 663 P.2d 1247 (Or. App. 983) (violation of Equal Privileges and Immunities Clause of Oregon Constitution), aff'd, 297 Or. 562, 687 P.2d 785 (1984); *Women's Health Ctr. of W. Va., Inc. v. Panepinto*, 446 S.E.2d 658 (W. Va. 1993) (relying on unique provisions of West Virginia Constitution to rule constitutional violation).

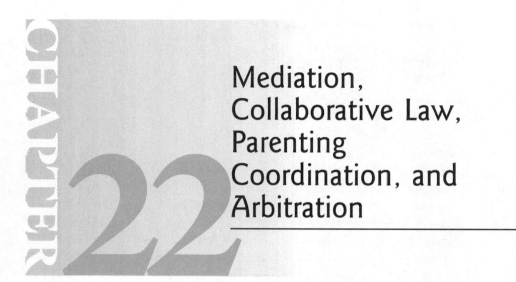

Mediation, Collaborative Law, Parenting Coordination, and Arbitration

22.1. Introduction

As a result of shifting societal values and expectations, the family court system and the process of divorce have changed remarkably over the last 40 years. Not surprisingly, the roles of family law professionals have been similarly transformed.

Families have widely embraced more cooperative and less adversarial divorce processes. Parents report that traditional adversarial divorce escalates conflict, takes too long, costs too much, and fails to yield parenting arrangements sufficiently tailored to meet their needs. Marsha Kline Pruett & Tamara D. Jackson, *The Lawyer's Role During the Divorce Process: Perceptions of Parents, Their Young Children, and Their Attorneys*, 33 Fam. L.Q. 283, 298 (1999). In light of research consistently showing that ongoing parental conflict harms children, parents began to seek divorce processes, such as mediation, designed to reduce conflict levels while also involving parents in creation of parenting plans specific to needs of their children. New societal norms about parenting were bolstered by research indicating that most children benefit from ongoing post-divorce contact with both parents. As a result of these trends, families flocked to processes that helped parents regularize their contact with each other for the purpose of parenting while keeping conflict to a minimum. Nancy Ver Steegh, *Family Court Reform and ADR: Shifting Values and Expectations Transform the Divorce Process*, 42 Fam. L.Q. 659 (2008). This chapter surveys several "alternative" processes and professional roles that have now become commonplace.

22.2. Choosing an Appropriate Process

Because of the proliferation of new divorce processes and services, some courts have developed protocols for matching families with resources that might be helpful to them. Some courts use a "linear" or "tiered" system in which families start in a less intrusive process such as mediation and progress through increasingly evaluative processes (potentially to trial) until the case is resolved. Other courts have adopted "triage" systems in which families are screened and referred to what is believed to be the appropriate level of service for them. Peter Salem, *The Emergence of Triage in Family Court Services: The Beginning of the End for Mandatory Mediation?*," 47 Fam. Ct. Rev. 371 (2009); Peter Salem, Debra Kulak & Robin M. Deutsch, *Triaging Family Court Services: The Connecticut Judicial Branch's Family Intake Screen*, 27 Pace L. Rev. 741 (2007). Family law attorneys should be prepared to counsel clients concerning various services and processes to ensure that clients are able to make informed choices.

MEDIATION

22.3. Definition Under the Model Standards

The Model Standards of Practice for Family and Divorce Mediation define *mediation* as

> A process in which a mediator, an impartial third party, facilitates the resolution of family disputes by promoting the participants' voluntary agreement. The family mediator assists communication, encourages understanding and focuses the participants on their individual and common interests. The family mediator works with the participants to explore options, make decisions and reach their own agreements.

Andrew Schepard, *An Introduction to the Model Standards of Practice for Family and Divorce Mediation*, 35 Fam. L.Q. 1, 3 (2001).

The process of family mediation assists couples in communicating and determining their own post-divorce outcomes. However, it is not intended to supplant either legal advice or therapy. The process keeps the needs of children in the forefront, while reducing the emotional and financial costs of divorce.

In practice, mediation programs differ significantly from each other. Some mediation takes place under the auspices of the court, and some mediation occurs in private practice settings. Other differences include the number of sessions offered, the qualifications of the mediator, and possible limitations on the issues considered. Mediators also adhere to different models of mediation. Consequently, when people refer to mediation, they may be discussing significantly different processes.

22.4. Mediation as an Interest-Based Process

The process of mediation focuses on the underlying needs and interests of the parties. Most couples have some common interests, such as the well-being of their children, and the mediation process encourages the participants to focus on ways they can work together to achieve common goals. Individual interests are also identified, and spouses consider how they can meet their own needs by also meeting the needs of the other person. For example, if one spouse feels strongly about continuing to live in the marital home and the other spouse is willing to move, the spouse staying in the home might agree to a division of assets that allocates liquid assets to the moving spouse so that he or she will be in a position to make a down payment on a new residence. Couples are thus encouraged to look for ways to "enlarge the pie" rather than becoming locked into a win-lose, rights-based orientation. Couples are discouraged from taking fixed positions and instead are encouraged to look for creative ways to satisfy important interests of both parties. Although the past actions of the parties can be relevant in trouble-shooting agreements, couples are encouraged to look forward rather than dwelling on past events.

Mediation is a structured problem-solving process that is likely to include the following steps: (1) identifying issues to be mediated; (2) gathering and documenting facts related to the issues; (3) reaching consensus on standards of fairness for each issue; (4) brainstorming possible solutions and considering the ramifications of each; and (5) making decisions about the issues. *See* Stephen K. Erickson & Marilyn S. McKnight, *The Practitioner's Guide to Mediation* 63 (2001). For example, if a couple is considering how to divide assets, they might first make a list of their assets and document the existence and value of each one. Next they would explore fair ways to divide the assets — for example, they might choose to divide their assets equally between themselves. With this information in mind, the couple is prepared to brainstorm about concrete plans for asset division, often with the use of a spreadsheet. After considering the pros and cons of each proposed plan, the couple would agree upon an option for dividing the assets.

Couples are encouraged to consider and define their own standards of fairness regarding particular issues. If both parties see their final agreement as being fair, they are more likely to comply with it and make it work. Of course, before the couple is divorced, their agreements are generally reviewed by attorneys and must be approved by the court.

22.5. Focus on Children's Needs

The focus on children's needs is a hallmark of the mediation process. Mediators continually ask parents to consider how their decisions will affect their children, and they encourage parents to build agreements around the particular needs of their children. Parents are given information about the impact of divorce on children, the developmental needs of children at various ages, and the effects of continuing parental conflict on children. In addition to encouraging parents to focus on the needs of children, new research indicates that more formal involvement of children in the mediation process (via separate consultation with a specialist) may improve relationships and boost child well-being. Jennifer E. McIntosh, Yvonne D. Wells & Bruce M. Smyth, *Child-Focused and Child-Inclusive Divorce Mediation: Comparative Outcomes from a Prospective Study of Postseparation Adjustment*, 46 Fam. Ct. Rev. 105 (2008).

Most mediation involves the preparation of a detailed "parenting plan." Typical parenting plans contain agreements about child-rearing practices, decision-making methods and authority, scheduling of physical residence and/or parenting time, budgeting and financial support, parental communication, and dispute resolution. Parenting plans focus on anticipating the needs of the children rather than enforcing the "rights" of the parents. Thus, where state law allows it, parenting plans avoid the use of custody labels because detailed parenting-time schedules and agreements about decision making obviate the need for these often contentious labels. The American Law Institute (ALI) adopted this approach, replacing the terms *custody* and *visitation* with the concept of *custodial responsibility*. ALI, *Principles of the Law of Family Dissolution: Analysis and Recommendations* §2.03(3) cmt. E, at 124 (2002). See Chapter 5 for a discussion of parenting plans.

Parties commonly develop a parenting plan and then implement it informally for a period of time before incorporating it into a final agreement or court order. This allows parents to "test-drive" arrangements and make desired changes prior to finalizing agreements.

22.6. The Role of the Mediator

The mediator functions as a neutral third party who facilitates the mediation process but generally does not express a point of view on the substantive issues. Instead, the mediator helps the participants reach their own decisions. This is quite different from the role of judges and arbitrators who make final decisions for the parties.

The mediator actively controls the mediation process by setting the agenda, deciding who will speak and in what order, creating ground rules, and framing the discussion. Through modeling and discussion, the mediator teaches the couple effective conflict-resolution and problem-solving skills. In addition, the mediator watches for power imbalance and uses techniques such as verifying facts, meeting in separate caucuses, and asking probing questions to ensure that couples make informed and voluntary decisions. Mediators carefully monitor the behavior of the participants and remain alert for lopsided agreements.

Research shows that mediation is most effective when the mediator actively structures the sessions, stays in "flexible control" of the process, "shapes" communication, and keeps the focus on problem solving and the parties' underlying interests. Joan B. Kelly, *A Decade of Divorce Mediation Research: Some Answers and Questions*, 34 Fam. & Conciliation Cts. Rev. 373, 382 (1996).

Example 22-1

Assume that P and D, who plan to divorce, disagree about issues such as parenting time and child support. The court appoints an attorney to act as a guardian *ad litem*, which entails functioning as an independent fact finder and evaluator who reports to the court regarding the best interests of the child. In the same order, the judge appoints the same lawyer to mediate the economic aspects of the divorce. As a guardian *ad litem*, the attorney criticizes some of P's parenting practices, and P contends that the attorney is biased toward her and consequently not a suitable mediator of economic issues. Was appointing the attorney to both roles in the same case improper?

Explanation

In the similar case of *Isaacson v. Isaacson*, 792 A.2d 525 (N.J. Super. 2002), the court found that the two roles were indeed incompatible. In New Jersey, the guardian *ad litem* functions as an independent fact finder and evaluator who reports to the court. That role was inconsistent with that of the mediator, who operates as a neutral party in a confidential setting. The court stated that "[w]e are not persuaded that the language limiting the role of [the attorney] as mediator to mediate economic issues and her role as guardian *ad litem* to protect the best interests of the children presents a defining distinction allowing her to serve in both capacities. Despite the seemingly disparate nature of the roles, they were not so distinct as to avoid the necessary overlap generating the conflict." *Id.* at 534.

22.7. Mediator Qualifications

The skill and experience of the mediator directly affect the quality of the mediation process. The Model Standards of Practice for Family and Divorce Mediation suggest that, at a minimum, family mediators should

1. have knowledge of family law;
2. have knowledge of and training in the impact of family conflict on parents, children, and other participants, including knowledge of child development, domestic abuse and child abuse and neglect;
3. have education and training specific to the process of mediation; and
4. be able to recognize the impact of culture and diversity.

Model Standards of Practice for Family and Divorce Mediation, Standard X (2001).

Family mediation is a multidisciplinary practice, and mediators are likely to be psychologists, social workers, and/or lawyers. Because mediators come from different professional backgrounds and mediation is a relatively new field, regulation and quality control have been controversial issues. Mediators and commentators continue to debate about how to effectively promote professional diversity and innovation while maintaining quality control. Despite disagreements over licensure, research shows that participants generally find that mediators are impartial, sensitive, and skilled. Joan B. Kelly, *A Decade of Divorce Mediation Research: Some Answers and Questions*, 34 Fam. & Conciliation Cts. Rev. 373, 378 (1996).

Example 22-2

P and D decided to divorce and were ordered by the court to attend mediation. After mediation concluded, the wife objected to the mediated agreement because during the mediation, the mediator (1) told the wife she would lose in court on an issue; (2) threw papers on the table and announced "that's it, I give up"; (3) threatened to report to the court that mediation had failed because of the wife; (4) guessed about the value of assets; and (5) applied time pressure, saying that "you guys have five minutes to hurry up and get out of here" after eight hours of mediation. The mediator argued that P was represented by counsel and could have objected to the process, terminated the mediation, or simply not agreed to the terms. Will the wife be successful in having the mediated agreement overturned?

Explanation

This mediator did not behave professionally during the mediation — the mediator should have remained neutral and should not have coerced the wife into agreeing to a settlement. A court will not adopt an agreement that is not made voluntarily and would not approve this one. *See Vitakis-Valchine v. Valchine*, 793 So. 2d 1094, 1099 (Fla. Dist. Ct. App. 2001).

Example 22-3

P and D mediate their divorce. Afterward, P claims that she was under duress because she had not slept during the 24 hours prior to the mediation, she was in pain from recent surgery, and she had a migraine headache. During the mediation, she took narcotic pain medication, an antidepressant, and a migraine-related injection. D presented evidence that (1) P was herself an experienced mediator who was represented by counsel at the mediation; (2) P appeared to understand what was transpiring; and (3) P did not seem confused or mentally incapacitated. Based on this evidence, the court ruled that P was not under duress. What is the likely result on appeal?

Explanation

In the similar case of *McMahan v. McMahan*, 2005 WL 3287475 (Tenn. Ct. App. 2005), the trial court found that P's testimony was "not persuasive." The appellate court did not overturn this finding on appeal and held that, based on the trial court's credibility finding, P's testimony did not rise to the level necessary to prove duress. *See also Ford v. Ford*, 68 P.3d 1258 (Alaska 2003) (agreement enforceable despite husband's poor health and desire to "get away from the intolerable stress of the mediation").

22.8. Mediator Testimony

The confidential nature of mediation allows participants to brainstorm and speak candidly during mediation sessions. Consequently, mediators object to being called as witnesses if mediation is unsuccessful and the parties return to court. For example, in *Marchal v. Craig*, 681 N.E.2d 1160, 1161 (Ind. Ct. App. 1997), the parties failed to reach a mediated agreement but stipulated that the mediator could testify as a witness for both parties. The husband later changed his mind, but the lower court allowed the mediator to testify. *Id.* at 1162. The appellate court found that the testimony violated Indiana ADR Rule 2.12, providing that a "[m]ediator shall not be subject to process requiring the disclosure of any matter discussed during the mediation, but rather, such matter shall be considered confidential and privileged in nature." *Id. But see Wilson v. Wilson*, 653 S.E.2d 702 (Ga. 2007) (mediator allowed to testify concerning husband's competency). State laws vary concerning the extent to which mediation sessions are protected. For a discussion of confidentiality and privilege under the Uniform Mediation Act, *see* Scott H. Hughes, *The Uniform Mediation Act: To the Spoiled Go the Privileges*, 85 Marq. L. Rev. 9 (2001); Ellen Deason, *The Quest for Uniformity in Mediation Confidentiality: Foolish Consistency or Crucial Predictability?*, 85 Marq. L. Rev. 79, 82

(2001) ("If a mediator can be converted into the opposing party's weapon in court, then her neutrality is only temporary and illusory."). *See also* ALI, *Principles of the Law of Family Dissolution: Analysis and Recommendations* §2.07(4), (5) (2000); *Lehr v. Afflitto*, 889 A.2d 462, 474-475 (N.J. Super. A.D. 2006) (courts should be especially wary of mediator testimony because "no matter how carefully presented, [it] will inevitably be characterized so as to favor one side or the other").

Example 22-4

A and B attended divorce mediation pursuant to a court order that specifically provided that the mediation process was to be confidential and "nonevidential." After the mediation ended, the parties disagreed about whether they had actually reached a settlement. A calls the mediator to testify on that question. A asserts that an agreement was reached and argues that the mediator was present when the agreement was made and that the mediator is in an ideal position to testify objectively about what occurred. B asserts that no settlement was reached and argues that the under the court order the mediation process was confidential and nonevidential and that mediator testimony would violate that order. Should the mediator be compelled to testify?

Explanation

In a similar case, the court recognized that the ability to be open and honest during mediation is key to the success of the process and that parties would be less likely to speak candidly if their statements could later be used in court. The court concluded that there had been no express waiver of the confidentiality provision and that mediator testimony was consequently improper. *See Lehr v. Afflitto*, 889 A.2d 462 (N.J. Super. 2006); *In re Marriage of Kieturakis*, 41 Cal. Rptr. 3d 119 (Cal. App. 2006).

22.9. Legal Advice in Mediation

Attorneys play different roles in mediation depending upon the model of mediation used. Sometimes lawyers attend mediation sessions with their clients and participate in the process. In other cases, the participants consult with their attorneys as needed between mediation sessions. Some people in mediation seek legal advice only after the mediation has concluded. A few people never consult an attorney and appear *pro se* in court. Mediators prefer that participants consult separate attorneys as needed throughout the process and also before a final divorce decree is entered in court. *See In re Approval of Application for Determination of Indigent Status Forms*, 910 So. 2d 194 (Fla. 2005) (mediators are not allowed to give legal advice); *Pappas v. Waggoner's Heating & Air, Inc.*, 108 P.3d 9 (Okla. Civ. App. 2004) (a mediator is not to "offer legal advice to parties").

22.10. Court Approval of Agreements

A divorce is not final until the mediated agreement is approved and a decree is entered by the court. Thus, even when private mediation is used, the court retrospectively oversees the process and may refuse to approve a mediated agreement for various reasons. For example, a court might refuse to adopt an agreement if the court believes that the parenting arrangements are not in the best interests of the children or if the mediated agreement departs substantially from state law without good reason. Under ALI section 2.06, courts are cautioned to reject parenting plans agreed to by parents if the agreement was not "knowing or voluntary" or if the plan would harm the child. *See* ALI, *The Allocation of Custodial and Decisionmaking Responsibility for Children* §2.06 (2000).

Example 22-5

P and D, who are divorcing, have one child. They attended mediation sessions, where they entered into an agreement under which D was to have sole physical custody of the child, but P was not ordered to pay any child support. Instead, D paid P a reduced amount of alimony. D later objected to the agreement on the basis that, under state law, child support could not be waived. P argued that the arrangement did not affect the amount of money available for support of the child; it just prevented the couple from exchanging unnecessary checks. Will a court adopt the mediated agreement?

Explanation

In the similar case of *Swanson v. Swanson*, 580 S.E.2d 526 (Ga. 2003), the court found that the right to child support belonged to the child and could not be waived by the parents in a mediated agreement. The court refused to incorporate the settlement agreement into a final decree, and the case was consequently reversed and remanded. *See also Esser v. Esser*, 586 S.E.2d 627 (Ga. 2003) (trial court not bound by an agreement regarding child support, nor is its obligation to determine whether the child support is sufficient simply by adopting the parties' agreement); *Hamilton v. Hamilton*, — A.2d —, 2009 WL 2392967 (Me. 2009) (Department of Health and Human Services (DHHS) had the right to seek child support from father, even though mother agreed at mediation that father would not have to pay any child support).

22.11. Mediation as Condition Precedent to Post-Decree Actions

If a final divorce decree requires the parties to mediate before filing post-decree motions in court, the provision is likely to be enforced by the court. For example, in *Gould v. Gould*, 523 S.E.2d 106, 107 (Ga. Ct. App. 1999), at the time of the divorce, the parties agreed to mediate conflicts prior to returning to court. Consequently, the court refused to hear a petition for modification and contempt until after mediation had taken place. *Id.* at 108. But *see Maurer v. Maurer*, 872 A.2d 326 (Vt. 2005) (claim by father that mediation was condition precedent to litigation was rejected by the court because the father was the party who refused to attend mediation).

22.12. Research on the Mediation Process

Research shows that mediated divorces generally take less time to complete than divorces that are not mediated. *See* Kenneth Kressel & Dean G. Pruitt, *Mediation Research: The Process and Effectiveness of Third-Party Intervention* 398 (1989); Jay Folberg, *Mediation of Child Custody Disputes*, 19 Colum. J.L. & Soc. Probs. 413, 431 (1985). In fact, some research shows that mediated divorce may be completed in half the time it would normally take the case to make its way through the court system. Joan B. Kelly, *A Decade of Divorce Mediation Research: Some Answers and Questions*, 34 Fam. & Conciliation Cts. Rev. 373, 376 (1996).

Studies show that mediated divorces are generally less expensive than traditional divorces. Kressel & Pruitt, *supra*; Kelly, *supra*. Couples save money on attorney fees and through the use of neutral experts — if expert opinions are necessary, couples hire one neutral expert to advise them rather than each hiring a "battling expert." The amount of money saved depends upon the type of mediation process used and how early the divorce is diverted from the adversarial system. *See* Connie J. A. Beck & Bruce D. Sales, *A Critical Reappraisal of Divorce Mediation Research and Policy*, 6 Psychol. Pub. Pol'y & L. 989, 1041 (2000).

Mediation settlement rates vary by program. Overall settlement rates range from 40 to 80 percent with an average settlement rate of 60 percent. Desmond Ellis & Noreen Stuckless, *Mediating and Negotiating Marital Conflicts* 103 (1996); Jeanne A. Clement & Andrew I. Schwebel, *A Research Agenda for Divorce Mediation: The Creation of Second Order Knowledge to Inform Legal Policy*, 9 Ohio St. J. Disp. Resol. 95, 99 (1993) (40% to 75%); Jay Folberg, *Mediation of Child Custody Disputes*, 19 Colum. J.L. & Soc. Probs. 413, 422 (1985) (58%).

Research indicates that participants express satisfaction with the mediation process in 60 to 93 percent of cases. Couples who reach settlement are predictably more satisfied than couples who do not settle. However, even among those who do not reach agreement, 81 percent would recommend the process to a friend. Ellis & Stuckless, *supra* at 93, Folberg, *supra* at 413, 424. Researchers have found that both men and women are more satisfied with mediation than with the adversarial divorce process. Ellis & Stuckless, *supra* at 95. Seventy-seven percent of mediating couples are pleased with the mediation process, but only 40 percent of litigating couples report satisfaction with the court procedure. Jessica Pearson & Nancy Thoennes, *Divorce Mediation: Reflections on a Decade of Research*, 437 in *Mediation Research* (Kenneth Kressel et al. eds., 1989). Mediation is seen as involving less pressure, protecting people's rights better, giving couples more control over decisions, and being less coercive. National Center for State Courts, *Multi-State Assessment of Divorce Mediation and Traditional Court Processing* 72 (1992).

Couples who mediate are more likely to comply with the agreements they have made. Not surprisingly, couples who participate in multiple mediation sessions have higher compliance rates than those participating in a single session. Ellis & Stuckless, *supra* at 116; Pearson & Thoennes, *supra* at 21. These higher compliance rates result from the voluntary nature of the agreements made in mediation and the thoughtful consideration given to various options before decisions are finalized.

While studies show that relitigation rates are lower for mediating couples, other studies limit this finding to the first few years following the divorce. *See* Ellis & Stuckless, *supra* at 115; Clement & Schwebel, *supra* at 95, 100.

Children whose parents attend mediation may have more long-term, ongoing contact with the nonresidential parent. In a study where families were randomly assigned to a divorce process (mediation or adversarial), 30 percent of nonresidential parents who mediated continued to see their children at least once per week 12 years after the divorce. In contrast, only 9 percent of nonresidential parents who participated in adversarial divorce had weekly face-to-face contact 12 years later. Similarly, 54 percent of the mediating nonresidential parents had weekly phone contact 12 years after the divorce compared with 13 percent of the adversarially divorced nonresidential parents. Robert E. Emery, David Sbarra & Tara Grover, *Divorce Mediation: Research and Reflections*, 43 Fam. Ct. Rev. 22 (2005).

22.13. Mandatory Mediation

Because mediation is cost-effective and reduces animosity, some states require divorcing couples to participate in mediation. For a state-by-state analysis, *see* Carrie-Anne Tondo et al., *Mediation Trends: A Survey of the States*, 39 Fam. Ct. Rev. 431 (2001). Proponents of mandatory mediation note high levels of satisfaction with the process and believe that all nonabusive couples can benefit from exposure to mediation. Andrew Schepard, *Children, Courts and Custody: Interdisciplinary Models for the Twenty-first Century* (2004).

In contrast, the Model Standards of Practice for Family and Divorce Mediation endorse the notion of informed consent by participants in mediation. Standard IIIC provides that "[a] mediator should not agree to conduct the mediation if the mediator reasonably believes one or more of the participants is unable or unwilling to participate." Because mediation is about self-determination, many mediators strongly object to the idea of requiring participation in mediation. *See* Ann Milne & Jay Folberg, *The Theory and Practice of Divorce Mediation: An Overview, in Divorce Mediation: Theory and Practice* 19 (Jay Folberg & Ann Milne eds., 1988); René L. Rimelspach, *Mediating Family Disputes in a World with Domestic Violence: How to Devise a Safe and Effective Court-Connected Mediation Program*, 17 Ohio St. J. Disp. Resol. 95, 102 (2001); ALI, *The Allocation of Custodial and Decisionmaking Responsibility for Children* §2.07 (2000).

22.14. Domestic Violence

Commentators express serious reservations about the use of mediation in cases involving domestic violence. Concerns include the possibility of coercion and retribution by the abusive partner as well as subjecting the victim to additional danger. Consequently, even states with mandatory mediation programs generally make an exception or have special provisions for cases involving domestic violence. Other states are "victim choice" states in that they have followed the Model Code on Domestic and Family Violence (1994), which provides

Section 407. Duty of the mediator to screen for domestic violence during mediation referred or ordered by court.

1. A mediator who receives a referral or order from a court to conduct mediation shall screen for the occurrence of domestic violence between the parties.

2. A mediator shall not engage in mediation when it appears to the mediator or when either party asserts that domestic or family violence has occurred unless:

   a. Mediation is requested by the victim of the alleged domestic or family violence;

   b. Mediation is provided in a specialized manner that protects the safety of the victim by a certified mediator who is trained in domestic and family violence; and

   c. The victim is permitted to have in attendance at mediation a supporting person of his or her choice, including but not limited to an attorney or advocate.

This approach allows victims of domestic violence to mediate if they choose to do so but does not require victims to engage in face-to-face negotiations with an abusive partner. *See also* ALI, *Principles of the Law of Family Dissolution: Analysis and Recommendations* §2.07 (2000).

If mediation goes forward, experienced mediators institute special safety precautions and ground rules, and they substantially modify the mediation process. Researchers Desmond Ellis and Noreen Stuckless have developed an empirically validated screening instrument that links risk level, violence predictors, and types and levels of abuse to specific modifications of the mediation process. Desmond Ellis & Noreen Stuckless, *Domestic Violence, DOVE, and Divorce Mediation*, 44 Fam. Ct. Rev. 658, 659 (2006). For a discussion of factors to be considered by victims of domestic violence in deciding whether to mediate their divorces and the special safety and procedural precautions that are needed, *see* Nancy Ver Steegh, *Yes, No, and Maybe: Informed Decision Making About Divorce Mediation in the Presence of Domestic Violence*, 9 Wm. & Mary J. Women & L. 145 (2003).

Example 22-6

Assume that P and D were divorced because during the marriage P was physically abusive to D and was arrested and convicted of assault and domestic violence. P and D return to court to resolve an issue related to parenting time, and the court orders them to attend mediation before a hearing date will be set. The jurisdiction has a statute providing that "[a]ny court of record may, in its discretion, refer any case of mediation services or dispute resolution programs . . . except that the court shall not refer the case to mediation services or dispute resolution programs where one of the parties claims that it has been the victim of physical or psychological abuse by the other party and states that it is thereby unwilling to enter into mediation services or dispute resolution programs." D objects to the mediation. What is the court likely to do?

Explanation

In most states the court will not require D to mediate with P if she objects to the mediation based on the occurrence of domestic violence. The statute clearly states that the court "shall not" refer to mediation if one of the parties "claims" to be a victim of domestic violence. Here, P has been convicted of assault and domestic violence, and D is opposed to mediating. *See Pearson v. District Court*, 924 P.2d 512 (Colo. 1996).

COLLABORATIVE LAW

22.15. The Collaborative Process

Building on the success and popularity of interest-based processes such as mediation, some lawyers have chosen to concentrate their practices on settlement. These lawyers may identify themselves as collaborative law practitioners who use interest-based problem-solving negotiation techniques to assist parties in reaching settlement. To participate, both parties must retain a collaborative law attorney and agree from the outset that the case will be resolved without going to court.

The parties and their lawyers typically engage in four-way meetings that sometimes involve other professionals such as child psychologists and financial planners. These professionals function as neutral advisors who assist the parties in better understanding their options going forward. Susan A. Hansen & Gregory M Hildebrand, *Collaborative Practice, in Innovations in Family Law Practice* 29 (Kelly Browe Olson & Nancy Ver Steegh eds., 2008).

22.16. The Disqualification Agreement

The disqualification agreement is a key distinguishing feature of the collaborative law process. In order to enhance commitment to the process and create a contained environment for negotiation, the parties agree that if the collaborative law process reaches an impasse and court activity begins, the collaborative lawyers will withdraw from representation and the parties will retain new litigation counsel. The disqualification agreement also reduces any financial incentive a lawyer might have to boost his or her fees by encouraging ongoing litigation. *See* Gary Voegele, Linda K. Wray & Ron Ousky, *Collaborative Law: A Useful Tool for the Family Law Practitioner to Promote Better Outcomes*, 33 Wm. Mitchell L. Rev. 971 (2007).

22.17. Ethical Concerns

In 2007 the American Bar Association Standing Committee on Ethics and Professional Responsibility issued an ethical opinion approving the collaborative law process so long as potential clients are advised of benefits and risks. American Bar Association Standing Committee on Ethics and Professional Responsibility, Ethical Considerations in Collaborative Law Practice, Formal Opinion 07-447 (August 9, 2007). The Committee viewed collaborative law practice as a limited scope representation under Model

Rule 1.2. It rejected the argument that a four-way agreement constitutes a non-waivable conflict of interest and concluded that the agreement to withdraw does not impair a lawyer's ability to represent the client.

States such as Colorado, Kentucky, Maryland, Minnesota, New Jersey, and North Carolina have issued ethical opinions concerning collaborative law. *See* John Lande, *Lessons Learned for Collaborative Lawyers and Other Dispute Resolution Professionals from Colorado Bar Associate Ethics Opinion 115*, Mediate.com. (2007), available at *http://www.mediate.com/articles/landeJ3.cfm* (last visited August 15, 2009) (analysis of Colorado opinion finding ethical violation in use of collaborative law).

22.18. Statutory Efforts

The National Conference of Commissioners on Uniform State Laws has proposed the Uniform Collaborative Law Act, available at *http://www.law. upenn.edu/bll/archives/ulc/ucla/2009am_approved.htm* (last visited August 15, 2009). The Act defines relevant terms and sets forth the contents of a valid collaborative law participation agreement. It discusses the application of the disqualification agreement in various contexts and creates a privilege against disclosure of collaborative law communications. Under the Act, collaborative law lawyers are required to "make reasonable inquiry" about the existence of domestic violence and special provisions apply in such cases.

In addition, several states have adopted statutes governing the use of collaborative law. Cal. Fam. Code §2013 (West 2007); N.C. Gen Stat. Ann. §50-7 et seq. (West 2007); Vernon's Tex. Stat. & Codes Ann. §§6.603, 153.0072 (West 2007).

22.19. Cooperative Law Compared

In part because of controversy related to the disqualification agreement, some lawyers practice under a slightly different model called "cooperative law." These lawyers use a process very similar to that found in collaborative law except that they do not enter into a disqualification agreement. Thus, if for any reason the parties decide to go to court, the cooperative lawyer does not need to withdraw from the case and be replaced by litigation counsel. Advocates of cooperative law believe that the model includes the benefits of collaborative law without potentially subjecting the parties to the added expense and delay that a change of counsel would entail. David A. Hoffman, *Cooperative Negotiation Agreements: Using Contracts to Make a Safe Place for a Difficult Conversation*, in *Innovations in Family Law Practice* 63 (Kelly Browe Olson & Nancy Ver Steegh eds., 2008).

PARENTING COORDINATION

22.20. The Role of the Parenting Coordinator

A parenting coordinator functions much like a special master might in a federal civil case. In essence, the judge delegates limited decision-making authority regarding a family to a professional with expertise in family dynamics and family law. The idea is to provide high-conflict families with additional oversight and faster access to decision-making assistance.

Parenting coordination is defined as

> [A] child-focused alternative dispute resolution process in which a mental health or legal professional with mediation training and experience assists high conflict parents to implement their parenting plan by facilitating the resolution of their disputes in a timely manner, educating parents about children's needs, and with prior approval of the parties and/or the court, making decisions within the scope of the court order or appointment contract.

Association of Family and Conciliation Courts Task Force on Parenting Coordination, *Parenting Coordination: Implementation Issues*, 41 Fam. Ct. Rev. 533 (2003).

Parenting coordinators typically help families resolve day-to-day matters such as scheduling, transportation, and child care. In some cases they facilitate communication between the parents; in other cases, they exercise limited decision-making authority. They are not empowered to make major decisions, such as those involved in modification of child custody or relocation. *See* Christine A. Coates et al., *Parenting Coordination for High-Conflict Families*, 42 Fam. Ct. Rev. 246 (2004); Matthew J. Sullivan, *Ethical, Legal, and Professional Practice Issues Involved in Acting as a Psychologist Parent Coordinator in Child Custody Cases*, 42 Fam. Ct. Rev. 576 (2004).

22.21. Courts and Legislatures Embrace the Role

Parenting coordination was initially conceptualized at a multidisciplinary meeting convened by the ABA's Family Law Section in 2000. Conference Report and Action Plan, *High Conflict Custody Cases: Reforming the System for Children, Wingspread Conference at Racine, Wisconsin*, September 8-10, 2000. By 2003 some 14 states had implemented the role, and by 2007 7 states (Oklahoma, Idaho, Oregon, Colorado, Texas, North Carolina, and Louisiana) had passed legislation governing it. Association of Family and Conciliation Courts Task Force on Parenting Coordination, *Parenting Coordination: Implementation Issues*, 41 Fam. Ct. Rev. 533, 534 (2003); Karl Kirkland & Matthew Sullivan, *Parenting*

Coordination (PC) Practice: A Survey of Experienced Professionals, 46 Fam. Ct. Rev. 622, 625 (2008).

The Colorado statute governing appointment of a parenting coordinators states as follows:

§14-10-128.1. Appointment of parenting coordinator

(1) Pursuant to the provisions of this section, at any time after the entry of an order concerning parental responsibilities and upon notice to the parties, the court may, on its own motion, a motion by either party, or an agreement of the parties, appoint a parenting coordinator as a neutral third party to assist in the resolution of disputes between the parties concerning parental responsibilities, including but not limited to implementation of the court-ordered parenting plan. The parenting coordinator shall be an individual with appropriate training and qualifications and a perspective acceptable to the court.

(2)(a) Absent agreement of the parties, a court shall not appoint a parenting coordinator unless the court makes the following findings:

(I) That the parties have failed to adequately implement the parenting plan;

(II) That mediation has been determined by the court to be inappropriate, or, if not inappropriate, that mediation has been attempted and was unsuccessful; and

(III) That the appointment of a parenting coordinator is in the best interests of the child or children involved in the parenting plan.

C.R.S.A. §14-10-128.1. *See also In re Marriage of Rozzi*, 190 P.3d 815 (Colo. App. 2008) (interpreting parenting coordination statute).

22.22. Common Practices

Despite the fact that parenting coordination is a new professional role, some practice trends are emerging. In a recent national survey of parenting coordinators researchers found that parenting coordinators are a multidisciplinary group of professionals including psychologists (44%), MSW social workers (19%), LPC counselors (15%), B.A.-level practitioners (11%), and attorneys (11%). All of the parenting coordinators surveyed work only by court order or under mutually signed consent decrees. Most use written parenting coordinator agreements that include the basis and scope of authority, advise that communications are not confidential, and clarify that the parenting coordinator will not provide therapy or give legal advice. Karl Kirkland & Matthew Sullivan, *Parenting Coordination (PC) Practice: A Survey of Experienced Professionals*, 46 Fam. Ct. Rev. 622 (2008).

Example 22-7

During the divorce process a mental health expert recommended that P and D work with a parenting coordinator. They consequently agreed to the entry of a court order appointing a parenting coordinator to assist with communications, resolve minor issues, monitor problems, and make recommendations about parenting time. The appointment was made pursuant to a state statute placing strict guidelines on the role. Despite having initially agreed, P later challenged the use of a parenting coordinator. She alleged that the parenting coordinator micro-managed the family and usurped her right to make decisions for her child. What is the likely result?

Explanation

In *Barnes v. Barnes*, 107 P.3d 560 (Okla. 2005), the court upheld the appointment of a parenting coordinator, noting that the role was a clearly limited one. The court held that the Oklahoma Parenting Coordinator Act did not violate equal protection and that P's substantive due process rights were not violated by the appointment.

ARBITRATION

22.23. Use of Arbitration in Family Cases

In arbitration a neutral third party selected by the parties hears evidence and in most cases makes a binding decision much like a judge would do. In recent years some spouses have attempted to arbitrate issues related to divorce in an effort to reduce costs and speed the divorce process.

States differ concerning the use of arbitration in family cases. For example, while agreements to arbitrate issues related to alimony will often be enforced, some courts are hesitant to delegate issues such as child custody, which traditionally involve court determination of the child's best interests. Elizabeth A. Jenkins, *Validity and Construction of Provisions for Arbitration of Disputes as to Alimony or Support Payments or Child Visitation or Custody Matters*, 38 A.L.R.5th 69 (2009). *See Toiberman v. Tisera*, 998 So. 2d 4 (Fla. App. 2008) (interpreting arbitration statute, court held that prohibition of arbitration of child-related issues foreclosed arbitration of other issues in the case). *But see Fawzy v. Fawzy*, 973 A.2d 347 (N.J. 2009) (only threat of harm to child justifies infringement on right of parents to choose dispute resolution method).

The Model Family Law Arbitration Act of the American Academy of Matrimonial Lawyers provides for *de novo* judicial review of arbitration awards involving child custody and child support. Model Family Law Arbitration Act, available at *http://www.aaml.org/go/library/publications/model-family-law-arbitration-act/* (last visited August 16, 2009). Several states have adopted statutes regarding matrimonial arbitration. Lynn P. Burleson, *Family Law Arbitration: Third Party Alternative Dispute Resolution*, 30 Campbell L. Rev. 297 (2008) (noting that Colorado, Connecticut, Indiana, Michigan, New Hampshire, New Mexico, and North Carolina have matrimonial arbitration statutes).

CHAPTER 23

Professional Responsibility

23.1. Introduction

This chapter focuses on issues of professional responsibility that are especially relevant to practitioners of family law. The changing role of the family attorney is also discussed.

23.2. Client Dissatisfaction with Family Law Attorneys

Unfortunately, some divorcing couples express dissatisfaction with their attorneys, and there is some evidence that more ethical complaints are filed against family attorneys than attorneys practicing in other areas. *See* Andrew Schepard, *The Evolving Judicial Role in Child Custody Disputes: From Fault Finder to Conflict Manager to Differential Case Management*, 22 U. Ark. Little Rock L. Rev. 395, 410 (2000); Susan Daicoff, *Lawyer, Know Thyself: A Review of Empirical Research on Attorney Attributes Bearing on Professionalism*, 46 Am. U. L. Rev. 1337 (1997). In one survey, divorcing parents reported that their attorneys lacked genuine interest in their cases and did not pay sufficient attention to their cases. These clients did not feel involved in important decisions and were concerned about the lack of attorney communication: "nobody hears you and nobody talks to you." Marsha Kline Pruett & Tamara D. Jackson, *The Lawyer's Role During the Divorce Process: Perceptions of Parents, Their Young Children, and Their Attorneys*, 33 Fam. L.Q. 283, 297 (1999). In partial explanation, attorneys point out that divorce clients sometimes have unrealistic expectations, are undergoing serious emotional stress, and may not have dealt with the legal system or an attorney before.

Of course, many divorce clients are pleased with the representation they receive. These clients report that their attorneys helped them keep perspective, "interpreted" the legal proceedings for them, and provided emotional support. Connie J.A. Beck & Bruce D. Sales, *A Critical Reappraisal of Divorce Mediation Research and Policy*, 6 Psychol. Pub. Pol'y & L. 989, 1014 (2000); Pruett & Jackson, *supra* at 294-295. In addition, lawyers serve an important function in protecting the interests of their clients.

SEXUAL RELATIONSHIPS WITH CLIENTS

23.3. Rule 1.8(j)

The 2008 Model Rules of Professional Conduct provide that "[a] lawyer shall not have sexual relations with a client unless a consensual sexual relationship existed between them when the client-lawyer relationship commenced." Rule 1.8(j). The comments following the rule explain the reasons for the prohibition of sexual relationships with clients. First, the attorney occupies a position of trust and has a fiduciary obligation to the client. The lawyer may not use this trust to disadvantage or exploit the client. Second, because of the nature of the relationship, the lawyer's independent professional judgment may be impaired. Third, it may be difficult to distinguish confidences protected by the attorney-client privilege from those that are not protected. Under these circumstances, the client is not considered able to give informed consent. *See In re Bash*, 880 N.E.2d 1182 (Ind. 2008) (attorney attempting to have sexual relations with client whom he represented in divorce action violated his ethical duty to client; failure to withdraw from representation following his sexual advances violated professional rules prohibiting lawyers from representing clients when such representation would be materially limited by a lawyer's self-interest, i.e., his desire to engage in a sexual relationship with client. Rules of Prof. Conduct, Rules 1.8(j), 8.4(a)); *Iowa Supreme Court Attorney Disciplinary Bd. v. Morrison*, 727 N.W.2d 115 (Iowa 2007) (attorney suspended for engaging in sexual relationship with client he was representing in marriage dissolution proceeding); *Disciplinary Counsel v. Engler*, 851 N.E.2d 502 (Ohio 2006) (public reprimand appropriate sanction for attorney's conduct in having two sexual encounters with client while representing her in divorce case); Gregory G. Sarno, Annotation, *Sexual Misconduct as Ground for Disciplining Attorney or Judge*, 43 A.L.R.4th 1062 (1986).

23.4. Existing Relationships Exception

Rule 1.8(j) provides for an exception when the lawyer and client have a preexisting sexual relationship. Even in this circumstance, the comments direct the lawyer to consider whether the relationship would materially limit the lawyer's ability to represent the client.

23.5. Special Concerns About Sexual Relationships in Family Cases

Sexual relationships with clients are especially problematic in divorce cases. If the client is involved in a custody dispute, the existence of an affair or cohabitation may adversely affect the outcome. The lawyer may, in fact, be called as a witness. At a minimum, the sexual relationship exacerbates an already emotionally charged situation, making resolution of the issues more difficult. Most people experiencing a divorce are more emotionally vulnerable than they normally would be, and exploitation is more likely to occur. *See Mann v. Saland*, 816 N.Y.S.2d 697 (N.Y. Sup. 2006) (in a dismantling marital relationship, the loss of love and intimacy, the bitter struggle over children, the marital home, and finances cause intense and conflicting feelings of anger, rejection, guilt, and vulnerability; litigants experience a state of despair and isolation equaled only upon the death of a loved one).

Example 23-1

A lawyer engages in a consensual sexual relationship with a client he is representing in a domestic relations matter, and she later files a disciplinary complaint against him. The attorney practices in a state with no specific rule prohibiting such a relationship, and he claims that he would not have engaged in the relationship if it were specifically barred. The attorney further argues that the former client has not presented any evidence of impaired representation. Does the attorney nevertheless have a conflict of interest?

Explanation

In a somewhat similar case, In re Application for Disciplinary Action Against Chinquist, 714 N.W.2d 469 (N.D. 2006), the court was not persuaded by either the absence of a "bright-line rule" prohibiting sexual relationships or the notion that evidence of impaired representation was necessary. The court found that the lawyer's relationship placed his interests above those of his client and was a conflict of interest.

Example 23-2

A lawyer has a sexual relationship with a woman, and while the relationship is ongoing, he undertakes representation of her in her divorce. If the jurisdiction doesn't have a specific rule forbidding this behavior, what other rules might apply?

Explanation

This behavior may violate rules related to (1) competent and diligent representation, (2) attorney acting as advocate and potential witness, and (3) conduct prejudicial to the administration of justice. In the similar case of *State ex rel. Oklahoma Bar Assn. v. Downes*, 121P.3d 1058 (Okla. 2005), the court noted that such behavior was adverse to the client's interest and added "even more hostility to an already acrimonious divorce."

REPRESENTING BOTH PARTIES

23.6. Dual Representation

Sometimes attorneys are asked to represent both parties in a divorce action. This is most likely to occur when the case is "uncontested." Unfortunately, once the lawyer starts to investigate the issues and assets, he or she is likely to uncover an issue or asset that the parties failed to consider and about which they disagree. Parties may also need to be advised concerning conflicting legal rights. Consequently, dual representation is ill advised, and the attorney should represent one party or the other in a divorce case. *See In re Disciplinary Proceedings Against Gamino*, 314 Wis. 2d 544, 753 N.W.2d 521 (Wis. 2008) (dual representation of husband and wife in their divorce proceeding absent obtaining any consent or waiver from husband or wife violated rule of professional conduct for attorneys governing conflicts of interest).

23.7. Representing Opposing Parties (Rule 1.7(b)(3))

Rule 1.7(b)(3) of the 2008 Model Rules of Professional Conduct disallows representation that involves "the assertion of a claim by one client against another client represented by the lawyer in the same litigation or other proceeding before a tribunal." Thus, the rule prohibits the representation of opposing parties in the same litigation. Comment [30] to Rule 1.7(b)(3) warns that the attorney-client privilege will not attach between commonly represented clients. If such representation proceeds and adverse interests surface, the attorney would have to withdraw from both representations, thus creating unnecessary hardship and expense for the clients. Comment [29] to Rule 1.7(b)(3).

Example 23-3

A lawyer met briefly with a husband about pending divorce proceedings and an action for a restraining order. The husband did not retain the lawyer to represent him and instead hired other counsel. Some time later, the lawyer was contacted by the wife, met with her, and agreed to represent the wife in the divorce proceeding. Was this a conflict of interest?

Explanation

Under similar facts, in *In re Conduct of Knappendberger*, 108 P.3d 1161 (Or. 2005), the court found that the lawyer did have a conflict of interest. The court characterized the husband as a former client in a significantly related matter.

CONTINGENT FEES

23.8. Forbidden Fee Arrangement (Rule 1.5(d)(1))

Sometimes potential clients are unable to pay hourly attorney fees and are interested in entering into a contingent fee arrangement.

Rule 1.5(d)(1) of the 2008 Model Rules of Professional Conduct forbids attorneys from charging or collecting "any fee in a domestic relations matter, the payment or amount of which is contingent upon the securing of a divorce or upon the amount of alimony or support, or property settlement in lieu thereof. . . ." Use of contingent fees in divorce cases goes against public policy because (1) the attorney would have a financial stake in the divorce proceeding and might promote divorce instead of encouraging reconciliation by the parties, and (2) a percentage fee might be unduly burdensome in the context of the work done and the financial circumstances of the parties. *See Maxwell Schuman & Co. v. Edwards*, 663 S.E.2d 329 (N.C. App. 2008) (contingent fee in child custody dispute was void).

23.9. Exceptions

Contingent fees are allowed in domestic relations cases involving collection of post-judgment amounts due "under support, alimony or other financial orders." Comment [6] to Rule 1.5(d)(1). *See Burns v. Stewart*, 188 N.W.2d 760 (Minn. 1971).

Example 23-4

Assume that P and D are divorcing. D is unemployed and cannot afford to pay an attorney an hourly fee. However, in the divorce, D expects to be awarded a parcel of land located on a lake. D agrees that if the land is awarded to D, D will sell it and give half of the payment received to the attorney. D is very happy with this arrangement because otherwise D will not be represented in the divorce. Is this an appropriate fee arrangement?

Explanation

This is the type of contingent fee prohibited under Rule 1.5(d)(1) because the arrangement gives the lawyer a financial interest in having D proceed with the divorce. The arrangement also gives the lawyer a vested stake in a certain outcome. If D decides to reconcile with P, or if D and P decide that P should have the lake property, the lawyer may have difficulty giving D objective advice because of the lawyer's own financial interest in the divorce.

COMMUNICATING WITH CLIENTS

23.10. Emotional Needs of Family Clients

Divorce clients often experience serious emotional turmoil as the legal action proceeds. Many clients have not been party to a lawsuit or dealt with an attorney before. As a result, most divorce clients have frequent questions and desire some level of emotional support. Clients experiencing serious distress should be referred for counseling. *See* Barbara Glesner Fines & Cathy Madsen, *Caring Too Little, Caring Too Much: Competence and the Family Law Attorney*, 75 UMKC L. Rev. 965 (2007) (discussing attorney competence in dealing with emotions). However, all clients are entitled to a reasonable amount of communication with their attorneys.

23.11. Informing and Consulting (Rule 1.4)

2008 Model Rule of Professional Conduct 1.4 provides as follows:

> a. A lawyer shall:
>
> 1. promptly inform the client of any decision or circumstance with respect to which the client's informed consent, as defined in Rule 1.0(e), is required by these Rules;
>
> 2. reasonably consult with the client about the means by which the client's objectives are to be accomplished;
>
> 3. keep the client reasonably informed about the status of the matter;
>
> 4. promptly comply with reasonable requests for information; and
>
> 5. consult with the client about any relevant limitation on the lawyer's conduct when the lawyer knows that the client expects assistance not permitted by the Rules of Professional Conduct or other law.
>
> b. A lawyer shall explain a matter to the extent reasonably necessary to permit the client to make informed decisions regarding the representation.

Example 23-5

Lawyer L agreed to represent P in a divorce from D. P was shocked when D filed for divorce and was extremely upset by the entire proceeding. At first, P called L four or five times a week to "check on the case." Lawyer L became weary of the calls and stopped returning them. L continued to ignore P's calls and only contacted P when L had a particular need to talk to P. P didn't hear from L for a period of two months, and P became distraught when P's calls were never returned. P finally filed a disciplinary complaint against L. Did L violate Rule 1.4?

Explanation

L should have referred P for counseling so that P could deal with the emotional aspects of the divorce more appropriately. L should also have had a conversation with P about the number of times P was calling the office — P needed information about how P could stay informed about the case and under what circumstances P should call. L's decision not to return calls or contact P for two months was unreasonable and violates Rule 1.4.

PRO SE LITIGANTS

23.12. Increasing Lack of Representation

In recent years, the number of unrepresented litigants in family cases has dramatically increased. A 1990 American Bar Association study conducted in Arizona found that at least one party was unrepresented in 88 percent of divorce cases. In contrast, a 1980 study found that one party was unrepresented in only 24 percent of cases. Steven K. Berenson, *A Family Law Residency Program? A Modest Proposal in Response to the Burdens Created by Self-Represented Litigants in Family Court*, 33 Rutgers L.J. 105, 109 (2001). This trend raises several issues for family practitioners.

23.13. Dealing with Unrepresented Parties (Rule 4.3)

Attorneys dealing with unrepresented parties have special obligations under Rule 4.3 of the 2008 Model Rules of Professional Conduct. First, the lawyer cannot imply that he or she is disinterested. Second, the lawyer should make reasonable efforts to correct the unrepresented person's misunderstandings of the lawyer's role. Third, the lawyer must not give legal advice to the unrepresented person but should advise the person to obtain counsel if there is a reasonable possibility that the person's interest will conflict with the client's interests. Within these guidelines, the Rule does not prohibit negotiating with an unrepresented person or explaining the lawyer's view of the meaning of documents prepared by the lawyer. *See* Comment [2] to Rule 4.3.

Example 23-6

Attorney L represents P in a divorce against D, who is unrepresented. P and D live in a jurisdiction where the sole custodian of a child can move to another state so long as the child is not endangered by the move. D is willing to agree to P having sole physical custody but does not want P to move from the state. D does not know that P could easily do so if D agrees to the sole custody arrangement. Attorney L wants to wrap up the case and allows D to continue to think that P can't permanently leave the state without D's permission. Has L violated Rule 4.3?

Explanation

L has likely violated Rule 4.3. Even though L had no obligation under the rule to give D legal advice, L should have strongly encouraged D to retain a lawyer. Furthermore, L's client, P, is not well served by making an agreement based on a misunderstanding.

23.14. Need for Pro Bono Representation (Rule 6.1)

All family law attorneys should provide pro bono representation to people who are unable to afford representation. Rule 6.1 of the 2008 Model Rules of Professional Conduct suggests that lawyers render at least 50 hours of pro bono representation each year.

Example 23-7

Assume that as part of an organized clinic, lawyers provide limited advice to people who can't afford to retain an attorney. These lawyers occasionally assist in preparing documents for filing, but they do not appear in court or establish an ongoing professional relationship. Clients are informed of the limited nature of the representation and that the attorneys will not make court appearances. Does this arrangement violate the rules of professional conduct?

Explanation

In Formal Opinion 2005-F-151 (2005), the Tennessee Supreme Court's ethics board concluded that such limited assistance was appropriate. Rule 1.2(c) allows lawyers to limit the scope of representation if reasonable under the circumstances. The board suggested that written client consent be sought and that documents drafted by the lawyers be labeled "Prepared with Assistance of Counsel." The board also cautioned lawyers to be mindful of potential conflicts of interest.

NEW AND CHANGING ROLES FOR LAWYERS

23.15. Dissatisfaction with Adversarial Divorce

Couples have increasingly expressed dissatisfaction with the adversarial approach to dissolution. Research shows that from 50 to 70 percent of litigants describe the adversarial process as "impersonal, intimidating, and intrusive." Mary R. Cathcart & Robert E. Robles, *Parenting Our Children: In the Best Interest of the Nation* 39 (1996). In another study, 71 percent of parents reported that the process escalated the level of conflict and distrust "to a further extreme." Marsha Kline Pruett & Tamara D. Jackson, *The Lawyer's Role During the Divorce Process: Perceptions of Parents, Their Young Children, and Their Attorneys*, 33 Fam. L.Q. 283, 298 (1999). This escalation of conflict makes it more difficult for parents to interact in the future and has long-term ramifications for children.

23.16. Attorney as Counselor

Attorneys practicing family law have begun to reexamine their traditional role as zealous advocates. Some have encouraged assumption of a more moderate role of attorney as counselor. *See* Nancy Ver Steegh, *Using Externships to Introduce Family Law Students to New Professional Roles*, 43 Fam. Ct. Rev. 138 (2005).

A group of commentators suggest that family attorneys have an ethical obligation to actively promote conflict resolution in the following ways:

1. counseling clients about the negative consequences of custody disputes and the availability of resources to reduce conflict;
2. discussing alternatives to litigation such as mediation;
3. encouraging cooperation with custody and mental health evaluations;
4. realistically evaluating cases and avoiding false expectations;
5. seeking early intervention in high-conflict cases and making referrals;
6. cooperating in narrowing the issues, procedures, and evidence needed to consider the best interests of the child;
7. maintaining a civil demeanor and encouraging clients to do so;

8. avoiding use of the media or protective services to exacerbate conflict;
9. seeking training in child development, abuse and neglect, domestic violence, family dynamics, and alternative conflict resolution and becoming knowledgeable about community resources; and
10. developing continuing legal education programs improving lawyers' ability to reduce conflict.

The Wingspread Report and Action Plan, *High Conflict Custody Cases: Reforming the System for Children*, 39 Fam. Ct. Rev. 146, 150 (2001). *See also* Andrew Schepard, *Children, Courts and Custody: Interdisciplinary Models for the Twenty-first Century* (2004).

23.17. Ethical Cautions for Lawyers Performing New Professional Roles

As discussed in Chapter 22, in addition to practicing in new forums lawyers may decide to assume new professional roles such as that of mediator, arbitrator, or parenting coordinator. Attorneys may also adopt new models of practice such as collaborative law, cooperative law, and/or provision of unbundled legal services. *See* Forrest S. Mosten, *Unbundling Legal Services to Help Divorcing Families*, in *Innovations in Family Law Practice* 117 (Kelly Browe Olson & Nancy Ver Steegh eds., 2008) (unbundling is a limited-scope representation wherein the client may contract for a specific aspect of representation such as drafting of documents, review of mediation agreement, advice only, etc.). As they take on different professional roles, lawyers must thoroughly understand the boundaries and ethical obligations of each role. In assuming new roles, lawyers may become subject to codes of ethics in addition to the Model Rules of Professional Conduct. *See* Model Rule of Professional Conduct 2.4, Lawyer Serving as Third-Party Neutral.

Example 23-8

A Texas lawyer is retained by a couple to mediate their divorce. Neither of the parties is represented by counsel. Mediation is successful, and the case is settled with respect to all issues. The parties ask the lawyer/mediator to draft the documents to be presented to the court. Should the lawyer/mediator agree to do so?

Explanation

In a similar situation, the Texas Bar Professional Ethics Committee, applying the Texas Disciplinary Rules of Professional Conduct, found that the lawyer/mediator could not draft the court documents to effectuate the divorce because the lawyer/mediator was prohibited from providing "both mediation and legal services" for the parties. *See* Texas State Bar Professional Ethics Comm., Op. 583, 9-08. *But see* Ohio Supreme Court Bd. of Commissioners on Grievances and Discipline, Op. 2009-4, 6-12-09, (lawyer/mediator may prepare legal documents on behalf of one party with written consent of both parties).

Jurisdiction

24.1. Introduction

There are two initial jurisdictional considerations associated with handling a marital dispute. The first is to determine whether the court assigned to hear the dispute has subject matter jurisdiction. The second assumes that subject matter jurisdiction exists but asks whether the court has personal jurisdiction over the parties. Absent subject matter jurisdiction, the court does not possess the power to hear any portion of the dispute. Without personal jurisdiction over both parties, a court with subject matter jurisdiction is limited in its ability to resolve all of the issues. For example, it may dissolve the relationship and issue a decree divorcing the couple. However, because personal jurisdiction is absent over one of the parties, it may not impose personal obligations such as alimony, child support, or attorney fees on the absent party. This chapter examines a variety of legal issues that involve these jurisdictional concepts.

SUBJECT MATTER JURISDICTION IN FEDERAL COURT

24.2. Domestic Relations Exception

Federal courts are courts of limited subject matter jurisdiction. *See, e.g.,* 28 U.S.C. §1331 (federal question); 28 U.S.C. §1332(a)(1) (diversity actions between citizens of different states involving matters in controversy exceeding $75,000 exclusive of costs and interest). Among long-standing limitations on federal court subject matter jurisdiction are the "domestic relations" and "probate" exceptions. Neither exception is compelled by the text of the Constitution or federal statutes; rather, they are judicially created doctrines stemming in large measure from "misty understandings of English legal history." *Marshall v. Marshall*, 547 U.S. 293, 299 (2006).

The decision that birthed the idea of the domestic relations exception in diversity matters can be traced to 1859. That year, the Supreme Court announced in *dicta* — without citation or discussion — that federal courts lack jurisdiction over suits for divorce or alimony. *Barber v. Barber*, 62 U.S. 582, 584 (1858). The *Barber* majority did not expressly tie its announcement of a domestic relations exception to the text of the federal diversity statute, but the *Barber* dissenters made the connection.

Since *Barber*, the Court has indicated that it agreed with the *dicta* of the dissenters in *Barber*, and has restated that the genesis of the exception is with the refusal of Congress to grant federal courts the statutory power to hear these disputes. *Ankenbrandt v. Richards*, 504 U.S. 689, 700 (1992). In addition, as a policy matter, federal courts recognize that they provide a difficult platform on which to adjudicate domestic disputes. *See Lloyd v. Loeffler*, 694 F.2d 489 (7th Cir. 1982). States have traditionally adjudicated marital and child custody disputes, and have developed competence and expertise in adjudicating such matters, which federal courts lack. *See Mansell v. Mansell*, 490 U.S. 581, 587 (1989) ("[D]omestic relations are preeminently matters of state law."); *Moore v. Sims*, 442 U.S. 415, 435, (1979) ("Family relations are a traditional area of state concern."). State courts are also thought to be peculiarly suited to enforce state regulations and domestic relations decrees involving alimony and child custody because such decrees often demand substantial continuing judicial oversight. *See Firestone v. Cleveland Trust Co.*, 654 F.2d 1212, 1215 (6th Cir. 1981). Furthermore, state courts have closer connections to local agencies than do federal courts, and these agencies are often involved in resolving conflicts resulting from domestic decrees.

One of the leading domestic relations exception decisions is *Ankenbrandt v. Richards, supra*, where the Court stated that federal courts are divested of the power to issue divorce decrees, alimony, and child custody orders. *Ankenbrandt*, 504 U.S. at 703. The Court stated that the exception is narrowly limited and that lawsuits affecting domestic relations are not within the exception unless the claim is one to obtain a divorce or establish alimony or child custody. This narrow construction led the Court to hold that the exception did not apply to the tort claims at issue in *Ankenbrandt v. Richards* despite their intimate connection to family affairs. 504 U.S. at 704.

Since *Ankenbrandt* federal courts have shown a reluctance to become involved in domestic disputes. For example, in *Cassens v. Cassens*, 430 F. Supp. 2d 830 (S.D. Ill. 2006), the federal district court rejected hearing an action that had been removed from state to federal court. The wife claimed that a prenuptial agreement that she entered into with her husband was void because it was procured through fraud. The court concluded that the relief she sought was in the nature of a request for a decree regarding the division of marital property and alimony, and the domestic relations exception to diversity jurisdiction divested the court of subject matter jurisdiction to hear the dispute.

Example 24-1

Assume that P, acting on behalf of himself and his severely disabled son, brought suit against P's former wife and the son's mother, D, alleging various tort claims arising from the former wife's care of the son while the couple were separated but still married. The parties were of diverse citizenship, and the amount of damages sought exceeded the minimum requirements of 28 U.S.C. §1332. D moved to dismiss the action on the ground that this was a domestic matter and outside the jurisdiction of the federal court. How will a federal court most likely rule on D's motion?

Explanation

The federal court will most likely find that it has subject matter jurisdiction to hear this case. While the action arises from the husband-wife relationship, it does not involve issuing a divorce decree, alimony, child support or custody. *See Dunn v. Cometa*, 238 F.3d 38 (1st Cir. 2001). One court has explained the application of the exception as follows:

> "The domestic relations exception has a core and a penumbra. The core is occupied by cases in which the plaintiff is seeking in federal district court under the diversity jurisdiction one or more of the distinctive forms of relief associated with the domestic relations jurisdiction: the granting of a divorce or an annulment, an award of child custody, a decree of alimony or child support." . . . "The penumbra of the exception consists of ancillary proceedings, such as a suit for the collection of unpaid alimony, that state law would require be litigated as a tail to the original domestic relations proceeding." Thus, the test of whether claims come within the core of the domestic relations exception to diversity jurisdiction is whether they "involve . . . distinctive forms of relief associated with the domestic relations jurisdiction."

Friedlander v. Friedlander, 149 F.3d 739 (7th Cir. 1998). Here, the claim does not clearly involve distinctive forms of relief associated with state-court domestic relations jurisdiction so as to fall within the core of the matters excluded from diversity jurisdiction by the domestic relations exception.

Example 24-2

Assume that P, who was not married at the time, began a relationship with D, who was married. P was employed as an elementary school teacher, a position she had held for some years. She resigned her teaching position allegedly in response to D's urging. She claimed that she quit so that she could be free to spend more time with D and travel around the world with him. She also claimed that she quit her job in reliance on D's promises to provide for her and that he would eventually marry her. D provided P with an extravagant lifestyle as a result of the relationship. She traveled around the world with him, and he provided her with sundry material benefits and comforts. He paid the rent on homes they shared in two different states, purchased and maintained her automobiles, allowed her the use of his luxury yachts, and presented her with lavish gifts. P states that she trusted D and believed that he would get a divorce. Occasionally, she and D discussed plans for their wedding. However, after ten years, D ended the relationship. P filed an action in federal district court relying on the court's diversity subject matter jurisdiction (citizens of different states and claims exceeding $75,000) and asserted claims involving the following: (1) promissory estoppel, (2) intentional infliction of emotional distress, (3) the tort of outrage, (4) fraud, and (5) breach of promise to marry. D brought a motion to dismiss on the ground the court lacked subject matter jurisdiction arguing that this was essentially a palimony case in which P was seeking distribution of property and support. How will the court most likely rule?

Explanation

The court will most likely reject the claim that it lacks subject matter jurisdiction. Despite the breadth of the phrase "domestic relations exception" and the potential reach of the exception's aim, *Ankenbrandt* made clear that the exception is narrowly limited. In general, lawsuits affecting domestic relations are not within the exception unless the claim at issue is one to obtain, alter or end a divorce, or to seek alimony, child custody, or child support. *Dunn v. Cometa*, 238 F.3d 38, 41 (1st Cir. 2001). Notwithstanding the fact that this hypothetical grows out of the breakdown of an intimate relationship, P's claims do not sound in family law, let alone the specific areas of divorce, alimony, child support, or child custody. Instead, P brought tort and contract claims. *See Norton v. McOsker*, 407 F.3d 501 (1st Cir. 2005).

24.3. Probate Exception

The probate exception has been discussed in a number of decisions by the Supreme Court. In *Markham v. Allen*, 326 U.S. 490 (1946), the Court stated the general principle that "a federal court has no jurisdiction to probate a will or administer an estate, the reason being that the equity jurisdiction conferred by the Judiciary Act of 1789, 1 Stat. 73, and §24(1) of the Judicial Code, which is that of the English Court of Chancery in 1789, did not extend to probate matters." 326 U.S. at 494. The exception is as applicable to federal-question cases as it is to the diversity cases in which it is usually invoked. *Jones v. Brennan*, 465 F.3d 304 (7th Cir. 2006).

In *Marshall v. Marshall*, 547 U.S. 293 (2006), the Court may have liberalized its probate perspective somewhat holding that the exception was not applicable to deprive a bankruptcy court of jurisdiction over a widow's claim that her stepson tortiously interfered with her expectancy of inheritance or gift from her deceased husband. The Court said that a ruling by a state probate court that it had exclusive subject matter jurisdiction over all of the widow's claims against her stepson did not deprive a federal district court of jurisdiction over the widow's tort claim against her stepson asserted in her bankruptcy proceeding.

Example 24-3

Assume that P filed a diversity action in federal district court against D, the administrator of her parents' estate. P alleged that D had breached its fiduciary duty by improperly paying inflated and fraudulent legal bills to the law firm that represented the administrator. D moved to dismiss the action on the ground the federal district court lacked subject matter jurisdiction. D contended that this was a probate matter within the exclusive jurisdiction of the state probate court. How will a court most likely resolve the issue?

Explanation

Under the probate exception set forth by the Supreme Court in *Marshall v. Marshall*, a federal court should decline subject matter jurisdiction only if a plaintiff seeks to achieve either administration or probate of an estate or a will, or to do any other purely probate matter. However, the probate exception should not bar P's claim in federal court against the executor of her parents' estate for breach of fiduciary duty. This claim is framed as an *in personam* tort action and does not directly implicate the *res* of the estate. It is not entirely intertwined with the issues of estate administration, consequently, the federal court will most likely accept jurisdiction and hear P's claim. *See Lefkowitz v. Bank of New York*, 528 F.3d 102 (2d Cir. 2007).

24.4. Federal Court Review of State Court Judgments

There has been an occasional effort to persuade a federal court to hear an appeal from a state court domestic relations judgment. However, federal courts have consistently held that they lack subject matter jurisdiction to review such judgments. *See, e.g., Exxon Mobil Corp. v. Saudi Basic Indus. Corp.*, 544 U.S. 280, 284 (2005); *Dist. of Columbia Court of Appeals v. Feldman*, 460 U.S. 462 (1983); *Staley v. Ledbetter*, 837 F.2d 1016, 1017-1018 (11th Cir. 1988) (district court lacked jurisdiction to hear a constitutional claim which essentially sought to reverse a state court's custody determination); *Sielck v. Sielck*, 202 Fed. Appx. 919 (7th Cir. 2006) (court rejected hearing claim that husband's misconduct throughout the divorce proceedings had resulted in a state court judgment that deprived her of "marital property" and custody of her children).

Example 24-4

Assume that P1 and P2 were the adoptive parents of child C. Assume that D, the State Department of Human Services, after an extensive investigation, brought an action in state court to terminate P1 and P2's parental rights to C. After a hearing, the state court judge issued an order terminating the rights of P1 and P2 to C. P1 and P2 then filed a civil rights action in federal district court against D alleging equal protection and due process violations and violations of Child Welfare Act of 1980 in connection with the termination. D has brought a motion to dismiss. How will a court most likely decide the motion?

Explanation

The matter will most likely be dismissed by the federal court. In effect, P1 and P2 are seeking to collaterally attack the state agency and court proceedings that terminated their parental rights. The federal court is being asked to reverse a state court's child custody determination. A federal court may not decide federal issues that are raised in state proceedings and are "inextricably intertwined" with the state court's judgment. *Staley v. Ledbetter*, 837 F.2d 1016 (11th Cir. 1988); *see Anderson v. State of Colorado*, 793 F.2d 262, 263-265 (10th Cir. 1986).

24.5. Federal Question Jurisdiction — Liberty Interest

Occasionally, a dispute may raise legitimate constitutional issues that appear, at least on the surface, as involving the domestic relations exception. If the claims are legitimate, a federal court may hear them. For example, the

Supreme Court has stated that under the Constitution, there is a protected liberty interest in familial relations. *Stanley v. Illinois*, 405 U.S. 645 (1972) (held that under the Due Process Clause of the Fourteenth Amendment, unwed father was entitled to hearing on fitness as parent before his children could be taken from him in dependency proceeding instituted by the state). Questions of the process used by a state in a particular setting where the parent or child challenge the process on constitutional grounds may implicate this liberty interest. *Winston v. Children and Youth Servs. of Del. County*, 948 F.2d 1380 (3d Cir. 1991) (parents have a fundamental liberty interest in the care, custody, and management of their children that is protected by the Due Process Clause of the Fourteenth Amendment). The adjudication of whether the state's process, which resulted in separating a child from a parent, may be challenged on due process grounds and is within a federal court's question jurisdiction. Resolution of a complaint about state procedures resulting in separation of child and parent do not necessarily entail any investigation by the federal court into the fitness of the parent to care for the child.

Example 24-5

Assume that state X enacts a statute that presumes that, on the death of an unmarried mother of a minor child, the father of the child is presumed to be unfit as the child's custodian. Under the statute, when the mother dies, the state, without conducting a hearing on the father's fitness, declares the child a ward of the state. In all other termination cases, the parties are provided with a pre-removal hearing. P, the father, challenges the statute as violating his due process rights by denying him a pre-removal hearing on the issue of his fitness. The state argues that P is challenging a termination proceeding, and therefore the federal court is without subject matter jurisdiction to hear the matter. How will a federal court most likely rule on P's challenge?

Explanation

P will most likely prevail. P is not asking the court to evaluate the legitimacy of the state ends; rather, P is asking the court to determine whether the means used to achieve these ends are constitutionally defensible. Under the statute, the state assumes custody of the children of married parents, divorced parents, and unmarried mothers only after a hearing and proof of neglect. The children of unmarried fathers, however, are declared dependent children without a hearing on parental fitness and without proof of neglect. The failure to afford P a hearing on his parental qualifications while extending it to other parents denied him equal protection of the law. Denying such a hearing to P and those like him while granting it to other parents is contrary to the Equal Protection Clause. *Stanley v. Illinois*, 405

U.S. 645 (1972) (under the Due Process Clause of the Fourteenth Amendment, unwed father was entitled to hearing on his fitness as parent before his children could be taken from him).

Example 24-6

Assume that P filed an action in federal district court against state M and the family court judge who heard the termination action. He claimed that he was unconstitutionally deprived of his right to a relationship with his son when the trial judge in state M terminated his parental rights. The state M judge held a full hearing at which P testified and was represented by counsel. The judge found that P willfully failed to contribute to the support of his child for one year and that it would be in the child's best interests to be adopted by his stepfather, with whom he had been living since his mother and stepfather's marriage. In the lawsuit filed in federal court, P does not attack state M's statute on termination of parental rights as unconstitutional, or claim that his rights were terminated without a due process hearing. Rather, P contends the court in state M did not have subject matter jurisdiction to terminate his parental rights because the custody of his child had previously been determined by a court in state Y, an argument P also made before the court in state M. The state brings a motion to dismiss the federal action. How will a court most likely rule?

Explanation

The federal court will most likely dismiss the lawsuit. It is true that the relationship between parent and child is constitutionally protected. As such, the state's power to legislate, adjudicate, and administer all aspects of family law, including determinations of custodial and visitation rights, is subject to scrutiny by the federal judiciary within the reach of the Due Process and/or Equal Protection Clauses of the Fourteenth Amendment.

It is clear, however, that the state has a compelling interest in the welfare of minor children and has authority to terminate parental rights under certain limited circumstances, so long as it makes that determination in the best interest of the child and after a hearing. *See Lassiter v. Dept. of Soc. Serv.*, 452 U.S. 18 (1981). Here, P appears to be relitigating issues identical to those raised in the state court. Under such circumstances, the federal court will most likely apply collateral estoppel to bar P's claim. *See Blair v. Supreme Court of State of Wyo.*, 671 F.2d 389 (10th Cir. 1982) (in proceeding for termination of parental rights, father raised jurisdictional claim in state trial court in Wyoming that custody of his child had previously been determined by a Colorado court, and because the jurisdictional claim was decided against him in Wyoming state trial court, he was precluded from relitigating such issue in federal court).

24.6. Abstention Doctrine

In some cases, where the federal courts have subject matter jurisdiction to hear a dispute, they may decide not to exercise their power by applying the "abstention doctrine." The United States Supreme Court, for example, has suggested that abstention might be relevant in a case involving elements of the domestic relationship even when the parties do not seek divorce, alimony, or child custody. The doctrine could, and most likely would, be applied when a case presents "difficult questions of state law bearing on policy problems of substantial public import whose importance transcends the result in the case then at bar." *Ankenbrandt*, 504 U.S. at 705 (quoting *Colorado River Water Conservation Dist. v. United States*, 424 U.S. 800, 814 (1976)).

One of the leading abstention doctrine cases is *Younger v. Harris*, 401 U.S. 37 (1971). In that case the Court agreed that a federal court may abstain from exercising its jurisdiction and deciding a matter when state proceedings are pending, state proceedings involve an important state interest, and the state proceeding will afford the party an adequate opportunity to raise the constitutional claims.

In *Middlesex County Ethics Comm. v. Garden State Bar Assn.*, 457 U.S. 423, 432 (1982), the Court applied *Younger* to noncriminal judicial proceedings where it concluded that important state interests are involved. In *Pennzoil Co. v. Texaco, Inc.*, 481 U.S. 1 (1987), the Court held that "federal courts must abstain from hearing challenges to pending state proceedings where the state's interest is so important that exercising federal jurisdiction would disrupt the comity between federal and state courts." 481 U.S. at 17. *See DeMauro v. DeMauro*, 115 F.3d 94 (1st Cir. 1997) (abstention not automatic in RICO claim by wife involving husband's alleged efforts to conceal real property or cash during divorce).

Example 24-7

Assume that state X has a domestic violence statute that enables domestic violence victims to seek and obtain *ex parte* civil protection orders (CPO) in a number of circumstances, including a divorce proceeding. The statute in state X states that a victim of domestic violence may "receive an *ex parte* CPO by filing a petition detailing (1) the nature and extent of the domestic violence, (2) the relationship between the respondent, the petitioner, and the victim, and (3) the relief requested." The statute also requires that the petition allege the "immediate and present danger of domestic violence," which constitutes good cause.

D obtained an *ex parte* order during the course of the divorce proceedings between P and D, and the order granted D exclusive possession of their residence and household furniture. While the divorce matter was being litigated in state court, P filed an action in federal district court and sought injunctive relief pursuant to 42 U.S.C. §1983. P alleged that service and execution of the CPO denied him due process. The federal court applied the abstention doctrine, finding that the pending divorce proceedings implicated important state issues regarding the resolution of domestic disputes and that the state court provided P with an adequate opportunity to present his constitutional challenges. P has appealed. How will the federal appellate court most likely treat the lower court's decision to abstain from hearing the civil rights claim?

Explanation

The appellate court will most likely affirm the decision to abstain. Here it is undisputed that a divorce case was pending at the time P filed his federal action. Therefore, the first element of *Younger* is satisfied.

State X also has a strong state interest in regulating domestic violence. The challenged statute affects the underlying divorce and involves important state interests, thus satisfying the second *Younger* criterion. Note that in *Ankenbrandt*, the Supreme Court narrowed the scope of the traditional domestic relations exception, but it did not overrule its prior decisions holding that domestic relations is an area of traditional state concern.

Finally, P has failed to prove the inadequacy of the courts in state X. There is no reason to question their ability or willingness to address P's constitutional issue. Because state X courts provide an adequate forum for P's constitutional claim, the third criterion of *Younger* is satisfied. Thus, most federal courts will abstain from ruling on the constitutionality of the statute. *See Kelm v. Hyatt*, 44 F.3d 415 (6th Cir. 1995) (*Younger* abstention was warranted on claims for injunctive relief alleging that Ohio provisions denied due process to husband).

SUBJECT MATTER JURISDICTION IN STATE COURT

24.7. Statutory Challenges — Residency Requirements

In *Sosna v. Iowa*, 419 U.S. 393 (1975), a challenge was brought in federal court to the constitutionality of Iowa's one-year residency requirement for a divorce. After the case was properly certified as a class action, the named plaintiff satisfied the residency requirement. By the time the case came before the Supreme Court, therefore, the named plaintiff's claim was moot. The Court concluded that, for the class as a whole, the issue was capable of repetition yet evading review, and therefore not moot.

The Court held that as long as the named plaintiff has a live claim at the time a suit is filed and at the time the trial court certified the class, mootness as to the named plaintiff is not a bar to considering the case on its merits as to the class.

The Court held that the durational requirement in the statute was constitutional. It rejected the argument that it established two classes of persons and discriminated against those who had recently exercised their right to travel to Iowa. It said that the requirement was reasonably justified on grounds of the state's interest in requiring those seeking a divorce from its courts to be genuinely attached to the state, and the state's desire to insulate its divorce decrees from the likelihood of successful collateral attack. The Court said that the durational residency requirement also does not violate the Due Process Clause of the Fourteenth Amendment on the theory that it denies a litigant the opportunity to make an individualized showing of *bona fide* residence. Rather, there is no total deprivation of access to divorce courts but only a delay in access to them.

24.8. Does Failure to Meet Residency Requirement Void a Divorce Decree?

Typically, state legislatures have enacted statutes governing divorce proceedings that require the moving party to show a minimum period of residency before a court has subject matter jurisdiction to hear the matter. The residence period may be from six weeks to two years. Usually, a person seeking a divorce offers proof that the residency requirement has been met. On a rare occasion, after the divorce decree has been entered, it is discovered that the petitioner failed to meet the statutory residency requirement. In theory, because the residency requirement was not met, the court was without subject matter jurisdiction, and the divorce decree is void. The theory is not, however, always applied in practice.

Courts appear loathe to vacate a divorce decree because of a failure to meet residency requirements — especially after several months or years have passed. When a collateral challenge to an existing decree is raised, a court will thoroughly examine the language of the residency requirement in the appropriate section of the statute to determine whether there is specific language stating that failure to meet the residency provision divests a court of subject matter jurisdiction. Without finding specific language, a court will most likely not vacate the judgment.

A second approach to get around vacating an existing divorce judgment is illustrated by the decision of the New York Court of Appeals in *Lacks v. Lacks*, 359 N.E.2d 384 (N.Y. 1976). In that case, the ex-wife asked the court to vacate a divorce judgment entered two years earlier on the basis the court lacked subject matter jurisdiction. The court held that the statutory residence requirements for maintaining an action for divorce go only to the substance of the cause of action, not to the competence of the court to adjudicate the cause. 359 N.E.2d at 879. It said that even if the court, which granted the final judgment of divorce in the instant case, made an error of law or fact in determining the issue of residence, the error did not deprive it of jurisdiction to render the judgment.

Example 24-8

Assume that the marriage of P and D breaks down. P serves D with a petition to dissolve the marriage. D does not appear, and the matter goes by default. Assume that the residency requirement for a divorce in this jurisdiction is one year. Furthermore, assume that two years following the divorce, D moves to vacate the judgment and decree divorcing the couple, claiming that the court lacked subject matter jurisdiction when it was entered because P had been a resident for only six months, which is true. Will a court most likely vacate the judgment?

Explanation

A court will most likely reject the argument for vacating the judgment. It will probably rule that the statutory residence requirements for maintaining an action for divorce go only to the substance of the cause of action, not to the competence of the court to adjudicate the cause, and accordingly, even if the court that granted the final judgment of divorce erred in determining the issue of residence, the error did not deprive it of jurisdiction to render the judgment, and the judgment was not subject to vacature on post-judgment motion made after the time for appeal had been exhausted.

PERSONAL JURISDICTION IN STATE COURT

24.9. State Jurisdiction to Grant *Ex Parte* Divorce — The Divisible Divorce Theory

The Supreme Court has stated that personal jurisdiction over a nonresident spouse is not necessary to dissolve a marriage because dissolution is a status determination. *Pennoyer v. Neff*, 95 U.S. 714, 735 (1877). The theory is that a state possesses *in rem* jurisdiction over the *res*, or "thing," which is the marriage itself. This theory, when coupled with *in personam* jurisdiction over one of the spouses, provides a court with power to grant a valid *ex parte* divorce on whatever basis it sees fit. A state is entitled, moreover, to give the divorce decree absolute and binding finality within the confines of its borders. This principle rests on the theory that every state possesses jurisdiction to determine the civil status and capacities of all its inhabitants and the authority to prescribe the conditions on which proceedings affecting them may be commenced and carried on within its territory. Consequently, a state is viewed as having an absolute right to prescribe the conditions upon which the marriage relation between its own citizens shall be created, and the causes for which it may be dissolved.

Under the theory of "divisible divorce," issues other than the dissolution of the marriage are severed from the divorce action when the court does not have personal jurisdiction over one spouse. *Conlon by Conlon v. Heckler*, 719 F.2d 788, 795-796 (5th Cir. 1983); *see also Vanderbilt v. Vanderbilt*, 354 U.S. 416, 418-419 (1957) (where wife not subject to Nevada jurisdiction, Nevada court could not extinguish right to support in another state even though not reduced to judgment in the other state).

The divisible divorce theory was developed by the United States Supreme Court in *Estin v. Estin*, 334 U.S. 541 (1948). In *Estin* the husband and wife were married and lived in New York until they separated. The wife brought an action in New York for separation, and the husband entered a general appearance. The New York court granted the separation and awarded the wife alimony. The husband then went to Nevada and instituted an action for divorce. The wife was notified of the action by constructive service, but entered no appearance. The Nevada court granted the husband a divorce, but made no provision for alimony. The Supreme Court found that the Nevada court did not have personal jurisdiction over the wife because she was not a resident of Nevada, nor had she voluntarily submitted to the jurisdiction of the Nevada court. The Court held that the absence of personal jurisdiction over the wife made the divorce "divisible" — accommodating the interest of both states but restricting each state to the matters of "dominant concern." 334 U.S. at 549. Based on this "divisible divorce," the Court held that the Nevada decree was effective only in changing the parties' marital status, but that the order had no effect on alimony, which was earlier entered by a New York court with both parties before it.

Example 24-9

Assume that P and D were married for ten years when their relationship broke down. They entered into a separation agreement in state X that provided that D was to pay P $750 per month for child support until their child reached age 18, plus $1,000 per month in alimony. The court in state X had subject matter and personal jurisdiction over the parties when it entered the order. Eight months later, D filed an action for divorce in state Y. P was served by constructive service. At the time, P was not a resident of state Y, was not served within state Y, and did not submit to the jurisdiction of state Y. The court in state Y granted a divorce, reduced D's child support to $250 a month, and eliminated any alimony payment. P challenges the decision from state Y in state X. How will a court in state X most likely treat the challenge?

Explanation

Based on *Estin v. Estin*, a separation order that is entered by a court in state X that had in *personam* jurisdiction over both parties, and that provided for alimony or child support, is not superseded by a subsequent divorce decree obtained in a foreign state where the foreign state did not have in *personam* jurisdiction over both parties. *See Burnett v. Burnett*, 542 S.E.2d 911 (W. Va. 2000) (West Virginia separation order, which directed former husband to pay former wife $750 per month for child support and alimony, was not superseded by later Arkansas divorce decree). The parties are legally divorced, but the absence of jurisdiction over P means that the child support and alimony awards made in state X remain in effect. The portion of the judgment and decree regarding support and alimony made by the court in state Y is of no effect.

24.10. *In Rem* Divorce

Occasionally a person seeks a divorce and despite his or her best efforts, the other spouse cannot be found and personal service of the divorce summons and petition cannot be effectuated. This does not mean, however, that the divorce cannot proceed because the spouse cannot be located.

In response to this situation, all jurisdictions have promulgated statutes containing specific requirements that if met, allow the divorce action to proceed. The legal action is usually labeled in *rem* and requires compliance with provisions relating to service of process and proper notice, with publication in a legal newspaper often acting as a surrogate for personal service of the summons and complaint. As noted earlier, in *personam* jurisdiction is not necessary to the dissolution of a marriage because such a proceeding affects only the status of the marriage itself. Because the divorce action is in *rem*, a valid judgment requires only that the *res* or status be before the court on proper notice. In re *Marriage of Breen*, 560 S.W.2d 358, 361 (Mo. App. 1977); *see Black's Dictionary* (8th ed. 2004) (*res* is defined as "an object, interest or status as opposed to a person"). In addition to dissolving the marriage, a proper in *rem* action may provide the court with the power to adjudicate interests in land located within that state, even though the person who claims an interest in it is not personally before the court.

Example 24-10

Assume that P desired to dissolve her marriage to D and be awarded title to the couple's home. D could not be located despite P's search for D at D's last place of employment and last known address. P checked the local telephone book and city directory, searched the Internet, and made inquiries of D's relatives without success. P's lawyer prepared a publication notice to be placed in a legal newspaper asking the state court to exercise in rem jurisdiction in the matter. The local statute states that service by publication notice for in rem civil actions shall include "a description of any property to be affected. When service is sought by means of constructive notice, strict compliance with the statute and rule allowing service by publication is required." Assume that a partial description of the property was included in the service by publication notice. The trial judge grants P an ex parte divorce and awards her all the interest in the home, which was in the name of P and D. P dies a year after the divorce. D suddenly appears and claims he was out of the country for the last two years and knew nothing of the divorce proceeding. D opposes providing P's heirs with any interest in the home. P's executor contends that the divorce action provided P with the real estate once owned by P and D and eliminated any interest D had in the property. How will a court most likely rule?

Explanation

Because the exact description of the property was not included in the service by publication notice, the defect constitutes a violation of the service by publication requirement set out by the statute. The theory is that the service by publication requirement was simply not met; therefore, the court was without jurisdiction to enter a judgment relating to the property. The court will sever the divorce from the award of the home. Most likely, the judgment divorcing the couple will remain untouched, but that portion of the judgment relating to the property will be considered wholly void.

24.11. State Long-Arm Statute Requirements

Before a state court can exercise personal jurisdiction over a nonresident who does not intend to voluntarily appear at a court proceeding after a resident has asserted a claim against the nonresident, two requirements must be met: First, there must exist a statute authorizing the state to seek out and serve the nonresident and mandates the nonresident to appear and respond to a particular claim. Such statutes are usually referred to as "long-arm statutes." Second, assuming the language of a state statute applies to the nonresident, there must be sufficient contacts between the nonresident and the state seeking to compel the nonresident's appearance to satisfy the constitutional standard of "traditional notions of fair play and substantial justice." *Milliken v. Meyer*, 311 U.S. 457, 463 (1940).

State legislatures have generated long-arm statutes that cover a variety of claims including domestic matters. However, because the statutes have sometimes been drafted quite narrowly, the legislative language in a long-arm statute must always be scrutinized to ensure that it applies to the facts of a particular dispute. A few states have passed broad long-arm statutes. For example, California's long-arm statute authorizes California courts to exercise jurisdiction on any basis not inconsistent with the Constitution of the United States or the Constitution of California. *Luberski, Inc. v. Oleficio F.LLI Amato S.R.L.*, 89 Cal. Rptr. 3d 774 (Cal. App. 2009).

The advent and growth of long-arm statutes represent attempts by states to provide a friendly litigation forum for the convenience of their own citizens at the expense of citizens of other states. Most agree that the use of such statutes is natural in a mobile, industrialized society that has effectively reduced the time and rigors of travel between states. *See* Annot., *Long-Arm Statutes: Obtaining Jurisdiction Over Nonresident Parent in Filiation or Support Proceeding*, 76 A.L.R.3d 708, 714-715 (1977).

Where domestic matters are concerned, courts have sometimes quite awkwardly applied commonly used phrases written into long-arm statutes such as "transacting business" or "tortious conduct" to encompass these disputes, even though such terms are generally understood as directed at personal injury claims or commercial activities. For example, in *Prybolsky v. Prybolsky*, 430 A.2d 804 (Del. Fam. Ct. 1981), the court held that it had acquired personal jurisdiction over a nonresident husband by means of the "doing business" provision of the Delaware long-arm statute. 430 A.2d at 807. The court reasoned that marriage is a contract and that support and other rights springing from a marriage contract have financial and business implications. (This decision was later overruled by statute. *See* T.L. v. W.L., 820 A.2d 506 (Del. Fam. Ct. 2003).)

States have sometimes struggled with their long-arm statutes when attempting to find a theory that provides them with personal jurisdiction over nonresidents who owe child support to a resident. One approach has been to construe the phrase "a tortious act" in a state's long-arm statute as encompassing a failure on the part of the nonresident to support a child following birth, which is viewed as an injury. Courts analogize the failure to pay child support to a typical tort injury and reason that the long-arm statute applies to a failure to pay child support just as it would apply to an injured accident victim involved in a crash with a nonresident.

Other state courts have approached the jurisdictional issue by defining the phrase "tortious act" as including any act committed in the forum state that involves a breach of duty to another where the nonresident's act has resulted in ascertainable damages. *See Poindexter v. Willis*, 231 N.E.2d 1 (Ill. Ct. App. 1967); *accord In re Marriage of Highsmith*, 488 N.E.2d 1000, 1003 (1986); *Black v. Rasile*, 318 N.W.2d 475, 476 (Mich. App. 1982); *State ex rel. Nelson v. Nelson*, 216 N.W.2d 140, 143 (Minn. 1974); *In re Custody of Miller*, 548 P.2d 542, 546 (Wash. 1976).

Example 24-11

Assume that P, a citizen of state X, alleges in a complaint filed in state X that she and D, a citizen of state Y, had a series of sexual encounters in state X that led to a pregnancy and the birth of a child. D denies he is the father of the child. P seeks to establish the child's paternity and obtain child support from D. The long-arm statute available in state X permits the exercise of jurisdiction over a nonresident "who transacts business in state X, causes tortious injury in it, or has an interest in real property there." When D is served in state Y via this statute, he challenges its application in state X to a domestic proceeding. In his motion to dismiss, he alleges that he dated P a half dozen times in state X but had protected intercourse with her. How will a court most likely rule on D's challenge in state X?

Explanation

First, the court will ask whether the language of the long-arm statute applies to these facts. Second, even if the statute applies, a question remains whether the contacts between D and state X are sufficient to meet the minimal due process requirements of the Constitution.

A court may rule that the language of the long-arm statute applies to these facts on the basis that a failure to support the child constitutes a tortious act. A "tortious act" is defined as including any act committed in the state that involved a breach of duty to another and resulted in ascertainable damages. *See Poindexter v. Willis*, 231 N.E.2d 1 (Ill. App. 1967) (establishing the *Poindexter* rule); *Lozinski v. Lozinski*, 408 S.E.2d 310 (W. Va. 1991).

However, some courts have refused to follow the *Poindexter* rule when the sexual intercourse occurred either within or outside the state, on the ground that the failure to support cannot be a tort until paternity, which gives rise to the duty to support, has been established. These courts further hold that even when the sexual intercourse occurs in the state, it is not a tort when it involves two consenting adults. *State ex rel. Garcia v. Dayton*, 695 P.2d 477 (N.M. 1985); *State ex rel. Larimore v. Snyder*, 291 N.W.2d 241 (Neb. 1980); *State ex rel. Carrington v. Schutts*, 535 P.2d 982 (Kan. 1975); *Barnhart v. Madvig*, 526 S.W.2d 106 (Tenn. 1975); *A.R.B. v. G.L.P.*, 507 P.2d 468 (Colo. 1973);

Anonymous v. Anonymous, 268 N.Y.S.2d 710 (N.Y. Fam. Ct. 1966); *Taylor v. Texas Dept. of Public Welfare*, 549 S.W.2d 422 (Tex. App. 1977).

P may find support from the Uniform Interstate Family Support Act, which has been adopted in some form in all states. That Act provides that a person who has sexual intercourse within a state submits to the jurisdiction of that state's courts with respect to a child who may have been conceived. Application of the Act always remains open to constitutional challenge, depending on the facts of each case.

Assuming a court applies its long-arm statute to these facts on a breach-of-duty theory, the question of the constitutional minimum contacts requirement remains open. At least one court has held that sexual contact in the state constitutes minimum contacts such that an action maintained there does not offend "traditional notions of fair play and substantial justice." *Bell v. Arnold*, 279 S.E.2d 449 (Ga. 1981). In this example, the defendant admits being in state X and having intercourse with P. This is probably sufficient to meet the minimum contacts requirement of the Constitution. The outcome depends more on the theory state X applied to its long-arm statute than on whether the Constitution has been satisfied.

24.12. Due Process Barriers to Application of Long-Arm Statutes

It is axiomatic that even though a state's long-arm statute applies to a domestic dispute, the Constitution may bar its application because the Due Process Clause of the Fourteenth Amendment operates as a limitation on the jurisdiction of state courts to enter judgments affecting the rights or interests of nonresident defendants. *Kulko v. Superior Court of California*, 436 U.S. 84 (1978). Under *Kulko*, the existence of personal jurisdiction depends upon the presence of reasonable notice to the defendant that an action has been brought and a factual showing that there exists a sufficient connection between the defendant and the forum state to make it fair to require the defendant to defend the action in the forum state.

In *Kulko*, for example, after the couple formally separated, the husband remained in New York, the state of marital domicile, and the wife moved to California. They executed a separation agreement in New York that provided that the parties' two children were to reside with Mr. Kulko in New York during the school year and with their mother during their Christmas, Easter, and summer vacations. Mr. Kulko also agreed to pay $3,000 a year in child support. The terms of this agreement were later incorporated into a Haitian divorce decree obtained by Mrs. Kulko.

Subsequently, the parties' daughter expressed a desire to live full-time with her mother. Mr. Kulko acquiesced and paid his daughter's airfare to California. A few years later, the couple's son expressed to his mother a desire to live with her. Without Mr. Kulko's knowledge, Mrs. Kulko sent the child a plane ticket, which he used to join his mother and sister in California.

With both children now living with her in California, Mrs. Kulko filed suit in that state seeking an increase in child support. Mr. Kulko was served with process under California's broad long-arm statute. He resisted the action on the ground that he did not have sufficient contacts to warrant the California court's assertion of personal jurisdiction over him. The California Supreme Court rejected this argument, reasoning that by his act of sending his daughter to reside permanently in California, Mr. Kulko had "purposely availed himself of the benefits and protections of the laws of California." 436 U.S. at 89.

The Supreme Court rejected the California court's analysis, reasoning that the mere fact that Mr. Kulko "acquiesced" in the desire of his daughter to live with her mother was not a sufficient contact with the state of California to warrant imposition of the unreasonable burden of having to litigate a child support action there. The Court observed that there was no other activity that would bring Mr. Kulko in contact with the state of California. The Court also said that Mrs. Kulko was not without a remedy, because she could initiate a proceeding under the Uniform Reciprocal Enforcement of Support Act (URESA) and have the merits of her support request adjudicated in New York, where the ex-husband continued to reside, "without either party's having to leave his or her own State." 436 U.S. at 86.

Example 24-12

Assume that P and D were married and lived in state X for five years. When P lost his part-time job at a local fast-food restaurant, he decided he needed more education. He applied and was accepted to graduate school in state Y. While D remained in state X because of her good job that helped pay for P's room, board, and tuition, P moved to state Y to attend the university. After seven months, D was served with a divorce petition begun by P in state Y. In it, P asked that the marriage to D be dissolved and that P be awarded alimony of $150 a month. D did not answer, and a decree of divorce was granted to P in state Y with the court awarding P $150 per month in alimony. After graduation, P moved back to state X and sought to enforce the judgment. D countered by asking the state X court to declare P's state Y divorce decree void. Most likely, how will a state X court rule?

Explanation

Recall from your Civil Procedure class *Pennoyer v. Neff*, where the Supreme Court said,

> The jurisdiction which every State possesses to determine the civil status and capacities of all its inhabitants involves authority to prescribe the conditions on which proceedings affecting them may be commenced and carried on within its territory. The State, for example, has absolute right to prescribe the conditions upon which the marriage relation between its own citizens shall be created, and the causes for which it may be dissolved.

95 U.S. at 714, 734-735 (1877). Therefore, so long as P has met the conditions state Y established for granting a divorce, P and D are divorced, and all sister states must recognize that the relationship is dissolved. Consequently, D's action to have the divorce portion of the judgment in state Y voided would be dismissed despite the fact that the divorcing court did not have personal jurisdiction over D.

However, that portion of the state Y judgment and decree dealing with the $150 monthly alimony payment will not be recognized in state X. This is a personal obligation, which is unrelated to the "status" of the couple's relationship. When the state Y court issued its decree, it did not have personal jurisdiction over D; therefore, it could not impose on D any personal obligations. Note that there is no suggestion in the example that D consented to or waived the personal jurisdiction defense.

Example 24-13

Assume that a statute in state X reads as follows: "In a proceeding to establish, enforce, or modify a support order or to determine parentage, a tribunal of this state may exercise personal jurisdiction over a nonresident individual or the individual's guardian or conservator if the child resides in this State as a result of the acts or directives of the individual." Assume that P, a citizen of state Y, was awarded custody of child C in a divorce five years ago in state Y. D, the child's mother, who was living in state X, did not appear in state Y but consented to the action. However, last month, P became angry with C, purchased a bus ticket, and sent C to live with D, who still lives in state X. Assume that D brought an action in state X asking for child support. P, who has never been to state X, challenges the court's exercise of personal jurisdiction over him on a constitutional basis. How will a judge in state X most likely rule on the challenge?

Explanation

This example is based on *Kulko v. Superior Court*. While the facts are not identical to those found in *Kulko*, they are not so dissimilar as to change the jurisdictional outcome. Here, regardless of the statutory language that provides the court with authority to bring a nonresident before it in a child support action, the Due Process Clause of the Fourteenth Amendment will bar the application of the long-arm statute. P does not have sufficient contacts with state X to satisfy the Constitution. D must seek to obtain child support under state X's Uniform Interstate Family Support Act, or proceed to state Y and initiate the child support action in that state.

24.13. Traditional View of Personal Jurisdiction

Personal jurisdiction may be exercised over an individual by virtue of being served with legal process while he or she is present within the forum state. This rule applies even if the person served is an out-of-state resident who comes into the forum state only briefly. *Burnham v. Superior Court*, 495 U.S. 604 (1990). In *Burnham*, the wife brought a divorce action in California and served her husband with divorce papers when he visited their children in that state. The Supreme Court ruled that his physical presence within the state conferred personal jurisdiction over him — no additional "minimum contacts" were required. 495 U.S. at 619.

Justice Scalia, writing for a plurality of four in *Burnham*, stated that "jurisdiction based on physical presence alone constitutes due process because it is one of the continuing traditions of our legal system that define the due process standard of 'traditional notions of fair play and substantial justice.'" *Id*. Three other Justices joined in a concurring opinion filed by Justice Brennan. In their view, tradition alone was not dispositive; they would judge the constitutionality of in-state service on a nonresident by examining contemporary notions of due process. 495 U.S. at 629-632 (Brennan, J., concurring). The Justices ultimately concluded that "as a rule the exercise of personal jurisdiction over a defendant based on his voluntary presence in the forum will satisfy the requirements of due process." 495 U.S. at 639. They reasoned that by visiting the forum state, a defendant avails himself of significant benefits, such as the protection of his health and safety. 495 U.S. at 637-638. Justice Stevens joined neither Justice Scalia's nor Justice Brennan's opinion, but concurred in the judgment based on considerations of history, fairness, and common sense.

Example 24-14

Assume that P asserts that D is the father of a child born out of wedlock. P is a citizen of state X and D a citizen of state Y. P initiates a paternity action in state X. D is served with a summons and complaint when D's private airplane touched down at a state X airport. The plane was traveling from Colorado to state Y when it made the 30-minute stop to refuel. D argues that state X does not have personal jurisdiction over him because the short stopover to refuel cannot meet the minimum contacts requirements of the Due Process Clause. How will a court most likely rule on the challenge?

Explanation

State X court has personal jurisdiction over D because D was served within the boundaries of state X. There is no basis for D's argument. *See In re Gonzalez*, 993 S.W.2d 147 (Tex. Ct. App. 1999) (personal service effected on father while his plane touched down in state for refueling authorized exercise of personal jurisdiction).

24.14. Continuing Jurisdiction

Most states take the view that they possess continuing jurisdiction over the parties to a dissolution if a court possessed personal jurisdiction over the parties at the time the divorce judgment was entered. Consequently, parties who move from a jurisdiction where a judgment was properly entered, and remain away for several years, cannot block modification or enforcement efforts on the ground the forum court lost personal jurisdiction once the party moved out of state. For example, in *Bjordahl v. Bjordahl*, 308 N.W.2d 817 (Minn. 1981), even though the husband had not resided in Minnesota for 22 years and the parties' children had reached age of majority, the Minnesota Supreme Court ruled that the court in which the divorce was granted under a stipulated judgment had continuing jurisdiction for modification and enforcement of the decree. *See Katz v. Katz*, 408 N.W.2d 835, 838 (Minn. 1987) (trial court's continuing jurisdiction extends to the modification or enforcement of the decree); *Angelos v. Angelos*, 367 N.W.2d 518, 519 (Minn. 1985) (domestic relationships, by their nature, continue under the jurisdiction of the court virtually throughout the lives of the parties).

Example 24-15

Assume that P and D divorced at a time when the court in state X had subject matter and personal jurisdiction over the parties. D left the jurisdiction and had remained away for ten years when P brought an action against D in state X to enforce provisions in the original divorce decree. P alleges that D has ignored provisions in the original decree relating to a car that was to be delivered in new condition but was delivered in used condition and five years late. P also asserts that certain insurance policies D was required by the divorce decree to keep in effect have lapsed, and that alimony and child support totaling $17,175 remain unpaid. D argues that state X cannot gain personal jurisdiction over him for these claims because of his long absence from that jurisdiction. How would a court most likely rule on these hypothetical facts?

Explanation

It is quite likely a court will agree with P and reject D's defense. Here state X was the original marital domicile. A due process argument can be made to support P as follows: The parties chose to resolve their marital dispute in state X, and thus D purposefully availed himself of the privilege of conducting activities within state X. At the time, it was entirely foreseeable that a future breach of the agreement could lead to D being called into a court in state X.

Furthermore, a court may reason that a finding that state X continues to have jurisdiction over the parties protects D from arbitrarily being sued in any other state. It may also reason that while D has not been a resident or transacted business in state X for ten years since the divorce decree, the obligations of that judgment have attached, and the obligations may constitute continuing contacts sufficient to satisfy due process.

24.15. Waiving Personal Jurisdiction

Personal jurisdiction may be conferred upon a party by a state because the party has waived the defense. The waiver may occur when the defendant appears in court and fails to properly raise the issue at the first opportunity to do so. *Mesenbourg v. Mesenbourg*, 538 N.W.2d 489, 492-493 (Minn. App. 1995) (finding that the appellant waived his right to challenge personal jurisdiction when he failed to do so in the district court). For example, if a defendant appears in a divorce action in a state court and fails to challenge the court's exercise of personal jurisdiction at the first opportunity, she may not subsequently collaterally attack the divorce decree for lack of personal jurisdiction. *Sherrer v. Sherrer*, 334 U.S. 343 (1948).

Waiver may also occur with the filing of a permissive counterclaim in response to a complaint. *Arch Aluminum & Glass Co., Inc. v. Haney*, 964 So. 2d 228 (Fla. App. 2007). However, a majority of jurisdictions will not treat a compulsory counterclaim as waiving a personal jurisdiction defense, because a compulsory counterclaim is waived if not asserted in the answer. *Babcock v. Whatmore*, 707 So. 2d 702, 704 (Fla. 1998) (defendant waived challenge to personal jurisdiction by seeking affirmative relief, but motion for relief from monetary judgments for special equities and child support arrearages did not waive his challenge to personal jurisdiction because it was not a plea for affirmative relief but rather a defensive motion seeking to avoid the judgments).

Example 24-16

Assume that P and D's marriage broke down and after several years of separation, P brought a divorce action in state X. D, who lives in state Y, appeared in state X through her lawyers. Following entry of the divorce decree, D believes that the court in state X did not have personal jurisdiction over her — that she never personally appeared — only her lawyers appeared on her behalf. The record of the divorce proceedings in state X show that D's lawyers contested the divorce in state X alleging that she was not a *bona fide* resident of the state as required by a statute in state X. The trial judge in state X expressly found that P was a *bona fide* resident of state X and granted the divorce. That ruling was not appealed by D's lawyers. D now collaterally attacks enforcement of the divorce action in state Y, claiming that the court in state X lacked personal jurisdiction over her. How will a court in state Y most likely rule?

Explanation

A court in state Y will most likely dismiss D's challenge. Once parties participate in a proceeding in person or by their lawyers, even if it is later discovered that the court lacked personal jurisdiction, the issue cannot be successfully raised collaterally. The reason for this is that the party has made an appearance, and the party has been afforded an opportunity to be heard. *See Sherrer v. Sherrer, supra,* at 350-351 of 334 U.S. In this example, D's lawyers made an appearance and failed to challenge personal jurisdiction. Rather, they contested the provisions of a statute that they said didn't apply to their client, they lost, and failed to appeal. This is sufficient to constitute a waiver of a challenge to personal jurisdiction.

STATUS AS A JURISDICTIONAL THEORY

24.16. Overview of Status Theory

Some jurisdictions have begun to more actively use status as a theory upon which to adjudicate family law issues without first obtaining personal jurisdiction over an out-of-state member of the family in the traditional fashion. The status theory originally sprang from actions where one spouse sought a divorce, and the other spouse could not be found. Acceptance of the theory allowed courts to grant an *in rem* divorce to the spouse who was before the court, even though the other spouse could not be found or chose not to participate in the divorce action.

The status theory has been extended by some courts to child custody disputes, which initially appears contrary to the Supreme Court's plurality view as expressed in *May v. Anderson*, 345 U.S. 528 (1953). In *May v. Anderson*, the Court held that a child custody decree of one state was not entitled to full faith and credit in another state when the decree was entered by a court that failed to possess personal jurisdiction over the nonresident parent.

However, application of the holding has been challenged in subsequent child custody disputes by many of the courts for a variety of reasons. For example, Tennessee rejected *May v. Anderson* on the ground that subsequent Supreme Court decisions had abolished the distinctions between *in rem* and *in personam* jurisdiction, and "recognized that exceptions can be made to the 'minimum contacts' standard" in "status" cases, such as child custody decisions. *Fernandez v. Fernandez*, 1986 WL 7935 (Tenn. Ct. App. 1986); *see also Brown v. Brown*, 847 S.W.2d 496, 499 n.2 (Tenn. 1993). The Tennessee court followed the rule that courts of a state "having the most significant connections with the child and his family have jurisdiction to make a custody adjudication, even in the absence of personal jurisdiction over a parent who does not reside in the forum state." *Fernandez*, 1986 WL 7935, at 2. *See also Roderick v. Roderick*, 776 S.W.2d 533 (Tenn. Ct. App. 1989).

Texas, when applying the status exception to custody disputes, has explained that "unlike adjudications of child support and visitation expense, custody determinations are status adjudications not dependent upon personal jurisdiction over the parents. Generally, a family relationship is among those matters in which the forum state has such a strong interest that its courts may reasonably make an adjudication affecting that relationship even though one of the parties to the relationship may have had no personal contacts with the forum state." *In re S.A.V.*, 837 S.W.2d 80, 84 (Tex. 1992); *see also In re Marriage of Los*, 593 N.E.2d 126 (Ill. App. 1992).

The status exception has also been extended by a few courts to parental termination proceedings. *See In re Appeal in Maricopa County, Juvenile Action No. JS-734,*

543 P.2d 454, 459-460 (Ariz. Ct. App. 1975) (in termination proceeding, court did not err in denying motion to dismiss for lack of jurisdiction, notwithstanding lack of *in personam* jurisdiction over the mother); *In re Interest of M.L.K.*, 768 P.2d 316, 319-320 (Kan. Ct. App. 1989) (proceeding for termination of parental rights was exception to "minimum contacts" rule for personal jurisdiction and thus personal jurisdiction over a parent who could not be located or over an unknown parent was not required to meet due process considerations); *In re Adoption of Copeland*, 43 S.W.3d 483, 487 (Tenn. Ct. App. 2000) (relying on status exception in parental rights termination proceeding against a father in prison); *Wenz v. Schwartze*, 598 P.2d 1086, 1091-1092 (Mont. 1979) (concluding personal jurisdiction over a parent is not necessary in order to terminate parental rights, without specifically discussing status exception), *cert. denied*, 444 U.S. 1071 (1980); *In re A.E.H.*, 468 N.W.2d 190, 198-200 (Wis. 1991) (focusing on child's contacts with the state in order to terminate parental rights), *cert. denied*, 502 U.S. 925 (1991).

The Oklahoma Supreme Court applied the status rationale to an adoption proceeding in *In re Adoption of J.L.H.*, 737 P.2d 915 (Okla. 1987). In that case, the children's natural father and stepmother petitioned Oklahoma for the non-consensual adoption of the father's children by the stepmother on the ground that their mother, a nonresident of Oklahoma, had willfully failed to pay child support. The adoption was allowed to proceed without the mother's consent or the court possessing personal jurisdiction over her. It relied upon *Williams v. State of North Carolina*, 317 U.S. 287 (1942), stating that "[a]ccording to *Williams*, judicial cognizance over personal status — be it one created by matrimony or by natural parentage — may be validly exercised by a court of the state in which only one party to the status is a *bona fide* domiciliary while the other party, whose bond is sought to be adversely affected by the litigation, is a resident of a foreign jurisdiction." 737 P.2d at 918-919.

In *Bartsch v. Bartsch*, 636 N.W.2d 3 (Iowa 2001), the court applied the status theory when a dispute arose over whether a wife could obtain what was essentially an *ex parte* protective order against her nonresident husband under Iowa's Domestic Abuse Act. The court majority agreed that Iowa did not possess personal jurisdiction over him, but ruled the protective order could be issued without having such jurisdiction because of the wife's status in the state. It relied heavily on *Williams, supra*, to buttress its status theory. It also observed that the Minnesota Supreme Court found no due process problems in a statute allowing *ex parte* restraining orders in domestic abuse cases, relying on (1) a state's strong interest in preventing abuse, (2) the necessity for prompt action, and (3) the protection provided by judicial scrutiny. *See Baker v. Baker*, 494 N.W.2d 282, 288 (Minn. 1992), *superseded in part by statute in Burkstrand v. Burkstrand*, 632 N.W.2d 206 (Minn. 2001). It reasoned that "the order here does not attempt to impose a personal judgment against the defendant. . . . [I]t deals with jurisdiction to enforce liability arising from status rather than with determination of status. The district court merely ordered the defendant to 'stay away from the protected party' and not assault or communicate with her, in furtherance of the State's strong interest in protecting Iowa residents from domestic abuse. If a court may constitutionally make orders affecting marriage, custody, and parental rights without personal jurisdiction of a defendant, it certainly should be able to do what the court did here — enter an order protecting a resident Iowa family from abuse." 636 N.W.2d at 10.

24.17. Restatement of Conflict of Laws — Status

The *Restatement of Conflict of Laws* discusses the traditional view of status but does not extend it beyond an *ex parte* divorce action. The *Restatement* uses the following illustration: Assume that "A leaves his home in State X and goes to State Y, where he becomes domiciled and there obtains an *ex parte* divorce from B, his wife. Assuming that the requirements of proper notice and opportunity to be heard have been met, this divorce is valid and must be recognized in State X under full faith and credit even though B was not personally subject to the jurisdiction of the State Y court and at all times retained her domicile in State X." *Restatement (Second) of Conflict of Laws* §71 cmt. a, illus. 1 (1971).

FULL FAITH AND CREDIT

24.18. State Recognition of *Ex Parte* Divorce — Full Faith and Credit

If one state's *ex parte* divorce decrees are to be accorded full faith and credit in the courts of a sister state, it is essential that the state issuing the decree have proper jurisdiction over the divorce proceedings. In addition to subject matter, a state must have jurisdiction over at least one of the parties to the *ex parte* proceeding. *See Vanderbilt v. Vanderbilt, supra,* at 422 of 354 U.S. With subject matter and personal jurisdiction over one party, the *ex parte* divorce is recognized by all other jurisdictions.

Example 24-17

Assume that P and D divorced in state Y and that, at the time, state Y had personal jurisdiction over both parties. Neither was awarded alimony, and alimony was not reserved. Two years following entry of the divorce decree, D moves to state X and remarries. P goes to state X and brings an action seeking alimony. D contends that the state X court may not hear the alimony action. How will a court most likely rule?

Explanation

D will most likely be successful in preventing the court from hearing the action. D will contend that the action in state Y is *res judicata* and must be enforced under the Full Faith and Credit Clause of the federal Constitution, which reads as follows: "Full Faith and Credit shall be given in each state to the public acts, Records, and Judicial Proceedings of every other state." U.S. Const. art. 4, §1. When there is nothing in the judgment and decree dissolving a marriage that reserves for a future date the question of alimony, most, if not all, jurisdictions will take the view that alimony was permanently waived.

24.19. State Recognition of Same-Sex Marriages (Defense of Marriage Act)

The Federal Defense of Marriage Act (DOMA) permits states to deny recognition of same-sex marriages originating in other states. It does not require that they do so. DOMA was enacted after the Supreme Court of Hawaii determined the state statute banning same-sex marriage fell under strict scrutiny, leading some to believe that constitutionalization of same-sex marriage was imminent.

The Federal DOMA declares that "No State . . . shall be required to give effect to any public act, record, or judicial proceeding of any other State . . . respecting a relationship between persons of the same sex that is treated as a marriage under the laws of such other State." 28 U.S.C. §1738C (Supp. 2000). The statute provides each state with the power to determine the validity of same-sex marriage within its own borders. The statute is, in effect, an exception to the Full Faith and Credit Clause of the United States Constitution. (See Chapter 2, *supra*, for additional discussion and citations.)

Some state courts, where same-sex marriages are not allowed, have shown a willingness to recognize same-sex marriages from states that do allow them. For example, in *Lewis v. New York State Dept. of Civil Service*, 60 A.D.3d 216 (N.Y.A.D. 2009), the court held that it would recognize the parties to a same-sex marriage as spouses if their marriage was valid in the jurisdiction where it was solemnized. The ruling allowed spouses of state employees access to the benefits provided under state health insurance program. The relationships are also recognized in New York for purposes of insurance law, "including all provisions governing health insurance." *In re Donna S.*, 871

N.Y.S.2d 883 (N.Y. Fam. Ct. 2009). Note, however, that a New York trial court held in July 2009 that a woman who entered into a civil union in Vermont with her same-sex partner was not entitled to the grant of her petition for the dissolution of their marriage in New York. The court explained that it could not treat the women's civil union as a marriage but had the authority to dissolve the civil union under its "general jurisdiction to hear and decide all equitable civil actions." It dismissed the marriage dissolution petition and advised the woman to return with a petition for dissolution of the civil union (B.S. v. F.B., N.Y. Sup. Ct., No. 09-10999, 7-15-09).

Other state courts have indicated they will not recognize a same-sex marriage validly entered in another jurisdiction. *Ghassemi v. Ghassemi*, 998 So. 2d 731, 738 (La. App. 2008) (marriage between persons of the same sex violates a strong public policy of Louisiana, and such a marriage contracted in another state shall not be recognized in this state for any purpose, including the assertion of any right or claim as a result of the purported marriage); *Chambers v. Ormiston*, 935 A.2d 956 (R.I. 2007) (a court of limited statutory jurisdiction is without jurisdiction to entertain divorce petition involving same-sex couple who were married in Massachusetts); *O'Darling v. O'Darling*, 188 P.3d 137 (Okla. 2008) (divorce vacated when information received that parties seeking divorce were of same sex); *Rosengarten v. Downes*, 802 A.2d 170 (Conn. App. 2002) (affirming trial court's dismissal of an action to dissolve a Vermont civil union for lack of subject matter jurisdiction — note, however, that Connecticut enacted a civil union statute in 2005, which gave couples the same rights and responsibilities as in marriage, but included a provision limiting marriage to a man and a woman. The limitation on the sex of persons who could marry in the statute was challenged in *Kerrigan v. State*, 957 A.2d 407 (Conn. 2008), and was found to be unconstitutional; Connecticut now recognizes same-sex marriage).

24.20. Full Faith and Credit for Child Support Orders Act

In 1996, Congress enacted the Full Faith and Credit for Child Support Orders Act, 28 U.S.C.A. §1738(B) (1996). The federal act is binding on all states and supersedes inconsistent provisions of state law. *In re Marriage of Carrier*, 576 N.W.2d 97, 98 (Iowa 1998). The Act ensures that only one child support order at a time is in effect, and it incorporates many of the concepts contained in the Uniform Interstate Family Support Act. For example, it requires that a state enforce a child support order made in another state at a time when that state had jurisdiction over both parties. The parties must be given reasonable notice and an opportunity to be heard. 28 U.S.C.

§1738B(c)(2). The Act supersedes any inconsistent provisions of the Uniform Interstate Family Support Act (UIFSA) as adopted by a particular state. *Witowski v. Roosevelt*, 199 P.3d 1072 (Wyo. 2009) (under the Supremacy Clause, Wyoming was obligated to enforce Virginia child support order, according to its terms, whether or not Virginia law differed from Wyoming law).

Example 24-18

Assume that P and D were divorced in state X. The court in state X ordered that P pay D $1,000 a month permanent maintenance and $600 a month child support. Shortly after the divorce, P moved to state Y, while D remained in state X. P had the original divorce judgment registered in state Y. A few months after registering the judgment, P lost his job and brought an action in state Y to modify the maintenance and child support ordered in the original judgment and decree. P stated at the modification hearing in state Y that he had discussed the matter with D and she did not necessarily object to the court hearing P's request. While written consent was not filed with the court in state Y, and D did not appear at the modification hearing, the trial judge believed that D had waived any challenge to the modification hearing's going forward. The judge in state Y reduced the support payments to $200 a month and suspended further maintenance payments. D has appealed the reduction in support. How will the appellate court most likely view the action?

Explanation

A literal application of the language in the Full Faith and Credit for Child Support Orders Act should result in a ruling that the court in one state did not have subject matter jurisdiction to modify the existing child support order. As a result, the lower court's judgment will most likely be vacated and the matter dismissed.

The reason for the dismissal is that when the Full Faith and Credit for Child Support Orders Act became effective, it generally deprived courts in state Y of subject matter jurisdiction to modify an amount of child support of an order entered by another state and registered under URESA (now UIFSA). *See, e.g., Paton v. Brill*, 663 N.E.2d 421 (Ohio App. 1995) (Ohio court did not have jurisdiction to modify child support order pursuant to original Maryland divorce decree). The Act requires each state to enforce a child support order made by a court of another state.

Pursuant to the statute, state courts are to refrain from modifying an existing order in another state unless the court of the other state no longer has continuing and exclusive jurisdiction of the child support order either because the child or any contestant is no longer a resident of the state, or each party has filed written consent in the original state, agreeing to permit the new state to modify the order. Here, D continues to reside in state X with the child and neither party filed written consent in state X that the matter could be heard in state Y.

SPECIAL SITUATIONS

24.21. Overview of Indian Child Welfare Act

The Indian Child Welfare Act (ICWA), §§1901 and 1911, gives tribal courts exclusive jurisdiction over proceedings concerning an Indian child who resides or is domiciled on an Indian reservation. 25 U.S.C. §§1901, 1911 (1978). In *Mississippi Band of Choctaw Indians v. Holyfield*, 490 U.S. 30 (1989), the Supreme Court held that custody and adoption decisions involving Indian children born off an Indian reservation to parents who were domiciled on the reservation at the time of birth, gave the tribe to which the parents belonged exclusive jurisdiction to decide those issues. Domicile was defined as physical presence with the intent to remain on the reservation. Minors will take the domicile of their parents because they are legally incapable of forming the requisite state of mind (intent) to create a domicile. The Court made it clear that parents could not defeat the intent of the ICWA absent changing their domicile.

A "child custody proceeding" is broadly defined by the ICWA, as referring to any proceeding involving foster care placement, termination of parental rights, preadoptive placement, or adoptive placement. 25 U.S.C. §1903(1) (1978). The only two exceptions to that definition are awards of custody to one of the parents in divorce proceedings and delinquency proceeding placements. 25 U.S.C. §1903(1) (1978).

24.22. Determining Ethnicity Under ICWA

The ICWA defines an "Indian child" as "any unmarried person who is under age eighteen and is either (a) a member of an Indian tribe or (b) is eligible for membership in an Indian tribe and is the biological child of a member of an Indian tribe." 25 U.S.C. §1903(4) (1978).

In *Matter of Petition of Phillip A.C.*, 149 P.3d 51 (Nev. 2006), the court, in the context of an adoption dispute, considered the issue of the type of evidence that may be used to determine whether a child is a Native American child under the ICWA. The child, Z.R.K., was adopted following a court hearing by Phillip. The child was the son of Phillip's ex-stepdaughter, Tarah K. Phillip. Soon after the district court granted the order of adoption, Tarah contacted the Central Council of the Tlingit & Haida Indian Tribes of Alaska, seeking assistance in overturning the adoption. Tarah claimed that she had signed the adoption consent under extreme duress and that Phillip had prevented her from attending the subsequent adoption hearing through deception. The parties agreed that ethnically, Tarah is 7/16ths Native American and Z.R.K. is 7/32nds Native American. They disagreed, however, as to whether Z.R.K. is a Native American child under the ICWA.

An affidavit of the tribal enrollment officer was submitted in which the officer stated that (1) she had served as the tribal enrollment officer for 15 years; (2) Tarah had been an enrolled member of the Tlingit & Haida Indian Tribes since 1989; (3) Z.R.K. was eligible for enrollment at the time of her adoption by Phillip on June 8, 2004; and (4) Z.R.K. had been an enrolled member of the tribes since February 16, 2005. The court found that Z.R.K. was a Native American child to whom the ICWA applied and that the adoption proceedings had violated part of the ICWA, 25 U.S.C. §1913(a), because no judicial certification had been entered. However, it remanded the case to allow Phillip the opportunity to challenge the authority of the tribal enrollment officer to speak for the tribe. 149 P.3d at 1297.

Example 24-19

Assume P and D are married and domiciled on an Indian Reservation in state X. For a variety of reasons, they decide that a child to be born to them in about two months should be put up for adoption. They move from the reservation to a town in state Y, where the infant is born. Six weeks later, non-Indians through a state Y court adopt the infant. Two months later, the tribe to which P and D belong bring an action in state Y to vacate the adoption decree on the ground that under the ICWA, exclusive jurisdiction was vested in the tribal court. The parents of the newly adopted infant respond that P and D waived the jurisdiction of the ICWA by word and act. They present a written waiver signed by P and D in which P and D state that their intention is to "waive any provisions of law under the ICWA that might prevent the adoption under state law." How should a court rule?

Explanation

Despite the efforts of P and D, the court will most likely rule that the adoption is void and that subject matter jurisdiction rests with the Indian tribe. *Mississippi Band of Choctaw Indians v. Holyfield*, 490 U.S. 30 (1989). The child was "domiciled" on the tribe's reservation within the meaning of the ICWA's exclusive tribal jurisdiction provision when it was born, thus the state court was without jurisdiction to enter the adoption decree. A child under the ICWA takes the reservation domicile of its mother at birth — notwithstanding that the child was born off the reservation.

Congress enacted the ICWA because of concerns going beyond the wishes of individual parents, finding that the removal of Indian children from their cultural setting seriously impacts on long-term tribal survival and has a damaging social and psychological impact on many individual Indian children. These concerns demonstrate that Congress could not have intended to enact a rule of domicile that would permit individual Indian parents to defeat the ICWA's jurisdictional scheme simply by giving birth and placing the child for adoption off the reservation.

24.23. Overview of Soldiers and Sailors Civil Relief Act — Servicemembers Civil Relief Act

The Soldiers and Sailors Civil Relief Act (SSCRA) of 1940 is essentially a reenactment of the 1918 statute, with a number of amendments. 50 U.S.C. app. §521. It was first amended in 1942, and again in 1991 as a result of the First Gulf War. In November 2002, Congress passed a law (the Veterans Benefits Act of 2002, Pub. L. No. 107-330 §305), which provides SSCRA protection to National Guard members called to state active duty under Title 32 if the duty is because of a federal emergency, the request for active duty is made by the president or secretary of defense, and the member is activated for longer than 30 days. An example of this would be the National Guard members who were activated by the states, at the request of the president, to provide security for airports after the attacks of September 11, 2001.

The Act states that a servicemember, who is either the plaintiff or the defendant in a civil lawsuit, may request a stay, or postponement, of a court proceeding in which he or she is a party and may request a stay at any point in the proceedings. See In re A.R., 88 Cal. Rptr. 3d 448 (Cal. App. 2009) (SCRA stay provision overrides state requirement to complete dispositional hearing within six months).

The statute was amended and given a new title in 2003. See 50 U.S.C. app. §501. It is now called the Servicemembers Civil Relief Act (SCRA). The SCRA protects servicemembers by providing for the "temporary suspension of judicial and administrative proceedings and transactions that may adversely affect the civil rights of servicemembers during their military service." 50 U.S.C. app. §502(2). The purpose of this protection is to enable servicemembers "to devote their entire energy to the defense needs of the Nation." 50 U.S.C. app. §502(1). SCRA also protects persons in military service from having default judgments entered against them without their knowledge. Judgments entered in violation of Soldiers and Sailors Civil Relief Act of 1940 are merely voidable and not void. They remain valid until properly attacked under the Act's provisions, and the challenge need be timely under the statute. *See Wilson v. Butler*, 584 So. 2d 414, 416 (Miss. 1991) (paternity judgment upheld where defendant did not invoke Soldiers and Sailors Civil Relief Act until 13 months after final judgment); *see Price v. McBeath*, 989 So. 2d 444 (Miss. App. 2008).

In general, courts take the view that the provisions of the Act are to be liberally construed toward protecting the rights of men and women in the service who have been obliged to drop their own affairs to take up the burdens of the nation. *Reed v. Albaaj*, 723 N.W.2d 50, 54 (Minn. App. 2006) (quoting *Boone v. Lightner*, 319 U.S. 561, 564 (1943)); *see Omega Industry, Inc. v. Raffaele*, 894 F. Supp. 1425 (Nev. Dist. Ct. 1995) (Civil Relief Act was intended to be liberally construed, and applied in a broad spirit of gratitude toward service personnel); 50 U.S.C. app. §512(1). However, the Act does not empower a court to collaterally review, vacate, or impede the decisions of a state court. *See Scheidegg v. Dept. of Air Force*, 715 F. Supp. 11, 13-14 (D.N.H. 1989); *Sarfaty v. Sarfaty*, 534 F. Supp. 701, 704 n.4 (Pa. D. & C. 1982). Judgments made in violation of the Act are subject to attack only in the courts that rendered the judgments. *See* 50 U.S.C. app. §520(4).

Members of the merchant marine are likely not covered by SCRA. The express definition of "servicemembers" in the SCRA makes the similarities between the merchant marines and branches of the armed services insufficient to grant a member of the merchant marines the protections of the Act. The "armed forces" are defined as the "Army, Navy, Air Force, Marine Corps, and Coast Guard." 10 U.S.C. §101(a)(4).

Example 24-20

Assume that P and D married and that P joined the U.S. Army. P got into difficulty with the Army and was incarcerated because he went AWOL (absent without leave). While P was incarcerated, D filed a divorce action in state X. P asked for a delay in the divorce proceedings arguing that he was protected by the Servicemembers Civil Relief Act (SCRA). D argues that he is not protected by SCRA because he was not on active duty as required by SCRA. D provides the court with several sections of SCRA including 10 U.S.C. §101(d)(1) (2000), which states that "active duty" means "full-time duty in the active military service of the United States. Such term includes full-time training duty, annual training duty, and attendance, while in the active military service, at a school designated as a service school by law or by the Secretary of the military department concerned." P also argues that he has been denied due process under the Fifth Amendment to the Constitution. How will a court most likely resolve P's issues?

Explanation

Most courts have concluded that the SCRA does not protect servicemembers who are incarcerated in military prison or who are AWOL, because such servicemembers are not on active duty and are not absent from duty on account of a lawful cause. *See, e.g., United States v. Hampshire*, 95 F.3d 999, 1005 (10th Cir. 1996); *Mantz v. Mantz*, 69 N.E.2d 637, 639 (Ohio Ct. Com. Pl. 1946) (stating that the SCRA does not protect "those who through their voluntary aggressions and conduct remove themselves from the role of servicemembers in active service or duty"); *Means v. Means*, 45 Pa. D. & C.2d 228, 231 (Pa .Ct. Com. Pl. 1968) (asking, "[c]an it be said in logic or reason that to permit [an AWOL servicemember's] wife to proceed with her divorce action prevents him from devoting his full energy to the defense needs of the Nation, or can it say that he has absented himself for any lawful cause?"). Because P was incarcerated in military prison for crimes that he committed while on active duty, he was not on active duty at the time of the dissolution proceeding and was, therefore, not entitled to benefit from the protections of the SCRA.

The court will also most likely reject the Fifth Amendment equal protection argument that the statute has created a class of servicemembers who are unable to use the protections of the SCRA. His argument that, other than his confinement, there is no legitimate basis on which to differentiate P from nonconfined active duty personnel will be rejected. The court will reason that a servicemember who is serving time confined in a military prison for crimes committed while in military service is not situated similarly to servicemembers not so confined. Therefore, P's confinement alone is not a legitimate basis to treat him differently from nonconfined servicemembers. The court will most likely conclude that because P has failed to show that he is being treated differently from similarly situated servicemembers, his equal-protection argument will fail. *See Reed v. Albaaj*, 723 N.W.2d 50 (Minn. App. 2006).

Example 24-21

Assume that P and D divorce and P is awarded custody of their two minor children by a judge in state X, where D and D's lawyer appeared. D, who is upset with the ruling and who is in the military, files a petition in federal district court asking that it issue an order staying the enforcement of the child custody order pending the end of D's military service in Afghanistan. A motion to dismiss the action has been brought by P. How will a court most likely rule?

Explanation

On these hypothetical facts, the federal court will most likely dismiss the request for injunctive relief. Note that under the Anti-Injunction Act, 28 U.S.C. §2283 (1948), a federal court may not stay a state court proceeding "except as expressly authorized by Act of Congress, or where necessary in aid of its jurisdiction, or to protect or effectuate its judgments." The Soldiers and Sailors Civil Relief Act does not contain language that expressly authorizes the federal court to issue a stay against a state court proceeding.

24.24. Child Custody Under SCRA

"Most states have a policy of providing for the best interests of the child when it comes to custody decisions. Reconciling the SCRA with state law, however, has produced a tremendous debate over which interests should take precedence: those of the child or those of the servicemember." Sara Estrin, *The Servicemembers Civil Relief Act: Why and How This Act Applies to Child Custody Proceedings*, 7 Law & Ineq. 211 (Winter 2009). It is believed that many individuals deployed in the United States Armed Forces often lose custody of their children partially as a result of their deployments. Some contend that this is a result of the deficiencies of the SCRA. *See* Christopher Missick, Comment, *Child Custody Protections in the Servicemembers Civil Relief Act: Congress Acts to Protect Parents Serving in the Armed Forces*, 29 Whittier L. Rev. 857 (2008). Since 2005, at least 12 states have amended their child custody statutes in an attempt to accommodate both the best interests of the child and the legal rights of the servicemember parent. *Estrin, supra,* at 226. *See Lenser v. McGowan,* 191 S.W.3d 423 (Ark. 2004) (husband's request for a stay in divorce proceeding, under the SCRA, did not deprive the trial court of jurisdiction to enter temporary custody order granting custody of child to wife).

In recognition that a national solution to the custody problem was needed when one spouse is in the military, Congress recently amended the SCRA and made it clear that a default judgment and stay provisions of the SCRA are applicable in child custody proceedings involving active-duty servicemembers. Pub. L. No. 110-181, §584, 122 Stat. 3, 128 (2008); *Estrin, supra,* at 238. However, because servicemembers are being treated differently depending on their state of residence, it is suggested that a new federal law be enacted that balances the competing interests of minor children and servicemember parents. *Id.* at 239.

The new federal amendment is criticized, however, as failing to adequately address the issue of whether the SCRA preempts state family law in child custody proceedings. It is suggested that Congress enact legislation that explicitly deals with the problem of staying child custody actions pursuant to the SCRA. *Id.*

Table of Cases

Table of Cases

Table of Cases

Table of Cases

Index

Index